Who Were the

Who Were the Rich?

A biographical directory of
British wealth-holders

Volume I
1809–39

William D. Rubinstein

British Library Cataloguing in Publication Data
A catalogue record of this book is available from the British Library

Printed and bound in the United Kingdom

ISBN-13: 978-1-904863-39-7

Social Affairs Unit
314–22 Regent Street
London W1B 5SA
www.socialaffairsunit.org.uk

CONTENTS

ABOUT THE AUTHOR

William D. Rubinstein is Professor of History at the University of Aberystwyth. He was born in New York and educated at Swarthmore College and Johns Hopkins University. Between 1976 and 1995 he lived in Australia and was Professor of Social and Economic History at Deakin University near Melbourne when he took up his present post.

He has written widely on British elites and wealth-holding, in such works as *Men of Property: The Very Wealthy in Britain Since the Industrial Revolution* (1981; revised edition 2006), and on a variety of other topics, including Jewish history and subjects which 'amateur historians' write about but which are ignored by academic historians, in such works as *Shadow Pasts: History's Mysteries* (2008). He is an elected Fellow of the Australian Academy of the Humanities, the Australian Academy of the Social Sciences and the Royal Historical Society.

INTRODUCTION

This work is intended to be the first of a series that will eventually offer biographical information, similar to that included in this volume, about everyone who left £100,000 or more in Britain between 1809, when the data about wealth at death first appear in a usable form, and 1914. The present volume comprises biographical information about all 881 persons who left £100,000 or more in Britain between 1809 and 1839.

The names and other basic information, including the valuation figures, for these persons have been taken from several probate sources. These are PROB 8, the probate calendars for estates left at death and probated in the Prerogative Court of Canterbury (PCC), which are held in the National Archives (formerly the Public Record Office) in Kew; the probate records of the Prerogative Court of York (York PC), held at the Borthwick Institute in York; the records of the Episcopal Consistory Court of Chester and the Court of the Archdeaconry of Richmond, covering Lancashire, held at the Lancashire Record Office; and the Scottish probate calendars, which begin in 1825, held at the Scottish Record Office in Edinburgh.

Prior to 1858, the probating of estates in England and Wales was wholly a monopoly of the Church of England, which established a wide-ranging ecclesiastical courts system for this purpose. All estates left at death, including estates left by all non-Anglicans and all intestacies, had to be probated in one of those courts. During the early nineteenth century, there were thirty-eight of them, most very minor, having jurisdiction over different diocesan areas in England and Wales. However, in all cases of any estate leaving £10 or more in both of the two archbishopric areas (Canterbury, covering the southern two-thirds of England plus Wales, and York, covering the northern third of England), and of all such persons who owned Bank of England stock ('consols'), the most common form of secure savings at the time, all such estates had to be probated in one or another of the two so-called prerogative courts, of Canterbury and of York. The PCC was by far the most important ecclesiastical court, and the great majority of wealthy estates were probated there. It is important to note that it was physically located not in Canterbury but at Doctor's Commons in Knightrider Street in the City of London, near St Paul's Cathedral and not far from the Inns of Court and law courts. (After the probating of estates became a wholly secular governmental matter, in 1858, the Principal Probate Registry, as it was then known, remained at Doctor's Commons until 1873, when it moved to Somerset House in the Strand, where it remained until the 1990s. It is now located at First Avenue House in High Holborn.) In all likelihood, more than 80 per cent of very large estates were probated in the PCC. A disproportionate share of all wealthy persons lived in or near London, and the best legal advice was available there. The York PC also saw the probate of some very large estates, but not many. I also searched the records of the two lower courts that covered Lancashire, the centre of the industrial revolution, for any large estates probated there. Scottish probate records begin at the national level in 1825 and were also searched by me. Pre-1858 Irish probate records were destroyed in the Four Courts fire during the Irish Civil War in 1922. It is possible that other local ecclesiastical courts contain the records of some other persons leaving £100,000 or more, although this is unlikely. It seems certain that I identified the great majority of large estates left in the period 1809–39 and that they are, accordingly, included in this work.

The valuation figures in these probate records are for the gross value of the unsettled personalty of each such person – that is, they exclude land and the value of any trust from which that person received an income but from which he or she could not touch the capital. The main exclusion is, of course, for land, although it will be seen that no fewer than 174 persons who have been classified by me chiefly as landowners, including dozens of landed aristocrats, did leave personal estates of £100,000 or more in this period. No statistics of landownership in Britain exist until the 1870s, when Parliament compiled the famous *Return of Owners of Land*, which recorded the acreage and gross annual income of all landowners in the United Kingdom except in London, which was excluded from the *Return.* In 1883, John Bateman collated and corrected these figures, publishing his *Great Landowners of Great Britain and Ireland,* which included the acreage and gross annual incomes of all landowners outside London at that time. Statistics from Bateman's 1883 work have been systematically included in the entries in this book. These statistics are, of course, indicative only, since they are relevant to our wealth-holders' descendants decades later; nevertheless, they still might have some descriptive validity. The capital value of land is normally taken to be thirty times the gross annual income; thus, the land of someone listed in Bateman as having an income of £20,000 was worth around £2 million. Great landowners, in fact, certainly remained the wealthiest men in Britain until the twentieth century. In 1987, the American scholar Peter Lindert published 'Who Owned Victorian England? The Debate Over Landed Wealth and Inequality' (*Agricultural History*, vol. 61, no. 4, pp. 25–51), which provided similar figures for the great London landowners for the 1890s. These have also been included in the entries in this work where relevant.

In other respects, the valuation figures are certainly accurate. As will be seen, very many celebrated businessmen deceased in the period 1809–39 are among the entries, including the millionaires Sir Robert Peel and Nathan Rothschild. Valuation figures were sworn to the nearest £10,000 or £20,000, rather than to an exact figure, in the case of estates in England and Wales until 1881 (when they were sworn to an exact figure). They were sworn, for example, 'Below £200,000' and so are actually worth slightly less than the sum noted. Estates sworn at the £100,000 level, the lowest in this study, have been included for completeness. Scottish estates were always given in precise figures. This data begins in a usable form in the somewhat strange year of 1809 because it was then that very large estates, over £100,000, were given a relatively precise figure rather than 'Upper Value', the term employed previously for such estates, and also because changes in the probate law at the time made the inclusion of the whole of the estate in the valuation figure mandatory. Previously, legacies to close relatives were generally excluded from the global valuation figure. Until the mid-nineteenth century, too, the term 'Upper Value' was often used to describe estates worth over £1 million, rather than giving such very large estates a more precise figure.

The probate calendars (as the annual lists of estate-leavers are known) give the name, address, date of probate, sometimes the occupation, and names of the executors of the deceased, including intestacies (where the deceased has left no will), and then the probate valuation of each. I personally went through all of the pre-1858 probate calendars included in this work in the early 1970s, when I began the research that led to my doctoral dissertation at Johns Hopkins University and to the publication of many works based upon this research. However, to identify each wealth-holder in the biographical detail aimed at in this work required much more research, in an endless variety of sources, over many years. Between about 1988 and 1995, when I lived in Australia and was an academic at Deakin University near Melbourne, I had a series of grants from the Australian Research Grants Scheme (ARGS) and from Deakin University to employ a full-time research assistant in London, Dr Carole M. Taylor, who carried out much of the research on these early wealth-holders from books and records held at the Institute of Historical Research, the Society of Genealogists and other archives in London. I am most grateful to these funding bodies and to Dr Taylor for their crucial assistance to me. Since taking up my present post at the University of Aberystwyth in 1995, I have carried on this research on my own and have completed the identification of all estate-leavers of £100,000 or more down to 1914 and even beyond, information which will be used in subsequent volumes. I am most grateful indeed to Michael Mosbacher and the Social Affairs Unit in London for agreeing to publish this and subsequent volumes. I have long hoped to make this information generally available to scholars, and this has given me the perfect opportunity to do so. It should also be noted that in the very recent past an extraordinary amount of new research material has become available via the Internet, material which was not available or was inaccessible earlier. In particular, the online edition of the *Oxford Dictionary of National Biography* (*ODNB*), published in 2004, makes it possible to find any reference in any article to any person instantaneously, a facility unimaginable before the internet age.

Most of the biographical information on these wealth-holders, it should be noted, was compiled long before this, from written and published sources. A number of key points ought to be made here. Before the earliest 'named' British Census, in 1841, and before the civil registration of births, marriages and deaths in 1836–7, there are simply no official sources that give the occupation or other salient information about the persons in this study. If these persons cannot be traced in any available published source, nothing further can be learned about their lives. One can read the will of each such individual, and, in the very recent past, all wills probated in the PCC can be read (PROB 11) online for a fee of £3.50 each. This has been done in several dozen cases (previously, one had to travel to Kew and order up the specific will), but in many of these cases biographical information about that person was not given in the will. Wills are simply official instructions concerning the posthumous disposal of one's property, not mini-autobiographies, and while, in some cases, something about the career of the testator can be directly or indirectly inferred from the will, in many cases such documents are not illuminating. They are also in many cases virtually unreadable, as PROB 11 contains the handwritten 'copywills' sent for deposit to the PCC, which are always written in an official courthand which is virtually illegible and almost entirely without punctuation, as well as often long, meandering and very complex. Indeed, so unreadable are these books of 'copywills' that the first time I tried to read one, in the 1970s at Somerset House (where they were kept at the time), I assumed at first glance that they were in Arabic and were the wills of British Levant merchants! It quickly became obvious that they were indeed in English but written in a virtually illegible fashion.

Most of the biographical information about each wealth-holder has come from a wide variety of printed sources, chiefly at the two outstanding open-shelf libraries in London which contain published works relevant to this study: the Institute of Historical Research (IHR) in the Senate House of London University and the Society of Genealogists in Clerkenwell. Just as it must be understood that there were no official sources for most of the period surveyed here, so it must be appreciated that newspapers at the time, even *The Times*, did not routinely carry obituaries. However, one monthly periodical, the *Gentleman's Magazine* (*GM*), did carry brief, but often extremely informative, obituaries of many of the people in this study. Most of these obituaries

were certainly submitted by the family of the deceased and generally listed his or her age and address, with, in some cases, a brief account of his or her career. All persons in this study were routinely checked in the *GM* indices, and any information given in the *GM* is noted in their entries. Another very important source of information are local directories, of which several hundred can be found on open shelf at the IHR. These are particularly good for London and contain the occupations of many hundreds of wealth-holders otherwise unidentifiable, although occupational designations such as 'merchant' are frustratingly vague. *Burke's Peerage* (*BP*) and *Burke's Landed Gentry* (*BLG*), available in many editions from the 1840s, also proved invaluable for genealogical information. *The Complete Peerage* (*CP*), which appeared in fifteen volumes, provides very comprehensive information about peers and their families. Alumni handbooks of the public schools, and the two alumni handbooks of the two old English universities, that for Oxford (*Alum. Oxon.*) compiled by John Foster, and that for Cambridge (*Alum. Cantab.*) compiled by J. A. Venn and one of the most remarkable collective biographies ever put together, far better than its Oxford counterpart, were also invaluable. The biographies of MPs in the various volumes of the *History of Parliament* (*HP*) are also very useful and particularly good for the occupational backgrounds of those included. Other useful sources include the *Law Lists*, containing brief information on all barristers and solicitors, and the many volumes of the *Victoria County History* (*VCH*) and of the *Survey of London*. The *ODNB* is now certainly the standard biographical reference work for the 56,000 persons it includes as well as for the thousands of others mentioned in passing and has been extensively used where this is possible. I should note that I have often discovered biographical information from other sources not included in its entries, or information that contradicts its assertions, and this have been used where apparently more accurate.

A work used often for Hull wealth-holders is K. S. Allison, *Hull Gent. Seeks Country Residence*, 1750–1850 (East Yorkshire Local History Society, 1981). Some other common abbreviations in the text below include:

d.s.p. (*decessit sine prole*): died without surviving children;

- DL: Deputy Lieutenant;
- FSA: Fellow of the Society of Antiquaries;
- FRS: Fellow of the Royal Society;
- JP: Justice of the Peace.

The base figure of £100,000 obviously has no special significance as such but represents a good and obvious round number to demarcate the lower limits of real wealth. In inflationary terms, it is the equivalent to about £8 million in today's (2008) money, although, in terms of the percentage of Britain's gross national product (GNP) it represents, and probably in terms of its real purchasing power, this sum is almost certainly much higher. The average wage of a skilled workman in 1820 was probably about £40–50 per year, perhaps 1/500th of the current salary of an equivalent person today, and it might be necessary to multiply very large fortunes or incomes by the same amount. It should always be kept in mind that all of the data in this work is for the *wealth* of the person concerned, not his or her *income*. If one received 3–5 per cent of any capital sum as one's income, an estate worth £100,000 would produce an income of £3,000–£5,000 per annum, although not all of the items included in this £100,000 fortune would produce an income. An income of the amount at that time would have made one extremely affluent, although not necessarily in the mega-rich class. The wealthiest single person deceased in Britain between 1809 and 1839 was almost certainly the first Duke of Sutherland, who was probably worth about £7 million including his lands, the equivalent, in inflationary terms, of about £560 million today. This, however, almost certainly does not really represent the real equivalent fortune of the man known as the 'Leviathan of Wealth' – he was certainly worth many billions in today's money.

Something must be said of the arrangement of the entries within each year, which are not listed either alphabetically or by size. They are listed in the order in which they occur in PROB 8: that source was arranged by the geographical area in which estates were probated, with those probated abroad and in remote parts of Britain usually found in the first part of each annual volume. These have generally been followed in the arrangement here by wealthy probates in York, Lancashire and Scotland. In fact, their arrangement within each year has no special significance whatever. Some estates would necessarily have been probated in the year of death, or, occasionally, several years after it. In some cases, the valuation figure is followed by the term 'Within Province', meaning that this was the size of the estate left in the area in which the PCC had jurisdiction. When the size of the estate left in the York PC or in Scotland is known, it has been added to this amount in a clearly indicated way. A comprehensive index of names has also been included.

For each wealth-holder, there are thirteen categories of information. They are:

1. **Name**, including the original name or maiden name of married women. Peerage titles are listed first in the case of aristocrats, followed by their actual name.
2. **Dates**. In some cases, the date of probate (from PROB 11) is known, but not the actual date of death. Dates have been ascertained from a variety of sources; readers should bear in mind again that for the most part there were no official sources in this period.
3. **Probate** valuation, with the name of the probate court. In some cases, especially millionaires' estates, informed estimates of the real size of the estate have been included, with their sources.

4. **Occupation** or source of wealth. These have been taken from a wide variety of sources, especially local directories, and then classified according to a schema of occupational distribution derived from the Standard Industrial Classification system, which is explained below. The geographical venue of the place in which wealth-holders earned their money is also given and then classified according to a geographical schema explained below. It must be emphasised that this is where wealth-holders actually earned their fortune, not where they lived. Some classes of wealth-holder cannot be readily assigned a geographical venue and have not been so classified. These include landowners, military officers and clergymen, although in one or two cases there was a strong, career-long association with a particular place that was clearly the locality in which the individual's fortune was earned; in these cases, the wealth-holder has been assigned a venue. Wives and the inactive children of business or professional wealth-holders have been put into the occupational category and venue where their inherited fortune was earned. Figures of landed acreage and income from Bateman's 1883 work *Great Landowners* and Lindert's study of London have also been included here as appropriate.
5. **Address**. Individuals' addresses have mainly been taken from the probate calendars, but those have been supplemented with other sources.
6. The name, dates and occupation of the **father**, with salient information about him and the birth order of the wealth-holder, where known.
7. Information about the **mother** of each wealth-holder, and her family where known.
8. Secondary, tertiary, and professional **education**.
9. Spouse, with date of **marriage** and information about her or his family background, their children and important descendants.
10. Original and final **religion**.
11. **Public** offices held and honours and titles received. Information about the party or political affiliation of MPs is given where known. Much information about MPs derives from Gerrit P. Judd IV, *Members of Parliament 1734–1832* (originally 1955; reprinted 1972), a very useful work (abbreviated Judd).
12. **Miscellaneous** information not provided elsewhere, comments and cross-references not under other headings.
13. **References** and sources.

All entries are kept in the same order and in the same format. Obviously, there are radically unequal amounts of information available on the 881 wealth-holders, who range in renown from former prime ministers and 'household names', often with lengthy biographies in the *ODNB* and other standard sources, to complete unknowns in the case of whom one is fortunate to be able to trace their occupations in local directories, if that. Regarding certain categories of information – for instance, the name of the mother of each wealth-holder, or the subject's secondary schooling – plainly no information exists in any surviving source, certainly without undertaking an infinite amount of research.

Further information about wealth-holding in Britain can be found in other works by me, especially *Men of Property: The Very Wealthy in Britain Since the Industrial Revolution* (originally 1981; revised edition 2006) and the essays in my *Wealth and the Wealthy in the Modern World* (1987).

I welcome any additions or corrections, sent to me c/o The Department of History, University of Aberystwyth, Penglais, Ceredigion SY23 3DY, UK (wdr @aber.ac.uk).

William D. Rubinstein
August 2008

OCCUPATIONAL CATEGORIES AND VENUES OF THE WEALTH-HOLDERS

As noted above, all wealth-holders are classified by their occupations and the venues in which they earned their fortunes. These are listed for each wealth-holder in the fourth item, 'Occupation' of their entries. The occupational categories derive from the *Standard Industrial Classification* (Central Statistical Office, 1968 revision) which separate manufacturing industry from commerce and the service sectors. They have been modified for the purposes of this study but, in general, are very close to the official categories.

I. LANDOWNERS

These are persons who apparently earned the bulk of their fortunes from income derived from land, including minerals and urban property. Plantation owners in the West Indies are also classified here. Persons whose fathers or grandfathers were in trade or the professions but who then purchased land would normally be classified with that trade or profession, although each case is judged on its apparent merits. Close relatives of landowners with no other apparent major sources of income are also classified here. Normally, titled landed aristocrats would automatically be classified here. However, colliery owners – businessmen who derived their incomes from working coalmines normally leased from a landowner – would not be classified here.

II. MANUFACTURING AND INDUSTRY

1. Coal mining. As noted, colliery proprietors are classified here, but the landowners who owned the land bearing the colliery or collieries (for instance Lord Londonderry) are classified in I.
2. Other mining.
3. Iron and steel manufacturing.
4. Shipbuilding.
5. Engineering and related trades.
6. Chemical manufacturing and related trades.
7. Cotton manufacturing.
8. Woollen manufacturing.
9. Other textile manufacturing.

10. Construction and building.
11. Other manufacturing.

III. FOOD, DRINK AND TOBACCO

12. Brewing and related, including maltsting, etc.
13. Distilling.
14. Tobacco manufacturing.
15. Foods and foodstuffs, including non-alcoholic beverages.

IV. COMMERCE AND FINANCE

16. Banking.
17. Merchant banking – comprises international bankers.
18. Other finance.
19. Foreign merchants – merchants trading abroad, import–export merchants, etc.
20. Retailing.
21. Other merchants, including warehousemen and 'merchants' not classified elsewhere. This category contains many wealth-holders described in directories as 'merchants' without any more specific information.
22. Insurance brokers.
23. Stockbrokers.
24. Shipowners.
25. Other commerce.

V. PUBLISHING AND MISCELLANEOUS

26. Newspaper proprietors.
27. Publishers.
28. Other miscellaneous.

VI. PROFESSIONALS, PUBLIC ADMINISTRATION AND DEFENCE

29. Lawyers and other legal professionals and officials.
30. Other professionals.
31. Public administration and defence, including government office-holders not classified elsewhere.

VII. OTHERS

Plainly, it is often difficult to classify some wealth-holders, given the lack of information about them and the fact that some had several sources of wealth, but the above categories are certainly broadly accurate.

VENUES

As noted, these are the places where wealth-holders apparently earned or

derived most of their fortune, according to the best information available. To reiterate, these venues are not necessarily where the wealth-holder lived.

1. City of London: that is, the historic 'Square Mile' centred around St Paul's Cathedral. Whether a business was literally in the City, or technically just outside of its boundaries, was sometimes difficult to ascertain. The Inns of Court are counted as being in the City of London.
2. Other London: other parts of central London, including Westminster, Mayfair, Southwark, the Docks, etc.
3. Outer London: the boundaries here are often somewhat arbitrary but are roughly coterminous with the outermost extent of the Underground system.
4. Greater Manchester, including neighbouring towns such as Bolton and Oldham.
5. Merseyside.
6. West Yorkshire – Leeds, Bradford and surrounding towns.
7. South Yorkshire – Sheffield and surrounding towns.
8. West Midlands – Birmingham, Wolverhampton and neighbouring towns.
9. Tyneside.
10. Clydeside.
11. East Anglia.
12. Bristol.
13. Other south-west England.
14. Other southern England.
15. Ribblesdale, including Preston and Accrington.
16. Mid-Lancashire, including Wigan and St Helens.
17. Nottingham-Derby-Belper.
18. Other Midlands, including the East Midlands.
19. Wales.
20. Teeside.
21. Humberside.
22. Other northern England.
23. Edinburgh.
24. Other Scotland.
25. Belfast.
26. Dublin.
27. Other Ireland.
28. Other and unclassified.
29. Overseas and foreign, especially India and the West Indies.

FINDINGS AND CONCLUSIONS

Numbers and gender

What does an analysis of the 881 wealth-holders who left £100,000 or more between 1809 and 1839 tell us about the structure of wealth-holding in Britain at that time? Some distinctive patterns clearly emerge.

Of the total of 881 wealth-holders, 214 were probated in the eleven-year period 1809–19, 308 in the decade 1820–9, and 359 in the decade 1830–9. There was, thus, a substantial rise in the number of large estates, a trend plainly consistent with the growth of the British economy at the time – although, as will be discussed, this certainly did not mean that the obvious growth areas in the British economy, especially the Industrial Revolution trades such as cotton-spinning and engineering, were well represented in this increase.

The great majority of wealth-holders in this study were, of course, males. Nevertheless, there were sixty-three women out of the grand total of 881 wealth-holders – 7.1 per cent. By decade, there were fourteen women wealth-holders in the eleven-year span 1809–19 out of the total of 214 (6.5 per cent), twenty-three out of 308 in 1820–9 (7.5 per cent), and twenty-six of 359 in 1830–39 (7.2 per cent). The majority were widows or 'spinsters', as unmarried women were normally described, but occasionally a married woman with a husband living left a fortune in her own right – for instance, the remarkable Harriot Mellon (whose entry appears below as 1838/35, which means that she is the thirty-fifth entry listed for 1838), widow of Thomas Coutts the great banker and, at the time of her death, the Duchess of St Albans, whose husband did not die until 1849. More than half of the wealthy women were widows, while another substantial percentage were spinsters. Both of these categories were themselves somewhat unusual, indicating that these women inherited great wealth in their own right (or expanded the size of their inheritance), rather than receiving an annual income paid out of a settlement, which they (or their current husbands) were unable to touch apart from the income it produced, as was certainly common for many female relatives of rich men.

The great majority of women wealth-holders left estates in the range of £100,000 to £200,000, rather than a higher sum. Five women, however, left estates of £500,000 or more. The wealthiest woman deceased in the period under consideration was Jane Innes (1748–1839; 1839/2), daughter and sister of wealthy Edinburgh bankers, who left £1,043,000. The four half-millionaires were Elizabeth Whittingstall (d. 1825; 1825/19), who inherited a Watford maltsting and brewing fortune; Lady Harriet Holland (1744–1825; 1825/23), daughter of a baronet and widow of the wealthy architect Sir Nathaniel Holland; Susannah Houblon Newton (née Archer, 1753–1837; 1837/28), who inherited a landed fortune and married into a Huguenot mercantile family; and the above-noted Harriot Mellon (1777–1837).

Extremes of wealth

While everyone in this study was, by definition, among the wealthiest persons of their time in Britain, some were even more extremely wealthy than others. Apart from the five women mentioned above, eight men left millionaire estates, and thirty-five men left half-millionaire estates: six in 1809–19, seventeen in 1820–9 and twelve in 1830–9. The eight millionaire estates were those left by the Hon. Henry Cavendish (1731–1810; 1810/2), the scientist, who inherited a landed fortune; Richard Crawshay (1739–1820; 1810/15), the ironmaster in south Wales; William Douglas, 4th Duke of Queensberry (1725–1810; 1811/9), 'Old Q', the notorious rake; Philip Rundell (1746–1827; 1827/25), goldsmith and jeweller in the City of London; Sir Robert Peel, 1st Baronet (1750–1830; 1830/17), the cotton manufacturer in Lancashire and father of his namesake the prime minister; George Leveson-Gower, 1st Duke of Sutherland (1758–1833; 1833/22), landowner; William Hollond (1750–1836; 1836/17), who made his fortune in the Bengal Civil Service; and Nathan Mayer Rothschild (1777–1836; 1836/25), the great merchant banker in the City of London. Of these, the Duke of Sutherland was certainly the wealthiest, with Rothschild probably the runner-up and richest businessman. It is worth making the point again that the value of land is excluded from these figures. It is likely that several dozen landowners, chiefly landed aristocrats, died in the period 1809–39 who were worth more than £1 million if the total value of their land is included with their personalty. Many of these – perhaps the majority – do appear in this study, however, since they left at least £100,000 in personalty.

Among the thirty-five male half-millionaires, twelve were active in the City of London, primarily as merchants, and six active chiefly in other parts of London. Seven were landowners who left personal estates in the half-millionaire class. Two (William Crawshay, 1764–1834 [1834/28], and Jonathan Peel, 1752–1834 [1835/1]) were industrialists or manufacturers in the new industrial areas, and one (Thomas Leyland, 1752–1827 [1827/5]) was a banker in Liverpool, but provincial businessmen were rare at this level of wealth. The remainder chiefly earned their fortunes overseas, usually in the West Indies or India.

Occupational distribution

The following is a table of the occupational distribution of the wealth-holders in this volume. It includes, where known, the most important occupation or source of wealth of each of these individuals, who include women and foreigners leaving large estates in Britain. By numbers deceased in each decade, the occupational distribution is as shown in Table 1.

The most striking finding of this occupational breakdown of the wealth-holders is, of course, the crucial importance of commercial and financial

Table 1

Occupation		1809–19	1820–9	1830–9	Totals	%
I. LAND		**50**	**54**	**70**	**174**	**22.1**
II. MANUFACTURING AND INDUSTRY						
1.	Coal mining		1	1	0	2
2.	Other mining		2	2	1	5
3.	Iron/steel		3	2	7	12
4.	Shipbuilding		2	2	2	6
5.	Engineering		1	0	0	1
6.	Chemicals		4	3	2	9
7.	Cotton		2	4	5	11
8.	Woollens		1	4	0	5
9.	Other textiles		5	3	2	10
10.	Construction		2	1	7	10
11.	Other manufacturing		4	10	11	25
Totals		**27**	**32**	**37**	**96**	**12.2**
III. FOOD, DRINK AND TOBACCO						
12.	Brewing and related		4	11	9	24
13.	Distilling		1	5	4	10
14.	Tobacco		0	1	1	2
15.	Foods		4	0	1	5
Totals		**9**	**17**	**15**	**41**	**5.2**
IV. COMMERCE AND FINANCE						
16.	Banking		24	21	31	76
17.	Merchant banking		2	0	2	4
18.	Other finance		3	2	3	8
19.	Foreign merchants		25	44	27	96
20.	Retailing		6	7	11	24
21.	Other merchants		31	19	38	88
22.	Insurance		2	3	1	6
23.	Stockbrokers		6	9	11	26
24.	Shipowners		1	0	3	4
25.	Other commerce		1	1	2	4
Totals		**101**	**106**	**129**	**336**	**42.7**
V. PUBLISHING						
26.	Newspapers		0	1	1	2
27.	Publishers		0	1	2	3
28.	Miscellaneous		0	0	0	0
Totals		**0**	**2**	**3**	**5**	**0.6**
VI. PROFESSIONALS AND PUBLIC ADMINISTRATION						
29.	Professions: law		10	13	24	46
30.	Other professionals		5	15	17	37
31.	Public administration/ defence		17	17	17	51
Totals		**32**	**45**	**58**	**134**	**17**
Totals		**219**	**256**	**312**	**786**	**99.8**

wealth, rather than manufacturing and industrial wealth. This conclusion was also reached in my previous study of the rich who left £500,000 or more, *Men of Property*. Although Britain was experiencing the world's first industrial revolution at that time, industrialists constituted only a small percentage of the wealthiest British people. The 'conservative' nature of Britain's wealth structure at that time is also evident from the very large number of wealthy landowners – even *without* the value of their land being included in the valuation figures – and the remarkable number of wealth-holders in the public-administration and defence categories, many of whom were a part of the world of 'Old Corruption' or the East India Company and military or naval figures as well as government civil servants and office-holders. If the landowners listed above are omitted, and only the known non-landed wealth-holders included (a total of 612 persons), 15.7 per cent were industrialists or manufacturers, 6.7 per cent in the food-drink-tobacco categories, 54.7 per cent in commerce and finance, 0.8 per cent in publishing and 21.9 per cent in public administration and defence.

Venues

These are arranged by the geographical venues in which each wealth-holder earned his or her fortune (not where he or she lived). Bearing in mind that many wealth-holders – landowners, military, most clerical figures, etc. – cannot readily be assigned to a venue, the 1809–39 wealth-holders can be assigned as shown in Table 2.

As with the occupational distributions of the wealth-holders – and, indeed, even more emphatically – the 'conservative' nature of Britain's wealth structure at this time is absolutely plain from the locational analysis, with London accounting for two-thirds of all large fortunes and another one-eighth earned overseas in the Empire and other trading entrepôts. In contrast, the new industrial cities and regions of Britain were the venues for only a small percentage of British fortunes. In provincial Britain, traditional and long-established trading and manufacturing areas such as Bristol and East Anglia were more likely than Manchester and Birmingham to have been the scene of large fortunes. If anything, this understates the importance of London for Britain's wealth elite at this time, for virtually all major landowners (not included with these statistics) spent much of each year in London and had houses there, as did many wealth-holders whose fortunes were earned elsewhere.

Social mobility

The number of wealth-holders who were 'self-made men' and the number who began in comfortable or affluent circumstances is an interesting and important question. Plainly, in a time of rapid economic change and the development of novel industries and of Britain's worldwide trading links, it is

Table 2

	Venue	1809–19	1820–9	1830–9	Totals	%
1.	City of London	81	95	108	284	44.4
2.	Other London	37	34	53	124	19.4
3.	Outer London	5	6	3	14	
	Total, London	*123*	*135*	*164*	*422*	*66.0*
4.	Greater Manchester	3	6	5	14	2.2
5.	Merseyside	1	4	11	16	2.5
6.	West Yorkshire	0	0	0	0	
7.	South Yorkshire	0	1	0	1	
8.	West Midlands	3	0	4	7	
9.	Tyneside	1	1	3	5	
10.	Clydeside	0	3	0	3	
11.	East Anglia	5	7	4	16	
12.	Bristol	3	4	9	16	
13.	Other south-west England	1	8	1	10	
14.	Other southern England	2	3	6	11	
15.	Ribblesdale	0	0	0	0	
16.	Mid-Lancashire	0	0	0	0	
17.	Nottingham-Derby-Belper	0	0	0	0	
18.	Other Midlands	0	8	5	13	
19.	Wales	3	1	4	8	
20.	Teeside	0	0	0	0	
21.	Humberside	0	4	0	4	
22.	Other northern England	0	1	2	3	
23.	Edinburgh	0	1	6	7	
24.	Other Scotland	0	0	0	0	
25.	Belfast	0	0	0	0	
26.	Dublin	0	0	1	1	
27.	Other Ireland	0	2	0	2	
28.	Nationwide	0	0	0	0	
29.	Overseas					
	West Indies	6	9	5	20	
	India	9	12	17	38	
	Portugal	3	4	2	9	
	Europe	1	0	2	3	
	North America	0	2	1	3	
	China	0	1	1	2	
	Total, overseas	*19*	*28*	*28*	*75*	*12.7*
	Totals	**166**	**217**	**256**	**639**	

to be expected that many persons outside the upper classes would be able to take advantage of new niches created by novel circumstances and to enrich themselves. Against this, it might be expected that the sons of already reasonably well-established families would be in a much better position to do so than those without any means, most of whom would have remained in the working classes.

Unfortunately, it is not possible, from the existing evidence, to give anything like a definitive answer about intergenerational social mobility. As will be seen, in many cases little or nothing is known about the occupation or social status of the father of the wealth-holder nor about the initial phases of the wealth-holder's careers. It is among this stratum of lesser-known wealth-holders that one might expect to find the most spectacular examples of upward social mobility. Prior to the named censuses (beginning in 1841) and the civil registration of births (from 1837), there are no consistent, official sources which might provide this information. On the other hand, we do have this information for most wealth-holders who started life in affluent circumstances, for instance all or virtually all hereditary peers. There were, however, certainly some very spectacular cases of intergenerational social mobility noted in this study, for example the judge Charles Abbott, Lord Tenterden (1752–1832; 1832/25) and Sir John Soane (1753–1837; 1837/4), the famous architect. Many wealthy businessmen whose biographies are known in detail appear to have emerged from relatively successful, but not enormously wealthy, backgrounds – probably a common pattern throughout British history. However, it should be stressed again that not enough information exists about the origins of a great many businessmen among the wealth-holders, making generalisations based on solid evidence very difficult. At a rough guess, my own estimate would be that about 15–25 per cent of all business wealth-holders in this study had fathers who, by occupation, were small shopkeepers or traders, or actually in the working classes. But this is just a guess, and further research might provide a different picture. It should also be stressed that it is difficult to see what further evidence exists on a comprehensive basis with which to address this question, especially for the large number of lesser-known merchants and the like who form such a large component of the wealth elite in this period.

Religion

Even more than with the statistics of intergenerational social mobility, information on the religious affiliations of most wealth-holders in this study simply does not exist. This information does exist for a segment of these wealth-holders, however, including persons who emerged from immigrant backgrounds, those from well-known families closely associated with a particular religion, such as members of the so-called 'Quaker Cousinhood' (Barclays, Bevans, Trittons, Gurneys, etc.) and Anglican clergymen or the close relatives of Anglican (or other) clergymen. In some cases, where the will of the wealth-holder has been read, there is direct information about his or her religious affiliation, while in other cases the wealth-holder is known to have had a Church of England funeral or a memorial inscription in an Anglican church. There is also the further complication that persons born into one religion might adopt another later in life: many Protestant Nonconformists probably became Anglicans as they moved up the social scale. All in all, however, religious affiliation cannot be traced for most of those in this study.

What information does exist, however, is of value to the historian. Social historians have long argued about the importance of religion in accounting for capitalist entrepreneurship and economic development. The most important work in this area was the famous publication by the great German sociologist Max Weber (1864–1920), *The Protestant Ethic and the Spirit of Capitalism* (1904–5), which argued that there was a salient causal connection between Protestantism (as opposed to Roman Catholicism) and the emergence of modern capitalism. According to Weber, Protestants no longer regarded the making of money as sinful but, on the contrary, as a sign of God's favour and practised what Weber described as 'this-world asceticism' – ploughing back profits into the firm and living frugally – and the rational organisation of businesses to maximise profits. Protestants ended the medieval ban on 'usury' (money-lending of any kind), while often favouring the reorganisation of legal and governmental frameworks to favour property-owners and businessmen. In the British context, historians such as T. S. Ashton have drawn a distinction between the established Anglican Church and Nonconformist sects such as Baptists, Congregationalists and Quakers who, they claim, 'sparked' the Industrial Revolution. Weber's famous work was written shortly before the right-wing German sociologist Werner Sombart (1863–1941) produced *The Jews and Modern Capitalism.* Sombart argued that the Jews had been chiefly responsible for the growth of capitalism in Europe.

As noted, the data on religious affiliation in this study is necessarily much sparser than one would wish for. As noted, for most wealth-holders, no direct information about religious affiliation is available. A number of important points ought, however, to be made. During most of the life spans of these wealth-holders, membership in the Church of England, the Church of Ireland (the Anglican church in Ireland) and the Church of Scotland was prerequisite for participation in most areas of public life, including membership of Parliament. Therefore, any wealth-holder associated in any way with public life or an official institution was likely to have been an Anglican (or member of the Church of Scotland). In all likelihood, and despite the fact that no direct information is available, most wealth-holders were Anglicans (or members of the Church of Scotland) rather than Protestant Nonconformists. On the other hand, it is also quite possible that a significant number of wealth-holders whose religious affiliation is unknown came from families that adhered to a sect in 'Old Dissent' which emerged in the seventeenth century. In most cases, unfortunately, there are no real markers (such as characteristic surnames) from which religious identity may be inferred.

Information, however, does exist about the religious identity of many wealth-holders. As noted above, in the case of persons of immigrant backgrounds, from well-known families associated with a particular religion and for clergymen and their relatives, this information is available, while direct information exists about other persons in this study. It is thus possible to produce some statistics, bearing in mind that the religious affiliations of very many wealth-holders remain unknown. In Table 3, no attempt has been made to enumerate all known Anglicans or Presbyterians, as their religious identity is known, if at all, only in a hit-or-miss way.

It will be seen from this table that, even given the limited data base available to the historian, there is no real evidence for any Nonconformist predominance in Britain's wealth elite at this time. Known Protestant Nonconformists made up around 7.6 per cent of all wealth-holders. While, given the large number of unknowns, this figure certainly understates the real Nonconformist total, it appears that historians who assign a special role to Nonconformists among Britain's most successful entrepreneurs are incorrect. Some Nonconformist sects certainly did produce many wealth-holders, most notably the Huguenots (French Protestant refugees and their descendants), who produced nearly 3 per cent of all wealth-holders, and the Quakers. There were only about 18,000 Quakers in Britain in 1821, a minute proportion of the population,

Table 3

Denomination, etc.	**1809–19**	**1820–9**	**1830–9**	**Total**
Anglican clergymen	5	13	12	30
Huguenots	8	5	9	22
Lutherans	4	4	0	8
Quakers	4	5	12	21
Unitarians	1	3	3	7
Moravians	1	0	0	1
Independents	1	0	0	1
Presbyterians in England	0	2	0	2
Baptists	0	1	0	1
Congregationalists	0	1	0	1
Methodists	0	2	0	2
'Dissenter'	1	0	0	1
Roman Catholics	6	4	7	17
Jews	2	3	4	9

but they accounted for nearly 3 per cent of all wealth-holders. The number identified as Quakers in this study almost certainly understates their actual strength, since we have identified as Quakers only such persons for whom actual biographical information exists. The number of Roman Catholics is probably higher than one would have supposed. Most were Spaniards, Portuguese or Latin Americans who left large fortunes in Britain, many connected with the wine trade or other mercantile activities. The number of wealthy Jews was very low, a fact which was almost certainly significant in explaining the low levels of antisemitism in Britain compared with the Continent, where Jews often played a much more prominent role in the local economy. Nevertheless, Nathan Rothschild (1777–1836; 1836/25) was perhaps the wealthiest single businessman in this study, while David Ricardo (1772–1823; 1823/7), the great economist (who became a Unitarian), made a fortune as a stockbroker. Perhaps the most striking single finding is the large number of Anglican clergymen who left enormous estates. Some of these were archbishops and bishops and other clergymen who benefited from astronomical salaries in their sees and clerical posts. Others were the sons of already wealthy families, generally landowners and aristocrats who inherited their fortunes.

Overall, the findings here might be seen as due to two factors. First, except in the case of small endogenous groups such as the Quakers, the religious distribution of the wealth-holders was probably something like a random sample of the entire British population, all of which has for centuries already been a part of what Thomas Carlyle termed a 'cash-nexus' society. Anglicans such as Sir Robert Peel, 1st Baronet, the earliest cotton millionaire – not just Protestant Nonconformists – certainly existed among very wealthy industrialists. Second, wealth-holding in this period appears to have centred around landowning, London-based mercantile activities, the Government–Empire nexus and 'Old Corruption', areas which probably strongly favoured Anglicans (and adherents of the Church of Scotland) rather than industrial and manufacturing activities where Dissenters might have been more prominent. This is a fascinating and important topic, which can be discussed here only in a superficial way.

Membership of Parliament

Most sons of titled aristocrats and other great landowners sat as Members of Parliament during the late eighteenth and early nineteenth centuries, as a matter of course. All holders of United Kingdom peerages and many (not all) holders of Scottish and Welsh peerages were, of course, members of the House of Lords. Wealthy businessmen, professionals and senior military figures also frequently sought election to the House of Commons. This process did not begin with the enfranchisement of the middle classes in the 1832 Reform Act but was certainly common long before that. Wealthy businessmen and others could 'buy' a pocket borough or be chosen as nominees of aristocrats and others who 'owned' a seat in Parliament. The City of London and other (but certainly not all) large cities and towns also returned MPs who were often wealthy businessmen.

Among the wealth-holders in this study, a total of eighty-two men who have been classified in occupational categories other than 'I. Landowners' served as MPs, out of a total of about 620 male British non-landowners (i.e. excluding all women, foreigners leaving fortunes in Britain and those classified as landowners), or about 15 per cent of this figure. This percentage was probably as high as among wealth-holders leaving £100,000 or more later in the nineteenth century. In 1809–19, twenty-seven of these men served as MPs, of whom eighteen can be classified as Tories (supporters of William Pitt or Lord Liverpool) and nine as Whigs. In 1820–9, there was a total of twenty-five such men, of whom seventeen were Tories, six Whigs and two 'Independents'. In 1830–9 there were thirty-four such MPs, of whom twenty-four were Tories and ten Whigs. The clear Tory predominance may seem surprising, given the widely held view of Whigs as allied to the 'rising' middle classes. This might have been the case in the mid-nineteenth century, but it was not a feature of late Georgian politics. The Tory government's patriotic, pro-British policies found favour with many businessmen and higher professionals, while the Whig party was seen as more narrowly aristocratic and anti-patriotic. Additionally, since Tory governments were in power throughout most of this period, many would-be placemen and contract-seekers would have supported them rather than the Opposition. The fact that Protestant Nonconformists were at least technically barred from election to Parliament until 1828 would also have worked against building up the Whig–radical coalition that formed one of the bases of mid-Victorian politics. The picture here is very consistent with the 'conservative' nature of the British wealth structure at that time found in other dimensions of the social analysis of these wealth-holders.

Directory

WEALTH-HOLDERS, 1809

Name **Heming, George** 1809/1
Dates Unknown: probated January 1809 but may have died 15 April 1807 at Stanmore, Middlesex (*GM*, April 1807, p. 388).
Probate £125,000 (PCC).
Occupation Goldsmith (Heming and Chawner) of New Bond Street: 1774 and 1793 directories. (Occupational categories II.11 and IV.20; venue 2.)
Address Lived Stanmore; owned the Banqueting House at Stanmore 'attributed to Chandos' in 1775.
Father Thomas Heming (stated in George Heming's will).
Mother Unknown.
Education Unknown.
Marriage To Ann née Gilroy (marriage date unknown); she died 9 June 1818, at Stanmore, leaving £120,000 (see 1818/16).
Religion Unknown, presumably Anglican.
Public None known.
Miscellaneous He owned the Banqueting House at Stanmore (*VCH Middlesex*, vol. 5, p. 66).
References Will PROB 11 online; above sources only.

Name **Chichester, Sir John, 6th Baronet** 1809/2
Dates c. 1752–30 October 1808.
Probate £100,000 (PCC).
Occupation Landowner in Devon. (In 1883, descendant owned 7,022 acres at £6,051 p.a.) (Occupational Category I.)
Address Lived in Devonshire and at Upper Grosvenor Street, Middlesex.
Father Sir John Chichester, 5th Baronet (1721–18 December 1784).
Mother Frances, daughter of Sir George Chudleigh of Haldon, Devon.
Education Unknown; Magdalen College, Oxford.
Marriage Unmarried.
Religion Anglican.
Public High Sheriff of Devonshire, 1788–9.
Miscellaneous Nothing known.
References *GM*, July 1808, p. 662; *BP.*

Name **Bull, Elizabeth** 1809/3
Dates c. 1749–20 April 1809, Northcourt House, Isle of Wight.
Probate £125,000 (PCC).
Occupation Probably widow of Richard Bull, MP; possibly Turkey merchant fortune. (If so, occupational category IV.19; venues 1 and 29?)
Address Northcourt House, Isle of Wight and Stratton Street, Westminster.
Father Unknown.
Mother Unknown.

Education Unknown.

Marriage To Richard Bull (marriage date unknown); he died 'lately' (*GM*, March 1806). Bull purchased North Shorwell (or North Court), c. 1795 from Robert Kekewich (*VCH Hampshire*, vol. 5, p. 280). In 1805, he lived at 10 Stratton Street and Northcote House. Richard Bull (c. 1725–1805) was MP for Newport, 1756–80. He was educated at Westminster and Trinity Hall, Cambridge. His father, Sir John Bull, was a wealthy Turkey merchant. There is no indication in *HP* of any other source of wealth. Richard Bull was also a 'foremost collector of prints'. It should be noted, however, that *HP*, 1754–90 gives Bull's wife as Mary, with no mention of an Elizabeth.

Religion Anglican.

Public None.

Miscellaneous Nothing known.

References *GM*, April 1809, p. 386; Judd; Venn.

1809/4 **Name** **Gardner, 1st Baron, Sir Alan Gardner, 1st Baronet**

Dates 12 April 1742, Uttoxeter, Staffordshire–31 December 1808.

Probate £125,000 (PCC).

Occupation Admiral of the Blue. (Occupational category VI.31.)

Address Lived various localities as naval officer.

Father (Lieutenant Colonel) William Gardner (1691–14 August 1762), 11th Dragoons, of Uttoxeter. (Third son.)

Mother Elizabeth (d. 1783), daughter of Valentine ffarington MD, of Preston, Lancashire

Education Unknown.

Marriage In 1769, to Susannah, daughter of Francis Gale of Liguania, Jamaica, and widow of Samuel Turner. (Seven sons, one daughter.)

Religion Anglican.

Public MP (pro-Pitt) Plymouth, 1790–6; Westminster, 1796–1806. Lord of the Admiralty, 1790–5. Created 1st Baronet 1794; 1st Baron (Irish peerage) 1800; 1st Baron (UK) 1806.

Miscellaneous Entered Royal Navy, 1755. Admiral, 1799; Major-General of Marines, 1794–death. Had a varied and controversial career and was Commander-in-Chief of the Irish Station in the early 1800s. Presumably benefited from placeman's money and prize money as well as inheritance and salary.

References *ODNB*; *BP*.

1809/5 **Name** **Sapte, Peter Anthony** (né Pierre Antoine)

Dates 1 October 1743, Leghorne (sic), Switzerland (sic)–28 October 1809, Bath.

Probate £125,000 (PCC).

Occupation Banker (Sapte, Guillemard and Brand, then C. W. Brand, of Coleman Street, City of London). Previously a merchant-banker (Peter Sapte & Co., of 7 Warnford Court, Throgmorton Street, City of London). (Occupational category IV.16; venue 1.)

Address Coleman Street, City of London, and Bath.

Father Francis Sapte (d. 4 July 1749) of Leghorn. (Second son.)
Mother Frances Desmaritz (d. 1769).
Education Unknown.
Marriage In 1787 to Mary Gamage.
Religion Presumably a Calvinist at birth; possibly later an Anglican.
Public None known.
Miscellaneous Naturalised UK, 1765 – unknown date of arrival. A 'merchant of great eminence in London' (*GM*). His brother, David Francis Sapte, was Private Secretary to Frederick the Great.
References *GM.*

Name **Monck, John** 1809/6
Dates 1734–12 November 1809, Marlborough Buildings, Bath.
Probate £125,000 (PCC).
Occupation Barrister. (Occupational category VI.29; venue 1.)
Address Formerly Lincoln's Inn then Cecil Street, Strand and Bath.
Father William Monck (b. 1692) of Cecil Street, Strand, barrister and Bencher, Reader and Treasurer of the Middle Temple.
Mother Dorothy, daughter of Rt. Hon. Thomas Bligh of Rathmore, County Meath, MP, and sister of John, 1st Earl of Darnley.
Education Westminster; Christ Church, Oxford (*BCL*, 1761); barrister Middle Temple, 1756, and Lincoln's Inn, 1758.
Marriage In 1767 to Emilia Snee (d. 1795) of London. (Five sons, one daughter.)
Religion Anglican.
Public None known.
Miscellaneous Presumably inherited legal and landed money. His son T. B. Monck of Reading, inherited £100,000 from him (*GM*). His legal career is unknown.
References *GM*; *BLG*, 'Monck of Coley Park'.

Name **Boulton, Matthew** 1809/7
Dates 3 September 1728, Snow Hill, Birmingham–18 August 1809.
Probate £150,000 (PCC).
Occupation The celebrated pioneer of steam power and partner of James Watt at Soho, Birmingham. Manufacturer, successively, of jewellery and buttons, then of steam engines at Soho, Birmingham, then coinmaker for the Mint from 1788. (Occupational category II.5; venue 8.)
Address Soho, Handsworth, Birmingham.
Father Matthew Boulton (d. 1759), hardware and toy manufacturer of Northampton and Birmingham.
Mother Christiana Peers (d. c. 1785) of Chester.
Education At the Academy of Revd Dr Hausted at Deritend, Warwickshire.
Marriage First in c. 1756 to Mary Robinson (d. c. 1760), daughter of Luke Robinson a 'wealthy mercer' of Lichfield. Second to her sister Anne (d. c. 1783). (One son, one daughter.)

Religion Anglican: buried Handsworth Church. Many in his circle had leanings towards Unitarianism.
Public None.
Miscellaneous Began as jewellery, button and luxury metal manufacturer, then famed as partner from 1769 with James Watt in pioneering steam-engine manufacturing works. From 1788, coinmaker for the Royal Mint. A founder of the famous Lunar Club and a friend of Joseph Priestley, Josiah Wedgwood, Erasmus Darwin and other intellectuals. FRS, a founder of the Royal Institution and the Society of Civil Engineers.
References *ODNB.*

1809/8 **Name** **Owen, Sir Hugh, 6th Baronet**
Dates 12 September 1782–8 August 1809.
Probate £175,000 (PCC).
Occupation Landowner, chiefly in Pembrokeshire; may have held urban interests in Pembroke. (Occupational category I.)
Address Orielton, Pembrokeshire.
Father Sir Hugh Owen, 5th Baronet (c. 1731–16 January 1786), MP, landowner, and Lord Lieutenant of Pembrokeshire.
Mother Anna (d. 11 April 1823), daughter of John Colby of Bletherston.
Education Raike's School, Neasden; Eton; Christ Church, Oxford.
Marriage Unmarried.
Religion Anglican.
Public MP (—) Pembroke Boroughs, 1809. Mayor of Pembroke, 1804; Sheriff of Pembrokeshire, 1804–5; of Anglesey, 1806–7. Lieutenant Colonel, Pembrokeshire Regiment.
Miscellaneous Succeeded to estates in Pembrokeshire, Anglesey, and (later) Tasmania, aged three. Disinherited his next of kin and left his estate to a distant cousin, Sir John Lord Owen (né Lord), later 1st Baronet.
References *BP; Complete Baronetage; GM;* Richard Rose, *Pembroke People* (2000), p. 233.

1809/9 **Name** **Littledale, Thomas**
Dates Baptised 24 October 1744–6 November 1809, Braywick Lodge, Berkshire.
Probate £200,000 (PCC).
Occupation Presumably banker/merchant in Rotterdam, then London. (Occupational category IV.17/19; venues 29 and 1.)
Address 'Of Rotterdam', then Wimpole Street and Portland Place, Middlesex, and Braywick Lodge, Berkshire.
Father James Littledale (1711–24 October 1744), 'mariner', then 'merchant' in Whitehaven, Cumberland, where he owned land and houses. (Fifth son.)
Mother Mary, daughter of Isaac Langton of The How, Ennerdale.
Education Unknown.
Marriage To (Anne Elizabeth) Susannah (d. 1809), daughter of Thomas Allen,

merchant of Rotterdam and Altona. Marriage date unknown; possibly 1772 (Family Search). (Three sons, three daughters; one daughter married Stephen Thornton, Director of the Bank of England.)
Religion Presumably Anglican.
Public None known.
Miscellaneous Presumably entered his father-in-law's mercantile/banking business in Rotterdam, then in business in London.
References *GM*, December 1809; *BP*, 1846.

Name **Liverpool, 1st Earl of, Sir Charles Jenkinson, Baronet** 1809/10
Dates 26 April 1729, Winchester–17 December 1808, at 26 Hertford Street, Mayfair.
Probate £200,000 (PCC).
Occupation Landowner and political placeman and office-holder. (Occupational categories I and VI.31; venue 2.)
Address Family estates in Oxfordshire, etc. Lived Mayfair.
Father (Colonel) Charles Jenkinson (1693– 23 June 1750), of an old Oxfordshire landed family; had estate at Burford, Oxfordshire.
Mother Aramantha, daughter of Wolfram Cornewall, RN, and relative of Speaker of the House Cornewall.
Education Charterhouse; University College, Oxford (MA); barrister, Lincoln's Inn, 1747.
Marriage First, in 1769, to Amelia (d. 1770), daughter of William Watts, Governor of Fort William, Bengal and then of Southall, Buckinghamshire. (One son.) Second, in 1782, to Catherine (d. 1827), daughter of Sir Cecil Bisshopp, 6th Baronet, and widow, Sir Charles Cope, baronet. (One son, one daughter.) Several of our wealth-holders were related to the Bisshopp family.
Religion Anglican.
Public MP (Tory) for Cockermouth, 1761–6; Appleby, 1767–72; Harwich, 1772–74; Hastings, 1774–80; Saltash, 1780–6. Under-Secretary of State, 1761; Secretary to the Treasury, 1763; Lord of the Treasury, 1767–73. In Cabinet from 1791 as President of the Board of Trade, etc. Created 1st Baron Hawkesbury, 1786; succeeded to uncle's baronetcy, 1789; created 1st Earl of Liverpool, 1796.
Miscellaneous Typical of well-placed politicians of the day, succeeded to landed estate and profited from East India money, political placeman's money, etc. His son by his first marriage, the 2nd Earl of Liverpool, was Prime Minister, 1812–27.
References *ODNB*; *BP*.

Name **Ancaster and Kesteven, 5th Duke of, Brownlow Bertie** 1809/11
Dates 1 May 1729, Swinstead–8 February 1809, Grimesthorpe.
Probate £175,000 (PCC).
Occupation Landowner. (Occupational category I.)
Address Principal seat was Grimesthorpe Castle, Lincolnshire.
Father Peregrine Bertie, 2nd Duke of Ancaster (1686–1 January 1742). (Third son.) Succeeded nephew as duke, 1779.

Mother Jane (d. 1736), daughter of Sir John Brownlow, 3rd Baronet, MP, of Great Humby, Lincolnshire.
Education Westminster School.
Marriage First, in 1772, to Harriet (d. 1763), daughter of George Norton Pitt, Governor in India, of Twickenham; second, in 1769, to Mary Anne (d. 1804), daughter of Peter Layard of Sutton Friars, Canterbury, d.s.p.
Religion Anglican.
Public MP (—) Lincolnshire, 1761–79; Lord Lieutenant of Lincolnshire.
Miscellaneous The dukedom became extinct with his death. Most of his property came to his relative, the Earl of Lindsey. The earldom of Ancaster was re-created in the late nineteenth century for a relative. In 1883, his kinswoman, Baroness Willoughby D'Eresby, owned 132,220 acres in Lincolnshire, etc., with an income of £74,006 p.a.
References *BP, CP.*

1809/12 **Name** **George, Augustin (sic; also given as Augustus) King**
Dates Unknown – probated March 1809.
Probate £100,000 (PCC).
Occupation 'Miller' (1791 Directory) of Enfield Mills, Enfield, Middlesex. (Occupational category III.15; venue 3.)
Address Unknown.
Father Unknown.
Mother Unknown.
Education Unknown.
Marriage Unknown.
Religion Unknown.
Public Nothing known.
Miscellaneous A large-scale miller, presumably of grain, at Enfield. Nothing could be traced of his career in any source. His forename was spelled 'Augustin' in the probate calendar.
References Above sources only.

1809/13 **Name** **Denne, Cornelius**
Dates c. 1736–13 April 1809. Probably identical with the Cornelius Denn (sic) listed on Family Search as baptised on 20 January 1737 at Spitalfields Christ Church, Stepney.
Probate £200,000 (PCC).
Occupation Banker at the Temple Bar (Denne & Co.) and 212 Strand, City of London. (Occupational category IV.16; venue 1.)
Address Lived Curzon Street, Mayfair.
Father Possibly John Denn (sic; Family Search).
Mother Possibly Anne (maiden name unknown) (Family Search).
Education Unknown.
Marriage Unknown.
Religion Possibly Anglican (see 'Dates' above).

Public Nothing known.
Miscellaneous 'For many years an eminent banker at the Temple Bar' (*GM*). Appears in 1771 London directory. Denne & Co. from 1774, then known as Snow, Denne, Denne & Sandby.
References *GM*, April 1809, p. 390.

Name **Cumberland, Simon** 1809/14
Dates Unknown–16 February 1809
Probate £150,000 (PCC).
Occupation 'Yarnmaker' at Bury St Edmunds (John and Simon Cumberland) (1791 directory). (Occupational category II.9? Venue 11.)
Address Lived Bury St Edmunds, Suffolk.
Father Unknown.
Mother Unknown.
Education Unknown.
Marriage Unknown.
Religion Unknown.
Public Nothing known; voted in Suffolk 1790 election.
Miscellaneous Nothing traced beyond this. In his will, mentions properties in Norwich and in the City of London.
References Directory only.

Name **Baker, Elizabeth** 1809/15
Dates Unknown–10 March 1809 Grosvenor Street, Middlesex.
Probate £150,000 (PCC).
Occupation She is described as a 'spinster' in the probate calendar and PROB 11. She was probably the daughter of John Baker, a silk weaver of the same address in Spitalfields. (Occupational category II.9; venue 2.)
Address 'Formerly of 12 Princes Street, Spitalfields, then Lower Grosvenor Street. Middlesex, and Mortlake, Surrey' (1805 directory).
Father Probably John Baker, a silk weaver of Princelet (sic) Street, Spitalfields in c. 1740–93. He was described in the 1763 London directory as a 'gold and silver brocade and flowered-silk weaver.' (See also *Survey of London*, vol. 27, p. 189).
Mother Unknown.
Education Unknown.
Marriage Unmarried.
Religion Unknown.
Public Nothing known.
Miscellaneous The date of death of John Baker could not be traced.
References *GM*, 1809, vol. I, p. 385 and above sources.

Name **Bolton, Duchess of, Katherine Powlett** (née Lowther) 1809/16
Dates c. 1726 or c. 1736 (*ODNB*)–21 March 1809, Grosvenor Square, Middlesex.
Probate £150,000 (PCC).
Occupation Land and West Indies money. (Occupational category I; venue 29.)

Address Estates in Westmorland, etc. Husband's seat was Hackwood House, Hampshire.
Father Robert Lowther (1681–September 1745), Governor of Barbados, of Maulds, Meaburn, Westmorland.
Mother Katherine (d. 1764), daughter of Sir Joseph Pennington.
Education Unknown.
Marriage In 1765, as his second wife, to (Admiral) Harry Powlett, 6th Duke of Bolton (1720–25 December 1794). (Two daughters.)
Religion Anglican.
Public None.
Miscellaneous Her brother was James, 1st Earl of Lonsdale (d. 1802), known as the 'richest commoner in England'. He had estates in Barbados, Cumberland and Westmorland. Her property passed to her grandson, William, 3rd Duke of Cleveland, of Raby Castle, Darlington. The Bolton dukedom became extinct upon her husband's death, and the existing honours passed to the Marquess of Winchester.
References *ODNB* for husband; *CP; BP.*

1809/17 **Name** **Berthon, Peter**
Dates 1739 Lisbon–8 July 1809, Leyton, Essex.
Probate £125,000 (PCC).
Occupation Merchant at Finsbury Square, City of London. (Occupational category IV.21; venue 1.)
Address Lived Lower Leyton, Essex at death.
Father Peter Berthon (1705–65), merchant in Lisbon.
Mother Jeanne Sauret.
Education Unknown.
Marriage In 1776, to Mary, daughter of John Harrison, of Charterhouse Square, Director of the Bank of England. (His second wife; no information about his first wife.)
Religion Originally Huguenot; presumably Anglican at death.
Public None known.
Miscellaneous Of an old Huguenot family that settled in Lisbon. He is noted as the first of his family to live in England. It is not clear what they dealt in, but many Lisbon merchants dealt in port and liquor.
References 1793, *Directory; BLG,* 1849; *Genealogical Magazine,* vol. 9 (1940–9), p. 500; Society of Genealogists.

1809/18 **Name** **Chauncey, Charles Snell** (né Snell)
Dates Unknown–6 July 1809.
Probate £125,000 (PCC).
Occupation Probably a West Indies merchant (William Snell & Co.) of 14 Austin Friars, City. (Occupational category IV.19?/ Venue 1.)
Address 'Formerly of Austin Friars, then Theobald's Herts' and Edmonton (*BLG*).
Father William Snell (1719–4 February 1779), 'merchant' of 14 Austin Friars, 'trading with the West Indies' (*BLG*).

Mother Martha (d. 1765), daughter of Charles Chauncey. Her brother, Charles Chauncey (1709–77), MD, FRS, is in the *ODNB*.
Education Unknown.
Marriage In 1781, to his cousin Amelia, daughter of Nathaniel Chauncey. (At least one son.)
Religion Presumably Anglican.
Public None known.
Miscellaneous Not listed in any directory as a merchant, but almost certainly connected with his father's firm, which traded with the West Indies. The father owned property in Grenada and St Vincent. Snell took the surname Chauncey possibly upon his marriage. His brother William (b. 1756) was also a merchant.
References *BLG*, 1846; Society of Genealogists.

Name **Normanton, 1st Earl of, Charles Agar; 1st Baron Somerton and Archbishop of Dublin** 1809/19
Dates 22 December 1736, Gowran Castle, County Kilkenny–14 July 1809, Marylebone.
Probate £175,000 (PCC).
Occupation Land plus Anglican clerical fortune. (Occupational categories I and VI.30; venue 26, etc.) In 1883, the Earl of Normanton owned 42,961 acres at £48,280 p.a. in Lincolnshire, Wilts, etc., and three Irish counties.
Address Family estate at Gowran Castle, County Kilkenny; lived in England at Great Cumberland Place, Middlesex.
Father Henry Agar, MP (d. 18 November 1746), landowner of Gowran Castle, County Kilkenny. (His brother was the 1st Viscount Clifden.)
Mother Anne, daughter of (Rt. Revd) Welbore Ellis, Bishop of Meath. (She married Second George Dunbar and she died in 1761.)
Education Westminster School; Christ Church, Oxford (MA; DCL).
Marriage In 1776, to Jane (d. 1826), daughter of William Benson, a merchant in Dublin, later of County Down. (Two sons; one daughter.)
Religion Anglican archbishop.
Miscellaneous 'Amassed an immense fortune' through clerical preferment and income. Chaplain to the Duke of Northumberland, Lord Lieutenant of Ireland, 1763; Dean of Kilmore, 1765; Bishop of Cloyne, 1768; Archbishop of Cashel, 1779; Archbishop of Dublin, 1801–9. Was also an influential political power broker in the Anglo-Irish Establishment. PC (Ireland) 1779; created 1st Baron Somerton (Irish), 1800; 1st Earl of Normanton, 1806. A striking example of 'Old Corruption'. He was buried in Westminster Abbey.
References *ODNB*; *CP*; *BP*.

Name **Winthrop, Benjamin** 1809/20
Dates c. 1737–7 October 1809. Probably the Benjamin Winthrop baptised on 13 January 1738 at Saint Stephen Walbrook, City of London (Family Search).
Probate £175,000 (PCC).
Occupation 'Merchant and Director of the Bank of England' (*ODNB* for son-in-

law); 'Merchant' at 16 John Street, Bedford Row (1794 directory). (Occupational category IV.21; venue 2.)

Address Lived Doughty Street, Bloomsbury, Middlesex.

Father Unknown. Possibly Stephen Winthrop (Family Search).

Mother Unknown. Possibly Frances née Davy, who married Stephen Winthrop on 17 July 1733 at St Mary Arches, Exeter, Devon (Family Search).

Education Unknown.

Marriage Wife's name and marriage date unknown. She was probably Elizabeth Neale, who married a Benjamin Winthrop on 12 January 1765 at St Mildred's Church, Bread Street, City of London (Family Search). Winthrop's daughter Elizabeth married William Mackworth Praed (1756–1835) of the Audit Office; their son was William Mackworth Praed (1802–39), the poet and literary figure, in the *ODNB.*

Religion Presumably Anglican. See 'Dates' above.

Public None known.

Miscellaneous A merchant, with his offices in Bloomsbury. Was a governor of the Bank of England, 1804–6, but was almost certainly not a banker.

References Directories and online source as above only. Son-in-law and grandson in *ODNB.*

1809/21 **Name** **Hill, Edmund**

Dates Unknown–9 November 1809.

Probate £350,000 (PCC).

Occupation Gunpowder manufacturer at Whitton (near Hounslow), Middlesex, with an office at Tower Hill. (Occupational category II.6; venue 3.)

Address Isleworth then Whitton, Middlesex.

Father Unknown.

Mother Unknown.

Education Unknown.

Marriage Unknown.

Religion Unknown, probably Anglican.

Public None known.

Miscellaneous A leading gunpowder manufacturer at Whitton, Middlesex, with an office at 1 Savage Gardens, Tower Hill (1794 directory). Hill is said to have begun as a journeyman breeches manufacturer and was then a master tailor at Brentford. He gained the monopoly on supplying gunpowder to the Turkish government and also dealt in Turkish goods as a merchant. He was rumoured to be worth £800,000. Hill was blind for many years and died without direct heirs – he is said to have left much of his property to his cousin, a clergyman.

References *GM,* November 1809, p. 1085; *Times,* 13 November 1809, p. 3, col. d; *VCH Middlesex,* vol. 3, pp. 42–3.

1809/22 **Name** **Bensley, Sir William, 1st Baronet**

Dates c. 1737–17 December 1809.

Probate £100,000 (PCC).
Occupation East India merchant and Director of the East India Company. (Occupational category IV.19; venue 29.)
Address Lived in Marylebone. Buried in Bletchingley, Surrey.
Father Unknown.
Mother Unknown.
Education Unknown.
Marriage Mary, daughter of Vincent Briscoe of London; marriage date unknown.
Religion Anglican: buried (with memorial monument) in St Mary's Church, Bletchingley, Surrey.
Public Created baronet 1801.
Miscellaneous Bensley was 'formerly in the Navy' but left it and went to the East Indies. He returned to London, and became a director of the East India Company. His career is very obscure, and he is not listed in any baronetage or other directory seen by me. He evidently left no heirs to the title. Bensley did not serve in Parliament, and why he received a baronetcy is unclear. He was, perhaps, related to the naval lieutenants John Bensely or Bensley (d. 1769) and/or William Bensely or Bensley (d. 1796).
References *GM.*

Name **Puget, John (or John David)** 1809/23
Dates August 1760–3 June 1805 (sic; probated in 1809).
Probate £175,000 (PCC).
Occupation Banker (Puget and Bambridge) at the Royal College of Physicians, Warwick Lane; later a director of the Bank of England. (Occupational category IV.16; venue 2.)
Address Lived at John Street, Bedford Row, and then at Russell Square, Middlesex.
Father John Philip Puget (1729–12 July 1768), merchant and banker (Puget & Sons), also gold refiner; lived Tonbridge, Kent.
Mother Esther (d. 1814), daughter of James Dunn, a 'prominent Dublin merchant'.
Education Unknown.
Marriage In 1786, to Catherine, daughter of Dr James Hawkins, Bishop of Raphoe. (One son, three daughters.)
Religion The family were originally Huguenots; the father was baptised Anglican, and the family were Anglicans.
Public None known.
Miscellaneous Puget was a banker whose offices were at the College of Physicians, Warwick Lane (1794–5 directories). It is not known what connection the firm had with the College of Physicians. He was later a director of the Bank of England and the 'Principal Agent for money transactions between the Government and Ireland'. Puget's brother (Captain) Peter Puget (1765–1822) was a prominent naval officer and explorer; the Puget Sound on the Canadian west

coast is named in his honour. It is not known why John Puget's estate was recorded in the probate records four years after he died.

References *GM,* June 1805, vol. I, pp. 75, 588; Percy G. Dawson, *The Puget Family in England* (1976).

1809/24 **Name** **Garratt, Francis**

Dates 11 October 1741–26 December 1808, Old Swan Stairs near Thring Street, City of London.

Probate £400,000 (PCC).

Occupation Tea merchant in the City of London. (Occupational category IV.21 and 20? Venue 1.)

Address Lived at Blackheath, and then Clapham. His offices were at Old Swan Stairs near Thring Street, City of London.

Father Unknown. 'Descended from a family settled in Derbyshire for many generations' (*GM*).

Mother Unknown.

Education Unknown.

Marriage Mary, daughter of John Mason of Lincoln. (Four sons, three daughters.) The wedding was apparently at St Margaret Lothbury, City of London, on 28 May 1781 (Family Search). Garratt's son John (1786–1859) was Lord Mayor of London and left £200,000 (1859/15).

Religion Almost certainly Anglican.

Public Member for the Bridge Ward on the City Common Council.

Miscellaneous An 'eminent tea dealer' in the City of London (*GM*). A 'wholesale tea dealer' at 7 Old Swan, London Bridge (1794 directory).

References *GM.*

1809/25 **Name** **Sprot, Mark**

Dates Unknown–17 December 1808.

Probate £250,000 (PCC).

Occupation Probably stockbroker in London; also landowner in Scotland. (Occupational category IV.23; venue 1.)

Address Lived at 4 King's Road, Gray's Inn and Bedford Row, Middlesex. Also owned a house at Garnick near Glasgow and land in Scotland.

Father Probably John Sprot (b. 1703) of Edinburgh.

Mother Probably Janet, daughter of Alexander Esplin.

Education Unknown.

Marriage Unknown. May be related to the family of Sprot of Riddell, listed in *BLG,* 1914, which records a Mark Sprot (possibly our man's uncle) as 'one of the founders of the London Stock Exchange'.

Religion Unknown; presumably Church of Scotland.

Public None known.

Miscellaneous Probably a stockbroker in the City. He also bought land in Scotland for £100,000. In his will he left money to two Goldsmids (bullion brokers) to buy rings. He also mentions his brothers Alexander and William and his

nephew John of Edinburgh. He could not be readily identified from London directories.

References *GM*, 1808, vol. II, p. 1134.

Name James, Robert 1809/26

Dates Unknown–30 July 1808.

Probate £500,000 (PCC).

Occupation 'Brandy merchant' at Mark Lane, etc., in the City of London. (Occupational Venue IV.20? Venue 1.)

Address Lived at (29) St Mary's Hill parish, in the City of London – presumably also his business address.

Father Unknown.

Mother Unknown.

Education Unknown.

Marriage Unknown.

Religion Unknown.

Public None known.

Miscellaneous A 'merchant' at 6 Little Tower Street and 29 St Mary Hill (1791 directory) and of Mark Lane in *GM*. Described as a 'brandy merchant' in his will. Little is known of his career or how he became so wealthy. *GM* describes him as 'a well-known eccentric character, especially on Custom House quays'.

References *GM*, 1808, vol. II, p. 658.

WEALTH-HOLDERS, 1810

1810/1 **Name** **Collingwood, 1st Baron, Cuthbert Collingwood**

Dates 26 September 1748, The Side, Newcastle upon Tyne–7 March 1810, Minorca.

Probate £125,000 (PCC).

Occupation Vice-Admiral of the Red. (Occupational category VI.31.)

Address Had two small estates in Northumberland but lived at sea most of his life.

Father Cuthbert Collingwood (1712–75), an 'impoverished' merchant of Newcastle upon Tyne. (First son.)

Mother Milcha (sic), daughter of Reginald Dobson of Darwess, Westmorland.

Education Newcastle Grammar School to age eleven, then entered Royal Navy.

Marriage In 1791, to Patience, daughter of (Alderman) Erasmus Blackett; she was 'apparently the granddaughter of Admiral Roddam'. (Two daughters.)

Religion Anglican; buried St Paul's Cathedral.

Public Created 1st Baron Collingwood in 1805 after Trafalgar. Curiously for a very senior admiral, he never received a knighthood.

Miscellaneous Nelson's second-in-command at Trafalgar. He sent back to England the celebrated dispatches reporting on the victory at Trafalgar and Nelson's death. A distinguished naval officer, later Commander-in-Chief, Mediterranean, 1805–death. Colingwood received a pension of £2,000 per year for life (with lesser sums to his widow and daughter after his death) for his part at Trafalgar.

References *ODNB*, etc.

1810/2 **Name** **Cavendish, (Hon.) Henry**

Dates 10 October 1731, Nice–10 March 1810, Clapham.

Probate 'Upper Value' (i.e. above £1 million) (PCC). Other reports of his holdings at death place his wealth at death at about £900,000.

Occupation Landed wealth. (Occupational category I.) The celebrated scientist.

Address Lived Great Marlborough Street, St James's; Clapham Common; 34 Church Row, Hampstead. Also had landed estates but lived almost entirely in London.

Father Eldest son of Lord Charles Cavendish (c. 1693–1783), Whig MP, son of William, 2nd Duke of Devonshire.

Mother Lady Anne, daughter of Henry, 1st Duke of Kent.

Education 'Pupil of Revd Dr Newcombe of Hackney Seminary'; Peterhouse, Cambridge.

Marriage Unmarried.

Religion Anglican.

Public None known.

Miscellaneous The celebrated scientist who discovered hydrogen and also many of the laws of electricity, many decades before later scientists identified them again. Led a solitary life; afraid of women and eschewed almost all human contact. Presumably became immensely wealthy by reinvesting his landed income and spending practically nothing.

References *ODNB*, etc.

Name **Morgan, James** 1810/3

Dates Unknown; estate probated on 25 September 1810.

Probate £300,000 (PCC).

Occupation Unknown; in his will mentions his son William of New London, New York. This would suggest that he was possibly a merchant in the American trade.

Address Lived Kensington Gore and then Bath.

Father Unknown.

Mother Unknown.

Education Unknown.

Marriage Unknown, but had sons William, a deceased son James, another son, Thomas, and three daughters, all unmarried.

Religion Unknown.

Public None known.

Miscellaneous Has proved difficult to trace. A James Morgan 'broker' is listed in the 1805 London directory at 13 Castle Street, Long Acre. There was also an 'attorney' of that name at Tottenham Court Road. A James Morgan, b. c. 1766, was at Eton from 1777 to 1780.

References Will only; not clearly listed in any source.

Name **Gillon, John** 1810/4

Dates c. 1750–14 December 1809.

Probate £125,000 ('within province') (PCC).

Occupation Planter in the West Indies. (Occupational category I; venue 29.)

Address 'Formerly of Dominica, West Indies, then of [60] Wellbeck Street, Marylebone' (will). Lived (1795) at the Adelphi; also owned an estate at Wallhouse, Linlithgowshire.

Father Alexander Gillon of Wallhouse (presumably Linlithgowshire).

Mother Eleanora Montgomery.

Education Unknown.

Marriage Catherina, daughter of Sir Andrew Agnew, Baronet, of Lochnaw; marriage date unknown.

Religion Presumably Church of Scotland.

Public None known.

Miscellaneous 'Went in early life to the West Indies where he acquired a considerable fortune.' (*GM*). Owned Wallhouse Plantation, Dominica. In 1795 lived in the Adelphi, London, where he signed a Merchant's Declaration. He may have been the head of John Gillon & Co. of 28 Wilson's Street, Finsbury Square (1808 directory).

References *GM*, 1810, vol. I, p. 89; *Caribbeana*, vol.1, p. 220.

1810/5 **Name** **Newman, Thomas**
Dates Unknown; probated 11 January 1810.
Probate £150,000 (PCC).
Occupation Unknown. A Thomas Newman, 'grocer' of 17 Shoreditch, is listed in the 1780 directory. He is apparently listed in the 1795 'Declaration of Merchants', but no occupation is listed. The fact that he lived in Spitalfields might indicate a connection with the silk trade.
Address Lived Church Street, Christ Church, Spitalfields.
Father Unknown.
Mother Unknown.
Education Unknown.
Marriage Unknown.
Religion Unknown.
Public None known.
Miscellaneous In his will, he left a legacy to his sister Elizabeth, married to a surgeon apothecary of Church Street, Christ Church, Middlesex. Cardinal John Henry Newman's father was a banker named John; there is no obvious connection.
References Will only.

1810/6 **Name** **Devaynes, William**
Dates c. 1730–29 November 1809.
Probate £175,000 (PCC).
Occupation Primarily banker (Crofts, Roberts, Devaynes & Dawes, of Pall Mall, Middlesex). Also had numerous other interests: was a 'big' government army contractor for victualling during the American Revolutionary War and was a director of the East India Company, 1770–85, and a director of the Globe Insurance Company from 1770. (Occupational category IV.16, etc.; venue 2.)
Address Lived Dover Street and Pall Mall; also owned Atherstone Manor, Barnstaple, Devon.
Father John Devaynes, 'peruke maker' of 9 St Martin-in-the-Fields.
Mother Mary, daughter of William Barker, banker and City Remembrancer.
Education Unknown.
Marriage First, to Jane Wintle, marriage date unknown. (One son, one daughter.) Second, in 1806, to Mary, daughter of William Wileman. Also had a mulatto son and daughter: he lived in Africa in early life.
Religion Presumably Anglican. His father's family were originally Huguenots.
Public MP (Tory) Barnstaple, 1774–80, 1784–96, 1802–6; Winchelsea, 1796–1802.
Miscellaneous Was also a Liverpool commissioner of the Africa Company, 1770–8, and a member of the London Dock Company, 1802–death. Held £100,000 in government stock. He was said to have inherited £50,000 from his brother John, the King's Apothecary, in 1801.
References *GM*, 1809, vol. II, p. 1181; *HP.*

1810/7 **Name** **Powell, David**
Dates 13 December 1725–31 January 1810. (Some sources say 30 March 1810.)

Probate £300,000 (PCC).
Occupation 'Merchant' (David Powell & Sons, 3 Little St Helens, City, 1793, 1802 directories). (Occupational category IV.21; venue 1.)
Address Lived at Little St Helens Place, and also at Homerton, Hackney, and at Hornton Kirby, Kent.
Father David Powell (1695–10 February 1784), merchant of Old Broad Street, London and of Wattisfield, Suffolk.
Mother Susannah (d. 1762), daughter of Edward Thistlethwayte of Winterslow, Wiltshire.
Education Unknown.
Marriage In 1761 to Laetitia (d. 1801), daughter of John Clark of St Botolph's, Bishopsgate. (Seven sons, seven daughters.)
Religion Anglican.
Public None known.
Miscellaneous A wealthy City merchant and the ancestor or relative of many famous Powells, including Baden Powell, the founder of the Boy Scouts. Treasurer of St Luke's Hospital 1794.
References *BP;* Richard Morris, *The Powells in Essex and Their London Ancestors* (2002).

Name **Filmer, (Revd) Sir Edmund, 6th Baronet** 1810/8
Dates Baptised 7 May 1727–27 June 1810, East Sutton.
Probate £100,000 (PCC).
Occupation Landowner. (Occupational category I.) In 1883, Sir Edmund Filmer, Baronet, owned 6,608 acres worth £9,395 p.a. in Kent.
Address East Sutton Park, Staplehurst, Kent.
Father Sir Edward Filmer, 3rd Baronet (1683–10 February 1755), landowner. The father had twenty children, and Sir Edmund succeeded two brothers, the second of whom died in 1805.
Mother Mary (d. 1761), daughter of John Wallis of Soundness, Oxfordshire. (Her grandfather was Savilian Professor at Oxford.)
Education Secondary school unknown; Corpus Christi College, Oxford.
Marriage In 1755, to Annabella (d. 1798), daughter of Sir John Honeyman, 3rd Baronet.
Religion Anglican.
Public None known.
Miscellaneous A wealthy landowner in Kent.
References *BP.*

Name **Walker, John** 1810/9
Dates c. 1740–2 September 1810, at Eydon Lodge, Northamptonshire.
Probate £150,000 (PCC).
Occupation 'Sugar refiner' at Hoxton and 21 Brick Lane, Spitalfields (will). (Occupational category III.15; venue 2.)
Address Formerly Bethnal Green, then Well Street, Hackney.

Father Unknown.
Mother Unknown.
Education Unknown.
Marriage Unknown – had a son, William, and daughters Ann and Hester.
Religion Unknown.
Public None known.
Miscellaneous A wealthy sugar refiner (presumably for breweries as well as a sweetener). Owned houses in Buckinghamshire, according to his will.
References Will only.

1810/10 **Name** **Baring, Sir Francis, 1st Baronet**
Dates 18 April 1740, Larkbear, Exeter–12 September 1810, Lee, Kent.
Probate £250,000 'within province' (PCC). (The *ODNB* states that he left £606,000 plus £70,000 in 'company holdings'. This includes the value of his land.)
Occupation Merchant banker in the City of London. (Occupational category IV.17; venue 1.)
Address Lived at Stratton Park, Hampshire, and at Lee, Kent.
Father John Baring (1697, Bremen–3 November 1748), woollen cloth merchant in Essex – naturalised 1723. (Third son.)
Mother Elizabeth (d. 1766), daughter of John Vowler, a 'prosperous grocer' of Exeter.
Education Educated 'in Exeter'; 'by Mr. Fargue of Hoxton'; and 'by Mr. Fuller of Lothbury'.
Marriage In 1767, to Harriet (d. 1804), daughter of William Herring of Croydon. (Five sons.) She was cousin of the Archbishop of Canterbury.
Religion Father was originally a German Lutheran, later an Anglican; the family were Anglicans.
Public MP (Whig) Grampound, 1784–90; Chipping Wycombe, 1794–6, 1802–6; Calne, 1796–1802. Created 1st Baronet, 1793.
Miscellaneous The founder, in 1762, of the celebrated merchant bank; Baring Brothers was later known as the 'sixth great power'. He was also a director of the East India Company, 1779–death, and its Chairman, 1792–3, and a director of the Royal Exchange Insurance Company, 1768–80. His descendants became a significant part of the Whig aristocracy and included the earls of Northbrook and of Cromer. Baring also began about 1790 to buy significant amounts of land in Hampshire and Kent. In 1883, his descendants owned about 19,000 acres worth c. £19,000 p.a. He was probably the most important merchant banker in England at his death.
References *ODNB*; *BP*; Philip Zeigler, *The Sixth Great Power: Baring Brothers 1762–1929* (1988).

1810/11 **Name** **Teissier, Charles**
Dates 1735, Bassishaw (sic), London–19 November 1810, Brighton.
Probate £125,000 (PCC).

Occupation 'Merchant' of 13 Austin Friars, City of London (1803 directory); also C. Loubier Teissier & Co., merchants, of same address. His brothers Stephen & Lewis Teissier, merchants, of 21 Old Broad Street, are listed in the 1755 and 1777 directories. (Occupational category IV.21? Venue 1.)
Address Lived at Austin Friars, then Lower Grosvenor Street, Middlesex.
Father Jacques de Teissier (1697, Geneva–1765, London). (Sixth son.)
Mother Charlotte Loubiens (1705, Geneva–1776, London).
Education Unknown.
Marriage Unknown.
Religion The parents were Huguenots; they were buried in the Huguenot chapel in London.
Public None known.
Miscellaneous Probably related to Stephen Teissier (1816/13).
References *GM*, 1809, vol. II, p. 591; Roots Web.

Name **Hawkes, Thomas** 1810/12
Dates c. 1745–10 December 1809, Piccadilly.
Probate £125,000 (PCC).
Occupation 'Army accoutrement maker' (will); 'Helmet, hat and cap maker to the King', of 17 Picadilly (Hawkes, Mosley & Co.) (1805 directory). (Occupational category II.11/IV.20; venue 2.)
Address His only address was 24 Piccadilly. His will states that he owned a leasehold in St Martin's-in-the-Field and an estate at Stourbridge.
Father Unknown.
Mother Unknown.
Education Unknown.
Marriage His wife, name unknown, predeceased him, according to his will.
Religion Anglican: owned an advowson, possibly at St Mary's, Birmingham, according to his will.
Public None known.
Miscellaneous An interesting example of a very lucrative luxury/niche market, not unknown at the time. This Thomas Hawkes may have been the man of that name who founded a dispensary for the poor at Christ Church, Birmingham with Joseph Moore (1766–1851). *ODNB* for Moore.
References *GM*, 1809, vol. II, p. 1182.

Name **Everett, Thomas** 1810/13
Dates 1739 or 1740–8 February 1810 at 19 Bedford Square.
Probate £100,000 (PCC).
Occupation 'Blackwell Hall factor' (a cloth wholesaler, named for Blackwell Hall at Basinghall Street, where cloth dealers traded) at Lawrence Lane, City of London (will), then a banker: co-founder of Newnham, Everett, Drummond, Tibbits & Tanner at 65 Lombard Street, and then Everett & Co., 9 Mansion House, City. (Occupational category IV.21 and IV.16; venue 1.)
Address 13 Bedford Square, Middlesex and Biddesden House near Andover,

Hampshire Also had an estate in Wiltshire. In 1883, his descendant owned 2,448 acres worth £3,279 p.a.

Father William Everett (d. 1792), a corn merchant of Heytesbury, Wiltshire. (First son.)

Mother Alice, daughter of Thomas Gale of Crawlbush near Andover.

Education Unknown.

Marriage In 1776, to Martha Dockson. (Two sons, three daughters.)

Religion Anglican. Buried in the Foundling Hospital Chapel, Bloomsbury.

Public MP (Tory) Ludgershall, 1796–1810.

Miscellaneous A merchant turned banker and MP.

References *GM,* 1810, vol. I, p. 186; *HP;* Ian R. Christie, *British 'Non-Elite' MP s, 1715–1820* (1995).

1810/14 **Name** **Hyde, John**

Dates Unknown; probated June 1810.

Probate £150,000 (PCC).

Occupation 'Cotton merchant' (John Hyde & Co., 3 Lothbury Street, City, 1802 directory; and at 35 Fenchurch Street, 1805 directory). (Occupational category IV.21; venue 1.)

Address The only address on his will is St Mary Pulteney, City of London.

Father Unknown.

Mother Unknown.

Education Unknown.

Marriage Unknown. His will does not mention a wife or children.

Religion Unknown.

Public None known.

Miscellaneous Little known about him. He may have had a Manchester connection, per an illegible portion of his will.

References None apart from the will.

1810/15 **Name** **Crawshay, Richard**

Dates September 1739, Normanton near Leeds–27 June 1810.

Probate 'Upper Value' (i.e. above £1 million). The *ODNB* states that his probate valuation was £1.5 million.

Occupation Ironmaster at Cyfarthfa, Glamorganshire; originally an iron merchant in the City of London. (Occupational category II.3; venue 19.)

Address Lived at Cyfarthfa Castle, near Merthyr Tydfil.

Father William Crawshay (1713–66), a farmer of Normanton. (First son.)

Mother Elizabeth Nicholson (d. 1774).

Education Unknown.

Marriage In 1763, to Mary (d. 1810), daughter of Ebenezer Bourne, 'stone grate maker' of St James's. (One son and probably one daughter.) Their son was William Crawshay, 1764–1834 [1834/28]). Richard Crawshay worked for Bourne and married 'the boss's daughter'.

Religion A 'devout' Anglican; endowed Sunday schools; is buried in Llandaff Cathedral.

Public None known.

Miscellaneous The great ironmaster and pioneer of the South Wales iron industry – 'Crawshay of Cyfarthfa'. Originally an iron merchant in the City and partner with James Bailey before founding his own mercantile business of Richard Crawshay & Co., 3 Cranes Stairs, Thames Street and other addresses. An ironmaster after about 1777 – originally a partner of Anthony Bacon. One of the earliest industrial millionaires; subsequently had many wealthy relatives. Was also one of the chief shareholders in the Glamorganshire Canal, which was very lucrative.

References *ODNB;* John P. Addis, *The Crawshay Dynasty* (1957); M. S. Taylor, *Crawshays of Cyfarthfa Castle* (1967).

Name **Jenner, Robert** 1810/16

Dates 7 April 1743–2 December 1810.

Probate £125,000 (PCC).

Occupation 'Deputy-Registrar of the High Court of Admiralty' (will), of Doctor's Commons in the City of London. (Occupational category VI.31; venue 1.)

Address Lived at Montagu Street, Middlesex and at Chislehurst, Kent.

Father Given in Foster, *Alum. Oxon.*, as Dr Robert Jenner, Doctor of Laws from Oxford, late of Doctor's Commons, died 1767; given in *BLG*, 1937 as Ven. Charles Jenner, Prebendary of Lincoln, DD (1707–2 February 1770).

Mother Mary (d. 1763), daughter of John Sawyer of Heywood, Berkshire.

Education Secondary schooling unknown; Merton College and Christ Church, Oxford (BA); Lincoln's Inn (entered 1770).

Marriage First, marriage date unknown, to Anne Belasis; second, in 1773, to Ann (d. 1823), daughter of Peter Birt of Armin, Yorkshire and Wenvoe Castle, Cardiff.

Religion Anglican.

Public None known.

Miscellaneous A London court official who presumably benefited from both his salary and the perquisites of his office. In 1883, Robert Francis Lascelles Jenner of Wenvoe Castle, Cardiff (b. 1826) owned 5,381 acres in Glamorganshire worth £5,200 p.a.

References *BLG*, 1937 and 1972, 'Jenner Fust of Hill Court'.

WEALTH-HOLDERS, 1811

1811/1 **Name** **Brown, Thomas**

Dates Unknown. Died 'at sea', presumably in 1810 or 1811; probated April 1811.

Probate £100,000 (PCC).

Occupation 'Chief Secretary to the Government in Bengal' (probate calendar). (Occupational category VI.31; venue 29.) He is described in the probate calendars as 'Senior merchant in the Civil Service of the United Company of Merchants Trading to the East Indies on their establishment at Bengal and at present Chief Secretary'.

Address Unknown, apart from Bengal.

Father Unknown.

Mother Unknown.

Education Unknown.

Marriage Unknown.

Religion Unknown.

Public None known.

Miscellaneous Virtually nothing could be traced of him. He may well be the Thomas Brown listed in the 1792 Bengal calendar as a 'senior merchant'. A Thomas Brown, Commercial Resident at Cossimbazar, was appointed in 1778.

References Will and above sources only.

1811/2 **Name** **Ellice, Alexander**

Dates Unknown–29 September 1805 (sic) in Bath. The reason for the long delay in probate is unknown, but presumably relates to his extensive North American holdings.

Probate £175,000 (PCC).

Occupation 'America and West Indies merchant' formerly of Schenectady, New York and then of Mark Lane, City of London. (Occupational category IV.19; venue 1, etc.)

Address Lived in America then in Mark Lane, City, and then of Bath.

Father William Ellice (d. 19 August 1756), who 'owned the estate of Knockleith' in Aberdeenshire.

Mother Unknown, but possibly Mary Simpson of Gartley.

Education Secondary schooling unknown; an advocate of the Scottish Bar.

Marriage Probably to Anne Russell; marriage date unknown. (Six sons, three daughters.) One son was Rt. Hon. Edward Ellice (1783–1863), cabinet minister and wealth-holder.

Religion Originally Church of Scotland, then Anglican; owned an advowson.

Public None known.

Miscellaneous Originally a merchant in what is now upstate New York, chiefly in the Canadian fur trade (Phyn, Ellice & Co.). Then a merchant in the City dealing in the North American trade. In 1883, 'Mrs. Ellice' of Glenquoich, Invernessshire owned 99,559 acres worth £6,771 p.a.

References *ODNB* for son; Robert Fleming, 'Phyn, Ellice & Co.' in *Contributions to Canadian Economic History*, vol. IV; J. C. Clarke, 'The Fortunes of the Ellice Family from Business to Politics, 1760–1860', Oxford D.Phil. thesis, 1974.

Name **Marwood, James Thomas Benedictus** 1811/3
Dates 1746–20 February 1811, Avishayes, Somerset.
Probate £200,000 (PCC).
Occupation Landowner. In 1883, his descendant Sir Edward Marwood-Elton, Baronet, owned 4,145 acres worth £4,918 p.a. in Devon and Somerset. (Occupational category I.)
Address Avishayes, near Chard, Somerset.
Father James Marwood (1702–3 April 1767), landowner of Avishayes. (First son.)
Mother Sarah, daughter of James Sealey.
Education Unknown.
Marriage Unmarried; his property came to his sister Frances.
Religion Anglican.
Public None known.
Miscellaneous 'One of the richest commoners in the west of England, having left property estimated to upwards of half a million pounds' (*GM*, obituary). 'An ancient family settled since Henry III's time.'
References *BLG*; *GM*, March 1811, p. 297.

Name **King, Richard** 1811/4
Dates Unknown; probated June 1811.
Probate £100,000 (PCC).
Occupation Unknown. Lived at Fowelscombe, Devonshire – near Modbury, 12 miles from Plymouth.
Address Of Fowelscombe, Devon.
Father Unknown.
Mother Unknown.
Education Unknown.
Marriage To Sarah, surname unknown; marriage date unknown. According to his will, he had nephews and nieces, including Thomas Amphlett Williams, and a brother, Robert King.
Religion Probably Anglican; the baptism of his infant great-niece Elizabeth Williams took place at Holne, Devon in 1807.
Public None known.
Miscellaneous Nothing more could be traced about him. His lengthy will of twenty-two pages provides no clue as to the source of his wealth. A Revd Richard King (d. 3 October 1810) 'divine', has an entry in the *ODNB*, but he lived in Shropshire and Cambridgeshire and had no connection with Devon. It is conceivable that there was a connection to the family of Admiral Sir Richard King, 1st Baronet (1730–1806), although he was born in Hampshire.
References Will (PROB 11 online); above sources only.

1811/5 **Name** **Holland, Sir Nathaniel, 1st Baronet** (né Dance)

Dates 18 May 1735, Chiswell Street, City of London–15 October 1811, Rollestone, Wiltshire.

Probate £250,000 (PCC).

Occupation A fashionable portrait painter and RA; inherited from his father, Clerk of the Works and Architect to the City of London; landed wealth inherited from his wife. (Occupational category VI.30, etc.; venue 2?)

Address Lived in London but had country seats at Cranbury Park, Hampshire and Rollestone near Salisbury, Wiltshire. In London, his studio was at 18 Tavistock Row, Covent Garden.

Father George Dance (c. 1694–11 February 1768), Clerk of the Works to the City of London, in *ODNB*. (Third son.)

Mother Elizabeth Gould (d. 1762) of Hackney.

Education Merchant Taylor's School; studied art in Rome.

Marriage In 1783, to Harriet, daughter of Sir Cecil Bishopp, 6th Baronet, and widow of Thomas Dumer of Cranbury Park and of Thomas Chamberlayne. His wife, sister-in-law of Sir Hugh Owen (1809/8), is said to have had a private income from land of £18,000 p.a. He died without issue.

Religion Anglican.

Public MP (Whig) for East Grinstead, 1790–1802 and 1807–11; Great Bedwin, 1802–6. Created baronet, 1800.

Miscellaneous A unique career as a fashionable portrait painter and member of the Royal Academy but also a politician and a wealthy man who inherited from several sources. In 1800, he took the name Holland after his wife's cousin Charlotte Holland. His wife Harriet was the sister of the second wife of Sir Charles Jenkinson, 1st Earl of Liverpool (see 1809/10).

References *ODNB*.

1811/6 **Name** **Hill, Jeremiah**

Dates c. 1820–23 July 1810, Clifton, Bristol.

Probate £125,000 (PCC).

Occupation Merchant in Bristol: Master of the Bristol Merchant Venturers' Company, 1785–6. (Occupational category IV.19? Venue 12.)

Address Lived at Clifton, Bristol – apparently had landed property in Gloucestershire. (Occupational category IV.19; venue 12.)

Father Unknown.

Mother Unknown.

Education Unknown.

Marriage Unknown.

Religion Presumably Anglican.

Public None known.

Miscellaneous Nothing could be traced of his career. In 1817, his property was sold to Sir C. Bethell Codrington, Baronet, for £45,000. In 1883, Codrington, Baronet, owned 4,218 acres in Gloucestershire worth £6,101 p.a.

References Probate calendar only.

Name **Alderson, Christopher** 1811/7
Dates Unknown–23 December 1810.
Probate £100,000 (PCC).
Occupation 'Mercer' at 6 Bridge Street West (presumably in the City of London; possibly Southwark). (1793 and 1795 directories.) (Occupational category IV.20; venue 1 or 2.)
Address Lived at Homerton, St John Hackney.
Father Unknown.
Mother Unknown.
Education Unknown.
Marriage Unknown. A Christopher Alderson married a Jane Wharton on 17 March 1772 at St Nicholas's Church, Rochester, Kent, and a Christopher Alderson, son of Jane and Christopher Alderson, was baptised on 27 January 1777 at St Martin-in-the-Fields, Westminster. A Christopher Alderson married an Elizabeth Hambelton on 12 July 1785 at St Anne's Church, Soho (Family Search).
Religion Unknown.
Public None known.
Miscellaneous Had brief obituary in *GM*, which noted that he was generous to the poor.
References *GM*, 1810, vol. II, p. 666.

Name **Stevens, (Revd) Thomas, DD** 1811/8
Dates c. 1749–13 June 1809 at Panfield Rectory, near Braintree, Essex.
Probate £120,000 (PCC).
Occupation Rector of Panfield and Vicar of Helions, Bumpstead, but how he accumulated his fortune is unknown.
Address Lived at Panfield Rectory at death.
Father Samuel Stevens of Quarndon near Derby.
Mother Unknown.
Education Wakefield School and Trinity College, Cambridge (MA, DD and Fellow); also Queen's College, Oxford (BD, 1772 and DD).
Marriage Unknown.
Religion Anglican clergyman.
Public None known.
Miscellaneous Was Whitehall Preacher at University, then rector at Panfield. How he accumulated £120,000 is unknown. His father's occupation is unknown.
References *GM*, 1809, vol. II, p. 679.

Name **Queensberry, 4th Duke of, Sir William Douglas** 1811/9
Dates 16 December 1725, Queensberry Lodging, Peeblesshire–23 December 1810 at 138 Piccadilly.
Probate 'Upper Value' (i.e. above £1 million) estimated in the *ODNB* at £900,000–£1.2 million.
Occupation Landowner. (Occupational category I.) Known as 'Old Q'.

Address Lived at Park Lane, Piccadilly (138 Piccadilly); Richmond; and at Drumlaurig, Peeblesshire.

Father William Douglas, 2nd Earl of March (1694–7 March 1731). (Only son.) Succeeded his first cousin as Duke of Queensberry, 1778.

Mother Lady Anne (d. 1748), daughter of John, Earl of Selkirk and Countess of Ruglen in her own right. (She married, second, Anthony Sawyer.)

Education Winchester.

Marriage Unmarried: had innumerable mistresses. His titles passed to the Earl of Wemyss and to the Duke of Buccleuch with the residue of his personalty coming to his illegitimate daughter Lady Yarmouth.

Religion Church of Scotland and (?) Anglican.

Public Representative peer for Scotland, 1761–88 (Tory); KT, 1763; Vice-Admiral for Scotland, 1766–76; First Lord of the Police, 1776–82; Lord Lieutenant of Peeblesshire from 1794. Created Baron Douglas of Amesbury (English peerage), 1786.

Miscellaneous The notorious rake 'Old Q', who 'dedicated himself to the pursuit of pleasure' throughout his life. One of the richest landowners in the country. Lived to be eighty-five despite dissipations. Also a patron of the arts, especially opera.

References *ODNB*. H. Blyth, *Old Q* (1967) and many other studies.

1811/10 **Name** **Cardigan, 5th Earl of, James Brudenell**

Dates 20 April 1725, London–24 February 1811, Grosvenor Square, Westminster.

Probate £175,000 (PCC).

Occupation Landowner. (Occupational category I.) In 1883, his heir the Marquess of Ailesbury owned 55,051 acres worth £59,716 p.a. At that time, the Countess of Cardigan (in her own right) owned 15,724 acres worth £35,357 p.a.

Address Main seat was at Hambleden, Buckinghamshire. Owned land in several counties.

Father George Brudenell, 3rd Earl of Cardigan (d. 5 July 1732). (Second son; succeeded brother 1790).

Mother Elizabeth (d. 1745), daughter of Thomas, 3rd Earl of Elgin.

Education Winchester and Oriel College, Oxford.

Marriage First, in 1760, to Anne (d.s.p., 1786), daughter of George Legge, Viscount Lewisham and sister of the 3rd Earl of Dartmouth. Second, in 1791, to Elizabeth (d.s.p., 1823 [see 1823/20]), daughter of John, 3rd Earl Waldegrave (left £100,000).

Religion Anglican.

Public MP (Tory) Shaftesbury, 1754–61; Hastings, 1761–8; Great Bedwin, 1768; Marlborough, 1768–80. Member of the Household of George III as Prince of Wales and King; Constable of Windsor Castle, 1791–1811. Created Baron Brudenell, 1780, when his brother held the earldom.

Miscellaneous An enormous landowner.

References *BP; CP.*

1811/11 **Name** **Grafton, 3rd Duke of, Augustus Henry Fitzroy**

Dates 28 September 1735–14 March 1811, Euston Hall, Thetford.

Probate £125,000 (PCC).
Occupation Landowner and Prime Minister. (Occupational category I.) In 1883, the Duke of Grafton owned 25,773 acres worth £39,284 p.a.
Address His main seat was at Euston Hall, Thetford.
Father Lord Augustus Fitzroy (1716–24 May 1741), Captain, RN. Succeeded grandfather, the 2nd Duke of Grafton, in 1757.
Mother Elizabeth (d. 1788), daughter of (Colonel) William Cosby, Governor of New York (she married, second, wedding date unknown, James Jeffreys).
Education Westminster school; Peterhouse, Cambridge (MA).
Marriage First, in 1756, to (Hon.) Anne (d. 1804), daughter of Henry, 1st Baron Ravensworth. (Two sons.) Divorced 1769: she then married John, Earl of Upper Ossory. Second, in 1769, to Elizabeth (d. 1822), daughter of (Revd) Sir Richard Wrottesley, 7th Baronet. (Four sons, five daughters.)
Religion Anglican, but in 1774 became a Unitarian (!), joining the Unitarian chapel in London.
Public MP (—) Bury St Edmunds, 1756–7. Secretary of State for the Northern Departments, 1765–6; First Lord of the Treasury and nominal head of the Chatham government, 1766–8; Prime Minister, 1768–70; Lord Privy Seal, 1771–5, 1782–3. KG, 1769. Chancellor of Cambridge University, 1769–death. Had a large library and was interested in theological questions.
References *ODNB; CP; BP.*

Name **Sims, William** 1811/12
Dates c. 1744–8 March 1811.
Probate £150,000 (PCC).
Occupation Rope manufacturer (William Sims & Sons, Shadwell, 1793 and 1802 directories). (Occupational category II.9; venue 2.)
Address His address on his will was Sun Tavern Fields, St George's parish, Middlesex.
Father Unknown.
Mother Unknown.
Education Unknown.
Marriage Unknown.
Religion Unknown.
Public None known.
Miscellaneous In all likelihood, he chiefly produced ropes for ships and ship-related uses.
References *GM,* April 1811, p. 397. Not in any other source.

Name **Devonshire, 5th Duke of, William Cavendish** 1811/13
Dates 14 December 1748–29 July 1811, Devonshire House, Piccadilly.
Probate £300,000 (PCC).
Occupation Landowner. (Occupational category I.) One of the greatest landowners in Britain. Was worth £36,000 p.a. from his lands in 1764 when he succeeded to the dukedom. In 1883, the Duke of Devonshire owned 198,572 acres worth £180,750 p.a.

Address Numerous houses and estates, especially Chatsworth, Chiswick House, and Devonshire and Burlington Houses, London, etc.
Father William Cavendish, 4th Duke of Devonshire (1720–2 October 1764). (First son.)
Mother Charlotte (d. 1754), Baroness Clifford in her own right, daughter of the Earl of Burlington. On her death, her son succeeded as 7th Baron Clifford.
Education Not at a public school or university.
Marriage First, in 1774, to Lady Georgiana (d. 1806), daughter of John, 1st Earl Spencer. (One son, two daughters.) She was the famous society hostess and subject of biographies. Second, in 1809, to Lady Elizabeth (d.s.p., 1824), daughter of Frederick, 4th Earl of Bristol. Devonshire also had several illegitimate children.
Religion Anglican.
Public Did not hold any government posts, although from a leading Whig family. Was Lord High Treasurer of Ireland and Governor of Cork, 1766–93 and Lord Lieutenant of Derbyshire, 1782–death. KG, 1782.
Miscellaneous Typical high Whig aristocrat. Accrued huge debts.
References *ODNB; CP; BP.*

1811/14 **Name** **Gurney, Richard**
Dates 1742–16 July 1811.
Probate £125,000 (PCC).
Occupation Banker in Norwich (partner, Gurney's Bank); also brewer in Norwich and London (Barclay, Perkins & Co.). (Occupational category IV.16; venue 11.)
Address Lived at Keswick, Norfolk and North Repps, Norfolk.
Father John Gurney (1715–70), woollen manufacturer of Norwich. (First son.)
Mother Elizabeth (d. 1788), daughter of Richard Kett of Norwich.
Education Unknown; presumably a Quaker education.
Marriage First, in 1773, to Agatha (d. 1776), daughter of David Barclay, banker and brewer, of Youngsbury, Hertfordshire. (One son, one daughter.) Second, in 1779, to Rachel, daughter of Osgood Hanbury of Holfield Grange, Essex. (One son, two daughters.) Richard Gurney's son Hudson (1775–1864) was a millionaire banker; his daughter Anna (1795–1857) was a scholar of Old English; both have entries in the *ODNB*.
Religion Quaker: prominent family.
Public None known.
Miscellaneous A member of one of the leading families of the 'Quaker cousinhood' centred in East Anglia. Also a 'keen sportsman and agriculturalist' (*GM*).
References *GM,* 1811, vol. II, p. 92; *ODNB* for relatives; Arthur Raistrick, *Quakers in Science and Industry* (1968).

1811/15 **Name** **Christie, William**
Dates c. 1745–14 October 1811, Bath.
Probate £100,000 (PCC).
Occupation 'Biscuit bakers' (William Christie & Co., 323 Wapping, 1793 direc-

tory; 'Biscuit bakers' of 15 Little Hermitage Street, Wapping, 1800 directory; 'baker' of 10 Lombard Street, Fleet Street, 1802 directory). (Occupational category III.15; venue 2.)

Address Lived at Wapping, Middlesex, then at Hoddesdon, Hertfordshire.
Father Unknown.
Mother Unknown.
Education Unknown.
Marriage Unknown.
Religion Unknown.
Public None known.
Miscellaneous From his business venue, probably made hardtack biscuits for sea voyages, as well as for home consumption.
References *GM*, 1811, vol. II, p. 488.

Name **Scott, William** 1811/16
Dates Unknown; probated May 1811.
Probate £250,000 (PCC).
Occupation 'Drysalters and merchants' at 8 Austin Friars (1791); 'merchant' there in 1802. (A 'drysalter' was usually a provision merchant for ships and overseas exports.) (Occupational category IV.21; venue 1.)
Address Lived at Austin Friars, City of London, and then at Bush Hill, Edmonton.
Father Unknown.
Mother Unknown.
Education Unknown.
Marriage Unknown.
Religion Unknown.
Public None known.
Miscellaneous Nothing more could be traced of him in any source.
References Probate calendar and directories only.

WEALTH-HOLDERS, 1812

1812/1 **Name** **Lamotte, John Lagier**

Dates Unknown–28 January 1812.

Probate £125,000 (PCC).

Occupation Probably a merchant in the City, although lived near Worcester in later life. (Occupational category IV.21 or 19? Venue 1?)

Address The address on his will is 'formerly Thornegrove near Worcester, then Brighton'.

Father Unknown. A John Lagier Lamotte, died 1792, is buried in the churchyard at Wanstead, Essex (*Environs of London,* vol. 4, pp. 231–44, online). This might obviously be his father. A John Lamotte married Frances Cooper on 28 December 1743 at St Anne's Church, Soho (Family Search).

Mother Unknown. Possibly Frances Cooper (see entry on father above).

Education Unknown.

Marriage Unknown. He was probably the John Lagur (sic; presumably misread by the transcriber) Lamotte who married Mary Davies on 29 September 1781 at St Luke's Church, Old Street, Finsbury, London (Family Search). His daughter Martha was married at Brighton in 1844.

Religion Presumably of Huguenot descent, and presumably an Anglican.

Public None known.

Miscellaneous Presumably a merchant in the City, or the son of one. He is mentioned in Holden Furber, 'The United Company of Merchants of England Trading to the East Indies, 1783–96', *Economic History Review* (1940), although this might be his father. His residence in Worcester is unclear.

References *GM,* 1812, vol. I, p. 192; online source as above.

1812/2 **Name** **Perry, John**

Dates 1743–7 November 1810.

Probate £100,000 (PCC).

Occupation Shipbuilder and dockyard owner at Blackwall. (Occupational category II.4; venue 2.)

Address Lived at Moor Hall, Essex and at Battersea.

Father John Perry (d. 20 January 1771), shipbuilder of Blackwall.

Mother Anne, daughter of Samuel Watlington of Watlington House, Reading.

Education Harrow School.

Marriage First to Elizabeth Browne (d. 1795). The wedding was probably that which took place between a couple of the same names on 19 March 1765 at St Dunstan's Church, Stepney (Family Search). (Four sons, four daughters.) Second, to Mary Green. The wedding was probably that which took place between a couple of the same names on 31 May 1798 at Old Church, Stepney (Family Search). (Three sons, two daughters; one son was Charles Perry, Anglican Bishop of Melbourne, Australia, in *ODNB.*)

Religion Anglican.

Public High Sheriff of Essex, 1798.
Miscellaneous The Perry family managed the Blackwall shipyard on the Thames from 1708. They introduced wet docks into East London. This man is an interesting example of a semi-gentrified industrialist very early. His relatives the Greens eventually gained control of his firm. He retired in 1803.
References *BLG*, 1846.

Name **Dingwall, John** 1812/3
Dates 1724–28 May 1812, Croydon.
Probate £250,000 (PCC).
Occupation Jeweller (Dingwall Baillieu) of 9 St James's, Westminster. (Occupational category IV.20 and II.11; venue 2.)
Address Of St James's and Croydon, and of Brucklay, Aberdeenshire.
Father William Dingwall (d. 1743) of Brucklay, Aberdeenshire.
Mother Anna, daughter of John Gordon of Nethermuir.
Education Unknown.
Marriage Patience Huddart (d.s.p.) of London; marriage date unknown.
Religion Presumably originally Church of Scotland.
Public None known.
Miscellaneous His estates came to his grandnephew.
References *BLG*, 1952.

Name **Hunter, Robert** 1812/4
Dates 1731–4 August 1812.
Probate £100,000 (PCC).
Occupation An 'eminent merchant' at 7 King's Yard, Coleman Street, City of London, then at Great St Helen's, City. (Occupational category IV.21 or IV.19; venue 1.)
Address In later life he lived at Kew Green, Surrey.
Father Unknown.
Mother Unknown.
Education Unknown.
Marriage In 1762, to Elizabeth, daughter of John Lowis, merchant of London. (His son William Hunter was MP for Ilchester 1802–3.)
Religion Presumably Anglican.
Public None known.
Miscellaneous Was 'Pitt's adviser on commercial affairs' (*GM*).
References *GM*, 1812, vol. II, p. 45.

Name **Perkins, John** 1812/5
Dates c. 1729–31 October 1812; killed at Brighton racecourse when kicked by a horse.
Probate £100,000 (PCC).
Occupation Brewer (Barclay & Perkins) in Southwark. (Occupational category III.12; venue 2.)

Address Lived at Camberwell and Brighton.
Father Unknown.
Mother Unknown.
Education Unknown.
Marriage To Amelia Bevan (marriage date unknown), widow of a Quaker merchant and related to David Barclay, his partner. Perkins had been married previously; his first wife's name is unknown.
Religion Might have been a Quaker but more likely to have been an Anglican.
Public None known.
Miscellaneous Was originally the manager of this famous brewery when it was owned by the Thrales. He and David Barclay bought it out in 1781 for £135,000. The auction of Thrale's brewery was conducted by Dr Samuel Johnson, who famously said that 'we were not here to auction a parcel of vats, but the prospect of wealth, beyond the dreams of avarice.' Perkins was a friend of Johnson and Boswell. The brewery stood near the site of the Globe Theatre on Southbank.
References *GM,* 1812, vol. II, p. 572.

1812/6 **Name** **Forester, George**
Dates 21 December 1735–13 July 1811.
Probate £175,000 (PCC).
Occupation Landowner – an 'ancient family'. In 1883, his heir, who had become Lord Forester, owned 15,615 acres worth £22,581 p.a. in Shropshire and Staffordshire. (Occupational category I.)
Address His seats were at Dothill and Willey Park, Shropshire.
Father Brooke Forester of Dothill (1716–8 July 1771), MP for Wenlock, landowner.
Mother Elizabeth (d. 1753), daughter of George Weld of Willey Park, Wenlock, Shropshire.
Education Unknown secondary school; Peterhouse, Cambridge.
Marriage Unmarried; had many illegitimate children.
Religion Anglican.
Public MP (Whig) for Wenlock, 1758–61, 1766–90.
Miscellaneous Was an early exploiter of iron and coal on his lands in the Black Country and had an early horse-drawn 'railway'.
References *GM.*

1812/7 **Name** **Schweitzer, John**
Dates Unknown–2 January 1812.
Probate £100,000 (PCC).
Occupation A 'tailor' (!) – 'for many years a considerable tailor in [12] Cork Street, Burlington Gardens' (*GM*). (Occupational category IV.20 and II.11; venue 2.)
Address Lived at Middlesex Place, New Road, Marylebone.
Father Unknown; he was 'a native of Germany'.
Mother Unknown.
Education Unknown.
Marriage Unknown.

Religion Unknown: presumably originally Lutheran, Calvinist or Catholic.
Public None known.
Miscellaneous An example of a fortune made in an unexpected way.
References *GM*, 1812, vol. I, p. 92.

Name **Cavendish, (Hon.) William** 1812/8
Dates 10 January 1783–14 January 1812; died accidentally, aged twenty-nine.
Probate £150,000 (PCC).
Occupation Landed. (Occupational category I.)
Address Lived in Piccadilly and at Savile Row, Middlesex.
Father Lord George Cavendish, 1st Earl of Burlington, MP (1754–4 May 1834), landowner.
Mother Lady Elizabeth (d. 1735), daughter of Charles, 7th Earl of Northampton.
Education Eton; Trinity College, Cambridge.
Marriage In 1807 to (Hon.) Louisa (d. 1863), daughter of Cornelius, 1st Baron Lismore. (Three sons, one daughter.)
Religion Anglican.
Public MP (Whig) Knaresborough, 1804; Aylesbury, 1804–6; Derby borough, 1806–12.
Miscellaneous Was the grandson of the 4th Duke of Devonshire. Captain and major in the Derbyshire militia.
References *BP.*

Name **Langston, John** 1812/9
Dates 1758–11 February 1812.
Probate £250,000 (PCC).
Occupation A banker at Cheapside in the City and a director of the Sun Life Office, 1794–death. His firm merged in 1811 with Roger & Co. (Occupational category IV.16; venue 1.)
Address Lived at Sarsden House, near Chipping Norton, Oxfordshire, and in Cavendish Square, Middlesex.
Father James Langston (d. 14 July 1795), wine merchant and banker (Langston, Towgood, and Amory, of Cheapside), and Deputy Governor of the Bank of England.
Mother Sarah (d. 1802).
Education Probably at Eton.
Marriage In 1774, to Sarah, daughter of John Goddard of Woodford Hall, Essex. (One son, four daughters.)
Religion Anglican.
Public MP (Tory) for Sudbury, 1784–90; Bridgewater, 1790–6; Minehead, 1796–1802; Portarlington, 1806; Bridgewater, 1806–7. High Sheriff of Oxfordshire 1804–5.
Miscellaneous Was 'said to be worth half a million' (*HP*).
References *HP; GM.*

1812/10 **Name** **Knight, Edward**

Dates c. 1734; probated June 1812.

Probate £125,000 (PCC).

Occupation Ironmaster at Wolverley, Worcestershire and in the Black Country. (Occupational category II.3; venue 8.)

Address Lived Wolverley, near Kidderminster, Worcestershire, and at 52 Portland Place, Middlesex.

Father Edward Knight (1699–1780), ironmaster of Wolverley, Worcestershire. (First son.) (He is in the *ODNB*, but not the son.)

Mother Elizabeth James (d. 1780), 'heiress' of Otton End, near Solihull.

Education Unknown.

Marriage Unmarried.

Religion Presumably Anglican.

Public None known.

Miscellaneous The family had been pioneering ironmasters in the Black Country since the Commonwealth period.

References *ODNB* for relatives; *GM*, 1812, vol. I, p. 598; *BLG*, 1952.

1812/11 **Name** **Gaussen, Samuel Robert**

Dates 27 February 1759–14 August 1812.

Probate £175,000 (PCC).

Occupation Banker in London. (Occupational category IV.16; venue 1.) His business address was probably at Little St Helens in the City.

Address Lived at Bedford Square, then at Brookman's Park, Kent (purchased in 1786) and at 3 Mansfield Street, Portland Place.

Father Peter Gaussen (1723–81). He migrated to England in 1739 and became a banker at Little St Helens in the City, a governor of the Bank of England (its first foreign-born governor) and a director of the East India Company. (Second son.)

Mother Anna Maria, daughter of Samuel Bosanquet, 'Turkey merchant' of Forest House, Essex.

Education Unknown.

Marriage In 1783, to Elizabeth, daughter of Jacob Bosanquet, 'Turkey merchant' of Broxbournebury. (Four sons, three daughters.)

Religion Originally Huguenot, but was certainly an Anglican in later life.

Public MP (Tory) Warwick, 1783–1802; High Sheriff of Hertfordshire, 1790–1.

Miscellaneous Besides his banking interests, was Director of the South Sea Company, 1782–death. Gaussen formed an important collection of eighteenth-century lansdscapes, now in a Canadian museum. In 1883, Robert George Gaussen of Brookman's Park owned 3,566 acres worth £4,246 p.a. Gaussen and his brother-in-law Joseph Bosanquet were important providers of information to the Pitt government on City opinion.

References *HP; GM; BLG.*

1812/12 **Name** **Uxbridge, 1st Earl of, and 9th Baron Paget, Henry Bayly Paget**

Dates 18 June 1744, at St George's, Hanover Square–13 March 1812.

Probate £150,000 (PCC).

Occupation Landowner. In 1883, his descendant, the Marquess of Anglesey, owned 29,737 acres worth £110,598 (sic) p.a. in Staffordshire, Anglesey, Derby and Dorset. (Occupational category I.)

Address His chief seat was apparently at Plas Newydd, Anglesey.

Father Sir Nicholas Bayly, 2nd Baronet (d. 9 December 1782), MP and landowner of Plas Newydd, Anglesey.

Mother Caroline (d. 1766), daughter of (Brigadier-General) Thomas Paget (son of the 6th Baron Paget).

Education Unknown. Received a DCL from Oxford University in 1773.

Marriage In 1767, to Jane (d. 1817), daughter of (Very Revd) Arthur Champagne, Dean of Clonmacnoise, Ireland. (Seven sons, five daughters.)

Religion Anglican.

Public Inherited barony of Paget in 1769 and was created 1st Earl of Uxbridge of the second creation in 1784; distant relatives had held the same title earlier. Lord Lieutenant of Anglesey from 1782 and Lord Lieutenant of Staffordshire from 1801.

Miscellaneous His son Henry (1768–1854) was the famous Napoleonic War general known as 'One Leg' and was created 1st Marquess of Anglesey.

References *CP; BP.*

WEALTH-HOLDERS, 1813

1813/1 **Name** **Hotham, 1st Baron, Sir William Hotham, 11th Baronet**
Dates 8 April 1736, Edenbury–2 May 1813, South Dalton, Yorkshire.
Probate £125,000 (PCC).
Occupation Admiral. (Occupational category VI.31.) Also landowner.
Address Lived in retirement at South Dalton, Yorkshire, near Hull.
Father Sir Beaumont Hotham, 7th Baronet (1698–September 1771), landowner. (Third son; succeeded two brothers and a nephew.) In 1883, Lord Hotham owned 20,352 acres worth £26,126, in Yorkshire.
Mother Frances (d. 1771), daughter of (Revd) Stephen Thompson of Thornthorpe, Yorkshire.
Education Winchester; Royal Naval Academy, Portsmouth.
Marriage Unmarried; succeeded by younger brother.
Religion Anglican.
Public Created 1st Baron Hotham in 1797 for naval exploits.
Miscellaneous Rear-Admiral, 1787; Vice-Admiral, 1790; Admiral, 1795; won two battles in the Mediterranean, 1795. One of a number of very wealthy admirals of the Napoleonic period.
References *ODNB.*

1813/2 **Name** **Palmer, Roger**
Dates c. 1739–6 October 1811, Paris (see 'Miscellaneous' below).
Probate £125,000 (PCC).
Occupation Landowner in Ireland. (Occupational category I.) In 1883, Sir Roger Palmer, Baronet, his successor, owned 98,954 acres worth £26,661 p.a., in County Mayo, etc.
Address Palmerstown, County Mayo; Rush House, County Dublin; Oxford Street, Middlesex.
Father Francis Palmer of Palmerstown, County Mayo, landowner.
Mother Elizabeth, daughter of Sir Robert Echlin, 2nd Baronet, of Kenure Park.
Education Educated 'in Germany'.
Marriage Unmarried.
Religion Anglican.
Public None known.
Miscellaneous A large landowner in Ireland. His estates passed to his cousin William Henry Palmer, who succeeded to the baronetcy awarded to his uncle. Roger Palmer mainly lived abroad and was 'detained' in Paris for ten years as a British national.
References *GM,* 1811, vol. II, pp. 403, 486; *BP.*

1813/3 **Name** **Hussey, William**
Dates 1 January 1725–26 January 1813.
Probate £125,000 (PCC).

Occupation Clothier at Salisbury; also inherited by fortunate marriages. (Occupational category II.8? Venue 13.)
Address Lived at New Sarum, Wiltshire; Upper Eldon, Hampshire; and The Hall, Salisbury, Wiltshire. Also owned estates at Compton Coombe and Compton Broomore, Wiltshire (purchased 1701, *VCH Wiltshire*, vol. 2, p. 120).
Father John Hussey (d. 1739), Mayor of Salisbury 1737; presumably woollen manufacturer and clothier.
Mother Margery, widow of Richard Rumsey of Salisbury.
Education Unknown.
Marriage First, in 1752, to Mary (d. 1754), daughter of John Eyre of Landford Lodge, Wiltshire. (One daughter.) Second, in 1758, to Jane, daughter of Robert Marsh, London merchant and Governor of the Bank of England. (One son, one daughter.)
Religion Anglican.
Public MP (anti-Pitt) St Germains, 1765–8; Hindon, 1768–74; Salisbury, 1774–1813. Mayor of Salisbury, 1759 (aged twenty-four) and Alderman – the 'doyen of Salisbury politics' (*HP*).
Miscellaneous 'Made a fortune' as a clothier in Salisbury (*HP*) and added to it by fortunate marriages.
References *HP.*

Name **Heyman, Henry** 1813/4
Dates Unknown–4 March 1813, Russell Square.
Probate £100,000 (PCC).
Occupation 'Merchant' (1793 directory and will) at 8 Old Jewry and Cateaton Street, City of London, then at 63 Lincoln's Inn Fields. (Occupational category IV.21? Venue 1.)
Address Lived at 21 Queen Street, Bloomsbury and at The Priory, Roehampton, Surrey.
Father Unknown.
Mother Unknown.
Education Unknown.
Marriage Unknown.
Religion Unknown.
Public None known.
Miscellaneous A merchant in the City. A Henry Heyman was naturalised by an Act of Parliament in 1766. A Sir Peter Heyman (d. 1641), politician, is in the *ODNB* – he had twelve children. It is unclear which of these, if either, was relevant to this man.
References Probate calendar only.

Name **Sir Charles Pole** (né Van Notten), **1st Baronet** 1813/5
Dates 14 January 1735–18 June 1813 at Wolverton Park, Hampshire.
Probate £250,000 (PCC).
Occupation Merchant trading with the Netherlands (Senior Partner, Van Notten

& Co.) and banker of Devonshire Square, Bishopsgate, City of London. (Occupational category IV.19 and 16; venue 1.) Also invested in the Hampstead estate and owned land there and in Hampshire. (In 1883, Van-Notten-Pole, Baronet, owned 2,827 acres worth £4,452 p.a. in Hampshire.)

Address Mayfair Street, Middlesex and Wolverton Park, Hampshire.

Father Charles Van Notten (1702–1 March 1750), a merchant of Amsterdam who settled in London c. 1720.

Mother Susanna, daughter of David Bosanquet of London, 'Turkey merchant'.

Education Unknown.

Marriage In 1769, to Millicent (d. 1818), daughter of Charles Pole of Holtcroft, MP for Liverpool. (Four sons, one daughter.) He changed his name to Pole in 1787, eighteen years after his marriage.

Religion The father was presumably originally Dutch Reformed; the mother came from a Huguenot family. He was buried as an Anglican.

Public High Sheriff of Hampshire 1791–2. Created 1st Baronet 1791.

Miscellaneous 'A successful merchant of London' (*Complete Baronetage*).

References *Complete Baronetage; BP.*

1813/6 **Name** **Aylesford, 4th Earl of, Heneage Finch**

Dates 4 July 1751, at Sion House–21 October 1812.

Probate £200,000 (PCC).

Occupation Landowner. (Occupational category I.) In 1883, the Earl of Aylesford owned 19,581 acres worth £32,620 p.a., in Warwickshire, Leicestershire and Kent.

Address His principal seat appears to have been Packington Hall near Coventry.

Father Heneage Finch, 3rd Earl of Aylesford (1715–9 May 1777), MP, landowner. (First son.)

Mother Charlotte (d. 1805), daughter of Charles, 6th Duke of Somerset. She is said to have brought 'a fortune of £50,000' to the marriage.

Education Westminster School; Christ Church, Oxford (MA, DCL).

Marriage In 1781 to (Hon.) Louisa (d. 1832), daughter of Thomas, 1st Marquess of Bath. (Six sons, six daughters.)

Religion Anglican.

Public MP (pro-Government) Castle Rising, 1772–4; Maidstone, 1774–7. Captain, Yeomen of the Guards, 1783–1804; Lord Steward of HM Household, 1804–death. PC, 1783.

Miscellaneous Also an art collector of note.

References *HP; CP; BP.*

1813/7 **Name** **Henley, Michael**

Dates 1742–11 September 1813, Friargate Street, Derby.

Probate £125,000 (PCC).

Occupation A 'coal merchant' (1793 directory) and then a shipowner at 344 Wapping, Middlesex. (Occupational category IV.24 and 21; venue 2.)

Address Later lived in Derby.

Father Probably Francis Henley, from Ireland, who lived in Rotherhithe and was buried in Bermondsey in February 1785.
Mother Unknown.
Education Unknown.
Marriage First, in 1765, to Mary Tonks (d. c. 1791). (Two sons, three daughters.) Second, in 1792, to Ann Lacey.
Religion Married as an Anglican.
Public None known.
Miscellaneous Has an entry in the *ODNB* as an important shipowner. Was apprenticed to a Thames lighterman and became a London waterman, then a coal merchant trading with Newcastle upon Tyne. He then built up a fleet of twenty-two ships trading with the Baltic, Mediterranean and Atlantic, of which he was the sole owner and used the vessels only for trading, both innovations.
References *ODNB*; *GM*, 1813, vol. II, p. 402.

Name **Baldock, William** 1813/8
Dates c. 1732–22 June 1813, Petham near Canterbury, Kent.
Probate £125,000 (PCC).
Occupation Unknown; possibly a 'coachmaster' at Canterbury or a land and property owner there. (Venue 14?)
Address Lived at Canterbury, Kent and then at Petham, near Canterbury.
Father Unknown.
Mother Unknown.
Education Unknown.
Marriage Unknown. A guide to Kent marriages lists a William Baldock of Canterbury, 'coachmaster and bachelor' as having married Elizabeth Jackson in July 1781, but that man appears to have been born in 1749 (1748 according to Family Search, which gives his date of death as 21 December 1812).
Religion Presumably Anglican.
Public None known.
Miscellaneous In 1883, a William Baldocks (sic) owned 700 acres worth £720 p.a. in Kent.
References *GM*, 1813, vol. I, p. 665, but does not discuss his occupation; other sources as above.

Name **Simeon, Edward** 1813/9
Dates Unknown–14 December 1812, Fitzroy Farm, Highgate.
Probate £150,000 (PCC).
Occupation 'Merchant' at Salvador House, Bishopsgate, in the City of London (1793 directory) and of Simeon & Co. (1802 directory). Also a director of the Bank of England, 1792–1812. (Occupational category IV.16 and 21? Venue 1.)
Address Lived in later life at St Johns, Isle of Wight; Cambridge; and Fitzroy Farm near Highgate.
Father Richard Simeon (d. 1784), solicitor of Reading. Two of Edward Simeon's

brothers are in the *ODNB:* Sir John, 1st Baronet (1755–1836), lawyer and politician, and (Revd) Charles (1759–1836), the famous Evangelical Anglican vicar.
Mother Elizabeth Hutton.
Education Eton College.
Marriage In 1792, to Harriet, daughter of Thomas Parry of Berners Street, Middlesex.
Religion Anglican.
Public None known.
Miscellaneous Possibly more heavily involved as a banker then as a merchant.
References *GM,* 1812, vol. II, p. 596.

1813/10 **Name Prime, Samuel**
Dates c. 1749–21 March 1813, Cambridge.
Probate £150,000 ('within province') (PCC).
Occupation Barrister in London. (Occupational category VI.29; venue 1.) Presumably inherited a legal fortune.
Address Lived at Whitton, Middlesex and in Upper Brook Street, Middlesex.
Father Sir Samuel Prime (1700–24 February 1777), Serjeant at Law and King's Serjeant, 1778, in *ODNB.*
Mother Hannah, daughter of E. Wilmot of Banstead and widow, John Sheppard of Ash Hall, Suffolk.
Education Eton; St John's College, Cambridge; barrister, Middle Temple and Lincoln's Inn, 1773.
Marriage In 1771, to Susan, daughter of Richard Holden of Field House, Yorkshire. (Two sons, three daughters.)
Religion Anglican.
Public None known.
Miscellaneous Presumably a full-time barrister who inherited a good deal from his successful father. There is no evidence that he had any other economic interests.
References *GM,* 1813, vol. I, p. 391; *BLG,* 1846.

1813/11 **Name Lucena, John Charles**
Dates c. 1751–2 June 1813 at 40 Upper Charlotte Street, Fitzroy Square, Middlesex.
Probate £100,000 (PCC).
Occupation 'Consul-General of Portugal in Britain' for thirty years. It is unclear whether he worked as a merchant in his own right, although he probably did – he is listed (1802–4 directory) as of Nicholas Lane in the City. The Portuguese wine trade was very lucrative: this was presumably one of the bases of his fortune. (Occupational category IV.19 or VI.31; venue 1?)
Address Nicholas Lane is the only traceable address.
Father Unknown. There was a Diego Carvalho de Lucena, born Lisbon 1720, died in London in the late eighteenth century, who was an 'Advogado da Casa da Suplicacao'.
Mother Unknown.

Education Unknown.
Marriage Unknown; he is known to have had at least one daughter.
Religion Presumably Roman Catholic, although his daughter Mary married Bartholomew Barnewell (1798–1828), presumably a Protestant (online Barnewell genealogy).
Public None known.
Miscellaneous Virtually nothing is known of his career.
References Probate calendar only.

Name **Bonar, Thomas** 1813/12
Dates 1742–30 May 1813. Murdered with his wife in their bedroom at Camden Place, Chislehurst by an Irish footman. There is some confusion here, as some accounts refer to him as 'Thomson Bonar' and his date of death as July 1814. This Thomson Bonar is also said to have lived at Chislehurst. Family Search lists the birth at Edinburgh on 25 November 1742 of a Thomson Bonnar (sic), son of Andrew Bonnar (sic) and Agnes Thomson. Family Search also lists two men (the names of their wives differ, neither being Ann, as in 'Spouse' below) named Thomson Bonar who died on 26 July 1814.
Probate £150,000 (PCC).
Occupation 'Merchant' at Old Bethlehem, City of London and then at Broad Street Buildings, City, then at New Broad Street, City. Possibly a Russia merchant. (Occupational category IV.19? Venue 1.)
Address Lived at Chislehurst, Kent in later life.
Father Andrew Bonar (1708–62), merchant and banker at Edinburgh.
Mother Agnes, daughter of John Thomson.
Education Unknown.
Marriage To Ann (murdered May 1813), daughter of Andrew Thomson of Roehampton; marriage date unknown. (Two sons; one was Colonel of the Kent local militia at the time of his parents' deaths.)
Religion Presumably originally Church of Scotland.
Public None known.
Miscellaneous A very confusing case. *Notes & Queries,* July 8, 1911 (p. 11) notes the case of Thomson (sic) Bonar, who 'made a fortune as a Russia merchant' at Old Broad Street, purchased Camden Place, Chislehurst, and was murdered there in July 1814 (sic) by his footman. However, *The Times* (1 June 1813) carries a report headed 'Horrible Murder of Mr. and Mrs. Thomson Bonar, of Chislehurst, Kent' which occurred on the night of 30–1 May 1813; they were struck in the head with a poker while in bed at Camden Place. A Thomson (sic) Bonar, 1743–1811 (sic), of Camden, County Kent, is also noted in *BLG,* 1846 and 1855. The man examined here definitely had his estate probated in 1813, and a brief obituary in *GM,* for that year.
References *GM,* 1813, vol. I, p. 657; online source as above.

Name **Barham, 1st Baron, Sir Charles Middleton, 1st Baronet** 1813/13
Dates 14 October 1726, Leith–17 June 1813.

Probate £150,000 (PCC).

Occupation Admiral of the Red and naval administrator. (Occupational category VI.31.)

Address Lived at Barham Court, near Canterbury, Kent in later life.

Father Robert Middleton, Collector of Customs at Bo'ness. (Second son.) His great-grandfather was Earl of Middleton and other ancestors were principals of King's College, Aberdeen.

Mother Helen, daughter of Charles Dundas of Arniston, Midlothian.

Education Unknown.

Marriage In 1761 to Margaret (d. 1792), daughter of James Gambier, barrister and Warden of Fleet Prison.

Religion Presumably originally Church of Scotland; in later life a 'keen Evangelical' Anglican; a friend of Wilberforce.

Public MP (Tory) Rochester, 1784–90; Comptroller of the Navy, 1778–90; later an important naval administrator. PC 1805; created 1st Baronet 1781 and 1st Baron Barham in 1805. Lord of the Admiralty, 1794–5.

Miscellaneous Entered Royal Navy in 1741. Rear-Admiral, 1781; Vice-Admiral, 1793; Admiral of the Blue, 1795; Admiral of the Red, 1805. Helped to organise the Trafalgar campaign and was noted for his administrative competence. Was a cousin of Henry Dundas, MP. His estates eventually passed to the earls of Gainsborough. He was also noted for his religiosity.

References *ODNB*, etc.

1813/14 **Name** **Denne, John**

Dates Unknown–November 1813.

Probate £125,000 (PCC).

Occupation Unknown. He was described on his marriage licence (1764) as a 'husbandman' (*Canterbury Marriage Licences*), and may have been related to the family of Denne of Lydd, Kent, listed in *BLG*, although he is not himself listed. A John Denne 'linen draper' of Canterbury is listed in a 1771 directory. He was apparently unrelated to Cornelius Denne (1809/13).

Address Of Canterbury and then of Chislet, near Canterbury, Kent.

Father Unknown. A John Denne 'gentleman' and Freeman of Canterbury is listed in a 1730 directory. A John Denne of Chislet, aged thirty-one, died 7 November 1781, leaving two sons.

Mother Unknown.

Education Unknown.

Marriage In 1764, to Elizabeth Hills of St Lawrence, Isle of Thanet.

Religion Unknown.

Public None known.

Miscellaneous Little could be traced as to how he made his fortune.

References *GM*, 1813, vol. II, p. 501.

1813/15 **Name** **Bogg, George**

Dates c. 1755–16 January 1813 at Doctor's Commons in the City of London.

Probate £125,000 (PCC).
Occupation 'Procurator-General of the Court of Arches' of Doctor's Commons, Knightrider Street, City of London. (A senior official of the Eccclesiastical Courts.) (Occupational category VI.31 and 29; venue 1.)
Address His only address is at Doctor's Commons in the City of London.
Father Robert Bogg (d. 1769), barrister of the Middle Temple and a procurator-general of the Arches Court of Canterbury.
Mother Unknown.
Education Secondary school unknown; entered the Middle Temple in 1769.
Marriage Unknown; probably unmarried.
Religion Anglican court official.
Public None known.
Miscellaneous A senior official of the Ecclesiastical Courts. 'For many years an eminent Proctor' (*GM*); he had 'no relatives to inherit his property'. (A 'proctor' in this context was usually a solicitor or attorney who administered court cases. The Ecclesiastical Courts remain very underexplored by historians.)
References *GM*, 1813, vol. I, p. 93.

Name **Heathcote, Michael** 1813/16
Dates c. 1735–8 January 1813, at Southampton Street, Bloomsbury.
Probate £125,000 (PCC).
Occupation 'Manchester warehouseman' at 25 Milk Street, City (usually, a wholesale or retail merchant dealing in textile goods). (Occupational category IV.21 and 20? Venue 1.)
Address Of 25 Milk Street, City, and then 8 Southampton Street, Bloomsbury.
Father Gilbert Heathcote (b. 1701). (See E. D. Heathcote, *The Heathcote Family*, chapter on 'The Heathcotes of Buxton and Hartington', Society of Genealogists.)
Mother Unknown.
Education Unknown.
Marriage Unknown. His daughter married Samuel Unwin.
Religion Unknown; presumably Anglican.
Public None known.
Miscellaneous Nothing could be traced of his career beyond these few facts. It is possible that he was related to Sir Gilbert Heathcote, Baronet.
References *GM*, 1813, vol. I, p. 184.

Name **Wyndham, Wadham** 1813/17
Dates 1737–16 December 1812, Charlotte Street, Bloomsbury.
Probate £125,000 (PCC).
Occupation Listed as 'Colonel Wyndham' – service in the Coldstream Guards; had a battalion in the Tower in the 1760s. Presumably landed wealth. (Occupational category I?)
Address Charlotte Street, Bloomsbury is the only address given, but probably had country properties.

Father Henry Wyndham (1709–80 according to *ODNB,* or 1788), of Compton Chamberlayne, Wiltshire, and of Salisbury.
Mother Arundel (d. 1780), daughter of Thomas Penruddock of Compton Chamberlayne.
Education Unknown.
Marriage To Sarah Leander (sic). The marriage date is unknown; indeed, there is some doubt as to whether the couple were married. (Three sons, six daughters.)
Religion Anglican.
Public None known.
Miscellaneous 'Inherited from his father Thomas of Hammersmith and from Wadham of Eversley, and became very comfortable.' See H. A. Wyndham, *A Family History, 1688–1837* (1950). His brother Henry Penruddock Wyndham (1736–1819) is in the *ODNB* as a 'topographer'. How Wadham Wyndham became so wealthy, apart from land, could not be traced. In 1883, William Wyndham of Dinton House, Salisbury, owned 23,708 acres worth £37,420 p.a.
References *GM,* 1812, vol. II, p. 596.

1813/18 **Name** **Stevenson, Robert**
Dates 1731–30 January 1813.
Probate £100,000 (PCC).
Occupation 'Merchant' (1795 declaration) and banker (*ODNB*), presumably of the City of London. (Occupational category IV.16 and 21? Venue 1?)
Address 'Formerly of Merton Hall, Chiswick and 26 Bedford Place, Middlesex, and also of Binfield Place, Bucks' (Probate calendar).
Father Unknown.
Mother Unknown.
Education Unknown.
Marriage In 1775, to Mary Cockburn, granddaughter of Thomas Holford of St Lawrence. (One son, one daughter.) Their son was George Stevenson, JP, DL. Their daughter Sophia married, in 1806, Sir Love Parry Jones Parry (1781–1853), army officer, in *ODNB.* Mary Stevenson married, second, Sir William Herne KCB (marriage date unknown).
Religion Presumably Anglican; mention of their 'family vault' at Binfield Place, Buckinghamshire.
Public None known.
Miscellaneous Little could be traced on him.
References *BLG,* 1914, but his ancestors are not listed; *GM,* 1813, vol. I, p. 188.

1813/19 **Name** **Goldschmidt, Benjamin Abraham**
Dates c. 1783–15 September 1813.
Probate £100,000 (PCC Special Probate).
Occupation Presumably of the financial family later known as Goldsmid. (Occupational category IV.16 or 18, if so; venue 1.)
Address Lived at Balham Hill, Surrey.
Father Presumably a relative of Benjamin, Abraham and Asher Goldsmid, finan-

ciers in the City of London. Abraham Goldsmid (c. 1756–1810) was a merchant, bullion broker and stockbroker, featured in the *ODNB*. They were the cousins of the wealthy financier Sir Isaac Lyon Goldsmid, 1st Baronet, who left over £1 million in 1859. It was a Jewish custom not to name a child for a living parent, so Asher is possibly the most likely father.

Mother Possibly Abraham's wife Jessie, daughter of Levien Salomons, East India merchant, but see the previous point.

Education Unknown.

Marriage Unknown.

Religion Jewish.

Public None known.

Miscellaneous Nothing could be traced about his career.

References *GM,* 1813, vol. II, p. 403; Albert M. Hyamson, *Anglo-Jewish Notabilities: Their Arms and Testamentary Dispositions* (London: Jewish Historical Society of England, 1949).

Name **Allen, Thomas** 1813/20

Dates Unknown; estate probated on 5 March 1813.

Probate £200,000 (Lancashire). This was the earliest estate in this study probated in an ecclesiastical court other than the PCC.

Occupation 'Dyer' at Macclesfield. (Occupational category II.6? Venue 4.)

Address Lived at Macclesfield.

Father Unknown.

Mother Unknown.

Education Unknown.

Marriage Unknown.

Religion Unknown.

Public None known.

Miscellaneous Thomas Allin (sic) 'dyer' is listed in the 1789 Macclesfield directory. A Thomas Allen, Junior was Mayor of Macclesfield in 1823.

References Probate calendar only.

Name **Yates, William** 1813/21

Dates c. 1739–1813, Spring Side near Bury.

Probate £175,000 (Lancashire)

Occupation Cotton manufacturer at Bury; partner with Sir Robert Peel, 1st Baronet, grandfather of the Prime Minister of the same name. (Occupational category II.7; venue 4.)

Address Lived at Spring Side near Bury in later life.

Father His father 'kept the Black Bull Inn' in Blackburn.

Mother Unknown.

Education Unknown.

Marriage Unknown. His daughter Ellen married Sir Robert Peel, 1st Baronet, his partner and one of the first cotton millionaires, and was the mother of the Prime Minister.

Religion Presumably Anglican.
Public None known.
Miscellaneous A partner with Peel and Haworth c. 1760 in Blackburn and Bury; later a cotton manufacturer on his own account. He started as a cotton-mill apprentice and began his business with £200 capital. Although his grandson became world-famous, few sources say much about his own life.
References *ODNB* for Sir Robert Peel, 1st Baronet; *GM*, 1813, vol. II, p. 501; Norman Gash, *Mr Secretary Peel* (1961).

Name **Bold, Anna Maria** (née Wentworth) 1814/1
Dates 1733–25 November 1813.
Probate £100,000 (PCC).
Occupation Presumably landowner or landed. (Occupational category I.)
Address Bold, near Widnes, Lancashire.
Father Godfrey Wentworth of Woolley Park, Yorkshire; presumably landowner.
Mother Unknown.
Education Unknown.
Marriage First, marriage date unknown, to (Revd) Edward Sylvester of Barthwaite. Second, marriage date unknown, to Peter Bold (1705–92) of Bold Hall, Prescot, Lancashire, Tory MP for Wigan and Lancashire, 1727–34, 1736–41, 1750–61. (Six daughters.)
Religion Anglican: buried in St Luke's Church, Widnes, Lancashire.
Public None known.
Miscellaneous From an 'ancient family'. Her estates passed to Peter Patten (d. 1819, later Peter Patten Bold), MP for Malmesbury. It is not clear, in Bateman, who owned these estates.
References *GM; PLG.*

Name **Wassenaer Obdam, Jacob, Count** 1814/2
(Given in the PROB 11 index as 'Jacob Unico Willem van Wassanaer, otherwise Van Vassanaer, otherwise Jacob Unico Willem Count Wassanaer Obdam, of Delden, Empire of France')
Dates Unknown; probated January 1814.
Probate £150,000 ('within province') (PCC).
Occupation Unknown: a Dutch nobleman. The Netherlands constituted part of the French Empire under Napoleon.
Address 'Formerly of The Hague, then Delden' (probate calendar).
Father Unknown.
Mother Unknown.
Education Unknown.
Marriage Unknown.
Religion Unknown, presumably Dutch Reformed.
Public None known.
Miscellaneous There was a Dutch barony of Obdam and a Dutch Admiral Obdam in the seventeenth century. The source of this man's wealth, or why he left a fortune in England, is unknown.
References Probate calendar only.

Name **Thompson, Henry** 1814/3
Dates c. 1743 or 1745–March 1814.
Probate £175,000 ('within province') (PCC).

Occupation Landowner in Yorkshire. In 1883, his descendant Meysey-Thompson, Baronet, owned 5,623 acres worth £10,600 p.a. in the North and West Ridings. (Occupational category I.)
Address Kirkby Hall, North Riding, Yorkshire.
Father John Thompson (b. 1701) of Kirkby Hall, North Riding, landowner.
Mother Elizabeth Croft (d. 1753) of Stillington.
Education Unknown.
Marriage In 1769, to Mary (d. 1843), daughter of Thomas Spence of Hurts Hall, Suffolk. (Four sons, three daughters.) Their daughter Mary (who died in childbirth in 1813) married Claudius Buchanan (1766–1815), East India Company chaplain, in *ODNB.*
Religion Anglican.
Public None known.
Miscellaneous A northern landowner; the family later became baronets.
References *BP.*

1814/4 **Name** **Meux, Richard**
Dates 4 October 1734–2 July 1813 at Castle Bar Hill, Ealing, Middlesex.
Probate £125,000 (PCC).
Occupation Brewer of Liquorpond Street (now Clerkenwell Road) and Leather Lane, City of London; known as Meux and Jackson in 1780. (Occupational category III.12; venues 1 and 2.) He does not appear to have been a landowner on any scale, but in 1883 Sir Henry Meux, Baronet, owned 15,110 acres worth £23,507 p.a. in Wiltshire, Hertfordshire, Middlesex, etc.
Address Lived at 26 Bloomsbury Square, Bloomsbury. From 1790, leased Castle Bar House, near Ealing (*VCH Middlesex,* vol. 7, 1982, pp. 128–31.)
Father (Revd) Richard Meux (d. 1751), rector of Weddington, Warwickshire. (First son.) The grandfather, Thomas Meux, was a London merchant who had married into the gentry.
Mother Hannah Bradshaw.
Education Unknown.
Marriage In 1767, to Mary (d. December 1812), daughter of Henry Brougham, and aunt to Henry Brougham, Lord Brougham, the Lord Chancellor. (Three sons, two daughters.) The couple's son (Sir) Henry Brougham (1770–1841) received a baronetcy; their grandson and great-grandsons were half-millionaires.
Religion Anglican.
Public None known.
Miscellaneous At the age of twenty-three (c. 1757) he acquired a 'run-down' brewery in Long Acre; this was rebuilt in 1763 in Liquorpond Street. By 1787, it was producing 50,000 barrels of porter and 100,000 by 1795. He allowed paying customers to walk inside his enormous vats, attracting much publicity. He took Andrew Reid (q.v.) and Sir Robert Wigram (1830/36) as partners. There was a fire on these premises in October 1814.
References *ODNB* and above sources.

Name **Long, Catherine** (spelt Katherine in PROB 11 online) 1814/5
Dates c. 1717 or 1720–20 (29?) January 1814, Wraxall near Trowbridge, Wiltshire.
Probate £175,000 (PCC).
Occupation Presumably landed, although how she became so wealthy in her own right is unclear. In 1883, Walter Hume Long of Wraxall, the Tory MP, owned 23,404 acres worth £23,213 p.a., chiefly in Wiltshire. (Occupational category I.)
Address Lived at Wraxall, Wiltshire.
Father Thomas Long (1678–28 January 1759), landowner.
Mother Mary Abbott (1687–18 July 1733).
Education Unknown.
Marriage Unmarried.
Religion Anglican: buried Whaddon Church.
Public None known.
Miscellaneous She is said to have died aged ninety-three, but her precise date of birth is unclear.
References *BP; GM.*

Name **Parsons, William** 1814/6
Dates c. 1721–23 December 1813, Bristol.
Probate £100,000 (PCC).
Occupation 'Linen merchant' (probate calendar) in Bristol, but apparently not listed in any Bristol directory. (Occupational category IV.21 and 20? Venue 12.)
Address Lived in Bristol.
Father Unknown.
Mother Unknown.
Education Unknown.
Marriage Unknown.
Religion Unknown.
Public None known.
Miscellaneous Nothing could be traced about him in any source. He died at the age of eighty-eight in Bristol, which suggests that his business activities must have occurred many years earlier.
References *GM;* probate calendar.

Name **Sheppard, (Revd) Thomas, DD** 1814/7
Dates c. 1727–22 or 29 January 1814. He was perhaps the Thomas Sheppard christened at Amport, Hampshire, on 12 October 1727, son of Thomas and Elizabeth (Family Search).
Probate £150,000 (PCC).
Occupation Anglican vicar and Fellow of Magdalen College, Oxford. (Occupational category VI.30; venue 14.)
Address Lived at Amport, near Andover, Hampshire, and Basingstoke; also Oxford.

Father (Revd) Thomas Sheppard of Amport, Hampshire.
Mother Unknown. Possibly Elizabeth (surname unknown): see 'Dates', above.
Education Secondary schooling unknown; Christ Church and Magdalen College, Oxford (MA, DD).
Marriage To Sophia (marriage date unknown), daughter of (Revd) Peter Routh and sister of Dr Martin Routh (1755–1854), the famous Oxford figure who coined the phrase 'one must always verify his references' and knew both Dr Johnson and W. E. Gladstone, dying at ninety-nine.
Religion Anglican clergyman.
Public Served as an alderman of Basingstoke in 1780 and 1798.
Miscellaneous Held 'the richest [Magdalen] College living for many years' – *ODNB* entry on (Revd) James Hurdis. Vicar of Asbury, Berkshire in 1758; Rector of Basingstoke and Quarley, Hampshire, 1768–death. Fellow and Vice-President of Magdalen College, Oxford. Presumably resigned his fellowship upon his marriage. Was also a benefactor of the college. Presumably his wealth stemmed largely from his fellowship income.
References *GM; Alum. Oxon.*

1814/8 **Name** **Neave, Sir Richard, 1st Baronet**
Dates 2 November 1731–28 January 1814, Brighton.
Probate £150,000 (PCC).
Occupation Was originally a merchant in London trading with America and the West Indies, and was Chairman of the Ramsgate Harbour Trust, the West Indies Merchants Committee, the London Dock Company, and a director of the Hudson's Bay Company. Later became a banker and was Governor of the Bank of England, 1783–85. (Occupational category IV.19 and 16; venue 1.) His office in later life was at Broad Street Buildings in the City of London.
Address Lived at Dagnam Park, near Romford, Essex (purchased 1772 and redeveloped) and at Brighton.
Father John Neave (1700–64) of London and Walthamstow, presumably a merchant. (First son.)
Mother Susannah (d. 1766), daughter of Thomas Trueman.
Education Unknown.
Marriage In 1761, to Frances (d. 1830), daughter of John Bristowe of Quindenham Hall, Norfolk, Sub-Governor of the South Sea Company and MP.
Religion Anglican.
Public High Sheriff of Essex, 1794; created baronet 1795.
Miscellaneous In 1883, Sir Thomas Neave, Baronet, of Dagnam owned 9,960 acres worth £10,599 p.a., of which more than half was in Anglesey. It is not clear how much of this was owned by Sir Richard in his lifetime.
References *BP; GM.*

1814/9 **Name** **Digby, (Admiral) (Hon.) Robert**
Dates 20 December 1732–25 February 1814.
Probate £100,000 (PCC).

Occupation Admiral of the Red; the 'Senior Admiral of the Royal Navy' at death. (Occupational category VI.31.)
Address Lived at Minterne Magna, Dorset, seat of Lord Digby.
Father (Hon.) Edward Digby (c. 1693–1796), MP, the son of William, 5th Baron Digby and uncle of his successor.
Mother Charlotte (d. 1733), daughter of Sir Stephen Fox and sister of the 1st Earl of Ilchester and of the 1st Baron Holland.
Education Unknown.
Marriage In 1784, to Eleanor (d.s.p.), daughter of Andrew Elliot, former Lieutenant-Governor of New York (he was brother of Sir Gilbert Elliot, Baronet) and widow of James Jauncey.
Religion Anglican.
Public None known.
Miscellaneous Entered Royal Navy, 1744. Captain, 1755. Second in command to Rodney at the Battle of St Vincent. Rear-Admiral, 1779; Vice-Admiral, 1787; Admiral of the Red, 1794. Never received a title. Was very well connected, although was inactive in later life.
References *ODNB; GM,* 1814, vol. I, p. 412.

Name **Wilson, Francis** 1814/10
Dates c. 1738–27 October 1814, Battersea Rise, Clapham Common.
Probate £125,000 (PCC).
Occupation 'Formerly of the Navy Pay Office, Somerset House' (probate calendar) – presumably a government pay official who must have profited from his post. (Occupational category VI.31; venue 21.)
Address Lived at Vauxhall, then at James Street, the Adelphi, and then at Clapham Common (probate calendar).
Father Unknown.
Mother Unknown.
Education Unknown.
Marriage Unknown.
Religion Presumably Anglican.
Public None known.
Miscellaneous Nothing more could be traced of his career.
References Probate calendar only.

Name **White, George** 1814/11
Dates Unknown–22 December 1814 at Newington House, Oxfordshire.
Probate £150,000 (PCC).
Occupation Unknown. He was probably the George White who was a merchant at 20 Rolls Building, Fetter Lane in 1793, but this isn't clear. (If so, occupational category IV.21; venue 2.) There was another George White, who was 'a highly respectable officer of the House of Commons' and 'Clerk of the Elections Committee of the House of Commons'; he had an obituary in *GM,* 1814, vol. II, p. 809. The man who left the fortune here lived at Park Street, Westminster, so this might

have been his obituary, although the date of death (22 December 1814) might rule him out. (If the subject of the obituary was the same man, occupational category VI.31; venue 2.)

Address Lived at Park Street, Westminster and Newington House, near Wallingford, Oxfordshire.

Father George White of Newington House.

Mother Unknown.

Education Unknown.

Marriage Unknown. His daughter Laetitia Mary married, in 1814, (Captain) John Forbes (b. 1780) of Binkfield Place, Berkshire (Family Search).

Religion Presumably Anglican.

Public None known.

Miscellaneous Owing to his common name he has proved difficult to trace.

References *GM,* as above; otherwise probate calendar only.

1814/12 **Name** **Evans, Thomas**

Dates c. 1723–1 (8?) March 1814.

Probate £300,000 (PCC).

Occupation Primarily a banker (Crompton, Evans & Co.) at Derby; also the owner of iron and lead mines and a cotton spinner – he provided the capital for the Arkwrights, and his daughter married the cotton manufacturer William Strutt. (Occupational category IV.16 and II.7; venue 17.)

Address Lived in Derby. Built a cotton mill at Darley Abbey, near Bakewell.

Father Edmund Evans (c. 1690–25 December 1746) leadmine-owner and ironmaster of Bonsell, Derbyshire.

Mother Rebecca, daughter of Thomas Gell of Middleton-by-Worksworth.

Education Unknown.

Marriage First, in 1751, to Sarah, daughter of William Evans, later Mayor of Derby (not a relative). (One [?] son, one daughter.) Second (marriage date unknown) to Barbara, daughter of John Stubbs of Ranton Abbey, Staffordshire. (Three sons, one daughter.) The third son of the second marriage, Walter Evans (see 1839/12) married the daughter of Jedediah Strutt. She had previously married Thomas Evans's eldest son. Thomas Evans's daughter married William Strutt, pioneering cotton manufacturer.

Religion Although possibly of Nonconformist background, he was an Anglican; his brother was a vicar.

Public Treasurer of Derbyshire.

Miscellaneous Branched out from the family mining business to become a major banker in Derby and a pioneer of the cotton industry, originally in partnership with two of his brothers.

References Jean Lindsay, 'An Early Industrial Community: The Evans' Cotton Mills at Darley Abbey, Derbyshire, 1783–1810', *Business History Review,* Autumn 1960; *BLG,* 1846.

Name **Biddulph, Robert Myddleton** 1814/13
Dates March 1761–30 August 1814, Cheltenham.
Probate £100,000 (PCC).
Occupation Banker at Charing Cross, London (Cocks, Biddulph & Co.), owned by his uncle. Had made a previous fortune in Bengal as a private contractor for bullocks. (Occupational category IV.16; venue 2; also IV.21; venue 29.) Also became a landowner in Denbighshire, owning Chirk Castle. (In 1883, Richard Myddleton-Biddulph of Chirk Castle owned 8,338 acres worth £11,742 p.a. in Denbighshire, Hereford, etc.). He had inherited Chirk Castle from his wife, who was also a distant relative of his.
Address Stanhope Street, Mayfair and Charing Cross, and Chirk Castle, Ruabon, Denbighshire at death.
Father Michael Myddleton (1725–6 December 1800), barrister of Crofton Hall and Ledbury, Hertfordshire. (First son.) The son, Robert Myddleton, added the name Biddulph in 1801 on succeeding to property.
Mother Penelope, daughter of John Dandridge of Balden Green, Malvern, Worcestershire.
Education Unknown.
Marriage In 1801, to Charlotte, daughter of Richard Myddleton of Chirk Castle, Denbighshire. (Two sons, one daughter.)
Religion Anglican.
Public MP (Independent Whig) Herefordshire, 1796–1802; Denbigh Boroughs, 1806–12. Was a common councillor of Denbigh 1809; Recorder of Denbigh 1795–96 and 1802–death.
Miscellaneous Also a lieutenant colonel in the Chirk Volunteers.
References *HP; BLG;* online sources.

Name **Taylor, John** 1814/14
Dates 20 February 1738–27 August 1814.
Probate £175,000 (PCC).
Occupation Banker in Birmingham; partner of Sampson Lloyd (Taylor & Lloyds). Later also a banker in the City of London (Taylor, Lloyd, Hanbury & Bowman, of 60 Lombard Street). (Occupational category IV.16; venue 8.)
Address Lived at Moseley Hall, Worcstershire and Bordesley Park, Warwickshire at death.
Father John Taylor of Bordesley Park (1711–27 March 1775), originally a button-maker and snuff-box manufacturer in Birmingham, then a banker and High Sheriff of Warwickshire; was regarded as very rich and is said to have left £200,000 (*VCH Warwickshire,* vol. 7, p. 95). He had been a partner of Sampson Lloyd.
Mother Mary Barker.
Education Unknown.
Marriage In 1778, to Sarah, daughter of Samuel Skey of Spring Grove, Worcestershire. (Three sons, three daughters.)
Religion Certainly an Anglican: there is no evidence that he was a Quaker, despite his partnership with the Lloyds.

Public High Sheriff of Warwickshire 1786; JP, DL, Warwickshire; JP, Worcestershire.

Miscellaneous A wealthy Birmingham banker.

References *BLG.*

1814/15 **Name** **Goddard, Henrietta Maria** (née Hope)

Dates c. 1740, Braintree, near Boston, Mass.–25 December 1814, Harley Street, Middlesex. She was a member of the Hope family, of Scottish origin, very important merchant bankers based in Amsterdam (see 'Mother' below and *ODNB* article on the Hope Family).

Probate £125,000 (PCC).

Occupation Her husband was a 'Rotterdam merchant' (*VCH Essex*, vol. 6, p. 345), and later a merchant in in London. (Occupational category IV.19; venue 1. Her family's occupational category was IV.17; venue 29.)

Address Lived at Woodford Hall, near Stratford, Essex, and later at Upper Harley Street, Midlesex.

Father Henry Hope, son of Rotterdam-born Archibald Hope (1664–1743) and brother of Thomas Hope (1704–79) and Adrian Hope (1709–81), of Hope & Co., the powerful merchant banking firm whose clientele included European rulers. Henry Hope had settled in Boston about 1730 (*ODNB* article on the Hope Family).

Mother Mary Willard, member of a family of Massachusetts clockmakers. Mary's sister Sarah was apparently Henry Hope's first wife and mother of his son Henry (1735–1811), who moved to England about 1748 to complete his education and joined Hope & Co. in 1760. Henry Junior was a bachelor, and Henrietta Maria Goddard's eldest daughter Anne (see 'Spouse' below) was his heiress.

Education Unknown.

Marriage In 1762, in Rotterdam to John Goddard of Woodford Hall (who probably died in 1800). (Three daughters.) He was originally a 'Rotterdam merchant', and then a merchant at Cannon Street, City of London (1774, 1795 directories). Henrietta Maria Goddard is described as a 'widow' in the probate calendar. The 1808 directory gives her address as Upper Harley Street. Her eldest daughter, Anne Goddard (1763–1820) married Cornish-born John Williams Hope (né Williams, 1757–1813); Anne was mother to Henrietta, wife of the 7th Earl of Athlone, and to wealthy eccentric William Williams Hope (1802–55) of Rushton Hall, Northamptonshire, and Paris. In 1808, Anne Williams Hope left her husband for Baron von Dopff, whom she married in 1813. The second Goddard daughter, Sarah (1765–1814) married William Markham (see 1815/2). The youngest Goddard daughter, Henrietta (1766–after 1830) married Admiral Sir Charles Morice Pole, 1st Baronet (*ODNB*).

Religion Presumably Anglican or Church of Scotland.

Public None known.

Miscellaneous See above for an account of her background.

References See above sources.

Name **Minet, Hughes** 1814/16
Dates c. 30 June 1731, Eythorne, Kent–23 December 1814, Westerham, Kent.
Probate £125,000 (PCC).
Occupation A 'merchant' (Minet and Fector) of 21 Austin Friars, City of London (1793, 1803 directories). Also owned the extensive Minet estate (109 acres) in the Camberwell area of south London, which became very valuable after his death. (*Survey of London*, vol. 26 (1956), pp. 141–5). (Occupational category IV.21 or 19; venue 1.) Additionally, he owned 502 acres in Hayes (*VCH Middlesex*, vol. 4, 1971, pp. 26–9).
Address 'Formerly of Austin Friars in the City of London, then of Fulham, and then of Westerham, Kent' (probate calendar).
Father (Revd) John Minet, Rector of Eythorne, whose father Isaac Minet was a Huguenot refugee.
Mother Alice Hughes (c. 1701–15 August 1778), daughter of Henry Hugh(e)s and Elizabeth Young. Married in 1724, she was a widow at her death, aged seventy-seven.
Education Unknown.
Marriage In 1761, to Mary Loubier (1737–21 November 1768), at St Mary's Undershaft, City of London (Family Search). Born in Moorgate, she was also of Huguenot background; her parents, Jean Antoine (John Anthony) Loubier and Charlotte Henriette Cazalet, married in the City of London in 1734 (Roots Web). Minet had an illegitimate daughter, Harriet Taylor, who married, in 1799 (Revd) James Hurdis (1763–1801), clergyman and poet, in *ODNB*.
Religion Of Huguenot descent; was probably an Anglican by the time he married.
Public None known.
Miscellaneous A merchant in London, of Huguenot descent.
References Above sources.

Name **Brand, Anne Mirabella Henrietta** (née Smyth) 1814/17
Dates c. 1732–probated February 1814.
Probate £100,000 (PCC).
Occupation Presumably a landowner or landed. (Occupational category I.)
Address Lived at Queen Anne Street, Middlesex and at Polestead Hall, Suffolk. (A 'Bland' is listed in the 1792 Court directory at 24 Queen Anne Street, Westminster.)
Father Sir Robert Smyth, 2nd Baronet, of Isfield (c. 1709–10 December 1773); lived Westminster; grandson of Lord Mayor of London, Sir James Smyth (c. 1633–1706), knighted by Charles II. Sir Robert's father, Sir James Smyth, (c. 1686–28 February 1716/17), Sheriff of Sussex, created a baronet on 2 December 1714, married Mirabella, daughter of Sir Robert Legard, one of the masters in Chancery.
Mother (Lady) Louisa Caroline Isabella Hervey (1714/15–11 May 1770), second daughter of John Hervey, 1st Earl of Bristol; she married Sir Robert Smyth in 1731. The couple's son, (Colonel) Sir Hervey Smyth, 3rd Baronet (1734–2 October 1811), General Wolfe's aide-de-camp at the siege of Quebec, died

unmarried and the baronetcy became extinct. (Burke's *Extinct Baronetage* (1844), p. 495: 'Smyth, of Isfield'.)

Education Unknown.

Marriage To William Beale-Brand (d. 1799), son of Jacob Brand (*VCH Essex*, vol. 10, 2001, pp. 27–30) Marriage date unknown. Jacob Brand had married Jane Beale in 1723. Anne Mirabella Henrietta Brand's estate came to the great-nephew, Thomas William Cooke of Cook's Hall, Netherall, West Bergholt, Essex.

Religion Presumably Anglican.

Public None known.

Miscellaneous Originally a mercantile and professional family, but apparently landed by her time.

References Probate calendar and above sources only.

1814/18 **Name** **Raikes, Thomas**

Dates 28 March 1741–29 December 1813.

Probate £150,000 (PCC).

Occupation 'An eminent merchant in London' (William and Thomas Raikes & Co., 3 Bishopsgate Yard, 1802 directory); later Governor of the Bank of England, 1797–9. (Occupational category IV.21? Venue 1.)

Address 'Formerly of New Bond Street, in the City of London, and then of Upper Grosvenor Street' (probate calendar).

Father Robert Raikes (1690–7 September 1757), printer and founder of the *Gloucester Journal.* (Third son.) Thomas Raikes's brother was Robert Raikes (1736–1811), the famous early promoter of Sunday schools, in the *ODNB.*

Mother Mary (d. 1779), daughter of (Revd) Richard Drew of Nailsworth, Gloucestershire.

Education Unknown.

Marriage In 1774, to Charlotte (d. 1810), daughter of (Hon.) Henry Finch and granddaughter of the Earl of Winchelsea. (Four sons, five daughters.) Their son Thomas Raikes, 'dandy and diarist', is in the *ODNB.* He may have been the uncle of Robert Raikes (see 1839/28), a City of London merchant.

Religion Anglican.

Public None known.

Miscellaneous William and Thomas Raikes (presumably brothers) 'succeeded to the business of their distant relative, – Nettleton, an eminent Russian merchant.' (*GM*). It is not clear whether Thomas Raikes was influenced by the strong religious views of his famous brother.

References *GM; ODNB* for relatives.

1814/19 **Name** **Sales, Joseph**

Dates c. 1737–4 March 1814, Gower Street, Bedford Square.

Probate £250,000 (PCC).

Occupation 'Wholesale tobacconist' (Sales & Pollard) of Aldersgate (1793 and 1802 directories). (Occupational category IV.21; venue 1.)

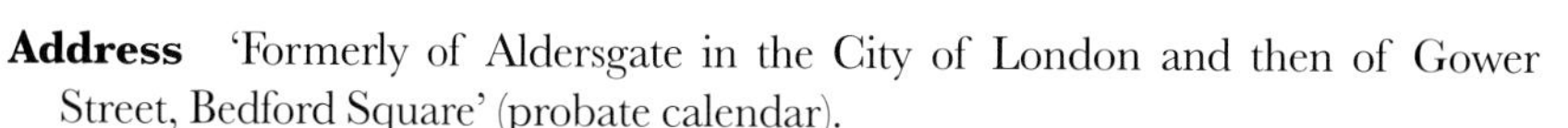

Address 'Formerly of Aldersgate in the City of London and then of Gower Street, Bedford Square' (probate calendar).
Father Unknown.
Mother Unknown.
Education Unknown.
Marriage Unknown.
Religion Unknown. The name might suggest a Sephardic Jewish origin, but there is no evidence for this.
Public None known.
Miscellaneous Evidently a major tobacco merchant in view of the size of his fortune.
References *GM,* 1814, vol. I, p. 413.

Name **Ailesbury, 1st Earl of, Thomas Brudenell (-Bruce)** 1814/20
Dates 30 April 1729–19 April 1814, Seamore Place, Mayfair.
Probate £150,000 (PCC).
Occupation Landowner. In 1883, the Marquess of Ailesbury owned 55,052 acres worth £59,726 p.a. in Wiltshire, Yorkshire, and Bedfordshire. (Occupational category I.)
Address The family's main seat was at Savernake near Marlborough, Wiltshire.
Father George, 3rd Earl of Cardigan (d. 5 July 1732). (Fourth son.)
Mother Elizabeth (d. 1745), daughter of Thomas Bruce, 3rd Earl of Elgin and 2nd Earl of Ailesbury of a former creation.
Education Winchester School.
Marriage First, in 1761, to Susannah (d. 1783), daughter of Henry Hoare, banker of Stourhead, Wiltshire and London; second, in 1788, to Anne (d. 1813), daughter of John, 1st Earl of Moira.
Religion Anglican.
Public Created Earl of Ailesbury of the second creation in 1776. Served as Treasurer of HM Household; PC; Lord Lieutenant of Wiltshire from 1780.
Miscellaneous Inherited and acquired titles and property in the usual complex way.
References *CP; BP; GM,* 1814, vol. I, p. 517.

Name **Prior, George** 1814/21
Dates c. 1734–23 April 1814, Sydenham.
Probate £120,000 (PCC).
Occupation Unknown. In his will he mentions his 'counting house' but does not specify the nature of his business. He does not appear to be listed in any London directory. As he was born in or about 1734, he might well have been in business during the period before trade directories were common.
Address 'Formerly of Whitechapel, then of Lewisham and Sydenham' (probate calendar).
Father Unknown.
Mother Unknown.

Education Unknown.
Marriage Mary, surname unknown. They had sons named Edward, John and William, and daughters named Mary and Amelia.
Religion Unknown.
Public None known.
Miscellaneous He does not appear to be listed in any source. The only relevant man in a contemporary directory is a George Prior, 'clock and watchmaker' of Sydenham in 1805–7. The Edward Prior (see 1859/31) of Regent's Park and Halse House, Somerset, may be his son.
References *GM,* 1814, vol. I, p. 518; will (PROB 11 online).

1814/22 **Name** **Franks, Jacob**
Dates Unknown–10 May 1814, Bath.
Probate £250,000 (PCC).
Occupation Probably of a family engaged in the American mercantile trade. (If so, occupational category IV.19; venue 1 or 29.)
Address 'Of Isleworth, then Bath and West Harling Park, Norfolk' (probate calendar).
Father Probably Jacob Franks (1688–1769) of New York, but see below.
Mother Probably named Bilhah (sic) Abigail.
Education Unknown.
Marriage To Priscilla (surname and marriage date unknown). She was probably Priscilla Franks; see 1832/23, left £400,000, but this isn't absolutely clear. In her will, she states that her late husband's sister married General Sir Henry Johnson, Baronet. According to the *ODNB,* he married Rebecca (d. 1823), daughter of David Franks of Philadelphia. According to her will, her husband was buried in St Michael's Church, Bath. She also states that her husband's brother was Moses Franks – see below.
Religion Of Jewish descent; he was an Anglican at death and was buried in Isleworth Church.
Public None known.
Miscellaneous The Frankses were prominent and wealthy merchants in colonial America. His uncle was Aaron Franks; Aaron's brother was Moses, Judge Advocate in Bermuda ('Coat of Many Colours', online). In his will, Jacob Franks mentions St Swithin's Lane in the City, presumably an office, but he is not listed in any directory, it seems. He also mentions his cousin in Philadelphia, Andrew Hamilton. Franks's cousin Oliver DeLancey (1749–1822) was an army officer and politician in America. Franks allegedly died 'of wounds received in the sortie from Bayonne' (*GM*).
References *GM,* 1814, vol. I, p. 625; above sources.

1814/23 **Name** **Dawkins, Henry**
Dates 24 May 1728–19 June 1814.
Probate £150,000 (PCC).
Occupation Planter in the West Indies: lived in Jamaica 1751–9 and owned

20,000 acres there. Later a landowner in Wiltshire and Oxfordshire. (Occupational category I; venue 29.)

Address 'Of Portman Square and Jamaica, and then of Over Norton, Oxfordshire and Standlynch, Wiltshire' (probate calendar).

Father Henry Dawkins (1689–1744) wealthy sugar planter in Jamaica and member of its House of Assembly.

Mother Elizabeth (d. 1757), daughter of Edward Pennant of Jamaica.

Education Secondary school unknown; St Mary's Hall, Oxford.

Marriage In 1759 to (Lady) Juliana (d. 1821), daughter of Charles, 2nd Earl of Portmore. (Eight sons, three daughters.)

Religion Anglican.

Public Member of the Jamaica House of Assembly, 1752–8 and of its Council, 1758–9. Then MP (Tory) Southampton Borough, 1760–8; Chippenham, 1769–74; Hindon, 1776–80; Chippenham, 1780–4.

Miscellaneous Relatives became Barons Penrhyn who, in 1883, owned 49,548 acres worth £71,018 p.a. Henry Dawkins wrote on Palmyra and Baalbek with his brother James (1722–57), who was the first Englishman to visit both; James is in the *ODNB* as 'antiquary and Jacobite sympathiser'.

References *GM,* 1814, vol. I; *BLG,* 1846, 1914; *HP.*

Name **Smith, Charles** 1814/24

Dates September 1756–9 May 1814.

Probate £125,000 (PCC).

Occupation Grain miller and merchant fortune at Barking, Essex and Stepney. (Occupational category III.15 and IV.21; venue 3.) Also possibly distillery inheritance in Stepney. (Occupational category III.13; venue 2.)

Address 'Formerly of Mile End, then of Suttons, Stapleford Tawney [near Romford], Essex' (probate calendar).

Father Charles Smith of Stratford, Essex (1713–8 February 1777), 'profitable' grain merchant and grain miller of Barking, Essex, in *ODNB* as 'writer on the Corn Laws'. His brother Nathaniel (d. 1794) was an MP.

Mother Judith, daughter of Isaac Lefevre, distiller of Stepney and Old Ford, Middlesex, of Huguenot descent.

Education Felsted School.

Marriage First, in 1791, to Susannah (d.s.p., 1796), daughter of John Devall of Marylebone. Second, in 1798, to Augusta, daughter of Joshua Smith, MP of Erlestoke Park, Wiltshire. (Three sons, six daughters.) One son became a baronet, Smith of Thring Park.

Religion Anglican; mother's ancestors were Huguenots.

Public MP (pro-Pitt) Saltash, 1796–1802; Westbury, 1802–6.

Miscellaneous Lived in Mile End in 1787, presumably in connection with the family's grain milling business, and then purchased the Suttons estate in 1787 and an estate at Stanford, Essex in 1796. Presumably his fortune derived from grain milling, but also possibly distilling. He invested in East India stock.

References *HP; GM,* 1814, vol. I, p. 525; *ODNB* for father.

1814/25 **Name** **Down, Richard**

Dates c. 1734–26 July 1814 at Colney Hatch, Middlesex.

Probate £100,000 (PCC).

Occupation A banker at 2 Bartholomew Lane, City of London (Down, Thornton & Co., 1803 directory). (Occupational category IV.16; venue 1.)

Address 'Of [2] Bartholomew Lane, City of London, and Colney Hatch, Middlesex' (probate calendar).

Father Unknown.

Mother Unknown.

Education Unknown.

Marriage In 1772, to Rose (d. 1832), daughter of Henry Neale, banker of the City of London and Halliwick Manor House. (Four sons, eight daughters.)

Religion Unknown.

Public None known.

Miscellaneous A City banker.

References *GM,* 1814, vol. II, p. 192; *BLG,* 1846.

1814/26 **Name** **Andrews, Miles Peter**

Dates 5 October 1742, City of London–18 July 1814.

Probate £175,000 (PCC).

Occupation Inherited a lucrative gunpowder works at Dartford, Kent from his brother and was in partnership there with his cousin Frederick Pigou from 1778 and later at Chester. (Occupational category II.6; venue 3.) Also was a noted playwright and a director of the Globe Insurance County from 1805–death.

Address Of Cleveland Row, St James's, Middlesex and Bignore near Dartford, Kent.

Father William John Andrews, a 'respectable drysalter and merchant' of Watling Street, London.

Mother Katherine, surname unknown.

Education In Utrecht (*ODNB*); intended for a business career.

Marriage Unmarried. Had numerous high-profile affairs with actresses.

Religion Anglican.

Public MP (pro-Tory) Bewdley, 1796–1814.

Miscellaneous A rather bizarre combination of activities. His gunpowder works were said to have been the largest in England (*ODNB*). Was a noted playwright in his day (wrote *The Election*) and was also a poet. Was also Lieutenant Colonel of the Prince of Wales Royal Volunteers, 1803, and was noted as the 'constant companion' of Lord Lyttelton (d. 1779) who 'haunted him as a ghost' (!) (*ODNB*).

References *ODNB* as 'playwright'; *HP.*

1814/27 **Name** **Ladbroke, Robert** (also spelled Ladbrooke in *GM*)

Dates c. 1739–1 July 1814, Pall Mall.

Probate £200,000 (PCC).

Occupation Banker at Lombard Street, City of London: partner with father and brother-in-law, Sir Walter Rawlinson. (Occupational category IV.16; venue 1.) Also owned the Ladbroke estate in North Kensington, then undeveloped, which he inherited from his brother Richard.

Address Of Pall Mall and Idlicote, near Shipton-on-Stour, Warwickshire.

Father Sir Robert Ladbroke (1713–73), banker 'at the sign of the Phoenix in Lombard Street', and also a distiller; Lord Mayor of London 1747–8, and M. for the City of London, 1754–73. Ladbroke, who was very wealthy, owned the Ladbroke Estate in North Kensington, then undeveloped. (*Survey of London*, vol. 37, 1973, pp. 194–200).

Mother Forename unknown, née Brown.

Education Unknown.

Marriage To Hannah, daughter of Robert FitzHardinge Kingscote of London. Marriage date unknown.

Religion Anglican.

Public MP (Whig) Warwick Borough, 1780–90; Okehampton, 1791–6; Winchelsea, 1802–6; Malmesbury, 1806–7.

Miscellaneous Owned a 'considerable' amount of government stock.

References *GM*, 1814, vol. II, p. 91; *BLG*, 1846.

Name **Ley, John** 1814/28

Dates c. 1733–13 June 1814, St Margaret's, Westminster.

Probate £125,000 (PCC).

Occupation Deputy-Clerk of the House of Commons for forty-seven years. (Occupational category VI.31; venue 2.) Also a barrister.

Address St Margaret's, Westminster.

Father John Ley (d. 1775) of Exeter, 'gentleman'.

Mother Grace, daughter of Henry Gaudy.

Education Secondary schooling unknown; Clare Hall, Cambridge (MA); barrister, Middle Temple, 1757.

Marriage Unmarried.

Religion Anglican.

Public None known.

Miscellaneous Presumably made most of his fortune from a very long career as Deputy-Clerk. His brother Henry (1744–1824; 1825/3 below) left £180,000.

References *GM*, 1814, vol. I, p. 700; *BLG*, 1846; Orlo Cyprian Williams, *The Clerical Organisation of the House of Commons 1801–1850* (1954).

Name **Brown, George** 1814/29

Dates Unknown–23 October 1814, Sun Court, Threadneedle Street, City of London.

Probate £175,000 (PCC).

Occupation 'Broker' at 3 Sun Court, Threadneedle Street (1795 directory) – presumably a stockbroker. (Occupational category IV.23; venue 1.) Also owned land at Clevedon, Somerset.

Address 'Of Stockton-on-Tees, County Durham and Sun Court, Threadneedle

Street, City of London' (probate calendar). The nature of his connection with Stockton-on-Tees is unknown.

Father Unknown.

Mother Unknown.

Education Unknown.

Marriage Unknown.

Religion Unknown.

Public None known.

Miscellaneous Little could be traced of his career.

References *GM,* 1814, vol. II, pp. 502–3.

Name **Atkinson, George** 1815/1

Dates 17 September 1764–11 May 1814.

Probate £140,000 (PCC).

Occupation 'Island Secretary for Jamaica and ADC to Lord Balcarres when Governor', then Agent-General for Jamaica in London (*BLG,* 1846). (Occupational category VI.31; venue 29.)

Address 'Formerly of Kingston, Jamaica, then Newcastle-upon-Tyne' (probate calendar); also of Morland Hall, Penrith, Westmorland and of Lee in Kent.

Father George Atkinson (1730–2 October 1781), Receiver-General for Cumberland and Westmorland.

Mother Bridget, daughter of Michael Maughan of Wolsingham.

Education Unknown.

Marriage In 1794, to Susan Mackenzie Dunkley (d. February 1830) of Clarendon, Jamaica. (Five sons, three daughters.)

Religion Unknown; presumably Anglican.

Public None known.

Miscellaneous An official in Jamaica. It is not known if he owned plantations or had other sources of income.

References *BLG,* 1856, 'Atkinson of Morland'.

Name **Markham, William** 1815/2

Dates 5 April 1760–30 December 1814 (*BLG* states 1 January 1815).

Probate £150,000, 'within province' (PCC).

Occupation 'Private Secretary to Warren Hastings' and 'subsequently resident for some time at Benares' (*GM*). (Occupational category VI.31? Venue 29.) His father was Archbishop of York and his maternal grandfather a wealthy English merchant in Rotterdam.

Address After India, his addresses were 'formerly of South Audley Street, Middlesex, and then of Becca Lodge, Aberford, West Riding and Montemore Street, Cavendish Square, Middlesex' (probate calendar).

Father (Rt. Revd) William Markham (1719–3 November 1807), Archbishop of York, 1777–death; previously Headmaster of Winchester, 1753–63; Bishop of Chester, 1771–7, in *ODNB,* which states he left about £10,000. The rich William Markham's younger brother John Markham (1761–1827) is also in the *ODNB* as a rear-admiral.

Mother Sarah (1765–1814), middle daughter of John Goddard of Rotterdam who brought her husband 'a considerable fortune'. Sarah's mother was Henrietta Maria Goddard (née Hope); see 1814/15.

Education Unknown.

Marriage In 1795, to Elizabeth (d. 1841), daughter of Oldfield Bowles of North Aston, Oxfordshire. (Five sons, three daughters.) She married, second (marriage date unknown), Alexander Mure.

Religion Anglican.
Public None known.
Miscellaneous Presumably a 'nabob', with Warren Hastings.
References *GM,* 1815, vol. I, p. 679; *BLG.*

1815/3 **Name** **Bennett, James**
Dates Unknown–8 January 1815, Cadbury, Somerset.
Probate £125,000 (PCC).
Occupation Unknown. Is unlisted in Bristol or London directories.
Address Of Cadbury House, North Cadbury, near Clevedon, Somerset – about fifteen miles from Bristol.
Father Unknown.
Mother Unknown.
Education Unknown.
Marriage In 1789, at Truro, to Mary, daughter of Thomas Clutterbuck of Marazion, Cornwall. (At least one son, James, JP, born 1793.)
Religion Unknown.
Public None known.
Miscellaneous Not listed in any source consulted. The implication is that he was a Bristol merchant, but there is no real evidence.
References *GM,* 1815, vol. I, p. 180, but provides no further information; *BLG,* 1871, 'Bennett of Cadbury'.

1815/4 **Name** **Wall, Charles**
Dates 1756–6 May 1815, Albury Park, Surrey: fell from a horse.
Probate £125,000 (PCC).
Occupation Banker: partner in Baring's Bank in the City. (Occupational category IV.16; venue 1.)
Address In later life lived at Norman Court, West Tytherley, Hampshire and at Albury Park near Guildford, Surrey.
Father Thomas Wall (1721–1812); a Thomas Wall, coal merchant, is listed in the 1811 London directory.
Mother Elizabeth Ellis.
Education Unknown.
Marriage In 1790 to Harriet (1768–5 March 1838), daughter of Sir Francis Baring, 1st Baronet, founder and head of the bank. She appears in the *ODNB* as a prominent Evangelical and a founder of the Irvingite movement. (One son, Charles Baring Wall, 1795–1853, MP.)
Religion Anglican.
Public None known.
Miscellaneous 'Married the boss's daughter' and was a Baring partner.
References *ODNB* for wife; *GM,* 1815, vol. I, p. 477; *BLG,* 1846, 'Wall of Norman Court'.

Name **Newberry, John** 1815/5
Dates c. 1750–13 August 1815.
Probate £175,000 (PCC).
Occupation Brewer with Henry Meux & Co., of Southwark. (Occupational category III.12; venue 2.)
Address Lived at Dulwich, Surrey.
Father Unknown.
Mother Unknown.
Education Unknown.
Marriage Unknown.
Religion Unknown.
Public None known.
Miscellaneous Little is known beyond his occupation as a brewer.
References *GM*, 1815, vol. II, p. 279.

Name **Porter, Thomas** 1815/6
Dates Unknown – probated December 1815.
Probate £120,000 (PCC).
Occupation In his will he notes that he owned estates in Tobago, Barbados and Demarara, as well as 'Negro slaves'. It is unclear whether he was also a merchant or shipowner in Exeter or elsewhere. (Occupational category I; venue 29+?)
Address Lived at Rockbeare House, East Burleigh, Devonshire, about seven miles from Exeter.
Father Unknown.
Mother Unknown.
Education Unknown.
Marriage To Sarah (surname and marriage date unknown). In his will he mentions his three sons, Thomas, Henry and William Porter, and two daughters, Christian and Eliza.
Religion Unknown.
Public High Sheriff of Devonshire in 1804.
Miscellaneous He is unlisted in any local directory. It appears that he was a West Indies plantation owner who then retired to Devon.
References Will (PROB 11 online); list of sheriffs of Devonshire (online).

Name **Harford, John Scandrett** 1815/7
Dates 10 April 1754–23 January 1815, Blaise Castle, near Bristol.
Probate £200,000 (PCC).
Occupation 'An eminent banker of Bristol.' (Occupational category IV.16; venue 12.) He was also an iron merchant and a partner in an ironworks and is listed, with his family, in the *ODNB*.
Address Bristol and Blaise (or Blaize) Castle, near Bristol.
Father Edward Harford (1720–28 April 1806), merchant and founder of the Bank, of Bristol. (Only son.)

Mother Sarah (d. 1776), daughter of John Scandrett of Yorkshire, a relative of the Lloyds of Lloyd's Bank.

Education Unknown.

Marriage In 1780 to Mary (d. 29 July 1830), daughter of Abraham Gray of Tottenham, Middlesex. (Five sons.) One son, John Scandrett Harford (1785–1866), was an MP.

Religion A Quaker, as well as his family. His son John became an Anglican.

Public None known. He built Blaize Hamlet for pensioners, designed by Nash, 1810–11.

Miscellaneous *ODNB; BLG; GM,* 1815, vol. I, p. 185.

1815/8 **Name** **Mathias, Lewis**

Dates 1740–1815, Haverfordwest, Pembrokeshire (exact death date unknown; an obituary appeared in *GM,* July 1815).

Probate £100,000 (PCC).

Occupation Landowner in Pembrokeshire. (Occupational category I.) No other source of wealth is known. In 1883, a Lewis Mathias of Lamphey Court, Pembrokeshire, owned 4,562 acres worth £4,113 p.a. in Pembrokeshire.

Address 'Formerly of Langwarren, Pembrokeshire, and then of Haverfordwest' (probate calendar).

Father John Mathias (c. 1694–1774), landowner, who added to the family estate.

Mother Margaret Thomas of Dyffryn.

Education Unknown.

Marriage Married but childless; succeeded by his nephew.

Religion Presumably Anglican, but his father is described as a 'Moravian' with 'Methodist leanings'.

Public High Sheriff of Pembrokeshire, 1811.

Miscellaneous A Welsh landowner.

References *Dictionary of Welsh Biography.*

1815/9 **Name** **Hughes, (Revd) Edward**

Dates 9 February 1738–1 June 1815, Kinmel Park, Denbighshire.

Probate £350,000 (PCC).

Occupation Essentially as the silent partner in Thomas Williams's great copper-mining ventures in north Wales, Cornwall and elsewhere, and in his processing works in London and elsewhere. (Occupational category II.2; venue 19, etc.) He was also an Anglican vicar, a landowner and a co-founder of the Chester and North Wales Bank in 1792.

Address 'Formerly of Lysdulas, Anglesey, and then of Kinmel Park, Denbighshire' (probate calendar).

Father Hugh Hughes (c. 1705–73) of Hereford and Lliniog in Anglesey, agent to (Dr) Edward Wynn of Boden Ryn and then a considerable landowner in Anglesey. (First son.)

Mother Unknown.

Education Secondary schooling unknown; Jesus College, Oxford.

Marriage In 1765, to Mary, daughter of (Revd) Robert Lewis, Chancellor of Bangor and landowner. Their son William Lewis Hughes (1767–1852), MP, was created 1st Baron Dinorben in 1831.
Religion Anglican clergyman.
Public None known.
Miscellaneous An interesting example of an Anglican clergyman who was an active industrialist and businessman, albeit as a 'silent partner' to Thomas Williams 'the Copper King'. Some of the copper deposits at Amlwch were on his property.
References *GM*, 1815, vol. I, p. 571; *ODNB* for Thomas Williams; *Dictionary of Welsh Biography*; J.R. Harris, *The Copper King* (1964); *BLG*, 1846.

Name **Ongley of Old Warden, 2nd Baron, Robert Henley-Ongley** 1815/10
Dates 3 October 1771–20 August 1814.
Probate £100,000 (PCC).
Occupation Presumably a landowner, but his grandfather, Sir Samuel Ongley (d. 1726), MP, was a linen merchant in Cornhill and a director of the South Sea Company. He was said to be 'very rich'. The subject's father, the 1st Baron, was an MP and barrister. (Occupational categories IV.21 and I? Venue 1?)
Address Lived at Old Warden, Bedfordshire.
Father Robert Henley-Ongley, 1st Baron Ongley of Old Warden (an Irish peerage) (c. 1720–23 October 1785), barrister and Whig MP, 1754–80 and 1784–5. (First son.)
Mother Frances (d. 22 January 1799), daughter of Richard Gosfright.
Education Unknown.
Marriage In 1801, to Frances (d. 1841), daughter of (Lieut. Gen.) Sir John Burgoyne, 7th Baronet. (Five sons, but the title became extinct in 1860.)
Religion Anglican.
Public None known apart from his peerage.
Miscellaneous Little is known about him. Presumably the large size of his personalty represents his inherited mercantile fortune.
References *CP.*

Name **Thorold, Sir John, 9th Baronet** 1815/11
Dates 18 December 1734–25 February 1815.
Probate £125,000 (PCC).
Occupation Landowner. (Occupational category I.) Described in the *ODNB* as 'landowner and book collector'.
Address Lived at Syston Park, Lincolnshire.
Father Sir John Thorold, 8th Baronet (1703–5 June 1775), landowner and Sheriff of Lincolnshire, 1751. (First son.) In 1883, Sir John Thorold, Baronet, owned 12,553 acres worth £17,652 p.a. in Lincolnshire.
Mother Elizabeth (d. 1779), daughter of Samuel Ayton of West Harrington.
Education Secondary schooling unknown; Hertford College, Oxford.
Marriage In 1771 to Jane (d. 1807), daughter of Millington Hayford of Oxton Hall, Nottinghamshire. (Three sons, one daughter.)

Religion Anglican.
Public MP (Whig) Lincolnshire, 1779–96. High Sheriff of Lincolnshire, 1778–9.
Miscellaneous Described as 'an independent country gentleman' in *HP;* was a great book collector.
References *HP; BP; ODNB.*

1815/12 **Name** **Beevor, John**
Dates c. 1726, Norwich–26 April 1815, Norwich.
Probate £100,000 (PCC).
Occupation 'Doctor in Physic' and physician in Norwich. (Occupational category VI.30; venue 11.)
Address Lived in Norwich.
Father Thomas Beevor (d. 1750), brewer of Norwich.
Mother Probably Hester, daughter of John Sharpe of Norwich.
Education Secondary schooling unknown; Caius College, Cambridge (Scholar; MB; MD, 1764; Fellow, 1750).
Marriage Unknown.
Religion Anglican.
Public None known.
Miscellaneous 'For many years an eminent [medical] practitioner' in Norwich (*GM*), and a founder of the Norwich Hospital. His brother was Sir Thomas Beevor, 1st Baronet (1726–1814), 'agriculturalist and prison reformer', in *ODNB.* Whether John Beevor had any other source of wealth is not known.
References *GM,* 1815, vol. II, p. 89; *Alum. Cantab.*

1815/13 **Name** **Baker, Peter William**
Dates c. 1756–25 August 1815, Spring Gardens, Middlesex.
Probate £150,000 (PCC).
Occupation Inherited a large building fortune from father, the builder who laid out Baker Street in the eighteenth century; also had a landed estate. Does not appear to have engaged in any other business, although was qualified as a barrister. (Occupational category II.10; venue 2.)
Address Lived at New Street, Spring Gardens, Middlesex and at Ranston, Dorset.
Father William Baker, 'a great London builder who made a large fortune' (*HP*), of Wick House, Middlesex and Bromley, Shropshire.
Mother Martha, daughter of Peter Stover of Highgate.
Education Eton and Trinity College, Cambridge; barrister, Lincoln's Inn.
Marriage In 1781, to Jane, daughter of James Clitheroe of Boston House, Middlesex (d.s.p.).
Religion Anglican.
Public MP (Whig) Arundel, 1781–4; Wootton Bassett, 1802–6; Corfe Castle, 1807–15; High Sheriff of Dorset, 1787–8.
Miscellaneous His estate came to his cousin Sir Edward Baker Littlehales. His heir in 1883 could not readily be traced.
References *GM,* 1815, vol. II, p. 281; *HP.*

Name **Morland, William** 1815/14
Dates 1739–14 July 1815, Pall Mall.
Probate £100,000 (PCC).
Occupation Banker (Morland, Ransom & Co.) of 57 Pall Mall, Middlesex. (Occupational category IV.16; venue 2.) His firm was patronised by the Prince of Wales and by Byron, among others. He was also Chairman of the British Fire Office Company and of Westminster Fire and Life Office.
Address Lived at 56 Pall Mall and at Lee, Kent.
Father John Morland, 'merchant' of Woolwich, Kent. (Some sources say that, his father having died young, William Morland was brought up by his grandfather, a shipwright of Sheerness; other sources state that his father died in 1799. Although a shipwright, the grandfather left him 'well provided for'.)
Mother Elizabeth Pratt.
Education Unknown.
Marriage In 1762, to Mary Ann, daughter of Austin Mills. (One daughter, who married Sir Scrope Bernard [later Morland], Baronet, MP, partner in the bank.)
Religion Anglican.
Public MP (Whig, then pro-Pitt) Taunton, 1786–1806. Joint Receiver of the Duchy of Cornwall, 1789–90.
Miscellaneous In early life travelled to Italy and collected art works. Treasurer of the British Institute for the Encouragement of Fine Arts.
References *HP; GM,* 1815, vol. II, p. 94.

Name **Bishop, Charles** 1815/15
Dates c. 1750–13 October 1815, Sunbury, Middlesex.
Probate £120,000 (PCC).
Occupation 'H.M. Procurator-General' (*GM,* and probate calendar) of Doctor's Commons, in the City of London. (Occupational category VI.29 and 31; venue 1.)
Address 'Formerly of Doctor's Commons and Russell Place, Middlesex, and then of Devonshire Place, Middlesex and Sunbury, Middlesex' (probate calendar).
Father Unknown.
Mother Unknown.
Education Unknown. May well be the Charles Bishop admitted to Trinity Hall, Cambridge in 1767 as a Scholar; *Alum. Cantab.* says 'perhaps admitted Proctor in the Court of Arches, 1771; died 1815'.
Education Unknown.
Religion Anglican.
Public None known.
Miscellaneous In the 1812 Law List, is apparently given under solicitors as 'King's Proctor, of 12 Doctor's Commons', along with Iltid Nicholls, proctors and notaries.
References *GM,* 1815, vol. II, p. 382.

Name **Anderson, James** 1815/16
Dates c. 1728–2 February 1815 Lamb's Conduit Street, Middlesex.

Probate £100,000 (PCC).
Occupation 'Merchant' of 73 Lamb's Conduit Street, Middlesex (1794 directory). (Occupational category IV.21? Venue 2.)
Address Lived at 73 Lamb's Conduit Street, Bloomsbury, Middlesex in 1811 and at death.
Father Unknown. The name suggests a Scottish origin.
Mother Unknown.
Education Unknown.
Marriage Name unknown. He had two sons, John and Simpson, and a daughter Charlotte. His wife was apparently deceased when he drew up his will. In view of the second son's name, she was possibly Mary Simpson, who married a James Anderson on 19 October 1767 at Allhallows, London Wall (Family Search).
Religion Unknown.
Public None known.
Miscellaneous As is so often the case, the nature of his mercantile activities is unclear.
References *GM,* 1815, vol. I, p. 188; will (PROB 11 online).

1815/17 **Name** **Gist, Samuel**
Dates c. 1724–16 January 1815 (*GM*).
Probate £150,000 (PCC).
Occupation Lloyd's broker in the City of London; previously a captain of a slaver and owned plantations in America (*GM*). Was apparently connected with Bristol in early life. He had been retired for twenty years when he died. (Occupational category IV.22; venue 1; also Occupational category I; venue 29.) It should be noted that a significantly different account of his life was given in Charles Roster, *The Fabulous History of the Dismal Swamp Company* (1999) – the 'Dismal Swamp' being an area in southern Virginia. According to the summary of this work online (www.melungeons.com), Gist was born in 1717 in Bristol, meaning that he was nearly ninety-eight at his death, and had been a business partner of George Washington. Claims from it have been added below.
Address Lived at Gower Street, Middlesex at death.
Father Unknown.
Mother Unknown.
Education Educated at the Free School, Bristol.
Marriage Unknown. Had two daughters. Melungeons.com states that he married, in 1747, Sarah (b. 1715), daughter of Thomas William Massey, and had four daughters. According to Family Search, his wife was Sarah Mary Massie, who married him, about 1747, in Virginia.
Religion Unknown. According to www.melungeons.com, he was (citing Royster) 'an old Jew' of Khazarian descent, and related to the Da Costa family. This claim (in particular) should be taken with many grains of salt.
Public None known.
Miscellaneous Was 'formerly the captain of a Carolina merchant ship' (i.e. a slaving vessel) and owned plantations in America with slaves whom he manu-

mitted in 1808 and resettled in a free settlement for former slaves in Ohio. In later life, was a successful Lloyd's broker who is 'said to have amassed more than half a million of money', although this is clearly an exaggeration. According to Royster (melungeons.com), he went to Virginia in 1739 as an indentured servant and owned a large plantation in the James Valley. In 1765, he became a tobacco merchant in London, with an office in America Square, City of London, and was a loyalist during the American Revolution. According to this source, he owned 274 slaves at his death. In my opinion, *GM* sounds more plausible, although further evidence is needed.

References *GM,* 1815, vol. I, p. 182; melungeons.com and other online sources about his freed slaves.

Name **Parker, Robert** 1815/18

Dates Unknown–21 July 1815, Stockport, Cheshire.

Probate £175,000 (York PC). This is the earliest York Prerogative Court estate of £100,000 or more to be identified.

Occupation Calico printer and manufacturer of Heaton Works near Stockport. Also – if this was the same man – he had works at 22 Cannon Street, Manchester and a house at 17 Piccadilly, Manchester (1808 Manchester directory). (Occupational category II.7; venue 4.)

Address Stockport and Manchester.

Father Unknown.

Mother Unknown.

Education Unknown.

Marriage Unknown.

Religion Anglican. Left money in his will to the Stockport Sunday School, the Established Church School and the British and Foreign Bible Society.

Public None known.

Miscellaneous An early cotton manufacturer at Stockport, five miles from Manchester, but little is known about his career.

References *GM,* 1815, vol. II, p. 187.

WEALTH-HOLDERS, 1816

1816/1 **Name** **Pattle, Thomas Charles**

Dates 1771 Bengal–26 November 1815, Macao. Will probated July 1816.

Probate £100,000 (PCC).

Occupation 'Civil Service of the East India Company in Canton' (probate calendar); 'a rich Canton merchant' – *ODNB* entry for Edward Gibbon Wakefield, who married his daughter (see 'Spouse' below). (Occupational category IV.19; venue 29.)

Address Lived in China most of his life. Having joined the East India Company in his native Bengal he was based in Canton from 1789, where he was Second Super-Cargo, 1807–10. Subsequently, in Macao, he was responsible for the export of the uncoined silver used by the Chinese as currency and grew rich from commissions. He was described as 'a man of remarkably convivial Habits and of great Conversational Powers'. Lindsay and May Ride, *An East India Company Cemetery: Protestant Burials in Macao,* edited by Bernard Mellor (1996, p. 124).

Father Thomas Pattle (1748–1818), a director of the East India Company, whose own father, Thomas, was also in the Company's service, on an Indiaman. (First son.) One of his brothers, James Pattle (1775–1845), was the father of celebrated photographer Julia Margaret Cameron (Roots Web).

Mother Sarah Hasleby (c. 1755–1813), who married Thomas Pattle in Bengal on 10 June 1770 (Family Search).

Education Unknown.

Marriage To Eliza Anne Frances Middleton (d. 1820) on 5 May 1795: India Office Ecclesiastical Returns, Bengal Presidency (Family Search). He had one daughter, Eliza, who married Edward Gibbon Wakesfield (1775–1845), the famous pioneer of colonisation. The daughter died in 1820, a year after eloping with Wakesfield.

Religion Presumably Anglican.

Public None known.

Miscellaneous The Pattles were related to Virginia Woolf, the writer, and to Sir James Brooke KCB (1803–68), 'White Rajah of Sarawak'.

References Probate calendar; *ODNB* for Wakefield; online sources.

1816/2 **Name** **Brunswick, Duke of, Frederick William**

Dates 9 October 1771–16 June 1815: killed at the battle of Quatre Bras fighting with Wellington's troops.

Probate £100,000 'within province' (PCC).

Occupation Foreign Royalty: Duke of Brunswick-Wolfenbuttel and Major-General. (Occupational categories VI.31 and I; venue 29, although this is indicative.)

Address In Brunswick; did not reside in Britain.

Father Charles Ferdinand, Duke of Brunswick (d. 10 November 1806), a general in the Seven Years' War.

Mother Princess Augusta Charlotte of Wales (1737–1813), sister of King George III.

Education Unknown.
Marriage In 1802, to Mary, daughter of Charles, Margrave of Baden. (Two sons.)
Religion Lutheran.
Public No positions in Britain. Became Duke of Oels in 1805.
Miscellaneous Why he left a large fortune in England is unclear, but his wealth here presumably stemmed from his British royal connections and his participation as an ally of Britain against Napoleon. A famous general in the Prussian Amy, known as the 'Black Duke'.
References *GM*, 1816, vol. II, p. 633; online sources.

Name **Antrobus, Philip** 1816/3
Dates c. 1754–27 January 1816, Lower Cheam, Surrey.
Probate £100,000 (PCC).
Occupation Stockbroker at 2 North Piazza, Royal Exchange, City of London (1793 directory). (Occupational category IV.23; venue 1.)
Address 'Formerly of Craven Street, Strand, then New Street, Spring Gardens, and Cheam, Surrey' (probate calendar).
Father Philip Antrobus (1720–4 November 1788) of Congleton. (Second son.) Sir Edmund Antrobus, 1st Baronet (d. 1826), a prominent banker, was the cousin of Philip (d. 1816), but apparently not a partner.
Mother Anne, daughter of John Vardon of Congleton.
Education Unknown.
Marriage Apparently unmarried.
Religion Presumably an Anglican.
Public None known.
Miscellaneous Little could be traced of his career. He might have been a banker, like his relative, as well as a stockbroker. The Baronet Antobuses owned nearly 11,000 acres of land, chiefly in Wiltshire, in 1883.
References *GM*, 1816, vol. I, p. 277.

Name **Weare, John Fisher** 1816/4
Dates c. 1746–23 January 1816.
Probate £300,000 (PCC).
Occupation 'Merchant', at 21 Queen Square, Bristol (1775 and 1793 directories). (Occupational category IV.19 or 21; venue 12.)
Address Bristol and Lower Ashton, Somerset.
Father William Weare. (He was probably the William Weare who died 15 January 1785 and was a member of the Bristol Corporation and Sheriff of Bristol.) His father was George Weare of Donyton and Bristol.
Mother Unknown.
Education Unknown.
Marriage In 1770, to Anne (d. November 1831), daughter of Samuel Gardner of Woodford, Essex.
Religion Anglican: purchased a living.

Public Member of Bristol Corporation, 1777–1816; Mayor of Bristol, 1794, also Sheriff.

Miscellaneous Was pro-slavery but advocated conciliation with the American colonies, 1775. He was probably the brother of William Weare (c. 1750–1836; see 1837/6, who left £100,000).

References *GM,* 1816, vol. I, p. 187; *BLG,* 1846.

1816/5 **Name** **Clagett, Horatio**

Dates c. 1756–19 December 1815, Clapham Rise, Surrey.

Probate £180,000 (PCC).

Occupation 'Merchant' of Clagett & Pratt, 1 America Square, City of London (1808 directory). (Occupational category IV.21 or 19? Venue 1.)

Address 'Formerly America Square, City of London and South Lambeth, and then Clapham Rise, Surrey' (probate calendar).

Father Unknown. A Horatio Clagett was born on or about 10 August 1756 in Prince George's County, Maryland, son of John and Sarah. If that is not him, he may have had connections with that American family, in which the forename Horatio seems to have recurred down the generations.

Mother Unknown.

Education Unknown.

Marriage Name unknown. His daughter Virginia (d. 1820) married, in 1814, Thomas Nash Kemble (1791–1833), sugar broker in the City (see 1833/16, left £120,000).

Religion Unknown.

Public None known.

Miscellaneous Nothing beyond the local directory.

References *GM,* 1815, vol. I, p. 643.

1816/6 **Name** **Rymer, John**

Dates Unknown – probated 1816.

Probate £160,000 (PCC).

Occupation 'Warehouseman' at 8 Basinghall Street, City of London (1793 directory) and also presumably of Mincing Lane, City. (A 'warehouseman' was usually a wholesale merchant, and sometimes a retail merchant.) (Occupational category IV.21; venue 1.)

Address 'Formerly of Mincing Lane, City of London, and then Barnwell Court and Streatham, Surrey' (probate calendar).

Father Unknown.

Mother Unknown.

Education Unknown.

Marriage Unknown.

Religion Unknown.

Public None known.

Miscellaneous Little could be traced about him.

References Probate calendar only.

Name Webster, Thomas, DD 1816/7
Dates 1731, probably at Dundee–6 July 1816, Bath.
Probate £120,000 (PCC).
Occupation He is listed as Thomas Webster, Doctor of Divinity, of Bath in the probate calendar. On 23 September 1755, in Clunie, Perthshire, he was ordained a minister of the Church of Scotland. On 26 July 1759 he became minister at Kinghorn, Fife, but was dismissed on 24 November 1779 'having given offence to his parishioners by not opposing the Catholic Toleration Bill'. He then went to live with his brothers at Clapham. This man was a relative of Sir Andrew Wedderburn, Baronet, a Scottish merchant in the City of London (*GM*). Several other London merchants with Scottish names are mentioned in his will, and he also noted there that he had estates in Scotland, although the will fails to shed light on his career.
Address Of Bath at death.
Father Probably George Webster (Family Search).
Mother Probably Beatrice Proctor (Family Search).
Education Secondary schooling unknown; graduated MA, St Andrews University, 1750.
Marriage On 8 June 1756, to Elizabeth (Betty) Meik (d. 23 June 1758), daughter of James Meik, portioner of West Banchory. (One daughter, Katherine, 14 September 1757–24 March 1772.)
Religion Church of Scotland; his religion at death is unknown.
Public None known.
Miscellaneous See above: a very odd case. It is possible that he had a second career as a City of London merchant, but there is no direct evidence.
References *GM,* 1816, vol. II, p. 94; will (PROB 11 online).

Name Penrhyn, Dowager Baroness, Susan Pennant (née Warburton) 1816/8
Dates 1745–1 January 1816.
Probate £120,000 'within province' (PCC).
Occupation Landowner: she owned the Penrhyn estate in Carnarvonshire and the Winnington Hall estate in Cheshire in her own right. (Occupational category I.)
Address Winnington Hall, Cheshire and Penrhyn Castle, Carnarvonshire.
Father (Lieut. Gen.) Hugh Warburton (1885–1771) of Winnington, Cheshire and Penrhyn. (Only daughter.)
Mother Susanna, daughter of Edward Norris MD who was MP for Liverpool, 1714–22.
Education Unknown.
Marriage In 1765, to Richard Pennant (c. 1737–21 January 1808), landowner and slate manufacturer; MP (Whig) Liverpool 1761–90, created 1st Baron Penrhyn in 1790. (He is in the *ODNB.*) Marriage childless: title extinct at his death. He also owned large estates in the West Indies and was connected with many leading West Indies planter families.

Religion Anglican.
Public None; see husband.
Miscellaneous She and her husband became major landowners and slate manufacturers; she had inherited large estates in her own right. The property went on her death to the husband's cousin's son, George Hay Dawkins, and a distant relative, Henry Dawkins, was created Baron Penrhyn of the second creation in 1866. In 1883, Lord Penrhyn owned 49,548 acres worth £71,018 p.a., chiefly in Carnarvonshire. (See also 1814/23.) By her will, 'she left pensions of £45 each to six of her horses' (*CP*).
References *CP; BP.*

1816/9 **Name** **Callan, 1st Baron, George Agar**
Dates 4 December 1751–29 October 1815 (29 October 1815, *GM*).
Probate £160,000 'within province' (PCC).
Occupation Presumably a landowner, but may also have had linen manufacturing interests. (Occupational category I.)
Address Chiefly Ringwood, County Kilkenny.
Father James Agar (d. 3 August 1769, killed in a duel with Henry Flood) of Ringwood, County Kilkenny. (His sister was the Countess of Brandon.)
Mother Rebecca, daughter of William Flower, 1st Baron, Castle Durrow (Irish peerage).
Education Eton and Trinity College, Cambridge (matriculated 1770).
Marriage Unmarried – the title became extinct.
Religion Anglican.
Public MP in the Irish Parliament for Callan, 1777–90. Created 1st Baron Callan (Irish peerage), 1790. Irish Representative Peer, 1801–15. PC (Ireland) 1789.
Miscellaneous His nephews were Viscount Clifden and the Earl of Normanton. In 1883, their heirs owned about 53,000 acres worth £33,000 p.a. in Ireland alone, chiefly in County Kilkenny.
References *GM,* 1815, vol. II, p. 475; *CP.*

1816/10 **Name** **Taylor, Sir Richard Brisset, 2nd Baronet**
Dates 15 October 1783 (October 1779, *GM*)–18 May 1815, Great Cumberland Place, Middlesex.
Probate £100,000 'within province' (PCC).
Occupation Jamaica fortune. (Occupational category I; venue 29.)
Address In England; lived at Great Cumberland Place, Middlesex.
Father Sir John Taylor, 1st Baronet (d. 8 May 1786), of Lysson Hall, Jamaica, planter. Created baronet 1778; FRS. (Only surviving son.)
Mother Elizabeth (d. c. 1821), daughter of Philip Houghton of Jamaica.
Education Unknown.
Marriage Unmarried.
Religion Anglican.
Public None known.
Miscellaneous Died young, probably aged thirty-one.

References *Complete Baronetage*, vol. V, p. 202.

Name **Harvey, Robert** 1816/11
Dates c. 1729–29 January 1816.
Probate £300,000 (PCC).
Occupation Banker in Norwich. (Occupational category IV.16; venue 11.)
Address Norwich.
Father Robert Harvey (1697–1773), banker in Norwich and Mayor, 1738.
Mother Lydia (d. 1759), daughter of John Black, Mayor of Norwich.
Education Unknown.
Marriage To Judith (d. 1810; marriage date unknown), daughter of (Captain) Onley, RN; presumably John Onley, made captain 1729; dismissed the service 1738 (David Syrett and R. L. DiNardo, eds, *The Commissioned Sea Officers of the Royal Navy 1660–1815*, 1994, pp. 338–3). (Three sons, one daughter.)
Religion Anglican.
Public Mayor of Norfolk, 1779 and 1809; JP, Norfolk.
Miscellaneous 'Alderman and father of the City of Norwich' who 'accumulated an immense property' (*GM*). Many of his relatives were part of the local civic elite. His son Charles Savill-Onley (1756–1843) was an MP from 1802 to 1826. The Harveys became baronets in 1868.
References *GM*, 1916, vol. 1, p. 278; *BP*, 1939.

Name **Sansom, Philip** 1816/12
Dates c. 1746–29 October 1815, Leytonstone, Essex.
Probate £140,000 (PCC).
Occupation Merchant (Philip Sansom & Sons) of 10 Finsbury Square, City of London (1811 directory), and probably also of Lombard Street. (Occupational category IV.21; venue 1.)
Address 'Of Lombard Street and Leytonstone, Essex' (probate calendar).
Father Unknown. *GM* states that he died at the age of sixty-nine, but a Philip Sansum (sic) was baptised 5 April 1752, St Botolph without Aldgate, London, son of Thomas and Frances (Family Search).
Mother Unknown.
Education Unknown.
Marriage Unknown.
Religion Unknown.
Public None.
Miscellaneous May have been one of the merchants involved with Wilberforce and John Clarkson in opposing the slave trade, 1787. (*ODNB* for Clarkson.)
References *GM*, 1815, vol. II, p. 636.

Name **Teissier, Stephen** 1816/13
Dates c. 1753–4 February 1816, Lower Grosvenor Street, Middlesex.
Probate £100,000 (PCC).
Occupation 'Merchant' of 13 Austin Friars, City of London (1793 directory).

The 1811 directory lists a Lewis Teissier at 2 Austin Friars. The 1802–4 directory lists a Charles Teissier, Loubier & Co., merchants of 27 Austin Frairs. (Occupational category IV.21? Venue 1.) In 1811, a Stephen Tiessier moved his residence to London from Dedham, Suffolk, where he owned a large house and 59 acres that he put up for auction (*Ipswich Journal*, 15 June 1811; Roots Web).

Address 'Of Austin Friars, City of London, and then Lower Grosvenor Street, Middlesex' (probate calendar).

Father Unknown. A Stephen Teissier was naturalised in 1728. An Etienne Tessier was baptised at Threadneedle Street French Huguenot Church on 4 May 1729, son of Jacques and Charlotte (née Loubier), and a Stephen (or Etienne) Teissier married an Elisabeth Loubier there in 1735 (Family Search, which shows the presence of a number of Teissiers in eighteenth-century London). Charles was possibly the brother of Lewis Teissier (b. 1736) of Woodcote Park, Surrey – see Titles of Foreign Nobility, 'De Teissier' in *BP.*

Mother Unknown.

Education Unknown.

Marriage Unknown.

Religion Presumably originally Huguenot.

Public None known.

Miscellaneous Probably a relative of Charles Teissier (1810/11).

References *GM,* 1816, vol. II.

1816/14 **Name** **Whitbread, Samuel**

Dates 18 January 1764, Cardington, Bedfordshire–6 July 1815; committed suicide by slitting throat.

Probate £200,000 (PCC).

Occupation Brewer in Southwark. (Occupational category III.2; venue 2.) Also a considerable landowner: in 1883, his successor owned 13,829 acres worth £21,790 p.a. in Bedfordshire and Essex. Was also the owner of the Drury Lane Theatre.

Address Southill, Bedfordshire and Dover Street, Middlesex.

Father Samuel Whitbread (1720–11 June 1796), MP for Bedfordshire, the largest brewer in England, who also became a large landowner in Bedfordshire. He was regarded as a millionaire. (Only son.)

Mother Harriet (d. May 1764, when her son was only three months old), daughter of William Hayton, solicitor of Ivinghoe, Buckinghamshire.

Education Eton; Christ Church, Oxford and then St John's College, Cambridge (BA, 1755).

Marriage In 1758, to Elizabeth, daughter of Sir Charles Grey (later 1st Earl Grey), sister of the Prime Minister.

Religion The family were originally Nonconformists; the father became an Anglican – he was a 'peculiar and forcible Anglican' (*ODNB*).

Public MP (radical Whig) Bedfordshire, 1790–1815. Whitbread was regarded as so 'erratic' that he never held office.

Miscellaneous Owned five-eighths of the largest brewery in London and was

also a substantial landowner, augmenting his land holdings in the 1790s. Very famous but was apparently clinically insane at the end of his life.
References *ODNB; BLG.*

Name **Tasker, John** 1816/15
Dates c. 1736–6 March 1816, Baker Street, Middlesex.
Probate £140,000 (PCC).
Occupation Unknown: may be the builder of this name of 59 Mortimer Street, Cavendish Square, in the 1802–4 and 1805 directories. (If so, occupational category II.10; venue 2.)
Address Lived at 8 Baker Street, Portman Square from c. 1808.
Father Unknown.
Mother Unknown.
Education Unknown.
Marriage Unknown.
Religion Possibly Roman Catholic – there was a well-known Catholic family called Tasker. The *Dictionary of Catholic Biography* includes a man, possibly his son, educated at Downside, described as a 'traveller'.
Public None known.
Miscellaneous Little could be traced about him.
References *GM,* 1816, vol. I, p. 373.

Name **Parry, Thomas** 1816/16
Dates 23 October 1732–9 April 1816, Berners Street, Middlesex.
Probate £160,000 (PCC).
Occupation Director of the East India Company from 1783 until his death. (Occupational category IV.19; venue 1?)
Address Berners Street, Middlesex and Banstead, Surrey.
Father Henry Parry of St Clement Danes, London.
Mother Unknown.
Education Unknown.
Marriage To Mary Oakes, sister of Thomas Oakes, 'member of the Company in India'. A Thomas Parry and a Mary Oakes married on 2 July 1767 at St Thomas's Church, Portsmouth (Family Search).
Religion Unknown, probably Anglican.
Public None known.
Miscellaneous His son Richard was a director of the East India Company. His grandson, Thomas Gambier Parry (1816–88), is in the *ODNB* as a 'benefactor and art collector'. A Thomas Parry (1768–1824) is in the *ODNB* as a merchant in Madras. It is not clear if they were related.
References *GM,* 1816, vol. I, p. 475; *BLG,* 1846, 1937.

Name **Conyngham, Ellen, Dowager Countess** (née Merrett) 1816/17
Dates c. 1725–15 June 1816, Lower Grosvenor Street, Middlesex.
Probate £140,000 'within province' (PCC).

Occupation Landowner. (Occupational category I.) In 1883, the Marquess Conyngham owned 166,710 acres worth £50,076, chiefly in Ireland.
Address Chiefly Hughenden, Bucks, which was later Disraeli's home, and Conyngham Hall, Knaresborough, Yorkshire, purchased 1796.
Father Solomon Merrett, 'merchant' of St Olave's, Hart Street, London.
Mother Rebecca, daughter of Robert Savage of London, 'a packer'.
Education Unknown.
Marriage In 1744, to Henry, 1st Earl Conyngham (1705–3 April 1781), member of the Irish Parliament and an Irish peer (created Baron, 1753; Viscount, 1756; Earl, 1781). He died childless, his titles passing to a nephew.
Religion Anglican.
Public See husband.
Miscellaneous Inherited Hughenden Manor from her husband. It is unclear how much of her fortune came from her merchant father.
References *GM*, 1816, vol. I, p. 573.

1816/18 **Name** **Tash, William**
Dates Unknown (but see 'References' below)–17 July 1816 Broomfield House, Southgate.
Probate £100,000 (PCC).
Occupation Urban property owner in Southgate, Middlesex – owned 502 acres on the borders of Southgate and Tottenham in Edmonton, the second largest estate in Edmonton (*VCH Middlesex*, vol. 5, p. 158). (Occupational category I.) He obtained this estate from his wife's family, which had owned it since before 1624. Any source of wealth apart from his ownership of this property is unknown. After his death, the estate was sold to Henry Philip Powys.
Address Lived at Broomfield House, Southgate and at Berkeley Court in Surrey.
Father Unknown. Possibly Thomas Tash (see 'References' below).
Mother Unknown. Possibly Honor Nicolson (see 'References' below).
Education Unknown.
Marriage To Mary Jackson, whose family had owned the Edmonton estate. Marriage date unknown.
Religion Unknown.
Public None known.
Miscellaneous The 1774 London directory lists a Thomas Tash, wine merchant, of 5 Suffolk Lane, Cannon Street. It is not known whether this man was a relative. A William Tash was baptised at Allhallows, London, in January 1746, son of Thomas and Honor Tash (Family Search). Honor Tash was presumably Honor Nicolson, who is known to have married a Thomas Tash. Honor was a daughter of Felix Calvert (1693–1756) of Furneux Pelham, near Bishops Stortford, Hertfordshire, and his wife Christian (d. 1759), daughter of Josias Nicolson of Clapham. Honor's brother Nicolson Calvert (1725–93) was High Sheriff of Hertfordshire in 1749 and MP for Tewkesbury 1754 and 1761 (*BLG*, p. 177, 'Calvert of Hunsdon').
References *GM*, 1816, vol. II, p. 137; *Middlesex Quarterly*, vol. 2, pp. 12–13.

Name **Watts, David Pike** 1816/19
Dates Baptised 7 February 1754, Allhallows, London–29 July 1816.
Probate £160,000 (PCC).
Occupation Inherited a wine-merchant fortune. (Occupational category IV.20? Venue 1?) Watts inherited the fortune of Benjamin Kenton (1719–25 May 1800), a wealthy wine merchant who was reported to have left £300,000. Watts was engaged to his daughter, who died of tuberculosis before their marriage. He had been employed as a clerk in Kenton's firm (*ODNB* for Kenton).
Address 'Formerly of Gower Street, the Portland Place, Middlesex.' He might also have owned an estate at Ilam Hall, Derbyshire.
Father Probably William Watts (1717–73), 'cooper' of London, who was also the grandfather of John Constable, the famous painter. Watts was Constable's uncle (*ODNB* for Constable).
Mother Jane; maiden name apparently Brickbeck (Family Search.)
Education 'By Alexander Cruden, author of a Concordance of the Bible.'
Marriage To Mary Ann Morison or Morrison of Durham. Marriage date unknown; possibly 1788 (Family Search). (Two sons, who both predeceased him; one daughter, Mary, who died in 1840, wife of Jesse Russell who lived at Ilam Hall, Derbyshire.) (See Watts-Russell, *BLG*.)
Religion Anglican – 'zealous', gave much to Anglican charities.
Public Was also noted as a 'wealthy connoisseur' and patron of writers. Was an ardent Tory of 'undeviating loyalty' to the 'Constitution of his country'.
References *GM*, 1816, vol. II, p. 182.

Name **Scott, Thomas** 1816/20
Dates 1723–probated October 1816
Probate £100,000 (PCC).
Occupation 'Brickmaker' (*HP*), probably at Shepperton, Middlesex. (Occupational category II.11; venue 2?) Also brewery fortune, from his father-in-law.
Address Lived at 2 Grafton Street, Piccadilly and at Shepparton, Middlesex. (1811 Court directory; probate calendar.)
Father Thomas Scott of Fulham.
Mother Unknown.
Education Unknown.
Marriage In 1782, to Susannah, daughter of Henry Thrale, brewer and MP, and widow of Arnold Nesbitt, MP.
Religion Anglican.
Public MP (Whig) Bridport, 1780–90.
Miscellaneous A wealthy brickmaker and MP.
References *HP.*

Name **Gildart, Thomas** 1816/21
Dates Baptised 25 April 1731, St Nicholas, Liverpool–30 October 1816 at Finchley.
Probate £150,000 (PCC).
Occupation West and East India merchant fortune in Liverpool. (Occupational

category IV.19; venue 5.) This fortune was made by his father and other relatives – he did not live in Liverpool.

Address Lived at Moss Hall, Finchley, Middlesex.

Father Richard Gildart (1670–25 January 1770, apparently aged ninety-nine), West India and East India merchant, MP for Liverpool, 1734–54; Mayor of Liverpool, 1731, 1736. Partner of his father-in-law.

Mother Mary, daughter of Sir Thomas Johnson, MP for Liverpool, 1701–23.

Education Unknown.

Marriage In 1759 to Sarah Meyer (d. 1767).

Religion Anglican.

Public None known.

Miscellaneous Is not known to have had business dealings in Liverpool in later life.

References *GM*, 1816, vol. II, p. 471; Society of Genealogists family trees.

1816/22 **Name** **Robarts, Abraham**

Dates 27 September 1745, Stepney–26 November 1816, Taplow.

Probate £350,000.

Occupation An 'eminent' banker (Robarts, Curtis, Robarts & Curtis of Lombard Street) and government loan contractor. (Occupational category IV.16; venue 1.) Also a 'West Indian factor and a director of the East India Company', a director of Royal Exchange Insurance and a partner in Lechmere's Bank, Worcester.

Address Lower Grosvenor Street, Middlesex and Worcester.

Father Abraham Robarts (1701–7 October 1761) of Stepney, occupation unknown. He had the title 'Captain'.

Mother Elizabeth (baptised 11 November 1708–November 1768), only daughter of Samuel Wildey (d. 1752 without male issue) of Stepney.

Education Unknown.

Marriage In 1774, to Sabine, daughter of Thomas Tierney and sister of (Rt. Hon.) George Tierney, MP. (Four sons, three daughters.) Their sons William Tierney Robarts (see 1820/24) and Abraham Wildey Robarts (1779–1858, q.v.). are also in the *ODNB*.

Religion Anglican.

Public MP (pro-Pitt) Worcester, 1796–1816; DL, City of London.

Miscellaneous Was also Colonel of the 1st Regiment of East India Volunteers. Had multiple lucrative interests, but was best known as a 'fortunate' loan contractor.

References *ODNB; HP; GM,* 1816, vol. II, p. 568.

1816/23 **Name** **Blicke, Sir Charles**

Dates 1745–30 December 1815, Bedford Place, Russell Square, Middlesex.

Probate £160,000 (PCC).

Occupation Surgeon to St Bartholomew's Hospital, London, who 'accumulated a large fortune through his practice in London' (*ODNB*). (Occupational category VI.30; venue 2.)

Address South Lambeth and Bedford Place, Russell Square.

Father Not stated in *ODNB* or any other printed source. According to Family Search, he was John Blicke.
Mother Elizabeth Seager (Family Search).
Education St Bartholomew's Hospital, London.
Marriage By licence, on 17 November 1777, to Jane Phelp (Family Search). His son Charles Tufton Blicke (1781–1827; see 1838/16), left £100,000. His daughter Frances (d. November 1834) married (General) Sir Loftus William Otway (d. 1834). She left £300,000 (1872/80).
Religion Presumably Anglican. According to Family Search his son Charles Tufton Blicke was baptised at All Hallows Staining, London, on 23 November 1781.
Public Knighted 1803.
Miscellaneous 'Surgeon to St Bartholomew's Hospital, 1787.' Governor of the College of Surgeons, 1801. Edited a work on yellow fever. A pupil thought him 'fonder of money-making than of science' (*ODNB*).
References *ODNB; GM,* 1816, vol. I, p. 89.

Name **FitzWilliam, 7th Viscount** (Irish peerage), **Richard FitzWilliam** 1816/24
Dates 1 August 1745, Richmond, Surrey–4 February 1816, Bond Street, Middlesex.
Probate £350,000 'within province' (PCC).
Occupation Landowner. (Occupational category I.) His property passed to the 11th Earl of Pembroke. In 1883, the Earl of Pembroke owned around 2,600 acres in Ireland, worth around £37,000 p.a. This enormous discrepancy suggests that it was urban land, docks or the like. His brother succeeded to the title.
Address Appears to have lived at Richmond, Surrey and at Bond Street, Middlesex.
Father Richard, 6th Viscount FitzWilliam (d. 25 May 1776), landowner.
Mother Catherine (1710–86), daughter of Sir Matthew Decker, Baronet, of Richmond, Surrey.
Education Charterhouse; Trinity Hall, Cambridge (MA, 1764).
Marriage Unmarried. Had numerous mistresses, and had three illegitimate children by a French ballerina.
Religion Anglican, but pro-Catholic Emancipation.
Public MP (—) Wilton, 1790–1806 (Irish peerage, could serve). Vice-Admiral of Leinster.
Miscellaneous Best known as the founder of the FitzWilliam Museum, Cambridge, which he founded in his will with a legacy of £120,000. FRS, 1789. Wrote the *Letters of Atticus.* Has an entry in the *ODNB* as a 'benefactor and musical antiquary', as was a noted musical scholar who had studied in Paris and Spain.
References *ODNB; CP.*

Name **Norfolk, 11th Duke of, Charles Howard** 1816/25
Dates 14 or 15 March 1746–16 December 1815, Norfolk House, Middlesex.
Probate £140,000 'within province' (PCC).
Occupation Landowner. In 1883, the Duke of Norfolk owned 29,866 acres

worth £75,596 p.a., plus land in London and mining royalties. He was, of course, one of the greatest aristocrats. (Occupational category I.)
Address Chiefly Arundel Castle, Sussex and Norfolk House, Middlesex.
Father Charles, 10th Duke of Norfolk (1720–31 August 1786).
Mother Katherine (d. 21 November 1784), daughter of John Brockholes of Claughton, Lancashire.
Education 'Roman Catholic tutors' and in France.
Marriage First, in 1767, to Mariana (d. 1768), daughter of John Coppinger of County Cork; second, in 1771, to Frances (d. 1820), daughter of Charles Fitzroy-Scuddamore.
Religion Roman Catholic until 1780, then Anglican.
Public MP (Whig) Carlisle, 1780–6. PC, 1783–98, when stripped of his positions after toasting 'The People' instead of 'The King'. Lord Lieutenant, West Riding, 1792–98. Lord Lieutenant, Sussex 1807–death. Deputy Earl Marshal, 1782.
Miscellaneous Was a Freemason after converting to Anglicanism; FRS, FSA.
References *ODNB; CP.*

1816/26 **Name** **Wynne, Sir William**
Dates 1729–1815.
Probate £180,000 (PCC).
Occupation 'Official Principal of the Court of Arches and Master of the Prerogative Court of Canterbury', of Doctor's Commons, City of London. (Occupational category VI.29 and 31; venue 1.) 'A judge of the Admiralty Court and Master of Trinity Hall, Cambridge from 1803 till his death (*Alum. Cantab.*).
Address London and Soughton Hall, Flintshire.
Father (Rt. Revd) John Wynne, DD (1667–15 July 1743), Bishop of Bath and Wells.
Mother Anne, daughter of Robert Pugh of Bennarth.
Education Secondary education unknown; Trinity Hall, Cambridge (admitted 1746; Scholar. LL.B, 1752; LL.D, 1757; Fellow, 1755–1803).
Marriage Probably unmarried; left property to his nephew Robert John Bankes (d. 1855) who is in *ODNB* as 'traveller and antiquary'.
Religion Anglican.
Public Knighted, 1788; PC, 1789.
Miscellaneous A senior official of the lucrative Prerogative Court and associated legal entities. Was Vicar-General of Canterbury from c. 1752; Advocate of the Court of Arches, 1757; King's Advocate-General, 1778; Dean of Arches, 1788–1809.
References *Alum. Cantab; Knightage.*

1816/27 **Name** **Lubbock, Sir John, 1st Baronet**
Dates Baptised 20 August 1744–24 February 1816.
Probate £120,000 (PCC).
Occupation Banker (senior partner, Lemon, Fuller & Lubbock of Mansion House Street, City of London), later known as Lubbock & Co. It began c. 1772 as

Robarts, Lubbock & Co. 'Settled in London, becoming an opulent merchant and banker there' (*HP*). (Occupational category IV.16; venue 1.)
Address Mansion House Street, City of London and St James's Place, Middlesex.
Father (Revd) William Lubbock (d. 20 April 1754) of Lamas, Norfolk, also described as 'a Cambridge don'. (First son.)
Mother Elizabeth, daughter of William Cooper of Calthorp.
Education Unknown.
Marriage In 1771, to Elizabeth (d. 1846), daughter of Frederick Commerell of Hanwell. (Since he died childless the baronetcy passed to his nephew.)
Religion Anglican.
Public MP (pro-Pitt, the pro-Whig) for Bossiney, 1796–1802, Leominster, 1801–12; created baronet, 1806.
Miscellaneous His relative was created 1st Baron Avebury.
References *HP; BP.*

Name **De la Torre, Don Manuel** 1816/28
Dates Unknown – probated October 1816.
Probate £120,000 (PCC).
Occupation Presumably of De la Torre and Emanuel, 'merchants' of 22 Finsbury Square, City of London (1814 directory). (Occupational category IV.19 or 21 and VI.31; venues 1 and 29.) Given in PROB 11 as 'Don Manuel de la Torre, Commissary Ordonnateur of the Royal Armies of His Catholic Majesty the King of Spain, of Finsbury Square, St Luke, Middlesex.'
Address Lived at Finsbury Square, City of London (probate calendar).
Father Unknown. A James Torre of Upper Montague Street, Montague Square, died 29 August 1816, aged sixty-eight (*GM*).
Mother Unknown.
Education Unknown.
Marriage Unknown.
Religion Unknown. Possibly Jewish, from the name of his partner. (See *Jewish Chronicle,* 25 November 1887, for a Jewish family of this name.) Also possibly Roman Catholic, a stronger possibility.
Public None known.
Miscellaneous He appears to have been an army contractor for the Spanish armies during the Napoleonic Wars.
References Probate calendar only.

WEALTH-HOLDERS, 1817

1817/1 **Name** **Bell, (Revd) William**

Dates 1731, Greenwich, Kent–29 September 1816 at Little Dean's Yard, Westminster.

Probate £120,000 (PCC).

Occupation Prebendary of Westminster, 1765; Treasurer of St Paul's Cathedral, 1810. (Occupational category VI.30; venue 1 and 2.) Decribed in the probate calendar as 'Prebendary of the Collegiate Church, St Peter's, Westminster'. Also Domestic Chaplain to Princess Amelia, daughter of King George III.

Address Various ecclesiastical residences in London; previously Cambridge.

Father William Bell, 'Esquire'.

Mother Unknown.

Education Greenwich School; Magdalene College, Cambridge (BA and 8th Wrangler; M., 1756). DD, 1767.

Marriage Unmarried.

Religion Anglican clergyman.

Public None known.

Miscellaneous He must have made the bulk of his fortune from his ecclesiastical income – no other source of income is known. He was also the vicar of St Bride's Church in the City of London, 1780–99, and a Fellow of Magdalene College, Cambridge, 1753–c. 1765. Bell was a well-known and respected author on population, arguing that 'luxury' decreased the birth rate, a bad thing, and on religion, advocating 'practical piety' (*ODNB*).

References *ODNB*.

1817/2 **Name** **Russell, William**

Dates 1734–8 June 1817.

Probate £140,000 (PCC) + £140,000 (York PC); i.e. £280,000. (This is one of several cases in which a wealthy person's estate was probated in part in the PCC and in part in the York PC. The assumption is that the real value of the estate is the total of the two figures.)

Occupation Colliery owner at Wallesend, County Durham. (Occupational category I.1; venue 9.) Also a merchant and banker at Sunderland.

Address Brancepeth Castle (purchased 1796), near Durham.

Father Robert Russell (1682–22 March 1757) of Rowenlands, possibly a merchant of Sunderland. (Second son.)

Mother Unknown.

Education Unknown.

Marriage First, in 1762, to Mary, daughter of Robert Harrison, 'a merchant of considerable wealth' of Sunderland; second (marriage date unknown) to Anne, daughter of (Admiral) Mark Milbanke and granddaughter of Sir Ralph Milbanke. His son Matthew Russell (1765–1822) was an MP, 1802–22; his daughter Margaret (d. 1852) married Sir Gordon Drummond (1772–1854), army officer, in *ODNB*.

Religion Anglican.
Public None known.
Miscellaneous After a career as a merchant and banker at Sunderland, 'made an immense fortune' from coal mines at Wallesend. (*HP* for son.) He 'raised infantry' in 1795. John Buddle (1773–1843), in *ODNB*, was his colliery manager. Russell purchased Brancepeth in 1796 for £75,000 from Sir Henry Vane Tempest. He should not be confused with William Russell (1740–1818), 'merchant and reformer', in *ODNB*.
References *HP; GM*, 1817, vol. I, p. 573.

Name **Close, (Revd) Samuel** 1817/3
Dates September 1749–probated October 1817.
Probate £120,000, 'within province' (PCC).
Occupation Probably a landowner in Ireland. (Occupational category I.) In 1883, Maxwell Charles Close of Drumbanagher, Newry owned 12,765 acres worth £13,441 p.a. Close was Rector of Keady, County Armagh and of Drakestown County Meath, but obviously did not accumulate his fortune from being an Irish clergyman.
Address Lived at Elm Park, County Armagh.
Father Maxwell Close (d. 1793) of Elm Park, High Sheriff of County Armagh, 1780. (First son.)
Mother Mary, daughter of (Captain) Robert Maxwell of Fellows Hall, County Armagh and brother of John, Lord Farnham.
Education Unknown, but was probably the Samuel Close who received a BA from Dublin University in 1769 and an MA in 1779.
Marriage In 1782, to Deborah (d. 1815), daughter of (Very Revd) Arthur Champagne, Dean of Clonmacnoise. (Four sons, three daughters.)
Religion Anglican clergyman.
Public None known.
Miscellaneous A Maxwell Close (1822–1903), geologist, is in *ODNB*.
References *Burke's Irish Gentry*, 1904, 'Close of Drumbanagher'; *BLG*, 1855.

Name **Carew, Richard** (né Gee) 1817/4
Dates c. 1745–18 December 1816. According to Family Search, a man of this name was born about 1741. The date c. 1745 comes from *GM*.
Probate £100,000 (PCC).
Occupation A large landowner near London in Surrey and Kent. (Occupational category I.) At his death, his property passed to his brother's widow and then to (Admiral) Sir Benjamin Hallowell (Carew) (d. 1834). It was eventually purchased by the wealthy brewer Cosmo Bonsor. It is not clear who owned his lands in 1883.
Address Of Orpington, Kent and Beddington Park, Surrey.
Father Richard Gee (d. 1791) of Beddington Park. His maternal ancestors had owned this property for several generations. His son inherited the property from his uncle in 1780 and changed his name.

Mother Possibly Elizabeth Holt (Family Search).
Education Unknown.
Marriage Unmarried.
Religion Presumably Anglican.
Public None known.
Miscellaneous Presumably the land was largely rural in his lifetime.
References *VCH Surrey*, vol. 3, p. 317; *GM*, 1816, vol. II, p. 573.

1817/5 **Name** **Groves, Paul**
Dates Unknown–27 January 1817, Stockwell, Surrey.
Probate £120,000 (PCC).
Occupation Stockbroker in London. (Occupational category IV.23; venue 1.)
Address 'Formerly of the Stock Exchange and the Stockwell, Lambeth' (probate calendar).
Father Unknown.
Mother Unknown.
Education Unknown.
Marriage Unknown. A Paul Groves married a Mary Briant on 28 November 1773 at St Clement Danes, Westminster, and a Paul Groves married a Jane Warman on 12 April 1783 at St Bride's, Fleet Street (Family Search).
Religion Unknown.
Public None known.
Miscellaneous Not listed in any London directory, 1793–1815, under his name.
References *GM*, 1817, vol. II, p. 184.

1817/6 **Name** **Ramsden, Elizabeth**
Dates Allegedly 1710 or 1711–probated June 1817, aged 106; died at Bath.
Probate £140,000 (PCC).
Occupation Unknown, probably landed. (Occupational category I.)
Address 'Formerly of Mansfield Wodehouse, Nottinghamshire, then of Bath' (probate calendar).
Father Possibly John Smyth of Heath, Yorkshire.
Mother Unknown.
Education Unknown.
Marriage Possibly (marriage date unknown) to Robert Ramsden of Carlton Hall, Nottinghamshire (1708–9 February 1769) (Rasmden in *BP* and *BLG*, but it is not clear whether this is the Elizabeth Ramsden listed in these sources. If so, her son was Robert Ramsden [1753–1830], but she would have been forty-two or more when he was born, assuming her advanced age at death is correct.)
Religion Unknown, presumably Anglican.
Public None known.
Miscellaneous Obviously her age at death – 106, so stated in *GM* – is probably an exaggeration. Nothing more could be traced about her. Mansfield Wodehouse is near Mansfield, Nottinghamshire
References *GM*, 1817, vol. I, p. 646.

Name **Parry, Richard** 1817/7
Dates c. 1776–30 June 1817, Banstead, Surrey.
Probate £160,000 (PCC).
Occupation Director of the East India Company. (Occupational category IV.19; venue 1?)
Address Berners Street, Middlesex and Banstead, Surrey.
Father Thomas Parry (1732–1816), Director of the East India Company, who left £160,000 (see 1816/16).
Mother Mary, daughter of Thomas Oakes.
Education Unknown.
Marriage To Mary (d. 1821; marriage date unknown), daughter of Samuel Gambier and niece of (Admiral) Lord Gambier. One son, Thomas Gambier Parry (d. 1888), who is in *ODNB*.
Religion Anglican.
Public None known.
Miscellaneous Continued in his father's career.
References *GM*, 1817, vol. I, p. 642; *ODNB* for son.

Name **Clavill, William** 1817/8
Dates Unknown – probated October 1817; died in Bath.
Probate £100,000 (PCC).
Occupation The only clue as to his occupation in his will is that he states that he was a member of the Drapers' Company in the City of London. He is not listed in any London or Bristol directories in this period.
Address 'Bath' is the only address given in the probate calendar.
Father Unknown.
Mother Unknown.
Education Unknown.
Marriage Ann, surname unknown. In his will, he states that he was 'living apart from her for many years on account of her base [. . .] conduct'. No children are mentioned. In his will, he mentions his cousins, John Beaumont and William Dyor, and his kinsman William Clavill Dyor, but with no indication as to their occupations.
Religion Anglican: in his will he gave instructions regarding his burial in a parish church.
Public None known.
Miscellaneous *GM*, 1817, vol. I, p. 619 lists a William Clavell (sic) who died 15 June 1816 aged sixty-two (*GM*, 1817, vol. I, p. 639). He was the son of William Richards and Margaret, daughter of Edward Clavell of Smedmore House, Dorset, whose family had owned this estate for centuries. He took the name 'Clavell' and was High Sheriff of Dorset in 1797. He married, in 1797, Sophia, daughter of (Captain) Richard Bingham. There is no mention of Bath in this obituary, nor of a wife named Ann. Smedmore is near Corfe Castle. No other person of this name could be traced in any printed source.

References Will (PROB 11 online) and above sources.

1817/9 **Name** **Haldimand, Anthony Francis**
Dates c. 1741–9 October 1817.
Probate £250,000 (PCC).
Occupation Banker and merchant in the City of London. (Occupational category IV.16 and 21; venue 1.) (Anthony Francis Haldimand & Sons, merchants, of 10 Bearbinder Lane, 1815 directory; 'merchants' at 51 St Mary Axe in 1808.) A founder of Morris, Prevost & Co., bankers.
Address Lived at Clapham Common.
Father François Louis Haldimand, 'a burgess of Yerdun, Switzerland and a merchant at Turin' (*ODNB*).
Mother Unknown.
Education Unknown.
Marriage In 1768, to Jane Pickersgill. (Seventeen children.) His son William (1784–1862), banker and MP, is in the *ODNB*, as is his daughter Jane Marcet (1769–1858), 'writer on science'.
Religion Presumably originally Huguenot or Calvinist, probably later an Anglican: he was married at St Mary's Church, Watford.
Public None known.
Miscellaneous He was also the heir of his uncle, (Lieut. Gen.) Sir Frederick Haldimand (1718–91), Governor General of Canada.
References *GM*, 1817, vol. II, p. 474; *ODNB* for relatives.

1817/10 **Name** **Marlborough, 4th Duke of, George Spencer**
Dates 26 January 1739–29 January 1817, at Blenheim Palace.
Probate £200,000 (PCC).
Occupation Landowner. (Occupational category I.) In 1883, the Duke of Marlborough owned 23,511 acres worth 336,557 p.a.
Address Chiefly Blenheim Palace, Oxfordshire and Marlborough House, St James's.
Father Charles Spencer, 3rd Duke of Marlborough, KG (1706–20 October 1758).
Mother Elizabeth (d. 1761), daughter of Thomas, 2nd Baron Trevor.
Education Eton. Received a DCL from Oxford University, 1763.
Marriage In 1762, to Caroline (d. 1811), daughter of John, 4th Duke of Bedford. (Three sons, five daughters.)
Religion Anglican.
Public Served as Lord Privy Seal, 1763–5. PC, 1762; KG, 1768. Lord Lieutenant of Oxfordshire, 1760–death. High Steward of Oxford, 1779.
Miscellaneous Was an officer in the Coldstream Guards, 1755–8.
References *ODNB*; *CP.*

1817/11 **Name** **Townsend, Richard**
Dates c. 1746–6 May 1817 at Newbury, Berkshire.

Probate £100,000 (PCC).
Occupation Unknown. London directories of the period list several possibilities, including a solicitor of Carey Street, a feather merchant of Ludgate Hill and the proprietor of a paper-hanging warehouse at Nightingale Lane. There is no clearly identifiable man of this name in any genealogical guide to the upper classes.
Address Newbury, Berkshire. *VCH Berkshire,* vol. 4, p. 61 states that his family obtained the patronage of the Ickford Church in the eighteenth century and the family retained it until 1890, but this is his only mention.
Father Unknown. A Richard Townsend was born and baptised at Wantage, Berkshire, in December 1749, son of Richard and Catherine (Family Search).
Mother Unknown.
Education Unknown.
Marriage Unknown. *GM* (1817, vol. II, p. 189) notes that a 'Mrs. Richard Townsend' of Upper Gower Street died 11 August 1817.
Religion Anglican.
Public None known.
Miscellaneous A mystery.
References *GM,* 1817, vol. I, p. 477.

Name **Fludyer, Henry** 1817/12
Dates Unknown – probated 1817. His estate is recorded in PROB 8, but not, strangely, in the online index for PROB 11.
Probate £100,000 (PCC).
Occupation Presumably a relative of Sir Samuel Fludyer, 1st Baronet (1704–68), clothier and merchant, reputedly worth £900,000 at death, in *ODNB.* The London directory of 1793 lists a Fludyer, Maitland & Co. of 79 Basinghall Street. (If Henry Fludyer was a merchant, his occupational category is IV.21? Venue 1.)
Address Lived at Wallingford, Berkshire (probate calendar).
Father Unknown.
Mother Unknown.
Education Unknown.
Marriage Unknown.
Religion Unknown.
Public None known.
Miscellaneous *GM,* 1819, vol. I, p. 91 states that a Henry Fludyer died 'lately' in Berkshire, leaving £1,000 to the Radcliffe Infirmary and dividends from £1,000 to the poor of Wallingford, but no other information is given. A John Fludyer of Abingdon, Berkshire matriculated at Pembroke College, Oxford in 1725 aged sixteen (BA, 1732; MA, 1735) (*Alum. Oxon.*)
References Probate calendar only.

Name **Elwes, John** 1817/13
Dates Unknown–10 April 1817.
Probate £250,000 (PCC).
Occupation The illegitimate son of John Elwes (d. 1789), a celebrated miser and

MP who allegedly left £800,000. This man apparently made his money from urban land – he owned the land in Marylebone on which Portman Square and Portland Place were built (*ODNB* for his descendant Henry John Elwes, 1846–1932). The senior Elwes also had brewing interests and owned land at Stoke, Suffolk. (Occupational category I?)

Address 'Formerly of Welbeck Street, Cavendish Square, then Colesbourne, Gloucestershire, Fingest Grove, Buckinghamshire, and Portman Sqaure, Middlesex' (probate calendar).

Father As noted, the illegitimate son of John Elwes (1714–89), MP for Berkshire, 1772–89, celebrated in his time as an eccentric and miser and said to be Dickens's original for Ebenezer Scrooge. He supposedly left his two sons more than £500,000 (*ODNB*).

Mother Elwes's housekeeper, Elizabeth Moren.

Education Was deliberately kept without formal education by his father, believing that education was instilled only to make a person ready to part with his money (an interesting insight!) (*ODNB* for father.)

Marriage To Sarah (marriage date unknown), widow of (Captain) Holmes. (Two sons.) Family Search lists the marriage on 23 December 1789 at St Anne's Church, Soho, of a John Elwes and a Sarah Haynes (the latter name may have been wrongly transcribed).

Religion Anglican.

Public None known.

Miscellaneous Was an officer in the Horse Guards. In 1883, Robert Elwes of Stoke Cottage, Suffolk, owned 3,441 acres worth £4,226 p.a., and John Henry Elwes of Colesbourne, Cheltenham, owned 4,549 acres worth £4,066 p.a.

References *GM,* 1817, vol. I, p. 381; *ODNB* for father and other relatives; *BLG.*

1817/14 **Name** **Pepys, Edmund**

Dates c. 1737–1 April 1817 at Russell Place, Fitzroy Square.

Probate £180,000 (PCC).

Occupation Unknown. Family Search lists an Edmund Pepys 'of the Inner Temple and Braiswick House, London', whose dates are given as 1738–1817; his parents are listed as John Pepys and Jane Smith. There is no listing of Edmund Pepys in the Law Lists or any other contemporary directory, although an *Edward* Pepys, 'attorney', of New Broad Street was listed in the 1760 directory. (If this was the same man, then Occupational category VI.29; venue 2?)

Address 'Formerly of Southampton Street, then Upper Charlotte Street and then Russell Place, Fitzroy Square' (probate calendar). He was living in Southampton Street in 1794.

Father As noted in 'Occupation' above, Family Search states John Pepys, although there is no direct evidence that this is correct.

Mother Family Search states Jane Smith.

Education Unknown.

Marriage In 1763, to Sarah Triquet. The wedding took place at St Anne's Church, Soho. The bride's dates are given as 1740–1806. There were several

Huguenot Triquets in eighteenth-century London, including daughters baptised Sarah, but she was apparently born at Spalding, Lincolnshire (Family Search).
Religion Presumably Anglican.
Public None known.
Miscellaneous There is no evidence that he was related to Samuel Pepys or to the Earls of Cottenham, whose name was Pepys.
References *GM,* 1817, vol. I, p. 379.

Name **Lombe** (né Hase)**, Sir John, 1st Baronet** 1817/15
Dates c. 1731–27 May 1817 at Great Melton Hall, near Dereham, Norfolk.
Probate £160,000 (PCC).
Occupation Inherited the fortune of his uncle Sir Thomas Lombe (1685–1739), who introduced silk-throwing machinery into England and was later Sheriff of London. Lombe's factories were at Derby. He supposedly made £120,000 from his inventions (*ODNB*). (Occupational category II.9; venue 17.) There is no evidence that Sir John Lombe was in trade, but he appears to have been a substantial landowner.
Address Lived at Bylaugh Hall, Great Melton, Norfolk. He purchased this estate in 1796.
Father John Hase of East Dereham, Norfolk: he took the name Lombe in 1763.
Mother Mary, daughter of Edward Lombe and heiress of Sir Thomas Lombe.
Education Unknown.
Marriage Unmarried. His title went to a relative, Sir Richard Paul Jodrell, Baronet (1745–1831), in *ODNB* as 'classical scholar and playwright', and some of his property to Edward Lombe né Beevor (d. 1852), a landowner and politician.
Religion Anglican.
Public Created baronet, 1783.
Miscellaneous In 1883, Henry Evans-Lombe of Bylaugh Hall owned 13,832 acres in Norfolk worth £17,789 p.a., and (Revd) Sir Edward Jodrell, Baronet, owned 5,972 acres worth £6,735 p.a., chiefly in Norfolk.
References *ODNB* for relatives; *GM,* 1817, vol. I, p. 571; *BP.*

Name **Harman, John** 1817/16
Dates 10 September 1738, Ealing, Middlesex–29 July 1817, Higham Hall, Walthamstow.
Probate £200,000 (PCC).
Occupation Merchant and banker at Old Jewry, City of London (Harman, Hoare & Co., 1793 directory; Harman & Co., merchants of Frederick Place, Old Jewry, 1802 directory). Presumably chiefly a banker. (Occupational category IV.16? Venue 1.)
Address Lived at Higham Hall, Walthamstow at death.
Father Jeremiah Harman (1707–41) 'merchant'.
Mother Hannah Gurnell (1715–95).
Education Unknown.
Marriage In 1760, to Elizabeth (d. 12 May 1821), daughter of Truman Harford of Bristol.

Religion Quaker, throughout his life, but 'one of the gay, tithe-paying Friends of Gracechurch Street' (*GM*).
Public None known.
Miscellaneous Part of the Quaker 'Cousinhood' of bankers and merchants.
References *GM*, 1817, vol. II, p. 185; Quaker sources.

1817/17 **Name** **Clements, John**
Dates c. 1732–9 August 1817.
Probate £120,000 'within province' (PCC).
Occupation Unknown. It is stated without evidence on Family Search that he was from County Cavan and was the son of John Clements. He might well have been a relative of the earls of Leitrim of Northern Ireland, whose name was Clements, but there is no direct evidence – he is not listed in *BP.* (In 1883, the Earl of Leitrim owned 56,852 acres worth £11,006 p.a.) A Henry John Clements (1781–1843) was an MP in 1805–18 and 1840–3. The Clements were also rich placemen in eighteenth-century Dublin, but there is no evidence that this man was related to them.
Address Of Upper Grosvenor Street (probate calendar); no other address given.
Father John Clements (1699–1746) of County Cavan, according to Family Search, but there is no direct evidence.
Mother Ruth Parr, according to Family Search.
Education Unknown.
Marriage In 1767, to Margaret Pulling, according to Family Search, but there is no direct evidence.
Religion Presumably Anglican or other Protestant.
Public None known.
Miscellaneous Cannot be identified with certainty.
References *GM*, 1817, vol. II, p. 189.

1817/18 **Name** **Hall, Benjamin**
Dates 1778–31 July 1817, Upper Brook Street, Middlesex.
Probate £100,000 (PCC).
Occupation Ironmaster: partner and son-in-law of Richard Crawshay (d. 1810) and a residuary legatee under his will. Owned the Rhymney Ironworks, purchased 1803. He sold his iron interests in 1816 to William Crawshay. (Occupational category II.3; venue 19.)
Address 'Of Hensol Castle, Llantrisant, Glamorganshire; Abercarn, Glamorganshire; and Upper Brook Street, Middlesex' at death (probate calendar).
Father (Revd Dr) Benjamin Hall, DD (1742–25 February 1825), Prebendary of Llandaff and Chancellor of Llandaff, a 'huge pluralist'.
Mother Elizabeth, daughter of Henry Grant of Knoll Castle, Glamorganshire.
Education Westminster School; Christ Church, Oxford (MA). Barrister, Lincoln's Inn, 1801.
Marriage In 1801, to Charlotte, daughter of Richard Crawshay of Cyfarthfa (see 1810/15), the millionaire ironmaster. She allegedly 'brought £40,000' to the

marriage (*HP*). Their son Benjamin (1802–67), MP, became Baron Llandover. He was the 'Big Ben' for whom Parliament's clocktower is named.
Religion Anglican.
Public MP (Tory) Totnes, 1806–12; Westbury, 1812–14; Glamorganshire, 1814–death. Despite his Tory affiliation, was said to have been 'the first great industrialist to enter the political field in Wales in opposition to the landed interest' (*Dictionary of Welsh Biography*).
Miscellaneous Was apparently active as an ironmaster from c. 1802 to 1816. Died at the age of thirty-nine.
References *Dictionary of Welsh Biography; ODNB* for relatives.

Name **Balfour, Arthur** 1817/19
Dates Unknown–14 November 1817, Portland Place, Middlesex.
Probate £160,000 (PCC).
Occupation Unknown. He is listed only in 'Court' directories (i.e. inhabitants of the wealthier areas, listed without an occupation) of London directories from 1796–1811. It is possible that he made a fortune overseas. There is no evidence that he was related to the family of Arthur James Balfour, the twentieth-century Prime Minister.
Address Lived at 31 Portland Place, Middlesex.
Father Unknown. In his will he mentions his brother John Balfour and his cousin Francis Balfour, as well as Sir George Atkinson and John Balfour Atkinson.
Mother Unknown.
Education Unknown.
Marriage Unmarried. His heir was his brother John.
Religion Anglican. Buried at New Church, Marylebone.
Public None known.
Miscellaneous Nothing more could be traced about him, or the origins of his wealth, in any source.
References *GM*, 1817, vol. II, p. 568.

Name **Taylor, Martha** 1817/20
Dates 22 March 1786–26 October 1817, Cheltenham.
Probate £120,000 (PCC).
Occupation Jamaica plantation fortune. (Occupational category I; venue 29.)
Address Lived at Great Cumberland Street, Middlesex and in Cheltenham.
Father Sir John Taylor, 1st Baronet (d. 1786) of Lysson Hall, Jamaica. She was the sister of Sir Richard Brisset Taylor, Baronet, d. 1816 (see 1816/10).
Mother Martha, daughter of George Taylor of Jamaica.
Education Unknown.
Marriage Unmarried.
Religion Presumably an Anglican.
Public None known.
Miscellaneous She had three elder sisters. How she accumulated such a large fortune is unclear.

References *GM,* 1817, vol. II, p. 565; *BP.*

1817/21 **Name** **Beauchamp, 1st Earl, William Lygon**

Dates 25 July 1747–21 October 1816, St James's Square, Middlesex.

Probate £700,000 (PCC) plus £60,000 (York PC); sec £760,000.

Occupation Landowner. In 1798, inherited the great estate of a relative, William Jennens, and inherited the Madresfield property from his father. (Occupational category I.) In 1883, Earl Beauchamp owned 17,634 acres worth £24,941 p.a. in Worcestershire and other counties.

Address Chiefly at Madresfield near Great Malvern, Worcestershire.

Father Reginald Lygon (né Pyndar; d. 25 December 1788) of Madresfield Court.

Mother Susannah, daughter of William Hannen of Bettisfield, Flintshire.

Education Secondary schooling unknown; Christ Church, Oxford (matriculated 1764).

Marriage In 1780 to Catherine (d. 1844), daughter of James Denn. (Four sons, six daughters.)

Religion Anglican.

Public MP (Pittite Tory) Worcestershire 1775–1806. Created Baron Beauchamp in 1806 and Earl Beauchamp in 1815.

Miscellaneous When he applied for an earldom in 1809, he 'claimed to have an income of £40,000 per year' (*HP*). He was rumoured to have paid £10,000 to the Prince Regent's Privy Purse for his title (*HP*).

References *ODNB; HP; CP.*

1817/22 **Name** **Champion, Benjamin**

Dates Unknown–13 June 1817 at New Broad Street.

Probate £160,000 (PCC).

Occupation Lloyd's insurance broker (Benjamin and Samuel Champion, 'merchants and insurance brokers' of 32 New Broad Street, 1811 directory). (Occupational category IV.22; venue 1.) His brother Samuel died 13 April 1817 (*GM*).

Address 'New Broad Street, City of London' (probate calendar). This was also his home, as his brother died there 'at his brother's house'.

Father Unknown. An Alexander Champion, possibly another brother, 'sent in regular reports of naval and political developments and shipping in the Baltic' to Lloyd's.

Mother Unknown.

Education Unknown.

Marriage Unknown.

Religion Unknown.

Public None known.

Miscellaneous Nothing more is known of him.

References *GM,* 1817, vol. I, p. 573.

Name **Cazenove, John Henry** 1817/23
Dates c. 1737–24 June 1817, at Savile Row, Middlesex.
Probate £100,000 (PCC).
Occupation Merchant (John Henry Cazenove, Frederick & Co., merchants of 11 Copthall Court, Throgmorton Street, City of London, 1793 directory). (Occupational category IV.21? Venue 1.) A director of Royal Exchange Assurance, elected 1792. His relationship to the other Cazenoves in the City, including the famous firm of stockbrokers, is unclear.
Address 'Formerly of Copthall Court, City of London the Savile Row, Middlesex and Waldron, Surrey' (probate calendar).
Father Unknown.
Mother Unknown.
Education Unknown.
Marriage Unknown.
Religion Possibly originally Huguenot or Calvinist.
Public None known.
Miscellaneous *ODNB* includes a Philip Cazenove (1798–1880), stockbroker, and a John Cazenove (1788–1879), merchant and political economist.
References *GM*, 1817, vol. I, p. 641.

Name **Jones, John** 1817/24
Dates Unknown–21 June 1817 at Brunswick Square, Middlesex.
Probate £160,000 (PCC).
Occupation 'Apothecary' at Gracechurch Street, City of London (probate calendar). The 1794 directory lists a 'Board and Jones, chymists [sic] and druggists' of 89 Gracechurch Street; also 1803, 1808 directories. (Occupational category II.6 and IV.20; venue 1.)
Address 'Formerly of Gracechurch Street, City of London, and then of Derry Ormond, Cardiganshire and Brunswick Square, Middlesex' (probate calendar).
Father Unknown.
Mother Unknown.
Education Unknown.
Marriage Probably in 1761 to Hannah, daughter of Andrew Smith of Gunston House, Hertfordshire. (Two sons, four daughters.) (*BLG*, 1871 and 1937, 'Inglis-Jones of Derry-Ormond', which states that he died in January 1815.) John Jones, who left £160,000 (see 1835/15) was probably his son.
Religion Unknown, presumably Anglican.
Public None known.
Miscellaneous Presumably a druggist, but may have sold chemicals for industrial processes, brewing, or the like. He may have come from Cardiganshire, where he acquired an estate.
References *GM*, 1817, vol. I, p. 640.

Name **Page, John** 1817/25
Dates Unknown – probated November 1817.

Probate £120,000 (PCC).

Occupation 'Formerly a naval agent' (probate calendar). (A naval agent ensured that prize monies due were paid to his officer-clients.) (Presumably occupational category IV.18 or 21; venue 2 or 1?) Possibly this man was a wholesale purchaser and supplier of naval goods. There is no evidence that he worked directly for the Government as an official.

Address Of 70 Great Russell Street, Middlesex.

Father Unknown.

Mother Unknown.

Education Unknown.

Marriage Unknown.

Religion Unknown; presumably an Anglican.

Public None known.

Miscellaneous Nothing more is known of him.

References Probate calendar only.

Name **Quintella, Baron de, Joaquin Pedro** 1818/1
(given as 'Baron Joaquin Pedro Quintela or Quintella or Baron Quintela or Baron de Quinitella, gentleman of the household' of the King of Portugal, in IR11)
Dates Unknown – probated February 1818.
Probate £400,000 (PCC).
Occupation Unknown. Lived Lisbon. He was apparently a Portuguese Court official. He might have been connected with the wine trade.
Address Of Lisbon. No other address given.
Father Unknown.
Mother Unknown.
Education Unknown.
Marriage Unknown.
Religion Presumably Roman Catholic.
Public None known.
Miscellaneous Nothing more could be traced about him. Why he left £400,000 in England is unknown.
References Probate calendar only.

Name **Campion, William** 1818/2
Dates c. 1738–28 February 1818, Lewes, Sussex.
Probate £140,000 (PCC).
Occupation Probably connected with the Portuguese wine trade as a merchant and also a landowner in Sussex, but occupation isn't clear. (If a Portugal merchant, then Occupational category IV.19; venue 29.)
Address Of Lewes, Sussex.
Father Probably William Campion (1700–75) of Hurstpierpoint, Sussex. (Second son.) In 1883, William Henry Campion of Danny Park, Hurstpierpoint, owned 6,832 acres worth £7,891 p.a. in Sussex, Essex and Kent.
Mother Probably Elizabeth, daughter of Edward Parteriche of the Isle of Ely.
Education Unknown.
Marriage First, to Catherine (d. 1763; marriage date unknown), daughter of Wiliam Dawson of Portugal. (One son.) Second, in 1774, to Priscilla, daughter of John Page of Oporto. (One son, three daughters.)
Religion Presumably Anglican.
Public None known.
Miscellaneous Both wives were the daughters of Englishmen, presumably wine merchants, in Portugal.
References *GM,* 1818, vol. I, p. 469; *BLG,* 1846, 1937.

Name **Combe, Harvey Christian** 1818/3
Dates 1752 Andover–4 July 1818.
Probate £140,000 (PCC).

Occupation Brewer. Began as corn factor in London. In 1787, acquired Gyfford & Co. brewers of Long Acre, Middlesex, later renamed Combe, Delafield & Co. His name is still known as part of Watney, Combe & Reid, brewers. Was also a director of the Globe Insurance Company (Occupational category III.12; venue 2).

Address Lived at Cobham Park, Surrey and Great Russell Street at death.

Father Harvey Combe (1716–2 August 1787), 'a prosperous attorney' of Andover. (Second son.)

Mother Christian Jarman (d. 1774), whose family had corn- and sugar-refining interests in London.

Education Apprenticed at an early age to his maternal uncle, Boyce Tree, 'a prosperous City corn and malt factor' (*ODNB*).

Marriage In 1780, to his cousin Alice (d. 1818), daughter of Boyce Tree. (Four sons, six daughters.)

Religion Anglican.

Public MP (Whig) for the City of London, 1796–1817; a friend of Fox, Sheridan, etc., Alderman of the City of London, 1790–1817; Sheriff of London, 1791–2; Lord Mayor of London, 1799–1800.

Miscellaneous Began as a successful corn factor in the City, as partner with his uncle, a major brewer at Long Acre. Bought Cobham Park in 1807.

References *ODNB; GM,* 1818, vol. II, p. 83.

1818/4 **Name** **Price, Sir Charles, 1st Baronet**

Dates 25 July 1748–19 July 1818, Spring Grove, Richmond, Surrey.

Probate £100,000 (PCC).

Occupation 'Oil, rum, and brandy merchant' (1793) at Snow Hill, City and then a 'general merchant' (from 1801) at William Street, Blackfriars; then a banker and partner Harrison, Price, Kaye, and Chapman (*HP*). (Occupational category IV.21 and 16; venue 1.)

Address 'Formerly of Snow Hill and William Street in the City of London, then Bedford Square, Middlesex and Spring Grove, Richmond' (probate calendar).

Father (Revd) Ralph Price (1715–20 November 1779), Vicar of Lyminge, Kent. (Third son.)

Mother Sarah (d. 1780), daughter of William Richardson of Smalley, Derbyshire.

Education Unknown.

Marriage In 1773, to Mary (d. 1838), daughter of William Runge of Conduit Street, Hanover Square. (Five sons, five daughters.)

Religion Anglican.

Public MP (moderate Tory) City of London, 1802–12; Alderman of the City of London, 1797; Sheriff of London, 1799, Lord Mayor of London, 1802, JP for London; Created baronet, 1804.

Miscellaneous Joined his uncle, an oil merchant in the City. Price was also a colonel of the London Volunteers and President of the Commercial Travellers' Association.

References *HP; BP; GM*, 1818, vol. II, p. 84.

Name **Bright, Lowbridge** 1818/5
Dates Baptised 12 April 1741, All Saints, Worcester. Probated October 1818.
Probate £100,000 'within province' (PCC).
Occupation 'Merchant' in Bristol – a prominent slave trader and West Indies merchant. (Occupational category IV.19; venue 12.) A 'merchant' of 1 Charlotte Street, Bristol (1775 directory); at Great George Street, Bristol, in 1793 'Gibbs, Bright & Co.' were West Indies merchants in Bristol.
Address Brockbury, Coddington, Herefordshire and Bristol (probate calendar).
Father Robert Bright (Family Search). Lowbridge Bright's uncle Henry Bright (1715–77) was a very prominent Bristol-based West Indies merchant, slave trader and shipowner, in *ODNB*. He reputedly left £50,000.
Mother Dorothy (baptised 9 October 1717), daughter of Edward Lowbridge (Family Search).
Education Unknown.
Marriage Unknown.
Religion Unknown. His parents were married in an Anglican church, the one where he and his mother were baptised. His uncle was a Congregationalist but was buried in an Anglican church. His cousin and business partner Richard, Henry's son (see 'Miscellaneous' below), was a Unitarian.
Public None known. His uncle was prominent in Bristol local politics.
Miscellaneous The designation 'within province' (i.e. of the Canterbury Prerogative Court) for his estate suggests that he had holdings in the West Indies. By 1765, his uncle Henry Bright's commercial interests in Jamaica were flagging somewhat, and he was sent out to revive them, soon entering into partnership with a Nathaniel Milward. Henry retired in 1775 owing to ill health, and his son Richard, recently come of age, went into partnership with Lowbridge, who thereupon based himself at Bristol. By the time of the American Revolution, 'the Bright family was considered in higher credit than any other house in England: the Brights were known to be men of large fortune' (Morgan, 'Bristol West India Merchants').
References I. V. Hall, 'Whitson Court Sugar House, Bristol, 1665–1824', *Trans. Bristol and Glouc. Arch. Soc.*, vol. 65 (1944); Kenneth Morgan, 'Bristol West India Merchants in the Eighteenth Century', *Transactions of the Royal Historical Society*, 1993; Trevor Burnard and Kenneth Morgan, 'The Dynamics of the Slave Market and Slave Purchasing Patterns in Jamaica 1655–1788', *William and Mary Quarterly*, vol. 58 (2001); *ODNB* for uncle.

Name **Howard** (né Bagot)**, Richard** 1818/6
Dates 18 November 1730, Blithfield, Staffordshire–12 November 1818, Ashtead Park, near Epsom, Surrey.
Probate £350,000 (PCC).
Occupation Landowner. (Occupational category I.) It is unclear who owned his estates in 1883. He inherited lands from Thomas, Earl of Berkshire.

Address 'Of Ashtead Park, Surrey; Castle Rising, Norfolk; Elford, Staffordshire; Livens, Westmorland; and Grosvenor Place, Middlesex' (probate calendar).
Father Sir Walter Wagstaffe Bagot, 5th Baronet, LL.D (1702–20 January 1768), MP. (Fourth son.) Richard Bagot changed his name to Howard in 1783, presumably upon his marriage.
Mother Lady Barbara Legge, daughter of William, 1st Earl of Dartmouth.
Education Secondary schooling unknown; Brasenose College, Oxford; All Souls College, Oxford (BCL, 1757; DCL, 1764).
Marriage In 1783, to (Hon.) Frances Howard (d. 1817), sister of Henry, 12th Earl of Suffolk. (One daughter, who married [Hon] Fulke Grevile Upton.)
Religion Anglican.
Public None known, but 'owned' the 'rotten borough' of Castle Rising (see *ODNB* for his nephew Sir Charles Bagot (1781–1843), MP).
Miscellaneous Was regarded as an 'excellent' landlord.
References *GM,* 1818, vol. II, p. 567; *VCH Surrey,* vol. 3, pp. 249, 292.

1818/7 **Name Sprot, John**
Dates c. 1775–9 July 1818, Clapham Common.
Probate £350,000 (PCC).
Occupation Stockbroker of the Stock Exchange (1811 directory and probate calendar). (Occupational category IV23; venue 1.) Might well have been the John Sprot of Edinburgh so described as the nephew of Mark Sprot (see 1809/25) in the latter's will.
Address 'Of the Stock Exchange and Clapham Common' (probate calendar).
Father James Sprot of Edinburgh.
Mother Frances Blair.
Education Unknown.
Marriage In 1801 to Mary (d. 1856), daughter of Benjamin Yule of Edinburgh. (Two sons, five daughters.) (Son James, d. 1882, see 1882/142; daughter Frances, see 1886/142).
Religion Presumably originally Church of Scotland.
Public None known.
Miscellaneous Presumably migrated to London from Edinburgh. Appears to have made his fortune quickly.
References *GM,* 1818, vol. II, p. 92; *BLG,* 1937.

1818/8 **Name Bengough, Henry**
Dates c. 1739–10 April 1818.
Probate £250,000 (PCC).
Occupation Solicitor in Bristol and founder of the Bristol City Bank. (Occupational category VI.29 and IV.16; venue 12.) Was termed the 'judicial steward of the corporate purse' in Bristol (*GM*).
Address 'Of Bristol and Perry Park, Westbury-upon-Trym' (probate calendar).
Father Unknown.
Mother Unknown.

Education Unknown.
Marriage Unknown. Possibly to Joanna Cadell, who married a Henry Bengough on 10 April 1760 at Christ Church, Bristol (Family Search).
Religion Left to Unitarian charities but buried as an Anglican.
Public Alderman of Bristol, 1797–1818; Mayor of Bristol, 1792–3, JP, Bristol.
Miscellaneous Left anonymous legacy to found a home for the aged and infirm, which accumulated until 1878, when 'Bengough's House, Bristol' was established. It still exists as an old-age home.
References *GM*, 1818, vol. I, p. 475; may be related to Bengough of the Ridge in *BLG*, 1937.

Name **Walsingham, 2nd Baron, William de Grey** 1818/9
Dates 14 July 1748–28 May 1818, Old Windsor.
Probate £200,000 (PCC).
Occupation Landed. (Occupational category I.) In 1883, Lord Walsingham owned 19,148 acres worth £16,578 p.a., chiefly in Norfolk. Also legal fortune, inherited from father. Was given a state pension of £2,000 p.a. by Parliament in 1814.
Address Merton Hall near Thetford, Norfolk.
Father William de Grey, 1st Baron Walsingham (1719–9 May 1781), Lord Chief Justice of the Common Pleas and Comptroller of First Fruits and Tenths.
Mother Mary (d. 1800), daughter of William Cowper of Hertingfordbury Park, near Hertford, Clerk of Parliament.
Education Eton; Trinity Hall, Cambridge; Middle Temple – admitted 1764.
Marriage In 1772 to Augusta (d. 1818), daughter of 1st Baron Boston. (Two sons, two daughters.)
Religion Anglican.
Public MP (Tory) Wareham, 1774; Tamworth, 1774–80; Lostwithiel, 1780–1; Under-Secretary for the Colonies, 1778–80; Joint Postmaster General, 1787–94; PC, 1783; Chairman of the Committee for Privileges in the House of Lords, 1794–1818.
Miscellaneous The family had been landed for several generations. He was an FRS.
References *ODNB*; *CP.*

Name **Brodie, Alexander** 1818/10
Dates 3 March 1748–15 January 1818.
Probate £120,000 (PCC).
Occupation East India merchant – East India Company Writer in Madras; a 'wealthy nabob', but lived in Britain for many years. (Occupational category IV.19; venue 29.)
Address 'Formerly Arnhall, and then Burn, Kincardineshire, then Savile Row and South Audley Street, Middlesex' (probate calendar). The Scottish properties were purchased in 1796 and sold in 1814.
Father James Brodie (d. 1756) of Spynie, Elginshire, advocate and landowner,

and Sheriff of Egin, although 'heavily encumbered'. (*HP* for Alexander's brother James, MP, died 1824.)

Mother Emilia, maiden name apparently Brodie (sic). The couple married in 1742 at Alves, Morayshire, where an Emilia Brodie was baptised in 1713, daughter of Thomas Brodie and Elizabeth Giles (Family Search).

Education Unknown.

Marriage In 1793, to Elizabeth (d. 1800), daughter of (Hon.) James Wemyss, MP; her mother was the daughter of the 16th Earl of Sunderland. Their daughter Elizabeth (d.s.p. 1864) married George, 5th Duke of Gordon.

Religion Church of Scotland.

Public MP (Pittite) Nairnshire, 1785–90; Elgin Burghs, 1790–1802. A friend of Henry Dundas.

Miscellaneous Presumably returned permanently from India before 1785.

References *GM*, 1818, vol. I, p. 92; *HP*.

1818/11 **Name** **Wyatt, Robert**

Dates Unknown – probated January 1818.

Probate £120,000 (PCC).

Occupation 'Currier and leather cutter' of 77 Coleman Street, City of London (1793 directory); 'curriers, etc.' (Wyatt, Burkitt, and Wyatt, of 77 Coleman Street), 1814 directory. (Occupational category II.11 and IV25; venue 1.) 'Currier of Coleman Street, City of London' (probate calendar).

Address 'Coleman Street, City of London, and Newington Green, Hornsey' (probate calendar).

Father Unknown.

Mother Unknown.

Education Unknown.

Marriage Unknown.

Religion Unknown.

Public None known.

Miscellaneous Presumably a large-scale leather merchant, possibly for the military and for coaches. Nothing else could be traced.

References Probate calendar only.

1818/12 **Name** **Northumberland, 2nd Duke of, Hugh Percy**

Dates 14 August 1742–10 July 1817.

Probate £600,000 (PCC) plus £60,000 (York PC); see £660,000.

Occupation Landowner – one of the greatest of landowners. (Occupational category I.) In 1883, he owned 186,397 acres worth £176,048 p.a., chiefly in Northumberland but also in Surrey and Middlesex, in addition to London properties and minerals. He is said to have had an annual income of £80,000 p.a. (*ODNB*). This man was also a senior army officer – General in 1793, etc. – and served in the American Revolutionary War.

Address Chiefly Alnwick Castle, Northumberland.

Father Hugh Percy (né Smithson), 1st Duke of Northumberland of the second

creation (1714–6 June 1783). Created duke, 1766.
Mother Lady Elizabeth, Baroness Percy (d. 1776), daughter of the 7th Duke of Somerset.
Education Eton and St John's College, Cambridge.
Marriage First, in 1764, to Annie, daughter of John, 3rd Earl of Bute (divorced 1779 after her adultery was proved; she remarried Baron von Poelnitz of Prussia). Second, in 1764, to Frances (d. 1820), daughter of Peter Burrell of Beckenham, Kent and sister, of the 1st Baron Gwydir. (Three sons, two daughters.)
Religion Anglican.
Public MP (Tory, later Oppositionist) for Westminster, 1763–76; Lord Lieutenant of Northumberland, 1786–99 and 1802–17; KG, 1788. Succeeded to the Percy barony 1776.
Miscellaneous A senior military officer: entered Army 1759, became Major-General in 1775 and full general in 1793. Fought at the battles of Lexington and Concord, etc., in American Revolution (FRS). Was notorious for his bad temper.
References *ODNB; CP,* etc.

Name **Kirkpatrick, James** 1818/13
Dates c. 1730–28 March 1818 at Hollydale, near Bromley, Kent.
Probate £120,000 (PCC).
Occupation Colonel in the East India Company: 'Formerly in the East India Company service' (*GM*). (Occupational category VI.31; venue 29.)
Address Hollydale, near Bromley, Kent.
Father Unknown.
Mother Unknown.
Education Unknown.
Marriage Unknown. Had an illegitimate son by 'Mrs. Booth, wife of a London solicitor', William Kirkpatrick (1754–1812), in *ODNB* as 'army officer in the East India Company officer, and diplomatist'.
Religion Presumably Anglican.
Public None known.
Miscellaneous Was known as 'the handsome colonel'. Presumably a 'nabob', with a fortune made in India.
References *GM,* 1818, vol. I, p. 474; *ODNB* for son.

Name **Pratt, Charles** 1818/14
Dates c. 1752–25 March 1818, Tottenham.
Probate £160,000 (PCC).
Occupation 'Mealman' at Tottenham Mills. (A 'mealman' is a dealer in meal and flour.) Also had coal wharfs at his oil mills. (*VCH Middlesex,* vol. 4, p. 337.) (Occupational category IV.21 and III.15; venue 3.)
Address 'Tottenham Mills and Tottenham High Crescent, Tottenham' (probate calendar).
Father Unknown.
Mother Unknown.

Education Unknown.
Marriage Unknown.
Religion Unknown.
Public None known.
Miscellaneous Presumably a large-scale dealer in meal and flour who presumably ground meal and flour at his mills near London. Was not known to have been related to Charles Pratt, 1st Earl Camden, Lord Chancellor.
References *GM,* 1818, vol. I, p. 473.

1818/15 **Name** **Baker, John**
Dates c. 1737–16 May 1818, at 80 Lower Grosvenor Street, Middlesex.
Probate £500,000 (PCC).
Occupation 'Gold and silver brocade and floured-silk weaver' (1763 directory) of Princelet Street, Spitalfields (*Survey of London,* vol. 27, p. 189). A 'merchant' in directories of 1740–4, possibly his father. (Occupational category II.9 and IV.21; venue 2.)
Address 'Formerly Christ Church, Middlesex, then Lower Grosvenor Street, Middlesex' (probate calendar). In the 1812 Court directory, he is listed as of '12 Lower Grosvenor Street and Mortlake, Surrey'. The Spitalfields address was given as 12 Prince's Street, Spitalfields in the probate calendar entry for his wife.
Father Unknown.
Mother Unknown.
Education Unknown.
Marriage To Elizabeth, surname unknown and marriage date unknown. She died 10 March 1809, leaving £150,000 (see 1809/15). She may have been Elizabeth Pick, who married a John Baker on 10 December 1798 at Spitalfields Christ Church, Stepney (Family Search).
Religion Unknown.
Public None known.
Miscellaneous Very elusive, considering the great size of his estate.
References *GM,* 1818, vol. I, p. 478.

1818/16 **Name** **Heming, Ann** (née Gilroy)
Dates Unknown–9 June 1818, Stanmore.
Probate £120,000 (PCC).
Occupation Widow of George Heming, goldsmith of New Bond Street, left £125,000 (see 1809/1). (Occupational category IV.20 and 25; venue 2.)
Address Stanmore, Middlesex – described (*GM,* 1818, vol. I, p. 508) as her 'stately home'.
Father Forename unknown; surname Gilroy. The surname suggests a Scottish or northern English origin. In addition to numerous Ann Gilroys baptised outside London in the eighteenth century, an Anna Joanna Lily Gilroy was baptised on 24 May 1761 at the Moravian Chapel, Fetter Lane, London; parents' names not recorded (Family Search).
Mother Unknown.

Education Unknown.
Marriage To George Heming (marriage date unknown).
Religion Unknown, presumably Anglican.
Public None known.
Miscellaneous Her husband purchased Stanmore around 1795; it was pulled down in 1820. (*VCH Middlesex*, vol. V, p. 93.)
References *GM*, 1818, vol. I, p. 574.

Name **Metcalfe, Philip** (Metcalf in *GM*) 1818/17
Dates 29 August 1733–26 August 1818.
Probate £250,000 (PCC).
Occupation Distiller (Bisson and Metcalfe, malt distillers) in West Ham, Essex. (Occupational category III.13; venue 3.)
Address 'Hill Street, Berkeley Square and Hawstead, Suffolk' (probate calendar).
Father Roger Metcalfe, MD, of London and Brighton (1680–after 1744).
Mother Jemima, daughter of Sir Philip Astley, 2nd Baronet, of Melton Constable, Norfolk.
Education Unknown.
Marriage Unmarried.
Religion Anglican.
Public MP (Tory) Horsham, 1784–90; Plympton, 1790–6, 1802–6; Malmesbury, 1796–1802.
Miscellaneous 'Had grown rich as a partner and eventually the head of a West Ham brewery (sic) [. . .] went blind after 1806' (*HP*). Metcalfe was a travelling companion of Dr Johnson and a friend and executor of Sir Joshua Reynolds.
References *GM*, 1818, vol. II, p. 379; *HP;* Ian Christie, *British Non-Elite MP s* (1995).

Name **Wilson, Lady (Jane)** (née Weller) 1818/18
Dates Unknown–17 August 1818.
Probate £180,000 (PCC).
Occupation Landowner in Kent; her family were, more importantly, the ground rent landlords in Hampstead. (Occupational category I.) Her husband was a general and 6th Baronet. (In 1883, Sir Spencer Maryon-Wilson owned 4,373 acres worth at least £3,418 p.a., plus his London lands.) The Hampstead holdings would, of course, have become immensely more valuable after her death.
Address Of Charlton House, Kent at death.
Father John Badger Weller, MB, physician (b. 1708), owner of the Hampstead ground rents.
Mother Margaret, niece and heiress of (Revd) John Maryon of Charlton Manor, Kent. According to Family Search, she was Margareta Maria Peers, baptised 12 May 1749 at Romford, Essex, who died 19 June 1777.
Education Unknown.
Marriage In 1767 to (General) Sir Thomas Spencer Wilson, 6th Baronet (1726–29 August 1798). (One son, three daughters.)

Religion Anglican.
Public None known.
Miscellaneous Founded a museum and constantly travelled all over England and Scotland (*GM*); was known for her charity and piety.
References *GM*, 1818, vol. I, p. 190; *ODNB* for relatives.

1818/19 **Name** **Bulkeley, Thomas**
Dates Unknown–2 December 1818, Montague Square, Middlesex.
Probate £160,000 (PCC).
Occupation 'Formerly of Lisbon' (*GM*) – probably the Thomas Bulkeley, baptised (Anglican) in Lisbon, 28 October 1762, who was connected with the British India trade. A banking firm in Lisbon (John Bulkeley & Son) existed in 1763. (Probably occupational category IV.19; venue 29.)
Address Of Montague (sic) Square, Middlesex at death.
Father Unknown; may be John Bulkeley, banker of Lisbon.
Mother Unknown. John Bulkeley of Lisbon married, on 4 February 1752 at Lisbon, Ann Masdam (Family Search). Her unusual surname, perhaps more plausibly Masham or Massam, has probably been misread from the original record.
Education Unknown.
Marriage Unknown.
Religion Presumably Anglican.
Public None known.
Miscellaneous Nothing more could be found.
References *GM*, 1818, vol. I, p. 643.

1818/20 **Name** **Fraser, Sir William, 1st Baronet**
Dates c. 1739–13 February 1818 at Bedford Square, Middlesex.
Probate £250,000 (PCC).
Occupation 'Hon East India Company naval service' (probate calendar). (Occupational category IV25? and VI29; venue 29.)
Address 'Formerly Queen Street, Bloomsbury, then Bedford Square' (probate calendar).
Father William Fraser 'heir to Ledeclune, Invernesshire' (*BP*); 'descended from a younger branch of the family of Fraser of Lovat'.
Mother Helen, daughter of William Ross of Mougnieth.
Education Unknown.
Marriage In 1795, to Elizabeth, daughter of James Farquharson, 'merchant' of London 'by whom he had twenty-eight children [!]' (*BP*).
Religion Presumably Church of Scotland.
Public Created baronet, 1806, for unknown reasons.
Miscellaneous Commanded two East India Company ships, *Lord Mansfield* (lost 1773) and the *Earl of Mansfield* (1771–85). Was FRS and an Elder Brother of Trinity House. May have inherited from his father-in-law.
References *GM*, 1818, vol. I, p. 379; *BP.*

Name **Anson, 1st Viscount, Thomas Anson** 1818/21
Dates 14 February 1767–31 July 1818, St James's Square, Middlesex.
Probate £120,000 (PCC).
Occupation Landowner. (Occupational category I.) His son was created 1st Earl of Lichfield. In 1883, the Earl of Lichfield owned 21,530 acres worth £42,042 p.a. in Staffordshire and Suffolk. Anson's son 'succeeds to a clear and unencumbered estate of £70,000 p.a.' (*GM,* 1818, vol. II, p. 375).
Address His chief seat was Shugborough, Staffordshire.
Father George Anson (né Adams) (1731–27 October 1789) of Shugborough and Orgrave, Staffordshire, MP, who inherited these estates from his uncle.
Mother Mary, daughter of George, 1st Viscount Vernon.
Education Eton.
Marriage In 1794, to Margaret (d. 1843), daughter of William Coke, 1st Earl of Leicester. (Five sons, five daughters.)
Religion Anglican.
Public MP (Whig) Lichfield, 1789–1806. Created 1st Viscount, 1806.
Miscellaneous Was probably related to George Anson, 1st Baron Anson (d. 1762), the admiral, but the relationship is not clear.
References *GM,* 1818, vol. II, p. 375; *HP; CP.*

Name **Martin, Francis Pitney** 1818/22
Dates Unknown – probated October 1818.
Probate £100,000 (PCC).
Occupation 'Merchant' of Fredericks Place, Old Jewry, City of London (1814 directory). (Occupational category IV.21? Venue 1.)
Address 'Fredericks Place, Old Jewry, City of London' (probate calendar).
Father Unknown.
Mother Unknown.
Education Unknown.
Marriage Unknown.
Religion Unknown.
Public None known.
Miscellaneous Nothing further could be traced.
References Probate calendar only.

Name **Main, Thomas** 1818/23
Dates Unknown–26 November 1818 at Great Russell Street, Bloomsbury, Middlesex. He was probably born in Scotland (see 'Occupation' below).
Probate £160,000 (PCC).
Occupation 'Merchant' (1793, 1802 directories) at the Crescent, Minories; 'merchant' of 10 Crescent, America Square in 1803. (Occupational category IV.19? Venue 1 or 2.) He was the nephew of John Hyndman, a Scot with Clydesdale connections who from about 1742 until moving to London in the mid-1750s had been a merchant in Virginia, representing James Buchanan (1696–1758), for whom see *ODNB.* Hyndman and Englishman Richard Lancaster were in business together

in London, trading as Hyndman, Lancaster & Co., merchants trading with Virginia and the West Indies. After Lancaster's death in about 1773, the firm was reorganised as John Hyndman & Co., Hyndman's partners being Robert Bunn and Thomas Main, both of whom had worked in Virginia. In 1775, the firm was the eleventh largest of the fifty-six London firms engaged in the tobacco trade. Undoubtedly owing to its substantial business interests with the West Indies, it comfortably survived the American Revolution, enduring until Hyndman's death in 1785. Bunn had left the City by 1788, subsequently resurfacing in Bromley, Kent as 'Robert Bunn, Esq.'. Main continued the business alone, until c. 1808–10. (Jacob M. Price, 'The Last Phase of the Virginia-London Consignment Trade: James Buchanan and Co., 1758–1768', *The William and Mary Quarterly*, vol. 43, 1986.)

Address Lived at Great Russell Street, Middlesex at death.

Father Unknown.

Mother Unknown.

Education Unknown.

Marriage Unknown.

Religion Unknown.

Public None known.

Miscellaneous Apart from the above, little could be found of his personal details.

References *GM*, 1818, vol. II, p. 642.

Name **Edwards, John** 1819/1
Dates c. 1745–probated May 1819.
Probate £180,000 (PCC).
Occupation Portuguese merchant' (probate calendar) who lived in Portugal much of his life. (Occupational category IV.19; venue 29.) He exported Yorkshire cloth to Portugal and imported dyestuffs, wines, etc. (Halifax Reference Library).
Address Lived at Northorodam House, Halifax, West Riding in later life; also had a house in Lisbon.
Father John Edwards (1706–9 December 1793, Lisbon), 'Portuguese merchant'.
Mother Mary Hargreaves.
Education Unknown.
Marriage Unknown.
Religion Parents married in an Anglican church; his brother buried in an Anglican church.
Public None known.
Miscellaneous Moved back to Halifax in later life.
References Information provided by the Halifax Reference Library.

Name **Meyrick, James** 1819/2
Dates Unknown–27 November 1818, Wimbledon.
Probate £180,000 (PCC).
Occupation 'Army Agents' (James and John Meyrick) of Parliament Street, Westminster (1793 directory) and of 17 Spring Gardens (1802 directory). (An 'army agent' generally handled the pay of army officers and men – his business operated as a kind of bank as well as a general agency.) (Occupational category IV.18; venue 2.)
Address 'Spring Gardens and Lower Grosvenor Street, and also Wimbledon' (probate calendar).
Father James Meyrick (1718–78) of Parliament Street, Westminster; presumably he was an army agent. (First son.)
Mother Mary Ann Whigges.
Education Unknown.
Marriage To Anne (marriage date unknown), daughter of Benjamin Whitelock; d.s.p.
Religion Presumably Anglican.
Public JP, DL (Surrey?).
Miscellaneous His brother and partner John 'of Bath' died in 1805.
References *BLG*, 1846; *GM*, 1818, vol. I, p. 642.

Name **Queen Charlotte Sophia** (consort of George III) 1819/3
(née Sophie Charlotte of Mecklenburg-Strelitz)
Dates 19 May 1744, The Palace, Mirow, Mecklenburg-Strelitz–17 November 1818, Kew Palace.

Probate £140,000 (PCC).
Occupation Queen of the United Kingdom from 1761 (except during the Regency period); Princess Charlotte of Mecklenburg-Strelitz. (Occupational category VI31; venue 2, although this is only indicative.)
Address Royal palaces.
Father Charles Louis Frederick, Duke of Mecklenburg-Strelitz (1708–52). (Second daughter.)
Mother Elizabeth of Saxe-Hildburghausen (1713–61).
Education Private tutors.
Marriage In 1761, to King George III (reigned 1760–1820, except during the Regency period). (Nine sons, six daughters; sons included George IV, William IV, and the Duke of Kent, Queen Victoria's father.)
Religion Originally Lutheran, later Anglican.
Public Queen of Great Britain.
Miscellaneous She had an official income as Queen of £40,000 p.a., rising to £100,000 p.a. Was also Electress of Hanover. Was noted for her intelligence and reading. It is interesting that a British queen's estate was probated in the ordinary way, with a valuation attached.
References *ODNB*, etc.

1819/4 **Name** **Everard, Edward**
Dates c. 1739–probated March 1819; died at Bath.
Probate £180,000 (PCC).
Occupation 'Merchant' in King's Lynn (so described in 1806 Poll Book); mentions in his will that he owned a shipyard, timber yard and brewery, and was 'co-partner' in a sailmaking business. (Occupational category II.4 [shipbuilding]; venue 11 – the occupational category is very tentative.)
Address 'Formerly of King's Lynn, Norfolk, then Middleton, Norfolk' (probate calendar).
Father Edward Everard (d. 1769) of King's Lynn.
Mother Mary, daughter of Benjamin Holley, Mayor of King's Lynn in 1707.
Education Unknown.
Marriage To Mary (d. 1794; marriage date unknown), daughter of Samuel Browne of King's Lynn and widow of P. Basham. (Four sons, five daughters.)
Religion Unknown, presumably Anglican.
Public None known.
Miscellaneous Like many from local elites in smaller towns, was multi-occupational.
References *BLG*, 1871.

1819/5 **Name** **Hardcastle, Joseph**
Dates 7 December 1752, Leeds–3 March 1819, Hatcham House, Surrey.
Probate £120,000 (PCC).
Occupation 'Merchant' (Joseph Hardcastle and Sons of 9 Old Swan Stairs, Thames Street, City of London, 1811 directory). A partner, as a merchant, with

Joseph Reyner at Duck Foot Lane near London Bridge, and then (from 1801) at Old Swan Stairs (*ODNB*). (Occupational category IV.21; venue 1.)
Address 'Of "The Old Swan", Thames Street, City, and Hatcham House, Surrey' (probate calendar). Lived at Peckham until 1798, then Hatcham House.
Father John Hardcastle of Leeds (fl. 1720–66). (Younger son.)
Mother Forename unknown; surname Snowden (died 1787).
Education Local schools in Leeds and London.
Marriage In 1777, to Anne (d. 1827), daughter of John Corsbie of Bury St Edmunds. (Three sons, four daughters.)
Religion Nonconformist: a member of the Independent Church at Bury Street, St Mary Axe; also attended Moravian and Evangelical Anglican services.
Public None known.
Miscellaneous A prominent Evangelical activist and anti-slavery campaigner. Came to London in 1766 to join his uncle Nathaniel, a merchant. Was a founder and Treasurer (1795–1816) of the London Missionary Society, a friend of members of the Clapham Sect and a director of the Sierra Leone Company. The nature of his mercantile business is unclear but presumably involved overseas import and exports.
References *ODNB; GM,* 1819, vol. I, p. 284.

Name **Cornwallis, (Hon.) Sir William** 1819/6
Dates 20 February 1744, Eye, Suffolk–5 July 1819.
Probate £100,000 (PCC).
Occupation Vice-Admiral; former Commander-in-Chief of the Channel Fleet. (Occupational category VI.31.)
Address Lived at Newland, Milford, Hampshire, purchased 1799.
Father Charles, 5th Baron and 1st Earl Cornwallis (1700–23 June 1762), Chief Justice in Eyre, South of the Trent, Constable of the Tower, etc. (Fourth son.)
Mother Elizabeth (d. 1785), daughter of Charles, 2nd Viscount Townshend.
Education Eton; entered Royal Navy 1755 aged eleven.
Marriage Unmarried.
Religion Anglican – a 'devoted' Churchman.
Public Combined naval career with being MP (Tory) for Eye, 1768–74, 1782–4, 1790–1807; for Portsmouth, 1784–90; GCB, 1815.
Miscellaneous Entered Royal Navy, 1755; Lieutenant, 1761; Captain, 1765; Commander-in-Chief, East Indies, 1788–94; Vice-Admiral, 1794; Commander-in-Chief, West Indies, 1796; Rear-Admiral, 1793; Vice-Admiral, 1814. In command of the Channel Fleet, on the tedious but necessary blockade duty that contributed hugely to Britain's success in the war against Napoleon; probably gained from prize money for ships taken in blockade duty, often very lucrative.
References *ODNB.*

Name **Parry, William** 1819/7
Dates Unknown – probated October 1819.
Probate £120,000 (PCC).

Occupation 'Merchants' (W. & T. Parry, of 17 Aldermanbury, City of London, 1803 directory; 'William Parry, merchants', of 10 Aldermanbury, 1793 directory). (Occupational category IV21; venue 1.)
Address 'Formerly of Aldermanbury, City of London, and then of Dulwich' (probate calendar).
Father Unknown: he is recorded as having a deed for lands in Glamorganshire, and could possibly have come from there. (Coleman Index 1750–99, online.)
Mother Unknown.
Education Unknown.
Marriage Unknown.
Religion Unknown.
Public None known.
Miscellaneous Nothing more could be traced.
References Probate calendar only.

1819/8 **Name** **Ripley, John Richard**
Dates c. 1754–2 October 1819, Clapham Common.
Probate £250,000 (PCC).
Occupation 'Broker' (Ripley, Wiss & Co., of 6 Lawrence Pountney Lane, City of London, 1808 directory; 'Ripley, Wiss, and Ripley, brokers', of same address, 1815 directory). He was presumably a stockbroker, but this isn't entirely clear. (Occupational category IV 23? Venue 1.)
Address 'Lawrence Pountney Lane, City of London, and Clapham Common, and Streatham' (probate calendar).
Father Unknown.
Mother Unknown.
Education Unknown.
Marriage Unknown.
Religion Unknown.
Public None known.
Miscellaneous Nothing more about him could be traced.
References *GM*, 1819, vol. II, p. 381.

1819/9 **Name** **East, Sir William, 1st Baronet**
Dates 27 February 1738 (1736 according to *BP*)–12 October 1819.
Probate £200,000 (PCC).
Occupation Legal fortune: father and grandfather were prominent lawyers. (Occupational category VI29; venue 1.) Also landowner – in 1883, Sir Gilbert Clayton-East, his descendant, owned 3,223 acres worth £5,869 p.a. in Berkshire.
Address Lived at Hall Place near Hurley, Berkshire.
Father William East (d. 1737) of the Middle Temple and Hall Place.
Mother Anne (1 April 1762), daughter of Sir George Cooke of Hadfield, Chief Prothonotary of the Court of Common Pleas.
Education Unknown. He was apparently not a lawyer.
Marriage First, in 1763, to Hannah, daughter of Henry Casmajor of Tokington,

Gloucestershire. (Two sons, one daughter.) Second, in 1768, to Miss Jackson. (One daughter.)

Religion Anglican.

Public Created baronet, 1766; High Sheriff of Berkshire, 1766–7.

Miscellaneous His own career is obscure. Why he received a baronetcy is unclear.

References *GM*, 1818, vol. II, p. 473; *CP*.

Name **Courtoy (or Courtois), John** 1819/10
(probably originally named Nicolas Jacquinet)

Dates Probably c. 1750–4, France–8 December 1818 'at an advanced age'.

Probate £250,000 (PCC).

Occupation One of the strangest cases among the wealth-holders. He was, wrote an obituarist, 'formerly for many years a hairdresser in the Metropolis. By dint of extraordinary exertions in various ways and through a most rigid system of economy in his expenditure, this man died immensely wealthy. Old Courtois was long well-known in the purlieus of St Martins and the Haymarket. His appearance was meagre and squalid, and his clothes, such as they were, were pertinaciously got up in exactly the same cut and fashion, and the colour always either a fawn or velvet.' Courtois, the same article added, met Lord Gage at at the Court Room of the East India Company, where they both had votes. After voting, Courtois cut Lord Gage's hair (*GM*)! It is almost certainly impossible for anyone to have made a fortune of £250,000 as a hairdresser simply by 'economy', and there must be more to Courtois's career than is stated here. (Occupational category VII? Venue 2?)

Research by an email correspondent in Australia, Judy Jenkins, a descendant of Courtois, reveals that his name was probably Nicolas Jacquinet, and that he was born in Jussey, Haute Saone, France in 1727–9. He was the son of Jean-Louis Jacquinet, occupation unknown, and Nicole Guiard, Roman Catholics. It is possible that this man came to England between 1750 and 1754 to escape having to share his fortune with his family, although the source of this 'fortune' is unknown. He was denizened in 1799 and described himself as a 'peruke maker' (a wigmaker) from Dijon. He purchased shares in the East India Company from 1765. He owned properties in James Street, Leicester Fields, St Martins and ran a hairdressing business at 43 Brewer Street. He may have retired in 1795. This man never married but fathered five children by Mary Anne Wooley. There were sharp disputes over his will. This still leaves unresolved the source of his fortune.

Address 'Formerly Oxenden Street, Middlesex, then Little Street, Martin Street, Leicester Square' (probate calendar).

Father Unknown, probably Jean-Louis Jacquinet of Jussey, France.

Mother Unknown, probably Nicole Guiard.

Education Unknown.

Marriage Unknown. Probably unmarried; had five children by Mary Anne Wooley.

Religion Unknown, probably originally Roman Catholic.

Public None known.

Miscellaneous His name is spelled Courtoy in the probate calendar but Courtois in *GM.* In 1795, he was the victim of an attempted robbery by Mary Benson, who was executed for wounding him (*GM,* vol. LXV, p. 344).

References *GM,* 1818, vol. II, p. 644; email correspondence with Judy Jenkins, 2007.

1819/11 **Name** **Boone, Charles**

Dates c. 1729–3 March 1819.

Probate £500,000 (PCC).

Occupation This is another case in which the origins of an enormous fortune are unclear. It is likely that most of the fortune derived from his father, who was Governor of Bombay, 1715–22, and a director of the East India Company, 1729–35. (If so, occupational category VI.31; venue 29.) It is also possible that some of it derived from his first wife, who was the granddaughter of Sir Ambroise Crowley, the famous ironmaster. Charles Boone does not appear to have had an occupation apart from being a landowner.

Address 'Formerly of Berkeley Square, then Grosvenor Square, then Stanhope Street and Lee Place, Kent' (probate calendar). Charles Boone succeeded his brother Daniel Boone (sic) MP at Lee Place in 1770. The family had owned Lee Place for several generations.

Father Charles Boone (d. 8 October 1735), MP, and see above.

Mother Mary, daughter of (Colonel) Thomas Garth of Hassold, Bedfordshire, and widow of George Evelyn, MP.

Education Eton; Trinity College, Cambridge.

Marriage First, in 1762, to Theodora (d. 1765), daughter of John Crowley, MP of Barking Hall (and see above). Second, to Harriet Wright (d. 1811; marriage date unknown) of Roehampton. No children.

Religion Anglican.

Public MP (pro-Lord North, then Pittite) Castle Rising, 1757–68; Ashburton, 1768–84; Castle Rising, 1784–96.

Miscellaneous His uncle Joseph was a planter in South Carolina. His brother Thomas (1730–1812), 'colonial governor and public official', is in *ODNB.* But the source of his great wealth is a mystery.

References *HP; BLG.*

1819/12 **Name** **Burrowes, Robert**

Dates Unknown–10 February 1819, Bolton Street, Piccadilly, Middlesex.

Probate £100,000 (PCC).

Occupation Unclear, but probably landed. He appears to have been from a landed family in County Cavan and is seemingly listed (although without dates) in *Burke's Irish Family Records* (1976). In his will, he mentions his 'family estates' in County Cavan. In 1883, Robert James Burrowes of Stradone House, Cavan owned 9,572 acres worth £5,426 p.a. Our Robert Burrowes also also left a legacy to Revd A. Burrowes, 'late of Bombay', and the family had other East India Company connections (see below). It is possible that the Burrowes family made its money in India, although this isn't clear. He does not appear to have had any professional or business links in London. (Occupational category I?)

Address '[25] Bolton Street, Piccadilly' (probate calendar and 1818 Court directory).

Father Apparently Thomas Burrowes of Stradone House, County Cavan, JP, High Sheriff 1743. (First son.)

Mother Apparently Jane (d. 1764), daughter of (Colonel) Thomas Nisbett MP of Lismore House, County Cavan.

Education Unknown.

Marriage Apparently Sophia, daughter of (Ven.) Joseph Story, Archdeacon of Kilmore. (One son, four daughters.)

Religion Anglican.

Public Apparently High Sheriff of County Cavan, 1773.

Miscellaneous His brother Thomas (1742–79) was a colonel in the East India Company. As noted, *Burke's Irish Family Records*, from which this genealogical information has been taken, does not give his dates, but it is virtually certain from those mentioned in his will that he was the same man. The family appears to have been part of the Anglo-Irish Anglican 'Establishment', although how Robert Burrowes became so wealthy isn't clear. Other relatives sat in the Irish Parliament during the eighteenth century.

References *GM*, 1819, vol. II, p. 188; will (PROB 11 online); *Burke's Irish Family Records* (1976).

Name **Tunno, John** 1819/13

Dates c. 1746–15 May 1819 at Devonshire Place, Middlesex. His birthplace was presumably Scotland (see 'Occupation' and 'Father' below).

Probate £500,000 (PCC).

Occupation 'Merchant' (Tunno & Houghman) of 8–9 New Broad Street, City of London; listed in 1791 and 1793 as at 13 America Square, City. (Occupational category IV.19 or 21; venue 1.) His brother Adam was 'situated in Carolina, USA', according to his will. Adam Tunno was one of the richest merchants in Charleston, South Carolina, and 'King of the Scotch' there, serving as President of the local St Andrew's Society until his death. A bachelor, he bought a notable mansion in Charleston in 1787, lived for forty years with a woman of colour, had two children by her and left her and their surviving child, a daughter, extremely well provided for with property that included slaves. He died in 1833 leaving $130,000 in loans, cash and investments. Frederic Cople Jaher, *The Urban Establishment: Upper Strata in Boston, New York, Charleston, Chicago, and Los Angeles* (1982), p. 338; Jonathan H. Poston, *The Buildings of Charleston* (1997), p. 103; Thomas H. Appleton and Angela Boswell, eds., *Searching for Their Places: Women in the South Across Four Centuries* (2003), p. 46. John Tunno was based in Charleston before moving to London. See 'Marriage' below and Henry R. Howland, 'A British Privateer in the American Revolution', *American Historical Review* (1902). Sir Thomas Baring was an executor of John's estate.

Address Devonshire Place, Middlesex at death.

Father Unknown. Of Scottish parentage. According to Family Search, a John Tunno was baptised at Stitchel, Roxburghshire, on 25 December 1740, son of William Tunno and Agnes Watson.
Mother Unknown.
Education Unknown.
Marriage On 18 October 1781, in St Philip's Church, Charleston, South Carolina, to Margaret Rose (Family Search). Her father, John Rose, was a Scottish-born Charleston merchant who married Hester Bond, of a Carolina landed family. Like John Tunno, John Rose was a loyalist; he left for Jamaica in 1782 but by 1784 was in London. He lived at Norfolk Street, Strand, dying on 16 June 1805 aged eighty-five. See Douglas Catterall, 'The Worlds of John Rose', in Angela McCarthy, ed., *A Global Clan: Scottish Migrant Networks and Identity since the Eighteenth Century* (2006), pp. 67–94. See also Robert S. Lambert, *South Carolina Loyalists in the American Revolution* (1987), pp. 279–81 for both Tunno and Rose. Tunno's son Edward Rose Tunno (1795–1863), MP (1816–32), had an estate of 3,500 acres.
Religion Presumably Presbyterian.
Public None known.
Miscellaneous He was a merchant in America and later in London.
References *GM,* 1819, vol. I, p. 493.

1819/14 **Name** **Barclay, George**
Dates c. 1759–8 June 1819, Harley Street, Middlesex.
Probate £140,000 (PCC).
Occupation Portuguese merchant in London. George Barclay & Co., 'merchants' of 84 Hatton Street, then Little Trinity Lane, Queenhithe (c. 1800) and 81 London Wall (1803 directory). (Occupational category IV.19; venue 1.) Was also a director of Royal Exchange Assurance, 1789–1809.
Address 'Burford Lodge [near Elstead] Surrey and Harley Street' (probate calendar).
Father Thomas Barclay (d. 1784), 'an unscrupulous Portuguese merchant' (*HP*) of Charterhouse Square. (First son.)
Mother Dorothy, daughter of Robert Thomson of Kilham, Yorkshire.
Education Unknown.
Marriage In 1782, to Rebecca, daughter of Benjamin Brockhurst of London. (Three sons.)
Religion Presumably Anglican: there is no evidence of a Quaker connection or any relationship with the Barclay's Bank family.
Public MP (Whig) Bridport, 1795–1807.
Miscellaneous Inherited £1,600 from his father. Bought Burford Lodge around 1800. 'Failed for £300,000' in 1803 but eventually paid 20 shillings in the pound and made another fortune.
References *HP.*

1819/15 **Name** **Solly, Elizabeth**
Dates c. 1796–14 July 1818 at Leyton (sic).

Probate £100,000.

Occupation Daughter of a 'stave and timber merchant' of 15 St Mary Axe. (Occupational category IV.21; venue 1.)

Address Walthamstow, Essex at death.

Father Isaac Solly (1768–1853) 'stave and timber merchant' of 15 St Mary Axe and Trinity Street, Rotherhithe. (Eldest daughter; he had ten children.)

Mother Mary, daughter of John Harrison, 'a London lawyer'. (*ODNB* for brother.)

Education Unknown.

Marriage Unmarried.

Religion Family were originally English Presbyterians, later Unitarians.

Public None known.

Miscellaneous Why a twenty-two-year-old woman should have a fortune of this size, when her father was still alive, is very unclear. Her niece Caroline Garrison Bishop (1846–1929), pioneer of kindergartens, is in the *ODNB*, as is her brother Henry Solly, social reformer (1813–1903), who died eighty-five years after her death.

References *ODNB* for relatives; *GM*.

Name **Vansittart, Emilia** (née Morse or Merse) 1819/16

Dates Baptised 27 May 1738, Fort St George, Madras–2 August 1819. Her baptismal name was recorded as Amelia (surname Morse) (Family Search).

Probate £120,000 (PCC).

Occupation Her husband was governor of Bengal, 1760–c. 1770), although he was in straitened circumstances at his death. According to *HP*, she was 'rumoured to have acquired a great fortune' after his death, but the source is unclear. (Occupational category VI.31; venue 29, although this is uncertain.)

Address Lived at Blackheath in later life.

Father Nicholas Morse (or Merse), Governor of Madras.

Mother Jane Goddard, who married him in Madras on 21 December 1730 (Family Search).

Education Unknown.

Marriage In 1754, to Henry Vansittart (1732–c. 1770), MP and Governor of Bengal of Foxley, Berkshire – he disappeared in late 1769 or early 1770 after his ship apparently foundered off Cape Town. He was a member of the Council of Madras, 1756, and a director of the East India Company, as well as MP for Reading, 1768 until his death. (Five sons, two daughters.) One son was Nicholas Vansittart (1766–1851), created 1st Baron Bexley in 1823.

Religion Anglican.

Public None known.

Miscellaneous 'Friends and relations' helped her after her husband's death (*HP*).

References *HP*.

Name **Harvey, Thomas** 1819/17

Dates c. 1757–8 November 1819 at Belmont, East Barnet.

Probate £100,000 (PCC).
Occupation Unknown. The only men of this name in a London directory were a 'lampblack manufacturer' of Shoreditch and a brushmaker of Borough, Southwark (1811 directory). Neither seems likely to have been him.
Address 'Formerly of Finchley then of Belmont, Barnet, and [16] Portland Place' (probate calendar). (Belmont was purchased in 1813.) In 1805, he lived at the Manor House, Finchley and Portland Place (court directory).
Father Unknown.
Mother Unknown.
Education Unknown.
Marriage Unknown.
Religion Unknown.
Public None known.
Miscellaneous Nothing further about him could be traced.
References *GM,* 1819, vol. II, p. 477.

1819/18 **Name** **Ellenborough, 1st Baron, Sir Edward Law**
Dates 16 November 1750, Great Salkeld, Cumberland–13 December 1818, at 13 St James's Square, Middlesex.
Probate £200,000 (PCC).
Occupation Lord Chief Justice, 1802–18 (Occupational category VI.29; venue 2.)
Address Lived at 13 St James's Square in later life.
Father (Rt. Revd) Edmund Law, DD, Bishop of Carlisle (1703–14 August 1787). (Fourth son.)
Mother Mary (d. 1762), daughter of John Christian of Unerigg, Cumberland.
Education Chaterhouse; Peterhouse, Cambridge (Third Wrangler and Fellow); Lincoln's Inn (called 1780).
Marriage In 1789, to Ann (d. 1843), daughter of (Captain) George Phillips Towry RN, of Shipley, Northumberland, 'Commander of the Naval Victualling Offices'. (Seven sons, six daughters.) In his youth, Ellenborough was a 'renowned womaniser' who fathered an illegitimate daughter (*ODNB*).
Religion Anglican.
Public MP (extreme Tory) for Newtown, Isle of Wight, 1801–2. King's Attorney General, County of Lancashire, 1793–1802; Attorney General, 1801–2; Lord Chief Justice, King's Bench, 1802–18; in Cabinet, 1806–7. Knighted, 1801; PC 1802; created baron, 1802.
Miscellaneous KC, 1787; Bencher, Lincoln's Inn, 1787; Reader, 1794; Treasurer, 1795. Was said to have 'acquired a fortune of £60,000' as a barrister. An extreme Tory.
References *ODNB.*

1819/19 **Name** **Shaddick, John**
Dates c. 1751–1 July 1818, at John Street, Bedford Row, Middlesex.
Probate £120,000 (PCC).

Occupation 'One of the sworn officers of the High Court in Chancery' (*GM*); a solicitor of Six Clerks Office, Chancery Lane (1805 directory). (Occupational category VI.29; venue 1.)
Address 'Of John Street, Bedford Row and Six Clerks Office, Chancery Lane' (probate calendar).
Father Unknown. A John Shaddick was baptised on 2 June 1750 at Clayhanger, Devon, son of Thomas and Mary. (Family Search).
Mother Unknown.
Education Unknown.
Marriage Unknown.
Religion Presumably Anglican.
Public None known.
Miscellaneous Another wealthy legal official. Nothing else could be found about him.
References *GM,* 1818, vol. II, p. 91.

Name **Croasdaile, Despard** 1819/20
Dates Unknown–28 January 1819 at Golden Square, Middlesex.
Probate £200,000 (PCC).
Occupation 'Army agent' (probate calendar) of Silver Street, Golden Square (1817 directory: not listed in previous ones). (Occupational category IV.18; venue 2.)
Address 'Golden Square, St James's' (probate calendar).
Father Unknown.
Mother Unknown.
Education Unknown.
Marriage In 1777, in St James's Westminster, to Charlotte Ann Fitter (Family Search).
Religion Presumably Anglican.
Public None known.
Miscellaneous An 'army agent' was chiefly a banker and agent to army officers serving overseas.
References *GM,* 1819, vol. I, p. 185.

Name **Dauncey, Philip** 1819/21
Dates Baptised 19 December 1759, Wotton-under-Edge, Gloucestershire–14 June 1819, Bedford Square, Middlesex.
Probate £120,000 (PCC).
Occupation 'King's Counsel' of 2 Holborn Court, Gray's Inn (1812 directory). (Occupational category VI.29; venue 1.)
Address 'Of Bedford Square and Gray's Inn' (probate calendar).
Father John Dauncey (d. 1788), 'gentleman' of Wotton-under-Edge, Gloucestershire. (First son.)
Mother Mary Vines, according to Family Search.
Education Secondary schooling unknown; Oriel College, Oxford (BA, matric-

ulated 1777). Barrister, Gray's Inn and Middle Temple (called at MT, 1785). Bencher, 1806; Treasurer and KC. Went the Oxford Circuit.
Marriage Unknown.
Religion Anglican.
Public None known.
Miscellaneous Was a senior barrister but held no official positions.
References *GM,* 1819, vol. I, p. 590.

1819/22 **Name** **Chatteris, William**
Dates c. 1738– 26 July 1819.
Probate £300,000 (PCC).
Occupation Banker (Fuller, Chatteris & Co.) of 24 Lombard Street, City of London (1802 directory); of Chatteris, Yapp & Co. (1812 directory). (Occupational category IV.16; venue 1.)
Address 'Lombard Street' (probate calendar) is the only address given.
Father Unknown.
Mother Unknown.
Education Unknown.
Marriage Unknown. His son William Poulett Broun Chatteris, JP (1808–89) left £155,142 (see 1889/22).
Religion Unknown.
Public None known.
Miscellaneous Nothing further about him could be traced.
References *GM,* 1819, vol. II, p. 186.

WEALTH-HOLDERS, 1820

Name **Adams, Alexander** 1820/1
Dates 28 August 1735–29 March 1817 (1819?).
Probate £140,000 (PCC).
Occupation 'Amassed a large fortune as an India merchant', probably in Calcutta, but lived in Newcastle upon Tyne (biographical notice of relative Thomas Naters). (Occupational category IV.19; venue 29 or 9.) Also partner in Northumberland Glass Company, formed 1780.
Address Lived at Northumberland Street, Newcastle upon Tyne at death.
Father Benjamin Adams (d. November 1737) of Acton near Alnwick.
Mother Elizabeth (d. 1782), daughter of Alexander Collingwood.
Education Unknown.
Marriage Unmarried. Left his estate to his illegitimate son William Adams, MD of Calcutta, whose mother was Barbara Carter. The son was said to have left 'half a million sterling' in 1822–3. He left his estate to his cousin Thomas Naters in Vermont, USA who then took the name Jacob von Naters and lived in Switzerland. He, in turn, left his estate to William Mather of Newcastle, a wealthy builder.
Religion Unknown.
Public None known.
Miscellaneous 'Succeeded his brother Thomas' in January 1813.
References Will mainly.

Name **Bridges, William** 1820/2
Dates Unknown–14 December 1819, Laverstoke, Hampshire.
Probate £120,000 (PCC).
Occupation Unknown.
Address Lived at Laverstoke, near Whitchurch, Hampshire.
Father Unknown.
Mother Unknown.
Education Unknown.
Marriage Unknown. His daughter Caroline married, in 1835, (Major-General) William Cooper Rogers (d. November 1857), son of Sir Frederick Rogers, 5th Baronet.
Religion Presumably Anglican.
Public None known.
Miscellaneous Nothing could be traced of him. Paper for the Bank of England's banknotes is made in Laverstoke, but this is likely to be coincidental. No one named Bridges or Rogers is listed in Bateman as owning a sizeable estate in Hampshire.
References Probate calendar; online genealogy sources.

Name **Hodson, Thomas** 1820/3
Dates c. 1751–25 January 1820, Plymouth.
Probate £120,000 (PCC).

Occupation Unknown. Presumably a merchant or other local notable in Plymouth, but virtually nothing could be traced of him. (Venue 13?)
Address Lived at Plymouth, Devon.
Father Unknown.
Mother Unknown.
Education Unknown.
Marriage To Mary Glanville (d. 1829; marriage date unknown). She left the dividends of £500 in 3 per cent stock for bread to be distributed twice yearly to the poor of the parish of King Charles the Martyr, Plymouth.
Religion Anglican; left £500 to the Household of Faith near Charles' Church, Plymouth (named for King Charles I) and £500 to the Church Missionary Society.
Public None known.
Miscellaneous His will is unilluminating, although one of his executors was Edward Snooks, a wharfinger of Tooley Street, Southwark. He also noted that he had East India Company stock.
References *GM,* 1820, vol. I, p. 188; will (PROB 11 online); online sources.

1820/4 **Name** **Gemmell, William**
Dates c. 1732–4 April 1820. Probated May 1820.
Probate £140,000 (PCC).
Occupation 'Merchant' of Weymouth Street, Marylebone (1793 directory). (Occupational category IV.21? Venue 2.)
Address 'Formerly of Bedford Square, Middlesex, then of Crofton House near Titchfield, Hants.' (probate calendar).
Father Unknown. The surname is Scottish.
Mother Unknown.
Education Unknown.
Marriage Unknown.
Religion Unknown.
Public None known.
Miscellaneous What kind of mercantile activity he was engaged in is unclear, or why his premises were in Marylebone rather than in the City.
References Local directory and probate calendar.

1820/5 **Name** **Barton, Henry**
Dates 6 November 1737–26 October 1818.
Probate £160,000 (York PC).
Occupation 'Merchant and cotton manufacturer' (Henry Barton and James Barton, of Manchester, 1791 and 1794 directories). (Presumably he was primarily a cotton manufacturer; if so, occupational category II.7; venue 4.)
Address Of Springwood, Lancashire, the location of which is unclear. There is a Springwood Hall near Stockport, Cheshire. At the end of the eighteenth century, he purchased the Swinton and War Hall estates.
Father George Barton (buried April 1740).
Mother Lucy (d. 1779), daughter of O. Segar of Catlow, Lancashire.

Education Unknown.
Marriage In 1769, to Mary (d. 1804), daughter of Joseph Bushell of Neston, Cheshire.
Religion Baptised as Anglican.
Public None known.
Miscellaneous An early cotton manufacturer (and presumably merchant), but little is known of him.
References *BLG*, 1914.

Name **Porcher, Josias DuPré** 1820/6
Dates c. 1761–25 April 1820, near Exeter.
Probate £180,000 (PCC).
Occupation 'East India Agents' (Porcher & Co., Devonshire Square near Bishopsgate, adjacent to the City of London). He was the Principal of the Company. (Occupational category IV.19; venue 1.) Had had a long career in Madras from 1778–1800: see below.
Address Lived at Hillingdon House, Middlesex, and Winslade House, near Exeter, Devon, at death.
Father Paul Porcher, 'planter' of Charleston, South Carolina.
Mother Esther DuPré.
Education Unknown.
Marriage In 1787, in Madras, to Charlotte, daughter of (Admiral) Sir William Burnaby, 1st Baronet, of Broughton Hall, Oxfordshire. (Four sons, one daughter.)
Religion Anglican; of Huguenot descent.
Public MP (pro-Tory) Bodmin, 1802–6; Bletchingley, 1806–7; Dundalk, 1807; Old Sarum, 1807–18.
Miscellaneous Previously had a long career in the East India Company: Writer at Madras, 1778; Deputy to the Paymaster of Madras, 1783–6; Member of the Board of Trade and Clerk to the Committee of Works, 1790; Mayor of Madras, 1791–2; Military Storekeeper at Madras, 1792–1800. His uncle was Alexander DuPré, 2nd Earl of Caledon (1777–1834). Another uncle was Josias DuPré, Governor of Madras, 1770–3.
References *HP.*

Name **Lowndes, Robert** 1820/7
Dates c. 1727–5 January 1820, Bristol.
Probate £140,000 (PCC).
Occupation Apparently a landowner, although he may have had mercantile inheritances from Chesterfield, Bristol, and possibly Liverpool. (Occupational category I?) In 1883, a George Alan Lowndes of Harlow owned 3,650 acres worth £4,387 p.a., chiefly in Essex.
Address 'Formerly of Chesterfield then Palterton, Derbyshire, then Bath' (probate calendar) and 'formerly of Lea Hall, Cheshire and sometime of Widcombe, Somerset.'
Father Robert Lowndes of Overton and Lea, Cheshire 'purchased Lea from his

niece Sarah'. (May be the 'Robert Lowndes Esquire' of Buckinghamshire, whose will was probated January 1783.)
Mother Mary Kenyon, widow of (Revd) W. Turton.
Education Unknown.
Marriage In 1761, to Elizabeth (d.s.p., 1769), daughter of Richard Milnes (1705–57) of Chesterfield. Elizabeth's sister Esther (1753–92) is described as an 'heiress from Chesterfield' in *ODNB* entry on her husband Thomas Day (1748–89), 'author and political campaigner'.
Religion Anglican.
Public None known.
Miscellaneous The origins of his fortune are elusive.
References *BLG*, 1914: 'Lowndes (now Gorst) of Castle Combe'; *GM*, 1820, vol. I, p. 89.

1820/8 **Name** **Hatsell, John**
Dates 22 December 1733–15 October 1820.
Probate £120,000 (PCC).
Occupation Chief Clerk of the House of Commons, 1768–1820, a 'lucrative office' (*GM*), and also Senior Bencher of the Middle Temple. (Occupational category VI.31 and 29; venue 2.)
Address Lived at Old Palace Yards, Cotton Gardens, Middlesex and Marden Park, Godstone, Surrey.
Father Henry Hatsell (1702–73), barrister of London. John's grandfather was Sir Henry Hatsell (1641–1714), Baron of the Exchequer.
Mother Penelope, daughter of Sir James Robinson, Baronet of Cranford Hall near Kettering.
Education Secondary schooling unknown; Queen's College, Cambridge (MA); barrister, Middle Temple (called 1757).
Marriage In 1778, to the daughter of (Revd) Jeffrey Elkins of Barton Seagrave, Northamptonshire, and the widow of (Major) Newton Barton of Northamptonshire. (She lived 1735–1804.)
Religion Anglican: buried in Temple Church.
Public No political offices.
Miscellaneous Wrote *Precedents of the Proceedings of the House of Commons* (5 vols., 1776–96). Master and Treasurer of Middle Temple.
References *ODNB; GM*, 1820, vol. II, pp. 372–3.

1820/9 **Name** **Levett, Thomas**
Dates Unknown–c. January 1820. (His death was announced in the *Staffordshire Advertiser* on 8 January 1820.)
Probate £180,000 (PCC).
Occupation Probably a landowner – his father was Town Clerk of Lichfield and a JP. Thomas Levett might also have been a barrister. He is listed as having become a member of the Inner Temple in 1753. In 1883, Theophilus John Levett owned 3,200 acres worth £5,500 p.a. in Staffordshire and Worcestershire. (Occupational category I?)

Address Packington, near Tamworth, Staffordshire and Whittington, near Stourbridge, Staffordshire.
Father Theophilus Levett (d. 1746), JP, Staffordshire, and Town Clerk of Lichfield, which suggests that he might have been a solicitor. His portrait was painted by the artist James Ward.
Mother Mary, daughter of John Babbington of Whittington, Staffordshire.
Education Unknown. (His brother John was educated at Westminster and the Middle and Inner Temples.)
Marriage In 1762, to Catherine, daughter of Charles Floyer of Hints Hall, Staffordshire.
Religion Presumably Anglican.
Public None known. His brother John (1721–99) was an MP, 1761–2.
Miscellaneous Probably local solicitors who became landowners, although this isn't clear.
References *BLG*, 1850, 1937.

Name **Tate, (Revd) Benjamin, DD** 1820/10
Dates c. 1751–22 November 1820.
Probate £120,000 (PCC).
Occupation Fellow, Bursar and Vice-President of Magdalen College, Oxford. (Occupational category VI.30; venue 14.)
Address Magdalen College, Oxford.
Father Benjamin Tate of Mitcham, Surrey.
Mother Unknown.
Education Secondary schooling unknown; University College and Magdalen College, Oxford (MA, BD, DD).
Marriage Unmarried.
Religion Anglican clergyman: has memorial in Magdalen College Chapel.
Public None known.
Miscellaneous Held Fellowship at Magdalen College, Oxford with rectory of Michaelston-y-Fedw, between Caerphilly and Newport; Bursar (1785) and Vice-President (1794) of Magdalen College and Dean of Divinity (1795). Held two shares in the Oxford Canal and was the 'stepgrandson' (sic) of President Butler of Magdalen.
References *Alum. Oxon.*; *GM*.

Name **Harvey, Robert** 1820/11
Dates 8 February 1753–13 January 1820.
Probate £250,000 (PCC).
Occupation Banker in Norwich. (Occupational category IV.16; venue 11.)
Address Catton in Norwich.
Father Robert Harvey (d. 1816), banker of Norwich (see 1816/11) who left £300,000.
Mother Judith (d. 1810), daughter of (Captain) Onley RN.
Education Unknown.

Marriage In 1781, to Anne (d. 1801), daughter of Jeremiah Ives, Mayor of Norwich. No children.
Religion Presumably Anglican.
Public Mayor of Norwich, 1785. JP, Norwich; JP, DL, Norfolk. Lieutenant Colonel, East Norfolk Militia.
Miscellaneous Of a well-established banking family in the local Norwich elite.
References *GM,* 1820, vol. I, p. 93. His nephew was created a baronet.

1820/12 **Name** **Dimsdale, 2nd Baron (of Russia), John Dimsdale**
Dates 11 March 1747–21 February 1820, Hampstead.
Probate £140,000 (PCC).
Occupation Banker (Baron Dimsdale Sons, Barnard, and Staples) in the City of London. (Occupational category IV.16; venue 1.) Also had medical fortune from his father and owned estates in Berkhampstead and Hertford. (In 1883, Baron Dimsdale owned 2,382 acres worth £3,641 p.a. in Hertfordshire, etc.)
Address Lived at The Priory, Hertford and in Hampstead.
Father Thomas Dimsdale, 1st Baron Dimsdale (of Russia) (1712–3 December 1800), of The Priory, Hertford, a famous Quaker physician who was given £10,000 and a £500 annuity by Empress Catherine the Great, as well as a Russian title, for inoculating her and her son against smallpox. Dimsdale later became a banker in London and an MP (*ODNB*).
Mother Anne (d. 1779), daughter of John Iles.
Education Unknown.
Marriage Unmarried.
Religion Buried as a Quaker.
Public None known.
Miscellaneous Continued the father's banking firm.
References *HP* and *ODNB* for father; *BP.*

1820/13 **Name** **Curzon, 1st Viscount, Assheton Curzon**
Dates 2 February 1729/30–21 March 1820, Lower Brook Street, Middlesex.
Probate £140,000 (PCC).
Occupation Landowner in Cheshire and Staffordshire. (No direct descendant is apparently listed in Bateman, but Lord Scarsdale, the descendant of his elder brother, in 1883 owned 9,929 acres worth £17,829 p.a. in Derbyshire, etc.) (Occupational category I.)
Address Penn House near Amersham, Buckinghamshire; Hagley, Staffordshire.
Father Sir Nathaniel Curzon, 4th Baronet, of Kedleston, Derbyshire (1675–16 November 1758), landowner, barrister and MP. The Curzons were 'at the apex of Derbyshire society' (*ODNB*) and also had colliery money and property in Westminster. (Second son; the elder brother was created Baron Scarsdale.)
Mother Mary (d. 1776), daughter of Sir Ralph Assheton, 2nd Baronet, MP of Middleton, Lancashire.
Education Westminster School and Brasenose College, Oxford.
Marriage First, in 1756, to Esther (d. 1764), daughter of William Hanmer of

The Fens, Flintshire. (One son, two daughters.) Second, in 1766, to Dorothy (d. 1774), daughter of Sir Robert Grosvenor, 6th Baronet, MP. Third, in 1777, to Anne, daughter of Amos Meredith and widow of (Alderman) Barlow Trevithick.
Religion Anglican.
Public MP (Tory) Clitheroe, 1754–80, 1792–4. Created 1st Baron Curzon (1794) and 1st Viscount Curzon (1802).
Miscellaneous The famous Marquess Curzon of Kedleston was descended from his elder brother.
References *ODNB; HP; BP.*

Name **Harewood, 1st Earl of, Edward Lascelles** 1820/14
Dates 7 June 1740, Barbados–3 April 1820.
Probate £250,000 (PCC).
Occupation 'An important West India proprietor' (*HP*), of a family connected with Barbados since the seventeenth century; was a plantation owner and sugar factor (Lascelles and Maxwell) there. (Occupational category I; venue 29.) Later succeeded to the Harewood estate, 1795. In 1883, the Earl of Harewood owned 29,620 acres worth £38,188 p.a., chiefly in Yorkshire.
Address Chiefly Harewood House near Leeds.
Father Edwin Lascelles (d. 1747). Collector of Customs at Barbados and plantation owner. (Eldest surviving son.)
Mother Frances, daughter of Guy Ball, member of the Council of Barbados.
Education Unknown.
Marriage In 1761, to Anne (d. 1805), daughter of William Chaloner of Guisborough, Yorkshire. (Two sons, two daughters.)
Religion Anglican.
Public MP (Whig, later Tory) Northallerton, 1761–74, 1790–6. Created 1st Baron Harewood in 1791 and 1st Earl of Harewood in 1812.
Miscellaneous A famous dynasty of West Indies planters who became leading English aristocrats.
References *ODNB* for relatives; *BP; HP.*

Name **Turner, Sir Gregory (Page-), 3rd Baronet** 1820/15
Dates 14 March 1748–4 (or 16) January 1805 (sic) at Bicester. Although his will was probated in 1820, there does not appear to be any other man of this name who died closer to that year. This identification is therefore tentative.
Probate £175,000 (PCC).
Occupation East India fortune; then landowner (occupational category IV.19 and also I; venue 29). His grandfather, Sir Edward Turner, 1st Baronet (d. 1735), was Chairman of the East India Company and an 'opulent merchant' in London. In 1883, Sir E. Page-Turner owned 6,065 acres worth £10,000 p.a. in Bedfordshire, Oxfordshire and Middlesex.
Address Battleden, near Woburn, Bedfordshire; Ambrosden, near Bicester, Oxfordshire; Portland Place, Middlesex.
Father Sir Edward Turner, 2nd Baronet (1719–31 October 1766), MP.

Mother Cassandra (d. 1779), daughter of William Leigh of Adlestrop, Gloucestershire. (It might be noted that Jane Austen's mother was also named Cassandra Leigh, and there might possibly have been a connection.)
Education Secondary schooling unknown; Hertford College, Oxford.
Marriage In 1785, to Frances, daughter of Joseph Howell of Elm, near Wisbeach, Norfolk (she died 1828).
Religion Anglican.
Public MP (Tory) Thirsk, 1784 until death; High Sheriff, Oxfordshire, 1783–4.
Miscellaneous The father inherited the landed estates of his uncle, John Turner of Sunbury, Middlesex, said to be worth over £100,000, and also inherited the fortune of his great-uncle Edward Turner. Sir Gregory, who added 'Page' to his name on inheriting from Sir Edward Page, 6th Baronet in 1775, was said to have had estates 'worth £24,000 per year' and £80,000 in government stock. Why his estate was not, apparently, probated until fifteen years after his death is unclear.

The *Universal British Directory* 1791 states of Bicester: 'At Ambrosden, a small village, 2 miles from Bicester, lately stood a magnificent edifice, (in the centre of an estate of 5000l. per year,) the seat of, and built by, the late Sir Edward Turner, Bart. deceased, at 100,000l. expence; but has lately been wholly taken down, and the materials sold by public auction, by his eldest son, Sir George Page-Turner, Bart. MP for Thirske, Yorkshire.'
References *HP; BP.*

1820/16 **Name** **Day, David**
Dates Unknown – probated June 1820.
Probate £120,000 (PCC).
Occupation Unclear, but was possibly/probably of Day & Nicholson, The Old Bank, Rochester, Kent. (If so, occupational category IV.16; venue 14.)
Address 'Formerly of Little Hermitage near Rochester, Kent and Rochester City, and then West Hill House near Rochester' (probate calendar). He built Little Hermitage around 1790 (*Arch. Cantiana.*, 1855).
Father Unknown.
Mother Unknown.
Education Unknown.
Marriage Unknown.
Religion Unknown.
Public None Known.
Miscellaneous Was connected with Rochester for his whole career, not London, so far as is known.
References Above and probate calendar only.

1820/17 **Name** **Higginson, William**
Dates Unknown–6 June 1812, Saltmarshe, Herefordshire. His will was probated in PROB 11 in 1812 but was recorded in PROB 8 in 1820.
Probate £140,000 (PCC).
Occupation A partner in Greenwood & Higginson of St Marylebone. It was

engaged in the export trade to the United States, from before the American Revolution, for instance with South Carolina. Greenwood & Higginson were among those who, being British loyalists, had their estates confiscated by the 'Rebel Assembly' of South Carolina convened at Jacksonburgh in 1782 (http://www.selway.net/hist/amrev/loyalists.html). He may also have been the William Higginson, 'merchant' of 35 Walbrook, City of London (1793 London directory) and 'merchant' of 2 New Court, Swithin's Lane, City (1808 directory). (Occupational Category IV.19; venues 2 and 1?)

Address Of 5 Berners Street, Middlesex (will) and Saltmarshe near Bromyarde, Herefordshire.

Father Unknown.

Mother Unknown.

Education Unknown.

Marriage Unknown. *BLG,* 1850, notes that Edmund Barneby (or Barnby) (b. 1802) was the 'devisee' of his great-uncle, William Higginson of Saltmarshe. His will makes no mention of a wife or children but mentions his brother Robert Higginson and his nephews John and Edward Barnby.

Religion Unknown.

Public None known.

Miscellaneous An export merchant in London.

References *GM,* 1812, vol. I, p. 604; will (PROB 11 online); Leger & Greenwood of Charleston, South Carolina – archives held by the University of Michigan, online.

Name **Russell, Jesse** 1820/18

Dates 31 August 1747–28 June 1820, Walthamstow.

Probate £500,000 (PCC).

Occupation 'Soapboiler' at Goodman's Yard, adjacent to the City of London and of Walthamstow, Essex (1770, 1799 and 1808 directories). (Occupational category II.6? Venue 1.) Presumably he was a soap manufacturer, or the manufacturer of chemicals.

Address Lived at Walthamstow. It is not clear whether he had a soapboiling works there as well.

Father John Russell (1699–1760) of Newcastle-under-Lyme, Staffordshire. (Fourth son.)

Mother Martha, surname unknown.

Education Unknown.

Marriage In 1772 to Elizabeth, daughter of Thomas Noble of Broughbridge, Yorkshire. (Three sons, two daughters.)

Religion Buried St Mary's Anglican Church, Walthamstow.

Public None known.

Miscellaneous How he accumulated £500,000 as a 'soapboiler' is unclear; he might have had government contracts.

References *BLG,* 'Watts-Russell'.

1820/19 **Name** **North, (Hon.) Brownlow, Bishop of Winchester**

Dates 17 July 1741, London–12 July 1820.

Probate £180,000 (PCC).

Occupation Successively Canon of Christ Church, Oxford, 1768; Dean of Canterbury, 1770; Bishop of Coventry, 1771; Bishop of Worcester, 1774, and Bishop of Winchester, 1781–death. (Occupational Category VI.30; venue 14, etc.)

Address Had an estate at Fareham Park, Hampshire.

Father Francis North, 1st Earl of Guildford (1704–4 August 1790). (Second son.)

Mother Elizabeth (1707–45), daughter of Sir Arthur Kaye, 3rd Baronet, and widow of George Legge, 1st Viscount Lewisham.

Education Eton; Trinity College, Oxford (BA, 1762); Fellow of All Souls.

Marriage In 1771, to Henrietta (d. 1796), daughter of John Bannister 'West India merchant'.

Religion Anglican clergyman.

Public Active politically in the House of Lords as a bishop.

Miscellaneous 'Accumulated preferment rapidly' (*ODNB*) owing to good family connections – an example of clerical 'Old Corruption'. 'It was calculated that twenty-six individuals [in his family or friends] received about seventy appointments to fifty churches' through his influence (*ODNB*). He was also noted as 'cultivated' and a collector of vases. He was, in addition, a promoter of the Three Choirs' Festival and a noted botanist and FSA.

References *ODNB*.

1820/20 **Name** **Thompson, Richard**

Dates Unknown–12 September 1820, Grosvenor Square, Middlesex.

Probate £250,000 (PCC).

Occupation The family were originally merchants in Hull, then land and mineral owners in the East Riding. In 1883, Lord Wenlock, who succeeded him, owned 26,080 acres worth £27,590 p.a. in the East Riding and Shropshire. (Occupational category I; if still in trade, occupational category IV.19; venue 21.)

Address 'Of Escrick, N.R., Yorkshire' (*GM*). Escrick is about six miles from York. Also lived at Grosvenor Square, Middlesex.

Father Unknown.

Mother Unknown.

Education Unknown.

Marriage Unknown. He was the uncle of Paul Beiby Thompson (né Lawley), 1st Baron Wenlock (1784–1852) who inherited Escrick on his (Richard Thompson's) death in 1820. Paul Thompson was created Baron Wenlock in 1839.

Religion Presumably Anglican.

Public None known.

Miscellaneous He was presumably a relative of Sir Henry Thompson, merchant and MP of York and Escrick in the late seventeenth century and a relative of Beilby Thompson (1742–99), MP, 1768–84. The family were originally 'leading exporters of cloth' in Hull. (Hull sources.) It is unclear whether Richard Thompson was engaged in trade.

References *GM,* 1820, vol. II, p. 285; *BP.*

Name **Gray, Thomas** 1820/21
Dates Unknown – probated October 1820.
Probate £120,000 (PCC).
Occupation 'Jeweller' of 42 Sackville Street, Piccadilly (1803 directory); 'jeweller and watchmaker' of the same address (1793 directory). 'Jeweller of Sackville Street, Piccadilly, Middlesex' (probate calendar). (Occupational categories IV.20 and II.11; venue 2.)
Address '[42] Sackville Street, Piccadilly and Earl's Court' (probate calendar).
Father Unknown.
Mother Unknown.
Education Unknown.
Marriage Unknown.
Religion Unknown.
Public None known.
Miscellaneous Nothing more could be found about him.
References Probate calendar and above only.

Name **Jones, Daniel** 1820/22
Dates c. 1746–11 October 1820, Fakenham, Norfolk.
Probate £120,000 (PCC).
Occupation Solicitor in Fakenham. (Occupational category VI.29; venue 11.) 'A very prominent Fakenham attorney' – was the agent for nearby large estates. (Basil Cozens-Hardy, *Norfolk Lawyers* [Norfolk, 1965]).
Address Fakenham (near East Dereham) Norfolk.
Father Unknown: probably was Daniel or David Jones (d. 1783) of Cranmer Hall. Our man's cousin was (Major-General) Sir John Jones, from whom he inherited the Cranmer Hall estate.
Mother Unknown.
Education Unknown.
Marriage Unknown.
Religion Unknown, presumably Anglican.
Public None known.
Miscellaneous Was active in enclosures in Norfolk (Cozens-Hardy).
References Probate calendar and above only.

Name **Gwydir, 1st Baron, Sir Peter Burrell** 1820/23
Dates 16 June 1754, Upper Grosvenor Street–29 June 1820, Brighton.
Probate £120,000 (PCC).
Occupation Land and 'Old Corruption' and mercantile fortune. (Occupational category I, etc.) His grandfather, Peter Burrell (d. 1756) had a lucrative victualling contract and was a director of the South Sea Company and the Royal Exchange. His father, an MP, was Surveyor-General of Crown Lands. His wife was Baroness Willoughby d'Eresby in her own right and succeeded to the Ancaster estates. In

1883, Baroness Willoughby d'Eresby owned 132,220 acres worth £74,006 p.a. in Lincolnshire, Perthshire, etc.

Address Gwydir, Carnarvonshire; Langley Park, Beckenham, Kent.

Father Peter Burrell (1724–6 November 1775), MP, 1759–74.

Mother Elizabeth (d. 1795), daughter of John Lewis of Hackney.

Education Eton; St John's College, Cambridge.

Marriage In 1779, to Lady Priscilla (d. 1828), daughter of Peregrine, 3rd Duke of Ancaster and Baroness Willoughby d'Eresby in her own right. (Three sons, one daughter.)

Religion Anglican.

Public MP (pro-government) Haslemere, 1776–80; Boston, 1782–96. Knighted, 1781; succeeded to the baronetcy of his uncle Sir Meyrick Burrell, 1787; created baron, 1796. PC, 1820.

Miscellaneous A very fortunate series of inheritances and marriages greatly benefited him. He was a member of White's Club and a well-known cricketer. His sister was the Duchess of Hamilton.

References *ODNB; HP; CP,* etc.

1820/24 **Name** **Robarts, William Tierney**

Dates 1786–9 December 1820.

Probate £120,000 (PCC).

Occupation Banker of Old Broad Street, City of London – a partner in his father's bank from 1810. He was also a director of the Bank of England from 1810–20. (Occupational category IV.16; venue 1.)

Address 'Old Broad Street, City of London, and John Street, Middlesex' (probate calendar). According to the *ODNB,* he lived at 49 Lower Grosvenor Street, Middlesex.

Father Abraham Robarts (1745–1816; see 1816/22, left £350,000), wealthy banker of the City of London. (Fourth son.)

Mother Sabine, daughter of Thomas Tierney and sister of Rt. Hon. George Tierney, MP.

Education Unknown.

Marriage Unmarried.

Religion Anglican.

Public MP (Whig), St Albans, 1818–20.

Miscellaneous His elder brother (Colonel) Abraham Wildey Robarts (1779–1858), MP (q.v.) was a partner in Watney, Combe & Reid, the brewers and a banker. William Tierney Robarts died at the age of only thirty-four. He had received about £30,000 from his father and had built up his fortune (*ODNB*).

References *ODNB; GM,* 1820, vol. II, p. 573, Judd.

1820/25 **Name** **Errington, Henry**

Dates c. 1738–15 December 1819, at The Stable Yard, St James's, Middlesex.

Probate £140,000 (PCC).

Occupation Owned land, minerals, collieries and smelting mills in Northumberland. (Occupational category I?) (No one of this name could be traced in Bateman, 1883.) Was also uncle to Maria Anne Fitzherbert (née Smythe), 'unlawful wife of George IV' (*ODNB* for Mrs Fitzherbert).

Address 'Sandhoe [near Hexham] Northumberland; Red Rice, Hants., and The Stable Yard, St James's, Middlesex' (probate calendar).

Father John Errington (1708–February 1741) of Beaufort, Northumberland. (Second son.)

Mother Maria, daughter of John Douglas of Newcastle upon Tyne.

Education Unknown.

Marriage In 1769, to Maria (d.s.p., 1813), daughter of Thomas Hill of Tern, Shropshire, widow of Sir Brian Broughton, Baronet, and sister of Lord Berwick.

Religion Roman Catholic.

Public None known.

Miscellaneous It is not clear whether he was primarily a businessman or a landowner – more information is needed.

References *ODNB* for Mrs Fitzherbert; online sources.

Name **Delafield, Joseph** 1820/26

Dates 14 May 1749–3 September 1820, Hastings.

Probate £100,000 (PCC).

Occupation Brewer in Castle Street, Long Acre, Middlesex. (Occupational category III.12; venue 2.) Assisted Samuel Whitbread from 1783 as manager of his Chiswell Street brewery. Later joined Gyfford & Co.'s Wood Yard brewery in Long Acre, which was later known as Combe, Delafield & Co. – presumably in partnership with his father-in-law.

Address Lived in Long Acre, Middlesex and at Camden Hill, Kensington.

Father John Delafield (1718–9 March 1763), 'cheesemonger' of White Cross Street, London. (Second son.)

Mother Martha (d. 1761), daughter of Jacob Dell of Aylesbury.

Education Unknown.

Marriage In 1789, to Frances, daughter of Hervey Christian Combe, MP, brewer of Cobham Park. (Four sons, two daughters.)

Religion The father was originally a Baptist but became an Anglican in 1757. He was an Anglican.

Public None known.

Miscellaneous One of the founders of a leading brewery.

References John Ross Delafield, *Delafield: The Family History* (1945), pp. 286 ff.

Name **Nanson, William** 1820/27

Dates c. 1745–27 September 1820, Hornsey.

Probate £100,000 (PCC).

Occupation Grocer and tea dealer – 'North, Hoare, Nanson & Simpson' of Fleet Street and New Bridge Street (1815 directory). In 1795 was a 'grocer' of Bridge Street. The 1808 directory lists a William Nanson, 'distiller', of 27 Stanhope Street, Clare Market. (Occupational category IV.20; venue 1.)

Address 'Bridge Street, Blackfriars, and then Russell Square, Middlesex' (probate calendar).
Father Unknown.
Mother Unknown.
Education Unknown.
Marriage Unknown.
Religion Unknown.
Public None known.
Miscellaneous Nothing more could be traced about him.
References *GM,* 1820, vol. II, p. 377.

1820/28 **Name** **Maitland, (Hon.) Sir Alexander, 1st Baronet**
Dates 21 March 1728–14 February 1820, Totteridge.
Probate £120,000 (PCC).
Occupation 'General in the Army' (probate calendar). 'The last survivor of the household of Frederick, Prince of Wales' (*GM*). (Occupational category VI.31.)
Address 'Formerly Welbeck Street, Middlesex, then Gray's Farm, Finchley, then Totteridge, Hertfordshire' (probate calendar).
Father Charles, 6th Earl of Lauderdale (d. 15 July 1744). (Sixth son.)
Mother Lady Elizabeth (d. 1778), daughter of James, 1st Earl of Findlater and 1st Earl of Seafield.
Education Unknown.
Marriage In 1754, to Penelope (d. 1805), daughter of (Colonel) Martin Madan, MP, Groom of the Bedchamber to Frederick, Prince of Wales. (Four sons, two daughters.)
Religion Originally Church of Scotland, then presumably Anglican.
Public Created baronet, 1818.
Miscellaneous Lieutenant in 1756 in 1st Foot Guards; Colonel, 1762; Major-General, 1772; Lieutenant General, 1777; General, 1793. One of the oldest army officers at his death.
References *GM,* 1820, vol. I, p. 282.

1820/29 **Name** **Warrender, Hugh**
Dates Unknown–8 June 1820, Edinburgh.
Probate £203,258 (Scottish probates: this is the earliest Scottish estate over £100,000 in their available records).
Occupation Solicitor – 'Writer to the Signet' in Edinburgh. (A 'writer to the signet' was a Scottish solicitor.) (Occupational category VI.29; venue 23.) He was 'H.M. Agent for Scotland and Deputy Keeper of the Signet' (*GM*).
Address Burntisland, Fife.
Father George Warrender of Burntisland, Fife. His father (Hugh's grandfather) was Sir George Warrender, Baronet, 'an eminent merchant' and Lord Provost of Edinburgh: the elder branch of the family succeeded to the baronetcy.
Mother Possibly Mary Boyd. A Hugh Warrender, son of George Warrender and Mary Boyd, was born in June 1746 in St Cuthbert's parish, Edinburgh (Family Search).

Education Unknown.
Marriage Unknown – married, but d.s.p.
Religion Presumably Church of Scotland.
Public None known.
Miscellaneous Succeeded to the business of John Davidson (d. December 1797), Writer to the Signet, whose chief clerk he had been. (*ODNB* for Davidson.)
References *GM. BP* for Warrender, Baronet.

WEALTH-HOLDERS, 1821

1821/1 **Name** **Chalie, Susannah** (or Susanna; née Suzanne Clarmont)

Dates Baptised 5 March 1736, St Martin Orgars French Huguenot Church, London–2 March 1821, St Cloud, France.

Probate £140,000 (PCC).

Occupation Widow of wine merchant in Mincing Lane. (Occupational category IV.20; venue I.)

Address 'Formerly Wimbledon, then Bedford Square, Middlesex; then Bathford, Somerset; then Rochester, Kent; then France' (probate calendar).

Father Mathieu Clarmont (Family Search). A Matthew Clarmont was Governor of the Bank of England, 1766–9.

Mother Marthe (surname unknown) (Family Search).

Education Unknown.

Marriage To John Chalie (d. 5 August 1803) of Bedford Square, 'a very opulent wine merchant' (*GM,* 1803, vol. II, p. 793). Their daughter Marianne married Henry Skrine, a wealth-holder. Chalie's business was John & Matthew Chalie, of 28 Mincing Lane, City of London (1795 and 1803 directories). The Chalies were also of Huguenot descent. A Jean Chalie was baptised in 1737 at the French Huguenot Church St Martin Orgars, London, and a Matthieu Chalie in 1747, sons of Jacques and Marianne Chalie (Family Search). Her husband's will was the subject of a well-known law case in 1804.

Religion Unknown.

Public None known.

Miscellaneous From a wealthy Huguenot background.

References *GM,* 1821, vol. I, p. 284; online source as above.

1821/2 **Name** **(Lane-) Fox, James** (Also given as Fox-Lane, e.g., in Judd)

Dates August 1756–7 April 1821.

Probate £120,000 (PCC).

Occupation Land: inherited his Yorkshire estates in 1773 from his uncle George Lane-Fox, 1st Baron Bingley (created 1762). (Occupational category I.) In 1883, George Lane-Fox, his successor, owned 39,069 acres worth £26,000 p.a. in the West Riding, Leitrim and Waterford.

Address Bramham Park, near Tadcaster, West Riding of Yorkshire.

Father Sackville Fox (d. 1 December 1760) of East Horsley.

Mother Ann Holloway of Birmingham.

Education Secondary schooling unknown; Christ's College, Cambridge.

Marriage In 1789 to (Hon.) Maria (or Marcia) (d. 1822), daughter of George Pitt, 1st Baron Rivers. (Four sons, one daughter.)

Religion Anglican.

Public MP (—) Horsham, 1796–1802.

Miscellaneous Was noted as a friend of George IV and was a lieutenant in the Dorset Militia. Presumably added Lane to his name when he inherited his uncle's estate.

References *BLG*, 1914; *HP.*

Name **Splidt (sic), Christian** 1821/3

Dates c. 1766–27 October 1821.

Probate £100,000 'within province' (PCC).

Occupation 'Russia merchant' of New Road, St George's in the East (1817 London directory); also 'rope makers' of New Road, St George's (1793 directory). A 'Philip Splidt & Co., hemp merchants' of 74 Cable Street, Wellclose Square is listed in the 1793 directory. (Presumably he imported hemp for ropes, used primarily for shipping, from Russia. If so, occupational category IV.19; venue 2.) In 1812, a Thomas Smith was tried and acquitted at the Old Bailey on a charge of stealing 30 pounds of bees wax valued at £3 from Christian Splidt, who, testified the Whitechapel beadle, 'dealt in articles of that sort'. See www.oldbaileyonline.org. Christian Splidt, Cable Street, St George's appears in *A List of the Names of the Members of the United Company of Merchants of England, Trading to the East Indies, 1815* (i.e. the East India Company): online.

Address 'Stratford Green, West Ham, Essex and Spitalfields' (probate calendar).

Father Unknown. Possibly Christian Split, baptised 10 October 1739 at St George's in the East, son of Philip and Martha. A Philip Split, born to the same parents, was baptised there on 29 April 1734 (Family Search). The name would obviously suggest a foreign origin, possibly German, Danish or Baltic.

Mother Possibly Elizabeth Smith, who married Christian Splidt on 13 December 1755 at St George's in the East, Stepney (Family Search).

Education Unknown.

Marriage To Mary Edis on 30 March 1793 at St Benet Fink, London (Family Search). He had at least two sons (Christian, baptised 31 March 1799, and Philip, baptised 4 June 1801), and at least two daughters, Elizabeth, baptised 23 December 1794, and Mary (b. c. 1801) (Family Search; Roots Web).

Religion Unknown.

Public None known.

Miscellaneous His 'town residence' was at Spitalfields (*GM*).

References *GM*, 1820, vol. II, p. 474.

Name **Forbes, John** 1821/4

Dates c. 1743–20 June 1821.

Probate £350,000 (PCC).

Occupation Merchant in Bombay (Forbes & Co.), then possibly of 16 New Broad Street, City of London (1803 directory). (Occupational category IV.19; venue 29.)

Address 'Newe, Strathdon, Aberdeenshire and Fitzroy Square, Middlesex' (probate calendar).

Father John Forbes (1707–91) of Bellabeg.

Mother Christian, daughter of (Revd) John Shepherd, Minister of Logie Coldstone.

Education A man of this name attended Aberdeen University, entering in 1758, but is unlikely to be this John Forbes.

Marriage Apparently unmarried.
Religion Church of Scotland.
Public None known.
Miscellaneous Went to India at an early age – originally a ship's purser. In Bombay, he established a 'most successful' mercantile house. He eventually took his two nephews into partnership. One was Charles Forbes (1773–1849), MP, in *ODNB* as a 'politician'; he served for twenty-four years in his uncle's mercantile house before returning to Britain in 1811. John Forbes returned and bought the Newe estate in Aberdeenshire. The family eventually received a baronetcy. In 1883, Sir Charles John Forbes, Baronet of Newe owned 29,238 acres worth £5,992 p.a. in Aberdeenshire.
References *GM*, 1821, vol. I, p. 574; A. N. Tayler & H. Tayler, *House of Forbes* (1937); *BP.*

1821/5 **Name** **Cattley, Stephen**
Dates 13 April 1721, Appleton, Yorkshire–5 February 1821.
Probate £140,000 (PCC).
Occupation 'Merchant' (John and Stephen Cattley, of 23 Garlick Hill, City) (1793 directory). Stephen Cattley is listed in 1795 as at Queenhithe, and, in 1817, John and Stephen Cattley are listed at 14 Queenhithe. He was previously the founder and head of Cattley & Co., import-export merchants, of St Petersburg, Russia, from 1777 to 1788. He was the father of Charles Robert Cattley (1816–55), diplomat (*ODNB*). (Occupational category IV.19; venues 1 and 29.) Robert Cattley (1 January 1748/9–22 January 1795), of Lime Street, was Stephen Cattley's brother; he was an insurance underwriter at Lloyds.
Address 'Formerly Lime Street then Fenchurch Street, then Brabant Court, Philpot Lane in the City of London and Camberwell' (probate calendar).
Father Robert Cattley (1720–98) of York, iron and deal (timber) merchant. He is described in the 1795 York directory as a 'raff merchant'. (Second son.)
Mother Dorothy (b. 1725), daughter of Richard Fowler of Colton, Yorkshire.
Education Unknown.
Marriage First, in February 1782, to Marianne (d. 25 February 1783 in childbirth at St Petersburg, aged twenty-three), daughter of Stephen Cattley of Kippax, Yorkshire. (One daughter.) Second, in 1793, to Ann 'Isabella', daughter of (Captain) Gilbert Lawson Reed of Trinity House. (Five sons, four daughters.)
Religion Unknown.
Public None known.
Miscellaneous A merchant in St Petersburg and then in London.
References Probate calendar and online sources.

1821/6 **Name** **Bridges, Robert**
Dates Probably 1758–1821 (probated April 1821).
Probate £100,000 (PCC).
Occupation Probably a land and property owner in Beddington and Ewell, Surrey, and also a gunpowder manufacturer. (If so, occupational category I and II.6;

venue 3.) It is not clear which was the more lucrative source of his wealth, if either.

Address Lived at Lower Tooting, Surrey.

Father Probably Alexander Bridges (1713–14 February 1781) of Langshott Manor and Ewell, Surrey. Bridges, who was already apparently wealthy, bought land and property at Ewell and, from 1754, owned a successful gunpowder manufacturing works there.

Mother Probably Joanna (d. 1788), daughter of William Bull.

Education Unknown.

Marriage Probably Margaret (d. 1823), daughter of Thomas Whittaker. (Two sons.)

Religion Probably Anglican: Alexander Bridges was a vestryman of Ewell Church.

Public None known.

Miscellaneous Sir Henry Bridges (1786–1859) may have been his son or nephew. Robert's son (Revd) Alexander Henry Bridges of Beddington House, in 1883 owned 5,412 acres worth £5,828 p.a. in Aberdeen, Surrey and Essex. The Bridges were Lords of the Manor of Beddington.

References *BLG*, 1914, 1952; 'Ewell Court, the Bridges Family and Ewell Powder Mills', online.

Name **Reid, John** 1821/7

Dates Unknown – probated May 1821.

Probate £120,000 (PCC).

Occupation Brewer at Liquorpond Street, Clerkenwell – a partner with Andrew Reid, Thomas (?) Meux, and others in Meux, Reid & Co., according to his will. (Occupational category II.12; venue 2.)

Address '48 Bedford Square and Kingswood Lodge, Egham, Surrey' (probate calendar).

Father Unknown. Presumably Andrew Reid and the Thomas Reid mentioned in his will were his brothers or cousins.

Mother Unknown.

Education Unknown.

Marriage Unknown.

Religion The family were from Scotland – presumably originally Church of Scotland.

Public None known.

Miscellaneous His role in the brewery is unclear, although he was a partner. The firm later became Meux's Brewery.

References Will (PROB 11 online).

Name **Clutterbuck, Daniel** 1821/8

Dates January 1744–11 June 1821.

Probate £120,000 (PCC).

Occupation Possibly a banker in Bradford-on-Avon, Wiltshire and a partner of

Sir Benjamin Hobhouse, Baronet, of Bath (which is nearby). (If so, occupational category IV.16; venue 13). Bradford-on-Avon is also noted as a centre of the wool trade. He may have been the partner, as a banker, of Sir Benjamin Hobhouse, Baronet. See *ODNB* for Timothy Brown (1743–1820), banker and radical. (If so, occupational category IV.16; venue 13.)

Address Bedford Leigh, Bradford-on-Avon, Wiltshire.

Father Thomas Clutterbuck (d. 15 June 1805) of Avening, a village near Stroud, Gloucestershire.

Mother Elizabeth, daughter of Thomas Webb of Avening.

Education Unknown.

Marriage In 1772 or 1773, to Elizabeth (d. 1826), daughter of Bryan Edwards, MP of Jamaica. (One son, who married the daughter of David Ricardo, MP, stockbroker and economist, 1823/7).

Religion Presumably Anglican; apparently owned an advowson.

Public None known.

Miscellaneous Little could be traced about his source of wealth.

References *BLG*, 1952; *VCH Wiltshire*, vol. 7, p. 74; *Wiltshire Notes and Queries*, vol. I (1893–5), p. 304.

1821/9 **Name Willes, Ann**

Dates Unknown – probated 1821. However, PROB 11 has no estate listed by anyone of this name in 1821 (or by any Anne Wells, Wills, or any other similar spelling). The closest PROB 11 estate was for an Anne Willes, spinster, of Uxbridge, Middlesex, probated in September 1815. The 1821 probate is from the PROB 8 calendar. The reason for the discrepancy is obscure.

Probate £120,000 (PCC).

Occupation A rather unclear case. She was probably the widow of John Willes, cornfactor of Whitechapel, resident in Dulwich, who has a memorial inscription in Wraysbury, Buckinghamshire. Her maiden name was Wright. *GM* lists two other possibilities: first, the widow of (Revd) William Willes, Archdeacon of Wells, who died at Bath, 17 January 1821 (*GM*, 1821, vol. I, p. 94); second, Anne Willes (the only daughter of J. Willes of Hungerford Place, Berkshire) who died at Hastings on 22 January 1820. The 1793 London directory lists: Pitman, Willes & Co., wholesale haberdashers of 18 Mark Lane; James Willes, cornfactor, of Mark Lane; and James Willes, brewer, of Lower Lambeth Marsh. Other persons named Willes have entries in the *ODNB*, but no identification with her could be made.

Address 'Dulwich, Camberwell' (probate calendar) is the only address known.

Father Possibly Thomas Wright of Dulwich (Gordon Gyll, *History of the Parish of Wraysbury, Ankerwyke Priory, and Magna Charta Island* [1862], p. 122.)

Mother Possibly Ann (d. 4 May 1809, aged eighty-two), daughter of William Gyll of Boxley, a village near Maidstone, Kent, and Elizabeth, daughter and heiress of John Lawrence. Elizabeth's maternal uncle, James Brooke of Lewisham, was High Sheriff of Kent 1731.

Education Unknown.

Marriage Possibly John Willes (marriage date unknown). The Dulwich mansion

Belair House, in Gallery Road (known as College Place in his day), was built for him about 1785.
Religion Unknown, but probably Anglican.
Public None known.
Miscellaneous See above.
References Probate calendar and above sources only.

Name **Alcock, Joseph** 1821/10
Dates c. 1758–2 August 1821, Roehampton, Surrey.
Probate £120,000 (PCC).
Occupation 'Late one of the Chief Clerks of H.M. Treasury' (*GM*). Ooccupational category VI.31; venue 2.)
Address 'Formerly Putney, then [Putney Heath], Roehampton' (probate calendar).
Father Unknown.
Mother Unknown.
Education Unknown.
Marriage Unknown.
Religion Presumably Anglican.
Public None known.
Miscellaneous Little could be learned of his career or if he had other sources of wealth.
References *GM*, 1821, vol. II, p. 188.

Name **Key, John** 1821/11
Dates Unknown–24 April 1819 (sic), Denmark Hill, Camberwell.
Probate £120,000 (PCC).
Occupation 'Stationer' (Keys [sic] Brothers, stationers, of 30 Abchurch Lane, Lombard Street, 1815 directory). Jonathan Key & Son, stationers, 38 Paternoster Row, City (1793 directory); of 30 Abchurch Lane, City (1803 directory). (Presumably a retail/wholesale stationer for City businesses, but might also have been involved in printing. Probably occupational category IV.20; venue 1.)
Address 'Abchurch Lane, City of London, and Denmark Hill, Camberwell' (probate calendar).
Father John (Jonathan?) Key. (Second son.)
Mother Unknown.
Education Unknown.
Marriage Unknown.
Religion Unknown.
Public None known.
Miscellaneous Nothing more could be learned of his career. There were presumably many stationers in the City, and it seems curious that one could have accumulated such a large fortune.
References *GM*, 1819, vol. I, p. 489.

1821/12 **Name** **White, Samuel**

Dates c. 1760–11 September 1821.

Probate £100,000 (PCC).

Occupation Unknown: presumably a landowner, but might have had interests in Poole, where he lived. Nobody named White, of Dorset, or named Driver (see below), is listed in Bateman. (Occupational category I?)

Address Charlton Marshall near Blandford, Dorset and Poole.

Father Samuel White (d. 1791) of Charlton Marshall.

Mother Anne Thomson, niece of Sir Peter Thomson, FRS, of Poole, MP for St Albans and High Sheriff of Surrey, 1745.

Education Unknown.

Marriage To Anne Linthorpe (marriage date unknown; d.s.p.). White's estate passed to his nephew William Driver, who took the name of White.

Religion Presumably Anglican.

Public None known.

Miscellaneous This man plainly inherited considerable means, but the source of his fortune, or his own occupation, could not be traced.

References *BLG*, 1846; *GM*, 1821, vol. II, p. 286.

1821/13 **Name** **Ames, Levi**

Dates Baptised 2 April 1739–16 December 1820.

Probate £120,000 (PCC).

Occupation Chiefly banker in Bristol. (Occupational category IV.16; venue 12.) His family also had interests in sugar trading and provisioning and was one of the leading commercial families of Bristol. Levi Ames was also a merchant who sold dyestuffs.

Address 'Clifton, Gloucestershire and Bristol' (probate calendar).

Father Jeremiah Ames (d. 3 April 1776), presumably a merchant in Bristol – Mayor of Bristol, 1759; Sheriff, 1742.

Mother Phoebe (d. 1779), daughter of Robert Collins of Horton, Somerset).

Education Unknown.

Marriage First, in 1770, to Anna Maria (d. 1792), daughter of Chauncey Poole of Bristol. Her mother was the sister of Sir Lionel Lyde, prominent Bristol merchant. (Six sons, four daughters.) Second, in 1796, to Elizabeth Wraxall (d. 1843) of Clifton.

Religion Described in some sources as a Unitarian but baptised as an Anglican.

Public Alderman of Bristol, 1792–1820, and previously a member of the Bristol Council, 1771–92; Mayor of Bristol, 1788–9.

Miscellaneous At the heart of the Bristol mercantile and civic elite of the time.

References Graham Bush, *Bristol and Its Municipal Government* (1976); *Transactions of the Bristol Historical Society*, 1968; *BLG*.

1821/14 **Name** **Kinnersley, Thomas**

Dates 8 December 1751–3 November 1819, Brighton.

Probate £140,000 (PCC).

Occupation Banker in Newcastle-under-Lyme. (Principal of the Newcastle and Staffordshire Bank, and agent of the Marquess of Stafford.) (Occupational category IV.16; venue 18.) He was also a glass manufacturer – partner in Davenport, Kinnersley & Grafton of Burslem.
Address 'Newcastle-under-Lyme and Clough Hall [near Tunstall] Staffordshire' (probate calendar).
Father William Kinnersley (1726–1 May 1788) of Newcastle-under-Lyme.
Mother Mary (d. 1781), daughter of William Ford of Ford Green, Staffordshire.
Education Unknown.
Marriage In 1778, to Mary (d. 1725), daughter of Edward Shepherd of Sheffield. (At least three sons, plus eight daughters.)
Religion Probably Anglican: apparently has a memorial in a local church.
Public None known. His son William Shepherd Kinnersley (c. 1780–1823) was MP for Newcastle-under-Lyme, 1818–23, and Mayor of Newcastle in 1810–11.
Miscellaneous He was 'succeeded' by his third son Edward, DL, a barrister (*BLG*).
References *GM,* 1819, vol. II, p. 568; *BLG,* 1846.

Name **Farley, Thomas** 1821/15
Dates Unknown – probated August 1821.
Probate £140,000 (PCC).
Occupation Probably a banker in Worcester city, in partnership with Benjamin Johnson (Worcestershire Record Office catalogue, online). (If so, occupational category IV.16; venue 18.)
Address Henwick Hall, Hallow (on the outskirts of Worcester), Worcestershire.
Father Unknown. A Thomas Farley was Mayor of Worcester in 1778.
Mother Unknown.
Education Unknown.
Marriage Unknown.
Religion Unknown. The name Farley is sometimes Irish, but there is no direct evidence of his ancestry. But this family may have owned an Anglican advowson (see *VCH Worcestershire,* vol. 3, p. 209).
Public None known, but see above.
Miscellaneous Little could be traced of him.
References Probate calendar only, and sources above.

Name **Wilson, William** 1821/16
Dates Unknown – probated October 1821.
Probate £250,000 (PCC).
Occupation 'Silk manufacturer' (Wilson & Moore, of 31 Milk Street City of London, 1815 directory); also owned a 'freehold warehouse' in Bow Lane, City (mentioned in his will). (Occupational category II.9; venue 1.)
Address 'Formerly of Milk Street, City of London, and then Nether Wharton, Oxfordshire' (probate calendar).
Father Unknown.

Mother Unknown.
Education Unknown.
Marriage Unknown.
Religion Anglican: mentions his ownership of an advowson in Walthamstow in his will.
Public None known.
Miscellaneous Exceptionally successful as a silk manufacturer, given the size of his fortune.
References Probate calendar only.

1821/17 **Name** **Pieschel, Charles Augustus**
Dates c. 1750–6 April 1821.
Probate £350,000 (PCC).
Occupation 'Merchant' (Pieschel and Schreiber of 11 Size Lane, Bridge Row, City of London, 1815 directory). (Occupational category IV.19 or 21; venue 1.)
Address 'Of Size Lane, City of London, then New Norfolk Street, Middlesex and Brighton' (probate calendar).
Father Unknown. An Augustus Pieschel was naturalised in 1798 by an Act of Parliament. A Charles Augustus Godfrey Pieschel is listed in Robert Chambers, *Index to Heirs at Law, Next of Kin, Names for Heirs in Chancery* (1857).
Mother Unknown.
Education Unknown.
Marriage Unknown.
Religion Unknown, possibly originally Lutheran.
Public None known.
Miscellaneous He left £20,000 in his will to the Duke of Gloucester.
References *GM,* 1821, vol. I, p. 382.

1821/18 **Name** **Boddington, Thomas**
Dates c. 1735–28 June 1821 at Lower Brook Street, Middlesex.
Probate £120,000 (PCC).
Occupation West India merchant of 17 Mark Lane, City of London (1795 directory, which describes him as a 'merchant'). (Occupational category IV.19; venue 1.) He was probably the brother of Benjamin Boddington, 'merchant' of the same address, who was a West India merchant 'with a turnover of half a million a year' in 1797 and a director of the South Seas Company (*HP* for Benjamin's son Samuel Boddington, 1766–1843). He was apparently the Thomas Boddington who was a slave trader, Director of the Bank of England and of the London Dock Company, who had worked at the Board of Ordnance from 1770. There he was the superior of Granville Sharp, the anti-slavery campaigner and was a noted philanthropist and campaigner for the repeal of the Test and Corporation Acts (Wikipedia).
Address 'Clapton, Middlesex and [8] Lower Brook Street, Grosvenor Square' (probate calendar).
Father Unknown.
Mother Unknown.

Education Unknown.
Marriage In 1764, at St John's Church, Hackney, to Maria Catherine, daughter of Peter John Fremeaux, Lord of the Manor of Hannington, Northamptonshire, which Boddington acquired in 1802 (Family Search; *VCH Northamptonshire,* vol. 4, pp. 172–4.) His daughter Elizabeth married, in 1805, Isaac Hawkins Browne (1745–1818), in *ODNB* as 'politician and industrialist'.
Religion Presumable Anglican.
Public None known.
Miscellaneous There is no evidence that he lived in the West Indies.
References *GM,* 1821, vol. II, p. 91.

Name **Stair, 6th Earl of, John Dalrymple** 1821/19
Dates 24 September 1749, Edinburgh–1 June 1821, Spring Gardens, Middlesex.
Probate £180,000 'within province' (PCC).
Occupation Landowner, also an ambassador. (Occupational category I.) In 1883, the Earl of Stair owned 116,370 acres worth £67,905 p.a. in Wigtownshire, Ayrshire, and Midlothian. The 6th Earl had 'extensive estates' in Galloway (*ODNB*).
Address His principal seat was Oxenfoord Castle, Dalkeith.
Father John Dalrymple, 5th Earl of Stair (d. 13 October 1789).
Mother Margaret, daughter of George Middleton of Erroll, a banker in London.
Education Eton; Edinburgh University. He went on the 'Grand Tour' and was praised by Voltaire.
Marriage Unmarried.
Religion Church of Scotland.
Public Representative Peer for Scotland (Whig), 1790–1807, 1820–1.
Miscellaneous Served as British Ambassador to Poland, 1782–4, and to Prussia, 1785–8. Was a captain in the 87th Foot and served in the American Revolutionary War.
References *ODNB; CP; BP.*

Name **Hollond (sic), Edward John** 1821/20
Dates Unknown–19 August 1821, Bologne.
Probate £600,000 (PCC).
Occupation A member of the 'East India Company at Madras' (probate calendar and *GM*). (Occupational category VI.31? Venue 29.)
Address Lived at Devonshire Place, Middlesex.
Father (Major) John (other sources say Richard) Hollond (1751 or 1756) 'in command of the East India Company's troops in Bengal' (*BLG,* 1914). (Third son.)
Mother Forename unknown. She was the sister of Edward Fowke of Horley, Kent. According to Family Search, a Sophia Fowke (1722–60) married John Hollond on 29 October 1741 at Fort St George, Madras.
Education Unknown.
Marriage Unmarried.
Religion Presumably Anglican.

Public None known.

Miscellaneous Another extremely wealthy man of this period of whom little could be traced: he was a very wealthy 'nabob', but few details could be found. The *ODNB* notes in the entry of a relative that Edward Hollond was of 'Anglo-Indian background', although it seems improbable, given his parentage, that he had Indian ancestry. Hollond's surname was spelled 'Holland' in some sources, but this is apparently a misspelling.

References *GM,* 1821, vol. II, p. 284; *BLG,* 1914, 1937.

1821/21 **Name** **Martin, Philip**

Dates 12 August 1733–buried 11 August 1821.

Probate £200,000 (PCC).

Occupation General in the Royal Artillery; landowner. (Occupational category VI.31 and I.) In 1883, Cornelius Wykeham-Martin of Leeds Castle owned 7,846 acres worth £12,162 p.a. in Kent, Warwickshire, etc.

Address Leeds Castle near Maidstone, Kent.

Father John Martin of Salts Place, Loose, near Maidstone, Kent.

Mother Unknown.

Education Unknown.

Marriage Unknown.

Religion Anglican.

Public Unknown.

Miscellaneous Martin fought at Gibraltar, 1779–83, was made a brevet major in 1782, a major in the same year, and then a general in the Royal Artillery. He apparently inherited Leeds Castle from Frances, the daughter of Thomas, 5th Lord Fairfax (1706–93), who lived in Virginia. Frances married a Denny Martin of Kent, apparently a relative of Philip. Whether the military, land or something else was the main source of Philip Martin's wealth is unclear, and this man is surprisingly obscure. He left £30,000 in his will for the restoration of Leeds Castle, which was left to a nephew of his mother.

References *GM,* 1821, vol. II, p. 188; Charles Wykeham-Martin, *History of Leeds Castle* (1869), p. 200; *BLG,* 1952, but Philip Martin is unlisted; online histories of Leeds Castle.

1821/22 **Name** **Nicholson, Robert**

Dates Unknown – probated October 1821.

Probate £100,000 (PCC).

Occupation 'Lieutenant General in the East India Company' (probate calendar). (Occupational category VI.31; venue 29.) Given on PROB 11 as 'Lieutenant General in the service of His Majesty and also of the Hon. East India Company, of Edinburgh, Midllothian'.

Address Lived at York Place, Portman Square, at the time of his death; also lived in Edinburgh.

Father Unknown.

Mother Unknown.

Education Unknown.
Marriage Unknown. A Robert Nicholson married an Elizabeth Barber on 21 September 1807 in Calcutta (Family Search).
Religion Presumably Church of Scotland or Anglican.
Public None known.
Miscellaneous Nothing more is known of his career – another case of a very obscure Indian fortune. A (Brigadier) John Nicholson was a prominent officer at the Siege of Delhi, 1757, but it is unclear if they were connected.
References Probate calendar only.

Name **Beauvoir, (Revd) Peter** 1821/23
Dates 1739–14 September 1822.
Probate £800,000 (PCC).
Occupation Owner of London urban land; East India Company money. (Occupational category I and IV.19; venue 29.) Beauvoir's family owned what is now DeBeauvoir Town in Hackney, which was just being developed at the time of his death. This man's father was a 'wealthy East India merchant'. The family also owned land in Essex and elsewhere. In 1883, Richard Benyon, his heir, owned 16,007 acres worth £20,004 in Berkshire, Essex and Hampshire. Peter Lindert credits the DeBeauvoir Estate in London (157 acres) with an assessed annual rental value of £68,231 p.a. in the 1890s, but this was long after the death of this man.
Address Downham Hall, Essex.
Father Osmond Beauvoir (1680–1757) of Downham Hall, Essex, a 'wealthy East India merchant'. The family originally came from Guernsey.
Mother Elizabeth Beard (d. 1772).
Education Secondary schooling unknown; Queen's College, Cambridge.
Marriage Apparently unmarried.
Religion Anglican clergyman: was Rector of Downham, Essex, 1760–1822.
Public None known.
Miscellaneous He left £720,000 and his land in his will to Richard Benyon, who was apparently unrelated to him. The reasons for this bequest are obscure. DeBeauvoir Town was largely developed after his death, although some building had already begun.
References *GM,* 1822, vol. II; Hackney sources; *BLG; VCH Middlesex,* vol. 10, 1995, pp. 33–5.

Name **D'Oyly, Sarah** (née Stanley) 1821/24
Dates 1725–28 November 1821.
Probate £100,000 (PCC).
Occupation 'Coheiress to large estates at Chelsea and elsewhere' (*HP* for husband). She inherited these from her famous maternal grandfather, Sir Hans Sloane. After her death, the lands went to Lord Cadogan and apparently formed the basis for much of the Cadogan estate. (Occupational category I.)
Address Lived at Charles Street and then Curzon Street, Mayfair, and at Twickenham.

Father George Stanley (d. 1734) of Paultons, Hampshire. (Younger daughter.)
Mother Sarah, daughter and co-heir of Sir Hans Sloane, Baronet, MD, of Chelsea.
Education Unknown.
Marriage In 1765, to Christopher D'Oyly (1717–20 January 1795; d.s.p.), attorney in the Court of Common Pleas and MP, 1774–84; he served as Under-Secretary in the Colonial Department, 1776–8, and was a prominent lawyer who acted as one of Clive's executors. He also inherited land at Walton-on-Thames.
Religion Anglican.
Public None known.
Miscellaneous It isn't clear if her husband was related to the D'Oyly Carte family.
References *ODNB* and *HP* for husband.

1821/25 **Name** **Fuller, Rose** ('Esquire', a male)
Dates c. 1748– 16 November 1821, York Street, Portman Square.
Probate £120,000 (PCC).
Occupation 'Merchant' (Rose and Augustus Fuller, 4 Church Court, Clements Lane, City of London, 1817 directory). He was probably a West India merchant. His uncle Rose Fuller Senior was a planter in Jamaica, and another uncle, Stephen Fuller, was an agent for Jamaica. (Occupational category IV.19; venue 1.)
Address (47) York Street, Portman Square, Middlesex, and Clements Lane in the City of London.
Father Probably Thomas Fuller, 'merchant' of London; he was the brother of Rose Fuller Senior (d. 1777), MP.
Mother Probably a Miss Ledgitter (sic) (*BLG,* 1871).
Education Unknown.
Marriage Unknown.
Religion Presumably Anglican.
Public None known.
Miscellaneous It is not known whether he lived in Jamaica at any time.
References 'Fuller-Meyrick', *BLG,* 1871; *GM,* 1821, vol. II, p. 478.

1821/26 **Name** **Perry, James** (né Pirie)
Dates 30 October 1756, Aberdeen–5 December 1821, Brighton.
Probate £100,000 (PCC).
Occupation Newspaper proprietor and editor in London. (Occupational category V.26; venue 2.) Was proprietor and editor of the *Morning Chronicle,* one of the most important Whig-radical newspapers of its time, from 1789 until his death. He was said to have had an annual income of £12,000 at his death and also owned £130,000 worth of properties in the London area (*ODNB*).
Address 'The Strand and Tavistock House, Tavistock Square, Middlesex' (later the home of Charles Dickens and now the headquarters of the BMA) (probate calendar).
Father Name unknown – a 'builder and joiner' in Aberdeen whose business failed at some point.
Mother Unknown.

Education Aberdeen High School; Marischal College, Aberdeen.

Marriage In 1798, to Anne (1773–1815), daughter of John Hull of Finsbury Square; she died soon after being captured and released by pirates off Portugal. (Eight children.) A son was Sir Thomas Erskine Perry (1806–62), judge in India.

Religion Originally presumably Church of Scotland; buried in an Anglican church.

Public None known.

Miscellaneous Began as a builder, draper and actor before coming to London in 1777 and working as a journalist. He was the first editor of the *European Magazine* (1782–3) and then of the *Morning Chronicle* from 1789. He was a famous and important radical journalist and editor, who was often in trouble with the authorities.

References *ODNB; Old and New London* (1878); online sources.

Name **Hope, Henry** 1821/27

Dates Apparently 1735, Boston, Mass.–1811, London. This is apparently the only possibility, although his estate was not probated until ten years after his death, presumably because of its international trading complexities.

Probate £500,000 (PCC).

Occupation Merchant banker and merchant (Hope Brothers, in the City of London). (Occupational category IV.17 and 19; venue 1.) Hope Brothers was the foremost merchant banking and mercantile house before the rise of the Barings and Rothschilds. It had vast international links, especially in the Netherlands and America, and was chiefly a merchant bank in London by the 1800s.

Address Lived at Southampton Row, Bloomsbury.

Father Henry Hope, son of Rotterdam-born Archibald Hope (1664–1743) and brother of Thomas Hope (1704–79) and Adrian Hope (1709–81), of Hope & Co., the powerful merchant banking firm whose clientele included European rulers. Henry Hope had settled in Boston about 1730 (*ODNB* article on the Hope Family). Our Henry Hope was the half-brother of Henrietta Maria Goddard (née Hope); see 1814/15.

Mother Apparently Sarah Willard, member of a family of Massachusetts clockmakers. Henry moved to England about 1748 to complete his education and joined Hope & Co. in 1760.

Education Unknown.

Marriage Unmarried. His half-sister Henrietta Maria Goddard's eldest daughter Anne was his heiress.

Religion Presumably Anglican.

Public None known.

Miscellaneous Joined Gurnell Hoare & Co., bankers, in 1754 and Hope Brothers in 1760; was its senior partner by the time of his death.

References *ODNB* for the Hope family; *BLG*, 1937, although this man is not included in the genealogy.

Name **Nettleshipp, William** 1821/28

Dates c. 1741–3 July 1821.

Probate £160,000 (PCC).

Occupation 'Merchant' (of the Tower of London [sic]), 1795 directory; a John Nettleshipp, merchant of Basinghall Street, presumably a relative, is also listed). (Occupational category IV.21; venue 1.) 'William Nettleshipp, Esq., Gower Street', appears in *A List of the Names of the Members of the United Company of Merchants of England, Trading to the East Indies*, 1815.

Address 'Formerly of the Tower of London, then Gower Street, Middlesex' (probate calendar). Possibly the Tower address meant that the firm was a government contractor of some kind, although this is unclear. There is no reason to suppose that he was a prisoner!

Father Unknown.

Mother Unknown.

Education Unknown.

Marriage Unknown.

Religion Anglican: there is a monumental inscription to him at the parish church at Charlton Kings, near Cheltenham, Gloucestershire.

Public None known.

Miscellaneous The 1808 directory lists T. & W. Nettleshipp, attorneys, of Grocer's Hall in the City; these may be his relatives.

References *GM*, 1821, vol. II, p. 92; online sources.

1821/29 **Name** **Lamb, Thomas Henry**

Dates Unknown – probated September 1821.

Probate £160,000 (PCC).

Occupation 'Army agent' at 2 Golden Square, Middlesex (1815 directory). (An 'army agent' usually acted as a banker and agent for officers overseas.) (Occupational category IV.18 or 16; venue 2.)

Address 'Of Golden Square, St James's and Tittenhanger Green, Hertfordshire' (probate calendar).

Father Unknown.

Mother Unknown.

Education Unknown.

Marriage Unknown.

Religion Unknown.

Public None known.

Miscellaneous As with many other such wealth-holders of the time, little or nothing could be traced.

References Probate calendar only.

1821/30 **Name** **Mansfield, Sir James** (né Manfield)

Dates 30 May 1733–23 November 1821, Russell Square, Middlesex.

Probate £100,000 (PCC).

Occupation Lord Chief Justice of the Court of Common Pleas, 1804–14. (Occupational category VI.29; venue 1.) (He should not be confused with William Murray, 1st Earl of Mansfield, 1705–93, the famous judge. They were unrelated.)

Address Lived at Russell Square, Middlesex.
Father John James Manfield (d. October 1762), solicitor, of Ringwood Manor House, Hampshire, and Under-Sheriff of Hampshire. (First son.)
Mother Elizabeth, surname unknown.
Education Eton; King's College, Cambridge (Scholar and Fellow; BA, 1755; MA, 1758). Barrister, Middle Temple, 1758. KC, 1772; Treasurer of the Middle Temple, 1785.
Marriage Unmarried, but is believed to have fathered five illegitimate children (*ODNB*).
Religion Anglican.
Public MP (pro-Tory) Cambridge University, 1774–84. Knighted, 1804; PC, 1804; Solicitor-General, 1780–2 and 1783.
Miscellaneous Changed his name to 'Mansfield' when at Cambridge. Chief Justice of Chester, 1789–1804. Practised at the common law and in Chancery; was an adviser to John Wilkes and prosecuted Lord George Gordon, 1781.
References *ODNB; GM,* 1821, vol. II, p. 572.

Name **Castle, Michael** 1821/31
Dates 1763–22 May 1821.
Probate £120,000 (PCC).
Occupation Probably a distiller ('rectifier') in Bristol. (Occupational category III.13; venue 12.)
Address Lived in Bristol.
Father Unknown. A Michael Castle and a Mary Tattle married on 7 January 1760 at St Philip and St Jacob, Bristol (Family Search).
Mother Unknown.
Education Unknown. His son Michael (d. 1845) was also a distiller. Michael was probably the father of Catherine Castle (see 1835/8, left £120,000).
Marriage Unknown.
Religion Unitarian.
Public Was a pro-Whig member of the Bristol Council, 1809–21. Mayor of Bristol, 1812. A Robert Castle was Mayor in 1802, dying in office 4 August 1803.
Miscellaneous Little else could be traced of him.
References Graham Bush, *Bristol and Its Municipal Government, 1820–51* (1976), p. 235; online sources.

WEALTH-HOLDERS, 1822

1822/1 **Name** **Jones, William**
Dates 1757–25 December 1821.
Probate £250,000 (York PC).
Occupation Banker in Manchester – partner, Jones, Loyd & Co., Manchester. (Occupational category IV.16; venue 4.)
Address Broughton Hall, Manchester.
Father James Jones (1713–75).
Mother Sarah, daughter of (Revd) Joseph Mottershead, Unitarian minister.
Education Unknown.
Marriage Unknown. He was the great-uncle of Samuel Jones Loyd, 1st Baron Overstone (1796–1883), the prominent banker and multimillionaire.
Religion Unitarian.
Public None known.
Miscellaneous One of the founders of the Manchester banking firm.
References *ODNB* for relatives; *BLG*.

1822/2 **Name** **Hopkinson, John**
Dates Unknown – probated March 1822.
Probate £100,000.
Occupation Presumably a sugar planter or merchant in Demarara (British Guiana). (Occupational category I and IV.19; venue 29.)
Address 'Formerly of Demarara and then Aigburth Hall near Liverpool' (probate calendar).
Father Unknown.
Mother Unknown.
Education Unknown.
Marriage Unknown.
Religion Unknown.
Public None known.
Miscellaneous Nothing more could be traced about him. A John Hopkinson appears in an online list of plantation owners on Demerara (www.Ancestry.com). Emilia Viotti da Costa, *Crowns of Glory, Tears of Blood: The Demerara Slave Rebellion of 1823* (1994), p. 26, mentions a 'mulatto' named John Hopkinson who owned the John and Cove and became 'relatively well to do'.
References Above sources only.

1822/3 **Name** **Russell, Matthew**
Dates 24 February 1765, Brancepeth, Durham–8 May 1822, London.
Probate £120,000 (PCC) + £100,000 (York PC): £220,000 total.
Occupation Colliery owner in County Durham. (Occupational category II.1; venue 9.)
Address Brancepeth Castle, Durham; Hardwicke Castle, Durham.

Father William Russell (1734–5 June 1817), banker, merchant and colliery owner (see 1817/2, left £280,000) at Sunderland. (First son.)
Mother Mary, daughter of Robert Harrison, merchant of Sunderland.
Education Secondary schooling unknown; University College, Oxford; Lincoln's Inn.
Marriage In 1793, to Elizabeth, daughter of George Tennyson of Bayon's Manor, Lincolnshire. (One son, one daughter.) The daughter, Emma (d. 1870) married Gustavus Hamilton, 7th Viscount Boyne. In 1883, Viscount Boyne owned 18,023 acres worth £76,865 p.a. in County Durham. This probably represents mainly Russell's land. The Boynes changed their surname to Russell-Hamilton.
Religion Anglican.
Public MP (Tory) Saltash, 1801–22.
Miscellaneous Was a captain and major in the Durham militia. The collieries were mainly at Wallsend-on-Tyne.
References *BLG; HP.*

Name **Dreghorn, Marion** 1822/4
Dates Unknown – probated August 1815 (sic). It is not known why the estate appears in PROB 8 in 1822.
Probate £175,000 (PCC).
Occupation The unmarried daughter of a wealthy Glasgow merchant and ship-owner in the Virginia trade. (Occupational category IV.19; venue 10.)
Address 'Of Blochairn' (PROB 11 online). 'Of Ruchill, Lanarkshire' (probate calendar).
Father Robert Dreghorn (1708–60), merchant in Glasgow along with his brother Allan.
Mother Isabella Bryson.
Education Unknown.
Marriage Unmarried: described as a 'spinster'.
Religion Presumably Church of Scotland.
Public None known.
Miscellaneous She lived quietly on inherited wealth and left most of her estate to her sister Margaret, wife of James Dennistoun of Dubbington and Colgrain. Her daughter Mary (1800–72) married Sir William Baillie, 1st Baronet. It is unclear why her will was probated in the PCC in 1822.
References Will (PROB 11 online); *Old Country Houses of Glasgow*, 'Ruchill', online.

Name **De Dopft, Baron Jean François** 1822/5
Dates Unknown – probated December 1822.
Probate £400,000 (PCC).
Occupation Unknown.
Address 'St John the Evangelist, Westminster; Bond Street, Middlesex; and Paris' (probate calendar).
Father Unknown.

Mother Unknown.
Education Unknown.
Marriage Unknown.
Religion Unknown.
Public None known.
Miscellaneous No information about him could be traced. His nationality – whether Dutch or French – is unclear, as is why he left such a large fortune in England.
References Probate calendar only.

1822/6 **Name** **Moffat, William**
Dates 7 March 1737–12 January 1822
Probate £200,000 (PCC).
Occupation Banker – partner in Wickenden, Moffat, Kensington & Boller, established in 1775 at 20 Lombard Street, City of London; senior partner, 1786–1807. Also connected with Williams, Son, Moffat & Burgess at 20 Birchin Lane, City, 'bankers and merchants'. (Occupational category IV.16; venue 1.)
Address Lived at 32 Queen Square, Bloomsbury, then at Wimbledon and at Painshill, Surrey.
Father John Moffat (d. April 1742), 'baillie' of Lauder, Berwickshire.
Mother Margaret (d. 1782), daughter of James Inglis of St Leonards, Lauderdale, Berwick.
Education Unknown.
Marriage First, in 1766, to Elizabeth (d. 1791), daughter of (Lieutenant Colonel) William Bowland. (One son, two daughters.) Second, in 1795, to Elizabeth (d.s.p., 1843), daughter of (Revd) John Harrington of Thruxton, Hampshire.
Religion Presumably originally Church of Scotland.
Public MP (Tory) Winchelsea, 1802–6.
Miscellaneous Described as 'an eminent banker at London'; his early life was 'obscure' (*HP*).
References *HP; GM,* 1822, vol. I, p. 93.

1822/7 **Name** **Chambers, Thomas**
Dates c. 1759–12 January 1822, at Walworth.
Probate £180,000 (PCC).
Occupation 'Silkman' (i.e. silk manufacturer and merchant) at 18 Iremonger Lane, Cheapside (1805 directory). (Occupational category II.9 and IV.20; venue 1; from the address, he appears to have been chiefly a retailer, although he may have been a manufacturer as well.)
Address 'Formerly Iremonger Row, City of London, then Charlotte Row, Walworth, Surrey' (probate calendar).
Father Unknown.
Mother Unknown.
Education Unknown.
Marriage Unknown.

Religion Unknown.
Public None known.
Miscellaneous Nothing more could be traced of him.
References Probate calendar and directory only.

Name **Hawes, Benjamin** ('or Haws', PROB 11) 1822/8
Dates 1770?–probated February 1822 (The *ODNB* entry for his father gives his dates as 1770–1861, but these are clearly wrong.)
Probate £120,000 (PCC).
Occupation 'Bluemaker' of Thames Street, City of London (so described in the probate calendar). ('Blue' was soap powder used by laundries.) (Occupational category II.6; venue 1.) His soapworks were 'opposite the [Inner and Middle] Temple' and 'a prominent London landmark' (*ODNB* for his son). ('T. & B. Hawes, soap makers, Old Barge House, Christ Church [Southwark]' – 1811 and 1817 directories.)
Address Thames Street, City of London, then Worthing, Sussex' (probate calendar).
Father William Hawes (1736–5 December 1808), in the *ODNB* as a 'philanthropist and physician'. He was a pioneer of resuscitation, a founder of the Royal Humane Society and a well-known physician in Spitalfields and elsewhere in London. (Third son.)
Mother Sarah, née Fox (1740–1814).
Education Unknown.
Marriage In 1796, to Anne, née Feltham. Their son was Sir Benjamin Hawes (1797–1862), Radical MP in 1832–47 and 1848–51, and Under-Secretary for the Colonies, 1846–7, in *ODNB*.
Religion His father was an Elder of the Presbyterian Church in Southwark but retained links to Anglicanism and was buried as an Anglican. He himself was married in an Anglican church, Christ Church, Spitalfields (Family Search).
Public None known.
Miscellaneous His son was regarded by many aristocrats in Parliament as uncouth and was noted as one of the first middle-class businessmen – he had entered the family soap business – to be given a government position.
References *ODNB* for relatives.

Name **Luther, Levina** (née Bennett) 1822/9
Dates Unknown – probated February 1822.
Probate £100,000 (PCC).
Occupation Widow of John Luther, MP (1739–86), a barrister of the Middle Temple who inherited from his maternal grandfather Hugh Chamberlain, MD, physician to Queen Anne. She was also the sister of Elizabeth Bull (c. 1749–1809; see 1809/3). She and her sister are described as owners of the Manor of Broad Clist or Clyst, near Exeter, having been 'devisees of the Rt. Hon. Humphrey Morice who died in 1784'. In 1808, the property was sold to Sir T. D. Acland, Baronet (Daniel and Samuel Lysons, *Magna Britannia*, vol. 6, 1822, online). Morice,

who lived 1723–85 (sic) was an MP from 1750 to 1780. His father was Governor of the Bank of England and a major African slave trader (*ODNB*). The relationship of Luther and Bull to him is unclear, as is the general source of her wealth.

Address 'Formerly Berkeley Square, Middlesex, then Lower Grosvenor Square, Middlesex, then Brighton' (probate calendar).

Father Bennet Alexander Bennet of Ongar; other sources say Wiltshire. She was the great-granddaughter of Sir Levinus Bennet, of Babtraham, Cambridgeshire *BLG*, 1838, 'Luther, of Myles's'.

Mother Possibly the daughter of Richard Bull (*HP* for husband) although this seems inaccurate.

Education Unknown.

Marriage To John Luther, MP, 1763–84 (marriage date unknown), d.s.p. *HP* says she was separated from her husband in 1764.

Religion Presumably Anglican.

Public None known.

Miscellaneous The actual source of her wealth is unclear.

References *HP* for her husband.

1822/10 **Name** **Blundell, Philip**

Dates c. 1767–probated April 1822.

Probate £120,000 (PCC).

Occupation Unknown – he was presumably a relative of Philip Blundell (d. 1601), an umarried clothier who founded Blundell's School, Tiverton. This man was 'a very wealthy merchant at Tiverton and London'. If this wealth-holder was a descendant, he appears to have been a landowner, although no further information about his career is known, and no one named Blundell is listed in Bateman as owning land in Devon.

Address (The Lodge or Zephyr Lodge), Tiverton, Devon.

Father Probably Peter Blundell of Tiverton (*Alum. Oxon.*), who was probably born c. 1733. There are several other possibilities, including Philip Blundell (b. c. 1724) and Philip Blundell (baptised at Tiverton on 21 June 1744).

Mother Unknown.

Education Unknown. A Philip Blundell of Tiverton was appointed the Blundell's Scholar at Balliol College, Oxford, matriculating in November 1785 aged eighteen. It would be remarkable if this were not the same man.

Marriage Unknown. A Philip Blundell married, in 1781, Catherine Archer (d. March 1810, aged forty-six, at Bath). She leased land in 1806 to a John Arden (online source).

Religion Almost certainly Anglican: he mentions (Revd) Henry Blundell in his will.

Public None known.

Miscellaneous A man of this name was made a Freeman of Tiverton in 1791. In his will he left money to his nephew Alan Nesbitt and the latter's son, Richard Blundell Nesbitt. The source of his wealth is unknown: it is unknown whether he engaged in trade.

References Probate calendar only, plus the above.

Name **Smith, John** 1822/11
Dates Unknown – probated April 1822.
Probate £100,000 (PCC).
Occupation 'Woollen draper' at Gracechurch Street and then a 'merchant' at Basinghall Street, City of London (presumably J. Smith & King, woollen drapers, 28 Gracechurch Street, City of London). (Occupational category IV.20; venue 1.) Given in PROB 11 as a 'merchant' of Basinghall Street, City of London.
Address 'Formerly of Gracechurch Street, City of London, then Basinghall Street, City of London, then Walworth, Surrey' (probate calendar).
Father Unknown.
Mother Unknown.
Education Unknown.
Marriage Unknown. He had a son named Archibald.
Religion Unknown.
Public None known.
Miscellaneous Obviously, the name makes tracing him difficult.
References Probate calendar only.

Name **Tate, George** 1822/12
Dates Unknown – probated June 1822.
Probate £120,000 (PCC).
Occupation Unknown. His will is unilluminating, but it states that he owned lands at Brompton and Chelsea and at Loughborough and elsewhere in Leicestershire. It also states that he had a daughter named Mary who was married to Sir Charles Rush or Firth – the name is hard to decipher and has not been identified. A George Tate (1746–12 February 1821) is in the *ODNB* as a 'naval officer in the Russian service', but he died at St Petersburg and had no known links with Hampshire. The Tate family of sugar refiners, who donated the Tate Gallery in Chelsea, only emerged much later.
Address Lived at Langdown near Southampton, Hampshire.
Father Unknown.
Mother Unknown.
Education Unknown.
Marriage Name unknown – at least one daughter.
Religion Unknown.
Public None known.
Miscellaneous The Soane Museum has a design for additions for an unidentified house for Mr Tate of Langdown, 1816. In 1849, a Miss Louisa Pinfold (d. 21 July 1861, aged eighty-six) of Wimpole Street and Burleigh Hall, Loughborough, took the additional name and arms of Tate, 'in compliance with an earnest wish expressed in the last will and testament of her cousin George Tate, late of Langdown, Esq., deceased'. Francis Watts, comp., *Bulletins and Other State Intelligence for the Year 1849* (1850), p. 648 (online).
References Will (PROB 11 online); online sources.

1822/13 **Name** **Brymer, Alexander**

Dates c. 1745, Scotland–27 August 1822, Ramsgate.

Probate £120,000 (PCC).

Occupation 'Agent, merchant, office holder, and politician' in Halifax, Nova Scotia (*Canadian Dictionary of Biography*). Lived in England after 1801 but does not appear to have been in trade. (Occupational category IV.19; venue 29.)

Address 'Formerly of Halifax, Nova Scotia, then Gower Street, Middlesex, the Great Pulteney Street, Bath' (probate calendar).

Father Unknown: little is known of his early life. The *Canadian Dictionary of Biography* suggests that Dundee might have been his birthplace. According to Family Search, an Alexander Brymer was baptised in Leith, the port of Edinburgh, on 21 September 1746, son of Robert Brymer and Elizabeth Fife.

Mother Unknown.

Education Unknown.

Marriage In 1796 in Preston, Lancashire, to Harriet Dobson née Parr. (Three sons.) His son (Revd) W. T. Brymer; see 1852/15.

Religion Presumably originally Church of Scotland.

Public JP and member of the Council in Nova Scotia.

Miscellaneous Emigrated to North America around 1770. Was a merchant in Boston, Mass., before 1772, then went to Halifax to join his uncle William Brymer, who had the naval victualling contract for North America. He remained in Nova Scotia from 1776 to 1801 and was a leading merchant there. He also received naval prize money. He lived in England thereafter. (*Canadian Dictionary of Biography*.)

References *Canadian Dictionary of Biography*.

1822/14 **Name** **Bulkeley, 7th Viscount, Thomas James Bulkeley** (then Warren-Bulkeley [Irish peerage])

Dates 12 December 1752–3 June 1822, Englefield Green.

Probate £100,000 (PCC).

Occupation Landowner. (Occupational category I.) In 1883, Sir Richard Williams-Bulkeley, Baronet, of Baron Hill owned 29,878 acres worth £21,138 p.a. in Anglesey and Carnarvonshire.

Address Baron Hill, near Beaumaris, Anglesey.

Father James, 6th Viscount Bulkeley (1717–23 April 1752). Thomas was born posthumously.

Mother Emma (d. 1770), daughter of Thomas Rowlands of Nant, Carnarvonshire. She married, second, Sir Hugh Williams, 8th Baronet (d. 1796).

Education Westminster School and Jesus College, Oxford.

Marriage In 1777, to Elizabeth (d. 1826), daughter of Sir George Warren of Poynton, Cheshire.

Religion Anglican.

Public MP (Whig) Anglesey, 1774–84. Received a UK barony, 1784. Lord Lieutenant of Carnarvonshire, 1781–death; Constable of North Wales from 1771; Constable of Beaumaris Castle.

Miscellaneous Despite his Irish peerage, does not appear to have had any connection with Ireland.
References *HP; CP; BP.*

Name **Whitchurch, Samuel** 1822/15
Dates Probably born 1748– probated November 1822.
Probate £120,000 (PCC).
Occupation A 'common brewer' at Salisbury (PROB 11). (Occupational category II.12; venue 13.)
Address 'New Sarum, Wiltshire' (probate calendar). His business was at Salisbury, and he held office there.
Father Probably James Whitchurch (c. 1704– 63) of Frome Selwood, Somerset and Bristol (*BLG*, 1846).
Mother Probably Ann, daughter of John Gresley of Drakelow, Derbyshire (*BLG*).
Education Unknown.
Marriage Probably to Mary Evans. (Four sons, six daughters.) (*BLG*.) A Samuel Whitchurch and a Mary Evans married in 1772 in St Michael's Church, Bristol (Family Search).
Religion Presumably Anglican.
Public An Alderman of Salisbury (*GM*).
Miscellaneous Although his father was from Bristol, there is no evidence that he had any business connection with that city. But a Samuel Whitchurch of Bristol was the father of George Gresley Whitchurch, who attended Oxford (*Alum. Oxon.*). George Gresley Whitchurch, son of Samuel and Mary, was christened at St Michael's, Bristol, on 6 May 1799 (Family Search).
References *GM*, 1822, vol. II, p. 478, where he is said to have died 'lately'.

Name **Sparrow, John** 1822/16
Dates 1736–17 December 1822.
Probate £180,000 (PCC).
Occupation Probably the owner of tinplate works (Sparrow & Co.) near Stafford; also described as a 'banker' and a 'cotton merchant' in online sources. (*VCH Staffordshire*, vol. 2, p. 174; vol. 8, p. 250; online sources.) (Occupational category II.3 and 11 and possibly IV.16; venue 18.) ('Tinplate' denotes iron sheets which have been coated in tin.)
Address Lived at Bishton Hall, near Colwich, Staffordshire.
Father Unknown.
Mother Unknown.
Education Unknown.
Marriage In 1779, to Elizabeth Moreton (c. 1742–October 1841). Their daughter Hannah Maria (d. 1860) married Sir George Chetwynd, 3rd Baronet.
Religion Unknown, presumably Anglican.
Public None known.
Miscellaneous It is possible that he was an ironmaster as well. The source of his

fortune is unclear and may well have derived from a number of business interests. A number of families named Sparrow are listed in various editions of *BLG*, but he does not appear to have been directly related to any of them.

References Above sources only.

1822/17 **Name** **Stephens, Richard**

Dates Unknown – probated February 1822.

Probate £100,000 (PCC).

Occupation Unknown. The only man of this name in London directories of the period was a 'tanner' of Bermondsey (1793 and 1805 directories). In his will he mentions his brother William and his nephews Charles, John and William, and his sister Mary, wife of Anna Carrick. He also noted that he owned lands in Berkshire, including Aldermaston, and in Hampshire. John Stephens (c. 1785–1847; see 1847/11) was probably his nephew. However, the will gives no real clue as to Richard's source of wealth.

Address Lived at Southcot near Reading, Berkshire.

Father Unknown.

Mother Unknown.

Education Unknown.

Marriage Unknown.

Religion Unknown.

Public None known.

Miscellaneous Nothing more could be traced about him.

References Will (PROB 11 online).

1822/18 **Name** **Homfray, Samuel**

Dates 16 February 1762–20 (22?) May 1822.

Probate £100,000 (PCC).

Occupation Ironmaster in South Wales. (Occupational category II.2; venue 19.) Also a partner in banks in Newport and Monmouth until 1813 and the chief promoter of the Glamorgan Canal in 1795.

Address 'Of Pennydarren, Monmouthshire' (probate calendar) and also lived at Coworth House near Windsor, Berkshire.

Father Francis Homfray (1726–December 1798), ironmaster, of Wollaston Hall, Worcestershire.

Mother Catherine (d. 1766), daughter of Jeremiah Caswell, ironmaster, of The Hyde, Staffordshire.

Education Unknown.

Marriage In 1793, to Jane (d. 1846), daughter of Sir Charles Gould Morgan, 1st Baronet of Tredegar, and widow of (Captain) Henry Ball, RN (d. 1792). (Two sons, three daughters.) Their daughter Amelia married William Thompson (1793–1854), wealthy businessman (q.v.).

Religion Anglican.

Public MP (Tory) Stafford, 1818–20; High Sheriff of Monmouthshire, 1813–24.

Miscellaneous Was a famous pioneering ironmaster in South Wales; was one

of the first to install Boulton and Watt steam engines and later Trevithick steam engines, and built a very early steam railway, 1804, the first to use a steam locomotive. Was also a major in the Pennydarren Volunteers, 1798. He was also a partner of Richard Crawshay (1810/15).
References *ODNB; HP.*

Name **Warner, Isaac** 1822/19
Dates c. 1742–3 January 1822, Blackheath.
Probate £300,000 (PCC).
Occupation 'Of the London Stock Exchange' (probate calendar). (Occupational category IV.23; venue 1.)
Address 'Formerly of New Cross, Deptford, then of Putney, and then of The Paragon, Blackheath, Kent' (probate calendar).
Father Unknown.
Mother Unknown.
Education Unknown.
Marriage Unknown.
Religion Unknown.
Public None known.
Miscellaneous An Edward Warner (see 1848/17) was a weath-holder 'of the Royal Exchange', and might have been a relative.
References Probate calendar only.

Name **Dresser, John** 1822/20
Dates 20 May 1746–18 February 1822.
Probate £160,000 (PCC).
Occupation Unknown. His will states that he had a nephew, John Day, in New York. A William Dresser (d. 1793) owned an India-muslin warehouse in Smithfield. John Dresser appears to have lived in Suffolk during his adult life.
Address Blyford (or Blythford), near Halesworth, Suffolk.
Father Richard Dresser (1721–6 July 1780) of Laxfield, near Framlingham, Suffolk.
Mother Mary, daughter of Gabriel Truson of Kelsale, Suffolk.
Education Unknown.
Marriage Unknown.
Religion Presumably Anglican.
Public High Sheriff of Suffolk, 1809.
Miscellaneous His source of wealth is very unclear. He might have been a local or London businessman, but there is no evidence that he was in trade.
References The *Ipswich Journal*, 23 February 1822, has a pedigree, per the Society of Genealogists.

Name **Gordon, James** 1822/21
Dates c. 1758, Antigua–18 February 1822, Hill Street, Berkeley Square – 'cut his throat'.

Probate £100,000 (PCC).

Occupation A 'practising' barrister of New Court, Inner Temple. (Occupational category VI.29; venue 1.) Also succeeded to the estates of his uncle James Gordon in Hertfordshire, Aberdeenshire and the West Indies, where the family had 'extensive connections'. He was said to have owned 1,400 acres in Antigua (*HP*). (It is unclear who had succeeded to the British lands in 1883.)

Address Lived at Hill Street, Berkeley Square, Middlesex and Moor Place, Much Hadham, Hertfordshire.

Father James Brebner Gordon (d. 1807), barrister and Chief Justice of Antigua.

Mother Anne, daughter of William Lavington, a judge of Antigua.

Education Winchester (other sources say Harrow); St John's College, Cambridge.

Occupation Barrister, Lincoln's Inn, admitted 1780.

Marriage In 1789, to Harriet, daughter of Samuel Whitbread, MP (1816/14).

Religion Presumably Anglican, although the father's family were Scots.

Public MP (pro-Government) Stockbridge, 1785–90; Truro, 1790–6; Clitheroe, 1808–12.

Miscellaneous From 'a Scottish family with extensive connections in the West Indies' (*HP*), but a successful practising barrister from 1796 to 1814. Why he committed suicide is unclear.

References *HP.*

1822/22 **Name** **Stuart, (Hon.) William, Archbishop of Armagh**

Dates 15 March 1755, London–6 May 1822, Hill Street, Berkeley Square, by 'accidental poisoning'. (Both he and the previous entry died in unusual circumstances in Hill Street, Berkeley Square within a few months of each other.)

Probate £250,000 (PCC).

Occupation Archbishop of Armagh, 1800–22. (Occupational category VI.30; venue 27.)

Address Lived in Armagh and at Hill Street, Berkeley Square, Middlesex.

Father John, 3rd Earl of Bute (1713–10 March 1792), the Prime Minister.

Mother Mary (d. 1794), daughter of Edward Wortley Montagu of Wortley. She was created Baroness Mount Stuart in her own right in 1761. Her mother was the famous Lady Mary Wortley Montagu.

Education Winchester; St John's College, Cambridge (MA, DD).

Marriage In 1796, to Sophia, daughter of Thomas Penn of Stoke Poges (a descendant of William Penn).

Religion Anglican Archbishop in Ireland.

Public Probably did not sit in the House of Lords, unless he did so as Bishop of St David's, 1793–1800.

Miscellaneous Was previously Vicar of Lutton and Canon of Christ Church, Oxford; Canon of Windsor, 1793; Bishop of St David's, 1793–1800. Obviously owed his ascent to his family connections. He knew Boswell and Dr Johnson.

References *ODNB.*

Name **Gaskell, William** 1822/23

Dates 21 July 1755, Worcester–25 May 1822, Chalfont St Peters, Buckinghamshire.

Probate £120,000 (PCC).

Occupation Possibly a wholesale linen draper (Gaskell & Evans) of 33 Cateaton Street, City of London (1793 directory), but this is far from clear as he had no London address at death. (If so, occupational category IV.21 or 20; venue 1 or 2?) His aunt, Ann Misenor, stated in her will of 1784 that William was then a linen draper in Oxford Street. The 1782–4 London directory gives his address as 81 Oxford Street. The aunt left her considerable estate to William and his twin brother George (1755–96).

Address Chalfont St Peters near Amersham, Buckinghamshire.

Father Probably John Gaskell (1714–66). (A younger son, with twin brother, George, who died in 1796.) Born in Manchester, the father apparently had a warehouse in Wood Street, London, for some time; after his marriage in Banbury in 1743, he moved to Worcester, where he was in business until shortly before his death as a 'London carrier' (www.gaskellfamily.com).

Mother Probably Elizabeth, née Barrett (c. 1720–7 August 1773), of Banbury.

Education Unknown.

Marriage On 31 December 1795, at Witham, Essex, to Elizabeth Kynaston (1768–10 January 1840). (At least one son; three daughters.) (Online source.)

Religion Anglican; father a churchwarden.

Public None known.

Miscellaneous He was an officer in the volunteer militia during the French Revolutionary War (www.gaskellfamily.com).

References Probate calendar and online sources.

Name **Hertford, 2nd Marquess of, Francis (Ingram-) Seymour-Conway** 1822/24

Dates 12 February 1743, London–17 June 1822, Hertford House, Manchester Square, Middlesex.

Probate £300,000 'within province' (PCC).

Occupation Landowner. (Occupational category I.) Also Ambassador to Berlin and Vienna, 1793–4. In 1883, the Marquess of Hertford owned 12,289 acres worth £18,392 p.a. in Warwickshire, etc. Also an important politician.

Address His chief seats were Ragley House, Alcester, Warwickshire and Hertford House, Manchester Square, Middlesex (now, of course, home of the Wallace Collection).

Father Francis Seymour Conway, 1st Marquess of Hertford (1718–14 June 1794).

Mother Lady Isabella (d. 1782), daughter of Charles, 2nd Duke of Grafton.

Education Eton; Christ Church, Oxford (MA).

Marriage First, in 1768 to (Hon.) Alice (d. 1772), daughter of Herbert, 2nd Viscount Windsor. (One daughter.) Second, in 1776, to (Hon.) Isabella (d. 1834), daughter of Charles, 9th Viscount Irwin. (One son.) Isabella was allegedly the mistress of George IV.

Religion Anglican.

Public MP (Irish Parliament), 1761–76; MP (British Parliament – Tory) Lostwithiel, 1766–8; Orford, 1768–94. Served as Lord of the Treasury, 1774–80; Master of the Horse, 1804–6; Lord Chamberlain, 1812–21; KG, 1807; PC, 1780; Lord Lieutenant of Warwickshire, 1816–death.

Miscellaneous Was known as 'Viscount Beauchamp' to 1794. Prefixed the name Ingram to his surname in 1807 in honour of his mother-in-law.

References *ODNB; CP; HP.*

1822/25 **Name** **Applebee, Josepha Martha**

(London Court directories list her surname as 'Appleby')

Dates Unknown–20 August 1822, Lower Grosvenor Place, Middlesex.

Probate £120,000 (PCC).

Occupation Unknown. Her will notes that she owned farms in Berkshire and Kent and buildings in the City of London (near Fleet market, Red Cross Street, Holborn Hill, etc.) and at Bermondsey Street, Surrey, but gives no indication of the source of her fortune. An Anthony Appleby (sic) was listed in the 1795 directory as of the Royal Exchange. He might be the woollen draper (Appleby & Co.) of 90 Cornhill in the 1793 directory, but there is no evidence of any connection with Miss Applebee. No one named Applebee is listed in any relevant London commercial directory. A well-known printer named Applebee died in 1750, but again there is no necessary connection. In her will she mentions her cousin Elizabeth, wife of William Sturck (?) of Bloomsbury.

Address Lived at 3 (30?) Lower Grosvenor Place, Middlesex.

Father Unknown. Family Search lists Josephine Mary Applebee, daughter of John and Mary, 'born [sic]' on 11 December 1745 at St Sepulchre's Church, London; it is possible that the forenames Josepha Martha were misread by the transcriber.

Mother Unknown.

Education Unknown.

Marriage Unmarried.

Religion Anglican. In her will she mention her nephew (Revd) John Applebee of East Thorp, Essex. Two men of this name attended Oxford (none Cambridge). The first, the son of Revd George Applebee of St Bride's, London, matriculated at St John's College in 1772. The second, the son of Charles James Applebee of Fulham, matriculated aged thirty at St Mary Hall, Oxford in 1818.

Public None known.

Miscellaneous In her will she left money for the upkeep of her cat.

References Will (PROB 11 online) and above sources.

1822/26 **Name** **Whittingstall, George**

Dates Unknown–15 September 1822, Watford.

Probate £500,000 (PCC).

Occupation A brewer in Watford; also had cornmeal contracts in the Napoleonic Wars. (Occupational category III.12 and 15; venue 3.) It is not clear which of these was the more lucrative.

Address Lived in Watford.
Father Henry Whittingstall, 'late' in 1807, corn miller near Hitchin, Hertfordshire. He had cornmeal contracts with the Government.
Mother Unknown.
Education Unknown.
Marriage Unknown. He is known to have been married and had two daughters.
Religion Unknown.
Public None known.
Miscellaneous His brothers James (1743–2 June 1807) and Henry (d. 1794) were known to have been very successful. Henry was credited with leaving £180,000. Although Henry is listed (*GM*) as his brother, he might have been his father. George Whittingstall was said to have left '£400,000 in funds and £300,000 in land' (*GM*). No one of this name appears to be listed in Bateman.
References *GM,* 1822, vol. II, p. 380. *BLG,* 'Fearnley-Whittingstall'.

Name **Onley, (Revd) Charles** 1822/27
Dates c. 1734–10 November 1822.
Probate £250,000 (PCC).
Occupation Probably a landowner in Essex, but the source of the fortune is unclear. (Occupational category I.) His property was chiefly left to Charles Harvey, son of Robert Harvey (1766–1843), the Norwich banker, who was married to his sister. Robert took the name Savill-Onley and was an MP between 1812 and 1826. In 1883, Savill-Onley of Stisted Hall owned 3,062 acres worth £4,617 p.a. in Essex, etc. It is unclear how much of this had been owned by (Revd) Charles Onley.
Address Stisted Hall near Braintree, Essex.
Father (Captain) John Onley, RN, who was 'dismissed from the service' in 1738.
Mother Name unknown; she was the 'daughter and co-heir' of Savill of Colchester.
Education Secondary schooling unknown; Pembroke College, Cambridge (MA and Fellow).
Marriage To Ann, née Savill (d.s.p.; marriage date unknown) of Colchester and Fordham, Essex – evidently a relative.
Religion Anglican clergyman.
Public None known.
Miscellaneous See above.
References *GM,* 1822, vol. II, p. 476; *Alum. Cantab.*

Name **Stainton, Matthew** 1822/28
Dates c. 1732–19 October 1822, Isleworth.
Probate £200,000 (PCC).
Occupation 'Warehouseman' (Stainton, Wilkinson & Co.) of Aldermanbury, City of London. (Occupational category IV.21; venue 1.) (A 'warehouseman' is a very ambiguous term, and could mean either a retailer or a wholesaler.)

Address 'Formerly of Aldermanbury in the City of London, and then of Isleworth, Middlesex' (probate calendar).
Father Unknown.
Mother Unknown.
Education Unknown.
Marriage Unknown.
Religion Unknown.
Public None known.
Miscellaneous His nephew was William Hodgson: there were subsequently several wealth-holders of this name.
References *GM,* 1822, vol. II, p. 477.

1822/29 **Name** **Heywood, John**
Dates Unknown – probated March 1822.
Probate £120,000 (PCC).
Occupation Unknown. He may have been the son of a linen draper who was an alderman of the City of London. John Heywood does not appear to be listed in any local directory, however. (Venue 1? because of his address.)
Address 'Formerly of Austin Friars in the City of London and of the Inner Temple and then of Coventry Street, St James's, Middlesex' (probate calendar).
Father Possibly James Heywood (1687–23 July 1776), a wholesale linen draper in Fish Street, City and of Austin Friars, and an Alderman for Aldgate, who also wrote poetry. He died at Austin Friars. A John Heywood was left a legacy by Bishop Hildesley, a friend of James, and a John Heywood was his pupil in 1772 (online sources).
Mother Unknown.
Education Unknown. A James Heywood (not John), son of James Heywood, was admitted to Trinity College, Cambridge in 1738.
Marriage Unknown.
Religion Presumably Anglican, if the above legacy refers to him.
Public None known.
Miscellaneous Despite his address at the Inner Temple, he is not listed in the Inner Temple Admission Book or in the 1812 or 1817 Law Lists. He could conceivably have been a solicitor.
References Probate calendar only.

1822/30 **Name** **Hunter, David**
Dates Unknown–22 April 1822 at Montague Street, Russell Square.
Probate £100,000 (PCC).
Occupation Probably a 'merchant' of 17 New Broad Street in the 1794 and 1817 directories. (If so, occupational category IV.21 or 19; venue 1.) The address given for him in the probate calendar, Old South Sea House (Threadneedle Street, City), would suggest that he was a merchant or financier.
Address 'Old South Sea House [Threadneedle Street] in the City of London and 2 Montague Street, Russell Square, Middlesex' (probate calendar).

Father Unknown.
Mother Unknown.
Education Unknown.
Marriage Unknown.
Religion Unknown.
Public None known.
Miscellaneous Nothing more could be traced about him.
References Probate calendar only.

Name **Oldham, James** ('otherwise James Oldham Oldham' – IR 11 online) 1822/31
Dates Unknown – probated July 1822.
Probate £400,000 (PCC).
Occupation 'Ironmonger to the Prince of Wales' of 142 Lower Holborn (1793 directory); 'furnishing ironmonger' (1805 directory); 'Patent stove manufacturer' (Oldham, Oldham & Son, Brooke House, Holborn, 1813 directory). (Occupational category II.11 and IV.20; venue 1.) (It is difficult to know which was the more lucrative side of the business.)
Address 'Formerly of Brooke House, Holborn, in the City of London, then Montague Place, Russell Square, Middlesex' (probate calendar).
Father Unknown.
Mother Unknown.
Education Unknown.
Marriage Unknown. His son James Oldham Oldham (sic) married in March 1820 (*GM*, 1820, vol. I, p. 272).
Religion Unknown.
Public None known.
Miscellaneous Nothing more could be traced about him.
References Probate calendar and directories only.

Name **Ffytche, Lewis Disney** (né Disney) 1822/32
Dates 9 October 1738–21 (22?) September 1822, Jermyn Street, Middlesex.
Probate £120,000 'within province' (PCC).
Occupation Probably primarily a landowner in Lincolnshire and Essex. (Occupational category I.) In 1883, J. L. Ffytche of Thorpe, Lincolnshire owned 2,909 acres worth £5,499 p.a. in Lincoln, Derby, etc. The wealth-holder might have inherited from his wife's father, the Governor of Bengal, and her uncle.
Address Swindersby, Lincolnshire, Danbury Place, near Chelmsford, Essex, and 39 Jermyn Street, Middlesex.
Father John Disney (1700–26 January 1771) of Swindersby and Lincoln City, Sheriff of Nottinghamshire 1733. The family 'could trace its descent back to the Normans' (*ODNB* for relative).
Mother Frances (d. 1791), daughter of George Cartwright of Ossington, Nottinghamshire.
Education Unknown.
Marriage In 1775, to Elizabeth, daughter of William Ffytche, Governor of Bengal, and heir to her uncle, Thomas Ffytche of Danbury Place, Essex.

Religion Anglican, but many of his relatives were prominent Unitarians.
Public None known.
Miscellaneous He took the name Ffytche on inheriting Danbury in 1775. His brother John Disney (1746–1816) was a prominent Unitarian minister, in *ODNB*. The brother was educated at Wakefield Grammar School. Our man's daughter Sophia married Dr John Disney (1779–1852), in the *ODNB* as a 'barrister and art collector'. The precise sources of Disney Ffytche's large estate are unclear.
References *GM,* 1846, vol. II, p. 379; *BLG,* 1846.

1822/33 **Name** **Goldsmid, Asher**
Dates c. 1751 Holland–30 October (1 November?) 1822.
Probate £250,000 (PCC).
Occupation 'Bullion broker to the Bank of England and the East India Company' (probate calendar) – partner with Abraham Mocatta. (Occupational category IV.18; venue 1.)
Address 'Formerly of Narwell Street, Goodman's Fields, then Leman Street, Goodman's Fields [technically, adjacent to the City but not in it], Middlesex, then Finsbury Square' (probate calendar).
Father Aaron Goldsmid (d. 3 June 1782) 'merchant' of Leman Street, Goodman's Fields and the City of London. He came from Holland to England, c. 1763.
Mother Catherine, daughter of Abraham DeVries, MD, of Amsterdam.
Education Unknown.
Marriage To Rachel (d. 1815; marriage date unknown), daughter of Alexander Keyser of London. (Four sons, two daughters.) A son was Sir Isaac Lyon Goldsmid, 1st Baronet (d. 1859) (q.v.), wealthy financier.
Religion Jewish.
Public None known.
Miscellaneous Became the leading bullion brokers in London. His brother Abraham (c. 1756–1810), merchant and financier, is in *ODNB*.
References *ODNB* for relatives; *BP;* Chaim Bermant, *The Cousinhood* (1971).

1822/34 **Name** **Coutts, Thomas**
Dates 7 September 1735, Edinburgh–24 September 1822, at 1 Stratton Street, Piccadilly.
Probate £600,000 (PCC). (Many sources credit him with a fortune ranging from £900,000 to over £1 million.)
Occupation Banker: the founder with his brother James in 1752 of Coutts Bank in the Strand, which catered to royalty and the aristocracy. He was sole partner from 1778. (Occupational category IV.16; venue 2.)
Address Lived at 1 Stratton Street, Piccadilly.
Father John Coutts (1699–1751, Naples), banker and merchant in Edinburgh; Lord Provost of Edinburgh, 1742–3.
Mother Jean (d. 1736), daughter of Sir John Stuart, 2nd Baronet of Allanbank, Berwickshire.
Education Edinburgh High School.

Marriage First, in 1763, to Susan Starkie (d. 1815), 'a servant of his brother'. (Three daughters, who married, respectively, the 3rd Earl of Guildford, the 1st Marquess of Bute, and Sir Francis Burdett, Baronet. The latter's daughter, who eventually inherited most of Coutts's fortune, was Baroness Burdett-Coutts, the celebrated philanthropist.) Second, in 1815, to Harriot Mellon (1777–1837) (1838/35), 'an actress', who famously ran Coutts's Bank after her husband's death and left her money to Burdett-Coutts; she married, second, in 1827, the 9th Duke of St Albans.

Religion Originally Church of Scotland; buried as an Anglican.

Public None known.

Miscellaneous The great banker. Worked in his father's import–export business in Edinburgh, and then in the City, before founding the bank with his brother; banker to King George II. Regarded as one of the richest men in Britain. Famous for leaving control of his bank and most of his fortune to his second wife, a former actress and a good businesswoman.

References *ODNB*.

WEALTH-HOLDERS, 1823

1823/1 **Name** **Turner, Ralph**

Dates c. 1752–23 April 1823.

Probate £140,000 (PCC).

Occupation 'Merchant' (probate calendar) in Hull. (Occupational category IV.21 or 19; venue 21.)

Address 'Formerly of Hull, then of Ferriby, E.R.' (probate calendar). He lived at Ladywellgate, Ferriby 1815–20 (K. J. Allison. *Hull Gent.*).

Father Unknown.

Mother Unknown.

Education Unknown.

Marriage To Mary (d. 9 September 1846; surname and marriage date unknown); she lived at Uplands, Ferriby (*GM*, 1846, vol. II, p. 557). (Four children.) She may have been Mary Ann Charlwood, who married a Ralph Turner (apparently of Hull) on 12 August 1791 (Family Search).

Religion Anglican: buried at All Saints' Church, North Ferriby with a memorial inscription.

Public None known.

Miscellaneous He left some of his money to Charles Turner, a wealthy Liverpool merchant, presumably a relative. Presumably Ralph Turner traded overseas from Hull, but this isn't clear.

References Online sources; Allison; above sources.

1823/2 **Name** **Crichton, James**

Dates Unknown – probated August 1823.

Probate £120,000 'within province' (PCC).

Occupation Presumably a merchant or East India Company official at Canton, China, from his address. (Occupational category IV.19 or VI.31; venue 29.)

Address 'Formerly of Canton, China, and then of Dumfries and Haddington in Scotland' (probate calendar). His entry in PROB 11 states that he lived at Friars Carse, Dumfriesshire, which he had purchased from a John Smith.

Father Unknown.

Mother Unknown.

Education Unknown.

Marriage To Elizabeth Grierson (from his will); marriage date unknown.

Religion Presumably originally Church of Scotland.

Public None known.

Miscellaneous A Captain James Crichton, of Addington Place, Camberwell and late of the East India Company's service, died at Stirling on 11 July 1819 (*GM*, 1819, vol. II, p. 93). This might well be the same man. His will states that he had a brother, John Crighton (sic) residing at Sangular in India. His wife might have been the daughter of Sir Robert Grierson, Baronet.

References Above sources only.

Name **Pearson, Allan** 1823/3
Dates Unknown – probated November 1823.
Probate £140,000 (PCC).
Occupation Merchant in Liverpool (Allan Pearson, 'merchant' of 93 Duke Street, 1805 directory). (Occupational category IV.21; venue 5.) In his will, he also mentions landed property he owned in Cumberland.
Address Lived in Liverpool.
Father Unknown. An Alan (sic) Pearson, son of Richard, was baptised at Isel, Cumberland, on 21 December 1740 (Family Search).
Mother Unknown.
Education Unknown.
Marriage Unknown.
Religion Unknown.
Public None known.
Miscellaneous Was described as a 'gentleman' of 103 Duke Street in the 1823 Liverpool directory. He left his property to his nephew Henry Thompson, his great-nephew Henry Testmaker (?) Thompson and to the children of Allan Thompson. They could not be traced.
References Will (PROB 11 online) and above sources.

Name **Drewe, William** 1823/4
Dates 10 July 1745–1821 (*BLG*, 1914). This is possibly a misprint for 1823.
Probate £120,000 (PCC).
Occupation Solicitor at 13 New Inn; also army agent (Drewe & Loxham) at 13 New Inn (New Inn is near today's Aldwych). (Occupational category VI.29 and IV.18; venue 2.)
Address 'Of the Grange [near Honiton], Devon; New Street, Spring Gardens; and 13 New Inn Chambers' (probate calendar). The London directories of 1811 and 1819 list him as of 18 New Street, Spring Gardens, Catherstone, Charmouth, Dorset, and of the Grange near Honiton, Devon.
Father Francis Drewe (1712–c. 1801) of the Grange near Honiton, Devon. (Younger son; succeeded elder brother.)
Mother Mary, daughter of Thomas Rose of Wootton Fitzpaine, Dorset.
Education Unknown.
Marriage Unknown – possibly unmarried. His property passed to his brothers John Rose Drewe and Samuel Drewe and his brother-in-law Francis Forones Luttrell of Clapham Common. William Rose Drewe appears to have been a solicitor in practice with him.
Religion Buried in the Anglican Church at Broad Hornbury, Devon.
Public None known.
Miscellaneous It is unclear if he was primarily a solicitor or an army agent.
References *BLG*, 1914; local directories.

Name **Tolcher, Henry** 1823/5
Dates Unknown–27 August 1823.

Probate £160,000 (PCC).
Occupation 'Customs Collector in the Port of Plymouth for fifty years' (*Holsworthy's Armagenious Families*). Presumably the family also had mercantile and landed wealth. (Occupational category VI.31; venue 13.)
Address Plymouth: probably of Colwell House, near Plymouth.
Father Probably Henry Tolcher, Mayor of Plymouth, 1739–40 and 1769–70. A Joseph Tolcher (1715–31 May 1794) was Mayor of Plymouth, 1771–2.
Mother Unknown.
Education Unknown.
Marriage Unknown.
Religion Presumably Anglican.
Public A Henry Tolcher was also Mayor of Plymouth, 1777–8.
Miscellaneous In 1759, a Henry Tolcher 'showed a specimen of James Northcote's drawings to Joshua Reynolds'. (Northcote, 1746–1831, was born in Plymouth; *ODNB*.)
References *Magna Britannica*, vol. 6, 1822.

1823/6 **Name** **Boughey, Sir John Fenton** (né Fletcher)**, 6th Baronet**
Dates 1 May 1784–27 June 1823.
Probate £120,000 (PCC).
Occupation Land and mineral owner in Staffordshire. (Occupational category I.) In 1883, Sir Thomas Fenton-Boughey, Baronet, owned 10,975 acres worth £16,715 p.a., chiefly in Staffordshire.
Address Aqualate House near Newport, Staffordshire; Betley Court near Newcastle-under-Lyme, Staffordshire.
Father Sir Thomas Fletcher, 1st Baronet (1747–14 July 1812), of Bexley Court, Staffordshire, JP, DL, High Sheriff 1783 and 1789; created Baronet 1795. (Only son.)
Mother Anne (d. 1821), daughter of John Fenton of Newcastle-under-Lyme.
Education Secondary schooling unknown; Christ Church, Oxford.
Marriage In 1808 to Henrietta (d. 1849), daughter of Sir John Chetwode, 4th Baronet, of Oakley, Staffordshire. (Eight sons, four daughters.)
Religion Anglican.
Public MP (—) Newcastle-under-Lyme, 1812–18; Staffordshire, 1820–3.
Miscellaneous Also inherited the estates of George Boughey of Audley, Staffordshire (d. 1788), a barrister, and added his name c. 1805. Was known as Boughey-Fletcher until 1808. He was apparently a land and mineral owner in the Black Country and a lieutenant colonel in the militia.
References *HP*; *BP*.

1823/7 **Name** **Ricardo, David**
Dates 19 April 1772, Broad Street Buildings, City of London–11 September 1823.
Probate £500,000 'within province' (PCC).
Occupation The celebrated economist; he made a fortune as a stockbroker and government loan contractor. (Occupational category IV.23 and 18; venue 1.)

Address Lived at 56 Upper Brook Street, Middlesex and Gatcombe Park near Stroud, Gloucestershire.

Father Abraham Israel Ricardo (1733, Amsterdam–24 March 1812), a wealthy stockbroker in the City of London. (First son.)

Mother Abigail (1753–1801), daughter of Abraham Delavalle, tobacconist of London.

Education Talmud Torah, Amsterdam.

Marriage In 1793, to Priscilla, daughter of Edward Wilkinson, a Quaker apothecary of Bow, Middlesex. (Three sons, five daughters.)

Religion Originally Jewish; was disinherited by his family when he married a gentile. He then became a Unitarian but was buried as an Anglican.

Public MP (Whig) Portarlington, 1819–23; High Sheriff of Gloucestershire, 1818–19.

Miscellaneous His estate at death was stated to be worth £675,000–775,000 (Sraffa and *ODNB*), but the probate figure was £500,000. He also owned land in Gloucestershire. He was a captain in the Volunteers, 1803. Ricardo died at the age of only fifty-one of an ear infection. He had become one of the most influential economists of his time.

References *ODNB*, etc.

Name **Angerstein, John Julius** 1823/8

Dates 1735, St Petersburg, Russia–29 January 1823, Woodlands, Kent.

Probate £500,000 'within province' (PCC).

Occupation Lloyd's insurance broker in London; also a loan contractor during the French Revolutionary Wars. (Occupational category IV.22 and 18; venue 1.)

Address Woodlands, near Blackheath, Kent, and 103 Pall Mall, Middlesex.

Father Unknown. Official sources give Peter Angerstein, a Lloyd's underwriter, as his father, but most sources, including the *ODNB*, state that the father was probably Andrew Poulett Thompson, a prominent English merchant in Russia, by the Empress Catherine the Great (!). Angerstein was the name of the doctor who delivered him. Poulett Thompson was supposedly given 100,000 gold rubles by the Empress. John Julius Angerstein's first job was as clerk to Poulett Thompson.

Mother Allegedly her name was Ever, and she died in St Petersburg in August 1807, aged ninety-three, but see previous.

Education Unknown.

Marriage Date unknown, to Anne (d. 1783), daughter of Henry Muilman 'of Dutch origin', and widow of Charles Crockett of Luxborough Hall, Essex. (One son, one daughter.) Second, in 1785 to Eliza Payton (d. 1800), widow of Thomas Lucas of Lee.

Religion Presumably Anglican; despite his name, there is no evidence that he had any Jewish or German ancestry (although Catherine the Great was of German descent).

Public None known. His son John was MP for Camelford, 1796–1837.

Miscellaneous Came to England c. 1750 and worked for Poulett Thompson; naturalised 1770 and retired 1811. Was known as the man who 'established the modern Lloyd's of London', and was on the Committee of Lloyd's, 1786–96. Was Chairman of the Lottery Loans during the Napoleonic Wars. Was a famous art collector whose collection was sold to the National Gallery for £57,000 after his death. 'Lived in princely style' at 103 Pall Mall.

References *ODNB.*

1823/9 **Name** **Burmester, Henry**

Dates c. 1745–10 March 1823.

Probate £160,000 (PCC).

Occupation Wine merchant (Burmester & Nash, 1805 directory) at 15 Bishopsgate and 4 Crosby Square, City of London; 'merchant' at 150 Bishopsgate Without (1793 directory). (Occupational category IV.21 and 20; venue 1.)

Address 'Formerly of Bishopsgate Street, City of London and then of Gwynne House, Woodford Bridge, Essex' (probate calendar).

Father Henry Burmester, Senior, from the north German town of Moelln. He founded a cereal-trading company in London c. 1730 and then moved to Portugal c. 1750 to establish a wine-shipping business.

Mother Unknown. A Henry Burmester, possibly a relative, married a Sarah Smith on 9 January 1716 at St Giles, Cripplegate (Family Search).

Education Unknown.

Marriage Unknown, forename probably Mary; had two sons. A Henry Burmester was baptised on 12 October 1780 at St Martin Outwich, Bishopsgate, London, son of Henry and Mary (Family Search).

Religion Probably originally Lutheran but presented plate to Woodford Anglican Church in his will.

Public None known.

Miscellaneous Established his own firm of wine shippers and merchants, c. 1799, and took his sons into partnership. He rebuilt Gwynne House, c. 1816.

References *GM,* 1823, vol. I, p. 285; online sources.

1823/10 **Name** **Cottrell, John**

Dates c. 1735–3 March 1823 at Lincoln's Inn.

Probate £140,000 (PCC).

Occupation 'One of the Sworn Clerks in Chancery' (*GM; BLG,* 1846). It is not clear precisely what type of position this was or if he was a solicitor or legally trained. The Six Clerks Office, his address, was at Chancery Lane. (Occupational category VI.29 or 31; venue 1.)

Address 'Lincoln's Inn and the Six Clerks Office, Chancery Lane' (probate calendar).

Father John Cottrell of Scarborough.

Mother Unknown.

Education Unknown.

Marriage Unknown.

Religion Presumably Anglican.

Public None known.

Miscellaneous Presumably made his money from the fees of his legal business rather than from his salary, but this isn't clear. Another beneficiary of 'Old Corruption', broadly defined.

References *GM,* 1823, vol. I, p. 184; *BLG,* 1846 under 'Powell of Brandesome Hall'.

Name **Martyn, Charles Fuller** 1823/11

Dates Unknown, Calcutta–Unknown, Paris. Probated March 1823.

Probate £140,000 (PCC).

Occupation Presumably an East India Company official or merchant in India; he had an illegitimate son, born in Calcutta – mentioned in his will. (Occupational category IV.19 or VI.31; venue 29.) 'Charles Fuller Martyn, Esq., Bengal' is listed in *A List of the Names of the Members of the United Company of Merchants of England, Trading to the East Indies, 1815* (online).

Address 'Formerly of the Albany, Piccadilly, then of New Bond Street, Middlesex' (probate calendar).

Father Unknown, but from his will the father might have been named Claudius Martyn. If so, the father was the half-brother of (Revd) Thomas Martyn (1735–3 June 1825), Professor of Botany at Cambridge, although this is far from clear.

Mother Unknown.

Education Unknown.

Marriage Unknown, possibly unmarried, but will mentions illegitimate son.

Religion Presumably Anglican.

Public None known.

Miscellaneous Nothing more could be traced about him. He probably made his fortune chiefly in India.

References Will and *ODNB* for possible relatives only.

Name **Read, John** 1823/12

Dates c. 1732–3 March 1823 at Walthamstow, Essex.

Probate £100,000 (PCC).

Occupation 'Merchant' (probably Read, Derby & Co., at 31 Old Jewry, City of London, 1803 directory). (Occupational category IV.21? Venue 1.)

Address 'Old Jewry, City of London' (probate calendar).

Father Unknown.

Mother Unknown.

Education Unknown.

Marriage Unknown. His daughter may have been Cordelia Angelica Read, baptised at St Pancras, 3 March 1801, daughter of John and Jane, died 6 December 1871 at Blackfriars, leaving £120,000 (see 1872/96), noted in Boase as 'very eccentric'.

Religion Unknown.

Public None known.

Miscellaneous A City merchant, who appears to have lived there until his death at ninety. Nothing else could be traced about him.

References *GM,* 1823, vol. I, p. 285.

1823/13 **Name** **Broadley, Elizabeth**

Dates c. 1733– 2 April 1823.

Probate £100,000 (PCC).

Occupation Widow of John Broadley, possibly a solicitor in Hull, and probably a landowner. The University of Hull Archives describes the Broadleys as 'the merchant family of Hull'.

Address Blyborough, Lincolnshire (40 miles south-west of Hull).

Father Unknown.

Mother Unknown.

Education Unknown.

Marriage Date unknown, to John Broadley (1730–25 October 1794 in Bath) of Blyborough. There was a solicitor in Hull of that name who died in 1837, possibly their son. He owned South Ella, Anlaby (K. J. Allison, '*Hull Gent. Seeks Country Residence', 1750–1850* [1981]). She was possibly related to the landed family of Broadley-Harrison, who, in 1883, owned 14,877 acres worth £23,378 p.a. in the East Riding, but no direct connection could be traced.

Religion Buried in an Anglican church with her husband.

Public None known.

Miscellaneous Nothing more could be traced.

References Oxoniensis (pseud.), *History of Blyton* (1901–4).

1823/14 **Name** **Chandless, Thomas**

Dates c. 1759–11 April 1823, Dorset Square, Middlesex.

Probate £160,000 (PCC).

Occupation Solicitor at 5 Whitehall (1805 directory) and at Golden Square, Middlesex (1793 directory). (Occupational category VI.29; venue 2.) He also bought land in Chelsea and built two houses at 7 and 9 Seymour Walk, near Fulham Road: *Survey of London*, vol. 41 (1983).

Address 'Formerly of York Place, Portman Square and then at Dorset Square, Middlesex' (probate calendar).

Father Unknown.

Mother Unknown.

Education Unknown.

Marriage Unknown; probably Sarah Ann Harrison. (Two possible marriages are listed on Family Search: those of Thomas Chandless and Sarah Ann Harrison in 1792 at St Bride, Fleet Street, and of Thomas Chandless and Mary Williams in 1794 at St Marylebone. Mary, daughter of the former couple, was baptised on 22 March 1795 at St Botolph's, Bishopsgate.) His daughter Mary (1797–1819) married Thomas Twisden Hodges of Hemstead, Kent. His son Thomas entered Gray's Inn in 1817 and became a QC; he married the daughter of Sir William Long.

Religion The daughter was buried in an Anglican churchyard.

Public None known.

Miscellaneous A wealthy solicitor, but little is known of his career.

References *GM,* 1823, vol. I, p. 383.

Name **Grenville, Richard** 1823/15
Dates 6 July 1742–22 April 1823, Hill Street, Berkeley Square, Middlesex.
Probate £120,000 (PCC).
Occupation 'General in the Army' (probate calendar). (Occupational category VI.31.)
Address Lived at Hill Street, Berkeley Square, Middlesex.
Father James Grenville (1715–83) of Butleigh Court, Somerset, MP, Deputy Paymaster of the Forces, Lord of the Treasury, Treasurer of Ireland, etc.
Mother Mary, daughter of James Smyth of South Elkington, Lincolnshire.
Education Eton.
Marriage Unmarried.
Religion Anglican.
Public MP (pro-Government) Buckingham, 1774–80.
Miscellaneous Was an ensign in the Army, 1759; Captain, 1761; Colonel, 1779; Major-General, 1782; General, 1801. He was also in charge of Prince Frederick's estate at Hanover, 1781–7, and was Controller of the Household to the Duke of York. His brother was created Baron Glastonbury in 1797. How much of his wealth came from inheritance from his Grenville relatives, how much from his salary and how much from the takings of his offices is unclear.
References *GM,* 1823, vol. I, p. 474; *HP; CP.*

Name **Owen, Lady (Anna)** (née Colby) 1823/16
Dates c. 1749–11 April 1823, Clifton. She was buried at Monkton, Pembrokeshire, 26 April 1832, 'aged 73' (Richard Rose, *Pembroke People,* 2000, p. 233.)
Probate £100,000 (PCC).
Occupation Landed. Her brother John Colby was a solicitor and administered the estates for her son when he was a minor. (Occupational category I.)
Address 'Formerly of Orielton [near Pembroke], Pembrokeshire, and then of Portman Square, Middlesex' (probate calendar).
Father John Colby of Bletherston, Pembrokeshire.
Mother Unknown.
Education Unknown.
Marriage In 1775, to Sir Hugh Owen, 5th Baronet (1729–16 January 1786), of Orielton, Pembrokeshire, MP, 1770–86, and Lord Lieutenant of Pembrokeshire, 1778–death. (One son, Sir Hugh, 6th Baronet, see 1809/8.) The estates later passed to a distant relative, barrister John Lord (d. 6 February 1861), who changed his name to Owen and was created a baronet. 'The story from that point is one of initial expense and the expansion of his estates for about ten years, followed by forty years of disposals, mortgages, the dwindling of landed property and the sale of furniture and plate. Election expenses, particularly those of the two County elections of 1831, bled his resources and by the date of his death his estate did not exceed £450' (Rose, *Pembroke People,* pp. 233–4). It is not clear who owned these estates in Bateman's time.
Religion Anglican.
Public None known.

Miscellaneous Presumably she inherited some land or personalty in her own right.
References *GM,* 1823, vol. I, p. 476; *HP; BP.*

1823/17 **Name** **Sowerby, John**
Dates 1745–20 January 1823, Putteridge Bury, Hertfordshire.
Probate £500,000 (PCC).
Occupation Both a 'warehouseman' at Cheapside (1815 directory) and an 'insurance broker' at Hatton Street, City (1795–1805 directories). He is also listed as a 'merchant' at 17 Hatton Gardens in 1805 and 1808, and a 'broker' at Old Broad Street (1780 directory). It is unclear which of these was the most lucrative. (Occupational category IV.21 and 22? Venue 1.)
Address Lived at Putteridge Bury, Hertfordshire. Was 'of Dalston' (presumably Cumberland) (*BLG,* 1952). Putteridge Bury Park is now owned by Luton University.
Father Name unknown: 'a farmer at Dalston, [near Carlisle], Cumberland' (*GM*). A John Sowerby was baptised at Dalston on 17 June 1746, son of Joseph Sowerby. There appear to have been two men of this name in Dalston at the time (Family Search).
Mother Unknown. Probably either Jane Topping, who married a Joseph Sowerby at Dalston in 1740, or Elizabeth Haugh, who married a man of that name there in 1743 (Family Search).
Education Unknown.
Marriage To Mary (d. 1812), surname and marriage date unknown. (Ten sons, six daughters.) She was perhaps Mary Marchant, who married a John Sowerby in 1774 at St Helen's Church, Bishopsgate. A Mary Lightfoot married a John Sowerby at St James's Church, Paddington, in 1771 (Family Search).
Religion Presumably Anglican.
Public High Sheriff of Hertfordshire 1796.
Miscellaneous An enormously wealthy merchant and businessman in the City, but one whose career is very obscure. According to an online history of Putteridge Bury, John Sowerby was a 'Cumberland farm labourer' who made a fortune through 'shrewd speculation'. His mansion there was rebuilt, after a fire in 1808, by John Claudius Loudon. In 1883, George Sowerby of Putteridge owned 6,001 acres worth £7,767 p.a. in Hertfordshire, Bedford, etc.
References *GM,* 1823, vol. I, p. 189; *BLG,* 1952.

1823/18 **Name** **Chaplin, Thomas**
Dates Unknown – probated June 1823.
Probate £100,000 (PCC).
Occupation Probably a maltster at Harlow, Essex (T. Chaplin, maltster, of High Street, Harlow, 1823 directory). Chaplin & Co., brewers of Harlow, existed from c. 1848–1926 (*VCH Essex,* vol. 7, p. 142). (Occupational category III.12; venue 11.) In PROB 11 he is listed as a 'farmer' of Harlow, Essex.
Address Lived at Harlow, Essex.

Father Unknown.
Mother Unknown.
Education Unknown.
Marriage Unknown.
Religion Unknown.
Public None known.
Miscellaneous A Mrs. T. Chaplin lived at 7 Grafton Street, Bond Street, Middlesex, in the 1811 and 1819 directories.
References Probate calendar and above sources only.

Name **Bridges, Thomas** 1823/19
Dates c. 1743–16 June 1823, Upper Wimpole Street, Middlesex.
Probate £120,000 (PCC).
Occupation Lieutenant General in the East India Company and a voting member (1794) of the East India Company. (Occupational category VI.31; venue 29.)
Address 'Formerly of Madras, then of Wimpole Street, Middlesex' (probate calendar).
Father Unknown.
Mother Unknown.
Education Unknown.
Marriage Unknown.
Religion Presumably Anglican.
Public None known.
Miscellaneous Major-General, 1795; Lieutenant General for the East Indies, 1802. 'Commanded the right wing of the army under Lord Harris at Seringpatam' (*GM*). In 1794, was listed as 'Colonel Thomas Bridges of Fort St. George and a voting member of the East India Company'. In 1798, was listed as 'Colonel Thomas Bridges of Hammersmith', if this was the same man. Like many East India Company figures, his early life is obscure.
References *GM*, 1823, vol. II, p. 187.

Name **Cardigan, Countess of, Elizabeth Brudenell** (née Waldegrave) 1823/20
Dates 26 May 1758, Kensington–23 June 1822, Seymour Place, Mayfair.
Probate £100,000 (PCC).
Occupation Landed. (Occupational category I.) In 1883, the Countess of Cardigan (in her own right) owned 15,724 acres worth £35,357 p.a. in the West Riding, Northampton, etc.
Address Deene Park, Northamptonshire, appears to have been the principal seat.
Father John, 3rd Earl Waldegrave (1718–22 October 1784), general, MP, and landowner.
Mother Elizabeth (1724–84), daughter of John, 1st Earl Gower.
Education Unknown.
Marriage In 1791, as his second wife, to James Brudenell, 5th Earl of Cardigan (1725–24 February 1811) (see 1811/10, left £125,000), landowner, Keeper of the

Privy Purse, etc. (d.s.p.).
Religion Anglican.
Public Lady of the Bedchamber to the Queen Consort, 1793–1809.
Miscellaneous How she became so wealthy in her own right is unclear.
References *CP; BP.*

1823/21 **Name** **Nollekens, Joseph**
Dates 11 August 1737–23 April 1823.
Probate £200,000 (PCC).
Occupation Sculptor: a fashionable sculptor, especially of busts. (Occupational category VI.30; venue 2.) He also successfully speculated on the Stock Market (*ODNB*).
Address Lived at Mortimer Street, Middlesex.
Father Joseph Nollekens the elder (1702–12 January 1748) (baptised as Corneille François Nollekens), sculptor. Came to England from Antwerp in 1733.
Mother Mary Anne LeSacq (Lesack). (She married Second Joseph William of Wales.)
Education 'At the studio of Peter Scheemakens in Antwerp.'
Marriage In 1774, to Mary (c. 1742–1817; d.s.p.), daughter of Saunders Welch, JP, of Westminster. She was a friend of Dr Johnson.
Religion Originally a Roman Catholic; buried as an Anglican.
Public None known.
Miscellaneous RA, 1772. A famous fashionable sculptor in London. Was reputed to be a miser and eccentric. He left most of his fortune to non-relatives, leading to several lawsuits. Some artists did leave large fortunes at around this time, although Nollekens's was plainly unusual.
References *ODNB.*

1823/22 **Name** **Taylor, Mary**
Dates Unknown–27 July 1822.
Probate £120,000 (PCC).
Occupation Probably inherited Jamaica plantation money. (Occupational category I? Venue 29?) Her executor was George Watson Taylor (1771–1841), an MP from 1816–32, and presumably her brother-in-law or nephew by marriage. He was born George Watson, the son of George Watson of Saul's River, Jamaica, and took the name Taylor in 1815 on succeeding to the property of his wife's brother. He had, in 1810, married Ann, the daughter of Sir John Taylor, Baronet (d. 1815) of Lysson Hall, Jamaica. It seems reasonable to assume that Martha Taylor was Ann's sister or another close relative.
Address Lived at Cumberland Place, Middlesex.
Father Probably Sir John Taylor, 1st Baronet (d. 1815), of Lysson Hall, Jamaica.
Mother Probably Lady Elizabeth Goodwin Taylor; so stated in her will.
Education Unknown.
Marriage Unmarried – described as a 'spinster' in her will.
Religion Presumably Anglican.

Public None known.
Miscellaneous Nothing more could be traced about her.
References *GM*, 1822, vol. II, p. 190; *Complete Baronetage; BP.*

Name **Burnley, Hardin** 1823/23
Dates 1741, Hanover, Virg.–27 November 1823, Brunswick Square, Middlesex.
Probate £120,000 (PCC).
Occupation 'Merchant' (Hardin & Burnley, 1817 directory) of 12 America Square, City of London. In 1795, was a 'merchant' of 10 Jamaica Square, City. The *ODNB* entry for his granddaughter notes that he was 'a proprietor of the East India Company' and had four votes in it. (Occupational category IV.19 or 21; venue 1.)
Address 'Formerly of [12] America Square in the City of London and then in Brunswick Square, Middlesex' (probate calendar).
Father Hardin Burnley (1703–70) of Virginia (Family Search).
Mother Ann Winston Terrell of Virginia (Family Search).
Education Unknown.
Marriage In 1759, to Catherine Maitland, in Virginia (Family Search). His daughter Mary married, in 1815, Joseph Hume, MP (1777–1855), the famous radical figure. Their daughter, Mary Catherine Hume-Rothery (1824–85) is in the *ODNB* as a 'campaigner for medical reform and anthropologist'.
Religion Unknown.
Public None known.
Miscellaneous Was apparently an independent merchant in the City trading with the East and possibly elsewhere.
References Above sources only.

Name **Bridgewater, 7th Earl of, John William Egerton** 1823/24
Dates 14 April 1753, St George's Hanover Square, Middlesex–21 October 1823, Ashridge Park near Berkhampstead, Hertfordshire.
Probate £700,000 (PCC).
Occupation Landowner. (Occupational category I.) Also owner of canals and a general in the Army.
Address Lived at Albemarle Street, Middlesex and Ashridge Park, Berkhampstead.
Father John Egerton, Bishop of Durham (1721–18 January 1787), brother of Francis, 3rd Duke of Bridgewater.
Mother Lady Anne (d. 1780), daughter of Henry, 1st Duke of Kent.
Education Eton; Christ Church, Oxford.
Marriage In 1783, to Charlotte (d.s.p., 1849), daughter of Samuel Haynes, MP, of Sunning Hill, Berkshire.
Religion Anglican.
Public MP (Tory) Morpeth, 1770–80, Brackley, 1780–1803; succeeded to earldom 1803 on the death of the 3rd Duke of Bridgewater.
Miscellaneous Cornet in the Army, 1771; Lieutenant, 1773; Captain, 1776;

Major, 1779; Major-General, 1795; Lieutenant General, 1802; General, 1812. FRS, 1808. His estates were said to be worth £70,000 p.a., and he was said by Faringdon (1803) to be the fourth richest man in England when he succeeded to part of the 'Canal Duke's' property.

References *ODNB* for brother, the Egerton of the Egerton Manuscripts; *CP*; *BP*.

1823/25 **Name** **Smith, Thomas**

Dates c. 1749–10 November 1823.

Probate £140,000 (PCC).

Occupation Presumably a distiller and brewer in Old Brentford. (Occupational category III.13 and 12; venue 3.) His brewery at St Mary, Old Brentford, existed in 1796 (*VCH Middlesex*, vol. 7, p. 151). He was also a partner in a distillery there with Thomas Harrison and Daniel Roberts. It was said to be 'the largest in England' in 1802 (Brentford: online sources). The distillery was sold to Booth's in 1817.

Address Of Old Brentford, Ealing.

Father Unknown.

Mother Unknown.

Education Unknown.

Marriage To Susannah (d. 1840, aged seventy-six), surname and marriage date unknown. Their son may have died in 1849, leaving £100,000 (see 1849/17).

Religion Buried in the Anglican Church, Brentford.

Public None known.

Miscellaneous A firm called T. & G. Smith, brewers of Whitechapel, were said to have 'paid the highest duty in England' in 1833 (*VCH Middlesex*, vol. 2, p. 127), but there appears to be no connection with this man.

References Above sources only.

1823/26 **Name** **Cornwallis, 2nd Marquess, Charles Cornwallis**

Dates 19 October 1774, Culford, Suffolk–9 August 1823, Burlington Street, Middlesex.

Probate £120,000 (PCC).

Occupation Landowner and presumably money from his father's positions. (Occupational category I.) No Lord Cornwallis is listed in Bateman.

Address Lived at Old Burlington Street, Middlesex. The family seat was at Culford, Suffolk.

Father Charles Cornwallis, 1st Marquess Cornwallis (1738–5 October 1805), Governor General of India and Lord Lieutenant of Ireland; famous or notorious for his military role in the American Revolutionary Wars.

Mother Jemima (d. 1779), daughter of (Captain) John Jones, 3rd Foot Guards.

Education Eton; St John's College, Cambridge (MA, 1794).

Marriage In 1797, to Lady Louisa (d. December 1850), daughter of Alexander, 4th Duke of Gordon. (Four daughters.)

Religion Anglican.

Public MP (Tory) Eye, 1795–6, Suffolk 1796–1805. Master of the Buckhounds, 1807–death.

Miscellaneous He was known as 'Viscount Brome' until 1805 and was a captain in the Suffolk Yeomanry.
References *ODNB* as 'landowner'.

WEALTH-HOLDERS, 1824

1824/1 **Name** **Maseres, Francis**

Dates 15 December 1731, London 19 May 1824, Church Street, Reigate.

Probate £100,000 (PCC).

Occupation Barrister and 'Cursitor Baron of the Court of Exchequer' (probate calendar). (Occupational category VI.29; venue 1.) The position was worth £300–£400 p.a.; he held it from 1773 until his death. He also inherited 'great wealth' from his father, a successful physician in London, and his bachelor brother John (*ODNB*).

Address King's Bench Walk, Inner Temple; Rathbone Place, Middlesex; The Barons, Reigate, Surrey.

Father Peter Abraham Maseres, a physician of Broad Street, Soho and then Rathbone Place, Middlesex.

Mother Magdalene, daughter of Francis du Pratt du Clareau.

Education 'At Kingston-upon-Thames'; Clare College, Cambridge (BA, Newcastle Medallist; Fellow; MA); barrister, Inner Temple (called 1758).

Marriage Unmarried.

Religion The family were Huguenots. He was a 'zealous Protestant' and fierce anti-Catholic, who leaned to Unitarianism. He was buried as an Anglican.

Public Attorney General of Quebec, 1766–9; Curistor Baron of the Court of Exchequer, 1773–death. Also Judge of the Sheriff's Court, London, 1773–death, and Common Pleader in the City of London, 1762–80.

Miscellaneous A well-known lawyer and also a mathematician and historian, in the *ODNB* as a 'colonial administrator and author'. Was a Bencher (1774) and Treasurer (1782) of the Inner Temple. Wrote important works on mathematics and history. An eccentric who 'wore clothes from the period of George II' (*ODNB*). He left virtually all of his fortune to an unrelated young friend (Revd) Robert Fellowes, who is said to have inherited £200,000, although Maseres left far less than this.

References *ODNB*.

1824/2 **Name** **Kinghorn, George**

Dates Unknown – probated February 1824.

Probate £120,000 (PCC).

Occupation 'Merchant' in Kingston, Jamaica. (Occupational category IV.19; venue 29.) There is no evidence that he was a plantation owner. His estate was probated in England, but no English address is given in the probate calendars.

Address Of Kingston, Jamaica.

Father Unknown. The surname is Scottish.

Mother Unknown.

Education Unknown.

Marriage Unknown.

Religion Unknown.

Public Was an Alderman of Kingston, Jamaica, in 1783 (*Times*); is listed as a Judge of the Surrey Assize Court, Jamaica, February 1793. He was also Treasurer of Wolmer's Free School, Kingston, Jamaica, established in 1729. In an essay entitled '"Important Truths" and "Pernicious Follies"', John W. Pulis describes him as 'a merchant in the slave trade': Kevin A. Yelvington, ed., *Afro-Atlantic Dialogues: Anthropology in the Diaspora* (2006), p. 209.
Miscellaneous Nothing more could be traced about him.
References Above sources only.

Name **Curtis, John** 1824/3
Dates c. 1765–28 December 1823, Herne Hill, Surrey.
Probate £120,000 (PCC).
Occupation 'Wholesale stationer' (probate calendar), presumably in the City of London, but could not be identified in any directory. (Occupational category IV.21; venue 1?)
Address 'Formerly of Camberwell then of Herne Hill, Lambeth' (probate calendar). He may be the John Curtis who lived at 20 Paradise Row, Stockwell (1817 directory).
Father Thomas Curtis, a 'wholesale stationer'.
Mother Unknown.
Education Unknown.
Marriage Unknown. His daughter Emily married, in 1832, Sir William Tite (1798–1873), the architect (*ODNB*). She was perhaps the Amelia (sic) Curtis, daughter of John and Elizabeth, baptised 4 September 1808 at St John Horsleydown, Bermondsey.
Religion Unknown.
Public None known.
Miscellaneous 'For many years an eminent wholesale stationer' (*GM*).
References *GM,* 1823, vol. II, p. 645.

Name **Irvine, Walter** 1824/4
Dates Unknown–7 January 1824, Luddington House, Egham, Surrey.
Probate £120,000 (PCC).
Occupation A sugar planter in Tobago. (Occupational category I; venue 29.)
Address 'Formerly of Tobago, and then of Wimpole Street, Middlesex and then of Luddington House, Egham, Surrey' (probate calendar).
Father Unknown. The surname is Scottish.
Mother Unknown.
Education Unknown.
Marriage Unknown. His daughter Elizabeth (d. 25 April 1864) married, in 1824, William Robert Keith Douglas (1783–December 1859), MP, 1812–32. Elizabeth's husband was the brother of the future Marquess of Queensbury. He 'owned sugar plantation estates in Tobago which formerly belonged to his father-in-law' (online source).
Religion Unknown, presumably Church of Scotland or Anglican.

Public None known.
Miscellaneous Nothing more is known of his career.
References *GM,* 1824, vol. I, p. 94.

1824/5 **Name** **King, Thomas**
Dates Unknown – probated February 1824.
Probate £120,000 (PCC).
Occupation 'Merchant' (probate calendar) in the City of London but could not be identified in any directory. (Occupational venue IV.21? Venue 1.)
Address 'Formerly of Stamford Hill, Middlesex and the City of London, and then of Bath' (probate calendar).
Father Unknown.
Mother Unknown.
Education Unknown.
Marriage Unknown.
Religion Unknown.
Public None known.
Miscellaneous Nothing more could be traced about him.
References Probate calendar only.

1824/6 **Name** **Pigott, (Revd) Wadham**
Dates c. 1749–25 December 1823.
Probate £140,000 (PCC).
Occupation Apparently he was a wealthy landowner of the wealthy Smyth-Piggott family, who became Lords of the Manor of Weston-super-Mare in 1696. (Occupational category I.) Brockley Court was built by him in the late eighteenth century. In 1883, John Piggott-Smyth-Piggott of Brockley Court owned 6,000 acres in Somerset worth £12,000 p.a. Brockley Court is eight miles from Bristol, suggesting that he owned land there.
Address Brockley Court, near Bristol, Somerset (*GM*); also The Grove, Somerset (*BLG,* 1846).
Father John Bigg Piggott of Brockley Court, Somerset.
Mother Ann, sister of Thomas Coward of Sparkgrove, Somerset.
Education Secondary schooling unknown; St Mary Hall, Oxford.
Marriage Unmarried.
Religion Anglican clergyman.
Public None known.
Miscellaneous Nothing more could be traced about his career.
References *GM,* 1824, vol. I, p. 188; *BLG,* 1846; online sources.

1824/7 **Name** **Sill, Joseph**
Dates Unknown – probated April 1824.
Probate £140,000 (PCC).
Occupation Presumably a merchant in Lisbon, Portugal, possibly in the wine trade. (Occupational category IV.19? Venue 29.)

Address 'Formerly of Lisbon, and then of Portland Place, Middlesex; died at Bath' (probate calendar).
Father Unknown.
Mother Unknown.
Education Unknown.
Marriage Unknown.
Religion Anglican; has an elaborate monument in Bath Abbey.
Public None known.
Miscellaneous He is not listed in any directory or Court guide; presumably he spent most of his career in Lisbon.
References Probate calendar only.

Name Owen, (Very Revd) John 1824/8
Dates c. 1753–4 June (July: *Cantab.*) 1824 at East Horsley, Surrey. *Cantab.* states that he was born in 1773, but *GM*, states that he died aged seventy.
Probate £100,000 (PCC).
Occupation Archdeacon of Richmond, Yorkshire and Chaplain-General to HM Forces. (Occupational category VI.30 and 31.) Whether he had any other sources of income is not known.
Address Lived at East Horseley, Surrey and presumably at Richmond, Yorkshire.
Father Thomas Owen of Llangurig, Montgomeryshire, 'gentleman' (*Cantab.*).
Mother Unknown.
Education Secondary schooling unknown; Hertford College, Oxford (BA); Christ's College, Cambridge (MA).
Marriage Unknown.
Religion Anglican clergyman.
Public None known.
Miscellaneous Was also rector of East Horseley and of St Benet's, Paul's Wharf, London. Little could be traced of his life in published sources.
References *GM*, 1824, vol. II, p. 188.

Name Cornwallis, 4th Earl, (Rt. Revd) James Cornwallis, Bishop of Lichfield and Coventry 1824/9
Dates 25 February 1742, Dover Street, Piccadilly–20 January 1824, Richmond, Surrey.
Probate £200,000 (PCC).
Occupation Bishop of Lichfield and Coventry from 1781 until death; also a landowner but succeeded his nephew as earl only in 1823. (Occupational category VI.30; venue 18?)
Address Lived at Lichfield and at Richmond, Surrey.
Father Charles Cornwallis, 1st Earl Cornwallis (1700–26 June 1762). (Third son; succeeded his nephew when he was eighty-one.)
Mother Elizabeth (d. 1785), daughter of Charles, 2nd Viscount Townshend.
Education Eton; Christ Church, Oxford (MA); admitted to the Inner Temple but did not complete. Received an Honorary DCL from Oxford, 1775.

Marriage In 1771, to Catherine (d. 1811), daughter of Galfridus (sic) Mann of Egerton, Kent and sister of Sir Horace Mann. (One son, two daughters.)
Religion Anglican clergyman.
Public None known: he presumably sat in the House of Lords for much of his career and was known as a Tory.
Miscellaneous Held livings in Kent, 1769–81; Dean of Salisbury, 1775; Dean of Windsor, 1791; Dean of Durham, 1794. Held the bishopric for forty-three years – another example of the colossal rewards of 'Old Corruption' in the Church of England.
References *ODNB*.

1824/10 **Name** **Clay, Joseph**
Dates 1756–probated July 1824.
Probate £160,000 (PCC).
Occupation Brewer and maltster, and then a banker, in Burton upon Trent. (Occupational categories IV.16 and II.12; venue 17.) Given as a 'banker' in PROB 11.
Address 'The Bank, Burton-upon-Trent, Staffordshire' (probate calendar).
Father Joseph Clay (d. 1800) 'a Derby maltster' (*VCH Staffordshire*, vol. 9, 2003).
Mother Unknown.
Education Unknown.
Marriage In 1791, to Elizabeth, daughter of Anthony Robinson. (Three sons, three daughters.) A daughter, Margaret, in 1828 married (Revd) Hastings Robinson (1792–1866), in *ODNB* as 'Evangelical Anglican clergyman'.
Religion Presumably Anglican.
Public None known.
Miscellaneous Was originally a maltster in Burton, then acquired an early brewery there and then 'opened one of the first banks in Burton' (*VCH Staffordshire*, vol. 9, 2003). It is not clear which of these was the most lucrative, although he is described as a 'banker' in his will and probate documents. The family malsting firm had been established in the 1750s.
References Sources noted above.

1824/11 **Name** **Whitehead, Richard**
Dates Unknown – probated September 1824.
Probate £100,000 (PCC).
Occupation Probably the owner of a cloth mill and dyeing business in Stroud, Gloucestershire. (Occupational category IV.8 and 6? Venue 13.)
Address Lived at Minchinhampton, Gloucestershire – about three miles from Stroud.
Father Unknown.
Mother Unknown.
Education Unknown.
Marriage Unknown.
Religion Unknown.
Public None known.

Miscellaneous He owned Peghouse (later Woodlands) Mill, which and his brother Thomas inherited in c. 1793 from Mary Fowler. He sold it in 1798. Any other source of his wealth could not be traced. (*VCH Gloucestershire*, vol. 11, 1976, pp. 70–9).
References Above sources only.

Name **Buller, Richard** 1824/12
Dates c. 1729–8 January 1824.
Probate £100,000 'Within province' (PCC).
Occupation 'Merchant' (Richard Buller & Co., 1795 directory) at 4 Crosby Square, Bishopsgate. The firm was a Lloyd's of London subscriber in 1787 and was presumably an insurance brokerage firm as well as a mercantile firm. (Occupational category IV.22 and 19; venue 1.)
Address 'Formerly of Crosby Square, Bishopsgate Street, City of London and then of Cumberland Street, Middlesex' (probate calendar).
Father Unknown.
Mother Unknown.
Education Unknown.
Marriage Unknown.
Religion Unknown.
Public None known.
Miscellaneous No connection with the titled Buller families could be traced.
References *GM*, 1824, vol. I, p. 283.

Name **Balfour (-Ramsay), James** 1824/13
Dates 1743–18 (or 19) March 1823, Bolton Row, Piccadilly.
Probate £250,000 (PCC).
Occupation General of the 83rd Regiment of Foot. (Occupational category VI.31.) Also landowner and colliery owner in Scotland: succeeded to the Whitehill estate in 1814 on the death of his brother Andrew (1741–1814), Vice-Dean of the faculty of Advocates and Judge of the Common Court. In 1883, Robert Balfour Wardlaw-Ramsay of Whitehill owned 7,500 acres worth £7,506 p.a. in Midlothian, etc., plus £2,312 p.a. from mines.
Address Whitehill, Midlothian and Balcurvie, Fifeshire, and Bolton Row, Piccadilly.
Father Robert Balfour(-Ramsay) (1698–1797, sic), land and colliery owner of Balbirnie, Fifeshire.
Mother Anne, daughter of Sir Andrew Ramsay, 4th Baronet of Whitehill.
Education Unknown.
Marriage Unmarried.
Religion Presumably Church of Scotland.
Public None known.
Miscellaneous Became a general in 1809; was known as both 'Ramsay' and 'Balfour-Ramsay'. It is not known how much of his fortune derived from his military salary and how much from land or other sources.
References *GM*, 1823, vol. I, p. 381; *BLG*, 1952.

1824/14 **Name** **Dowson, Joseph**
Dates Unknown – probated March 1824.
Probate £120,000 (PCC).
Occupation 'Ship and insurance broker' (Joseph Dowson & Sons, 4 Warnford Court, Throgmorton Street, City, 1795 directory), and also of Simpson Gardens, Wapping, a business address. (Occupational category IV.22; venue 1.)
Address 'Stratford Green, Stratford, Bow, Essex and Simpson Gardens, Wapping' (probate calendar). He might thus also have been a shipowner or broker. PROB 11 gives his address as Warnford Court, City of London.
Father Unknown.
Mother Unknown.
Education Unknown.
Marriage Unknown.
Religion Unknown.
Public None known.
Miscellaneous Nothing more could be traced of his career.
References Above sources only.

1824/15 **Name** **Orde, Sir John, 1st Baronet**
Dates 22 December 1751, Nunnykirk, Morpeth–19 February 1824, Gloucester Place.
Probate £180,000 (PCC).
Occupation 'Admiral of the Red.' (Occupational category VI.31.)
Address Gloucester Place, Portman Square, Middlesex, and also of Burwash near Battle, Sussex.
Father John Orde (1704–84 or 1786), landowner, JP, DL, of Morpeth. (Third son.) Sir John's elder brother Thomas Orde-Powlett was created 1st Baron Bolton. In 1883, Lord Bolton owned 29,221 acres worth £27,552 p.a. in Hampshire and the North Riding.
Mother Anne (d. 1788), daughter of Ralph Marr of Morpeth and widow of (Revd) William Pye of Morpeth.
Education Morpeth Grammar School.
Marriage First, in 1781, to Margaret (d. 1790; d.s.p.), daughter of Richard Stephens of South Carolina. Second, in 1793, to Jane (d. 1829), daughter of John Frere of Roydon, Norfolk. (One son, one daughter.)
Religion Anglican.
Public MP (Whig) Yarmouth, 1807–24. Created baronet, 1790.
Miscellaneous Entered the Royal Navy, 1766; Captain, 1778; Rear-Admiral, 1795; Vice-Admiral, 1799; Admiral of the Blue, 1805; Admiral of the White, 1809; Admiral of the Red, 1814. Was also Governor of Dominica, 1783–93.
References *ODNB*.

1824/16 **Name** **Auriol, James Peter**
Dates Baptised in Lisbon, Portugal, 1753–probated July 1824.
Probate £120,000 (PCC).

Occupation 'Former Secretary to the Supreme Council of India' – *ODNB* for his relative, Archbishop Robert Hay Drummond. He was cross-examined by Burke during the impeachment trial of Warren Hastings. In London, he was apparently a merchant ('Peter James Auriol, merchants, of 1 Devonshire Square [near Bishopsgate in the City]', 1795 directory. Other mercantile firms headed by a J. P. Auriol also existed, including Auriol & Bowyer, merchants, of 24 Pall Mall. He was also apparently Secretary of the Royal Institution of Great Britain from 1801 to 1811. There may well be some confusion among several different men with similar names here, but it seems likely that he was primarily a merchant in London. (Occupational category IV.19? Venue 1.) Revd Sabine Baring-Gould, in his *Family Names and Their Story* (1910, p. 284), states: 'James and Peter Auriole [sic] were [Huguenot] refugees. James became a wealthy merchant in Lisbon, whence he went from London. His eldest son, James Peter, as well as his brother, obtained lucrative appointments in India. The second, Charles, became a General in the royal service. James Peter was the father of Edward Auriol, Rector of St Dunstan's, in the West of London, and Prebendary of St Paul's.'

Address 'Formerly of Stratford Place, then of Park Street, Grosvenor Square and of Pall Mall' (probate calendar).

Father James Auriol, a merchant in Lisbon and London (see 'Occupation' above).

Mother Unknown.

Marriage Unknown. Peter Auriol's daughter Henrietta married, in 1749, Robert Hay Drummond (1711–76), later Archbishop of York.

Religion Of Huguenot descent, but presumably an Anglican from his apparent relationship with an archbishop.

Public None known.

Miscellaneous In 1792, he was one of the proprietors of the Whitchurch Bridge in Oxfordshire (online sources). The 1796 London directory includes a J. P. Auriol of 6 Portugal Street and Woodcote, Oxfordshire. It is unclear whether this is the same man. It seems likely that, as noted, several men with similar names, presumably relatives, have been highlighted in this entry, and it is difficult to disentangle them without further information.

References Sources as noted above.

Name **Gunman, James** 1824/17

Dates Unknown–29 June 1824, Dover.

Probate £120,000 (PCC).

Occupation His grandfather was a 'merchant' in Dover and Mayor of Dover, 1737. James Gunman owned Shebbertswell Manor, near Dover in 1800, and appears to have been primarily a landowner, but the precise source of his wealth is unclear. His wife's father owned Doddington Hall, Lincolnshire. In 1883, a relative who owned Doddington Hall, George Eden Jarvis, owned 4,720 acres worth £5,824 p.a. in several counties including Kent. James Gunman owned lands in Dover and elsewhere in Kent.

Address Dover, Kent.

Father Christopher Gunman (d. 1781), 'Collector of Customs at Dover'. His father, James Gunman, was a merchant at Dover and Mayor in 1737 (*Arch. Cantiana*, 1917). He seems to have been the Captain James Gunman RN (d. 30 June 1756) who was Treasurer of Greenwich Hospital, 1742–54. Captain Gunman, of Dover, obtained the manor of Buckland, in Kent, through his marriage with the daughter of Edward Wivell (six times Mayor of Dover); it passed to Christopher and then to James. (W. H. Ireland, *England's Topographer: Or a New and Complete History of the County of Kent*, vol. II, 1829, p. 124).
Mother Unknown.
Education Unknown.
Marriage In 1805, to Sarah (see 1825/21, left £120,000), daughter of Edward Hussey Delaval of Seaton Delarole, Northumberland and Doddington, Lincolnshire.
Religion Anglican.
Public Member and Freeman of the Dover Corporation. A James Gunman was Mayor of Dover 1776, 1784 and 1789.
Miscellaneous There is no direct evidence that he was active in trade.
References *GM*, 1824, vol. II, p. 94; above sources.

1824/18 **Name** **Josselyn, James**
Dates Unknown – probated July 1824.
Probate £120,000 (PCC); above sources.
Occupation Possibly a land agent and landowner, although the family is not listed in Bateman.
Address 'Formerly of Rivers Hall [near Boxted], then of Great Horkesley, then of Boxted Hall [near Colchester], Essex.'
Father Probably John Josselyn (d. 20 February 1819) of Copdock, Suffolk, and formerly of Nedging, Suffolk, apparently a farmer. (Probably third son.) (*BLG*, 1952, although this family's genealogy is very confusing, with several men of the same name and approximate dates.) The will of a James Josselyn of Little Horkesley, Essex was probated (PCC) in September 1787.
Mother Probably Sarah (d. 29 October 1816), daughter of Simon Sparrow of Ipswich.
Education Unknown.
Marriage He may be the James Josselyn who married, in July 1774, at Little Horkesley, Margaret Lay. However, he left much of his property to a John Josselyn of Bury St Edmunds, possibly a more distant relative rather than his son.
Religion The family might at one time have been Quakers.
Public None known.
Miscellaneous The family was prominent in Essex, but the source of his wealth is unclear. He is described in the probate calendar as a 'gentleman'. He is apparently not listed in any London directory. The family is apparently descended from Thomas Josselyn (d. 1636), who worked in the King's Remembrancer's Office.
References *BLG*, 1952.

Name **Perry, John** 1824/19
Dates 1768–5 July 1824.
Probate £140,000 (PCC).
Occupation Shipbuilder at Blackwell. (Occupational category II.4; venue 2.)
Address 'Formerly of Blackwall and of Brunswick Square, Middlesex, and then of Moor Hall near Harlow, Essex' (probate calendar).
Father John Perry (1743–7 November 1810) of Moor Hall, shipbuilder, educated at Harrow and High Sheriff of Essex, 1798.
Mother Elizabeth Browne (d. 1795).
Education Unknown.
Marriage Unknown; apparently unmarried.
Religion Anglican.
Public None known.
Miscellaneous The family had been shipbuilders at Blackwall since 1708. John Perry was a partner with his brother and brother-in-law Richard Green but sold the business to Green (1767–1849) in 1798. He also owned the Blackwall Estate, which was sold to the East India Dock Company in 1803. Green's son Richard Green (1803–63) carried on the business (*ODNB*).
References *ODNB* for Richard Green.

Name **Hampden, 3rd Viscount and 6th Baron Trevor, John Hampden-Trevor** 1824/20
Dates 24 February 1749, London–9 September 1824, Berkeley Square, Middlesex.
Probate £250,000 (PCC).
Occupation Landowner. (Occupational category I.) But he held the title for only three weeks, succeeding his brother (see 1824/24) on 20 August 1824, and was also an ambassador. In 1883, Lord Trevor owned 23,694 acres worth £17,700 p.a. in Ireland, Salop, Flintshire, etc.
Address The main seat of the family was apparently at Glynde, near Lewes, Sussex, but this man seems to have lived chiefly in London.
Father Robert Hampden-Trevor, 1st Viscount Hampden and 4th Baron Trevor (1706–22 August 1783), diplomat and Joint Postmaster-General. (Second son.)
Mother Constantina, daughter of Peter Anthony de Huybert, Lord van Kruyningen of The Hague.
Education Westminster School; Christ Church, Oxford (MA).
Marriage In 1773, to Harriet (d.s.p., 1829), daughter of (Revd) Daniel Burton, DD, Canon of Christ Church, Oxford.
Religion Anglican.
Public PC, 1797.
Miscellaneous Served as British Minister at Munich, 1780–3, and at Turin, 1783–98. The father took the additional name of Hampden in 1754 on succeeding to the Hampden estate. As noted. John Hampden-Trevor held the titles for only three weeks. He was also noted as a friend of Burke, Horace Walpole, Gibbon and other writers (*ONDB*).
References *ODNB* as 'diplomatist'.

1824/21 **Name** **Walker, John**

Dates 1766–9 May 1824.

Probate £200,000 (PCC).

Occupation Brewer at Southgate, Middlesex. (Occupational category III.12; venue 3.)

Address Bedford Square and Arnos Grove, Southgate, Middlesex. (His father had purchased Arnos Grove in 1777.) In 1900, the family owned 600 acres at Southgate.

Father Isaac Walker (1725–1804), linen merchant and Quaker. It is not clear whether he was also engaged in brewing.

Mother Unknown.

Education Unknown.

Marriage To Sarah, surname and marriage date unknown. Their descendants became famous cricketers, including Vyell Edward Walker (1837–1906), in the *ODNB* as a cricketer and also a very wealthy brewer.

Religion Quaker; he opened a charity school in 1812 on the Walker estate. The descendants were certainly Anglicans.

Public None known.

Miscellaneous His brewery later became Taylor Walker Brewery. He had an important garden on his estate and corresponded about plants with famous scientists; he was FRS and FSA.

References *GM,* 1824, vol. I, p. 476; W. A. Bettesworth, *The Walkers of Southgate* (1900); *ODNB* for descendant.

1824/22 **Name** **Gillow, Thomas**

Dates 5 March 1756–16 September 1824.

Probate £100,000 (PCC).

Occupation Apparently the owner of gunpowder mills at the Isle of Thanet, Kent leased to Miles Peter Andrews (1814/26) to make gunpowder for the East India Company. The family also apparently owned land in Kent, including Buckland near Faversham but is unlisted in Bateman. However, little of a definite nature could be identified regarding their source of wealth. They were apparently unrelated to the famous Gillow family of cabinetmakers, listed in the *ODNB,* who had no connection with the Isle of Thanet. (Occupational category II.11? Venue 14?)

Address St Nicholas Atwade, Isle of Thanet, Kent.

Father Thomas Gillow (1727–26 June 1797) of St Nicholas Atwade. (First son.)

Mother Anne (1734–9 January 1816), daughter of (Captain) Robert Eason Jnr., his father's cousin.

Education Unknown.

Marriage In 1788, to Elizabeth Bridges (1761–6 November 1831). (Six sons, two daughters.)

Religion Anglican; his sister married a clergyman.

Public None known.

Miscellaneous Whether he was in trade is unclear.

References Online sources and above sources only.

Name **Wilshere, William** 1824/23
Dates 6 September 1754–2 September 1824, Hitchin, Hertfordshire
Probate £140,000 (PCC).
Occupation Solicitor and estate steward in and near Hitchin, Hertfordshire (Occupational category VI.29; venue 3.) He was also a landowner – in 1883, Charles Wiles Wilshere of The Frythe owned 3,449 acres worth £6,347 p.a. in Hertfordshire, Bedfordshire, and Cambridge.
Address Lived at The Frythe, Hitchin, Hertfordshire. Also owned the manors of Great and Little Wymondley, near Hitchin, purchased in 1802.
Father William Wilshere (1730–1 November 1798) of The Frythe, Hitchin, Hertfordshire.
Mother Susannah, daughter of Simon Browne of Wendon Lofts, Essex.
Education Unknown.
Marriage In 1785 to Martha Wortham (d.s.p.).
Religion A Congregationalist; known as a 'very kind friend to the poor'.
Public Deputy-Sheriff of Hertfordshire. Also JP and Chairman of the Bedfordshire Quarter Sessions.
Miscellaneous Was a captain in the Hitchin Loyal Volunteers. He was described at his death as an 'attorney and steward of many copyhold manors, and acquired much wealth and influence'. (Cited in R. L. Hine, *Hitchin Worthiest: Four Centuries of English Life*, 1932, vol. II, p. 424.)
References *BLG*, 1952; above sources.

Name **Hampden, 2nd Viscount and 5th Baron Trevor, Thomas Trevor-Hampden** 1824/24
Dates 11 September 1746, The Hague–20 August 1824, Green Street, Grosvenor Square.
Probate £160,000 (PCC).
Occupation Landowner. (Occupational category I.) Elder brother of 1824/20 – see his entry for details.
Address Apparently lived at Glynde, Sussex and in London.
Father Robert Hampden-Trevor, 1st Viscount Hampden and 4th Baron Trevor (1706–83). (First son.)
Mother Constantia, daughter of Peter Anthony de Huybert Baron van Kruyningen of The Hague.
Education Westminster School (?); Christ Church, Oxford.
Marriage First, in 1768, to Catherine (d.s.p., 1804), daughter of David Graeme MP of Braco, Perthshire. Second, in 1805, to Jane (d.s.p., 1824 or 1833), daughter of George Brown of Ellistoun, Scotland.
Religion Anglican.
Public MP (Whig, then Tory) Lewes, 1768–74. Contested Bedford, 1774.
Miscellaneous Chiefly a landowner; see brother for details.
References *GM*, 1824, vol. II, pp. 274–5; *CP*; *BP*.

1824/25 **Name** **Montefiore, Abraham**
Dates 1788–25 August 1824, Lyons, France.
Probate £500,000 (PCC).
Occupation Stockbroker in London. (Occupational category IV.23; venue 1.) Was the stockbroker for the Rothschilds. Had earlier made a fortune as a silk merchant and then was head of Montefiore Brothers, stockbrokers.
Address Lived at Stamford Hill, Middlesex. (Now the centre of the Strictly Orthodox Jewish community in London, appropriately enough.)
Father Joseph Elias Montefiore (1759–11 January 1804), 'Italian merchant' in London: he sold straw hats and marble.
Mother Rachel, daughter of Abraham Lumbrozo de Mattos Mocatta.
Education Unknown.
Marriage First (marriage date unknown) to Mary, daughter of George Hall, a stockbroker. (One daughter.) Second, in 1815, to Henrietta, daughter of Meyer Anselm Rothschild of Frankfurt and sister of Nathan Mayer Rothschild. (Two sons, two daughters.)
Religion Jewish – one of the founders of the so-called Anglo-Jewish 'Cousinhood' of intermarried Montefiores, Mocattas, Rothschilds and others that dominated Anglo-Jewish life until the First World War. He was the brother of the great Anglo-Jewish leader Sir Moses Montefiore (1784–1885) (q.v.).
Public None known.
Miscellaneous He was apprenticed to silk merchants in Watling Street and made a 'small fortune' as a silk merchant before becoming a leading stockbroker. His first wife was evidently not Jewish – this was very unusual at the time, as was his second marriage, between members of Sephardic and Ashkenazi Jewish families.
References Chaim Bermant, *The Cousinhood* (1971); Jewish sources; *BLG*, 1952; *GM*, 1824, vol. II, p. 564.

1824/26 **Name** **Sorrell, Robert**
Dates Unknown–1823 (will probated January 1824).
Probate £160,000 (PCC).
Occupation 'Surgeon' (probate calendar) in Holborn, London. (Occupational category VI.30; venue 1.)
Address 'Formerly of Thavies Inn [London] then of Holborn, then of The Lane, Holborn, and formerly of Ingatestone [near Chelmsford], Essex' (probate calendar).
Father Unknown.
Mother Unknown.
Education Unknown; was an 'M.D.', according to the probate calendar.
Marriage Unknown, but probably unmarried.
Religion Unknown.
Public None known.
Miscellaneous His fortune was 'acquired [. . .] by rapid accumulation, owing to a disposition to [. . .] save [. . .] lived in obscure lodgings'. He was supposed

to be worth £200,000 (*GM*). How he accumulated so much as a surgeon is unknown.

References *GM*, 1823, vol. II, p. 571.

Name **Reid, Sir Thomas, 1st Baronet** 1824/27

Dates 26 October 1762–29 February 1824.

Probate £300,000 (PCC).

Occupation East India merchant in the City of London ('Chairman of the Court of Directors of the East India Company' and head of Reid, Irvine & Co., 'merchants' of Broad Street Buildings, City of London). (Occupational category IV.19; venue 1.)

Address 'Broad Street Buildings, City of London and Ewell Grove, Surrey' (probate calendar).

Father James Reid (d. 20 May 1775), 'a merchant of Dumfriesshire' (*GM*).

Mother Helen, daughter of John Davidson of Woodside, Dumfriesshire.

Education Unknown.

Marriage In 1791, to Elizabeth (d. 1829), daughter of John Looke Goodfellow of Newbury, Berkshire. (Two sons, two daughters.) His daughter Helen married (Revd) Benjamin Winston. Their son, Charles Winston (1814–64) is in the *ODNB* as a 'barrister and stained glass historian'.

Religion Presumably originally Church of Scotland.

Public Created baronet, 1823.

Miscellaneous It is not known whether he visited India or spent time there.

References *GM*, 1824, vol. I, p. 646; BP.

Name **West, William** 1824/28

Dates c. 1763–16 May 1824.

Probate £160,000 (PCC).

Occupation Wholesale merchant – owned a 'wholesale leather warehouse', chiefly for bookbinders, at 24 Bridle Lane, Fleet Street (1808 and 1817 directory). (Occupational category IV.21; venue 1.)

Address Lived in Bedford Square, Middlesex.

Father Unknown.

Mother Unknown.

Education Unknown.

Marriage To the daughter (name and marriage date unknown) of the former owner of the business, a Mr Avery. (One son, one daughter.) West became Avery's partner and successor.

Religion Unknown.

Public None known.

Miscellaneous Nothing further could be traced about him.

References *GM*, 1824, vol. I, p. 645.

Name **Wood, Sir George** 1824/29

Dates 13 February 1743, Roystone, Yorkshire–7 July 1824.

Probate £120,000 'within province' (PCC).
Occupation Judge – Baron of the Exchequer, 1807–23. (Occupational category VI.29; venue 1.) Also purchased lands in Yorkshire.
Address 'Formerly Gower Street, then Bedford Square, Middlesex' (probate calendar); also Moor Grange, East Riding – he built it in 1813.
Father (Revd) George Wood (1704–81), Vicar of Roystone near Barnsley, Yorkshire.
Mother Jane, daughter of John Matson of Roystone.
Education 'In Yorkshire'; Middle Temple (called 1775).
Marriage To Sarah (1754–18 December 1839; d.s.p.), surname and marriage date unknown.
Religion Anglican: buried in Temple Church.
Public MP (Pro-Pitt) Haslemere, 1796–1806; knighted in 1807.
Miscellaneous Was apprenticed to a solicitor and then read for the Bar. Was a Special Pleader on the Northern Circuit and was later known as 'the father of the English Bar' – Ellenborough, Erskine, and Scarlett were among his pupils. Appointed Serjeant-at-Law in 1807, and then a judge, and was a Bencher (1802) and Reader (1806) of the Middle Temple. He was said to be worth £300,000 at his death (*ODNB*).
References *ODNB; GM,* 1824, vol. I, p. 645.

1824/30 **Name** **Dulany, Daniel**
Dates c. 1750, Annapolis, Md.–12 August 1824.
Probate £160,000 'within province' (PCC).
Occupation Probably a merchant trading with America, although he is not listed in any directory. (If so, then occupational category IV.19; venue 1 or 2?) His extraordinary address – 11 Downing Street – is also a mystery.
Address Lived at 11 Downing Street, Middlesex.
Father Daniel Dulany (1722–97), a leading barrister and politician in Maryland before the Revolution (*ODNB*). He was also an investor in the Baltimore Ironworks Company. His property was confiscated after the Revolution since he was regarded as neutral or pro-British.
Mother Rebecca (1724–1822), daughter of Benjamin Tasker, President of the Governor's Council of Maryland.
Education Unknown.
Marriage Unknown.
Religion The father was buried as an Anglican.
Public None known.
Miscellaneous No information about his career could be found in any source or directory. The fact that his estate was sworn 'within province', i.e. of the Canterbury Prerogative Court, suggests that he had property overseas, presumably in America.
References *GM,* 1824, vol. II, p. 189; *ODNB* for father; online sources.

1824/31 **Name** **Ewart, William**
Dates 26 February 1763, Troqueer, Kirkcudbrightshire–6 (or 8) October 1823.

Probate £180,000 (PCC).
Occupation Foreign merchant (senior partner, Ewart, Ruston & Co.), a general commission merchant dealing especially with America and the East Indies, in Liverpool. (Occupational category IV.19; venue 5.)
Address Lived in Liverpool.
Father (Revd) John Ewart (c. 1716–5 September 1799), Church of Scotland minister of Troqueer and author.
Mother Mary, daughter of Joseph Corrie of Carlingwark, Kirkudbrightshire.
Education Unknown.
Marriage To Margaret (marriage date unknown), daughter of Christopher Jacques of Yorkshire. (Four sons, three daughters.) His son William (1798–1869) is in the *ODNB* as a 'politician' (see 1869/33; left £180,000).
Religion Church of Scotland.
Public None known.
Miscellaneous He was the godfather of William Ewart Gladstone (1809–98), the Prime Minister, who was named for him. He was one of many successful Scottish-born merchants trading overseas from Liverpool, as was Gladstone's father.
References *ODNB* for son; *BLG*, 1914.

Name **Smith, Thomas** 1824/32
Dates c. 1745–6 December 1824.
Probate £180,000 (PCC).
Occupation Apparently a plantation owner in Jamaica. These are mentioned in his will. (If so, occupational category I; venue 29). His brother, Sir John Smith(-Burges), 1st Baronet (c. 1734–24 April 1803) was 'for upwards of thirty years a director of the East India Company'; and was a lieutenant colonel of the 3rd Battalion of the East India Volunteers. He received a baronetcy in 1793. Since he died without surviving children, Thomas Smith probably also inherited some of his property. His widow Margaret remarried the 4th Earl Powlett.
Address Lived at New Norfolk Street, Middlesex and Bearsted Lodge near Bognor, Sussex.
Father John Smith, 'merchant' of Lambeth, Surrey.
Mother Mary, daughter of Griffin Ransom of Lambeth.
Education Unknown.
Marriage To Susannah Mackworth Praed (d.s.p., 13 October 1856), daughter of William Mackworth Praed, MP (marriage date unknown).
Religion Anglican: gave a shield to St John's Anglican Chapel, Bognor.
Public None known.
Miscellaneous In his will, he states that Spencer, Earl Compton was his great-nephew and that he was a relative of the Earl of Mayo, but little more could be found about him.
References *GM*, 1825, vol. I, p. 93; *BLG*, for Mackworth Praed; *Burke's Complete Baronetcy* for brother.

WEALTH-HOLDERS, 1825

1825/1 **Name** **Roberts, Thomas**

Dates c. 1747–5 May 1825.

Probate £350,000 (PCC).

Occupation Stockbroker in London – 'For many years a member of the Stock Exchange' (*GM*). (Occupational category IV.23; venue 1.)

Address 'Formerly of the Stock Exchange, then of Russell Square, Middlesex, and then of Hampstead' (probate calendar).

Father Unknown.

Mother Unknown.

Education Unknown.

Marriage Unknown.

Religion Unknown. He was a governor of Christ's Hospital, the charity public school, which was connected with the Church of England.

Public None known.

Miscellaneous A very wealthy stockbroker, but nothing more could be learned about him.

References *GM,* 1825, vol. I, p. 476.

1825/2 **Name** **Robertson, Ebenezer**

Dates Unknown – probated September 1825.

Probate £100,000 (PCC).

Occupation A former planter or merchant in Jamaica, but nothing could be learned about his career. He then lived in Beverley, Yorkshire. (Occupational category I? Venue 29.)

Address 'Kingston, Jamaica and Beverley [East Riding], Yorkshire' (probate calendar).

Father Unknown. He might have had a Scottish background, judging from the number of exact namesakes with links to Scotland listed on Family Search.

Mother Unknown.

Education Unknown.

Marriage Unknown.

Religion Unknown.

Public None known.

Miscellaneous He left £250 in his will for the poor patients of the Lying-in Hospital in Beverley, Yorkshire. Its income continued to be paid until 1911 (*VCH Yorkshire: East Riding,* vol. 6, 1989, pp. 161–70). He appears to have owned the Craig Mill Plantation, St George parish, Jamaica, the mortgage of which he assigned in December 1801 to a Thomas Jameson: see Kenneth E. Ingram, *Sources for the History of the West Indies* (2000), p. 243.

References Probate calendar and above sources only.

Name **Ley, Henry** 1825/3
Dates 1744–18 (29?) December 1824.
Probate £180,000 (PCC).
Occupation Brother of John Ley (1733–1814) (see 1814/28), who left £125,000, and was Deputy-Clerk of the House of Commons for forty-seven years. John Ley was unmarried, and his brother presumably inherited much of his estate. (Occupational category VI.31? Venue 2.) Henry Ley does not appear to have had any occupation of his own, although he is noted as having lived 'formerly' in Exeter. He was probably also a landowner. In 1883, J. H. F. Ley of Trehill, Devon, owned 2,996 acres worth £4,500 p.a. in Devon.
Address 'Formerly of Exeter and then of Trehill [near Exeter], Devonshire' (probate calendar).
Father John Ley (d. 1775) of Trehill, Devon. (Second son.)
Mother Grace (d. 1772), daughter of Henry Gandy of Exeter.
Education Unknown.
Marriage In 1773, to Mary (d. 1834), daughter of (Captain) Smith, RN. (One son, who married a daughter of the 7th Marquess of Tweedale.)
Religion Presumably Anglican.
Public None known.
Miscellaneous See above. It is possible that the family had mercantile or legal interests in Exeter.
References *GM,* 1824, vol. II, p. 645; *BLG,* 1914.

Name **Baker, Sir Edward, 1st Baronet** (né Littlehales) 1825/4
Dates Unknown–4 March 1825.
Probate £160,000 (PCC).
Occupation Inherited the building fortune of his cousin Peter William Baker (c. 1756–1815) (see 1815/13), who left £150,000. This man's father, William Baker, constructed Baker Street and other parts of London. (Occupational category II.10; venue 2.) Sir Edward Baker was a lieutenant colonel in the Army and apparently a landowner, although his successor in 1883 could not be traced in Bateman. He changed his name from Littlehales to Baker in 1817.
Address 'Formerly of Dublin and then of Ranston near Blandford, Dorset' (probate calendar). He also had a seat at Ashcombe, Sussex.
Father Baker John Littlehales (1732–30 October 1785), barrister of Mousley, Surrey and Lincoln's Inn.
Mother Maria (d. November 1796), daughter of Bendall Martyn.
Education Unknown.
Marriage In 1805, to Lady Elizabeth (d. 1857), daughter of William, 2nd Duke of Leinster. (Four sons, four daughters.)
Religion Anglican.
Public Created a baronet in 1802, possibly owing to his ducal connections.
Miscellaneous He served as an army officer for most of his adult life.
References *BP; GM,* 1825, vol. I, p. 464.

1825/5 **Name Cooper, Isaac**
Dates Unknown – probated May 1825.
Probate £120,000 (PCC).
Occupation 'Stockbroker' (probate calendar) in London. (Occupational category IV.23; venue 1.)
Address 'Of the Stock Exchange, City of London, and Stockwell, Surrey' (probate calendar).
Father Unknown.
Mother Unknown.
Education Unknown.
Marriage Unknown.
Religion Unknown.
Public None known.
Miscellaneous He does not appear to be listed in any directory under his own name.
References Probate calendar only.

1825/6 **Name Hollingsworth, William**
Dates c. 1752–19 July 1825, at Nine Elms, Battersea.
Probate £140,000 (PCC).
Occupation A lime merchant ('Hollingswoth & Pass, lime merchants, of Nine Elms, Battersea', 1802 directory) in Battersea. (Occupational category IV.21? Venue 2.)
Address Of Nine Elms, Battersea – no other address is given.
Father Unknown.
Mother Unknown.
Education Unknown.
Marriage Unknown.
Religion Unknown.
Public None known.
Miscellaneous It is not clear whether he was also engaged in manufacturing lime, which presumably would have been used chiefly in making mortar for construction purposes, or was purely a merchant.
References *GM,* 1825, vol. II, p. 93.

1825/7 **Name Everett, John Gale**
Dates Unknown–14 August 1825, Biddesden near Andover, Hampshire.
Probate £100,000 (PCC).
Occupation Probably a clothier of Heytesbury near Warminster, Wiltshire. (Occupational categories II.8? and IV.16? Venue 13.) He is described as a 'clothier' and the owner of a grist mill near Heytesbury, in *VCH Wiltshire,* vol. 8 (1965), pp. 61–74. A 'clothier' was presumably a woollen manufacturer. He is also described as a 'banker in Warminster' in *GM,* 1830, vol. II, p. 87. His relatives are also described in *HP* as bankers.
Address Heytesbury, near Warminster, Wiltshire.

Father Probably William Everett (d. 1792), corn merchant of Heytesbury, Wiltshire. John Gale Everett was probably the brother of Thomas Everett (1740–1810) of Biddesden House, an MP from 1796–1810. He is described in *HP* as a 'Blackwell Hall factor' in Lawrence Lane in the City of London – that is, a clothing wholesaler in London.

Mother Probably Alice, daughter of Thomas Gale of Crawlbush, or Crawlboys, in the parish of Ludgershall near Andover.

Education Unknown.

Marriage Unknown; he had a son named Joseph.

Religion Presumably Anglican. A nephew was an Anglican clergyman.

Public None known.

Miscellaneous He voted in the 1772 Wiltshire election, indicating that he must have been born prior to c. 1751.

References *GM,* 1825, vol. II, p. 189; 1830, vol. II, p. 87; *HP* for Thomas Everett; *BLG.*

Name **Sutton, Sir John** 1825/8

Dates c. 1758–8 August 1825 at Ramsgate.

Probate £100,000 (PCC).

Occupation 'Admiral of the White' (probate calendar). (Occupational category VI.31.)

Address Lived at Ham Common, Surrey.

Father Thomas Sutton (d. 1789) of Moulsey, Surrey, High Sheriff of Surrey. Sir John Sutton's brother, Sir Thomas Sutton (c. 1755–1813), created a baronet in 1806, was an MP in 1812–13.

Mother Jane, daughter of Sir Thomas Hankey, Alderman of London.

Education Unknown.

Marriage In 1797, to (Hon.) Frances, daughter of Beaumont, 2nd Baron Hotham and sister of (Vice-Admiral) Sir Henry Hotham.

Religion Anglican.

Public Created KCB, 1815.

Miscellaneous Lieutenant in 1778 – served in the American Revolution; captain in 1782. Was with Nelson at Corsica and with Jervis in 1797. Captain of the Channel Fleet, 1801. Rear-Admiral, 1804; Vice-Admiral, 1809; Admiral, 1819; Admiral of the White, 1825. Served as Commander-in-Chief, Halifax. He clearly had wealthy relatives and might well have inherited from them, thus augmenting his naval income.

References *GM,* 1825, vol. II, p. 563.

Name **Vivian, Alice** (née Vivian) 1825/9

Dates 1752, Kea, near Truro, Cornwall–18 August 1825.

Probate £140,000 (PCC).

Occupation Presumably benefited from the family's copper-mining and smelting fortune and was also a landowner. (Occupational category II.2 and I; venue 13.) In 1883, Lord Vivian owned 8,269 acres worth £8,719 p.a. in Cornwall, Anglesey, etc.

Address Lived at Penkalenick near Truro, Cornwall.
Father Matthew Vivian of Penelewey, Cornwall.
Mother Jane Bennett (Family Search).
Education Unknown.
Marriage In 1771, to her cousin, (Revd) John Vivian (1743–27 December 1801) of Camborne and Truro, Cornwall. (At least one son, John, a barrister who died in 1817.) Their uncle, James Vivian, was High Sheriff of Cornwall in 1772. They were almost certainly cousins of John Vivian (1750–1826), in the *ODNB* as a 'copper mining and smelting entrepreneur', who founded the well-known mining concern.
Religion Anglican.
Public None known.
Miscellaneous See above. She was the sister of John Vivian (see 1828/21), who left £180,000.
References *BLG,* 1871; *GM,* 1825, vol. II, p. 188; online source as above.

1825/10 **Name** **Hordern, James**
Dates Unknown–3 April 1825, The Old Deanery, Wolverhampton.
Probate £120,000 (PCC).
Occupation Banker in Newport, Shropshire and possibly then Wolverhampton. (Occupational category IV.16; venue 18 or 8.) He founded his banking business with his brother Joseph in Newport, Shropshire in 1791 (Hordern & Hill). It then became known as the Shropshire Banking Company and was absorbed by Lloyd's Bank in 1789. It financed, in particular, the iron industry and canals in Shropshire.
Address Oxley Manor, Shropshire (near Wolverhampton), and then The Old Deanery, Wolverhampton. These addresses suggest that he conducted business chiefly from Wolverhampton in later life.
Father Joseph Hordern (d. March 1807), a 'yeoman' of Bushbury, Shropshire. (Second surviving son.)
Mother Margaret Eggington (d. 1812) of Featherstone.
Education Unknown.
Marriage To Jane, surname and marriage date unknown. (Two sons, at least one daughter.)
Religion Anglican: buried in Bushbury Church.
Public High Sheriff of Staffordshire in 1823.
Miscellaneous His parents were married in 1751, so he must have been born after that date.
References *GM,* 1825, vol. I, p. 477. Some of the family are listed in *BLG,* 1846.

1825/11 **Name** **Hall, William**
Dates 1740–probated May 1825.
Probate £120,000 (PCC).
Occupation A 'brewer' (PROB 11) in Oxford. (Occupational category III.12; venue 14.) Described as 'the Oxford brewer' who 'improved' Barton Abbey' in

1811–13 (*VCH Oxfordshire*, vol. 12, 1990, pp. 117–20). *Jackson's Oxford Journal*, the local newspaper, was also owned by a family named Hall.
Address 'St Thomas's, Oxford and Barton Abbey [near Steeple Ashton], Oxfordshire' (probate calendar).
Father William Hall (1682–1769). (Third son.)
Mother Hester, surname unknown.
Education Unknown.
Marriage To Elizabeth, daughter of William Green; marriage date unknown. (One son, one daughter.) The son, Henry, d. 1862 (see 1863/29) married the daughter of Lord Bridport; she was the granddaughter of Nelson's brother. Henry's son, Alexander William Hall (1838–1919) of Barton Abbey, was Conservative MP in 1874–80 and 1885–92. He is described in Stenton as 'a brewer at Oxford'.
Religion Anglican; owned the advowson of Steeple Barton Church.
Public None known.
Miscellaneous The family was prominent in Oxford for several generations. This man, however, did not attend Oxford or Cambridge.
References *BLG*, 1914, 1871; Stenton 1886–1918.

Name **Hill, Thomas** 1825/12
Dates Unknown – probated June 1825.
Probate £120,000 (PCC).
Occupation Possibly a nail manufacturer at Old Swinford near Stourbridge, Worcestershire, or perhaps a glass manufacturer there (Dennis glass house, Amblecote, Old Swinford [*VCH Worcestershire*, vol. 3, 1913, pp. 213–23). (If the former, occupational category II.11; venue 18.)
Address Lived at Dennis, Old Swinford, Staffordshire, near Stourbridge. (Old Swinford is now, it seems, in Worcestershire.)
Father Unknown.
Mother Unknown.
Education Unknown.
Marriage Unknown.
Religion Presumably Anglican as he apparently appointed the vicar of Old Swinford (online sources).
Public None known.
Miscellaneous Described as a 'nailmaker' in online sources, although there is no confirmation and his name makes precise identification difficult. Family Search lists a Thomas Hill, born 1773, the son of William Hill and Anne Jones, of Old Swinford.
References Probate calendar and above sources only.

Name **Maynard, Anthony Lax** (né Lax) 1825/13
Dates 30 April 1742–2 (3) July 1825, Chesterfield.
Probate £100,000 (PCC).
Occupation Apparently a landowner in the Chesterfield area and also in the

Cleveland area of Yorkshire. (Occupational category I.) There is no trace of a successor named Lax or Maynard in Bateman.

Address Of Chesterfield, Derbyshire, and Harsley Hall, Yorkshire.

Father John Lax (1705–10 December 1783) of Eryholme (near Darlington, North Riding), Yorkshire. (First son.) He was granted a Coat of Arms in 1775.

Mother Sarah (d. 18 April 1812), daughter of John Jefferson. She was the granddaughter of John Maynard of Kirklevington and Yarmouth, Yorkshire; he evidently left his property to Anthony Lax, who changed his name to Maynard.

Education Unknown.

Marriage In 1766, to Dorothy (d.s.p., 1811), daughter of (Revd) Ralph Heathcote, Rector of Morton, Derbyshire.

Religion Anglican.

Public JP, DL, Derbyshire 'upward of fifty years' (*GM*).

Miscellaneous His nephew, Charles Maynard, who succeeded him, was a 'pioneer of the Cleveland [Yorkshire] ironstone' mining industry. Presumably this was on the basis of lands owned by Anthony Lax Maynard.

References *GM,* 1825, vol. II, p. 93; *BLG,* 1846.

1825/14 **Name** **Hulbert, George Redmond**

Dates Baptised 30 January 1774, St Nicholas Church, Rochester–c. August 1825, near Southampton.

Probate £120,000 (PCC).

Occupation Naval agent in Jamaica, Bermuda and Nova Scotia, where he was a Prize Agent, 1812–14. (Occupational category VI.31; venue 29.) Hulbert 'acted as an admiral's secretary and prize agent in the early nineteenth century' (National Maritime Museum online catalogue). He was secretary to Sir John Borlase Warren in 1804 on the North American Station and with Admiral Bartholomew Samuel Rowley on the Jamaica Station, 1808–9. He was then Prize Agent at Halifax, 1812–14. He afterwards bought a country seat near Derby.

Address Lived at Aston Lodge, six miles south of Derby but described in PROB 11 as 'of Southampton, Hampshire'.

Father George Hulbert (Family Search); he 'ran a local guesthouse' in Rochester 'frequented by naval officers' (Gutridge).

Mother Mary, surname unknown (Family Search).

Education Unknown.

Marriage Unknown. According to Family Search, a George Redmond Hulbert and a Mary Daintry married on 27 May 1812 in Prestbury, Cheshire.

Religion Unknown; presumably Anglican.

Public None known.

Miscellaneous He appears to have profited considerably from prize money of captured ships during the Napoleonic Wars. No other source of wealth could be traced. He died in a coaching accident near Southampton. One online source states that 'he joined Nelson's navy and earned large sums of money working as a Naval Prize Agent in the West Indies'. It also notes that in 1825 Hulbert's widow sold The Lodge to the canal entrepreneur James Sutton (www.astonontrenthistory.org.uk).

References Anthony Gutridge, 'George Redmond Hulbert: A Prize Agent on the North America Station 1812–1814', *Bermuda Journal of Archaeology and Martime History*, vol. 2 (1990), pp. 105–26; Anthony Gutridge, 'George Redmond Hulbert: Prize Agent at Nova Scotia, 1812–14', *Mariners's Mirror*, vol. 87 (2001), pp. 30–42; *GM*, 1825, vol. II, p. 285; online source.

Name **Fairlie, William** 1825/15
Dates 15 September 1754, Kilmarnock (Family Search)–19 January 1825.
Probate £300,000, 'within province' (PCC).
Occupation East India merchant and agent, 'formerly of Calcutta' (*GM*). ('Fairlie, Bonham & Co., East India agents, 9 Broad Street Buildings, City of London', 1822 directory.) (Occupational category IV.19; venue 1 and 29.) According to Michael Greenberg (*British Trade and the Opening of China 1800–42* [1951, repr. 1969], pp. 35–6), Fairlie and John Fergusson went to India in the 1780s. During the 1790s they were in partnership with David Reid, who moved to Canton. Fairlie's Calcutta firm was known successively as Fairlie Fergusson & Co., Fairlie Gilmore & Co. and Fergusson Clark & Co. Fairlie returned home in 1812, the London house of David Scott & Co. becoming Fairlie Bonham & Co. (and, in 1832, Fairlie, Clark, Innes & Co.). David Scott, a director of the East India Company, was an MP; Henry Bonham, one of the directors of the East India Dock Company, was also an MP. Fairlie was a major figure in the Calcutta mercantile world and has a street named after him in that city.
Address 'Of [9] Broad Street Buildings, City of London, and of Park Crescent, Portland Place, Middlesex' (probate calendar).
Father John Fairlie (1717–11 May 1757) of Irvine, near Kilmarnock. (Third son.)
Mother Agnes, surname unknown, of Bruntwood. A John Fairlie married an Agnes Muir in 1741 in Kilmarnock (Family Search).
Education Unknown.
Marriage In 1798, in Fort William, Calcutta, to Margaret (d. 1845), daughter of John Ogilvy of Myrtle. (Three sons, two daughters.)
Religion Presumably Church of Scotland.
Public None known.
Miscellaneous An important Scottish-born merchant in Calcutta and then in London.
References *GM*, 1825, vol. I, p. 188; *BLG*, 1937; online source as above.

Name **Wray, Lady Esther** (Hester [GM]) (née Summers) 1825/16
Dates c. 1735/6)–1 February 1825 at Summer Castle near Lincoln.
Probate £120,000 (PCC).
Occupation Landed. (Occupational category I.) At her death her lands passed to her husband's nephew, the son of John Dalton. In 1883, John Dalton of Ripon owned 5,600 acres worth £8,037 p.a. in Lincolnshire and the North Riding. She apparently inherited her husband's 'large estates' in Lincolnshire, Yorkshire and Norfolk.
Address Lived at Pall Mall and at Summer Castle, Lincolnshire.

Father James Summer.
Mother Unknown.
Education Unknown.
Marriage Around 1760, to Sir Cecil Wray, 13th Baronet (1734–10 January 1805) of Fillingham, Lincolnshire; MP (Radical pro-Whig) East Retford, 1768–80; Westminster, 1782–death (d.s.p.).
Religion Anglican.
Public None known.
Miscellaneous It is not clear what, if anything, she inherited from her father or other relatives.
References *ODNB* for husband; *GM*, 1825, vol. I, p. 477.

1825/17 **Name** **Buggin, Sir George**
Dates c. 1759–12 April 1825, at Great Cumberland Place.
Probate £100,000 (PCC).
Occupation Probably a West India merchant of Crutched Friars, City of London, or the relative of one, but the source of his fortune is very obscure, as is information about him, despite being a knight. The 1793 directory lists a Barrington Buggin, 'West India merchant', of Cowper's Row, Crutched Friars, City of London. Sir George was presumably a relative but is not listed directly. (If so, occupational category IV.19; venue 1.)
Address Lived at Great Cumberland Place, Middlesex, and Wellington Place, Tunbridge Wells.
Father Unknown; nothing about the background of this man could be traced.
Mother Unknown.
Education Unknown.
Marriage First, unknown, though possibly Jane Tapps, who married a George Buggin in Marylebone in 1790 (Family Search); second, in 1815, to Cecilia Letitia (1793–1873), daughter of Arthur Saunders, 2nd Earl of Arran (d.s.p). Cecilia married, second, in 1831, Augustus, Duke of Sussex, sixth son of King George III, and, in 1840, was created Duchess of Inverness in her own right! The marriage with the Duke of Sussex was legal but contrary to the Royal Marriages Act.
Religion Anglican.
Public Knighted in 1797.
Miscellaneous An extremely curious case. Nothing could be learned about his background, the real source of his fortune, or why he was knighted. The dukedom created for his widow is also extraordinary.
References *GM*, 1825, vol. I, p. 475.

1825/18 **Name** **Meyrick, Owen Putland**
Dates c. 1752–24 March 1825, Upper Harley Street, Middlesex.
Probate £140,000 (PCC).
Occupation Landowner. (Occupational category I.) He was Lord of the Manor of Morden, Surrey, which he inherited from his mother, was said to have an income of £11,000 p.a. from his Welsh lands, and was reputedly worth £600,000 'in

funded property' (*GM;* this was a great exaggeration). In 1883, Sir George Tapps-Jervis-Meyrick, Baronet, who apparently inherited his lands, owned 21,201 acres worth £16,641 p.a. in Anglesey and Hampshire.

Address Bodorgan, Anglesey and Upper Harley Street, Middlesex.

Father Owen Meyrick (1705–March 1790) of Bodorgan, Anglesey, MP, 1761–70, landowner.

Mother Hester, 'a wealthy heiress', daughter of John Putland of London.

Education Westminster School and BNC, Oxford.

Marriage In 1774, to Clara, daughter of Richard Garth of Morden, Surrey. (One daughter – her husband later took the name of Meyrick.)

Religion Anglican.

Public None known.

Miscellaneous A wealthy but rather obscure landowner.

References *GM,* 1825, vol. I, p. 471.

Name **Whittingstall, Elizabeth** 1825/19

Dates Unknown – probated April 1825.

Probate £600,000 (PCC).

Occupation Brewery family; she apparently inherited her father's corn mills and most of her brother George's brewing interests (see 1822/26). He left £500,000 from his brewery and corn mills in Watford. (Occupational category III.12; venue 3.) The family also apparently has maltsting interests. It is possible, however, that she was the widow or daughter of George Whittingstall.

Address Watford and Hitchin, Hertfordshire.

Father Apparently Henry Whittingstall, corn miller in Hitchin, Hertfordshire, but see above.

Mother Unknown.

Education Unknown.

Marriage She is described as a 'spinster' in her will, although *BLG* (1952) states that she had been married to Edmund Fearnley, who predeceased her. This is almost certainly incorrect.

Religion Unknown, presumably Anglican. She left money to almshouses in Hitchin, Hertfordshire.

Public None known.

Miscellaneous She must have been one of the wealthiest women in England in her own right but is virtually unknown. It is possible that there is a confusion here between George Whittingstall's sister, widow and daughter, and further research is needed to properly identify her.

References *BLG,* 1914.

Name **Glastonbury, 1st Baron, James Grenville** 1825/20

Dates 6 July 1742, St Giles-in-the-Field, Middlesex–26 April 1825, Hill Street, Berkeley Square, Middlesex.

Probate £250,000 (PCC).

Occupation Landowner and government office-holder. (Occupational category

I.) His property came to his kinsman (Very Revd) George Neville Grenville, Dean of Windsor (d. 1854). In 1883, it was owned by Ralph Neville-Grenville of Burleigh Court, who owned 3,434 acres worth £5,770 p.a. in Somerset.

Address Of Burleigh Court near Glastonbury, Somerset and Hill Street, Berkeley Square, Middlesex.

Father (Rt. Hon.) James Grenville (1715–14 September 1783), MP of Burleigh Court. His uncle was the 1st Duke of Buckingham and Chandos, and his grandmother was the Countess Temple.

Mother Mary (d. 1757), daughter of James Smyth of South Elkington, Lincolnshire.

Education Eton; Christ Church, Oxford. Entered Lincoln's Inn in 1760.

Marriage Unmarried.

Religion Anglican.

Public MP (Whig) Thirsk, 1765–8; Buckingham, 1770–90; Buckinghamshire, 1790–7. Was a Commissioner of the Board of Trade, 1784–death, and a Lord of the Treasury, 1782–3. PC, 1780; Created baron 1797.

Miscellaneous One of the powerful Grenville family. It is not clear how much he inherited and how much was made from his official positions. He does not have an entry in the *ODNB*.

References *GM,* 1825, vol. II, p. 479.

1825/21 **Name** **Gunman, Sarah Hussey** (née Hussey-Delaval)

Dates Unknown – probated May 1825.

Probate £120,000 (PCC).

Occupation Widow of James Gunman of Dover, Kent (d. 29 June 1824; see 1824/17, left £120,000), apparently a merchant in Dover, but this isn't certain.

Address Lived at Upper Seymour Street, Portman Square at death.

Father Edward Hussey-Delaval of Seaton Delavale in Northumberland and of Doddington, Lincolnshire, landowner. He also owned property in Coventry and Worcestershire.

Mother Unknown.

Education Unknown.

Marriage In 1805, to James Gunman (see 1824/17, left £120,000). The property came to (Colonel) George Jarvis (d. 1851). She left Doddington and property in Warwickshire to her friend (and reputed lover) Colonel George Ralph Payne Jarvis (d. 14 June 1851) (www.lincolnshire.gov.uk).

Religion Presumably Anglican.

Public None known.

Miscellaneous She probably inherited from both her father and husband.

References Probate calendar only.

1825/22 **Name** **Morgan, Mary**

Dates Unknown – probated May 1825.

Probate £160,000 (PCC).

Occupation Unknown. Her will gives few clues as to the source of her wealth.

In her will she mentions her sisters Sarah Eyles and Harriet (Morgan?) and her brothers Francis and Thomas Morgan, but none could be definitively traced. A Francis Morgan was a 'millowner' in St Petersburg, Russia, a partner in 1792 with Charles Baird (1766–1843), an ironmaster, gun manufacturer and pioneer of steam machinery in Russia (*ODNB*). But it is not clear if this was the same man.
Address Lived at Upper Seymour Street, Portman Square, Middlesex.
Father Unknown.
Mother Unknown.
Education Unknown.
Marriage Unmarried.
Religion Unknown.
Public None known.
Miscellaneous Nothing more is known of her. Possibly she inherited from her father, but he could not be traced.
References Will (PROB 11 online).

Name **Holland, Lady Harriet** (née Bisshopp) 1825/23
Dates 1744–1825.
Probate £500,000 (PCC).
Occupation Landowner, and also inherited architectural and building money. (Occupational category I.) She was 'said to have an income of £18,000 p.a.' upon her marriage to Sir Nathaniel Holland. Some or all of her fortune came to her nephew, Robert, Earl of Cardigan. In 1883, the Countess of Cardigan (in her own right) owned 15,724 acres worth £35,357 p.a.
Address Lived at Cranbury, near Winchester, Hampshire, and at Piccadilly Terrace, Middlesex.
Father Sir Cecil Bisshopp, 6th Baronet (d. 15 June 1778), MP, of Parham Park, Sussex, whose family was connected with several of our wealth-holders.
Mother Ann (d. 1749), daughter of Hugh Boscawen, Viscount Falmouth.
Education Unknown.
Marriage First, in 1766, to Thomas Dummer (c. 1739–81), MP, 1768–81, of Cranbury, Hampshire (d.s.p.); second, in 1783, to Sir Nathaniel Dance (late Holland), 1st Baronet (MP, 1790–1811), artist and son of George Dance, architect and Clerk of Works to the City of London (see 1811/5, left £250,000) (d.s.p.).
Religion Anglican.
Public None known.
Miscellaneous A wealthy heiress who became even wealthier.
References *ODNB* for husband; *HP* for relatives; *BP*.

Name **Walsham, Charles** 1825/24
Dates c. 1752–2 June 1825 at Green Street, Grosvenor Square, Middlesex.
Probate £100,000 (PCC).
Occupation Distiller and brandy merchant in the City of London (Walsham & Co., distillers of 58–9 Aldersgate, 1803 directory; Walsham & Bishop, distillers and brandy merchants of 12 Finsbury Place, City, 1817 directory). (Occupational

category III.13 and IV.21; venue 1.)
Address 'Formerly of Ashted Lodge, Surrey, and then of Green Street, Grosvenor Square, Middlesex' (probate calendar).
Father Unknown.
Mother Unknown.
Education Unknown.
Marriage Unknown.
Religion Unknown.
Public None known.
Miscellaneous Was active as a distiller before 1795. Whether he was primarily a distiller or a merchant is unclear. In 1813, at the trial of a porter in his employ convicted of stealing a pint of brandy from him and his partners (James Bishop Senior, James Bishop Junior, and George Bishop), he described himself as 'a distiller, and wine manufacturer' (www.oldbaileyonline.org).
References *GM,* 1825, vol. I, p. 572.

1825/25 **Name** **Vernon, John**
Dates Unknown–30 April 1825 at 3 Tilney Street, Middlesex.
Probate £120,000 (PCC).
Occupation Either a KC or a solicitor – there is an ambiguity. The 1797 and 1805 directories list a John Vernon Junior, KC, of Vernon, Elderton & Vernon, 10 Lincoln's Inn Fields. The 1820 directory lists John Vernon and William Francklin (sic), solicitors to the Mint, of 10 Lincoln's Inn, New Square. No John Vernon is listed as a lawyer after 1824. (In either case, occupational category VI.29; venue 1.)
Address 'Of Lincoln's Inn' (probate calendar) and 'Buckhurst Hill, Berkshire' (*GM*). The London directory lists him as of 21 Bedford Square in 1811 and of 3 Tilney Street in 1819.
Father Unknown. The Lincoln's Inn Admission Books list a John Vernon, only son of John Vernon of Southampton Buildings, Chancery Lane, as entering in December 1770 and another John Vernon, born around 1758, the eldest son of George Vernon of Clontarf (or Clontarf Castle), Ireland, as entering in 1774. It is not clear whether either was identical to this man.
Mother Unknown.
Education Unknown.
Marriage Unknown.
Religion Unknown, presumably Anglican.
Public None known.
Miscellaneous His exact identity remains to be ascertained.
References *GM,* 1825, vol. I, p. 475.

1825/26 **Name** **Hoare, Samuel**
Dates 29 May 1751–13 (14?) July 1825.
Probate £250,000 (PCC).
Occupation Banker – partner in Barnett, Hill, Barnett & Hoare of Lombard

Street, City of London. (Occupational category IV.16; venue 1.)
Address 'Formerly of Lombard Street in the City of London and then Hampstead, Middlesex' (probate calendar).
Father Samuel Hoare (1716–30 August 1796), Quaker merchant from Cork who then became a merchant (Gurnell, Hoare, Harman & Co.) in the City of London. (First surviving son.)
Mother Grizell (she died 1756), daughter of Jonathan Gurnell, merchant of Ealing.
Education At a 'seminary under John Riveaux of Grange Road' until the age of fourteen.
Marriage First, in 1776, to Sarah (d. 1783), daughter of Samuel Gurney of Norwich. (One son, one daughter.) Second, in 1788, to Hannah (d. 1856), daughter of Henry Sterry of Hatton Gardens, London. (One son, three daughters.)
Religion Quaker family and still a Quaker at the time of his first marriage, but was not listed in the *Quaker Monitor* as a member at his death.
Public None known.
Miscellaneous The founder of the well-known bank, later merged with Lloyd's. He was apprenticed to Henry Gurney in Norwich and was later a prominent banker in Lombard Street. He was the ancestor of Sir Samuel Hoare and other prominent members of this family.
References *GM,* 1825, vol. II, p. 92; *BP* and *BLG; ODNB* for relatives.

Name **Moore, Thomas Joseph** 1825/27
Dates c. 1755–20 June 1825.
Probate £100,000 (PCC).
Occupation 'Currier' (Thomas and Joseph Moore, curriers, of 412 Strand, 1793 directory; 'currier and leather cutler', at 14 Newcastle Street, Strand, 1817 directory). (Occupational category II.12? Venue 2; this assumes that Moore was primarily engaged in actually dressing leather and making leather goods, not primarily in retailing leather goods.)
Address 'Formerly Newcastle Street, Strand, Middlesex, and then Stratford House, Turnham Green, Middlesex' (probate calendar).
Father Unknown.
Mother Unknown.
Education Unknown.
Marriage Unknown.
Religion Unknown.
Public None known.
Miscellaneous Nothing more is known of him, or how he made so much money – possibly through government contracts during the Napoleonic Wars, although this is pure speculation.
References Probate calendar and above sources only.

Name **Smith, John** 1825/28
Dates c. 1760–21 July 1825.
Probate £100,000 (PCC).

Occupation 'Coffin maker and undertaker' of 4 John Street, Oxford Street, 1817 directory. (If primarily a coffin maker, his occupational category is II.11; if primarily an undertaker, V.28? Venue 2.)
Address 'John Street, Oxford Street, Middlesex, and Nottingham Terrace, New Road, [Marylebone], Middlesex' (probate calendar and *GM*).
Father Unknown. Obviously, in view of his name, he is not the easiest person in the world to trace.
Mother Unknown.
Education Unknown.
Marriage Unknown. His sons and executors were named Benjamin, William and George.
Religion Unknown.
Public None known.
Miscellaneous It is not clear how he became so wealthy as either a coffin-maker or an undertaker – presumably there was much competition.
References *GM,* 1825, vol. II, p. 187.

1825/29 **Name** **Barne, Miles**
Dates 22 May 1746, Grosvenor Square–8 September 1825, Sotterley Hall, Suffolk.
Probate £400,000 (PCC).
Occupation Presumably land, as well as London mercantile and East India Company wealth. (Occupational category I?) In 1883, Frederick Barne of Sotterley Hall owned 7,642 acres worth £9,471 in Suffolk and Kent. Miles Barne's grandfather was a London merchant, and his great-grandfather was Lord Mayor of London in 1580. Barne's maternal grandfather was an official in the East India Company at Madras.
Address Sotterley Hall, near Beccles, Suffolk and May Place, Crayford, Kent.
Father Miles Barne (1718–20 December 1780), MP, 1747–67, of Sotterley Hall. (First son.)
Mother Elizabeth (d. 1747), daughter of Nathaniel Elwick of May Place, Kent, Governor of Fort St George, Madras, India.
Education Secondary schooling unknown; Peterhouse, Cambridge; entered Lincoln's Inn, 1764. Barne made the 'Grand Tour' in 1769–71.
Marriage Unmarried.
Religion Anglican.
Public MP (Tory) Dunwich, Suffolk, 1791–6. High Sheriff of Suffolk, 1790–1.
Miscellaneous His property passed to his half-brother, Michael Barne (d. 1836). Whether Miles Barne had mercantile interests is unclear.
References *HP; BLG; GM,* 1825, vol. II, p. 280.

1825/30 **Name** **Berens, Joseph**
Dates 21 February 1745–19 December 1825.
Probate £160,000 (PCC).
Occupation Merchant. Berens was a director of the South Sea Company and of

the Hudson's Bay Company and was a member of the latter's Committee from 1776 to 1795. He also owned paper mills in Kent. (Occupational venue IV.19, etc.; venues 1 and 3.) He was also a landowner. In 1883, Richard Benyon Berens of Kevington, Kent owned 3,438 acres worth £3,937 p.a. in Kent and Essex.

Address Kevington, St Mary Cray, Kent. He had lived at Hextable, Kent.

Father Herman Berens (d. 1795), a 'merchant' of London (Halsted). He was a member of the Committee of the Hudson's Bay Company, 1765–94. His father, also Herman Berens, had emigrated from Amsterdam.

Mother Regina, daughter of Stephen Riou of London. Stephen Riou, who came from a mercantile Huguenot family which had migrated from Switzerland, was a notable writer on architecture and relative of the famous Captain Edward Riou, RN, in whose will (proved after his death at the Battle of Copenhagen in 1801) our man featured: 'My dear Cousin Joseph Berens Esquire of Kivington in the County of Kent holds of mine some small matter of stock in the 3 Pr Cents reduced in his name, I believe it amounts now to two thousand Pounds 3 Pr Cents.' (Online source cited in 'References' below.)

Education Unknown.

Marriage In 1772, to Elizabeth (d. 27 April 1827), daughter of Sir Edward Hulse, 1st Baronet, a prominent physician. (Four sons, three daughters.)

Religion Anglican, but his name and ancestry obviously indicates foreign origin. Later, the family names would indicate Jewish background, but it is unlikely (but not impossible) that Dutch Jews would have had these names in the eighteenth century, and it is more likely that his father was of German Protestant background. His mother appears to have been of Huguenot descent.

Public None known.

Miscellaneous His son Joseph Berens (1773–1853), a barrister, married the daughter of Richard Benyon of the wealthy landowning family.

References *GM,* 1825, vol. II, p. 647; *BLG,* 1937; Hasted, *Kent,* vol. 2, p. 119; 'The Men Who Sailed with Captain James Cook' (online; segment on Edward Riou).

Name **Budd, Richard** 1825/31

Dates c. 1750–8 July 1824 (sic), Tunbridge Wells.

Probate £180,000 (PCC).

Occupation Stockbroker in London. (Occupational category IV.23; venue 1.)

Address 'Formerly of the Stock Exchange, and then of Russell Square, Middlesex' (probate calendar).

Father Unknown.

Mother Unknown.

Education Unknown.

Marriage Unknown.

Religion Unknown.

Public None known.

Miscellaneous He is not listed in any directory. The *ODNB* lists a Richard Budd (1746–1821), a prominent physician, who was the son of a banker in Newbury,

Berkshire, and once employed the future Lady Hamilton as a nursemaid. There is no direct evidence that he had any connection with Richard Budd, however.

References *GM,* 1824, vol. II, p. 94.

1825/32 **Name** **Hecker, John Henry**

Dates c. 1747–14 January 1825, Finsbury Square, City of London. (*Annual Register 1825,* p. 219.)

Probate £120,000 (PCC).

Occupation 'Merchant' of 17 Coleman Street, City (1793 directory) and of 47 Finsbury Square, City (1803, 1817 directories). (Occupational category IV.21? Venue 1.)

Address 'Finsbury Square' (probate calendar).

Father Unknown. The name suggests a German background.

Mother Unknown.

Education Unknown.

Marriage Unknown.

Religion Unknown.

Public None known.

Miscellaneous Nothing more could be traced about him. He left his property to Samuel Henry Teuch (c. 1780–1854), a merchant, on condition the latter affixed the surname Hecker to his name (online source).

References *GM,* 1825, vol. I, p. 187; other sources as above.

1825/33 **Name** **Jackson, Samuel**

Dates Unknown–6 March 1825 at Great Pulteney Street.

Probate £160,000 (PCC).

Occupation Probably a 'currier' of Little Windmill Street, Golden Square, Middlesex (1817 and 1822 directories). In his will, he mentions that he owned 'workshops' at Golden Square and also property at Berwick Street, Soho. (If so, occupational category II.11; venue 2.) It is also possible that he was a 'ship and insurance broker' (Jackson & Andrews, 1 Church Court, Old Jewry, City of London, 1817 directory). In his will, he notes that his 'workshops' were 'occupied' by him and a John Andrews. It is difficult, however, to see why an insurance broker in the City would need 'workshops' in Golden Square.

Address Lived at Great Pulteney Street, St James's (probate calendar).

Father Unknown.

Mother Unknown.

Education Unknown.

Marriage Unknown. The *ODNB* lists a Randle Jackson (1757–1837), barrister, the third son of Samuel Jackson of Paddington, who was educated at Oxford. It is possible that he was this man's brother.

Religion Anglican: in his will he asked to be buried in Paddington Church (see previous) with his sister and brother.

Public None known.

Miscellaneous Nothing more could be found about him.

References *GM*, 1825, vol. I, p. 284.

Name **Nash, George Augustus** 1825/34
Dates c. 1770–22 August 1825, Brighton.
Probate £100,000 (PCC).
Occupation 'Glass manufacturer' (Andrew & George Nash) of 75 Cornhill (1817 directory). He was listed as a 'merchant' there in the 1795 directory. (Occupational category II.11; venue 1.)
Address Of 'Finsbury Square and Cornhill, City of London' (probate calendar). He may have lived at Edmonton before his death.
Father Unknown.
Mother Unknown.
Education Unknown. Educated 'at Edmonton, Middlesex' (www.thepeerage.com).
Marriage In 1796, to Lydia Watson. His son (Revd) Andrew John Nash (1807–88; see 1888/78) left £157,000. His daughter Augusta (c. 1800–65) married Frederick Septimus Leighton (1800–92), a physician. Their son was Lord Leighton (1830–1916), the famous painter. Their daughter Alexandra Orr (1828–1903) is listed in the *ODNB* as a 'biographer'.
Religion Presumably Anglican: married in St Michael's, Cornhill.
Public None known.
Miscellaneous Nothing more could be traced about him.
References *GM*, 1825, vol. II, p. 190; *ODNB* for descendants.

Name **Colvin, Robert Sharp** 1825/35
Dates Unknown – probated December 1825.
Probate £120,000 (PCC).
Occupation Presumably a merchant or stockbroker, as was of 'Threadneedle Street, City of London', but there is no trace of him in any directory, 1795–1825. There was a Blackwell & Colvin, printer's ink manufacturers, but they were of Goswell Street in 1807. The *ODNB* lists a John Russell Colvin, who was connected with the London and Calcutta mercantile firm of Colvin, Bazett & Co. (Venue 1.)
Address 'Formerly of Threadneedle Street, City of London and then of Percival Street, and then of King Street, St John's Clerkenwell' (probate calendar).
Father William Colvin (*BLG*, 1914).
Mother Elizabeth, sister of William Sharp of Half Moon Street (*BLG*, 1914).
Education Unknown.
Marriage Susannah (d. 18 October 1835), daughter of James Dyson, whose family evidently owned the Booths Hill estate. (William Robinson, *The History and Antiquities of the Parish of Tottenham*, 1840, p. 74; www.turtlebunbury.com.)
Religion Unknown.
Public None known.
Miscellaneous He remains elusive. No one of this name is listed in any London directory, it would seem, despite his City address. He inherited two acres of land from his brother Beale Blackwell Colvin (d. 1817) (www.turtlebunbury.com).

References Probate calendar and above sources only.

1825/36 **Name** **Crawford, 23rd Earl of and 6th Earl of Balcarres, Alexander Lindsay**

Dates 18 January 1752, at Kilconquhar, Fifeshire–27 March 1825, at Haigh Hall near Wigan, Lancashire.

Probate £100,000 (Lancashire Record Office: Episcopal Consistory Court of Chester).

Occupation Land and mineral owner. (Occupational category I.) In 1883, the Earl of Crawford and Balcarres owned 13,480 acres worth £39,252 p.a., chiefly in Lancashire. The 23rd Earl was also a lieutenant general in the Army and Lieutenant Governor of Jamaica, 1794–1801.

Address His chief residence was Haigh Hall near Wigan.

Father James, 5th Earl of Balcarres (1691–20 February 1768). (First son.)

Mother Anne (1727–1820), daughter of Sir Robert Dalrymple of Castleton.

Education Joined the Army at fifteen.

Marriage In 1780, to Elizabeth (1759–1816), daughter of Charles Dalrymple of North Berwick. (Four sons, two daughters.) She inherited the valuable Lancashire property of the Haighs of Lancaster, with enormous colliery deposits.

Religion Originally Church of Scotland; buried as an Anglican.

Public Scottish Representative Peer, 1784–96, 1820–5. He was a Tory but favoured Catholic 'emancipation'.

Miscellaneous Was a professional army officer. He joined the Army in 1767 and was wounded at Ticonderoga in the American Revolution, where he was taken prisoner. He became a major-general in 1793, a lieutenant general in 1798 and a full general in 1803. He also served as Commander of Jersey. There are several oddities about his estate. It was probated in the Chester Consistory Court, not the PCC or York PC. This was very odd indeed for a wealthy aristocrat. As well, although he was of a famous Scottish noble family, his wealth came chiefly from Lancashire, where his chief residence was located.

References *ODNB* as 'army officer and colonial governor'.

1825/37 **Name** **McInroy, James**

Dates Unknown–12 July 1825.

Probate £172,913 (Scottish probate – these were sworn to an exact figure rather than a round number, as in England.)

Occupation Originally a sugar planter in Demerara, then a West Indies merchant in Glasgow (McInroy, Parker & Co.). (Occupational category I and IV.19; venues 29 and 10.)

Address Lived at Lude near Blair-Atholl, Perthshire, in later life.

Father Unknown.

Mother Unknown.

Education Unknown.

Marriage Unknown.

Religion Presumably Church of Scotland.

Public None known.

Miscellaneous Came to Demerara (British Guiana, now Guyana) in 1782 as a sugar planter and then became head of a firm of sugar merchants in Glasgow. In Demerara, he became a partner with Samuel Sandbach, Charles Stewart Parker and George Robson. The partners also opened a branch in Liverpool in 1804 as Sandbach, Tinne & Co., a well-known firm, and he was also a partner in the Demerara branch, McInroy, Sandbach & Co.

References Institute of Commonwealth Studies holdings (online).

WEALTH-HOLDERS, 1826

1826/1 **Name** **Gould, Garrett**

Dates Unknown, in Ireland–3 December 1825, Lisbon.

Probate £140,000 (PCC).

Occupation Wine and port shipper in Lisbon and Oporto. (Occupational category IV.19; venue 29.)

Address Lived in Lisbon, Portugal from 1797.

Father Unknown.

Mother Unknown.

Education Unknown.

Marriage Unknown.

Religion Roman Catholic. His sister Hannah became a boarder in a Catholic convent in Doneraile, Ireland.

Public None known.

Miscellaneous Emigrated from Ireland after the 1797 uprising and established a leading wine- and port-shipping concern, Gould Brothers, there. (The name of the firm indicates that he had a brother or brothers in Portugal, but these have not been traced.) After his death, the firm became known as Gould Campbell and is still a leading Portuguese wine-exporting firm.

References National Archives of Ireland online index; online sources; *GM,* 1826, vol. I, p. 95.

1826/2 **Name** **Stephens, John James**

Dates 22 January 1747, Exeter–12 November 1826, Lisbon.

Probate £600,000 'within province' (PCC).

Occupation Glass manufacturer in Lisbon, Portugal. His brother William Stephens (1731–11 May 1803) became a favourite of the Portuguese royal family and was given a monopoly on the manufacturing of glass in Portugal, plus exemption from taxation. John Stephens took over the firm and became remarkably wealthy. His fortune passed to his cousin, Charles Lyne Stephens, who was even wealthier. (Occupational category II.11; venue 29.)

Address Lived in Lisbon for most of his adult life.

Father Oliver Stephens (1689–1753), 'schoolmaster'. (Fourth son.) His brother (John James's uncle) was John Stephens (1690–1767), a merchant in Lisbon.

Mother Jane Smith (1710–55).

Education Christ's Hospital.

Marriage Apparently unmarried.

Religion Anglican. His grandfather (Revd) Lewis Stephens was an Anglican clergyman.

Public None known.

Miscellaneous His glassworks were confiscated by the French in 1807 but then returned. On his death, he left the glassworks to the 'Portuguese nation'.

References *ODNB* for brother; Jenifer Roberts, *Glass: The Strange History of the Lyne Stephens Fortune* (2003), *passim.*, and genealogical table, pp. xvi–xvii.

Name **Garland, George** 1826/3
Dates 1753–28 December 1825.
Probate £120,000 (PCC).
Occupation Merchant (Benjamin Lester & Co.; and then Garland, Simonds & Linthorne) in Poole, Dorset. It specialised in the Newfoundland trade. (Occupational category IV.19; venue 13.)
Address Lived at Poole and at Leeson House, Purbeck, Dorset.
Father Joseph Garland, merchant of Poole. (Third surviving son.)
Mother Mary; her surname was probably Lillington.
Education Unknown.
Marriage In 1779, to Amy (d. 1802), daughter of Benjamin Lester, merchant and MP, of Poole. (Eight sons, two daughters.) A son, John Bingley Garland (1791–1875) became the first Speaker of the Newfoundland House of Assembly.
Religion Anglican.
Public Sheriff of Poole 1784 and Mayor of Poole 1788 and 1810; MP (Tory) Poole, 1801–7. High Sheriff of Dorset, 1824–5.
Miscellaneous Was employed in the offices of Benjamin Lester, a leading Poole merchant, married his daughter and became head of the firm.
References *HP;* online sources.

Name **Rutherford, John** 1826/4
Dates Unknown – probated January 1826.
Probate £120,000 (PCC).
Occupation Stockbroker in London. (Occupational category IV.23; venue 1.)
Address 'Formerly of the Stock Exchange and then of Chester Place, Surrey [Middlesex?]' (probate calendar). PROB 11 states that he lived at St Mary Lambeth, Surrey.
Father Unknown.
Mother Unknown.
Education Unknown.
Marriage Unknown.
Religion Unknown. The name suggests a Scottish background.
Public None known.
Miscellaneous Nothing more could be traced about him.
References Probate calendar only.

Name **Bulkeley, Dowager Viscountess, Elizabeth Harriet Warren-Bulkeley** (née Warren) 1826/5
Dates c. 1759–23 February 1826, Englefield Green.
Probate £250,000 (PCC).
Occupation Widow of the 7th Viscount Bulkeley (d. 1822; see 1822/14) and daughter of Sir George Warren, landowner. (Occupational category I.) In 1883,

Sir Richard Williams-Bulkeley, Baronet of Baron Hill owned 29,878 acres worth £21,138 p.a. in Anglesey and Carnarvon.

Address Baron Hill, Anglesey and Englefield Green, Surrey.

Father Sir George Warren (1735–31 August 1801), MP, of Stockport and Poynton, Cheshire. (Only daughter and heir.) He reportedly had estates worth £6,500 p.a. in Cheshire and Lancashire (*HP*).

Mother Jane, daughter of Thomas Revel, MP, of Fetcham, Surrey.

Education Unknown.

Marriage In 1777, to Thomas, 7th Viscount Bulkeley (1752–3 June 1822), MP, created 1st Viscount Bulkeley (GB peerage) in 1784.

Religion Anglican.

Public None known.

Miscellaneous It is not clear what happened, after her death, to the estates she inherited from her father.

References *BP; HP; GM,* 1826, vol. I, p. 285.

1826/6 **Name** **Leman, (Revd) Thomas**

Dates 29 March 1751, Kirkstead Hall, Norfolk–17 March 1826, Bath.

Probate £160,000 (PCC).

Occupation Anglican clergyman and Chancellor of Cloyne, 1796–1802, although the full source of his fortune is unclear. (Occupational category VI.30?)

Address Wenhaston Hall, East Suffolk; Lower Crescent, Bath; he lived chiefly at Bath in adult life.

Father (Revd) John Leman (1705–June 1777) of Wenhaston Hall, Suffolk. (Only son.) Possibly landed wealth. No one of this name is listed in Bateman, however.

Mother Anne (d. 1796), daughter of Clement Reynolds of Cambridge.

Education 'At a school at Uggeshall, Suffolk'; Emmanuel College, Cambridge (BA, 1770; MA, 1778); Fellow of Clare College and of Emmanuel College.

Marriage First, in 1796, to Frances (d. 1818), daughter of William Nind, barrister, and widow of (Colonel) Alexander Champion of Bath. Second, in 1819, to Frances, daughter of Sir Robert Deane, Baronet, and widow of (Colonel) John Hodges (d.s.p.).

Religion Anglican clergyman.

Public None known.

Miscellaneous Was 'for many years in receipt of a considerable fortune' (*GM*), although its exact nature is not clear. He benefited from clerical pluralism, but there were almost certainly other sources. He is in the *ODNB* as a well-known 'antiquary', who wrote widely on Roman roads in Britain. He was an FSA and a founder of the Bath Institution.

References *ODNB; GM,* 1826, vol. II, p. 373; 1828, vol. II, p. 183.

1826/7 **Name** **Whittaker, Thomas**

Dates c. 1750–16 March 1826, Bath.

Probate £120,000 (PCC).

Occupation Probably 'chemist and druggist' (T. Whittaker, chemist and druggist,

of Chiswell Street, City of London, 1811 directory; of 68 Chiswell Street, Moorfields, 1793 directory). (If so, occupational category II.6 and 11; venue 1.)
Address 'Clapham, then Bath' (probate calendar).
Father Unknown.
Mother Unknown.
Education Unknown.
Marriage Unknown.
Religion Unknown.
Public None known.
Miscellaneous He presumably supplied pharmaceuticals to the Moorfield Hospital, although what he dealt in – assuming that he was the 'chemist and druggist' noted above – and how he became so wealthy are unclear.
References *GM,* 1826, vol. I, p. 382.

Name **Morgan, Elizabeth** 1826/8
Dates Unknown–17 December 1824, Loudwater near Rickmansworth, Hertfordshire, although her will was not probated until January 1826 (PROB 11 online).
Probate £100,000 (PCC).
Occupation Unknown. In her will she mentions her brother James Morgan and his illegitimate children James and Sophia Hayward. Her executor was Edward Whitmore of Lombard Street, banker. She apparently had no connection with Mary Morgan (see 1825/22).
Address Loudwater, near Rickmansworth, Hertfordshire.
Father Unknown.
Mother Unknown.
Education Unknown.
Marriage Unmarried: she is described as a 'spinster' in the probate calendars.
Religion Unknown.
Public None known.
Miscellaneous Nothing further could be traced about her.
References *GM,* 1825, vol. II, p. 647; will (PROB 11 online).

Name **Antrobus, Sir Edmund, 1st Baronet** 1826/9
Dates Unknown–26 February 1826.
Probate £250,000 (PCC).
Occupation Banker in London – partner (from 1779) in Coutts & Co. in the Strand. (Occupational category IV.16; venue 2.) In 1883, Sir Edmund Antrobus, Baronet, owned 10,673 acres worth £13,224 p.a. in Wilts, Roxburgh, etc., and John Coutts Antrobus of Eaton Hall, Congleton owned 3,051 acres worth £5,806 p.a. in Cheshire and Staffordshire. Presumably some of this had been owned by Sir Edmund.
Address 'Of the Strand; Hyde Park Corner; and Antrobus Hall near Lymm, Cheshire' (probate calendar).
Father Philip Antrobus (1720–4 November 1788) of Congleton. (Fourth son.)

Mother Mary (1720–29 September 1791), daughter of Thomas Rowley of Overton, Staffordshire.
Education Unknown.
Marriage Unmarried.
Religion Anglican.
Public Created baronet, 1815.
Miscellaneous His property came to his nephews, Sir Edmund Antrobus, 2nd Baronet and Gibbs Crawford Antrobus. Sir Edmund was an FSA and FRS. His date of birth, oddly, could not be traced.
References *GM*, 1826, vol. I, p. 187.

1826/10 **Name** **Wilson, John**
Dates Unknown – probated February 1826.
Probate £120,000 (PCC).
Occupation 'Ribbon and silk manufacturer' at 124 Wood Street, Cheapside (1817 directory). (Occupational category II.9; venue 1.)
Address 'Wood Street, Cheapside, City of London, and Highbury Place, then Upper Street, Islington' (probate calendar).
Father Unknown.
Mother Unknown.
Education Unknown.
Marriage Unknown.
Religion Unknown.
Public None known.
Miscellaneous Nothing more could be traced about him.
References Probate calendar and above only.

1826/11 **Name** **Mills, Charles**
Dates 13 July 1755–29 January 1826.
Probate £120,000 (PCC).
Occupation Banker (Glyn Mills & Co.) in the City of London and also Chairman of the East India Company, 1801–2. (Occupational category IV.16; venue 1.)
Address Of Barford, near Warwick, Warwickshire and Manchester Square, Middlesex; also 12 Mansfield Street, Marylebone, Middlesex.
Father (Revd) John Mills (1712–21 March 1791) of Barford and Oxhill, Warwickshire. (Second son.)
Mother Sarah (d. 1807), daughter of (Revd) William Wheler, Vicar of Leamington Hastings, Warwickshire.
Education Rugby School.
Marriage In 1810, to Jane (d. 1841; d.s.p.), daughter of (Hon.) Wriothesley Digby of Meriden, Warwickshire.
Religion Anglican.
Public MP (Whig) Warwickshire, 1802–26.
Miscellaneous Succeeded his uncle William Mills (1714–82) at the London

bank, and was succeeded by his nephew Sir Charles Mills (1792–1872). Sir Charles's son was created 1st Baron Hillingdon.
References *ODNB* and for his family; *GM,* 1826, vol. I, p. 366.

Name **Barrington, (Hon.) Shute, Bishop of Durham** 1826/12
Dates 26 May 1734, Becket, Berkshire–25 March 1826, Cavendish Square, Middlesex.
Probate £120,000, 'within province' (PCC).
Occupation Bishop of Durham, 1791–1826; previously Bishop of Llandaff, 1769–82 and of Salisbury, 1782–91. (Occupational category VI.30; venue 22, etc.)
Address Lived in London at Cavendish Square.
Father John Shute Barrington, 1st Viscount Barrington (1678–28 December 1734), barrister and landowner. (Sixth son.)
Mother Ann (d. 1763), daughter of Sir William Daines, MP.
Education Eton; Merton College, Oxford (MA, DCL, DD).
Marriage First, in 1761, to Lady Diana (d. 1766; d.s.p.), daughter of Charles, 2nd Duke of St Albans. Second, in 1770, to Jane (d. 1807; d.s.p.), daughter of Sir John Guise, 4th Baronet.
Religion Anglican bishop.
Public Presumably sat in the House of Lords.
Miscellaneous Was King's Chaplain 1761, Canon of Christ Church 1761 and Resident Canon of St Paul's and of Windsor before becoming a bishop at the age of thirty-four. Held the 'rich see' of Durham for thirty-five years. He was, however, an excellent churchman, widely admired by both evangelicals and High Church partisans, and was a pioneer of Sunday Schools and friendly to Roman Catholics.
References *ODNB; GM,* 1826, vol. I, p. 284.

Name **Erskine, Stewart** 1826/13
Dates c. 1751–31 July 1826, Bromley Lodge, Kent.
Probate £140,000 (PCC).
Occupation Unknown. His paternal grandparents were Sir Alexander Erskine (1663–1727), 2nd Baronet of Cambo, Lyon King of Arms, and Anna (née Erskine), daughter of the 3rd Earl of Kellie, but the source of his wealth is unclear, as is the occupation of his father, Thomas Erskine. He may have been the Stewart Erskine who was the 'deputy on the Thames' of Duncan Campbell (1726–1803), a successful West India merchant. Campbell, who held the position of overseer of Thames prison hulks from 1776 to 1801, is best known today for organising the transport of convicts to New South Wales and elsewhere (on-line, State Library of New South Wales). However, even if this was the case, it is unclear how Erskine accumulated his fortune.
Address 'Formerly of Park House, Maidstone, Kent, and then of Bromley Lodge near Bromley, Kent' (probate calendar).
Father Thomas Erskine (1699–2 February 1783). He was the son of Sir Alexander Erskine, 2nd Baronet (see 'Occupation' above). (Third son.)

Mother Jean Rue.
Education Unknown.
Marriage To Mary Reid or Reed (see 1837/30, left £120,000); marriage date unknown.
Religion Presumably originally Church of Scotland.
Public None known.
Miscellaneous He was a relative of the Erskines, Earls of Kellie.
References *GM,* 1826, vol. II, p. 189; BP, 'Earls of Kellie'.

1826/14 **Name** **Ramsden, John**
Dates c. 1740–18 May 1826, Hammersmith.
Probate £140,000 (PCC).
Occupation Unknown; he is not listed in any directory, etc. A John Ramsden, son of John, of Southowram, Yorkshire, entered University College, Oxford in March 1761 aged eighteen. A John George Ramsden entered Lincoln's Inn in 1837, the son of John of Twickenham, of the East India Company. There is no real evidence they were connected with this man, however.
Address 'Formerly of [17] Tavistock Square, Middlesex, and then of Hammersmith' (probate calendar). He lived in Tavistock Street, Bedford Square, in 1796.
Father Unknown.
Mother Unknown.
Education Unknown.
Marriage Unknown.
Religion Anglican; buried in the Anglican church of St Lawrence, Slough.
Public None known.
Miscellaneous Nothing further could be traced about him.
References *GM,* 1826, vol. I, p. 476.

1826/15 **Name** **Pearson, John**
Dates 3 January 1758, York–12 May 1826.
Probate £140,000 (PCC).
Occupation Surgeon – an 'eminent surgeon' (*ODNB*) and Surgeon to London Hospital, 1782–1818. (Occupational category VI.30; venue 2.)
Address Lived at Golden Square, Middlesex. In 1785, lived at Air Street, Middlesex.
Father John Pearson of Coney Street, York.
Mother Unknown.
Education 'Apprenticed at sixteen to a surgeon in Morpeth, Northumberland' (*ODNB*). Diploma of Surgeon's Company, 1781.
Marriage In 1784, to Sarah (1763–10 September 1826), daughter of Robert Norman of Lewisham. Their son was (Revd) John Norman Pearson (1787–1865), in the *ODNB* as a clergyman.
Religion Presumably Anglican. Married at St James's, Westminster.
Public None known.
Miscellaneous Studied in Leeds under Dr William Hey (d. 1819), the 'great sur-

geon', and came to London 1780 to work under Dr John Hunter. FRS; Fellow of the Linnaean Society, etc.

References *ODNB; GM,* 1826, vol. I, p. 476.

Name **Shedden, Robert** 1826/16

Dates 1741–26 September 1826.

Probate £120,000 (PCC).

Occupation 'Merchant' (Robert Shedden & Sons, of 35 Gower Street, etc.), traded with the Mediterranean and North America. (Occupational category IV.19; venue 2.) He settled in Virginia in 1759, and was then at Bermuda from 1776, then at New York, and in London from 1783 (*BLG*). There was a Hawthorn & Shedden, West India merchants, at 5 Lime Square, City of London.

Address Lived (and traded from) 35 Gower Street, Middlesex and also had a house, Slatwoods, at East Cowes, Isle of Wight.

Father William Shedden (1708–51) of Aughingree, Ayrshire and Kerse, Renfrewshire. (First son.)

Mother Beatrix, daughter of Robert Dobbie Chamberlain of Giffen.

Education Unknown.

Marriage In 1767, to Agatha (d. 1837), daughter of John Goodrich of Nansemond Plantation, Virginia. (Five sons, three daughters.)

Religion Presumably originally Church of Scotland but was buried in an Anglican church in Paulerspury, Northamptonshire.

Public None known.

Miscellaneous He appears to have traded chiefly with the Mediterranean, but also with North America, where he had lived.

References *BLG,* 1914; *Mariner's Mirror,* 1958, vol. 44, p. 2, on his family; University of London archives online.

Name **Balfour, Ann** 1826/17

Dates Unknown–13 January 1826.

Probate £118,161 (Scottish probate).

Occupation Unknown. *BLG,* 1914 lists two possibilities: the second daughter of John Balfour of Balbirnie (1738–1833) by Ellen, daughter of James Gordon of Ellon; and the third daughter of John Balfour of Kilmany (1727–October 1805) by Margaret (d. 1824), daughter of Alexander Balfour. In neither case are dates given, and there is no evidence that either was identical with this Ann Balfour. Her executor was Robert Wardlaw Ramsay of Whitehill (d. 1837), who was married to the daughter of the 6th Earl of Balcarres.

Address Lived at St John Street, Canongate, Edinburgh.

Father Unknown.

Mother Unknown.

Education Unknown.

Marriage Unmarried.

Religion Presumably Church of Scotland.

Public None known.

Miscellaneous Nothing more could be traced.
References Probate calendar and above only.

Name **Preston, (Revd) Thomas** 1827/1

Dates c. 1748 (1742 in other sources)–21 February 1827.

Probate £180,000 'within province' (PCC).

Occupation Anglican vicar; probably also landowner. (Occupational category I?) In 1883, Thomas Henry Preston of Moreby Hall, Yorkshire, owned 5,348 acres worth £7,325 p.a. in East and West Riding. The family had been Leeds merchants in the early eighteenth century. An ancestor, John Preston (d. 1710) was Mayor of Leeds in 1692. Whether they were still in trade in Revd Thomas Preston's father's generation is unknown.

Address Moreby Hall, near York.

Father Thomas Preston of York.

Mother Unknown.

Education Educated 'in York' and at Trinity College, Cambridge (BA).

Marriage Unknown.

Religion Anglican clergyman.

Public JP, East Riding.

Miscellaneous Was vicar of Scalby-cum-Cloughton from 1773 until death. He inherited property and probably land, but it isn't clear if his father was in trade. His property passed to his nephew, Henry Preston (d. 12 August 1857) of Moreby.

References *GM,* 1827, vol. I, p. 376; *Alum. Cantab.; BLG,* 1914; University of Hull online catalogue of the family's papers.

Name **Foster, John** 1827/2

Dates 1759, Liverpool–27 April 1827.

Probate £180,000 (PCC) + £60,000 (Lancashire Probates): £240,000.

Occupation Surveyor and architect – Surveyor to the Liverpool Corporation from c. 1790 to 1824. (Occupational category VI.30; venue 5.) He was retained for over thirty years at a salary of £500 p.a., but was also in business as a large-scale builder and modernised the Liverpool Docks. He built the Athenaeum, the Town Hall and the Theatre Royal in Liverpool and collaborated with James Wyatt on the Liverpool Exchange.

Address Lived in Liverpool.

Father John Foster (c. 1730–1801), 'master joiner' and builder in Liverpool.

Mother Unknown.

Education Unknown: he 'bought the freedom of Liverpool for 12 guineas' in 1773, aged fourteen (*ODNB*).

Marriage Name unknown. His son Thomas (d. 1836) became Town Clerk of Liverpool in 1832, his son John became the second Municipal Architect, and his son William became Secretary to the Dock Committee (*ODNB*).

Religion Presumably Anglican.

Public None known.

Miscellaneous Erected 'well-built houses' throughout Liverpool. Had to resign all his municipal positions in 1824 when it was found he had overcharged in building Prince's Dock, but no charges were pressed.

References *ODNB;* Howard Colum, *A Biographical Dictionary of British Architects, 1600–1840* (1978).

1827/3 **Name** **Peel, Lawrence**

Dates 1756–June 1827.

Probate £90,000 (PCC) + £160,000 (York PC): £250,000.

Occupation 'Calico printer' at Manchester (Occupational category I.7; venue 4.) He was the brother of Sir Robert Peel, 1st Baronet (d. 1830, 1830/17), and the uncle of Sir Robert Peel the Prime Minister.

Address 'Ardwick near Manchester and then at Elmfield near Doncaster, Yorkshire' (probate calendar).

Father Robert Peel (1723–12 September 1795) of Burton-on-Trent and Ardwick near Manchester, founder of the cotton-spinning dynasty, allegedly left £140,000.

Mother Elizabeth (d. 1796), daughter of Edmund Haworth of Lower Darwen, Lancashire.

Education Unknown.

Marriage First, in 1781, to Alice (d. 1807), daughter of Jonathan Haworth, his cousin. (Four sons, seven daughters.) Second, in 1822, to Elizabeth (d.s.p., 1855), daughter of Richard Creswick of Sheffield.

Religion Anglican.

Public None known.

Miscellaneous A pioneering cotton-spinner in Manchester, not Blackburn, unlike his brother.

References *BP; GM,* 1827, vol. II, p. 647; *ODNB* for relatives.

1827/4 **Name** **Morgan, Samuel**

Dates Unknown – probated November 1827. (According to Family Search, a Waterford man of the same name was born in 1728 and died on 26 January 1825.)

Probate £100,000 (PCC).

Occupation Unknown; lived Waterford, Ireland. Presumably a merchant there, but cannot be readily traced. PROB 11 describes him as an alderman of Waterford. (Venue 27.)

Address Waterford, Ireland.

Father Unknown. A Samuel Morgan was Mayor of Waterford in 1779 and also in 1801 and 1817. The earlier one may have been his father or uncle.

Mother Unknown. A Samuel Morgan (possibly his father) married a Margaret Brothers in Waterford in 1736 (Family Search), but see 'Dates' above.

Education Unknown.

Marriage Unknown.

Religion Presumably Church of Ireland or possibly Protestant Nonconformist.

Public None known.

Miscellaneous A Samuel Morgan voted for Cornelius Bolton (twice Mayor of Waterford) in the 1807 Waterford election. Nothing else could be traced of him.
References Online sources and probate calendar only.

Name **Leyland, Thomas** 1827/5
Dates c. 1752–20 May 1827, Walton Hall, Liverpool.
Probate £600,000 (Lancashire probates) + £200,000 (PCC): £800,000. (One source gives the exact figure as £756,531.)
Occupation Merchant and banker in Liverpool – a general merchant with world-wide interests, including slaves, and then a banker, providing capital to Liverpool merchants. (Occupational category IV.19 and 16; venue 5.) According to the *ODNB* and other sources, Leyland was employed by a cooper in Liverpool in 1768 when he won £20,000 in a lottery and became a merchant. He went into banking around 1802.
Address Walton Hall, Liverpool.
Father Richard Leyland of Knowsley, Lancashire (Only son.)
Mother Unknown.
Education Unknown.
Marriage In 1773, to Ellen (d.s.p., 1839), daughter of Edward Bridge, a 'cooper'. Leyland's property passed chiefly to his nephews Richard and Christopher Bullin.
Religion Anglican.
Public Mayor of Liverpool in 1788, 1814 and 1820.
Miscellaneous 'Altogether a self-made man': H. R. Fox-Bourne, *English Merchants* (1866), vol. II, p. 294.
References *ODNB*; *BLG*, 1914.

Name **Bonham, Thomas** 1827/6
Dates c. 1754–15 December 1826.
Probate £120,000 (PCC).
Occupation Brewer in Petersfield, Hampshire. (Occupational category III.12; venue 14.) Also a landowner – in 1883, John Bonham-Carter, his successor, owned 5,622 acres worth £6,260 p.a., in Hampshire.
Address Castle House, Petersfield, Hampshire.
Father John Bonham of Castle House, Petersfield, brewer and landowner.
Mother Ann, daughter of William Pike, 'brewer', who is said to have left £100,000 in 1797.
Education Unknown.
Marriage Unmarried. The property passed to his cousin, John Carter, who took the name Bonham-Carter and founded the well-known family of that name.
Religion Dissenter, probably a Unitarian. His cousin John Carter was a Unitarian.
Public None known.
Miscellaneous He was said to have been a shareholder in the family brewery but not an active manager.
References *ODNB* for relatives; Victor Bonham-Carter, *In a Liberal Tradition: A Social Biography, 1700–1950* (1960); *BLG*, 1914.

1827/7 **Name** **Hodges, Benjamin**

Dates c. 1749–2 April 1827, at Dunstable House, Richmond.

Probate £100,000 (PCC).

Occupation Distiller in Millbank, Lambeth (Hodges & Chamberlain, distillers of Millbank, 1808 directory; B. Hodges & Sons, distillers and importers, 6 Church Lane, Lambeth – 1822 and 1826 directories). (Occupational venue III.13; venue 2.)

Address 'Formerly of Millbank and of Hanwell, Middlesex, and then of Richmond, Surrey' (probate calendar).

Father Unknown. A Henry Hodges, distiller of Millbank, possibly his father, is listed in the 1793 directory.

Mother Unknown.

Education Unknown.

Marriage To Catherine (marriage date unknown), daughter of William Reeve of Harts, Gloucestershire. His daughter married Joseph Mazzinghi (1765–1844), a composer in the *ODNB* who was created a papal count. Another daughter married George Thomas Whitgreave (b. 1787), of a family listed in *BLG*, 1846.

Religion Unknown. The daughter's husband would suggest a Roman Catholic connection, but there is no direct evidence for this.

Public None known.

Miscellaneous Nothing further could be traced.

References *GM*, 1827, vol. I, p. 477.

1827/8 **Name** **Daubeny, (Ven.) Charles**

Dates Baptised 16 August 1745–10 July 1827, North Bradley, Wiltshire.

Probate £120,000 (PCC).

Occupation Archdeacon of Sarum, Wiltshire, but appears to have inherited from his father, a sugar refiner and distiller in Bristol, who 'left a considerable fortune' (*DNB*). (Occupational category VI.30 and III.13 and 15; venue 12.) His brother George (1742–1806) was a leading businessman in Bristol, who was a sugar refiner, a partner of Stevens & Co., glass manufacturers, one of the founders of Ames, Cave & Co., the bankers, and an MP (*HP*).

Address Lived at North Bradley, Wiltshire.

Father George Daubeny (1713–20 January 1760), sugar refiner and distiller of Bristol, a Warden of the Merchant Venturers, 1750–1. (Second son.)

Mother Mary Jones (d. 1764) of Bristol.

Education Winchester; New College, Oxford (BCL, DCL, 1822).

Marriage In 1778, to Elizabeth (d. 1823), daughter of William George Barnston of Woodford, Essex. (Two sons, one daughter.)

Religion Anglican clergyman.

Public None known.

Miscellaneous Vicar of Bradley, Wiltshire and Archdeacon of Salisbury from 1804. He was a well-known Anglican controversialist and has an entry in the *ODNB*. This entry states that he left 'several thousands of pounds', which is incorrect. It is unclear how much of his fortune came from his clerical income and how much was inherited.

References *ODNB; GM,* 1827, vol. II, p. 274; *Annual Biography and Obituary, 1828; HP* for brother.

Name **Nicholson, Samuel** 1827/9
Dates c. 1737–26 October 1827 at Ham Common, Surrey.
Probate £180,000 (PCC).
Occupation 'Haberdasher' (S. Nicholson & Sons, of Cateaton Street near Milk Street, Cheapside, City of London, 1793 directory). 'Warehouseman' (Nicholson & Nephews, of Cateaton Street, 1812 directory). (Occupational category IV.20 and 21; venue 1.)
Address 'Formerly of Cateaton Street and Kings Arms Yard, City of London; then Ham Common, Surrey' (probate calendar).
Father Possibly George Nicholson of Finsbury Square and Guildford.
Mother Unknown.
Education Unknown.
Marriage Unknown. His daughter Caroline married (Revd) Thomas Hackin Kingdon (1775–1853). Their daughter Emmeline Maria Kingdon (1817–90) is in the *ODNB* as the Headmistress of the Royal School, Bath.
Religion Presumably Anglican.
Public None known.
Miscellaneous Nothing more could be traced.
References *GM,* 1827, vol. II, p. 476.

Name **Pretyman-Tomline, Sir George, 5th Baronet, Bishop of Winchester** (né Pretyman) 1827/10
Dates 9 October 1750–14 November 1827, at Kingston Hall, Wimbourne.
Probate £200,000 (PCC).
Occupation Bishop of Winchester, 1820–death; previously Bishop of Lincoln and Dean of St Paul's from 1787. The King refused to make him either Archbishop of Canterbury or Bishop of London. He was well known as William Pitt's tutor and wrote a major biography of Pitt. (Occupational category VI.30.) In 1883, Colonel George Tomline, MP, of Orwell Park, Woodbridge, Suffolk owned 26,914 acres worth £35,542 p.a. in Suffolk and Lincolnshire.
Address He had country seats at Bacton, Suffolk and at Riby Grange, Lincolnshire, and lived in Winchester.
Father George Pretyman (1728–12 December 1810), a 'tradesman' in Bury St Edmunds, who inherited land in Suffolk. In 1823, the Bishop inherited a dormant baronetcy and became 5th Baronet. In 1803, Bishop Pretyman inherited 'out of the blue' the property of Marmaduke Tomline, who was not related to him and whom he had met only a few times, and changed his name to Pretyman-Tomline.
Mother Susan (d. 1807), daughter of John Hubbard of Bury St Edmunds.
Education Bury St Edmunds Grammar School; Pembroke College, Cambridge (Senior Wrangler, Smith's Prizeman, Fellow, MA, DD).
Marriage In 1784, to Elizabeth (d. 1827), daughter of Thomas Maltby of Germans, Buckinghamshire. (Three sons.)

Religion Anglican clergyman.
Public Sat in the House of Lords. Was very influential with Pitt in his lifetime.
Miscellaneous An interesting case of upward mobility and clerical 'Old Corruption'.
References *ODNB*; *GM*, 1828, vol. I, pp. 201–4; *BLG*.

1827/11 **Name** **Penoyre, Francis Rigby Broadbelt Stallard** (né Broadbelt)
Dates 1771–1827.
Probate £120,000 (PCC).
Occupation Jamaica money from his father, a prominent physician there, close to the slave-owning estate-owners, then a landowner in Hereford. In 1883, Thomas J. Stallard-Penoyre of the Moor, Hereford, owned 2,035 acres worth £1,680 p.a. (Occupational category I; venue 29?)
Address Lived at The Moor, Hereford, then at Bath Easton Villa near Bath and Hardwick Court, Hereford.
Father (Dr) Francis Rigby Broadbelt (1746–95), of Spanish Town, Jamaica, physician to wealthy plantation-owning families. (First son.)
Mother Anne (1751–6 September 1827), daughter of Thomas Penoyre. She is in the *ODNB* for the famous letters she wrote about life in Jamaica and the plantation gentry. She later lived in Bath.
Education Unknown.
Marriage Unknown.
Religion Anglican.
Public None known.
Miscellaneous At some stage he took the surname Penoyre (his mother's maiden name), but the circumstances are unknown. He was presumably chiefly a landowner in England. It is not clear how he came to amass a fortune of £120,000, unless his father or another relative was a plantation owner in Jamaica.
References *ODNB* for mother; *BLG*, 1914.

1827/12 **Name** **Gardiner, Samuel**
Dates 13 September 1755–4 July 1827.
Probate £140,000 (PCC).
Occupation 'For many years the Military Secretary to the East India Company's government at Calcutta, under the Marquess of Hastings' (*BLG*, 1914). (Occupational category VI.31; venue 29.)
Address Lived at Coombe Lodge near Whitechurch, Oxfordshire, England.
Father Samuel Gardiner (1724–4 January 1794) of Woodford, Essex. (First son.)
Mother Jane Ann Parkinson (d. 1781) of London.
Education Unknown.
Marriage In 1782, to Mary (d. 1813), daughter of Charles Boddam of Enfield and widow of George Boddam of Bombay. (Her father was descended from Oliver Cromwell's daughter Bridget and her husband Major-General Henry Ireton.) Samuel and Mary Gardiner's son was Rawson Boddam Gardiner (1788–1863) of the East India Company, who married Margaret, daughter of William Baring

Gould. Their son (Samuel Gardiner's grandson) was Samuel Rawson Gardiner (1829–1901), the famous historian.
Religion Anglican.
Public High Sheriff of Oxfordshire in 1794.
Miscellaneous It is not clear when he returned to England from India.
References *BLG*, 1914.

Name **Hurd, Richard** 1827/13
Dates c. 1749–6 October 1827, at the Episcopal Palace, Worcester.
Probate £120,000 (PCC).
Occupation Inherited the wealth of Richard Hurd, Bishop of Worcester (1720–1808), formerly Bishop of Coventry, his uncle, who died unmarried. (Occupational category VI.30.)
Address Lived at The Palace, Worcester. Presumably he was allowed to remain there after his uncle's death.
Father Unknown.
Mother Unknown.
Education Unknown.
Marriage Unknown.
Religion Anglican.
Public None known.
Miscellaneous He edited his uncle's writings. He does not appear to have had a profession or trade.
References *GM*, 1827, vol. II, p. 195; *ODNB* for uncle.

Name **Spode, Josiah** 1827/14
Dates 8 May 1755, Stoke-on-Trent–16 July 1827, The Mount, Penkhull, Stoke-on-Trent, Staffordshire.
Probate £250,000 (PCC).
Occupation Pottery manufacturer at Stoke-on-Trent – 'Potter to the King'. (Occupational category II.11; venue 18.) He also opened a warehouse and retail outlet at Fore Street, Cripplegate (Spode & Copeland) and at Lincoln's Inn Fields.
Address The Mount, Stoke-on-Trent, Staffordshire in later life.
Father Josiah Spode (1733–97), founder of the pottery business.
Mother Ellen Finley (1726–1802).
Education 'Learned his trade in his father's workshop' (*DNB*).
Marriage In 1775, to Elizabeth Barker (d. 1782 or 1797), daughter of a pottery manufacturer. (Two sons, three daughters.)
Religion Buried as an Anglican.
Public None known.
Miscellaneous The famous pottery manufacturer (founder of bone china in England) – probably the second most famous English potter after Josiah Wedgwood.
References *DNB*; *ODNB*; *GM*, 1827, vol. II, pp. 93 and 470.

1827/15 **Name** **Davidson, Henry**

Dates 1771–7 January 1827, at Rosslyn House, Hampstead.

Probate £500,000 (PCC).

Occupation West India merchant in London (Davidson, Barclay & Co., of 6 Lime Square, City of London). Also owned plantations and slaves in Jamaica and Grenada. (Occupational category IV.19 and I; venue 1 and 29.) In 1883, Duncan Davidson of Tulloch owned 36,130 acres worth £6,093 p.a. in Ross-shire.

Address 'Formerly of Bedford Square, Middlesex; then of Tulloch [near Dingwall], Scotland, Cavendish Square, and Lime Square in the City of London' (probate calendar).

Father Duncan Davidson, JP, DL and MP (1733–99), merchant in London and landowner of Tulloch, purchased by his brother in 1763. (Only son.) Duncan was a merchant at 14 Fenchurch Street Buildings. He presumably owned West Indies plantations.

Mother Louisa, daughter of Thomas Spencer.

Education Unknown.

Marriage In 1798, to Caroline, daughter of John Diffnell. (Four sons, three daughters.) His niece in 1792 married Sir Robert Dallas (1756–1824), judge, in *ODNB.*

Religion The father was buried as an Anglican. Presumably the family were originally Church of Scotland.

Public JP, DL, presumably in Ross-shire.

Miscellaneous An enormously wealthy West India merchant in London and plantation owner in Jamaica and Grenada. Whether he ever lived in the West Indies is unknown. He became a partner in his father's mercantile business in 1793.

References *GM,* 1827, vol. I, p. 92; *BLG,* 1914.

1827/16 **Name** **Frederick, Duke of York and Albany**

Dates 16 August 1763, St James's Palace–5 January 1827 at the Duke of Rutland's house, Arlington Street, Piccadilly.

Probate £180,000 (PCC).

Occupation Royal Duke; was also the Bishop of Osnabruck, 1764–1803 (despite being a Protestant!). He was created Duke of York and Albany and Earl of Ulster in 1784. He was also a field marshal, 1793, and Commander-in-Chief of the Army. 'The Grand Old Duke of York.' (Occupational category IV.31.)

Address Apparently lived chiefly in St James's Palace.

Father The second son of King George III (d. 1820). He was heir presumptive to the Throne and would have succeeded had he lived another three years.

Mother Charlotte, daughter of the Grand Duke of Mecklenburg-Strelitz.

Education Private tutors.

Marriage In 1791, to Frederica, Princess Royal of Prussia (1767–1820; d.s.p.). They quickly separated. He lived with his mistress, Mary Anne Clarke (1776–1852).

Religion Anglican and Lutheran.

Public KB, 1767; KG, 1771; created Duke of York, 1784. He sat in the House of Lords from 1787 onwards.

Miscellaneous Although known for 'marching up to the top of the hill and marching down again', he is regarded as a very efficient and reforming commander-in-chief who founded the forerunner of Sandhurst. The famous nursery rhyme may predate him by centuries. It is interesting to note that the estates of royal dukes are recorded in the probate calendars (although not those of sovereigns).
References *ODNB; GM,* 1827, vol. I, p. 69–85, etc.

Name **Bayly, John** 1827/17
Dates Unknown – probated March 1827. A 'Captain J. Bayly of Stamford Hill' is listed in *GM,* 1827, vol. I, p. 283 as having died on 21 February 1827, aged sixty-one. He is presumably this man. If so, he was born c. 1765.
Probate £140,000 (PCC).
Occupation Unknown. If he was 'Capt. J. Bayly', this suggests a possible East India Company connection. A John Bayly, boot and shoemaker, of 11 Rotherhithe Street, was listed in the 1826–7 London directory. A Nathaniel Bayly (1726–98), MP, of Epsom, Surrey and Abingdon, Berkshire was a Jamaica planter. There is no real evidence of any connection with this John Bayly. There seems to have been no captain or commander of this name in the Navy List.
Address 'Formerly of Hackney and then of Stamford Hill' (probate calendar). 'Of Tottenham, Middlesex' (PROB 11).
Father Unknown.
Mother Unknown.
Education Unknown.
Marriage Elizabeth, surname unknown. No children are mentioned in his will. He left legacies to his sister Mary Potts and to his nephews William and George Potts.
Religion Probably Anglican: he left a legacy in his will to the Church Missionary Society.
Public None known.
Miscellaneous His will, generally unilluminating, notes that he owned shares in the West India Docks.
References Will (PROB 11 online) and above sources.

Name **Kerrison, Matthias** 1827/18
Dates 1742–12 April 1827.
Probate £250,000 (PCC).
Occupation Owned the navigation rights on the River Waveney from Yarmouth to Bungay in Suffolk, an area that traded in coal, corn and wood (*Beccles & Bungay Journal,* vol. 24, online, which states that he 'became a millionaire as a result'. This is difficult to classify). (Occupational category IV.25 'Other Commerce' seems most relevant, as he does not appear to fall under any other occupational heading; venue 11.) He was probably engaged before this in 'trade', but its exact nature is unclear, and he also became a landowner. In 1883, his descendant Sir Edward Kerrison, Baronet, owned 11,861 acres worth £28,608 p.a. in Suffolk and Norfolk.

Address Lived at Hexne Hall near Bungay, Suffolk in later life.

Father Roger Kerrison (1711–73) of Broke, Norfolk. Matthias Kerrison was 'born in an inferior station' in life, rose by 'trade', left 'little less than a million sterling' and 'invested in the fine estates of Lord Maynard and the Marquess Cornwallis' (*GM,* 1827, vol. I, p. 477). The estimate of his wealth here is clearly wrong. The *Beccles & Bungay Journal* stated that he began as a 'carpenter'.

Mother Mary, daughter of John Osborn of Kirkstead, Norfolk.

Education Unknown.

Marriage In 1772, to Mary (d. 1815), daughter of Edward Barnes of Barnham, Suffolk. His only son was Sir Edward Kerrison, 1st Baronet (1776–1835), an MP and army general, with an entry in the *ODNB.*

Religion Presumably Anglican.

Public None known.

Miscellaneous Clearly there is a story of upward mobility here, but its details are unclear.

References *GM,* 1827, vol. I, p. 477 and above sources.

1827/19 **Name** **Shrewsbury, 15th Earl of, Charles Talbot**

Dates 8 March 1753, Hill Street, Berkeley Square–6 April 1827, Stanhope Street, Middlesex.

Probate £500,000 (PCC).

Occupation Landowner. (Occupational category I.) In 1883, the Earl of Shrewsbury owned 35,382 acres worth £62,382 p.a. in Staffordshire, Cheshire, etc.

Address His main seats appear to have been Heythrop, Oxfordshire and Alton Abbey, Staffordshire.

Father Charles Talbot (1721–11 April 1766) of Horecross, Yoxhall, Staffordshire. (First son.) He succeeded his uncle, George, 14th Earl, who died in 1787.

Mother Mary, daughter of Sir George Mostyn, 4th Baronet of Talacre, Flintshire.

Education Secondary schooling unknown; University College, Oxford (despite being a Catholic).

Marriage In 1792, to Elizabeth (d.s.p., 1847), daughter of James Hoey, a 'printer' of Dublin. This was an extraordinary marriage choice in 1792. The title passed to his nephew, the 16th Earl, who is in the *ODNB* as a 'patron of the Gothic revival'.

Religion Roman Catholic; from a leading aristocratic Catholic family.

Public None known – presumably his religion debarred him from all offices.

Miscellaneous He was not a well-known public figure, despite his immense wealth.

References *BP; GM,* 1827, vol. I, pp. 463–4.

1827/20 **Name** **Cholmondeley, 1st Marquess and 4th Earl of, George James Cholmondeley**

Dates 11 May 1749, Hardingstone, Northamptonshire–10 April 1827, Piccadilly.

Probate £140,000 'within province' (PCC).

Occupation Landowner. (Occupational category I.) Also a colonel in the Army from 1779 and Envoy to Berlin, 1782. In 1883, the Marquess of Cholmondeley owned 33,991 acres worth £41,288 p.a. in Cheshire and Norfolk.
Address Cholmondeley Castle, Nantwich, Cheshire, was the main seat.
Father George Cholmondeley, Viscount Malpas, MP (1724–15 March 1764). (First son.) The 1st Marquess succeeded his grandfather, the 3rd Earl, as 4th Earl in 1770; the 3rd Earl's name was 'a byword for insane vices'.
Mother Hester, daughter of Sir Francis Edwardes, 3rd Baronet.
Education Unknown.
Marriage In 1791, to Georgiana (d. 1838), daughter of Peregrine, 3rd Duke of Ancaster and Kesteven. (Two sons, one daughter.)
Religion Anglican.
Public Served as Captain, Yeomen of the Guards, 1783. Was Chamberlain to the Prince of Wales, 1795–1800; Lord Steward of the Household, 1812, 1821. PC, 1783. Was originally a Whig, later supported the Tories. Created a marquess, 1815; KG, 1822. Lord Lieutenant of Cheshire, 1770–83.
Miscellaneous As noted, was also a diplomat.
References *BP, CP.*

Name **Lyon, David** 1827/21
Dates c. 1754– 26 June 1827, Portland Place, Middlesex.
Probate £600,000 'within province' (PCC).
Occupation West India merchant in London (David Lyon & Co., of Lime Street Square, City of London). Also lived in Jamaica, and was presumably a planter there. (Occupational category IV.19; venue 1; also [?] Occupational category I; venue 29.)
Address Lived at Portland Place, Middlesex. *BLG,* 1914, states that he also had lived in Jamaica.
Father John Lyon of Castle Lyon, Perthshire and Kinnaird, Fifeshire. (Second son.)
Mother Jane, daughter of Alexander Ochterlony of Pitforthy, Angus. (Her niece was Sir David Ochterlony, Baronet, East India Company.)
Education Unknown.
Marriage In 1787, to Isabella, daughter of John Reid of Cairney. (Five sons, five daughters.) Their son William Lyon (1807–92) was briefly an MP in 1831–2, and was one of the last survivors of the pre-1832 Parliament. Their daughter married Lord Kilmaine. Another daughter, Isabella, married James Wedderburn (d. 1831) of Jamaica.
Religion Presumably Church of Scotland. Their daughter Isabella married in an Anglican ceremony.
Public None known.
Miscellaneous An enormously wealthy West India merchant who had lived in Jamaica.
References *GM,* 1827, vol. I, p. 646; *BLG,* 1914.

1827/22 **Name** **Stephens, Mary Bryanna** (née Bulkeley)
Dates Baptised 27 May 1764–9 July 1827, Montagu Square, Middlesex.
Probate £140,000 (PCC).
Occupation She was the sister-in-law of John James Stephens (1747–1826; see 1826/2), glass manufacturer in Lisbon who left £600,000. Her husband was a merchant in Lisbon. (Occupational category IV.19 and II.11; venue 29.)
Address 'Formerly of Upper Seymour Street, Middlesex, and then Montagu Street, Middlesex' (probate calendar). She married in Lisbon and presumably had resided there.
Father John Bulkeley.
Mother Elizabeth, surname unknown.
Education Unknown.
Marriage In 1779, in Lisbon to Lewis Stephens (1744, Exeter–6 September 1795, Lisbon), 'merchant and member of the British Factory [i.e. commercial trading area] in Lisbon' (*GM*). He was the brother of John James Stephens.
Religion Anglican: married and buried as an Anglican.
Public None known.
Miscellaneous She presumably benefited from her brother-in-law's enormously lucrative glassworks in Lisbon.
References *GM,* 1827, vol. II, p. 91; Jenifer Roberts, *Glass: The Strange History of the Lyne Stephens Fortune* (2003).

1827/23 **Name** **Fletcher, Henry**
Dates Unknown–15 July 1827.
Probate £180,000 (PCC).
Occupation Shipbuilder in Shadwell and Limehouse (Henry Fletcher & Sons, shipbuilders of Shadwell Docks and Union Docks, Limehouse – 1793 and 1805 directories). (Occupational category II.4; venue 2.)
Address 'Formerly of St John, Wapping, then of Shadwell Docks' (probate calendar).
Father Unknown.
Mother Unknown.
Education Unknown.
Marriage Unknown. His firm was known as 'Fletcher & Son' in 1820.
Religion Nonconformist – either Independent or Congregationalist. He bought Clare Hall (later Chapel House) in Wapping as a Nonconformist chapel, 1801. Joseph Fletcher, a 'shipbuilder of Shadwell Docks', presumably a close relative, was a trustee (*VCH Essex,* vol. 4, 1956, pp. 35–7).
Public None known.
Miscellaneous Presumably he built merchant ships, not naval vessels.
References *GM,* 1827, vol. II, p. 91.

1827/24 **Name** **Baker, Richard**
Dates February 1743–probated December 1827 (died 'lately', *GM,* 1827, vol. II, p. 91 – the July issue).

Probate £180,000 (PCC).
Occupation Barrister in London and landowner. (Occupational category VI.29 and I; venue 1.) In 1883, his heir, Digby Wingfield-Baker of Orsett Hall, Essex, owned 8,545 acres worth £11,791 p.a. in Essex.
Address Orsett Hall near Romford, Essex and Portland Place, Middlesex.
Father Richard Baker (c. 1707–22 April 1751), 'merchant and ropemaker' of Stepney, who purchased Orsett Hall in 1746 (Thurrock Historical Society, online).
Mother Unknown.
Education Charterhouse and Peterhouse, Cambridge (BA, 1763). Admitted to Lincoln's Inn, October 1759. Called at the Inner Temple, 1766.
Marriage Unknown. His estate went to his nephew, William Wingfield.
Religion Anglican.
Public None known.
Miscellaneous Was a leading barrister at Tanfield Court, Inner Temple. Bencher (1800), Reader (1806) and Treasurer (1808) of the Inner Temple. Was also a wealthy landowner.
References *GM,* 1827, vol. II, p. 91; *Alum. Cantab.; Charterhouse Register 1769–1872.*

Name **Rundell, Philip** 1827/25
Dates 15 January 1746, Norton near Bath–17 February 1827 'at the house of his mistress' near Regent's Park.
Probate 'Above £1 million' (PCC). (Estates until the later nineteenth century probated in England worth more than £1 million were not generally sworn to an approximate figure but stated to be worth 'Above £1 million' or 'Upper value'.)
Occupation Goldsmith (Rundell, Bridge & Rundell) at Ludgate Hill, City of London and 'diamond jeweller to the Royal Family'. (Occupational category IV.20 and V.28? Venue 1.)
Address 'Of [32] Ludgate Hill and [The Crescent], New Bridge Street, City of London' (probate calendar). He had a house at South Bank, Regent's Park, Middlesex, near his mistress.
Father Richard Rundell, a 'victualler and maltster in extensive trade' (*Annual Biography and Register* obituary of Philip Rundell) in Bath.
Mother Ann Ditcher. Her uncle was Philip Ditcher, an eminent surgeon at Bath who was married to the daughter of Samuel Richardson the writer.
Education 'At Bath', and then 'apprenticed to William Rogers, the eminent jeweller and goldsmith' there.
Marriage Unmarried – he lived with mistress in later life. His property went to his sister's grandson, Joseph Neeld.
Religion Anglican.
Public None known.
Miscellaneous Came to London aged twenty-one and entered Alderman Pickett's jewellery firm on Ludgate Hill. He then went into partnership with Mr Bridge for many years – he was the manufacturer, Bridge the retailer – and became one

of the richest men in England. He was very well known, and has an entry in the *ODNB*.

References *ODNB; GM,* 1827, vol. I, p. 563.

1827/26 **Name** **Jennings, William**

Dates c. 1748–17 February 1827.

Probate £100,000 (PCC).

Occupation Unknown – he is not listed in any London directory or any other source apart from an obituary notice in *GM.* This suggests he was primarily occupied elsewhere, possibly overseas.

Address (26) Bloomsbury Square, Middlesex–1811 Court Guide.

Father Unknown.

Mother Unknown.

Education Unknown.

Marriage Unknown.

Religion Unknown.

Public None known.

Miscellaneous Nothing more could be traced about him.

References *GM,* 1827, vol. I, p. 187.

1827/27 **Name** **Perkins, John**

Dates c. 1747–6 March 1827, Gerrard Street, Middlesex.

Probate £140,000 (PCC).

Occupation Stockbroker in London (1808 directory). (Occupational category IV.23; venue 1.)

Address 'Pendell [Plenwell?] Court near Bletchingley, Surrey; 38 Gerrard Street, Middlesex; and the Stock Exchange, City of London' (probate calendar).

Father Unknown.

Mother Unknown.

Education Unknown.

Marriage Unknown.

Religion Unknown.

Public None known.

Miscellaneous Nothing further could be traced about him.

References *GM,* 1827, vol. I, p. 283.

1827/28 **Name** **Gist, Samuel**

Dates Unknown – probated 1827 (PROB 8), but no one of this name is recorded as having an estate probated in 1827 or any adjacent year. This entry might be the second probating of the estate of Samuel Gist (1815/17), or another man of the same name whose estate, for whatever reason, is not recorded or his will available on PROB 11.

Probate £150,000 'within province' (PCC).

Occupation Tobacco merchant of 37 Gower Street, Bedford Square, Middlesex (1805, 1808 directories). (Occupational category IV.21 or 19; venue 2.) He was presumably a relative, probably the son, of Samuel Gist (1724–1815; see 1815/17), the Lloyd's broker who left £150,000. This Samuel Gist had been the captain of a Carolina merchant ship and lived in Gower Street. He is, however, listed as having had two daughters – there is no mention of a son.

Address (37) Gower Street. The 1811 directory states that he also lived at Wormington Grange, Gloucestershire.

Father Unknown.

Mother Unknown.

Education Unknown.

Marriage Unknown.

Religion Unknown.

Public None known.

Miscellaneous *BLG*, 1894 (Gist of Wormington) states that a Josiah Gist of Wormington and Stanton, Cheltenham in 1791 married an Anne Placeway. They had a son, Samuel Gist Gist Jnr. (sic), but he died in 1845.

References Probate calendar and above sources only.

Name **Pembroke, 11th Earl of, and Montgomery, 8th Earl of, George Augustus Herbert** 1827/29

Dates 10 September 1759, Wilton House, Salisbury–26 October 1827, Pembroke House, Whitehall.

Probate £600,000 (PCC).

Occupation Landowner. (Occupational category I.) In 1883, the Earl of Pembroke and Montgomery owned 44,806 acres worth £77,720 p.a. in Wiltshire, County Dublin, etc. He was also Ambassador to Vienna, 1807, Governor of Guernsey, 1807–death, and a general in the Army.

Address Wilton House, Salisbury was his principal seat.

Father (Lieutenant General) Henry Herbert, 10th Earl of Pembroke (1734–26 January 1794). (Only son.)

Mother Elizabeth (d. 1831), daughter of Charles, 3rd Duke of Marlborough.

Education Harrow. Made the Grand Tour, 1775–80.

Marriage First, in 1787, to Elizabeth (d. 1793), daughter of Topham Beauclerk (his cousin). (Three sons, one daughter.) Second, in 1808, to Catherine, daughter of Simon Count Wornzow, Russian Ambassador to Britain. (One son, one daughter.)

Religion Anglican.

Public MP (Whig, then Pittite) Wilton, 1780–4 and 1788–96. PC, 1784. Served as Vice-Chamberlain, 1784–94. KG, 1805. Lord Lieutenant of Wiltshire, 1794–1827.

Miscellaneous Greatly increased his rent-rolls by agricultural improvements. He declined a marquessate. He left much of his property to his son by his second marriage, the Cabinet minister Lord Herbert of Lea.

References *ODNB* as 'army officer and landowner'; *BP; GM*, 1827, vol. II, p. 557.

1827/30 **Name** **Gordon, 4th Duke of, Alexander Gordon**

Dates 29 June 1743, Gordon Castle–17 June 1827, at Mount Street, Berkeley Square.

Probate £122,677 (Scottish probate).

Occupation Landowner. (Occupational category I.) He was regarded as 'the greatest subject in Britain in the extent of his rent roll and of the number of persons depending on his rule and protection' (*DNB*). In 1883, he had two successors, the Duke of Richmond and Gordon, who owned 286,411 acres worth £79,683 p.a., of which about 258,000 acres worth about £80,000 p.a. were in Scotland; and the Marquess of Huntly, who owned 85,711 acres worth £19,860 p.a.

Address Gordon Castle, Banffshire, was his chief seat.

Father Cosmo George Gordon, 3rd Duke of Gordon (c. 1720–5 August 1752).

Mother Catherine (d. 1779), daughter of William Gordon, 3rd Earl of Aberdeen. (She married, second, Staats Long Morris, who died in 1800.)

Education Eton; made the Grand Tour.

Marriage First, in 1767, to Jane (d. 1812), daughter of Sir William Maxwell, 3rd Baronet. (Two sons, five daughters.) The couple were 'estranged'. Second, in 1820, Mrs Jane Christie (d. 1824) of Fochabers 'by whom he had previously had four children'.

Religion Church of Scotland.

Public Keeper of the Great Seal of Scotland, 1794–1806, 1807–27. Lord Lieutenant of Aberdeenshire, 1794–1808. A Scottish Representative Peer from 1767. KT, 1775. Created Earl of Norwich and Baron Gordon of Huntly (British peerage), 1784.

Miscellaneous Chancellor of King's College, Aberdeen, 1793–1827, and was an FRS. His younger brother was Lord George Gordon. His property was divided between the Duke of Richmond and the Marquess of Huntly.

References *ODNB; CP.*

1827/31 **Name** **Sykes, Nicholas**

Dates Unknown – probated 1827. His will (without a valuation) is also available on PROB 11. It was probated in PCC in June 1827.

Probate £100,000 (York PC).

Occupation A merchant in Hull. (Occupational category IV.19 or 21; venue 21.)

Address Ferriby near Hull, East Riding. He also owned West Ella Hall in Hull, purchased in 1756, possibly by his father. 'Of Ferriby, Kingston-upon-Hull, Yorkshire' (PROB 11).

Father Possibly Joseph Sykes (d. 1805), a merchant in Hull (K. J. Allison, *'Hull Gent. Seeks Country Residence', 1750–1850*). According to Family Search, a Nicholas Sykes, son of Joseph Sykes, was baptised on 27 August 1763.

Mother Unknown. Possibly Dorothy Twigge or Twiggs (Family Search).

Education Unknown.

Marriage Unknown. Possibly in 1790 to Mary Cam (Family Search). His son Daniel was a barrister and Recorder of Hull. His daughter Martha married in 1829 (Revd) Henry Venn (1796–1873), missionary society administrator, in *ODNB*.

Religion Presumably Anglican.

Public None known.

Miscellaneous Presumably was an export or shipping merchant in Hull.

References K. J. Allison, *'Hull Gent. Seeks Country Residence', 1750–1850'* (1981).

WEALTH-HOLDERS, 1828

1828/1 **Name** **Firth, John**

Dates Unknown – probated February 1828.

Probate £120,000 'within province' (PCC).

Occupation Wholesale hosier in the City of London ('M Pope and J. Firth, wholesale hosiers', of 28 Friday Street, City of London, 1820 directory; M. Pope and J. Firth, 'Manchester warehouse', of same, 1803 directory). (Occupational category IV.21; venue 1.) Described as a 'merchant of Friday Street, City of London' in PROB 11.

Address 'Friday Street, Cheapside, City of London, and Rose Hill near Rotherham, Yorkshire' (probate calendar).

Father Unknown. There is no direct evidence that he was related to the famous family of steel manufacturing Firths of Sheffield, although his Rotherham address suggests that he probably was. The *DBB* entry on Mark Firth (1819–80) states that the firm was founded c. 1842. Mark's father Thomas Firth (1789–1850) was the chief smelter in a steelworks in Sheffield.

Mother Unknown.

Education Unknown.

Marriage Unknown.

Religion Unknown.

Public None known.

Miscellaneous Nothing further could be traced about him.

References Probate calendar and above sources only.

1828/2 **Name** **Brandenburg-Anspach, Margravine of, Lady Elizabeth** (née Berkeley)

Dates 17 December 1750, Spring Gardens, Middlesex–13 January 1828, Naples.

Probate £120,000 (PCC).

Occupation Landed and European aristocratic wealth. (Occupational category I.)

Address Brandenburg House, Hammersmith and The Cravens, Benham Valence, Berkshire.

Father Augustus Berkeley, 4th Earl of Berkeley (1716–9 January 1755), KT. (Second daughter.)

Mother Elizabeth (1719–29 June 1792), daughter of Henry Drax of Charborough, Kent. (She married, second, Earl Nugent.)

Education Unknown.

Marriage First, in 1767, to William Craven, 6th Earl Craven (1738–26 September 1791); they separated in 1780. (Five children.) Second, at Lisbon in 1791, to Christian, Margrave of Brandenburg-Anspach (1736–5 January 1806). In 1792, he sold (sic) his principality to the King of Prussia and settled in England. He allegedly left £150,000 at his death.

Religion Anglican.
Public None known.
Miscellaneous Known for her scandals and for her writings – *Journey Through the Crimea to Constantinople; Memoirs* (1826), plays, etc. Her property passed chiefly to her third son, the Hon. R. K. Craven, and then to her nephew, Sir George Berkeley.
References *ODNB; GM,* 1828, vol. I, p. 466.

Name **de la Torre, Don Jose Ignacio** ('Don Jose Ygnacio or Ignacio De la Torre, Honorary member of the Chamber of Commerce of the Province of Lievana in the mountains of Santander, Spain' – PROB 11) 1828/3
Dates Unknown – probated June 1828.
Probate £160,000.
Occupation PROB 8 states that he lived in Bordeaux, suggesting that he was connected with the wine trade, but PROB 11 (above) describes him as a Spaniard.
Address Bordeaux, France (PROB 8); Lievana, Santander, Spain (PROB 11).
Father Unknown.
Mother Unknown.
Education Unknown.
Marriage Unknown.
Religion Presumably Roman Catholic.
Public None known.
Miscellaneous Is not directly listed in any directory, but the 1802 London directory lists a Count de la Tour de Pin, of 9 Thayer Street. *GM,* 1829, vol. I, p. 268, notes a Don Manuel De la Torre, late of Devonshire Street, Middlesex, who married, at Richmond, Miss Anne Jones Harrison. (See also 1816/28.)
References Probate calendar only.

Name **Walker, John** 1828/4
Dates Unknown – probated June 1828.
Probate £120,000 'within province' (PCC).
Occupation 'Cotton merchant' of Manchester (PROB 11). (Occupational category IV.21; venue 4.) He may be the John Walker listed in the 1816–17 Manchester directory as a 'cotton manufacturer' (rather than a merchant) of Back Piccadilly, although there are many other John Walkers listed. (If so, occupational category II.7; venue 4.)
Address Manchester (probate calendar). His specific street address is not noted.
Father Unknown.
Mother Unknown.
Education Unknown.
Marriage Unknown.
Religion Unknown.
Public None known.
Miscellaneous Nothing more could be traced about him.
References Probate calendar only.

1828/5 **Name** **Thompson, Thomas**

Dates 5 April 1754–14 September 1828, Paris.

Probate £120,000 (PCC).

Occupation Banker in Hull (Partner, Smith & Thompson; and Samuel Smith's Bank, Hull). (Occupational category IV.16; venue 21.) He was also a partner in Sykes & Co., metal merchants of Hull, from 1788. (See Nicholas Sykes, 1827/31.)

Address Lived in Kingston-upon-Hull and at Cottingham Castle, Yorkhire.

Father Name unknown – a 'yeoman of Owborough Grange near Hull, who died in debt in France' (*HP*). According to Family Search, a Thomas Thompson (presumably this man) was baptised at Swine, near Hull, on 9 April 1754, son of Francis Thompson.

Mother Unknown. Probably Ann Torrington, who married Francis Thompson at Swine, near Hull, in 1750 (Family Search).

Education 'By Revd William Stead, Vicar of Swine' (*HP*).

Marriage In 1781, to Philothea, daughter of William Briggs of Shoreditch, Middlesex. (Three sons, one daughter.)

Religion Wesleyan Methodist – a 'stalwart' (*HP*). But he presumably regarded himself as sufficiently within the Church of England to serve in Parliament.

Public MP (Tory) for Midhurst 1807–18 (a pocket borough of Lord Carrington).

Miscellaneous Was a clerk in Wilberforce & Smith, Baltic merchants in Hull; then manager for Abel Smith, the banker and relative of Lord Carrington, in Nottingham; then a leading banker in Hull. He was Chairman of the Hull Dock Committee in 1812 and had mercantile interests. Was an FSA.

References *HP; GM,* 1829, vol. I, p. 94.

1828/6 **Name** **Buccleuch, Dowager Duchess of, Elizabeth Scott** (née Montagu)

Dates 29 May [9 June, *GM*] 1743, St George, Hanover Square–21 November 1821, Richmond, Surrey.

Probate £160,000 (PCC).

Occupation Landed wealth. (Occupational category I.)

Address Dalkeith Castle, near Edinburgh was the principal seat.

Father George Brudenell Montagu, 1st Duke of Montagu and 4th Earl of Cardigan (1712–23 May 1790). (Only daughter.)

Mother Mary (d. 1751), daughter of John, 2nd Duke of Marlborough.

Education Unknown.

Marriage In 1767, to Henry Scott, 3rd Duke of Buccleuch and 5th Duke of Queensberry, KG, KT (1746–11 January 1812). (Three sons, four daughters.)

Religion Anglican.

Public None known.

Miscellaneous *GM,* stated that 'no female . . . possessed equal patronage, wealth, or power'. She was noted for her 'munificence'. The Duke of Buccleuch was one of the wealthiest landowners in Scotland.

References *GM,* 1828, vol. I, pp. 176–7; *CP; ODNB* for husband.

Name **Holland, Swinton Coulthurst** 1828/7
Dates 27 November 1777, Roehampton–December 1827 (1828, *BLG*).
Probate £180,000 (PCC).
Occupation Apparently of a landowning family in Cheshire and Lancashire. He owned real estate at Toxteth Park, Liverpool. (Occupational category I?) The family may well also have had Liverpool mercantile wealth – *ODNB* has a Samuel Holland (1803–92), industrialist and railway promoter, the son of Samuel Holland (1768–1851), a Liverpool merchant. The family was also related to Sir Henry Holland, 1st Viscount Knutsford (1809–99), the politician, whose ancestors had owned land in Lancashire and Cheshire 'for centuries' (*ODNB*). It does not, however, appear to be listed in Bateman.
Address Lived at The Priory, Roehampton, Surrey. He does not appear to have lived in Cheshire or Lancashire in later life.
Father Samuel Holland (1734–26 May 1816) of Sandlefored near Knutsford, Cheshire.
Mother Anne (d. 1814), daughter of Peter Swinton of Knutsford.
Education Unknown.
Marriage In 1805, to Anne (d. 1845), daughter of (Revd) William Willets of Newcastle-under-Lyme. (Three sons.) (His son was George Henry Holland; see 1892/112.)
Religion Presumably Anglican.
Public None known.
Miscellaneous Josiah Wedgwood was one of his executors. The source of his wealth is unclear, apart from land.
References *BP; BLG.*

Name **Vaughan, George** 1828/8
Dates 3 July 1755–7 February 1828.
Probate £100,000 (PCC).
Occupation Hat manufacturer in Blackfriars, Southwark (Vaughan, Plank & Co., of 1 Gravel Lane, Southwark). (Occupational category II.11; venue 2.)
Address 'Of [1] Gravel Lane, Southwark' (probate calendar).
Father George Vaughan (1714–27 November 1780) – he 'owned an estate' at Gravel Lane and at Greenwich (*Genealogical Magazine*). (Second son.)
Mother Elizabeth King (1717–6 January 1789).
Education Unknown.
Marriage First, in 1785, to Mary Bunn (d.s.p., 11 November 1786). Second, marriage date unknown, to Elizabeth Andrews (1771–2 May 1852). (Two sons, one daughter.) Their son, Henry Vaughan (1809–99), is in the *ODNB* as an 'art collector'. He donated Constable's *Hay Wain* to the National Gallery, as well as many other bequests, and left £230,000. He is described as the son of George Vaughan, who 'carried on a successful business as a hat manufacturer'. Their daughter Mary Sanction founded almshouses in Southwark.
Religion His parents married in the Anglican church of St Thomas, Southwark.
Public None known.

Miscellaneous He might have owned urban land in London as well, as per his father.
References *GM*, 1828, vol. I, p. 187; *Genealogical Magazine*, August 1903, pp. 164–5.

1828/9 **Name** **Connolly, Charles**
Dates c. 1760–7 April 1828.
Probate £160,000 (PCC).
Occupation Probably a landowner in Somerset, from an Irish landowning family, but this isn't entirely clear. He is described in *GM* as 'an opulent and untitled country gentleman'. His Lincoln's Inn address suggests that he was also a barrister – see below. (Occupational category I?) Nobody of his name owning land in England is listed in Bateman, but it does list a Thomas Connoly (sic) of Castletown, County Kildare, who owned 26,853 acres worth £12,611 p.a. in three Irish counties.
Address 'Formerly of Lincoln's Inn, and then of Tatchbury, Hampshire, and then of Midford Castle [near Bath], Somerset' (probate calendar).
Father Charles Connolly, 'a near relation of the Connollys of Castletown, County Dublin [sic]' (*GM*).
Mother Dorothy Rogers.
Education Unknown. He may well have been the Charles Connolly who was admitted to Lincoln's Inn in November 1781, the son of Charles Connolly of Hendon (*LI Admissions Book*).
Marriage In 1784, to Maria Rebecca, daughter of Thomas Bourke. (One son, two daughters.)
Religion There is no evidence that he was a Roman Catholic. He was probably an Anglican. He married at the Anglican church of St Anne, Soho.
Public None known.
Miscellaneous How he became so wealthy is unclear.
References *GM*, 1828, vol. II, p. 183.

1828/10 **Name** **Hoy, Michael**
Dates c. 1758–26 June 1828, Midenbury, Hampshire.
Probate £140,000 (PCC).
Occupation A Russia merchant of 10 Crosby Square, Bishopsgate Street, City of London (1802 directory). (Occupational category IV.19; venue 1.)
Address 'Walthamstow and Midenbury House, Hampshire' (probate calendar).
Father Unknown.
Mother Unknown.
Education Unknown.
Marriage To Elizabeth (marriage date unknown), daughter of Andrew Hawes Dyne of Gore Court, Kent.
Religion Unknown, probably Anglican.
Public 'One of the Sheriffs for London and Middlesex' (*GM*).
Miscellaneous Nothing further could be traced about him.
References *GM*, 1828, vol. I, p. 647; *BLG*, 1846 in Bradley of Gore Court.

Name **Manners-Sutton, Charles, Archbishop of Canterbury** 1828/11
Dates 14 February 1755–21 July 1828.
Probate £180,000 (PCC).
Occupation Archbishop of Canterbury 1805–28. (Occupational category VI.30; venue 2?)
Address Lived at Lambeth Palace as Archbishop.
Father Lord George Manners-Sutton (d. 1723–83), son of the 3rd Duke of Rutland. (Fourth son.) The Archbishop's maternal grandfather was Lord Lexington – the Duke inherited his estates.
Mother Diana (d. 1767), daughter of Thomas Chaplin of Blankney, Lincolnshire.
Education Charterhouse; Emmanuel College, Cambridge (15th Wrangler; AA, DD).
Marriage In 1778, to Mary (d. 1832), daughter of Thomas Thoroton of Screveton, Nottinghamshire (Two sons, ten daughters.) Their son Charles Manners-Sutton, later 1st Viscount Canterbury (1780–1845), was Speaker of the House.
Religion Anglican clergyman.
Public In the House of Lords for much of his adult life.
Miscellaneous Was Dean of Peterborough, 1791–4; Dean of Windsor, 1794; Bishop of Norwich, 1792–1805, then Archbishop of Canterbury. A governor of Charterhouse. He received an enormous income from his clerical appointments. His brother Thomas (1756–1842) was Lord Chancellor of Ireland.
References *ODNB.*

Name **Dulany, Ann** 1828/12
(Given in a lengthy online genealogical source about the Dulany family as Rebecca Ann 'Nancy' Dulany, with the same address and date of death.)
Dates c. 1754, Annapolis, Md.–2 October 1828.
Probate £140,000 (PCC).
Occupation According to the online source on the Dulany family, she was the sister of Daniel Dulany (1750–1824; see 1824/30). If so, she inherited American mercantile and legal money, but the full source of this family's wealth is unclear.
Address Lived at Grand Parade, Brighton at death.
Father Daniel Dulany (1722–97), a prominent lawyer and businessman in pre-Revolutionary Maryland, in *ODNB.* (Only daughter.)
Mother Rebecca (1724–1822), daughter of Benjamin Tasker.
Education Unknown.
Marriage Unmarried.
Religion Her father was buried as an Anglican.
Public None known.
Miscellaneous Presumably inherited from her father or brother.
References *GM,* 1828, vol. II, p. 381; 'Descendants of the Sept. O'Dubhshlaine-Dulaney' (sic; online).

Name **Butterworth, Joseph Henry** 1828/13
Dates Unknown–27 October 1828, Geneva, Switzerland.

Probate £100,000 (PCC).
Occupation Publishers and law booksellers of London (J. Butterworth, booksellers, of 43 Fleet Street – 1803 and 1817 directories). (Occupational category V.27 and IV.20; venue 1.)
Address 'Fleet Street, City of London, and Clapham Common, Surrey' (probate calendar).
Father Joseph Butterworth (c. 1770–30 June 1826), law publisher of Fleet Street and Bedford Square, and MP, 1810–18 and 1820–6, in *ODNB*.
Mother Anne, daughter of John Cooke, 'clothier' of Trowbridge, Wiltshire.
Education Unknown.
Marriage To Marianne (marriage date unknown), daughter of Thomas Stock, 'sugar refiner' of Bristol.
Religion The father was a prominent Wesleyan Methodist and one of the first Methodist MPs.
Public None known.
Miscellaneous *ODNB* states that he 'predeceased' his father, but this is incorrect. He must, however, have been a young man when he died. The business went to Joseph's brother Henry, who continued it – the firm still exists as a major law publisher.
References *GM*, 1828, vol. II, p. 478; 'Memoir of the Late H. Butterworth', *GM*, 1861, vol. I; *ODNB* for the father.

1828/14 **Name** **Jones, Elizabeth**
Dates Unknown–6 December 1827, Clifton, Gloucestershire.
Probate £180,000 (PCC).
Occupation She may have been the daughter of the James Jones of the Merchant Venturers Company, Bristol, who died on 21 March 1795 (A.B. Beaven, *Bristol Lists: Municipal and Miscellaneous*, 1899). (If so, occupational category IV.19? Venue 12.)
Address Clifton, Gloucestershire.
Father She was stated to be 'the last surviving child of James Jones of Portland Square, Bristol' (*GM*, 1827, vol. II, p. 572).
Mother Unknown.
Education Unknown.
Marriage Unmarried: she is described in the probate calendars as a 'spinster'.
Religion Presumably Anglican.
Public Unknown.
Miscellaneous The father was presumably a leading Bristol merchant.
References *GM*, only.

1828/15 **Name** **Wilkins, Walter**
Dates 14 or 15 November 1741–17 March 1828, Oxendon Street, Haymarket.
Probate £250,000 (PCC).
Occupation Merchant in India – 'gained a fortune in India under the East India Company' and returned to England in 1772 and purchased the Maesllwch estate

in Radnorshire. (*ODNB* for grandson.) (Occupational category IV.19; venue 29.) In 1883, his grandson and heir, Walter de Winton of Maesllwych Castle, Hay, owned 9,600 acres in Radnor, Glamorgan, and Brecon worth £15,642 p.a.

Address Maesllwch, Radnorshire and Wallsworth Hall, Gloucester.

Father John Wilkins (d. 1784), solicitor of The Priory, Brecon.

Mother Sybil, daughter of Walter Jeffries of Lywel, Brecon, a relative of Lord Camden.

Education Christ's College, Brecon; Winchester; and Reeve's Academy, Bishopsgate Street, City of London.

Marriage In 1777, to Catherine, daughter of Samuel Hayward of Wallsworth Hall. (One son, one daughter.) Their son, Walter Wilkins (1809–40), MP, 'enjoyed a princely income' (*ODNB*). Their grandson was Sir Francis de Winton, in *ODNB*.

Religion Anglican.

Public MP (Independent) for Radnorshire, 1796–1828. High Sheriff of Radnorshire, 1774–5; for Brecon, 1778–9.

Miscellaneous Was a Writer employed by the East India Company in Bengal, 1758; a Resident at Lakipur, 1768; Senior Merchant and Governor of Chittagong, 1771; Member of the Supreme Council, 1772. Returned to Britain that year with a fortune. Was Lieutenant Colonel of the Brecon Volunteers, 1809.

References *GM*, 1828, vol. I, p. 371; *HP*; *ODNB* as noted.

Name **Smith, Thomas Assheton** 1828/16

Dates c. 1752–12 May 1828, Tidworth House, Hants.

Probate £180,000 (PCC).

Occupation Land and mineral owner, who developed the slate quarries on his Welsh estates. (Occupational category I.) In 1883, his successor Thomas Duff-Assheton-Smith of Vaynol, Bangor owned 34,482 acres worth £43,022 p.a., chiefly in Carnarvonshire.

Address 'Portman Square, Middlesex; South Tidworth, Hants.; Vaynol [near Bangor], Carnarvonshire; and Ashley Hall, Cheshire' (probate calendar).

Father Thomas Assheton Smith (1725–16 April 1774) of Ashley, Cheshire, landowner. (First son.)

Mother Mary Clayton, the 'heiress of Brymbo Hall, Denbighshire' (*HP*).

Education Eton.

Marriage In c. 1776 to Elizabeth (d. 1814), daughter of Watkin Wynne(e) of Foelas, Carnarvonshire. (Three sons, five daughters.) (Their son Thomas Assheton Smith (1776–1858) is in the *ODNB* as a 'quarry owner and sportsman'.

Religion Anglican.

Public MP (pro-Government) Carnarvonshire, 1774–80; Andover, 1797–1821. Lord Lieutenant of Carnarvonshire, 1822–death. High Sheriff of Carnarvonshire, 1774–5, 1783–4; of Anglesey, 1784–5.

Miscellaneous A member of one of the great untitled landowning families, who was important in developing the Welsh slate quarry industry. He enclosed 2,500 acres of common land (*HP*). The family was extremely wealthy into the twentieth century.

References *HP; GM,* 1828, vol. I, p. 476.

1828/17 **Name** **Cook, Thomas Valentine** (*GM,* spells the surname Cooke)

Dates c. 1766–14 August 1828, Horsham, Sussex.

Probate £120,000 (PCC).

Occupation 'Distiller' (probate calendar) (T. V. Cooke [sic], lived at 21 Hertford Street, Middlesex, 1819 Court directory; he is unlisted in any London directory as a distiller). (Occupational category II.13; venue 1 or 2?)

Address 'Formerly of Hertford Street, Middlesex, and then Sunninghill, Berkshire' (probate calendar).

Father Unknown.

Mother Unknown.

Education Unknown.

Marriage Unknown. *GM,* 1829, vol. I, p. 557 states that Margaret, third daughter of George Valentine Cooke of Hertford Street, London, married, at Wargrave, Berkshire, Edmund, the son of J. E. Currie of Standlake Park. London-born Thomas Valentine Cooke (1786–1840), possibly his son, served on the frigate *Naiad* at Trafalgar and was promoted Lieutenant RN in 1815. Robert Holden Mackenzie, *The Trafalgar Roll* (1913), p. 297.

Religion Unknown.

Public None known.

Miscellaneous Nothing further could be traced about him.

References *GM,* 1828, vol. II, p. 190.

1828/18 **Name** **Agace, Daniel**

Dates c. 1750–28 April 1828. According to Family Search, a Daniel Agace was baptised at the French Huguenot Church, Threadneedle Street, in 1747, son of Abdias Agace and Jeanne (née Pilon), and a Daniel Agace, with the same parents, was baptised there in 1751.

Probate £180,000 (PCC).

Occupation Silk weaver in Spitalfields, City of London. (Occupational category II.9; venue 1.)

Address Lived at Ascot Place, Winkfield, Berkshire. Also lived at 26 Gower Street, Middlesex. (Court guides from c. 1793.) He still had the Gower Street address in 1826. Ascot Place was purchased from King George III's trustee in 1819 and is known for its grounds.

Father Obadiah Agace (1709–87), silk weaver of Spitalfields and of Stratford, Essex. See also 'Dates' above.

Mother Jane (d. 1780), daughter of Daniel Pilon, 'silk weaver' of Spitalfields. See also 'Dates' above.

Education Unknown.

Marriage Unknown.

Religion Huguenot descent. The father was a director of the French Hospital in Victorian Park, regarded as a prestigious position in the Huguenot community. The father was, however, buried as an Anglican.

Public High Sheriff of Berkshire, 1803, although this was before he purchased Ascot Place, it seems.

Miscellaneous It is not clear whether he was in trade after his early life, or if he had other sources of wealth besides the family silk-weaving business.

References *Notes & Queries*, 28 April 1928 contains a genealogy. *GM*, 1828, vol. I, p. 476; *VCH Berkshire*, vol. 3 (1923), pp. 85–91.

Name **Peters, Henry** 1828/19

Dates Baptised 17 December 1762, St Botolph's, Bishopsgate, London–21 December 1827, Park Street, Grosvenor Square, Middlesex.

Probate £140,000 (PCC).

Occupation Banker in the City of London (Partner, Masterman & Co., Nicholas Lane, Lombard Street, City of London). (Occupational category IV.16; venue 1.)

Address 'Betchworth Castle, Surrey; 50 Park Street, Middlesex; White Hart Court, Lombard Street, and then Nicholas Lane, Lombard Street, City of London' (probate calendar). Peters employed Sir John Soane as an architect at Betchworth Castle.

Father George Peters (d. 1797) a 'wealthy' Russia merchant in the City of London and Governor of the Bank of England, 1785–7, of Hendon Place, Middlesex. (Second son.)

Mother Sarah Jager, whom George Peters married at the British Chaplaincy at St Petersburg on 25 February 1755 (www.allnames.co.uk).

Education Secondary schooling unknown; St John's College, Cambridge; admitted to Lincoln's Inn.

Marriage In 1785, to Charlotte Mary, daughter of (Lieutenant General) George Morrison of Sion Hill near Barnet, Hertfordshire. (Five sons, five daughters.)

Religion Anglican.

Public MP (Independent) for Oxford, 1796–1802. High Sheriff of Surrey, 1818–19.

Miscellaneous A wealthy banker. He contributed £60,000 to the Loyalty Loan for 1797 and was a captain in the Volunteers. His elder brother was a linen merchant.

References *HP*; *GM*, 1827, vol. II, p. 646.

Name **Sladen, Joseph** 1828/20

Dates Baptised 5 December 1736–27 December 1827, Folkestone, Kent.

Probate £180,000 (PCC).

Occupation Unknown. He was Mayor of Folkestone three times, but nothing about his career could be traced. (Venue 14?)

Address Of Folkestone, Kent and Ripple Court, near Deal, Kent.

Father John Sladen (c. 1715–2 June 1747).

Mother Hannah, daughter of Joseph Bayley.

Education Unknown.

Marriage In 1767, to Elizabeth (c. 1742–27 September 1811), daughter of Thomas Baker. (At least three daughters.) Their daughter Sarah (1773–c. 1848) married Lawrence Banks (1763–1824/30 (online genealogy). A grandson was Sir Charles Sladen (1816–84), solicitor, who migrated to Melbourne, Australia and became a prominent politician and businessman.

Religion Anglican: buried in Folkestone Church.

Public JP, Folkestone; Mayor of Folkestone in 1787, 1803, 1808.

Miscellaneous Nothing more could be traced about him.

References Online sources and will, PROB 11, online; *BLG*, 1952, whose genealogy begins with his brother John Sladen (1745–5 February 1830).

1828/21 **Name** **Vivian, John**

Dates Baptised 1756–8 (3?) January 1828, Portland Place, Middlesex.

Probate £180,000 (PCC).

Occupation Barrister and 'Solicitor of the Excise of England' (*GM*). (Occupational category VI.29; venue 2?)

Address 'Formerly of Bedford Square, Middlesex, then of Lincoln's Inn Fields, then of Portland Place, Middlesex and of Claverton near Bath, Somerset' (probate calendar).

Father Matthew Vivian (d. 1771 or 1773) of Penalewey and Kea, Cornwall. (Only son.) He was presumably related to the wealthy Vivian family of copper smelters.

Mother Janes (d. 1784), daughter of Matthew Bennett.

Education Secondary schooling unknown; St Mary's Hall, Oxford (MA). Barrister, Inner Temple, called 1785.

Marriage In 1792, to Marianne, daughter of Samuel Edwards of Cotham Lodge, Bristol. His daughter is listed in *BLG*, 1846, 'Rattray'.

Religion Anglican: buried in the Middle Temple vaults.

Public None known.

Miscellaneous Was a Reader of the Inner Temple, 1788. Nothing more is known of his career. He was the brother of Alice Vivian (see 1825/9), who left £140,000.

References *GM*, 1828, vol. I, p. 92; J. L. Vivian, *Pedigree of Vivian* (1884), p. 19; *BLG*, 1846, 'Rattray'.

1828/22 **Name** **Parker, Rogers (sic)**

Dates 8 June 1744–10 April 1828.

Probate £140,000 (PCC).

Occupation Probably inherited landed property in the Peterborough area through his father's family and land in Hertfordshire through his mother's uncle, John Rogers, a London mercer. (If so, occupational category I.) His land passed after his death to his niece, Mary Hibbert. Her father, George Hibbert (1757–1837) is in the *ODNB* as a dock owner and MP. The land eventually passed to Sir Henry Holland, 1st Viscount Knutsford (1825–1914), the politician, who had married a Hibbert relative. He owned about 1,100 acres in c. 1900. None of these is listed in Bateman.

Address Munden, near Ware, Hertfordshire. It had been bought in 1715 by John Rogers, a London mercer, and inherited by his niece, Rogers Parker's mother.

Father Armstead Parker (1699–February 1777) of Peterborough. (Only son.) Rogers Parker's grandfather, Charles Parker, MP (1663–1750), 'held property in Peterborough' (*HP*).
Mother Elizabeth (d. 1787), daughter of (Captain) Francis Roberts (d. 1725), Keeper of the Wardrobe to King James II.
Education Secondary schooling unknown; Trinity Hall, Cambridge (admitted 1761).
Marriage Unmarried.
Religion Anglican: baptised in Peterborough Cathedral.
Public None known.
Miscellaneous If he had other sources of wealth, these have not been traced. He does not appear in any London directory.
References Cussar, *Hertfordshire; VCH Hertfordshire;* sources listed above.

Name **Pusey, (Hon.) Philip** (né Bouverie) 1828/23
Dates 14 April 1828–8 October 1746.
Probate £140,000 (PCC).
Occupation Inherited mercantile and landed fortunes. (Occupational categories IV.21 and 1; venue 1.) In 1883, Sidney Edward Bouverie-Pusey of Pusey, Faringdon, owned 5,022 acres worth £7,082 p.a. in Berkshire, while the heir of his half-brother, the Earl of Radnor, owned 24,870 acres worth £42,900 p.a., including 4,334 acres worth £7,500 p.a. in Berkshire.
Address Pusey House, near Faringdon, Berkshire and Grosvenor Square, Middlesex.
Father Sir Jacob de Bouverie, 1st Viscount Folkestone (1694–17 February 1761), 'formerly a merchant in London' and an MP; created a viscount in 1747. (Younger son.) Philip Pusey changed his surname from Bouverie to Pusey in 1784 upon inheriting the estates of Pusey of Pusey, Berkshire (*GM*). This apparently consisted of about 5,000 acres in Berkshire.
Mother Elizabeth (d. 1782), daughter of Robert Marsham, 1st Baron Romney.
Education Eton; Christ Church, Oxford.
Marriage In 1798, to Lucy (d. 1858), daughter of Robert, 4th Earl of Harborough and widow of Sir Thomas Cave, 4th Baronet (Three sons, two daughters.) Their son was (Revd Professor) Edward Bouverie Pusey (1800–82), the celebrated leader of the Oxford Movement and the 'Puseyites'. Another son, Philip (1799–1855) is in the *ODNB* as an 'agriculturalist'.
Religion Anglican.
Public None known.
Miscellaneous He was almost certainly never engaged in trade and was always a landowner, although his father's fortune was mercantile.
References *GM*, 1828, vol. I, pp. 565–6; *ODNB* for relatives; *HP* for father.

Name **Taddy, James** 1828/24
Dates Unknown – probated August 1828.
Probate £140,000 (PCC).

Occupation Tobacco and snuff merchant in the City of London (Taddy, Tomlin & Co., 45 Minories, 1820 directory). He is listed as a 'tobacconist' in the 1793 directory. (Occupational category II.14 and IV.20; venue 1.)

Address 'Formerly of Fenchurch Street and then of [45] Minories in the City of London, and Hartsdown near Margate, Kent' (*GM*). He is described as of 'Minories, City of London' in PROB 11.

Father Unknown. According to *GM,* he came 'of an old and respectable family in the Isle of Thanet, well-known as the principal supporters of the sea-bathing infirmary and other benevolent institutions'. A John Taddy (d. 22 March 1773) was Mayor of Canterbury in 1772. Westgate Manor near Birchington was 'alienated to James Taddy of St John's, whose surviving sons were James and Edward Taddy' (Hasted, *Kent*).

Mother Unknown.

Education Unknown.

Marriage Unknown.

Religion Anglican – he gave money for the Anglican church at Margate.

Public None known.

Miscellaneous Tobacco firms named 'Taddy' continued into the twentieth century, but it is not clear whether his family were still connected with them.

References *BLG,* 1914 and 1937 has a 'Taddy of Caldecote Lodge', but he is not directly listed. *GM,* 1828, vol. I, p. 647; Edward Hasted, *Hasted's History of Kent,* ed. Henry H. Drake (1886); Samuel Lewis, *Topographical Dictionary of England* (1848), pp. 253–7.

1828/25 **Name** **Tillard, James**

Dates c. 1755 (but see 'Mother' below)–1 September 1828, Ramsgate.

Probate £180,000 (PCC).

Occupation Apparently a mercantile fortune plus urban property in London, but this isn't entirely clear. There is no evidence that he was in trade. (Possibly occupational category IV.21 and 1; venue 1.)

Address Street End House, Peltham (near Canterbury), Kent.

Father Probably William Tillard, brother of Sir Isaac Tillard, a London merchant who was knighted in 1722. A James Tillard, presumably our man, owned the Blossom Estate in Spitalfields (*Survey of London,* vol. 27, 1957, pp. 87–9). Tillard was also apparently the grandson of the 1st Viscount Bateman (*BLG).*

Mother Unknown. According to Family Search, a James Tillard was baptised in 1764 at Great Stanmore, son of William and Ann.

Education Unknown.

Marriage Unknown. He died childless (*BLG*).

Religion Presumably Anglican. The family, from Devon, was apparently of French origin (*BLG*).

Public None known.

Miscellaneous No one of his name is listed in Bateman.

References *BLG,* 1846; *GM,* 1828, vol. II, p. 284; Edward Hasted, *Hasted's History of Kent,* ed. Henry H. Drake (1886), p. ix.

Name **Bosanquet, Jacob** 1828/26
Dates c. 1756–30 July 1828, Broxbournbury, Broxbourne, Hertfordshire.
Probate £100,000 (PCC).
Occupation Chairman of the East India Company three times (1797, 1802, 1810) and junior partner in the mercantile firm owned by his cousin William (Bosanquet and Willermin, of Throgmorton Street); also Deputy Governor of the Levant Company and a member of Lloyd's, all in the City of London. (Occupational category IV.19; venue 1.)
Address Broxbournbury, Hertfordshire – purchased in 1790.
Father Jacob Bosanquet (1713–9 June 1767), importer of goods from the East and Governor of the East India Company. (First son.)
Mother Elizabeth (d. 1799), daughter of John Hanbury of Kelmarsh, Northamptonshire.
Education Eton.
Marriage In 1790, to Henrietta (1767–18 October 1797), daughter of Sir George Armytage, Baronet of Kirklees, and widow of Thomas Grady of Harley Street. (Two sons, two daughters.)
Religion The father's family were Huguenots who came to England in 1685. He was an Anglican, although a director of the French Hospital, a major Huguenot institution.
Public High Sheriff of Hertfordshire, 1803.
Miscellaneous He was a governor of Christ's Hospital and a senior trustee of Morden College. His brothers were bankers. He was part of the important 'Huguenot Cousinhood' in England – the Bosanquets produced many notable figures.
References *GM,* 1828, vol. II, p. 435; *BLG,* 1952; G. L. Lee, *The Story of the Bosanquets* (1966) and Louisa C. Meyer, *Genealogy of the Bosanquets,* at the Society of Genealogists.

Name **Du Boulay, Francis Houssemayne** 1828/27
Dates 30 (12?) June 1759–28 October 1828, Bath.
Probate £300,000 (PCC).
Occupation Strangely, the source of his wealth isn't clear. He was possibly a stockbroker in the City of London. His brothers-in-law John and Philip Cazenove were stockbrokers. A P. Du Boulay of Threadneedle Street signed the 1795 Merchant's Declaration. Francis Du Boulay does not appear to be listed under his own name in any directory. (Occupational category IV.23? Venue 1?, although this is uncertain.)
Address Forest House, Walthamstow.
Father Benjamin François Houssemayne du Boulay (d. June 1765), Pastor of the French Church in Threadneedle Street, City of London.
Mother Louise (1736–1825), daughter of Jean Lagier Lamotte of Grotto House, Berkshire and Thorne Grove, Worcestershire.
Education Unknown.
Marriage In 1798, to Elizabeth (d. 1814), daughter of John Paris of Wanstead. (Two sons.)

Religion Huguenot. His religion at death is unclear.
Public None known.
Miscellaneous The size of his fortune suggests that he was a successful businessman.
References *BLG*, 1914, 1937. Another man of his name (1837–1914) was an important naturalist in Australia.

1828/28 **Name** **Taylor, John Vickers**
Dates c. 1747–11 September 1828.
Probate £160,000 (PCC).
Occupation Brewer in Limehouse (John Vickers Taylor & Co., of Fore Street, Limehouse, 1822 directory). (Occupational category III.12; venue 2.) A J. V. Taylor of Old South Sea House signed the 1795 Merchant's Declaration. A firm called A. & J. V. Taylor, corn factors, of 8 Great St Helen's, City of London, is listed in the 1793 directory.
Address 'Fore Street, Limehouse, and Southgate, Norfolk' (probate calendar).
Father Robert Taylor.
Mother Sarah Simonds.
Education Unknown.
Marriage In 1797, to Sophia, daughter of Nicholas Donnithorne of St Agnes, Cornwall. Their daughter Sarah married Isaac Walker, a wealthy Quaker brewer of Arnos Grove; their son Vyell Edward Walker (1837–1906) is in the *ODNB* as a 'cricketer' and was also a millionaire brewer. The Walkers were renowned cricketers.
Religion Possibly of Quaker background, although he is not listed at marriage or death in the *Quaker Monitor*.
Public None known.
Miscellaneous The family is listed in *BLG*, although it is apparently unlisted in Bateman.
References *BLG*, 1952.

1828/29 **Name** **Baillie, James**
Dates 1771–probated January 1828.
Probate £250,000 (PCC).
Occupation 'Merchant' of 45 Bedford Square (1822, 1825 directories). He might have been a West Indies merchant. (If so, occupational category IV.19; venue 2.)
Address 45 (14?) Bedford Square is the only known address.
Father Possibly the illegitimate son of Alexander Baillie (d. 1798) of Dochfour, Inverness-shire. (Wyldbore-Smith Collection.) James Baillie was probably the nephew of James Baillie (c. 1737–93), MP, of Bedford Square and Ealing Grove. His brother Evan (c. 1741–1835) of Bristol was an 'eminent' West Indies merchant there. Peter Baillie, MP (d. 1811) was also possibly a relative.
Mother Given (Wyldbore-Smith Collection) as 'Mrs. Sarah Smith'.
Education Unknown.
Marriage Unknown.
Religion Unknown: presumably originally Church of Scotland.

Public None known.

Miscellaneous Nothing else could be traced about him. He might have been connected with the Baillies mentioned in S. G. Checkland, 'Finance for the West Indies, 1780–1810' (*Economic History Review*, ns, vol. 10, no. 3, 1954, p. 469) and in Douglas J. Hamilton, *Scotland, the Caribbean and the Atlantic World, 1750–1820* (2005).

References Wyldbore-Smith Manuscript Genealogical Collection (Box 2, I) at the Society of Genealogists.

Name **Leader, William** 1828/30

Dates 19 October 1767–18 January 1828.

Probate £300,000 (PCC).

Occupation Malt distiller of Wandsworth (partner with John Falconer Atlee and James Langdale); 'By the time of his death' also had an 'interest' in Pellatt & Green, wholesale china, glass and earthernware dealers of St Paul's Churchyard, City (*HP*); and was also a coach and harness maker at 9 Three King Street, Lombard Street, City. He is described in the *ODNB* entry for his son as a 'coach builder, distiller, and glass manufacturer'. (Occupational categories II.11, III.13, and IV.21; venues 1 and 2.) He also owned real estate, but the family is not listed in Bateman. It is difficult to know which of these was his primary interest. His father was 'coachmaker to the Prince of Wales'.

Address '[14] Queen Square, Westminster; Lower House, Putney Hill' (probate calendar).

Father William Leader (d. 1798), 'Coachmaker to the Prince of Wales', of 37 Liquor Pond Street, St Andrews, Holborn and 32 Bedford Row, Middlesex' (*HP*).

Mother Mary, surname unknown – possibly Lucas.

Education Eton.

Marriage To Mary, surname unknown (1762–1838; other sources state that she died on 7 May 1833, aged seventy-two). She was perhaps Mary Bond, who married a William Leader in 1797 in St Martin-in-the-Fields, Westminster (Family Search). (Two sons, four daughters.) Their son John Temple Leader (1810–1903) is in the *ODNB* as a 'politician and connoisseur of the arts'; he left £279,000.

Religion Anglican.

Public MP (pro-Whig) for Camelford, 1812–28, Winchelsea, 1823–6.

Miscellaneous Described as 'a wealthy London merchant'. (*ODNB* for his son.) His nephew was William Leader Maberley, MP.

References *ODNB* for son; *HP*; J. T. Leader, *Rough and Rambling Notes on My Early Life* (1890).

Name **Dick, James** 1828/31

Dates Baptised 6 February 1743 at Forres, Morayshire–24 May 1828, Bunhill Fields.

Probate £140,000 (PCC).

Occupation West Indies merchant, formerly of Jamaica, then of Finsbury Square, City of London. (Occupational category IV.19; venue 1 and 29.)

Address '[19] Artillery Place, Finsbury Square, City of London, and then Finsbury Square' (probate calendar). Lived in Jamaica, c. 1762–82.
Father Alexander Dick (d. 1783), 'shoemaker and town councillor' of Forres (*ODNB*).
Mother Elizabeth, surname unknown.
Education Rafford (near Forres) Grammar School.
Marriage In c. 1762 to Jane Anderson, 'a servant'. (One son, one daughter.)
Religion Presumably Church of Scotland.
Public Made a Freeman of Forres, 1783.
Miscellaneous Went to the West Indies aged nineteen as a clerk in a merchant's house in Kingston, Jamaica, and remained twenty years before becoming a London-based merchant. Became famous for endowing the 'Dick Bequest' in his will, for poor Scottish schoolmasters, who had to pass rigorous exams in order to double their salaries. His bequest is said to be responsible for raising educational levels in Scotland (*ODNB*). He was the uncle of Quintin Dick (d. 1858), a half-millionaire West Indies merchant.
References *ODNB; GM,* 1828, vol. I, p. 572.

1828/32 **Name** **Hobson, Edward**
Dates c. 1759–8 September 1828, Hope Hall, Eccles, Lancashire.
Probate £140,000 (York PC).
Occupation Probably a woollen manufacturer in Manchester ('Edward Hobson, woollen manufacturer', of 2 South Parade, Manchester, 1803 directory). (If so, occupational category II.8; venue 4.)
Address Lived at Hope Hall, Eccles, near Manchester.
Father Unknown.
Mother Unknown.
Education Unknown.
Marriage Unknown. *GM,* 1828, vol. II, p. 638, notes the marriage of Edward Hobson of Hope Hall, Lancashire (presumably his son) to Esther Reade, daughter of (Revd) H. Quarterley of Wicken, Northamptonshire.
Religion Presumably Anglican.
Public None known.
Miscellaneous The 1818–20 Manchester directory also lists a Hobson & Taylor, 'merchants' of 7 Worsley's Court, Market Street, Manchester.
References *GM,* 1828, vol. II, p. 284 and above sources.

1828/33 **Name** **Rawson, William**
Dates 1748–25 August 1828.
Probate £160,000 (York PC).
Occupation Banker in Halifax (Rawson, Rhodes & Briggs, then Rawson Brothers). (Occupational category IV.16; venue 7.) The bank was opened by his brother John. The brothers John, William and Christopher were partners in Rawson Brothers.
Address Lived at Millhouse, near Halifax, West Riding.

Father Christopher Rawson (1712–80), woollen textile manufacturer of Stonyroyd, Halifax. (Fourth son.)
Mother Grace, daughter of Jeremiah (John?) Rawson of Beckfoot and Cottingley.
Education Unknown.
Marriage In 1791, to Elizabeth (d.s.p., 23 December 1837), daughter of (Revd) Samuel Threlkeld. Her mother was the sister of William Wordsworth's grandfather.
Religion Anglican.
Public JP, DL, West Riding.
Miscellaneous His bank was also known as the Halifax New Bank.
References *BLG; Halifax Antiquities Society,* 1909.

Name **Walker, Thomas** 1828/34
Dates Unknown–15 April 1828, Bath.
Probate £200,000 (York PC).
Occupation 'Ironmaster' (probate calendar) in Mansfield, Nottinghamshire. (Occupational category II.3; venue 17.)
Address Berry Hall, Mansfield, Nottinghamshire.
Father Samuel Walker (1716–12 May 1782), founder of the ironworks in Mansfield.
Mother Unknown.
Education Unknown.
Marriage In 1783, to Mary (d.s.p.), daughter of Samuel Need, of Arnold, Nottinghamshire.
Religion Presumably Anglican.
Public High Sheriff of Nottinghamshire, 1809. He appears to have been the Samuel Walker who was the first Chairman of the Mansfield Improvement Commissioners in 1823.
Miscellaneous An early local ironmaster.
References *BLG,* 1846.

Name **Hibbert, James** 1828/35
Dates Unknown. Probated 12 May 1828.
Probate £100,000 (Chester Consistory Court).
Occupation He was probably the James Hibbert, 'fustian manufacturer', of 13 St John's Street, Manchester, listed in the 1793 directory. (If so, occupational category II.7 or 9; venue 4.)
Address Broughton, Manchester.
Father Unknown.
Mother Unknown.
Education Unknown.
Marriage Unknown.
Religion Unknown.
Public None known.

Miscellaneous Nothing more could be traced about him.
References Probate calendar only.

Name **Jauncey, William** 1829/1

Dates Unknown (possibly 1744 New York). Probated July 1829.

Probate £250,000 'within province' (PCC).

Occupation Apparently a merchant and property owner in New York City. He had previously lived in London, but his career here is unclear. He was presumably a merchant. (If so, occupational category IV.19? Venues 29 and 1, but this is uncertain.)

Address 'Formerly of Charlotte Street, Portland Place, Middlesex, and then of New York City' (probate calendar).

Father Unknown. According to Family Search, a William Jauncey was baptised at the First and Second Presbyterian Church, New York, on 25 December 1744. According to Rootsweb.com, the family came from Stretton Grandison, Hereford. His father is listed as James Jauncey (d. 6 February 1790 in London). The father was possibly born in Bermuda and is described on this site as 'rich'. William Jauncey was his eldest son. The father left about £52,000 at his death.

Mother Possibly Maria or Mary, daughter of William Smith (Roots Web).

Education Unknown.

Marriage Unknown.

Religion Unknown.

Public None known.

Miscellaneous A Jauncey residence near Broad Street in lower Manhattan was built by William Jauncey 'soon after the Revolution'. He moved to 24 Broadway in 1815 or 1816 (*Wall Street Ninety Years Ago*, 1921, online). Jauncey owned real estate in Manhattan valued at $100,000–$200,000 (£20,000–£40,000) in 1828 and was one of the wealthier men in New York. (Edward Pessen, 'Did Fortunes Rise and Fall Mercurially in Antebellum America?', *Journal of Social History*, Summer [1971].) The family apparently emigrated from England to Bermuda to New York and then back to London.

References Above sources only.

Name **Smithson, James Lewis** (né James Louis Macie) 1829/2

Dates '[E]arly 1764 Paris'–27 June 1829, Genoa, Italy.

Probate £120,000 (PCC). (The value in American dollars was $508,318.)

Occupation Apparently inherited the landed fortune of his mother, who was an heiress of the Hungerfords of Studley, and money from his father, the 1st Duke of Northumberland. (Occupational category I.) Other sources state that he received the fortune of his half-brother Henry Louis Dickinson. Smithson is world-famous for having established the Smithsonian Institute in Washington, DC, in his will.

Address 'Clarges Street, Middlesex, then Manchester Street and St James's Place, Middlesex; late of Genoa' (probate calendar).

Father The illegitimate son of Henry Percy Smithson, 2nd Earl and 1st Duke of Northumberland (1712–6 June 1786), one of the richest landowners in Britain.

Mother Elizabeth (1728–1800), daughter of Henry Keate. She was the widow of a Mr Dickinson and then of James Macie (1720–61), a country gentleman of Weston near Bath, who inherited the properties of the Hungerfords of Studley from his brother.

Education Probably Charterhouse, although he is not recorded in its Register (*ODNB*); Pembroke College, Oxford (matriculated as James Ludovic Macie, 1782; MA, 1786).

Marriage Unmarried.

Religion Anglican, although his father was a Roman Catholic at the time of his birth.

Public None known.

Miscellaneous An eminent geologist and mineralogist, FRS. He established the Smithsonian Institute in his will with a bequest of £104,960. No one knows why he established an American body, although his experiences in the French Revolution, when he was arrested, apparently made him despair of the Old World. He had apparently never visited America. His body, originally buried in Paris, was reinterred at the Smithsonian Institute.

References *ODNB; GM,* 1830, vol. I, p. 275.

1829/3 **Name Bagwill, John**

Dates c. 1750–25 January 1828, Newington Place, Surrey.

Probate £140,000 (PCC).

Occupation Stockbroker in London. (Occupational category IV.23; venue 1.)

Address 'Of the Stock Exchange and Newington Place, Surrey' (probate calendar).

Father Unknown.

Mother Unknown.

Education Unknown.

Marriage Unknown. Possibly Hester Bull, who married a John Bagwell (sic) in 1781 at St George's, Hanover Square, Westminster (Family Search).

Religion Anglican; buried St Margaret's, Westminster.

Public None known.

Miscellaneous Nothing further could be trace about him.

References *Notes & Queries,* 21 November 1931, notes his memorial inscription at St Margaret's, Westminster, but provides no further information.

1829/4 **Name Liverpool, 2nd Earl of, Sir Robert Bankes Jenkinson, 8th Baronet**

Dates 7 June 1770–4 December 1828, Coombe Wood near Kingston, Surrey.

Probate £120,000 (PCC).

Occupation Inherited landed estates and money from his maternal grandfather, the Governor of Fort William, Bengal, and was Prime Minister. (Presumably occupational categories I and VI.31.)

Address His chief house was Coombe Wood near Kingston, Surrey; also official residences.

Father Sir Charles Jenkinson, 7th Baronet (1729–17 December 1808), created 1st

Baron Hawkesbury in 1786 and, in 1796, 1st Earl of Liverpool. Landowner, MP and Cabinet minister. (First son.)

Mother Amelia (d. 1770, aged nineteen), daughter of William Watts, Governor of Fort William, Bengal, who subsequently resided at South Hill, Ascot, Berkshire.

Education 'Parson's Green, Fulham'; Charterhouse; Christ Church, Oxford.

Marriage First, in 1795, to Lady Theodosia (d.s.p., 1821), daughter of Frederick, 4th Earl of Bristol and Bishop of Derry. Second, in 1822, to Mary (d.s.p.), daughter of (Revd) Chales Chester (né Bagot).

Religion Anglican.

Public MP (Tory) for Rye, 1790–1803. PC, 1790. Held office as Master of the Mint, 1799–1801; Foreign Secretary, 1801–4; Home Secretary, 1804–6, 1807–9; War and Colonial Secretary, 1809–12; Prime Minister 1812–death. Lord Warden of the Cinque Ports, 1807–19, etc.

Miscellaneous His estates passed to his brother. No obvious heir is listed in Bateman. Norman Gash's entry on him in the *ODNB* states that he was not wealthy by the standards of his day, but he obviously was.

References *ODNB; GM,* 1828, vol. I, pp. 81–6.

Name **Poore, Charlotte** 1829/5

Dates c. 1739–24 March 1829, Bath.

Probate £140,000 (PCC).

Occupation Presumably inherited land and a legal fortune. She is described in Bell's article as 'a wealthy lady who owned extensive properties in Wiltshire and Hampshire'. (If so, occupational category I.) Her relative Sir Edward Poore inherited her property, but no one named Poore appears in Bateman.

Address 'Formerly of High Hall, Wimborne, Dorset, and then Bath' (probate calendar).

Father Edward Poore (c. 1704–19 May 1780), MP, of Salisbury, Wiltshire. Bencher and Treasurer of Lincoln's Inn and a Welsh judge, 1753–death.

Mother Rachel, daughter of George Mullins, MD, of Salisbury.

Education Unknown.

Marriage Apparently unmarried.

Religion Anglican.

Public None known.

Miscellaneous Apart from her landed holdings, she owned 4 The Circus, Bath. Presumably her fortune represented chiefly landed income left to accumulate, but this is unclear. *VCH Wiltshire* (16 [1999], pp. 120–6) gives an account of this family's holdings at Chute Forest, Wiltshire.

References Robert D. Bell, 'The Discovery of a Buried Georgian Garden in Bath', *Garden History,* 18, 1 (1990); *VCH Wiltshire,* 16 (1999), pp. 120–6; *GM,* 1829, vol. I, p. 381.

Name **Ward, George** 1829/6

Dates 31 August 1751–18 February 1829, Northwood Park, Isle of Wight.

Probate £200,000 'within province' (PCC).

Occupation A Spanish and Mediterranean merchant in the City of London (John and George Ward, merchants, of Old Pay Office, Broad Street, City; or George Ward 'merchant' of 34 New Broad Street, Bishopsgate, 1817 directory). (Occupational category IV.19; venue 1.) He was also 'a large landowner in the Isle of Wight and Hampshire' (*BLG*). In 1883, William George Ward, of Freshwater, Hampshire, presumably a descendant, owned 10,000 acres worth £11,000 p.a.

Address Northwood Park, Isle of Wight. In 1817, he lived in St Anne's, Westminster.

Father John Ward, 'a merchant of Spain', 'of the Garrison at Gibraltar', who settled in England in 1782 and lived in Westminster (*BLG*). John Ward 'combined the comfortable office of chief clerk to the Ordnance with his trade as a Spanish merchant' (*Blackwood's Edinburgh Review*, August [1850], p. 200). (First son.)

Mother Rebecca Raphael of Gibraltar, described as 'a Spanish Jewess' (*Blackwood's Edinburgh Review*, August [1850], p. 200). Her family were Sephardim from Spain who had settled in Genoa. (*ODNB* entry on Robert Plumer-Ward, her sixth son.)

Education Unknown.

Marriage In 1784, to Mary (d. 1814), daughter of Thomas Woodfall (given as Henry Samson Woodfall in *GM*). (Six sons, five daughters.) (Their son, William Ward, was MP for the City of London, 1826–31, and a director of the Bank of England.)

Religion Presumably Anglican. His mother was Jewish.

Public None known.

Miscellaneous Described in *BLG*, as 'a merchant of great eminence in the City of London'. He possibly traded with or supplied British troops, given his Gibraltar connection. His brother Robert Plumer-Ward (d. 1846) was also an MP.

References *GM*, 1829, vol. I, p. 185; *BLG*, 1937; *HP* for brother and son; *Blackwood's Edinburgh Review*, August (1850), pp. 199–216, and *ODNB* for his brother Robert Plumer-Ward.

1829/7 **Name** **Bolland, John**

Dates c. 1742–7 June 1829, Clapham.

Probate £120,000 (PCC).

Occupation Hop merchant at 106 Upper Thames Street (1791 directory) and later at Mark Lane; retired c. 1825 (*HP*). (Occupational category IV.21 and III.12? Venue 1.)

Address Lived in Clapham.

Father John Bolland, 'linen draper' of Cheapside (*HP*). A James Bolland, 'linen draper', 108 Cheapside; Bolland & Prestwidge, hop merchants, 30 Mincing Lane is listed in the 1794 directory.

Mother Unknown. She was perhaps Ann (surname unknown): a John Bolland, son of John and Ann, was baptised at St Mary's, Marylebone, on 26 January 1742. A child of the same name, son of John and Elizabeth, was baptised at St Luke's, Finsbury, on 10 June 1744 (Family Search).

Education Unknown.

Marriage In 1778, to Elizabeth, daughter of Henry Gipps of Canterbury. (One son, six daughters.) Their daughter Sophia (d. 1852) married John Lonsdale, Bishop of Lichfield (1788–1867); their daughter Elizabeth married her cousin Sir William Bolland (1771–1840), lawyer and book collector; their daughter Sarah married Sir William Reid (1791–1858), meteorologist and army officer (all *ODNB*).
Religion Anglican.
Public MP (Whig) Bletchingley, 1814–18.
Miscellaneous He acted as London agent for his wife's uncle George Gipps, MP, in a Canterbury election. He subscribed to the Loyalty Loan, 1797.
References *HP; GM,* 1829, vol. I, p. 572; *ODNB* for relatives.

Name **Currie, William** 1829/8
Dates 26 February 1756–3 June 1829.
Probate £140,000 (PCC).
Occupation Banker at 29 Cornhill, City of London. His firm was known as Currie, Lefevre, Yallowby & Co., then Lefevre, Currie and then Currie & Co. It was later associated with Glyn, Mills & Co. (Occupational category IV.16; venue 1.)
Address 'Of Cornhill, in the City of London, and East Horsley, Surrey' (probate calendar); also lived at Upper Gatton, near Reigate, Surrey. East Horsley was purchased in 1784.
Father William Currie (1721–10 November 1781), banker of Cornhill; lived at Bow near Stratford, Essex. (First son.)
Mother Madeline, daughter of Isaac Lefevre, banker of London and partner in the firm.
Education Unknown.
Marriage In 1794, to Percy, daughter of (Colonel) Francis Gore, first Governor of Grenada. (Five sons, two daughters.) Their daughter Percy married Horatio Powys, Bishop of Sodor and Man (1805–77), who has an entry in the *ODNB.*
Religion Anglican. His mother was of Huguenot descent, it would seem.
Public MP (Whig, then Tory) Gatton, 1790–6; Winchelsea, 1976–1802.
Miscellaneous A prominent City banker.
References *HP; GM,* 1829, vol. I, pp. 568, 652; *BLG.*

Name **Thornton, Thomas** 1829/9
Dates Unknown–3 May 1829.
Probate £160,000 (PCC).
Occupation Brewer, of Cooper's Row, Crutched Friars, City of London (1793 directory). (Occupational category III.12; venue 1.)
Address 'Formerly of the Red Lion Brewhouse; Lower East Smithfield; and then Springfield near Horsham, Sussex' (probate calendar).
Father Unknown.
Mother Unknown.
Education Unknown.

Marriage To Ann Christian (marriage date unknown). They had a son named Thomas.
Religion Unknown.
Public None known.
Miscellaneous There is no evidence that he was related to either the well-known Thornton banking family or to the very wealthy Russia merchants named Thornton.
References *GM,* 1829, vol. I, p. 477.

1829/10 **Name** **Hunt, William**
Dates c. 1751–23 September 1829.
Probate £250,000 (PCC).
Occupation 'Silkman' at 117 Bishopsgate, City of London. He was apparently a 'silk merchant' (1817 directory), not a manufacturer, although more information is needed. (Occupational category IV.21? Venue 1.) He is also described as a 'silk merchant' in the online history of University of London-Guy's Hospital, of which he was a benefactor.
Address 'Bishopsgate Street, City of London, and then Petersham, Surrey' (probate calendar).
Father Unknown.
Mother Unknown.
Education Unknown.
Marriage Unknown.
Religion Presumably Anglican; he is buried in the vaults at Guy's Hospital.
Public None known.
Miscellaneous He gave the money for Hunt's House at Guy's Hospital.
References *GM,* 1829, vol. II, p. 381; Guy's Hospital online sources.

1829/11 **Name** **James, Sir Walter James, 1st Baronet** (né Head)
Dates 8 February 1759–8 October 1829.
Probate £200,000 (PCC).
Occupation Apparently chiefly a landowner. In 1883, Sir Walter Charles James Baronet owned 6,617 acres worth £12,949 p.a. in Northumberland, Kent and Durham. (Occupational category I.) He was also Warden of the Mint to 1798. Sir Walter, his grandson (1816–93) became 1st Baron Northbourne (*ODNB*).
Address 'Formerly of Langley Hall, Hampstead and Norris, Berkshire, and then Freshford House, Somerset' (probate calendar).
Father Sir Thomas Head (1715–October 1780) of Langley Hall, High Sheriff of Berkshire, 1744. Sir Walter took the name James in 1778 when he inherited from John James of Denford Court, his uncle.
Mother Jane, daughter of Rowland Holt of Redgrave Hall, Suffolk. (Her sister was Mary, Countess of Haddington; they were nieces of Lord Chief Justice Holt.)
Education Secondary schooling unknown; Trinity College, Cambridge (DCL, 1788).

Marriage In 1780 (1788?) to Lady Jane Pratt (d. 1825), daughter of Charles, 1st Earl Camden, Lord Chancellor. (Two sons, four daughters.)
Religion Anglican.
Public Created baronet, 1791.
Miscellaneous Apparently a well-connected landowner, with holdings near London, although the sources of his wealth are not entirely clear.
References *GM,* 1829, vol. II, pp. 368–9; *BP.*

Name **Blades, John** 1829/12
Dates c. 1752–10 November 1829, at Brockwell Hall near Dulwich, Surrey.
Probate £140,000 (PCC).
Occupation 'The great Glassman at Ludgate Hill' (*GM*); John Blades, glass manufacturers, of 5 Ludgate Hill, St Paul's, City of London, 1820 directory. (Occupational category II.11 and IV.20; venue 1.) He also owned 'considerable' landed property, especially at St Bride's Avenue, Fleet Street; Brixton; and at Shooter's Hill Tower (*GM*).
Address '5 Ludgate Hill, City of London and Brockwell Hall, Surrey' (probate calendar).
Father Unknown.
Mother Unknown.
Education Unknown.
Marriage In 1786, to Hannah Hobson. Their daughter Caroline married (Revd) Edwin Prodgers of Trinity College, Oxford.
Religion Anglican; married and buried St Bride's Church, City of London.
Public Sheriff of London and Middlesex, 1812–13.
Miscellaneous Held Royal Warrants as glass-cutters and sellers to the British and Persian courts. It isn't clear whether he chiefly sold glass vessels and artefacts, mirrors, or windows, or all of these.
References *GM,* 1829, vol. II, pp. 476, 653.

Name **Beech, James** 1829/13
Dates 1763–29 October 1828.
Probate £120,000, 'within province' (PCC).
Occupation Pottery manufacturer in Burslem, Staffordshire. (Occupational category II.11; venue 18.) The family also acquired land. In 1883, James Beech, of Brandon Lodge, Coventry, owned 4,159 acres worth £6,090 p.a. in Staffordshire and Warwickshire.
Address Lived at Kingsley, near Cheadle, Staffordshire.
Father John Beech (1726–20 October 1767) of Tideswell and The Shawe, Staffordshire. (First son.) He inherited The Shawe from his aunt, Mary Stubbs.
Mother Hannah, daughter of Edward Swann of Fairfield, Derbyshire.
Education Unknown.
Marriage In 1799, to Esther (d. 1835), daughter of Richard Sutton of Shawe House, Staffordshire. (One son, four daughters.)
Religion Presumably Anglican.

Public High Sheriff of Staffordshire, 1811.
Miscellaneous In 1838, James Beech (presumably his son) 'Owned substantial potteries, including Sandyford Pottery in Staffordshire' (*VCH Staffordshire*).
References *BLG*, 1846, 1952; *VCH Staffordshire*, vol. 8, p. 99; online sources.

1829/14 **Name** **East, Sir Gilbert, 2nd Baronet**
Dates 17 April 1764, Hall Place–11 December 1828.
Probate £300,000 (PCC).
Occupation Legal fortune inherited from his father, also land. (Occupational categories I and VI.29; venue 1.) In 1883, Sir Gilbert Clayton-East, Baronet, owned 3,223 acres worth £5,869 in Berkshire. There is no evidence that Sir Gilbert East practised law.
Address Fairfield and Hall Place, Berkshire.
Father Sir William East, 1st Baronet (1737–12 October 1819), of Hall Place, Hurley, Berkshire (see 1819/9, left £200,000), legal fortune. (First son.)
Mother Hannah, daughter of Henry Casamajor of Tokington, Gloucestershire.
Education Secondary schooling unknown; Queen's College, Oxford (matriculated 1783). He apparently entered the Middle Temple in 1769, although, from the date, this might well have been another man of his name. He apparently was not called to the Bar.
Marriage In 1788, to Eleanor (d.s.p., 1838), daughter of William Joliffe MP, of Petersfield. Having died childless, the property passed to his nephew, who became Clayton-East, Baronet.
Religion Anglican.
Public High Sheriff of Berkshire, 1822–3.
Miscellaneous He appears to have been chiefly a landowner in Berkshire.
References *GM*, 1829, vol. I, pp. 173–4; *BP.*

1829/15 **Name** **Evans, George Freke**
Dates c. 1742–19 July 1829, Laxton Hall, Northamptonshire.
Probate £120,000 (PCC).
Occupation Landowner. He was the cousin of Lord Carbery and married his widow, who had 'brought a fortune of £6000 p.a.' to Lord Carbery, possibly East India Company money. He also apparently inherited from his parents, landowners in Ireland and Scotland. How he became so wealthy is, however, not entirely clear, since he was the second son. (Occupational category I.) In 1883, Lord Carbery owned 21,246 acres worth £12,850 p.a. in Ireland, Northamptonshire and Dorset.
Address Laxton Hall, near Stamford, Northamptonshire, and Bulgaden Hall, County Limerick.
Father Sir John Freke (né Evans), 1st Baronet (d. 20 March 1777), Irish MP and Sheriff of County Wexford, 1774, of Castle Freke, County Cork. (Second son.) (George Freke Evans apparently changed his name back to Evans at some point.)
Mother Elizabeth (d. 1776), daughter of Arthur, 1st Earl of Arran.
Education Unknown.
Marriage In 1808, to Susan (d. October 1828), daughter of Henry Watson,

Chief Engineer at Bengal, and widow of George Evans, 4th Baron Carbery (d. 1804), his cousin.
Religion Anglican.
Public None known.
Miscellaneous As noted, the sources of his fortune aren't very clear, apart from some land.
References *GM,* 1829, vol. I, p. 2; vol. II, p. 188; *BP;* A. P. W. Malcolmson, *The Pursuit of the Heiress* (1982), pp. 19–20.

Name **Fitzroy, Lord Charles** 1829/16
Dates 17 July 1764–20 December 1829.
Probate £100,000 (PCC).
Occupation 'General in the Army' (probate calendar). (Occupational category VI.31.)
Address 'Formerly of Salcey Forest, Newport Pagnall, Berks., and then Wicken, Northamptonshire' (probate calendar).
Father Augustus Fitzroy, 3rd Duke of Grafton (1735–14 March 1811). (Second son.)
Mother (Hon.) Anne, daughter of Henry, 1st Baron Ravensworth. (She divorced her husband and married, second, John, 2nd Earl of Upper Ossory, and died in 1804). She left Lord Charles Fitzroy £60,000, it is said.
Education Harrow; 'Hackney'; Trinity College, Cambridge (MA).
Marriage First, in 1795, to Frances (d. 1797), daughter of Edward Miller Mundy of Shipley, Derbyshire. (One son.) Second, in 1799, to Frances (d. 1810), daughter of Robert, 1st Marquess of Londonderry. (Two sons, one daughter.) Two of his sons are in the *ODNB:* Sir Charles Augustus Fitzroy (1796–1858), colonial governor, and Robert Fitzroy (1805–55), hydrographer and meteorologist.
Religion Anglican.
Public MP (pro-Whig), Bury St Edmunds, 1787–96, 1802–18.
Miscellaneous Ensign, 1782; Captain, 1787; Lieutenant Colonel, 1789; Colonel, 1799; Lieutenant General, 1804; General, 1814; Aide-du-Camp to the King, 1795.
References *ODNB; HP; GM,* 1830, vol. I, pp. 78–9.

Name **Curtis, Sir William, 1st Baronet** 1829/17
Dates 25 January 1752, London–18 January 1829, Ramsgate.
Probate £140,000 (PCC).
Occupation Primarily a banker (founder and partner in Roberts, Curtis & Were of Cornhill). (Occupational category IV.16; venue 1.) He was also a shipowner, especially in whale fisheries, an East India merchant, a government contractor, and he continued his father's trade of manufacturing ships' biscuits. As well, he was a director of the West India and East India Docks and a director of Pelican Life Assurance. Most sources describe him primarily as a banker.
Address Cullands Grove, Southgate, Middlesex; Cliff House, Ramsgate, Kent.
Father Joseph Curtis (1715–21 March 1771), manufacturer of ships' biscuits, of Wapping. (Third son.)

Mother Mary (d. 1759), daughter of Timothy Tennant of Wapping.
Education Unknown.
Marriage In 1776, to Anne (d. 1833), daughter of Edward Constable. (Four sons, two daughters.)
Religion Anglican. His father was known to be a Presbyterian.
Public MP (pro-Government) City of London, 1790–1818 and 1820–6; Bletchingley, 1819–20; Hastings, 1826. Alderman in the City of London, 1785–death; Sheriff of London, 1788–9; Lord Mayor of London, 1795–6. Also held many other City offices. Created baronet 1802.
Miscellaneous A major member of the London civic elite, who had multiple economic interests, although chiefly a banker. He was also President of Christ's Hospital.
References *ODNB; GM,* 1829, vol. I, p. 273; *HP; BP.*

1829/18 **Name** **Johnston, John**
Dates c. 1745–24 December 1828, Danson (Park), Kent.
Probate £120,000 (PCC).
Occupation Merchant in the City of London (H. J. Johnston & Co., merchants, of 6 Scott's Yard, City of London, 1818 directory). The firm was apparently primarily engaged as West Indies merchants. Johnston had lived at Tobago. He was apparently originally a corn merchant and banker in London (online genealogy). (Occupational category IV.19; venue 1.)
Address 'Formerly of [94] Newman Street and Scott's Yard, Cannon Street, City of London, then of Danson [Park near Bexleyheath], Kent' (probate calendar). The 1818 directory lists a John Johnston of 94 Newman Street as the proprietor of an 'Italian oil warehouse' there.
Father Charles Johnston (d. 1776). (Second son.)
Mother Margaret Smith.
Education Unknown.
Marriage In 1790, to Anna Smyth (1767–14 November 1860). (Four sons, two daughters.) (Their son was Thomas Edward Homan Johnston; see 1884/68).
Religion Presumably Anglican.
Public None known.
Miscellaneous According to an online genealogy source, he was 'originally of Tobago and Scarborough' and was a captain in the 2nd Regiment. He joined his brother Hugh (b. 1742) as a corn merchant and banker in London, but he was primarily a West Indies merchant in London. Danson Park, which he purchased, is a well-known Palladian mansion described in 1995 as the 'single most significant building' in London threatened with demolition. It was saved and restored in 2003 and is open to the public (online account of Danson Park).
References Above sources only.

1829/19 **Name** **Nash, Andrew John**
Dates Probably baptised 31 July 1768, St Martin-in-the-Fields, Westminster–18 January 1829, Hyde House, Edmonton (Family Search; *The Times,* 20 January 1829).

Probate £100,000 (PCC).
Occupation Glass manufacturer (Andrew & George Nash, 1817 directory) of 75 Cornhill, City of London. (Occupational category II.11; venue 1.) Presumably he was a retailer as well.
Address Hyde House, Edmonton, Middlesex, and 75 Cornhill, City of London.
Father Andrew Nash (d. c. 1789) (Family Search; http://memberscoxnet/ghgraham/andrewnashhtml). (First son.)
Mother Augusta Neunburg (http://members.cox.net/ghgraham/andrewnash.html).
Education Unknown. He perhaps attended Merchant Taylor's School like his brother George Augustus (for whom see 'Miscellaneous' below).
Marriage In 1793 to Susanna Horne. (Six sons, two daughters.)
Religion Presumably Anglican: baptised and married in Anglican churches.
Public None known.
Miscellaneous Nothing further could be traced about him. His brother George Augustus Nash (1770–1825), a glass merchant, was Master of the Merchant Taylor's Company, 1817–18.
References Above sources only.

Name **Todd, George** 1829/20
Dates c. 1761–4 January 1829, Belsize, Hampstead.
Probate £120,000 (PCC).
Occupation Presumably a merchant or banker in the City of London, given his address, but, strangely, he could not be readily traced in any directory. The nearest likely entries in any London directory include George Todd, 'linen draper' at 450 Strand (1802); George Todd & Co., 'coal merchants' of Ratcliff Cross (1825); and Kenneth Tod (sic) 'merchant' of Old Broad Street (1808). There is no evidence that any of these are connected with this George Todd. (Venue 1.)
Address 'Formerly of St Swithin's Lane, Old Broad Street, City of London, and then Belsize, Hampstead, Middlesex' (probate calendar).
Father Unknown.
Mother Unknown.
Education Unknown.
Marriage Unknown.
Religion Unknown.
Public None known.
Miscellaneous He occupied a mansion at Belsize in 1818 (*VCH Middlesex*, vol. 9, 1989, pp. 51–60).
References Above sources only.

Name **Oakes, James** 1829/21
Dates 7 November 1741 (Family Search)–31 January 1829.
Probate £180,000 (PCC).
Occupation 'Banker' (probate calendar) at Bury St Edmunds, Suffolk. (Occupa-

tional category IV.16; venue 11.) He also had other lucrative interests there as a yarn manufacturer and receiver-general of land taxes.

Address Bury St Edmunds, Suffolk and Nowton Court, Suffolk.

Father James Oakes (b. 1701) a 'prosperous linen draper' of Bury St Edmunds, originally from Manchester. (Only son.)

Mother Susan, daughter of Orbell Ray.

Education Unknown.

Marriage In 1764 to Elizabeth (d. 1802), daughter of Christopher Adamson of Wareham, Norfolk. (Two sons, one daughter.)

Religion Anglican.

Public Mayor of Bury St Edmunds, 1772–3 and 1786–7, and senior member of the town corporation. A James Oakes, presumably his father, was Mayor in 1758–9. JP, DL, Suffolk and Bury St Edmunds.

Miscellaneous He inherited the yarn-manufacturing business of his uncle, was Receiver-General of Land Taxes for Suffolk from 1787 (an office given to him by the Duke of Grafton) and then opened the Bury & Suffolk Bank in 1794. His family were prominent in Bury St Edmunds for many years. His *Diaries*, an important source, were printed in 1990. They cover the period from 1778 to 1820.

References *GM*, 1829, vol. I, p. 189; Jane Fiske, ed., *The Oakes Diaries* (2 vols., 1990).

1829/22 **Name** **Perceval, (Hon.) Edward**

Dates 21 April 1744–1829. (The exact date does not appear to be given in any source.)

Probate £120,000 (PCC).

Occupation Landed. (Occupational category I.) In 1883, the Earl of Egmont owned 34,972 acres worth £35,510 p.a. in Sussex, Surrey, County Cork, etc. He was the brother of Spencer Perceval, the assassinated Prime Minister.

Address Formerly of Stroxford [Stroxton?] Hall, Lincolnshire and Charles Street, Berkeley Square, Middlesex, and then Hamels Park near Watford, Herts.' (probate calendar).

Father John Perceval, 2nd Earl of Egmont (1711–20 December 1770), MP and Cabinet Minister, created Baron Lovel and Holland, 1762. (Fourth son.)

Mother Catherine (d. 1752), daughter of James, 5th Earl of Salisbury.

Education Unknown.

Marriage In 1775, to Sarah (d. 1808), daughter of John Howarth. (Three daughters.)

Religion Anglican.

Public None known.

Miscellaneous Surprisingly little is known about his career, or why he left a fortune as a younger son.

References *BP.*

1829/23 **Name** **Strutt, Isaac**

Dates Unknown – probated March 1829.

Probate £140,000 (PCC).
Occupation Unknown. He does not appear to be related to any of the well-known Strutts, Barons Belper or Barons Rayleigh. (Venue 11?)
Address Groton, near Hadleigh, Suffolk.
Father Unknown.
Mother Unknown.
Education Unknown.
Marriage Unknown.
Religion Unknown.
Public None known.
Miscellaneous There is an online listing for a Robert Lay Strutt (1815, Polstead, Suffolk, January 1876), the son of an Isaac and Susannah Strutt, but it is not clear whether this is the same man. Our man was presumably a landowner or merchant in the Hadleigh area.
References He is not listed in Charles Richard Strutt, *The Strutt Family of Terling* (1939). Above sources only.

Name **Denn, Robert** 1829/24
Dates c. 1756 (1758, online sources)–21 December 1828, Brandon, Suffolk.
Probate £250,000 (PCC).
Occupation Unknown; he was apparently a landowner in Suffolk, but little could be traced of his career. His father, of High Ongar, Essex, might have been a London merchant.
Address 'Formerly of Dunham Lodge, Norfolk, then of Brampton, Huntingdonshire, then Tempsford Hall, Bedfordshire, then Brandon Hall [near Thetford] Suffolk' (probate calendar).
Father Thomas Denn (b. 1723) of High Ongar, Essex.
Mother Hannah Vincent.
Education Unknown.
Marriage Unmarried.
Religion Anglican.
Public None known.
Miscellaneous There is some information about him in online sources, but nothing about how he became so wealthy, or why he had so many houses. His will gives no clue as to his source of wealth. In it, he mentions his 'late uncle' William Denn.
References *GM,* 1828, vol. II, p. 649; online sources.

Name **Gibson, Atkinson Francis** 1829/25
Dates 20 January 1763, Saffron Walden (Family Search)–22 January 1829.
Probate £100,000 (PCC).
Occupation Brewer in Saffron Walden, Essex (Atkinson F. Gibson & Sons, brewers, of High Street, Saffron Walden, 1826 directory). (Occupational category II.12; venue 11.) In 1883, George Stacey Gibson (b. 1818) of Hill House, Saffron Walden, presumably a relative, owned 3,300 acres worth £3,400 p.a., chiefly in

Essex, 'exclusive of £2000 for house property'. This would suggest that Atkinson Gibson moved into land and property ownership.

Address Saffron Walden, Essex, is the only address.

Father George Gibson (Family Search).

Mother Ann (surname unknown) (Family Search).

Education Unknown.

Marriage In 1789, to Elizabeth Wyatt (Family Search).

Religion Unknown.

Public None known.

Miscellaneous He developed 'superb gardens' at Bridge End, Saffron Walden (online sources).

References Above sources only.

1829/26 **Name** **Fleming, John**

Dates 1747–17 May 1829, Gloucester Place, Middlesex.

Probate £160,000 (PCC).

Occupation 'Doctor of Medicine' (probate calendar); formerly Head Surgeon of the East India Company at Bengal. (Occupational category VI.30; venue 29.) He has an entry in the *ODNB* as a 'surgeon and naturalist'. He lived in England from c. 1813.

Address 'Formerly of Fitzroy Square and then of 104 Gloucester Place, Middlesex' (probate calendar).

Father Described in *HP* as 'an orphan brought up by a maternal uncle, John Cleghorn, Professor of Anatomy at Trinity College, Dublin'. His entry in the *ODNB* has no information whatever about his parentage, and its author has not read Fleming's *HP* entry. The *ODNB* does have an entry on a George Cleghorn (1716–69), Professor of Anatomy at Trinity College, Dublin, born Scotland, who 'brought up the nine children of his deceased brother', but there is no trace of any relative named Fleming.

Mother Presumably né Cleghorn, but see previous entry.

Education He 'may have attended' Edinburgh University (*ODNB*). He received an MD from Edinburgh University in 1804.

Marriage Unmarried.

Religion Presumably originally Church of Scotland.

Public MP (pro-Government, but sometimes voted with the Opposition) Gatton, 1818–20; Saltash, 1820–6.

Miscellaneous He entered the Indian Medical Service in 1768, aged about twenty-one, and was Assistant Surgeon of the East India Company at Bengal, full Surgeon in 1771, and Head Surgeon from 1786. He was a Member (from 1786) and President (1810–11) of the Medical Board of Calcutta. He returned permanently to England in 1813. He was known as a 'keen scholar and naturalist', especially interested in botany, who corresponded with Sir Joseph Banks. It is unclear where his fortunes came from, apart from medicine, but presumably involved dealings with the East India Company.

References *ODNB; HP; GM,* 1829, vol. I, p. 475.

Name **Wicke, (Johann) George** 1829/27

Dates c. 1751–21 April 1829, Stratford Green, Essex.

Probate £180,000 (PCC).

Occupation 'Sugar refiner' at Church Lane, Whitechapel (1822 directory). (Occupational category III, 15 and 12; venue 2.) He had 'leasehold sugar houses' in Wellclose Square, Whitechapel (will).

Address 'Church Lane, Whitechapel and Stratford Green, Essex' (probate calendar).

Father Unknown – born Germany. His brother, Johann Jost Wicke, lived in Unshaussen, Germany (will).

Mother Unknown.

Education Unknown.

Marriage Apparently unmarried – no wife or children are mentioned in his will.

Religion Lutheran; left money to the 'German Chapel' in London and was buried in the German Chapel in Hooper Square.

Public None known.

Miscellaneous A German immigrant who became a successful sugar refiner. This commodity was used both as a sweetener and in brewing, etc.

References *GM*, 1829, vol. I, p. 475; above sources.

Name **Wilson, Thomas** 1829/28

Dates Unknown. *GM* lists a Thomas Wilson as having died on 15 June 1829, probably this man.

Probate £120,000 (PCC).

Occupation 'Merchant' of 6 Warnford Court, Throgmorton Street, City of London (1817 directory). Listed as 'merchant and Consul for Denmark', 1829 directory. (Occupational category IV.19 or 21? Venue 1; he was presumably a genuine 'merchant', not a banker or retailer.)

Address '6 Warnford Court, Throgmorton Street, City of London and [12 Montagu Street,] Portman Square, Middlesex' (probate calendar).

Father Unknown.

Mother Unknown.

Education Unknown.

Marriage Unknown.

Religion Unknown.

Public None known.

Miscellaneous Nothing more could be traced about him.

References Probably *GM*, 1829, vol. I, p. 572.

Name **Turnor (sic), Edmund** 1829/29

Dates Baptised 13 December 1754 (1755?), Lincoln–13 December 1829, Stoke Park.

Probate £160,000 (PCC).

Occupation Landowner. (Occupational category I.) In 1883, Christopher Turnor of Stoke Rochford owned 20,664 acres worth £27,513 p.a. in Lincolnshire. The family had also profited from customs farming.

Address Panton House and Stoke Rochford, near Grantham, Lincolnshire.

Father Edmund Turnor (c. 1719–22 January 1805), landowner of Stoke Rochford. (First son.)

Mother Mary (1731–1818), daughter of John Disney of Lincoln.

Education Stamford school; Trinity College, Cambridge (BA, 1777; MA, 1781); barrister, Lincoln's Inn (called 1775); made the Grand Tour.

Marriage First, in 1795, to Elizabeth (1773–1801), daughter of Philip Broke of Nacton, Suffolk. (One daughter.) Second, in 1803, to Dorothy (d. 1854), daughter of (Lieutenant Colonel) Martin Tucker. (Five sons, two daughters.)

Religion Anglican.

Public MP (Tory) Midhurst, 1802–6; High Sheriff of Lincolnshire, 1810–11.

Miscellaneous 'A Lincolnshire country gentleman and antiquary' (*HP*). An 'eminent antiquary' (FSA, FRS) – wrote on London and Lincolnshire. Has an entry in the *ODNB* as 'landowner and antiquary'.

References *ODNB; HP; GM,* 1829, vol. I, pp. 566–8; *BLG.*

1829/30 **Name** **Hollond (sic), Edward**

Dates Baptised 5 November 1773 Fort St George, Madras–7 December 1829 Cavendish Square.

Probate £160,000 (PCC).

Occupation East India Company fortune from father and possibly other relatives, then a landowner. (Occupational category VI.31; venue 29.) In 1883, (Revd) Edmund Hollond of Benhall Lodge owned 4,243 acres worth £6,071 p.a. in Suffolk, Norfolk and Dorset.

Address 'Formerly of Grosvenor Place, Middlesex, and then of Benhall [Place, Saxmundham,] Suffolk and Cavendish Square, Middlesex' (probate calendar). He also had a house at Bexington, Dorset.

Father John Hollond (c. 1744–31 January 1806), Acting Governor of the East India Company in Madras.

Mother Eliza (Anne?), daughter of John (Joseph?) Henchman.

Education Harrow.

Marriage Unmarried.

Religion Anglican.

Public None known.

Miscellaneous Many in his family were prominent in the East India Company and made substantial fortunes from it. His uncle or brother William Hollond (1750–1836) of the Bengal Civil Service left £1 million. It is not clear how sums of this size were made. Edward Hollond purchased the Benhall Lodge estate in 1808.

References *GM,* 1829, vol. II, p. 648; *BLG;* online sources.

1829/31 **Name** **Willoughby de Eresby, Baroness, Priscilla Barbara Elizabeth Heathcote-Burrell** (né Bertie) **and Dowager Baroness Gwydir**

Dates 16 February 1761–29 December 1828, Whitehall.

Probate £100,000 (PCC).
Occupation Landed fortune. (Occupational category I.) In 1883, Baroness Willoughby de Eresby owned 132,220 acres worth £74,006 p.a. in Lincolnshire, Perth, Carnarvon, etc.
Address The chief residence appears to have been at Grimsthorpe, Bourne, Lincolnshire.
Father Peregrine Bertie, 3rd Duke of Ancaster (1714–12 August 1778), Lord Lieutenant of Lincolnshire, etc. The daughter is said to have brought her husband an income of £60,000 p.a. on their marriage. She succeeded to 'the greater part' of her father's estates and became Baroness Willoughby de Eresby in her own right in 1779.
Mother Mary, daughter of Thomas Panton of Newmarket, 'Master of the King's Running Horses'. She was Mistress of the Robes to Queen Charlotte, 1761–93.
Education Unknown.
Marriage In 1779, to Sir Peter Burrell, 2nd Baronet (1754–29 June 1820), MP, Master of the Horse, created Baron Gwydir in 1796. (Three sons, one daughter.)
Religion Anglican.
Public She was Hereditary Lord Chamberlain in her own right.
Miscellaneous One of the richest women landowners and aristocrats in Britain.
References *BP; ODNB* for husband; *HP* for husband.

Name **Williams, Bigoe (sic) Charles** 1829/32
Dates Baptised 2 June 1770, Epsom, Surrey (Family Search)–15 September 1829.
Probate £300,000 (PCC).
Occupation Solicitor at 9 New Square, Lincoln's Inn Fields (1820 Law List) with Robert Whitmore and others, and Side Clerk in Exchequer (1805 Law List). (Occupational category VI.29; venue 1.)
Address 'Formerly of Bedford Row, and then of Lincoln's Inn Fields' (probate calendar).
Father Thomas Williams (Family Search).
Mother Mary (surname unknown) (Family Search).
Education Unknown.
Marriage Unknown.
Religion Unknown, presumably Anglican.
Public None known.
Miscellaneous He might have been related to the family of Bigoe, Huguenot glass manufacturers of Stepney.
References *GM,* 1829, vol. II, p. 283, which spells his first name 'Bigot'.

Name **Gardiner, Joseph** 1829/33
Dates Unknown. Probated December 1829.
Probate £120,000 (PCC).
Occupation 'Stationer' (probate calendar) of Newgate Street, City of London. (Occupational category IV.21 and 20? Venue 1.) (Thomas & Joseph Gardiner,

'wholesale stationers' of 49 Newgate Street, 1830 directory.)

Address Newgate Street, City of London is the only address given.

Father Unknown.

Mother Unknown.

Education Unknown.

Marriage Unknown.

Religion Unknown.

Public None known.

Miscellaneous Nothing more could be traced about him.

References Probate calendar only.

1829/34 **Name** **Parker, Charles Stewart**

Dates Unknown–1825 (sic), but registered in the Scottish probate records on 5 January 1829 and in PROB 11 in November 1828.

Probate £105,893 (Scottish probates).

Occupation West Indies merchant in Glasgow (*BLG*, 1914). Described as a 'merchant' in the Scottish probate records. (Occupational category IV.19; venue 10.)

Address Blochairn, Glasgow.

Father James Parker (1728–1813), 'a planter in Virginia and an officer in the King's service in the American War' (*BLG*). (First son.)

Mother Margaret Elligood, of Huguenot descent.

Education Unknown.

Marriage In 1797, to Margaret, daughter of (Revd) George Rainy, Minister of Crieth, Sutherlandshire. (Four sons, two daughters.) Their daughter Annie married Edward Cardwell, 1st Viscount Cardwell (1813–66), the politician. Their grandson Charles Stewart Parker (1829–1910) is in the *ODNB* as a 'politician'. He is given there as the son of Charles Stewart Parker, a partner in Sandbach, Tinne & Co., merchants in Liverpool.

Religion Presumably Church of Scotland.

Public None known.

Miscellaneous It is not known whether he ever lived in the West Indies.

References *BLG*, 1914 and above sources.

1829/35 **Name** **Gordon, John**

Dates Unknown–1828 (registered in the Scottish probates on 11 August 1829).

Probate £118,543 (Scottish probates).

Occupation West Indies merchant in Glasgow (Somervell, Gordon & Co., then Stirling, Gordon & Co.) (Online sources in accounts of Aikenhead.) (Occupational category IV.19; venue 10.) He also owned properties in Glasgow and land near Glasgow.

Address Lived at Aikenhead, Cathcart, near Glasgow, and was 'the largest heritor in the parish' (online description of Aikenhead). He also owned a house on Buchanan Street, Glasgow.

Father Alexander Gordon, a property owner in Glasgow. (Second son.)

Mother Isabel, daughter of John Fleming, a 'brewer' of Glasgow.

Education Unknown.

Marriage First, in 1800, to Anne, daughter of John Alston, 'merchant and banker' of Glasgow. (One daughter.) Second, in 1813, to Janet, daughter of Gilbert Hamilton, Provost of Glasgow. (One son, one daughter.)

Religion Presumably Church of Scotland.

Public None known – he was known to be pro-Tory.

Miscellaneous It is unclear if he ever lived in the West Indies.

References *Old Country Houses of the Glasgow Gentry* (1878), online; other online sources.

WEALTH-HOLDERS, 1830

1830/1 **Name** **Cumming, Patrick**
Dates Unknown – probated May 1830.
Probate £120,000 'within province' (PCC).
Occupation Unknown. He presumably had mercantile or other interest in Riga, then in Russia, but nothing about them could be traced. In his will, he mentions two brothers, James and Henry, both of Liverpool. The 1805 Liverpool directory lists 'James and Henry Cumming, merchants, Counting House, 2 Goree Piazzas and of 10 Queen Anne Street'. No Patrick Cumming is listed in any Liverpool directory of that period. (Venue 29?, but this is very tentative.)
Address 'Dover Street, Piccadilly and East Cliffe Lodge, Isle of Thanet, Kent and Riga, Russia' (probate calendar).
Father Unknown. The name suggests a Scottish background.
Mother Unknown.
Education Unknown.
Marriage To Elizabeth Christina, surname and marriage date unknown.
Religion Unknown.
Public None known.
Miscellaneous East Cliffe Lodge had been owned by Admiral Lord Keith and later would be owned by Sir Moses Montefiore.
References Probate calendar only.

1830/2 **Name** **Shaw, John**
Dates Unknown – probated August 1830.
Probate £70,000 (PCC) + £60,000 (Chester Consistory Court): £130,000.
Occupation Presumably a 'merchant. in Liverpool ('Counting house' at 7 Great Charlotte Street, 1805 directory). (Occupational category IV.19? Venue 5.)
Address 'Liverpool' only.
Father Unknown.
Mother Unknown.
Education Unknown.
Marriage Unknown.
Religion Unknown.
Public A John Shaw was Mayor of Liverpool in 1800–1.
Miscellaneous He may have been the John Shaw who owned the Shaw Street area of Everton, which was built upon around 1830. This man was 'a Liverpool councillor, whose father had inherited through marriage the extensive Everton estate of the Halsall family' and who built 'prestigious' houses there. (Online account of Liverpool street names). There is no direct evidence that this was the same man, however.
References Above sources only.

Name **Douglas, Edward Bullock** 1830/3
Dates 28 June 1774–7 July 1830.
Probate £100,000 (PCC).
Occupation Probably landed. (Occupational category I?, although his source of wealth is unclear.)
Address 'Formerly of Abercrombie Place, Edinburgh, then Bradbourn Place, Kent and Montpellier, France' (probate calendar).
Father Charles James Sholto Douglas (b. 1741). He was the son of Sir John Douglas, 3rd Baronet (1733–13 November 1778) and Christian Cunninghame (d. 1741). He was a relative of the Marquesses of Queensberry.
Mother Mary Bullock.
Education Unknown.
Marriage In 1811, to Harriet (d. 2 November 1850), daughter of (Revd) Richard Bullock. (One son, who became a Roman Catholic priest.)
Religion Presumably originally Church of Scotland, but the above and the French address suggest that he might have been a Roman Catholic.
Public None known.
Miscellaneous A mysterious case – the source of his wealth is unclear.
References Online genealogy and above sources only.

Name **Donaldson, James** 1830/4
Dates 10 December 1751, Edinburgh–16 December 1830.
Probate £100,000 (PCC).
Occupation Founder of the *Edinburgh Advertiser* (a pro-Tory biweekly) and a partner in his father's business of bookseller and publisher in Edinburgh. (Occupational category V.26 and 27; venue 23.)
Address Broughton Hall, Edinburgh, and a house on Princes Street, Edinburgh.
Father Alexander Donaldson (1727–94), bookseller and publisher of Edinburgh. He 'incurred the wrath' of many writers, including Dr Johnson, by taking advantage of differing copyright laws in England and Scotland, to the detriment of authors. He is said to have left £100,000.
Mother Ann Marshall.
Education Unknown.
Marriage In 1792, to Jean Gillespie (d.s.p., 1828).
Religion Church of Scotland.
Public None known.
Miscellaneous Was said to have doubled his father's fortune of £100,000 by 'judicious investments'. He was said (*ODNB*) to have left £220,000, but there is no evidence for this figure. He apparently left £89,957 in Scotland. It is puzzling that his estate was probated in the PCC. He is most famous as a philanthropist and as the founder of Donaldson's Hospital for destitute children, later a hospital for the deaf. He was 'invariably dressed in the costume of the eighteenth century' (*DNB*).
References *ODNB*.

1830/5 **Name** **Chamberlayne, William**

Dates 4 December 1760–10 October 1829, Cranbury Park.

Probate £250,000 (PCC).

Occupation Apparently an 'Old Corruption'/legal-type fortune: his father was Solicitor to the Treasury for nineteen years. (Occupational category VI.29; venue 2.) The family were also extensive landowners. In 1883, Tankerville Chamberlayne of Cranbury Park, Winchester, owned 12,363 acres worth £19,000 p.a. (It might be more accurate to list them as occupational category I.)

Address Cranbury Park, near Winchester, Hampshire; Weston Grove, Hampshire; Dunmer, Leicestershire.

Father William Chamberlayne (1703–99), Solicitor to the Treasury for nineteen years and previously Solicitor to the Mint, of Coley Park, Berkshire. (First son.)

Mother Hariott, daughter of Sir Cecil Bisshopp, 5th Baronet.

Education Winchester; New College, Oxford; barrister, Middle Temple (called 1778).

Marriage Unmarried. His estate went to his sister Charlotte (d. 1831; see 1831/6).

Religion Anglican.

Public MP (Radical, pro-Whig), Christchurch, 1800–2; Southampton, 1818–29.

Miscellaneous He was a first cousin of the Earl of Liverpool. He succeeded the widow of Sir Nathaniel Holland (1811/15) to the Dunmer estate in Leicesteshire (*VCH Leicestershire,* vol. 5, 1964, pp. 153–7).

References *HP; BLG,* 1937.

1830/6 **Name** **Goring, Charles**

Dates 1743 or 1744–3 December 1829.

Probate £250,000 (PCC).

Occupation Landowner. (Occupational category I.) In 1883, (Revd) John Goring of Wiston owned 14,139 acres worth £13,705 p.a. in Sussex. Charles Goring is said to have had an income of £12,000 p.a. from his land.

Address Wiston Park, near Steyning, Sussex.

Father Sir Charles Matthew Goring, 5th Baronet (1731–August 1769). (Second son: by his second wife.)

Mother Elizabeth (d. 1784), daughter of Sir Robert Fagg(e), 4th Baronet of Wiston. Charles Goring inherited Wiston from his mother.

Education Unknown.

Marriage First, in 1779, to Sarah (d.s.p., 1797), daughter of Ralph Beard of Hurstpierpoint, Sussex. Second, in 1798, Elizabeth (d. 1811), daughter of Edward Luxford. (Three daughters.) Third, in 1812, to Mary (d. 1845), daughter of (Revd) John Ballard DD, Fellow of Winchester. (Two sons, one daughter.)

Public Anglican.

Public None known.

Miscellaneous His elder half-brother inherited the baronetcy. Charles Goring was described (*GM*) as 'a singular specimen of the old English gentleman of the highest Tory principles'.

References *BLG*, 1937; *GM*, 1830, vol. I, p. 87.

Name **Medley, Jane** (née Waldo) 1830/7
Dates c. 1737–14 December 1829.
Probate £180,000 (PCC).
Occupation Her husband was a wine and spirit merchant in Portugal who had 'immense property'. Her father was apparently a London merchant, who owned the famous Hever Castle in Kent from 1749 until his death. She inherited it from him. If she was primarily a landowner, then occupational category I. In 1883, E. Meade-Waldo, of Stonewall, Kent, the owner of Hever Castle, owned 2,798 acres worth £3,837 p.a.
Address Felsted Place and Buxted Park, Felbridge, Surrey; Hever Castle, Kent. The probate calendar gives her address as 'Clapham'.
Father Sir Timothy Waldo (d. 1786) of Hever, Kent and Clapham, Surrey. His knighthood was created in 1769. It is not clear how he had earned his money, but he was apparently a London merchant.
Mother Catherine Wakefield.
Education Unknown.
Marriage In 1782, to George Medley (1720–96; d.s.p.), MP, 1768–80 and 1783–90, of New Burlington Street, Middlesex and East Grinstead, Sussex. He was a wine and spirit merchant in Lisbon, Portugal with 'immense property', but he lost 'much' of it in the Lisbon earthquake of 1755.
Religion Anglican.
Public None known.
Miscellaneous Upon Jane Medley's death, Hever Castle passed to her cousin Jane Waldo. Jane Medley's property 'came to the daughters of the Earl of Liverpool, in the right of their mother, Julia Evelyn Medley, only daughter of Sir George Shuckburgh Bt., by Julia, daughter of James Evelyn and Annabella, sister of George Medley, the husband of the old lady now deceased' (*GM*).
References *GM*, 1829, vol. II, p. 649; Hever Castle, online history; *HP* for husband.

Name **Pepys, Sir Lucas, 1st Baronet** 1830/8
Dates 24 May 1742, London–17 June 1830, Park Street, Grosvenor Square, Middlesex.
Probate £120,000 (PCC).
Occupation Medical fortune: he was President of the Royal College of Physicians, 1804–10, and Physician-in-Ordinary to King George III from 1784. He also had 'a large practice' (*ODNB*). (Occupational category VI.30; venue 2.)
Address Park Street, Grosvenor Square, Middlesex; Mickleham, Surrey.
Father William Pepys (1698–September 1743) 'banker' of London and Ridgeley, Cheshire and uncle of the 1st Earl of Cottenham.
Mother Hannah (d. 1761), daughter of Richard Russel (sic) of Lewes, Sussex, and widow of Alexander Weller.
Education Eton; Christ Church, Oxford (BA, 1764; MB, 1770; MD, 1771);

trained at Edinburgh University. FRCP, 1775; later served four times as its Censor, and as its Treasurer, 1788–98.

Marriage First, in 1772, to Jane Leslie (d. 1810), Countess of Rothes. (Two sons, one daughter.) Second, in 1813, to Deborah (d. 1848), daughter of Dr Anthony Askew.

Religion Anglican.

Public Created baronet 1784.

Miscellaneous A famous physician, renowned as the physician to King George III during his madness. He practised in Brighton and then in London and was also Physician-General to the Army from 1794. He was an early supporter of vaccination.

References *ODNB; GM,* 1830, vol. II, p. 274.

1830/9 **Name Oliveira, Dominick (sic)**

Dates Probated September 1830.

Probate £400,000, 'within province' (PCC).

Occupation 'Merchant', listed at 67 Tower Street, City of London (1794 directory); 67 Gower Street (1808); 40 Upper Seymour Street, Portman Square (1815); and 4 Great Cumberland Street (1825). The 1815 directory lists him as 'D. Oliveira, Junior'. (Occupational category IV.19 or 21? Venue 1 and 2?)

Address 'Formerly of Gower Street and then Upper Seymour Street and Great Cumberland Street, Middlesex, and Hastings, Sussex' (probate calendar).

Father Unknown.

Mother Unknown.

Education Unknown.

Marriage Unknown.

Religion Unknown.

Public None known.

Miscellaneous In a court case brought in 1835 regarding his will, he was described as 'at the time of his death, an alien, and a native of Portugal' (Peregrine Bingham, comp., *New Cases in the Court of Common Pleas, and Other Courts,* vol. I (London, 1835), pp. 490–2. His name at birth was, therefore, probably Domingos Oliveira or de Oliveira.

References Probate calendar and above sources only.

1830/10 **Name Digby, Robert**

Dates Unknown – probated 1830 (PROB 8). There is no listing in 1830 or adjacent years for a man of this name in PROB 11. The only listing in PROB 11 for a relevant man of this name is for Robert Digby, 'Admiral of the Red', of Mintern Magna, whose estate was probated in May 1814. It is likely that the 1830 wealth-holder was Admiral Robert Digby. (If so, occupational category VI.31.)

Probate £100,000 (PCC).

Occupation Unknown. Admiral Robert Digby (1732–1814), lived at Minterne Magna, Dorset after his retirement. He had no children. His widow Elizabeth died 5 August 1830 at Minterne Magna. (Revd Hon.) Robert Digby (10 April 1775–25 September 1830) was the son of Henry Digby, 1st Earl of Digby (d.

1793), but he was a vicar in Warwickshire, and PROB 8 does not state that he was a clergyman, while the vicar did not live in Dorset. The only people with the surname Digby owning land in Dorset listed in Bateman were George Digby Wingfield-Digby of Sherborne Castle, Dorset, who owned 26,883 acres worth £46,092 p.a., of which 21,230 acres worth £36,106 p.a. were in Dorset, and, more relevantly, Lord Digby of Minterne House, Cerne, who owned 39,505 acres worth £15,968 p.a., of which 1886 acres worth £2,291 p.a. were in Dorset.

Address Minterne Magna, Dorset.

Father Unknown.

Mother Unknown.

Education Unknown.

Marriage Unknown.

Religion Presumably Anglican.

Public None known.

Miscellaneous If this is indeed Admiral Robert Digby (20 December 1732–25 February 1814; d.s.p.), then he was the son of Edward Digby (c. 1693–1746), MP for Warwickshire and Charlotte, sister of Sir Stephen Fox, MP. He was the grandson of the 5th Baron Digby. He went to sea in 1744, and became a post-captain in 1755, reaching flag-rank in 1779, and becoming Admiral of the Red in 1805. In 1784, he married Mrs Eleanor Jauncy, daughter of Andrew Elliot and niece of Sir Gilbert Elliot, 3rd Baronet (*ODNB*).

References *GM*, 1830, vol. II, p. 379, although it is not clear if this reference is to the same man.

Name **Barclay, Robert** 1830/11

Dates 15 May 1751–22 October 1830.

Probate £160,000 (PCC).

Occupation Banker in the City of London (Barclay, Bevan & Bening, of Lombard Street); also a brewer, of the Anchor Brewery, Southwark. (Occupational categories IV.16 and III.12; venues 1 and 2.)

Address Bury Hill, Dorking, Surrey, and Worthing, Sussex.

Father Alexander Barclay (1711–71) of Philadelphia, apparently a merchant. His father David Barclay was a well-known 'apologist for the Quakers'.

Mother Ann Hickman.

Education Unknown.

Marriage First, in 1775, to Rachel, daughter of John Gurney of Keswick. (Four sons, four daughters.) Second, to Margaret Hodgson. His son Charles Barclay (1780–1835) was an MP in 1815–18, 1826–30 and 1833–7.

Religion Quaker, and related to many famous Quaker families, although his MP son was presumably an Anglican.

Public None known.

Miscellaneous His uncle, David Barclay (1729–1809), took him into banking and brewing. Silvanus Bevan (see 1830/24) was a cousin. Barclay purchased Bury Hill in c. 1805. It is not clear whether his banking or brewing interests were the more important.

References *ODNB; BLG,* 1914 and 1937; *GM,* 1830, vol. II, p. 477.

1830/12 **Name** Grevile (Greville in some sources), (Revd) Edward Colston

Dates c. 1755–18 October 1830.

Probate £140,000 (PCC).

Occupation 'Rector of St Stephen's, Bristol and Vicar of Clevedon, Somerset' (*GM*). Also a landowner – inherited Edgewater Manor, Gloucestershire, from Thomas Westfaling (né Brereton; d. 1814): *VCH Gloucestershire,* vol. 11, 1976, pp. 42–4. It is still unclear how he made his fortune. His father is described as a 'gentleman' of Bristol. There is no evidence from any genealogical guide that he was related to the Earls of Warwick, the Lords Broke or any other aristocratic family of his surname. (Occupational category I? Venue 12?, although this is tentative.)

Address 'Bristol and Clevedon, Somerset' (probate calendar).

Father Giles Grevile of Bristol, described as a 'gentleman' in the 1774 Bristol poll book. It is possible, indeed likely, that he had a mercantile background, but there is no direct evidence.

Mother Unknown.

Education Secondary schooling unknown; Pembroke College, Oxford (BA, 1777; MA, 1781).

Marriage Unknown. It is known that he had seven children (*VCH Gloucestershire,* vol. 11, 1976, pp. 42–4).

Religion Anglican clergyman.

Public None known.

Miscellaneous Some of his wealth might have come from his clerical income, but any mercantile source is unclear.

References *GM,* 1830, vol. II, p. 474; *Alum. Oxon.*

1830/13 **Name** **Forman, William**

Dates Baptised 6 June 1767–23 July 1829, Cornwall Terrace, Regent's Park.

Probate £140,000 (PCC).

Occupation Ironmaster in South Wales. (Occupational category II.3; venue 19.) He had also been engaged in the family ordnance trade in London.

Address Pen y Darran, Merthyr Tydfil, Glamorganshire; North Cornwall Terrace, Regent's Park, Middlesex.

Father Richard Forman (1733–94), Clerk in the Board of Ordnance at the Tower of London, and 'proof master' during the American Revolutionary Wars.

Mother The father was married twice, to Mary Baines and Elizabeth Crewe. It is not clear who was the mother.

Education Unknown.

Marriage In 1789, to Mary Seaton, 'daughter of a Lancashire landowner'. (Three sons.) One son, William Henry Forman (1794–1869), was a millionaire ironmaster; another son; see 1851/9.

Religion Anglican.

Public None known.

Miscellaneous Developed the Glamorganshire iron industry with (Alderman) William Thompson (1793–1854, q.v.) after buying the mines and works from the Homfray family. He had a three-eighths share in the Pen-y-Daren works and other ironworks.
References *ODNB* for the 'Forman family'; *GM*, 1831, vol. II, p. 92.

Name **Brooke, Sir Richard Brooke De Capell, 1st Baronet** (né Supple) 1830/14
Dates 6 January 1758–27 November 1829, Great Oakley, Northamptonshire. (Some sources state 1830 as the year of death.)
Probate £100,000 'within province' (PCC).
Occupation Landowner; also barrister. In 1883, his successor owned 6,593 acres worth £8,472 p.a. in Northamptonshire, County Cork, Rutland, etc. (Occupational category I; also VI.29; venue 1.)
Address Lived at Great Oakley, near Kettering, Northamptonshire.
Father Richard Supple (d. 5 March 1797) of Great Oakley and Aghadoo, County Cork, apparently a landowner.
Mother Mary (d. 1782), daughter of Arthur Brooke and niece and heiress of Wheeler Brooke of Great Oakley. Sir Richard inherited Great Oakley from his great-uncle and apparently changed his surname in 1797.
Education Unknown; barrister, Inner Temple (called 1787).
Marriage In 1788, to Mary (d. 1846), daughter of (General) R. Worge. (Two sons, four daughters.)
Religion Anglican.
Public Created baronet 1803.
Miscellaneous Is listed as a Bencher of the Inner Temple, implying a highly successful legal career, but he cannot be traced in the Law Lists. He was a colonel in the Northamptonshire Militia and an FRS. He appears to have been primarily a landowner.
References *BP.*

Name **Stephens, William** 1830/15
Dates Unknown – probated February 1830.
Probate £180,000 (PCC).
Occupation 'Brewer' (probate calendar) at Aldermaston Wharf, Berkshire. (This is one mile from Aldermaston and near Padworth.) (Occupational category III.12; venue 14.)
Address 'Aldermaston Wharf, Berkshire, and then Padworth, Berkshire' (probate calendar).
Father Unknown.
Mother Unknown.
Education Unknown.
Marriage Unknown. His son John lived at Caversham Place, near Reading, Berkshire.
Religion Unknown.
Public None known.

Miscellaneous Nothing further could be traced about him.
References Probate calendar only.

1830/16 **Name** **Spode, Josiah**
Dates 1777–6 October 1829 at The Mount near Newcastle-under-Lyme, Staffordshire.
Probate £140,000 (PCC).
Occupation China pottery manufacturer in the famous family firm at Stoke-on-Trent. (Occupational category II.11; venue 18.) He had also been connected with the family's 'warehouse' (showroom and retail shop) in London.
Address 'Formerly of Great Fenton and then of The Mount, Stoke-on-Trent, Staffordshire' (probate calendar).
Father Josiah Spode (1754–16 July 1827; see 1827/14, left £250,000), the famous china pottery manufacturer. (Second son.)
Mother Elizabeth Barker.
Education Unknown.
Marriage In c. 1815 to Mary Williamson. (One son.)
Religion Anglican.
Public None known.
Miscellaneous He had his arm amputated in 1803 as a result of an engine accident at the Spode works. He retired from 1815–27, but became the head of the firm again after his father's death.
References *ODNB* for father; 'The Spode Family and Early Company History', Spode Museum, Stoke-on-Trent, online.

1830/17 **Name** **Peel, Sir Robert, 1st Baronet**
Dates 25 April 1750, near Lancaster–3 May 1830.
Probate 'Upper Value' (i.e. above £1 million. A common estimate was £1.5 million) (PCC).
Occupation Cotton manufacturer at Bury, Lancashire (occupational category II.7; venue 4).
Address Bought an estate at Fazeley, near Tamworth, Staffordshire in the 1790s and lived there. He had previously lived in Blackburn and Bury, Lancashire.
Father Robert Peel (1723–95), calico printer at Peele Fold and Blackburn, Lancashire. He was a partner of William Yates from the 1760s. He is said to have left £140,000. (Third son.)
Mother Elizabeth (d. 1796), daughter of Edmund Haworth.
Education Blackburn Grammar School, then apprenticed to William Yates.
Marriage First, in 1783 to Ellen (1766–1803), daughter of William Yates (six sons, three daughters. Their eldest son was, of course, Sir Robert Peel, 2nd Baronet (d. 1850; the Prime Minister); second, in 1895 to Susannah (d.s.p., 1824), daughter of Francis Clerke.
Religion Anglican.
Public MP (Tory) Tamworth, 1790–1820. Created baronet in 1800 after donating £10,000 towards raising troops to stem a French invasion.

Miscellaneous After his apprenticeship, briefly worked in London and was a partner at Bury with William Yates from c. 1773. In 1803, he employed 15,000 men in his cotton factories and paid £40,000 p.a. in excise taxes. He introduced the spinning mule and other innovations to cotton manufacturing. He and Richard Arkwright (d. 1843) were the richest cotton manufacturers during this phase of the industrial revolution. He was also a governor of Christ's Hospital. He set out, successfully, to found a dynasty.
References *ODNB; HP; GM,* 1830, vol. I, p. 551.

Name **Harcourt, Sir William, 3rd Earl Harcourt** 1830/18
Dates 20 May 1742–18 June 1830, at St Leonard's Hill near Windsor.
Probate £180,000 (PCC).
Occupation Field-Marshal; also landowner on a small scale. (Occupational category VI.31 and 1.)
Address Lived at an estate at St Leonard's near Windsor, Berkshire, which he had purchased in 1782. This apparently consisted of the 681 acres worth £1,000 p.a. in 1883 that his heir Edward Venables Harcourt owned. (He owned in all 8,200 acres worth £13,000 p.a.).
Father General Sir Simon Harcourt (1714–16 September 1777), Ambassador to Mecklenburg and Lord of the Bedchamber, 1735–51 (second son), in the *ODNB.*
Mother Rebecca (d. 1765), daughter of Charles LeBas of Pipewell Abbey, Northamptonshire.
Education Unknown.
Marriage In 1778, to Rebecca (1749–1833; d.s.p.), daughter of (Revd) William Danby DD of Farnley, Yorkshire, and widow of Thomas Lockhart of Craighouse, Scotland.
Religion Anglican.
Public MP (Tory) Oxford, 1768–74. Created GCB, 1820. Served as Master of the Robes, 1808–9. He succeeded his elder brother as Earl, 1809. He was Master of the Horse to the Queen, 1809–18.
Miscellaneous Entered 1st Foot Guards, 1759; Captain, 1760: Lieutenant Colonel, 1764; Colonel, 1779; Major-General, 1782; General, 1798; Field-Marshal, 1821. Served as Aide-de-Camp to the King, 1777, and served in the American Revolutionary and French Wars. First Governor of Royal Military College, Marlow and Sandhurst, 1799–1808; Governor of Portsmouth from 1811. His estates passed to his cousin, Edward Venables Harcourt, Archbishop of York. Presumably his wealth came in large part from his military pay, but this isn't clear.
References *ODNB; GM,* 1830, vol. II.

Name **Filmer, (Revd) William** 1830/19
Dates c. 1762–17 July 1830.
Probate £120,000 (PCC).
Occupation Unclear. His family was landed. In 1883, Sir Edmund Filmer, Baronet, owned 6,608 acres worth £9,395 p.a. in Kent, but (Revd) William Filmer was a second son.

Address Lived at Heyford Purcell (also known as Lower Purcell), eleven miles from Oxford.
Father (Revd) Sir Edmund Filmer, 6th Baronet (d. 27 June 1810) of Bedford Row, Middlesex and East Sutton, Kent. (Second son.)
Mother Annabella, daughter of Sir John Honywood, 3rd Baronet.
Education Secondary schooling unknown; Corpus Christi College, Oxford (MA, BD) and Senior Proctor in 1794.
Marriage Apparently unmarried.
Religion Anglican clergyman.
Public None known.
Miscellaneous Was presented to the living of Lower Heyford, Oxfordshire, by Oxford University in 1794. Filmer presumably inherited much of his fortune and may have made a substantial amount from his clerical income, but none of this is clear.
References *BP; Alum. Oxon.*

1830/20 **Name** **Oddie, Henry Hoyle**
Dates Baptised 24 April 1744, Gisburn, Yorkshire (Family Search; Roots Web says born at Stirk House, Gisburn)–29 July 1830 (probated August 1830), 'of St Clement Danes, Westminster'.
Probate £100,000 (PCC).
Occupation Solicitor (Oddie, Hoyle & Co., Carey Street, Middlesex) in London near the Law Courts. (Occupational category VI.29; venue 2.)
Address Carey Street, Middlesex, and Barnwell, Northamptonshire.
Father John Oddie.
Mother Unknown.
Education Unknown.
Marriage To Jane (c. 1745–9 February 1825; marriage date unknown), daughter of John Yarker of Middleham, Yorkshire. (At least two sons and three daughters.)
Religion Presumably Anglican.
Public None known.
Miscellaneous He was a solicitor at Carey Street from before 1785 until at least 1820, according to directories and the *Law List.*
References *BLG*, 1846; online sources as above.

1830/21 **Name** **Muckleston, Joseph**
Dates c. 1756–November or December 1830, Prescott, Shropshire (probated December 1830).
Probate £180,000 (PCC).
Occupation Apparently a landowner, although his father and his ancestors were, it appears, solicitors in Shrewsbury. (Occupational category I or VI.29? Venue 18, but these are very tentative.) Nobody of this name is listed in Bateman.
Address Prescott near Shrewsbury, Shropshire. PROB 11 gives his address as Baschurch, Shropshire.

Father Richard Muckeston, probably a solicitor in Shrewsbury. An ancestor was Recorder of Oswestry in c. 1630.
Mother Mary, daughter of William Hawkins of Burton-on-Trent.
Education Unknown.
Marriage Unmarried.
Religion Anglican. He endowed the living of Holy Trinity Church, Burton-on-Trent: *VCH Staffordshire*, vol. 9, 2003.
Public High Sheriff of Shropshire, 1788.
Miscellaneous He purchased the Merrington, Shropshire, estate from his cousin, (Revd) John Fletcher Muckeston DD of Christ Church, Oxford.
References *GM*, 1830, vol. II, p. 647; *Burke's Commoners*, vol. 2, 1835, p. 168.

Name **Browne, Margaretta** 1830/22
Dates Unknown – probated January 1830.
Probate £120,000 (PCC).
Occupation Unknown. Her will mentions her brother, Thomas Browne, who predeceased her, her cousin (Revd) Richard Townsend Andrews and her cousin John Daniel Andrews, a 'merchant'. Richard Townsend Andrews (1770–20 May 1849) was the son of (Revd) Townsend Andrews and was educated at Merchant Taylor's and Trinity Hall, Cambridge. John Daniel Andrews apparently does not appear in any London directory, and Thomas Browne could not be traced definitively. A 'wine merchant' named Thomas Browne, of Gould Street, Crutched Friars, was listed in the 1793 London directory.
Address Bromley St Leonard, Middlesex (i.e. the Bromley which is two miles east of Whitechapel).
Father Unknown.
Mother Unknown.
Education Unknown.
Marriage Her will states that she was a 'spinster'. However, she was described as 'Mrs. Margaretta Browne' in the *Topographical Dictionary of England* (1848), pp. 317–20 (online), which notes that she left money in her will for the poor of Bromley.
Religion Anglican; she requested that she be buried in the Church of St Mary Aldermary, Watling Street, City of London, next to her brother. Her will is very religious, with strong Christian terminology and many charitable bequests.
Public None known.
Miscellaneous It is unclear whether she was a native of Bromley or the wife or daughter of a Londoner, or what the source of her wealth might have been. In her will she left a legacy to Charles Kingsley Junior. This may well have been Charles Kingsley (1819–75), the writer, whose father was also named Charles.
References Will (PROB 11 online) and above sources.

Name **West, James** 1830/23
Dates 1750–24 December 1829, Bryanston Square, Middlesex.
Probate £100,000 (PCC).
Occupation 'Commissioner of the East India Company's Ships' (probate calen-

dar). This post was presumably in London, not India, but nothing more is known about it. (Occupational category VI.31; venue 2?)

Address 'Formerly of Wimpole Street, then of [37] Bryanston Square, Middlesex' (probate calendar).

Father Unknown.

Mother Unknown.

Education Unknown.

Marriage Unknown.

Religion Unknown; presumably Anglican.

Public None known.

Miscellaneous Nothing further could be traced about him.

References *GM,* 1829, vol. II, p. 649.

1830/24 **Name** **Bevan, Silvanus**

Dates 2 August 1743–25 January 1830, Brighton.

Probate £350,000, 'within province' (PCC).

Occupation Banker of the City of London (Barclay, Bevan & Benning, of Lombard Street); also a brewer of the Anchor Brewery, Southwark. (Occupational category IV.16 and III.12; venue 1 and 2.) He was also a landowner. In 1883, his grandson Robert Cooper Lee Bevan of Forbery House owned 3,913 acres worth £3,576 p.a., of which 2,227 acres worth £1,679 p.a. were in Wiltshire.

Address Fosbery House, near Hungerford, Wiltshire, and Gloucester Place, Middlesex. He bought Fosbery Place in 1810, *VCH Wiltshire,* vol.16, 1899, pp. 222–6.

Father Timothy Bevan, originally of Swansea. He moved to London and founded the family bank. (Men of this name died in 1773 and 1786.)

Mother Elizabeth, daughter of David Barclay of Bury Hill.

Education Unknown.

Marriage First, in 1769, to Isabella Wakefield (d.s.p.); second, in 1773, to Louisa Kendall (d. 1838). (Seven sons.) His grandson, Robert Cooper Lee Bevan (1809–90) was a millionaire banker, in *ODNB,* as are other relatives.

Religion Originally a Quaker, but was disowned in 1773 for marrying his non-Quaker second wife.

Public None known.

Miscellaneous The cousin of Robert Barclay (see 1830/11) and a member of the Quaker 'Cousinhood', although expelled for marrying out.

References *ODNB* for grandson; *GM,* 1830, vol. I, p. 189; *BLG,* 1937.

1830/25 **Name** **Perry, Philip**

Dates c. 1769–19 January 1830, Upper Berkeley Street, Middlesex.

Probate £250,000 (PCC).

Occupation Shipbuilder at Blackwall. (Occupational category II.4; venue 2.) 'A member of the family of the great shipbuilders at Blackwall' (*GM*). He was also said to have owned £100,000 worth of freehold estates, but the family is not listed in Bateman. His brother was John Perry (1768–1824; see 1824/19, who left £140,000.

Address Moor Hall, Harlow, Essex.
Father John Perry (1743–7 November 1810), shipbuilder of Blackwall and Walthamstow, Essex.
Mother Elizabeth Browne (1746–95), or Anne, daughter of Samuel Watlington of Reading.
Education Unknown.
Marriage Unmarried.
Religion Anglican; buried St Matthias's Church, Blackwall (*Survey of London Poplar*, 1994).
Public None known.
Miscellaneous The family apparently retired from shipbuilding around 1810.
References *BLG*, 1846; *ODNB* for relatives; *GM*, 1830, vol. I, pp. 91 and 652.

Name **Norman, George** 1830/26
Dates 1756–probated February 1830.
Probate £140,000 (PCC).
Occupation Timber merchant in Blackfriars, City of London ('George Norman & Sons, merchants, of 23 Earl Street, Blackfriars', 1825 directory). A 'timber merchant' who 'specialised in the Baltic timber trade' and also had banking and insurance interests. *ODNB* for son. (Occupational category IV.19; venue 1.) He is described in PROB 11 as a 'merchant'.
Address 'Bromley Common, Kent and Earl Street, Blackfriars, City of London' (probate calendar).
Father James Norman (1713–87) of Bromley, Kent.
Mother Henrietta Wroughton.
Education Unknown.
Marriage In 1792, to Charlotte, daughter of (Revd) Edwards Beadon DD, Rector of Stoneham, Hampshire. (Five sons, four daughters.) A son was George Warde Norman (1793–1882), in *ODNB* as 'financial writer and merchant banker'; see 1882/92. A grandson was Charles Lloyd Norman, a wealthy banker. A great-grandson was Montagu Norrman, 1st Baron Norman, famous Governor of the Bank of England. A brother was Richard Norman (c. 1758–1847), MP, 1804–6).
Religion Anglican.
Public High Sheriff of Kent, 1793.
Miscellaneous One of the founders of a famous banking dynasty. He was only peripherally involved in banking.
References *BLG*, 1952; *ODNB* for relatives.

Name **Bazzelgette, (Jean) Louis** (sic; usually spelled Bazalgette) 1830/27
Dates 5 October 1750, France–16 February 1830, Eastwick Park, Surrey.
Probate £250,000 (PCC).
Occupation 'Tailor to the Prince of Wales' at 22 Lower Grosvenor Stret, Middlesex; also merchant and moneylender. (Occupational category IV.25? Venue 2.)
Address Eastwick Park near Leatherhead, Surrey and 86 Gloucester Place, Middlesex.

Father Etienne Bazalgette (1709–22 September 1757), 'tailor of suits at Ispagna, France'.
Mother Jeanne (b. 1715), daughter of George Deleize.
Education Unknown.
Marriage First, in 1779, to Catherine Metrivier (d. 1785). (Four sons.) Second, in 1787, to Frances, daughter of Daniel Bergman. (Two sons, two daughters.) His grandson was Sir Joseph Bazalgette (1819–91), the celebrated civil engineer who built the Thames Embankment.
Religion Baptised Roman Catholic, but his family were 'probably closet Protestants' (Charles Bazalgette, online). He appears to have been an Anglican in England. He was not a Huguenot, since he was not a religious refugee.
Public None known.
Miscellaneous Arrived in London c. 1775 as a 'silk merchant' or high-class tailor and became the principal tailor to the Prince of Wales. His workshops were in his original house at 22 Lower Grosvenor Street. He was also a moneylender and merchant in the French community. His probate valuation is very high, and there might well have been other sources of income.
References Charles Bazalgette, 'Merchant Tailor, Adventurer, or Rags to Riches, Being the Life of Jean Louis Bazalgette' (online); Sir Joseph Bazalgette in *ODNB*.

1830/28 **Name** **Harvey, Sir Eliab (sic)**
Dates 5 December 1758, Chigwell, Essex–20 February 1830, Rolls Park, Chigwell, Essex.
Probate £120,000 (PCC).
Occupation 'Admiral of the Blue' (probate calendar) and landowner. (Occupational category VI.31.) He succeeded to his father's landed property upon the death of his elder brother in 1830, but no one named Harvey with land in Essex is listed in Bateman.
Address Lived at Rolls Park, Chigwell, Essex.
Father William Harvey (1714–63) MP, of Rolls Park, Chigwell, Essex. (Second son.)
Mother Emma, daughter of Stephen Skynner of Walthamstow.
Education Westminster and Harrow to 1774.
Marriage In 1783 (1784?) to Lady Louisa, daughter of the 1st Earl Nugent. (Six daughters.)
Religion Anglican.
Public MP (Tory) Malden, Essex, 1780–4; Essex, 1802–12, 1820–30. Created KCB, 1815, GCB, 1825.
Miscellaneous Entered Royal Navy, 1770, and fought in the American Revolutionary War; Lieutenant, 1779; Post-Captain, 1783; Rear-Admiral, 1805; Vice-Admiral, 1810; Admiral, 1819. At the Battle of Trafalgar he commanded the *Téméraire*, later immortalised in Turner's famous painting *The Fighting Téméraire*. A colourful character, he allegedly lost £100,000 (later reduced to £10,000) at a single game of hazard and, in 1809, was dismissed from the Navy after being court-martialled for insulting Admiral Lord Gambier but was reinstated the following year.
References *ODNB*.

Name **Allen, Thomas** (possibly né Greenhalgh) 1830/29
Dates Unknown – probated April 1830.
Probate £500,000 (PCC).
Occupation Apparently urban property: he was Lord of the Manor of Finchley and apparently owned much property there and in the nearby Manor of Bibbesworth (*VCH Middlesex*, vol. 6, 1980, pp. 55–9). For a man of his great wealth he is very obscure, and very little could be traced about him, even his dates of birth and precise date of death. (Occupational category I?)
Address Lived at Henrietta Street, Cavendish Square, Middlesex and at Finchley.
Father Thomas Allen Greenhalgh (d. 1780) who changed his surname to Allen in 1774.
Mother Anne (d. 1796), surname unknown.
Education Unknown.
Marriage Possibly to Elizabeth (d.s.p.), daughter of Dudley Loftus (*BLG*, 1846).
Religion Anglican; buried at St Mary's Church, Finchley, with a monument.
Public None known.
Miscellaneous An ancestor, Edward Allen (d. 1642), a London Alderman, bought the Manor of Finchley around 1622. His son Sir Thomas Allen owned 'extensive Middlesex estates'; he was Thomas Allen's great-grandfather. After our Allen's death without children, his will was disputed by (Revd) Edward Cooper and by descendants of Edward Allen.
References Information from Barnet Public Library, 29 October 1993; above sources.

Name **Taylor, Martha** 1830/30
Dates Unknown – possibly 4 July 1829. However, the only Martha Taylor of Great Cumberland Place whose estate is listed in PROB 11 in this period was probated in December 1817. The identity of this person is thus unclear.
Probate £120,000 (PCC).
Occupation Unclear, but possibly a West Indies fortune. She was possibly the daughter (d. 4 July 1829) of Sir John Taylor, Baronet, a West Indies planter and sister of Sir Simon Taylor (1740, Jamaica–1813) who lived at Great Cumberland Place, Middlesex. (If so, occupational category I; venue 29.). However, her forename is given as Maria, not Martha. Moreover, no one of this name had an estate probated in 1830 or any adjacent year and listed in PROB 11.
Address Lived at Great Cumberland Place, Middlesex.
Father Possibly Sir John Taylor, whose dates could not be traced.
Mother Unknown.
Education Unknown.
Marriage Presumably unmarried.
Religion Presumably Anglican.
Public None known.
Miscellaneous A very mysterious case; her identity cannot be traced with certainty.
References Taylor records, Institute of Commonwealth Affairs index, online; *GM*, 1829, vol. II.

1830/31 **Name** **Martin, Thomas**

Dates Unknown – probated July 1830.

Probate £140,000 (PCC).

Occupation 'Warehouseman' (probate calendar) at King Street, Cheapside ('Manchester factor' at 20 King Street, Cheapside, 1820 directory; 'Thomas Martin & Sons and Hughes', of the same address, 1822 directory). He was apparently a cotton-goods wholesaler in the City. (Occupational category IV.21; venue 1.)

Address 'King Street, Cheapside and Enfield, Middlesex' (probate calendar).

Father Unknown.

Mother Unknown.

Education Unknown.

Marriage Unknown – he apparently had 'sons'.

Religion Unknown.

Public None known.

Miscellaneous Nothing more could be traced about him.

References Above sources only.

1830/32 **Name** **Tibbits, Charles**

Dates Unknown–19 July 1830, Bryanston Square, Middlesex.

Probate £120,000 (PCC).

Occupation Apparently a landowner in Northamptonshire. (Occupational category I?) In 1883, J. B. Tibbits of Barton Seagrave, Northamptonshire, owned 2,117 acres worth £3,838 p.a. If he had any other sources of wealth, these have not been traced.

Address Barton Seagrave near Kettering, Northamptonshire and 44 Bryanston Square, Middlesex.

Father Probably Richard Tibbits of Barton Seagrave. His occupation or source of wealth is unclear.

Mother Unknown.

Education Unknown.

Marriage In 1791, to Mary (b. 1763), daughter of John Woodyeare, JP, DL, of Crookhill, West Riding. (Their son Richard John Tibbits matriculated at Christ Church, Oxford in October 1812, aged eighteen.)

Religion Presumably Anglican.

Public DL, Northamptonshire 1767, although, from the date, this might relate to a namesake (*Northampton Mercury* online).

Miscellaneous He or his ancestors might have been local lawyers or merchants, although nothing more could be traced. The 1793 directory for Kettering lists a Tibbets (sic), Belcher & Co., weavers and merchants, of Milk Street, but no one named Tibbits.

References *BLG,* 1846; *GM,* 1830, vol. II, p. 92; online source as before.

1830/33 **Name** **Bebb, John**

Dates Unknown – probated October 1830.

Probate £180,000 (PCC).
Occupation Chairman of the East India Company, 1817–18, and a director of the East India Company seven times between 1804 and 1829. (Occupational category VI.31 and IV.19; venue 1.)
Address Donington Grove near Newbury, Berkshire and 13 Gloucester Place, Portman Square, Middlesex.
Father Unknown.
Mother Unknown.
Education Unknown.
Marriage Name unknown (d. 1850).
Religion Presumably Anglican.
Public None known.
Miscellaneous Described as 'an East India Company official' in an online description of Donington Grove, which he purchased in 1795. His background and career are very obscure.
References Office-holders of the East India Company, online, and above sources.

Name **Lett, Thomas** 1830/34
Dates 1770–probated October 1830.
Probate £160,000 (PCC).
Occupation 'Timber merchant' (Thomas Lett & Sons, of Commercial Road, Lambeth – 1815 and 1825 directories). (Occupational category IV.20 and 21; venue 2.)
Address 'Commercial Road, Lambeth and St Peter's, Isle of Thanet, Kent' (probate calendar).
Father Unknown.
Mother Unknown.
Education Unknown.
Marriage Unknown; he presumably had 'sons' (see 'Occupation' above).
Religion Anglican; his bust can be found in St Mary-at-Lambeth Church (online description of this church).
Public High Sheriff of Surrey, 1817.
Miscellaneous Nothing further could be traced about him.
References Above sources only.

Name **Cholmondeley, George James** 1830/35
Dates 22 February 1752–5 November 1830.
Probate £180,000 (PCC).
Occupation 'Receiver-General of Excise' (*BP*). This was apparently a lucrative 'Old Corruption' office which he secured courtesy of his important relatives. (Occupational category VI.31; venue 2?) He does not appear in John Wade's *Black Book*, published in 1832, just after his death.
Address Great Cumberland Street, Middlesex.
Father (Revd Hon.) Robert Cholmondeley (1727–5 June 1804), Rector of St

Andrew's, Hertfordshire. (First son.) Robert was the younger son of the 3rd Earl of Cholmondeley.

Mother Mary (d. 1811), daughter of Arthur Woffington and sister of Margaret ('Peg') Woffington 'the celebrated actress'.

Education Unknown.

Marriage First, in 1790, to Marcia (d. 1805), daughter of John Pitt of Encombe, Dorset. (One son.) Second, in 1814, to Catherine (d. 1827), daughter of Sir Philip Francis. Third, in 1825, to (Hon.) Mary (1794–25 December 1847), daughter of John, 2nd Viscount Sydney. (One daughter.) Mary married, second, in 1832, Charles, 2nd Earl of Romney (1777–1845).

Religion Anglican.

Public None known, apart from the above office.

Miscellaneous Little about his career could be traced.

References *BP.*

1830/36 **Name** **Wigram, Sir Robert, 1st Baronet**

Dates 30 January 1744, Wexford–6 November 1830.

Probate £400,000 (PCC).

Occupation Multiple interests but primarily a shipbuilder, shipowner and drug importer in Crosby Square, Bishopsgate and Blackwall. (Occupational categories II.4, IV.19 and 24; venues 1 and 2.) He was also a director, and Chairman in 1810, of the East India Company, and a director of the East India Docks, as well as a landowner, although no one named Wigram or FitzWygram is listed in Bateman.

Address 'Crosby Square, City of London and Walthamstow House, Essex' (probate calendar). He also had an estate at Belmont Lodge, Worcester.

Father John Wigram ('lost at sea, 1746'), Master of the privateer *Boyne*, of Wexford.

Mother Mary, daughter of Robert Clifford of Wexford.

Education Apprenticed to a surgeon in Wexford.

Marriage First, in 1772, to Catherine (d. 1786), daughter of Francis Broadhurst of Mansfield, Nottinghamshire. (Four sons, two daughters.) Second, in 1787, to Eleanor (d. 1841), daughter of John Watts, Secretary of the Victualling Office, and widow of Captain Agnew. (Thirteen sons, four daughters.) Four of the sons have entries in the *ODNB*, including Joseph Wigram, Bishop of Rochester (1798–1867).

Religion Originally Anglican but became a Unitarian after marrying his first wife, a Unitarian. One of his sons, as noted above, was an Anglican bishop.

Public MP (Tory) Fowey, 1802–6; Wexford, 1806–7. High Sheriff of Essex 1812–13. Created baronet 1805.

Miscellaneous His successors as baronet changed their name to FitzWygram. He was brought up in Wexford by a maternal uncle and apprenticed to a surgeon. He served as a surgeon in the East India Company and then became a drug merchant. He returned to London, where he became 'one of the greatest importers of drugs in England' (*DNB*). Wigram then became a shipowner and in 1805 became a leading shareholder in Green's Blackwall shipbuilding firm. He was a director and Chairman of the East India Company and was involved in many other business pursuits, still finding time to serve as an MP and father seventeen sons and six daughters with two wives!

References *ODNB; BP; HP.*

Name **Levy, Moses Lyon** (His middle name appears as Lionel in the *ODNB* entry on his son; name given in PROB 11 as 'Moses, otherwise Lyon Levy, of Goodman's Fields, Middlesex') 1830/37

Dates c. 1765–probated February 1830.

Probate £100,000 (PCC).

Occupation 'Money broker and agent' of 18 Great Alie Street, City of London, 1827 directory. (Occupational category IV.18; venue 1.)

Address Great Alie Street, Goodman's Fields, City of London.

Father Unknown.

Mother Unknown.

Education Unknown.

Marriage To Helena (Leah?) (1790–1861), daughter of J. Moses. Marriage date unknown. (In view of her age, this might have been a second marriage.) J. Moses's brother Henry Moses (see 1836/34) left £100,000. His son Joseph Moses Levy (1811–88) was the proprietor of the *Daily Telegraph* and is in the *ODNB*. His grandson was Edward Levy Lawson, 1st Baron Burnham (1833–1916).

Religion Jewish – 'Orthodox' (*ODNB* entry on son.)

Public None known.

Miscellaneous Apparently a successful moneylender in the City.

References *ODNB* for son; *BP.*

Name **Baker, Sir Frederick Francis, 2nd Baronet** 1830/38

Dates 13 May 1773, Jermyn Street, Middlesex–1 October 1830, Hastings.

Probate £120,000 (PCC).

Occupation Medical fortune – inherited much of the estate of his father, Sir George Baker, Physician to King George III. (Occupational category VI.30; venue 2.) He does not appear to have had any other occupation.

Address Jermyn Street, Middlesex.

Father Sir George Baker, 1st Baronet (1723–15 June 1809), Physician to King George III, FRS; in *ODNB*. (First son.)

Mother Jane (d. 12 July 1813), daughter of Roger Morris.

Education Secondary schooling unknown; Balliol College, Oxford (BA, 1792; MA, 1796).

Marriage In 1814, to Harriet (d. 15 November 1845), daughter of Sir John Simeon, 1st Baronet, MP. (Three sons, one daughter.)

Religion Anglican.

Public None known.

Miscellaneous He appears to have lived quietly in London and was an FRS (1811) and FSA. Suffering from myopia, he was accidentally killed when he walked into the blades of a windmill at Hastings.

References *GM,* 1830, vol. II, p. 469; *BP.*

1830/39 **Name** **Milward, John**
Dates c. 1736–27 September 1830.
Probate £140,000 (PCC).
Occupation Unclear. Despite his Westminster address, he could not be identified with confidence in any directory. He might have been the John Milward who is listed in the 1803 directory as a 'mealman' (merchant and dealer in grain) of Bromley, Middlesex, but this is unclear. The 1808 directory lists a 'Charles and John Milward, mealmen and maltsters, of Bromley, Middlesex'. A John Milward, 'coal merchant', of Redcross Wharf, London Bridge, is listed in the 1829 directory. In view of his great age, he was presumably in business or a profession chiefly during the eighteenth century, before the time when directories were common. His will is also unclear. It names a Henry Milward and properties in Bishopsgate and Houndsditch, but nothing could be determined regarding his occupation.
Address 'Artillery Place, St Luke's parish, Middlesex' (probate calendar). This is in Westminster, off what today is Victoria Street. PROB 11 gives his address as of 'St Luke Old Street, Middlesex'.
Father Unknown.
Mother Unknown.
Education Unknown.
Marriage Unknown – his will does not mention a wife or children. *Environs of London,* vol. II, 1795, under 'Edmonton' notes that a Susannah Milward was buried in Edmonton Church in 1792.
Religion Anglican – his will requests that he be buried in the Church of England, Edmonton along with his father and brother.
Public JP, Middlesex.
Miscellaneous Two John Milwards, deceased in 1829 and 1830, are listed for two families in *BLG,* 1937, but neither has the right date of birth or any London association. It is possible that he was a lawyer or some kind of government functionary in a lucrative post.
References *GM,* 1830, vol. II, p. 374; will (PROB 11 online).

1830/40 **Name** **Newton, John**
Dates Unknown – probated October 1830.
Probate £140,000 (PCC).
Occupation 'Wine and brandy merchant' (probate calendar) of the City of London; ('H. & J. Newton, wine and brandy merchants, of 47 Aldgate High Street, City of London' – 1815 and 1817 directories). (Occupational category IV.20 and 21; venue 1.)
Address '[47] Aldgate High Street, City of London, and Chingford Lodge, Essex' (probate calendar).
Father Unknown.
Mother Unknown.
Education Unknown.

Marriage Unknown.
Religion Unknown.
Public None known.
Miscellaneous Nothing more could be traced about him.
References Probate calendar and directories only.

WEALTH-HOLDERS, 1831

1831/1 **Name** **Peto, Henry**

Dates 4 May 1774–15 September 1830.

Probate £120,000 (PCC).

Occupation 'Builder' (probate calendar). Building contractor in the City of London, the founder of a well-known building dynasty. (Occupational category II.10; venue 1.) His office was at 31 Little Britain, Smithfield, in 1825.

Address 'Highbury Terrace, Islington and York Row, Lambeth' (probate calendar).

Father James Peto (1732–12 May 1816), apparently a tenant farmer of Cookham, Berkshire.

Mother Unknown.

Education Unknown.

Marriage Unmarried. He left his firm to his nephews, Sir Samuel Peto, a leading Victorian builder, and to Thomas Grissell.

Religion The family were 'strict Congregationalists'.

Public None known.

Miscellaneous He built the Custom House in the City. His nephew built Nelson's Column, Paddington Station, and many other famous sites.

References *ODNB; DBB;* Sir Henry Peto, *Sir Morton Peto* (1893).

1831/2 **Name** **Robarts, James Thomas**

Dates Unknown – probated July 1830.

Probate £120,000 (PCC).

Occupation Of the 'East India Company in China' (probate calendar), although his exact occupation is unclear. (Presumably occupational category IV.19; venue 29.)

Address He appears to have been resident in China at the time of his death.

Father Abraham Robarts (1745–1816; see 1816/22), who left £350,000. He was a director of the East India Company. In 1821, when he and his wife were granted coats of arms, James Thomas Robarts was described as 'of Wimpole Street', the 'third son' of Abraham Robarts. W. Bruce Bannerman (ed.), *Miscellanea Genealogica et Heraldica*, 4th series, vol. 5 (London, 1914), pp. 46–7.

Mother Sabine, daughter of Thomas Tierney.

Education Unknown.

Marriage In 1814, to Charlotte, daughter of Martin Allen Lloyd.

Religion Presumably Anglican. Married in an Anglican church.

Public None known.

Miscellaneous Nothing further could be traced about him. He is mentioned in Hosea Ballou Morse, *The Chronicles of the East India Company trading to China 1654–1834* (Oxford, 1926).

References Probate calendar; other source as above.

1831/3 **Name** **Booth, Frederick**

Dates c. 1748–2 May 1831, at New Street, Spring Gardens, Middlesex.

Probate £350,000 (PCC).
Occupation 'Solicitor for the Affairs of Taxes and Vestry Clerk to St Martin's-in-the-Fields', of 3 Lincoln's Inn (1809 directory). (Occupational category VI.29 and 31; venues 1 and 2.)
Address 'New Street, Spring Gardens, Middlesex' (probate calendar).
Father Unknown.
Mother Unknown.
Education Unknown.
Marriage In 1813, to Anna Maria, daughter of Robert Bristow (1712–76), MP.
Religion Presumably Anglican. Married in an Anglican church, the same one that employed him.
Public None known, apart from his legal position.
Miscellaneous Apparently a solicitor who enjoyed a lucrative official position.
References *GM*, 1831, vol. I, p. 475; *BLG*, 1846, 'Bristow of Broxmore Park'.

Name **Somerville, Jane** (née Seaman) 1831/4
Dates c. 1755–3 December 1830.
Probate £120,000 (PCC).
Occupation A landowner in Wiltshire and Somerset, but little could be traced about her fortune. No one named Somerville is listed in Bateman. She also possibly inherited clerical money from her father, grandfather and husband. (Occupational categories I? and VI.30?)
Address 'Formerly of Bibury, Gloucestershire, then Dinder House [near Wells], Somerset and Gay Street, Bath' (probate calendar).
Father (Revd) Lionel Seaman, DD, Archdeacon of Taunton and Wells.
Mother Jane, daughter of Edward Willes, DD, Bishop of Bath and Wells.
Education Unknown.
Marriage In 1777, to (Revd) William Somerville (1732–25 June 1803), of Dinder House, Prebendary of Wells, Vicar of Bibury and Rector of Aston Somerville, Gloucestershire. On her death without issue her property passed to a relative, James Somerville Somerville, (b. 1769).
Religion Anglican.
Public None known.
Miscellaneous She owned land in Upton Scudamore, Wiltshire (*VCH Wiltshire*, vol. 8, 1965), and presumably also in Gloucestershire.
References *BLG*, 1846.

Name **Batt, John Thomas** 1831/5
Dates c. 1746–8 March 1831, New Hall, Wiltshire.
Probate £120,000 (PCC).
Occupation Barrister and 'Auditor of Irish Accounts' (*GM*). (Occupational categories VI.29 and 31; venues 2 and 1.)
Address 'New Hall, near Salisbury, Wiltshire' (probate calendar). His legal offices were at New Square, Lincoln's Inn. In 1811, he also lived at 12 South Audley Street, Middlesex.

Father John Thomas Batt (d. 1762), MD of Downton, Wiltshire.
Mother Unknown.
Education Westminster School; Christ Church, Oxford (MA); barrister, Lincoln's Inn (called 1763).
Marriage Unknown; probably unmarried.
Religion Anglican.
Public JP, DL, Wiltshire.
Miscellaneous Also inherited land from his uncle, presumably in Wiltshire. No one of his name is listed in Bateman as having owned land in Wiltshire, however.
References *GM,* 1831, vol. I, p. 274.

1831/6 **Name** **Chamberlayne, Charlotte**
Dates Unknown – probated April 1831.
Probate £160,000 (PCC).
Occupation Sister of William Chamberlayne (see 1830/5) who left £250,000, mainly to her. He was a landowner and inherited 'Old Corruption' and legal money. (Occupational category I, etc.)
Address Weston Grove, Hampshire.
Father William Chamberlayne (d. 1799), Solicitor to the Treasury and to the Royal Mint, etc.
Mother Harriot, daughter of Sir Cecil Bisshopp, 5th Baronet. Yet another of Bisshopp's relatives married to a wealth-holder.
Education Unknown.
Marriage Unmarried.
Religion Anglican.
Public None known.
Miscellaneous Whether she was very wealthy in the brief time between her brother's death and her own is unknown; probably she was not.
References *BLG,* 1846.

1831/7 **Name** **Choumert, George**
Dates c. 1745–5 March 1831.
Probate £140,000 (PCC).
Occupation 'Tanner' of Russell Street, Bermondsey (1811 directory); 'Tanner' of 1 Five Foot Lane, Bermondsey (1794 directory). (Occupational category II.11? Venue 2.) There is a Choumert Road and a Choumert Square in Peckham, implying that he owned land or property there.
Address 'Formerly of Russell Street, Bermondsey, and then Peckham, Surrey' (probate calendar).
Father Unknown. He was naturalised in 1796 and was possibly of French or Swiss birth.
Mother Unknown.
Education Unknown.
Marriage Unknown; she was a daughter of Elizabeth (née Fendall; d. 1795). From his wife and her sister he acquired the estate in Bermondsey that belonged

to their father Richard Fendall (d. 1753). He sold several parts of it during his lifetime; the remainder (said to be worth £6,000 p.a. in rental at the time of his death) was auctioned in 123 lots. (G. W. Phillips, *The History and Antiquities of the Parish of Bermondsey* [1841], pp. 112–13.)
Religion Unknown.
Public None known.
Miscellaneous Nothing more could be traced about him. In 1783, he was granted a patent 'for his Invention of a Machine for cutting, splitting, and dividing Hides and Skins, as well as in the Pelt before dressed as when dressed into Leather, severing the Grain-side from the Flesh-side': *The Repertory of . . . Patent Inventions* (1796), pp. 104–6.
References *GM,* 1831, vol. I, p. 282; other sources as above.

Name **Spicer, John** 1831/8
(so stated in the probate calendar, but his name is given in *BLG,* 1952 as John William Spicer)
Dates Unknown – probated April 1831. *BP* gives his date of death as 1831.
Probate £120,000 (PCC).
Occupation 'Of the Stock Exchange' (probate calendar). (Occupational category IV.23; venue 1.)
Address 'Hanover Square, Middlesex and Esher Place, Surrey' (probate calendar).
Father John Spicer.
Mother Unknown.
Education Unknown.
Marriage In 1816, to Hannah, daughter of Philip Smith Webb of Milford House, Witley, Surrey. Her mother was the daughter and heiress of Sir Robert Baker, 1st Baronet, of Godalming. (At least one son, John William Gooch Spicer, JP, DL, q.v.).
Religion Presumably Anglican.
Public None known.
Miscellaneous He purchased Esher Place in 1805. A wealthy stockbroker who possibly also inherited money.
References *BLG,* 1952.

Name **Leaf, William** 1831/9
Dates 1758–late 1830 (probated April 1831).
Probate £250,000 (PCC).
Occupation 'Merchant' (probate calendar) of Old Change, City of London. ('Leaf, Sons & Coles, wholesale haberdashers, of 39 Old Change', 1825 directory; Leaf & Co., founded in 1790, was the largest firm of London wholesale and export merchants dealing in silks, ribbons and velvets.) (Occupational category IV.21; venue 1.)
Address 'Old Change, City of London and Goose-in-Green, Camberwell, Surrey' (probate calendar).
Father William Leaf of Bishop Monckton, Yorkshire. (First son.)

Mother Elizabeth, daughter of John Bradshaw.
Education Unknown.
Marriage First, in 1790, to Susanna Ladler (d. 1792) of Cripplegate, London. (One son.) Second, in 1795, to Elizabeth Horsnell of Guildford, Surrey. (Two sons, three daughters.) Walter Leaf (1852–1927), the well-known banker and classical scholar, in the *ODNB*, was his grandson.
Religion Anglican.
Public None known.
Miscellaneous A self-made silk- and cotton-goods wholesaler and exporter.
References *BLG*, 1970; *ODNB* for grandson.

1831/10 **Name Lopes, Sir Manasseh Massey, 1st Baronet**
Dates 27 January 1755, Jamaica–26 March 1831, Maristow House, Devonshire.
Probate £160,000 (PCC).
Occupation Sugar planter's fortune in Jamaica, and then a large landowner in and near Plymouth. (Occupational category I; venue 29.) He also was a director of the Rock Life Assurance Company. In 1883, Sir Massey Lopes owned 12,103 acres worth £10,668 p.a. in Devon and Wiltshire. He took the middle name Massey (or Masseh) in 1805.
Address 'Maristow House [near Roborough,] Devonshire and Arlington Street, Piccadilly' (probate calendar).
Father Mordechai Rodriguez Lopes (d. 1796), a sugar planter in Jamaica and then of Clapham, Surrey. He was 'extremely wealthy' (*HP*). (Only son.)
Mother Rebecca, daughter of Manasseh Perera of Jamaica.
Education Unknown. He was stated (*HP*) to be 'uneducated'.
Marriage In 1795, to Charlotte (d. 1833), daughter of John Yeates of Monmouthshire. (One daughter, who predeceased him; his baronetcy passed to his nephew.)
Religion Originally Sephardic Jewish. He was baptised as an Anglican in 1802.
Public MP (pro-Pitt) New Romney, 1802–6; Evesham, 1807–8; Barnstaple, 1812–19; Westbury, 1823–9. JP, Devonshire and Wiltshire. High Sheriff of Devonshire, 1810–11. Recorder of Westbury, 1810–death. Created baronet, 1805.
Miscellaneous Regarded as one of the richest men in England and stated to be worth 'over £800,000' when his land was taken into account (*ODNB*). He was said to have owned 'immense' landed acreage near Plymouth. It is likely that these claims are somewhat exaggerated, given that he left £160,000 in personalty. Much of this was said to be in 'India and government stock'. In 1819, Lopes was found guilty of bribery, jailed and fined £10,000, but recovered. He was also an early example of a successful Jewish entrant into the elite, after his baptism.
References *GM*, 1831, vol. I, p. 465; *ODNB; HP; BP.*

1831/11 **Name Nation, William**
Dates Unknown – probated July 1831.
Probate £160,000 (PCC).

Occupation 'Wholesale linen draper and snuff maker' of High Street, Exeter (1791 directory). He is also described as a 'banker' of Exeter in the *ODNB* entry on (Revd) William Adams. (Occupational categories IV.16 and 21 and III.14; venue 13.)
Address Lived in Exeter.
Father Unknown.
Mother Unknown.
Education Unknown.
Marriage Unknown. His daughter Eliza (d. 1841) was the mother of (Revd) William Adams (1814–48), 'Church of England clergyman and author', in *ODNB*. She had married Serjeant John Adams of St Pancras, Assistant Judge at the Middlesex Sessions.
Religion Unknown, probably Anglican.
Public None known.
Miscellaneous What his main source of wealth consisted of is unclear.
References Above sources and probate calendar only.

Name **Wilson, John** 1831/12
Dates c. 1771–14 January 1830 at Market Drayton. His estate was not probated until 1831, it seems.
Probate £120,000 (PCC).
Occupation Canal and engineering contractor. He 'built part of the Shropshire Union Canal' near Market Drayton, and had previously worked for Thomas Telford (1754–1834) 'on the Pontycysyllte Aquaduct, on the Holyhead Road in North Wales, and on various of his works in Scotland' ('Salop. Routes to Root', online, which states that he died in 1831). (Occupational category II.10.)
Address Grove House, Drayton-in-Hales, near Market Drayton, Shropshire.
Father Unknown.
Mother Unknown.
Education Unknown.
Marriage Unknown.
Religion Unknown.
Public None known.
Miscellaneous It is not known how long he lived in Shropshire, but he owned a substantial mansion there.
References *GM*, 1830, vol. I, p. 92 and above sources.

Name **Wilkins, Walter** 1831/13
Dates Unknown–1 May 1830, Maeslough Castle, Radnorshire.
Probate £250,000 (PCC).
Occupation Apparently an East India fortune, inherited from his father, plus land. (Occupational category IV.19 and 31 and 1; venue 29.) In 1883, Walter DeWinton of Maeslough Castle, who inherited his property, owned 9,900 acres worth £15,642 p.a. in Radnor, Glamorgan, Brecon, etc.
Address 'Cambridge Terrace, Regent's Park, Middlesex and Maeslough, Radnorshire' (probate calendar).

Father Walter Wilkins (1741–17 March 1828; see 1828/15; left £250,000) East India Company official and merchant and MP. (Only son.)
Mother Catherine, daughter of Samuel Hayward of Walsworth Hall, Gloucestershire.
Education Unknown.
Marriage In 1806, to Catherine (d. 1856), daughter of George Devereux, Viscount Hereford.
Religion Anglican.
Public None known.
Miscellaneous Inherited his father's considerable fortune but died only two years later.
References *GM*, 1830, vol. I, p. 478; *BLG*, 1846, 'DeWinton of Maeslough Castle'; *HP* for father.

1831/14 **Name** **Headfort, 1st Marquess of and 2nd Earl of Bective, Sir Thomas Taylour (Taylor)** (given in the probate calendar as the Earl of Bective)
Dates 18 November 1757–24 October 1829, Lausanne.
Probate £250,000 (PCC).
Occupation Landowner. (Occupational category I.) In 1883, the Marquess of Headfort owned 42,754 acres worth £39,606 p.a. in Ireland, Westmorland and Lancashire.
Address His principal seat was Headfort House, Kells, County Meath.
Father Sir Thomas Taylor, 1st Earl of Bective (1724–14 February 1795), Irish MP and landowner, whose Irish peerage was created in 1760. (First son.)
Mother Jane, daughter of Rt. Hon. Hercules Langford Rowley.
Education Secondary schooling unknown; Trinity College, Cambridge.
Marriage In 1778, to Mary (d. 1842), daughter of George Quin of Quinsborough, County Clare.
Religion Anglican.
Public Created a marquess in the Irish peerage, 1800, and was an Irish Representative Peer, 1801–29. He had been a member of the Irish Parliament, 1776–95. Created KP, 1806. High Sheriff, County Meath, 1786.
Miscellaneous A wealthy Irish aristocrat. FSA, 1808. His will was not probated until October 1830 and appears only in the 1831 probate calendar.
References *BP*; *CP*.

1831/15 **Name** **Gurney, Joseph**
Dates 1757–25 December 1830, Lakenham Grove, Norwich.
Probate £120,000 (PCC).
Occupation 'Banker' (probate calendar). Partner in Gurney's Bank in Norwich. (Occupational category IV.16; venue 11.) In 1883, two members of the Gurney family owned 11,714 and 8,703 acres worth £6,229 p.a. and £8,965 p.a., in Norfolk, Scotland, etc.
Address Lakenham Grove, Norwich.

Father John Gurney (1715–70) yarn manufacturer of Norwich and Keswick. He 'introduced the manufacture of handspun yarn into Norwich from southern Ireland' (*BLG*).
Mother Elizabeth (d. 1788), daughter of Richard Kett of Norwich.
Education Unknown.
Marriage In 1784, to Jane (d. 1841), daughter of Abel Chapman of Whitby. (Five daughters.) Their daughter Elizabeth married, in 1802, Robert Barclay (1787–1853) of Knott's Green. Other daughters married into the Pease, Birkbeck and Backhouse families.
Religion Quaker – a part of the Quaker 'Cousinhood'.
Public None known.
Miscellaneous He was also a director of the Norwich Union Fire Office.
References *BLG; GM,* 1830, vol. II, p. 647.

Name **Hope, Thomas** 1831/16
Dates 30 August 1769, Amsterdam–3 February 1831.
Probate £180,000 (PCC).
Occupation Mercantile and banking family in Amsterdam, although he played no role in the family business after his early twenties, and is in the *ODNB* as an 'art collector and connoisseur'. (Occupational category IV.16 and 19; venue 29.) In 1883, Mrs Hope of Deepdene owned 21,773 acres worth £22,138 p.a. in County Monaghan, Surrey, Gloucestershire and Warwickshire.
Address Lived at Duchess Street, Middlesex and Deepdene near Dorking, Surrey, which he purchased in 1807.
Father John Hope (1737–84) merchant and banker in Amsterdam, who was 'immensely wealthy' (*ODNB*). The Hopes were regarded in the same class as the Barings or Rothschilds two generations later.
Mother Philippina Barbara (1738–89), daughter of Elias Van der Hoeven.
Education Unknown.
Marriage In 1806, to (Hon.) Louisa (d. 1851), daughter of (Rt. Revd) Lord Decies, Bishop of Tuam. (Three sons, one daughter.) A son was Alexander Beresford Hope (1820–87), the novelist, in *ODNB.* The family were later known as Beresford-Hope. (Louisa married second, in 1832, Field Marshal Viscount Beresford.)
Religion Presumably Anglican, although his Dutch relatives were presumably Dutch Reformed. He 'abandoned Christianity' while visiting Turkey (*ODNB*).
Public None known.
Miscellaneous Travelled around Europe, and then, from 1795, became a famous patron of the arts and art collector in London, with a 'Temple of Art' at his Duchess Street home to which one was admitted by ticket. He wrote a novel and a *History of Architecture,* and was an RA and member of the Dillettanti Club.
References *ODNB; GM,* 1831, vol. I, p. 368; *BLG,* 1937.

Name **Hambrough, John** 1831/17
Dates 1753–8 May 1830.
Probate £120,000 (PCC).

Occupation 'Gunpowder merchant' at 11 Savage Gardens (near Fenchurch Street in the City of London, 1808 directory). (Occupational category IV.21 and II.11? Venue 1.)

Address Lived at 16 Hereford Street, Park Lane, Middlesex (purchased in the late 1820s) and at Marchwood Lodge, near Southampton, Hampshire. He also owned the Steephill estate at Ventnor, Isle of Wight.

Father Unknown.

Mother Unknown.

Education Unknown.

Marriage Unknown.

Religion Apparently an Anglican: he held the patronage of the Anglican church at Hayes, Middlesex (*VCH Middlesex,* vol. 4, 1971).

Public None known.

Miscellaneous Little could be traced about his career. He presumably did well during the Napoleonic Wars.

References *GM,* 1830, vol. I, p. 475. *BLG,* 1855, has a genealogy for the Hamboroughs of Steephill Castle, Isle of Wight, but does not directly list him.

1831/18 **Name** **Harrington, Sir John Edward, 8th Baronet**

Dates 30 September 1760–9 June 1831.

Probate £120,000 (PCC).

Occupation 'For some time in India, in the service of the Company' (*GM*). 'In the civil service of the East India Company at Fort William in Bengal' (*Complete Baronetage*). His family is not listed in Bateman. (Occupational category VI.31; venue 29.)

Address Lived at Berkeley Square, Middlesex, and is described (*GM*) as of Ridlington, Rutlandshire.

Father Sir James Harrington, 7th Baronet (1726–17 January 1793), presumably a landowner. His remote ancestors were London merchants. (First son.)

Mother Anna (d. 1812), daughter of James Ashenhurst of Park Hall, Staffordshire.

Education Unknown.

Marriage In 1787 at Fort William, Calcutta, to Marianne (d. 1824), daughter of Thomas Philpot. (Four sons, one daughter.)

Religion Anglican.

Public None known.

Miscellaneous What happened to the family's land is unclear.

References *GM,* 1831, vol. II, p. 177; *Complete Baronetage.*

1831/19 **Name** **Harris, William**

Dates Unknown – probated July 1831.

Probate £100,000 (PCC).

Occupation 'Auctioneer' (probate calendar). Possibly of Harris, Sharpe & Co., auctioneers, of Gracechurch Street, City of London. (Occupational category IV.21; venue 1?)

Address Lived at 27 Norton Street, Fitzroy Square, Middlesex.
Father Unknown.
Mother Unknown.
Education Unknown.
Marriage Unknown.
Religion Unknown.
Public None known.
Miscellaneous Nothing more could be traced about him.
References Probate calendar only.

Name **Christie, John** 1831/20
Dates Unknown – probated August 1831.
Probate £160,000 (PCC).
Occupation Rather remarkably, it has proven impossible to trace this man satisfactorily. In the 1827 Court directory he is listed as of 6 Queen Street, Mayfair, and Quenby Hall (near Hungarton), Leicestershire. In 1819, he was listed as of Queen Street only. Quenby Hall was rented out on a casual basis at that time (online history of Quenby Hall). John and Robert Christie, merchants of 52 Mark Lane, City of London, are listed in the 1815 directory. The famous auction house was headed at that time by a James Christie. He is not listed in any genealogical or school guide.
Address 'Queen Street, Mayfair.' Christie died at Cowes, Isle of Wight.
Father Unknown.
Mother Unknown.
Education Unknown.
Marriage Charleotte, surname unknown. (At least three sons and two daughters.)
Religion Unknown.
Public None known.
Miscellaneous His will is unilluminating. He had at least three sons, named Thomas, Edgar and Peter, but they could not be readily traced.
References Probate calendar, will (PROB11 online).

Name **Hobhouse, Sir Benjamin, 1st Baronet** 1831/21
Dates 29 March 1757, Bristol–14 August 1831.
Probate £250,000 (PCC).
Occupation Multiple interests. His father was an apparently wealthy Bristol merchant. Our man was a barrister on the Western Circuit and invested £33,000 in Whitbread's Brewery. The father of his first wife was a banker in Bradford. He was also a landowner, but the family is not listed in Bateman. It appears that he should be classified as wealthy from mercantile interests and as a barrister. (Occupational categories IV.19 and VI.29; venues 12 and 1? If he was also a brewer, the occupational category III.12 and venue 2.)
Address 'Whitton Park, Middlesex and Berkeley Square, Middlesex' (probate calendar). He also had an estate at Westbury, Gloucestershire and at Bradford, Wiltshire.

Father John Hobhouse (1712–21 May 1787), merchant of Bristol.
Mother Mary Medley (d. 1759) of Hereford, widow of Mr Smith.
Education Bristol Grammar School; Brasenose College, Oxford (BA, 1778; MA, 1781); barrister, Middle Temple (called 1781).
Marriage First, in 1785, to Charlotte (d. 1791), daughter of Samuel Cam, banker of Bradford, Wiltshire. (Three sons, two daughters.) Second, in 1793, to Amelia, daughter of Joshua Parry, Presbyterian Minister of Cirencester. (Four sons, ten daughters.) A son was John Cam Hobhouse, 1st Baron Broughton (see 1869/14), the radical politician.
Religion Originally Anglican, but was pro-Unitarian later in life.
Public MP (Radical and Whig) Bletchingley, 1797–1802; Gampound, 1802–6; Hindon, 1806–18. Secretary to the Board of Control, 1806; Chairman of the Committee for Supplies, 1805. Created baronet, 1812.
Miscellaneous Was also an FRS, FSA and Vice-President of the Royal Society of Literature. As a schoolboy, had been awarded a school prize, a copy of Milton, by Edmund Burke, the local MP.
References *ODNB* as 'politician'; *GM,* 1831, vol. II, p. 371; *BP.*

1831/22 **Name Claypon, Bartholomew**
Dates 1750–4 September 1830, Worthing.
Probate £140,000 (PCC).
Occupation Banker in Boston, Lincolnshire (Claypon, Garfit & Claypon, High Street, Boston, 1822 directory). The oldest bank in Boston, it was founded in 1774 when Benjamin Claypon had become a partner with William Garfit. (Occupational category IV.16; venue 18.)
Address Boston, Lincolnshire.
Father Unknown. Bartholomew became a bank partner at the age of twenty-four, which suggests that he was reasonably affluent at the time. According to an obituary of his daughter in *GM,* the family name had been Claypole, and they were lineal descendants of Oliver Cromwell's daughter Elizabeth and her husband John Claypole.
Mother Unknown.
Education Unknown.
Marriage Unknown.
Religion Unknown. A Charlotte Claypon witnessed a deed he signed in 1805. His daughter Elizabeth (d. 1863, aged seventy-seven) married Boston banker Henry Clarke (founder with Thomas Gee of the firm later known as Gee, Wise & Gee); their daughter Elizabeth Clarke (c. 1810–87) married Sir Alan Edward Bellingham, 3rd Baronet, of County Louth, Ireland.
Public None known.
Miscellaneous Nothing further could be found about him. He and C. W. Sibthorpe were 'the principal proprietors' of Thorpe, Lincolnshire (Oldfield); he was 'active in the [Lincolnshire] land market' (Holderness).
References *GM,* 1831, vol. II, p. 285; *GM,* 1863, vol. I, p. 580, for daughter; Edmund Oldfield, *A Topographical and Historical Account of Wainfleet* (1829), p. 302;

B. A. Holderness, 'The English Land Market in the Eighteenth Century: The Case of Lincolnshire', *Economic History Review*, n.s., vol. 27, no. 4, 1974, p. 567; online sources.

Name Isacke, Matthew 1831/23

Dates c. 1758–29 August 1831. A Matthew Isacke, son of Gabriel and Sarah (see 'Father' and 'Mother' below) was born on St Helena on 16 November 1767 (www.leavesonatree.org).

Probate £120,000 (PCC).

Occupation 'Merchant' of 10 George Yard, Lombard Street, City of London (1825 directory). A Captain Matthew Isacke was employed in the East India Company service in 1808 (*Naval History of Great Britain*, online). His son was described as 'Captain Isacke of the East India Company's service' in *BLG*, 1846. His sister lived on St Helena, according to his will. (Occupational categories IV.19 and VI.31; venues 1 and 29?) He also owned lands in the Isle of Thanet and in Kent, and a leasehold in Greenwich.

Address 'Croom's Hill, Greenwich and North Forland, Kent' (probate calendar).

Father Unknown. Possibly Gabriel Isacke, born on St Helena in 1717 to a father from Lincolnshire and a mother born on the island.

Mother Unknown. Possibly Sarah Whaley, born on St Helena in 1737.

Education Unknown.

Marriage In 1802 to Margaret Steell (sic; d. 1848) (abstract of his will and online genealogy sources). They had two sons, Captain Robert Matthew Isacke and Frederick James Isacke, and two daughters. Robert married Matilda (d. 1841), daughter of Henry Scrymgeour-Wedderburn (*BLG*, 1846). They also had two daughters.

Religion Presumably Anglican.

Public Unknown.

Miscellaneous Apparently an East India Company mercantile captain who became a merchant in London, although this may represent a confusion between two different men.

References *GM*, 1831, vol. II, p. 282; Society of Genealogists: abstract of will; online sources.

Name Roberts, Roger Elliot 1831/24

Dates c. 1783–9 August 1831, Upper Grosvenor Street, Middlesex.

Probate £100,000 (PCC).

Occupation Unknown. There is no clue in his will regarding his occupation or source of wealth. He owned property at Hampstead. In *GM*, he is described as 'Colonel Roberts'.

Address 'Upper Grosvenor Street' (probate calendar).

Father Unknown.

Mother Unknown.

Education Unknown.

Marriage Marianne (d. 21 September 1842), daughter of Sir William Wake, 8th Baronet. Marriage date unknown. They had at least three children: two sons,

Elliot Roberts Roberts and Lawrence Roberts, and a daughter, Sophia Frances Lamprier. Elliot was born c. 1805 and educated at Eton and Christ Church, Oxford (matriculated January 1822).

Religion Anglican. He was buried in the family vault at Stoke Poges Church and left money for the British and Foreign Bible Society.

Public None known.

Miscellaneous Nothing more could be traced about him. He is not listed in any obvious genealogical or alumni source consulted. His description as 'Colonel Roberts' might suggest a connection with the East India Company, but there is no direct evidence.

References *GM*, 1831, vol. II, p. 187; Will (PROB 11, online).

1831/25 **Name** **Daubuz, John Theophilus**

Dates Baptised 22 September 1757 (Family Search). Probated October 1830, although his estate was recorded in PROB 8 in 1831.

Probate £120,000 (PCC).

Occupation The 1772 directory has a Theophilus Daubuz, 'merchant' of 4 Devonshire Square, in Bishopsgate, adjacent to the City of London. The 1763 directory has a Theophilus Daubuz, 'Italian merchant' of the same address. John Theophilus Daubuz was presumably the son of this man. (Occupational category IV.19? Venue 1?) Our man also owned an estate at Leyton in Essex (*VCH Essex*, vol. 6, 1973), but the family is not listed in Bateman.

Address (The Great House,) Leyton, Essex.

Father Unknown, but see 'Occupation' above. According to Family Search, the John Theophilus Daubuz baptised on 22 September 1757 was the son of Theophilus and Magdalen Judith. A Lewis Charles Daubuz, son of the same parents, was christened in 1755.

Mother Unknown. Possibly Magdalen Judith, maiden surname unknown (see 'Father' above).

Education Unknown.

Marriage Unknown. William Daubuz (see 1854/7) was a wealthy tin-smelter in Cornwall. A Captain John Theophilus Daubuz died in 1887.

Religion Originally Huguenots, who came to England around 1685.

Public None known.

Miscellaneous Presumably a London merchant who became a landowner in Essex.

References Above sources only. There is a privately printed history of the Daubuz family by M. L. Savell, but no copy could be located by me.

1831/26 **Name** **Dawson, William**

Dates Unknown – probated October 1831.

Probate £100,000 (PCC).

Occupation 'Grocer and tea dealer' (probate calendar) of 65 and 96 Piccadilly (1825 directory). (Occupational category IV.20; venue 2.)

Address 'Formerly of Piccadilly, and then of Turnham Green, Middlesex' (probate calendar).

Father Unknown.
Mother Unknown.
Education Unknown.
Marriage Unknown. She was presumably the 'Mrs. Dawson, of Albemarle Street, relict of William Dawson, of Turnham-green, esq.' who died 7 March 1839, aged fifty-six; that man's 'youngest surviving son', William Dawson of Albemarle Street, died 19 December 1840 (*GM*, 1839, vol. I, p. 552, and *GM*, 1841, vol. I, p. 215).
Religion Unknown.
Public None known.
Miscellaneous Presumably a leading tea and grocery retailer catering for the affluent.
References Above sources only.

Name **Williams, Richard** 1831/27
Dates Unknown–1831. (He was presumably the Richard Williams of Albemarle Street, Middlesex, whose estate was probated in October 1831.)
Probate £120,000 (PCC).
Occupation Unknown. He inherited land near Shrewsbury, but the origin of the fortune is unclear.
Address In 1827–30, he is listed in the Court directory as of 29 Albemarle Street, Middlesex and Eaton Hall, Shrewsbury. His addresses are given in the probate calendar as 'Pall Mall East and Eaton Mascot, Shropshire', five miles from Shrewsbury. A Richard Williams, solicitor to the Westminster Life Office, of 9 Lincoln's Inn New Square, is listed in the 1812 Law List, but of course this name is very common. No one named Williams and owning land in Shropshire is listed in Bateman.
Father Edward Williams (d. 1824), who bought Eaton Mascot in 1771. According to the *ODNB* entry for Richard's brother (Revd) Edward (1762–1833), 'antiquary', the father 'was said to have been a coachman by trade', but this is surely inaccurate.
Mother Barbara, daughter of John Mytton (d. 1796) of Halston and widow of John Corbet.
Education Unknown. His brother was educated at Repton and Oxford, but Richard Williams was not educated at Repton or at either university.
Marriage Name unknown. He was known to have had two sons, Edward Hosier Williams (d. 1844) and Richard Williams.
Religion Anglican.
Public None known.
Miscellaneous His name makes identification difficult.
References Above sources only.

Name **FitzGerald, Keane** 1831/28
Dates c. 1749–14 October 1831, Barnet, Hertfordshire.
Probate £140,000 (PCC).

Occupation Barrister – Bencher of the Inner Temple, 1808. (Occupational category VI.29; venue 1.)
Address 'Formerly of Charles Street, St James's Square, Middlesex, and then Dover Street, Middlesex and Barnet, Hertfordshire' (probate calendar).
Father Keane FitzGerald of St Anne's, Westminster.
Mother Unknown.
Education Secondary schooling unknown; Queen's College, Oxford (matriculated 1765; MA); barrister, Inner Temple (called 1773).
Marriage Unknown.
Religion Presumably Anglican, despite his Irish surname.
Public None known.
Miscellaneous He was an FRS; he wrote on thermometers (sic) and corresponded with Sir Joseph Banks (online sources). He retired as a barrister in 1817.
References *GM,* 1831, vol. II, p. 380.

1831/29 **Name** **Halford, James**
Dates Unknown–18 October 1831, Piccadilly.
Probate £140,000 (PCC).
Occupation Probably a stockbroker ('James and Thomas Halford, stockbrokers, of 12 Finch Lane, Cornhill', 1817 directory). (Occupational category IV.23? Venue 1?)
Address 'Norfolk Street, Strand; Piccadilly; and Laleham, Norfolk' (probate calendar). The 1819 Court directory lists him as of 20 Piccadilly and Laleham, Norfolk.
Father Unknown. The 1793 directory lists a John Halford, stockbroker, of 19 Cornhill.
Mother Unknown.
Education Unknown.
Marriage Name unknown. His son (Revd) Thomas (see 1857/28), educated Cambridge, left £140,000. His daughter Eleanor (d. 1841) married Sir Thomas Fuller Elliott-Drake, Baronet. He also had a son named Charles.
Religion Anglican.
Public None known.
Miscellaneous Nothing further could be traced about him.
References *GM,* 1831, vol. II, p. 379.

1831/30 **Name** **Migoni, Francis De Borja**
(given in *GM* as 'Don Francisco De Borja Migoni')
Dates Unknown–7 December 1831.
Probate £120,000 (PCC).
Occupation 'Merchant' in the City of London (probate calendar). 'The first Mexican Agent in England, appointed in 1823 by the Government of Mexico' (*GM*). He had previously been Consul-General for Mexico. The 1825 directory lists him as a 'merchant' of 5 Old Broad Street, City of London. (Occupational category IV.19; venue 1 and 29.)
Address 'Tokenhouse Yard in the City of London and Craven Street, Middlesex' (probate calendar).

Father Unknown.
Mother Unknown.
Education Unknown.
Marriage Unknown.
Religion Presumably Roman Catholic.
Public See above.
Miscellaneous He was apparently an important figure in the Mexican independence movement, and Mexican sources might well give more information about him.
References *GM*, 1831, vol. II, p. 570.

Name **Neill, John** 1831/31
Dates Unknown – probated December 1831.
Probate £120,000 (PCC).
Occupation 'Cornfactor' (probate calendar). He is listed in the 1794 directory as a 'factor and warehouseman' at 20 Surry (sic) Street, Strand, and in the 1825 directory as a 'Scotch factor' at 20 Surry Street, Strand. He appears to have been a wholesale merchant of some kind. Surrey (sic) Street runs between the Strand and the Embankment. (Occupational category IV.21? Venue 2.)
Address 'St Clement Danes, Middlesex' (probate calendar).
Father Unknown.
Mother Unknown.
Education Unknown.
Marriage Unknown. Possibly Isabella Kane, who in 1786 married a John Neill at St Clement Danes, Westminster (Family Search).
Religion Unknown. The name and occupation suggest a Scottish background.
Public None known.
Miscellaneous Nothing more could be traced about him.
References Above sources only.

Name **Shaw, John** 1831/32
Dates Unknown – probated January 1831.
Probate £100,000 (PCC).
Occupation 'Warehouseman' of 4 King Street, Cheapside (1815 directory); 'Manchester warehouseman' of the same address (1825 directory). (Occupational category IV.21 or 20; venue 1.) He may have been a retailer or wholesaler, or both. The Cheapside address suggests that he was probably mainly a retailer.
Address '[4] King Street, Cheapside, City of London' (probate calendar).
Father Unknown.
Mother Unknown.
Education Unknown.
Marriage Unknown.
Religion Unknown.
Public None known.
Miscellaneous Nothing more could be traced about him.

References Above sources only.

1831/33 **Name** **Smith, William**

Dates Unknown – probated 1831. (Owing to his common name the date of his probate could not be identified in PROB 11.)

Probate £300,000 (PCC).

Occupation Apparently the owner of a plant nursery and land at Brompton Park, now the area of the Victoria & Albert Museum. The Brompton Park Nursery, as it was known, had been in the Smith family since 1714 (*Survey of London*, vol. 38, 1975, pp. 3–8). His fortune thus presumably came from agricultural and urban land, although there might have been other sources. The Brompton Park Nursery was described as the 'noblest nursery of the world' (*Survey of London*, vol. 38, 1975, pp. 3–8). (Occupational category I.)

Address 'Curzon Street, Middlesex and Brompton Park House, Kensington Gore, Middlesex' (probate calendar).

Father Unknown. As noted, the family had owned the Nursery and surrounding lands since 1714.

Mother Unknown.

Education Unknown.

Marriage Name unknown. He had at least three sons, named Bright (sic), Jason [James?] and John.

Religion Unknown.

Public None known.

Miscellaneous Nothing more could be found, in part because of the difficulty in tracing so common a name. Two William Smiths are listed in *GM* as having died in 1830: one at Fairy Hall near Mottingham, Kent, on 13 October, and one, aged fifty-eight, in Great Russell Street, on 4 March. None is listed as having died in 1831.

References Above sources only.

1831/34 **Name** **Robins, John**

Dates Unknown – probated June 1831.

Probate £120,000 (PCC).

Occupation 'Auctioneer' (probate calendar). The 1815 directory lists him as an 'upholsterer and auctioneer' of Warwick Street, Golden Square, Middlesex; the 1825 directory lists him at 170 Regent Street, Middlesex. Henry and John Robins are given in the 1815 directory as having an office in the Great Piazza, Covent Garden. (Occupational category IV.21; venue 2.)

Address 'Regent Street, Middlesex' (probate calendar).

Father Possibly John Robins (1766–1821), who began as an auctioneer in Covent Garden in 1790, although his birth date might be too late for him to have been this man's father. It is possible that the source (*ODNB*) has confused 1821 and 1831, in which case this John Robins was identical with the man here. He is noted in the entry for his nephew, George Henry Robins (1777–1847), a flamboyant auctioneer who became legendary. He owned the Montpelier estate at St Mary's,

Westminster, which he bought in 1824 for £6,000. (*Survey of London* [45], 2000). George Henry Robins (1766–1821) was the son of Henry Robins (1753–1821), who established the auctioneer business with John.

Mother The mother of John Robins (1766–1821; see 'Father' above) was Ann Marless (1746–1820): *ODNB* entry on George Henry Robins.

Education Unknown.

Marriage Unknown.

Religion Unknown, probably Anglican – George Henry Robins was buried in Kensal Cemetery.

Public None known.

Miscellaneous A 'J. Robins' of Charmouth, Dorset died on 7 September 1831, aged eighty-five (*GM,* 1831, vol. II, p. 379). He is the only plausible man of this name listed in *GM* for 1830–1. John Robins (possibly not this man) was a business associate of Sir John Soane, who built Norwood Hall, Southall for him in 1801–3.

References *ODNB* for George Henry Robins, which notes a privately printed work by M. Robins, *Gleanings of the Robins Family* (1908).

Name **Strahan, Andrew** 1831/35

Dates 15 January 1750 at 10 Little New Street, Gough Square, City of London–25 August 1831, at the same address.

Probate £800,000 (PCC).

Occupation 'King's Printer' (probate calendar) at Little New Street, City of London. (Occupational category V.27; venue 1.)

Address 'Little New Street[, Gough Square], City of London' (probate calendar).

Father William Strahan (1715–9 July 1785), the 'King's Printer', and MP, 1774–84. He was said to have left £95,000 (*ODNB*). He was praised by Dr Johnson, a close neighbour. (Third son.)

Mother Margaret (d. 1785), daughter of (Revd) William Elphinston of Edinburgh.

Education Unknown.

Marriage Unmarried.

Religion Presumably originally Church of Scotland, then Anglican.

Public MP (pro-Government) Newport, Hampshire, 1797–1802; Wareham, 1802–7; Carlow, 1807–12; Aldeburgh, 1812–18; New Romney, 1818–20.

Miscellaneous Amassed a vast fortune as the official printer to the Government. His printing rights passed to his nephews the Spottiswodes, and the firm eventually became Eyre & Spottiswode.

References *ODNB* with his father; *GM,* 1831, vol. II, p. 274; C. H. Timperley, *A Dictionary of Printers and Printing* (1839), p. 918.

Name **Beaumont, Diana** (née Blackett) 1831/36

Dates Unknown–10 August 1831.

Probate £180,000 (York PC).

Occupation Land and minerals. In 1883, Sir Edward Blackett, 6th Baronet, owned 17,476 acres worth £16,183 p.a. in Northumberland; West Riding, etc., and Wentworth Blackett Beaumont (created Baron Allendale in 1906) of Bretton Hall owned 24,098 acres worth £34,670 p.a. in the same counties. (Occupational category I.)
Address Bretton Hall, near Wakefield, West Riding.
Father The illegitimate daughter of Sir Thomas Wentworth Blackett, 5th Baronet (né Wentworth; 1726–10 July 1792) of Bretton Hall. With her two sisters she was his heiress.
Mother Unknown. The father was unmarried.
Education Unknown.
Marriage In c. 1786 to (Lieutenant Colonel) Thomas Richard Beaumont (1758–31 July 1829), MP, 1795–1818 (see 1833/25, left £120,000). Lord Allendale was their grandson.
Religion Anglican.
Public None known.
Miscellaneous Inherited very lucrative lands and coalfields in the north of England as her father's illegitimate daughter.
References *BP; GM,* 1831, vol. II, p. 189; *HP* for father and husband.

WEALTH-HOLDERS, 1832

Name **Clegg, Arthur** 1832/1
Dates Unknown: 'lately' in October 1831; probated February 1832 (*GM*).
Probate £180,000 (PCC) + £200,000 (York PC): £380,000.
Occupation Cotton merchant in Manchester ('cotton merchant' of 1 Crow Alley, 1804 directory; of 8 Bank Street, Manchester, 1815 directory). Presumably he was a 'merchant' rather than a manufacturer. (If so, occupational category IV.21; venue 4.)
Address 'Formerly of Manchester and then of Irwell Bank near Manchester' (probate calendar). The 1804 directory states that he had a house at 8 Charlotte Street, Manchester.
Father Unknown. The 1797 directory lists him as 'Arthur Clegg, Junior'. He might have been related to the Clegg family of timber merchants who owned land at Caley Bangs, Manchester.
Mother Unknown.
Education Unknown.
Marriage Name unknown. His son was Joseph Clegg, of Peplow Hall, Shropshire. Joseph's daughter Anne (d. 1891), who inherited his property, married in 1831 Rowland, 2nd Viscount Hill.
Religion Presumably Anglican.
Public None known.
Miscellaneous *GM* states that he left 'property to the value of nearly half a million' to his eighteen-year-old granddaughter. He was apparently a very successful early cotton merchant in Manchester.
References *GM,* 1831, vol. II, p. 380.

Name **Upton, John** 1832/2
Dates Unknown–6 January 1832, Ingmire Hall, West Riding.
Probate £100,000 (PCC).
Occupation Apparently a landowner. In 1883, his great-grandson Charles Walter Cottrell-Dormer, who had apparently inherited his land, owned 7,853 acres worth £8,322 p.a., of which about 5,500 acres worth £5,800 p.a. were in Westmorland and Yorkshire. (Occupational category I.)
Address Ingmire Hall, Sedbergh, West Riding.
Father John Upton (1718–22 October 1767), barrister, landowner and MP, of Middleston Hall, Westmorland and Ingmire Hall, West Riding.
Mother Mary, daughter of George Noble of Weston, County Durham.
Education Unknown.
Marriage First (marriage date unknown) to Dorothy, daughter of Christopher Wilson, DD, Bishop of Bristol. (One son.) Second, in 1799, to Florence, daughter of Thomas Smyth and sister of Sir John Smyth, 4th Baronet, of Ashton Court, Somerset. (One son.)
Religion Anglican.

Public None known.

Miscellaneous The sources of his wealth are not entirely clear, but he was a landowner in the north of England. He might have inherited from the families of his wives.

References *GM*, 1832, vol. I, p. 94; *BLG*, 1846, 1937.

1832/3 **Name** **Walker, James**

Dates Unknown – probated November 1832.

Probate £100,000 (PCC).

Occupation 'Merchant' (probate calendar) in the City of London (James Walker & Co., 'merchants', of 1 Artillery Place, Finsbury Square, City of London – 1811 and 1817 directories). (Occupational category IV.21? Venue 1.)

Address 'Formerly of Artillery Place, Finsbury Square, City of London, and then of Woodland near Dumfries, Scotland' (probate calendar).

Father Unknown.

Mother Unknown.

Education Unknown.

Marriage Unknown.

Religion Probably originally Church of Scotland, from his address.

Public None known.

Miscellaneous The nature of his mercantile activities is unclear.

References Probate calendar and above sources only.

1832/4 **Name** **Brecknell, Benjamin**

Dates c. 1752–19 November 1831, Brighton.

Probate £160,000 (PCC).

Occupation Tallow chandler and soap manufacturer on the Haymarket, Middlesex (Brecknell & Turner, 'wax, spermaceti, and tallow chandlers to His Majesty, Their Royal Highnesses and the Prince and Princess of Saxe-Coburg and the Duke of Sussex', of 31 Haymarket, 1817 directory; Brecknell & Turner, 'wax chandlers' of 31 Haymarket, 1825 directory.) He 'made candles, soap, and saddle soap' (*ODNB* for Benjamin Brecknell Turner [1815–94], photographer, the son of his partner). (Occupational categories II.11 and IV.20; venue 2.)

Address 'Formerly of the Haymarket and then of Tavistock Square, Middlesex and Brighton' (probate calendar).

Father Unknown.

Mother Unknown.

Education Unknown.

Marriage Unknown.

Religion Unknown.

Public None known.

Miscellaneous His business apparently dealt with an upper-class clientele.

References *GM*, 1831, vol. II, p. 573.

Name **Borrer, William** 1832/5
Dates 7 March 1753–18 January 1832, Brighton.
Probate £250,000 (PCC).
Occupation Apparently a landowner in Sussex. (Occupational category I.) No one of his name is listed in Bateman. Described in his son's entry in the *ODNB* as a 'landowner and sometime High Sheriff of Sussex'.
Address 'Hurstpierpiont and Kenton, Kenton parish, Sussex, and then Brighton' (probate calendar).
Father William Borrer (1724–21 January 1797), a landowner who bought Parkyns, Sussex in 1797 (*VCH Sussex*, vol. 7).
Mother Barbara (d. 1795), daughter of Edward Hardres of Albourne House.
Education Unknown.
Marriage In 1780, to Mary (d. 1807), daughter of Nathaniel Lindfield of Dean House. (Three sons, two daughters.) Their son, William Borrer (1781–1862), is in the *ODNB* as a 'botanist'.
Religion Anglican.
Public High Sheriff of Sussex 1801–2; JP, DL, Sussex.
Miscellaneous He may have owned properties in Brighton, since Hurstpierpoint is nearby.
References *GM*, 1832, vol. I, p. 94; *BLG*, 1855.

Name **Surtees, William** 1832/6
Dates 6 September 1750–1 January 1832.
Probate £120,000 (PCC).
Occupation Banking and mercantile fortune in Newcastle upon Tyne, and also a landowner. (Occupational categories IV.16 and 21 and I; venue 9.) In 1883, Henry Edward Surtees owned 9,456 acres worth £7,102 p.a. in Durham, Hertfordshire, etc.
Address 'Formerly of Montagu Square, Middlesex, and then of Weymouth and then of Hastings' (probate calendar). He also built Benwell Hall, Newcastle upon Tyne, and had a house at Seatonburn near Newcastle.
Father Aubone (sic) Surtees (1711–30 September 1800), 'a leading merchant and banker at Newcastle-upon-Tyne' and Receiver-General for Durham and Northumberland, known as 'the Father of the Corporation of Newcastle' (*BLG*). (First son.)
Mother Elizabeth, daughter of John Stephenson of Knaresdale Hall.
Education Unknown.
Marriage In 1775, to Elizabeth (d. 1833), daughter of (Very Revd) John Lewis, MA, Dean of Ossory. (Five sons, seven daughters.)
Religion Anglican.
Public Sheriff of Newcastle upon Tyne, 1781–2.
Miscellaneous He does not appear to have been directly related to the writer Robert Smith Surtees. His family is best known for the fact that his sister Elizabeth (Bessie) eloped with John Scott, the future Earl of Eldon, the famous Lord Chancellor. This caused a great scandal, as Scott was young and impecunious. William

Surtees appears to have lived without working, although he may have had banking or mercantile interests in Newcastle as a young man.

References *BLG*, 1846.

1832/7 **Name** **Rogers, John**

Dates 15 August 1750–22 February 1832.

Probate £120,000 (PCC).

Occupation Landowner in Cornwall. (Occupational category I.) In 1883, John Peverell Rogers of Penrose owned 6,214 acres worth £5,812 p.a. According to the *ODNB* entry for his son, John Rogers 'succeeded to the Penrose and Helston estates', of 10,000 acres, all in Cornwall, and to tin mines. John Rogers was also a barrister and Recorder of Helston.

Address 'Penrose [near Helston] Cornwall' (probate calendar).

Father Hugh Rogers (1729–17 June 1773), of Treassowe, Cornwall, High Sheriff of Cornwall, 1770. He bought the Penrose estate in 1770. (Only son.)

Mother Anne, daughter of James Bishop of Lower Trekyninge.

Education Secondary schooling unknown; Trinity College, Oxford. Barrister, Inner Temple (called 1771).

Marriage In 1776, to Margaret (d. 1842), daughter of Francis Basset of Tehidy, Cornwall, and sister of Francis, Baron de Dunsterville. (Six sons, twelve [sic] daughters.) Their son (Revd) John Rogers (1776–1856) is in the *ODNB* as a 'Church of England clergyman and Biblical scholar'.

Religion Anglican; owned an advowson.

Public MP (pro-Godolphin) West Looe, 1775–80; Penrhyn, 1780–2; Helston, 1784–6. JP, DL, Cornwall.

Miscellaneous It is likely that he owned property in Helston. He also owned tinmines.

References *BLG*, 1846, 1914.

1832/8 **Name** **Elliott, Charles**

Dates 1751–probated November 1832.

Probate £120,000 (PCC).

Occupation 'A rich and successful Cabinet maker with a Royal warrant' (*ODNB* for son); 'a Bond Street silk merchant'. (*ODNB* for daughter.) 'C. Elliott & Co., upholsterers of 97 New Bond Street', 1808 directory. (Occupational categories IV.20 and II.11; venue 2.)

Address '[Grove House] Clapham, then Brighton' (probate calendar). At one time he rented out his house to Lord Nelson.

Father Unknown. He appears to have been of Scottish background, a relative of the Elliots (sic), Earls of Minto.

Mother Unknown.

Education Unknown.

Marriage First wife's name and marriage date unknown; second, in 1785 to Eling (sic) (1758–1843), daughter of (Revd) Henry Venn, the Evangelical author of *The Complete Duty of Man*, and sister of (Revd) John Venn. (Six children.) Their daughter Charlotte Elliott (1789–1871), 'the third daughter of six children' (Duffield), is in the *ODNB* as a 'poet and hymn writer'; their sons (Revd) Edward Bishop Elliott (1793–1875) and (Revd) Henry Venn Elliott (1792–1865), are also in the *ODNB*. Charles Elliott was the great-uncle of Sir Leslie Stephen, founder of the *ODNB* and great-great-uncle of Virginia Woolf.

Religion Anglican – a member of the Clapham Sect and a strong Evangelical, apparently owing to the influence of his second wife.

Public None known.

Miscellaneous He clearly saw no inconsistency between his upper-class Bond Street business and his religious beliefs. It is not clear whether he was primarily a 'cabinet maker' or a 'silk merchant'. According to Samuel Willoughby Duffield, *English Hymns: Their Authors and History* (London, 1886), p. 368, his daughter Charlotte was born at Westfield Lodge, Brighton (cf. *ODNB*).

References Above sources only.

Name **Galton, Samuel** (given in *BLG*, 1855, as Samuel John Galton) 1832/9

Dates 18 June 1753–19 June 1832

Probate £140,000 (PCC).

Occupation Banker in Birmingham. (Occupational category IV.16; venue 8.)

Address Lived at Duddeston House, Aston, near Birmingham.

Father Samuel Galton (1720–99) of Duddeston House, Aston. His occupation could not be traced, but, given his address, he must have been successful. (Only son.)

Mother Mary, daughter of Joseph Farmer.

Education Unknown.

Marriage In 1777, to Lucy (d. 1817), daughter of Robert Barclay, MP of Kincardine. (Six sons, four daughters.) (Their daughter Mary Anne Schimmelpennick, 1778–1856, is in the *ODNB* as an 'author'.)

Religion A Quaker, who brought up his children 'strictly' (*ODNB* for daughter).

Public None known.

Miscellaneous FRS. He was related to the Darwins and to Sir Francis Galton (1822–1911).

References *GM*, 1832, vol. I, p. 647; *BLG*, 1855, 1914.

Name **Holmes, (Revd) Thomas** 1832/10

Dates c. 1758, Brooke Hall, Norfolk–22 February 1832.

Probate £100,000 (PCC).

Occupation Apparently a landowner. (Occupational category I?) In 1883, G. J. Holmes of Brooke Hall owned 2,932 acres worthy £4,121 p.a. in Norfolk.

Address Brooke Hall (near Loddon), Norfolk.

Father Thomas Holmes (d. 1761) of Brooke Hall.

Mother Sarah (d. 1760), daughter of Thomas Seaman of Brooke Hall.

Education Wyverstone School; St John's College, Cambridge (BA, MA).

Marriage First, in 1787, to Charlotte (d. 1810), daughter of Edmund Lyon of Liverpool. (Three sons; one daughter.) Second, in 1812, to Margaret (d. 1876), daughter of John Tuthill of Halesworth, Suffolk. (One son, one daughter.) His daughter Margaret (d. 1880) married (Revd) Joseph Williams Blakesley, Dean of Lincoln, in the *ODNB*. Another daughter, Martha (1801–77), married (Revd) Sir Thomas Combe Miller, Baronet.

Religion Anglican clergyman.

Public None known.

Miscellaneous He was apparently a well-off landowner who became a clergyman, but little more could be traced about his fortune. He was Rector of Woolton, Norfolk and of Holbrook, Suffolk.

References *BLG*, 1914.

1832/11 **Name** **Bishop, Marianne** (née Fremantle)

Dates Unknown – probated May 1832.

Probate £100,000 (PCC).

Occupation Her husband, Charles Bishop (1750–13 October 1815), educated at Trinity Hall, Cambridge, was HM Procurator-General, a legal position in the Court of Arches. She presumably inherited from him. (If so, occupational category VI.29 and 31; venues 1 and 2.)

Address 'Of 1 Devonshire Place, Portland Square, Middlesex and Sunbury, Middlesex' (probate calendar).

Father John Fremantle (d. c. 1784) of Aston Abbots, Buckinghamshire. (Sixth daughter.) He was the son of John Fremantle, a merchant of Lisbon.

Mother Frances, daughter of John Edwards of Bristol.

Education Unknown.

Marriage In 1790, to Charles Bishop (see 'Occupation' above). Their daughter Marianne (d. 1876) married, in 1815, Sir East George Clayton East, Baronet (1794–1851).

Religion Anglican. Married at Old Church, St Pancras, London (Family Search).

Public None known.

Miscellaneous Her husband was King William IV's Proctor. It is unclear whether she inherited money chiefly from her ancestors or her husband.

References GM, 1815, vol. II, p. 382 and *Alum. Cantab.* for her husband; Debrett's *Baronetage* (1839), p. 406.

1832/12 **Name** **Robinson, (Revd) Sir John, 1st Baronet** (né Freind [sic])

Dates 15 February 1754, Witney, Oxfordshire–16 April 1832, Hall Barn, Buckinghamshire.

Probate £120,000 (PCC).

Occupation Landowner and clerical money, and also inherited clerical and medical money. He was Prebendary of Armagh in 1778 and Archdeacon of Armagh in 1787. (Occupational categories I and VI.30). In 1883, Sir J. Robinson, Baronet of Rokeby, Louth, owned 2,941 acres worth £2,733 p.a.

Address 'Of Rokeby Hall, Louth, Lincolnshire' (*GM*); 'Albemarle Street, Middlesex and Hall Barn, Buckinghamshire' (probate calendar).

Father (Very Revd) William Freind, DD, Dean of Canterbury (1715–26 November 1766). He was 'extremely well off' from 'inheriting the greater part of the estate of his uncle, John Freind, M.D. (1675–1728), MP' (*ODNB*).

Mother Grace (d. 28 December 1776), daughter of Sir William Robinson, 1st Baronet, of Rokeby, Yorkshire and sister of (Revd) Richard Robinson, Archbishop of Armagh, created 1st Baron Rokeby. Sir John Robinson 'succeeded to his estates', and apparently changed his surname as a result, in 1793 (*ODNB*).

Education Westminster School (Scholar); Christ Church, Oxford (BA, MA).

Marriage In 1786, to Mary Anne (d. 1834), daughter of James Spencer of Rathangan. (Six sons, twelve daughters.)

Religion Anglican clergyman.

Public Created baronet 1819.

Miscellaneous He had multiple sources of wealth. It is difficult to say which was the most important.

References *GM*, 1832, vol. I, p. 462; *BP*; *ODNB* for father.

Name **Williams, Owen** 1832/13

Dates 19 July 1764–23 February 1832.

Probate £120,000 (PCC).

Occupation Inherited a copper and banking fortune made chiefly in Anglesey, North Wales. His copper firm had its offices at Upper Thames Street, City of London. (Occupational category II.2 and IV.16; venues 19 and 1.)

Address 'Temple House, Bisham, Berkshire and Berkeley Square' (probate calendar).

Father Thomas Williams (1737–29 November 1802), the 'copper king' of Llanidanin, Anglesey and Temple House, Berkshire, later a banker and shipowner in North Wales and London and MP. He is said to have left £500,000 (*ODNB*).

Mother Catherine, daughter of John Lloyd of Anglesey.

Education Westminster School.

Marriage In 1792, to Margaret (d. 1821), daughter of (Revd) Edward Hughes (q.v.) of Kenmel Park, Denbighshire. She was the sister of 1st Baron Dinorben (q.v.).

Religion Anglican.

Public None known.

Miscellaneous He appears to have had little or no active involvement in business, although he seems to have had banking interests in London.

References *GM*, 1832, vol. I, p. 366; *ODNB* for father; *BP*.

Name **Bevan, Charles** 1832/14

Dates 5 March 1782 (1781?)–13 May 1832, Devonshire Place, Middlesex.

Probate £120,000 (PCC).

Occupation His father was a wealthy banker and brewer in London. (Occupational categories IV.16 and II.12; venues 1 and 2.)

Address Lived at Devonshire Place, Middlesex.

Father Silvanus Bevan (1743–25 January 1830), banker and brewer of Gloucester Place, Middlesex and Forsbury House, Wiltshire (see 1830/24, left £350,000). (Fourth son.)

Mother Louisa Kendall (d. 1838).
Education Unknown.
Marriage In 1808, to Mary (d. 1854), daughter of James Johnstone. (Five sons, two daughters.)
Religion The father had been a Quaker but was disowned when he married an Anglican. Charles Bevan was apparently an Anglican.
Public None known.
Miscellaneous He was presumably active in the family banking business in the City of London, but there is no direct evidence.
References *GM,* 1832, vol. I, p. 475; *BLG,* 1914.

1832/15 **Name** **Dimsdale, Anne**
Dates 14 February 1755–June 1832.
Probate £250,000 (PCC).
Occupation Inherited part of a medical fortune earned in Russia and London. (Occupational category VI.30; venues 2 and 29.)
Address Lived in Hertford.
Father Thomas Dimsdale, 1st Baron Dimsdale of the Russian nobility (1712–December 1800), physician to the Russian Empress Catherine and then a fashionable physician in London and MP, in the *ODNB.* (Second daughter.)
Mother Anne (d. 1779), daughter of John Iles.
Education Unknown.
Marriage Unmarried.
Religion Quaker – the family were Quakers (despite the father accepting a foreign title and serving in Parliament), and she was buried as a Quaker.
Public None known.
Miscellaneous She apparently lived quietly with her family.
References *ODNB* for father; *BP* for foreign titles.

1832/16 **Name** **Hornby, John**
Dates 5 July 1764–7 May 1832, Portland Place, Middlesex.
Probate £160,000, 'within province' (PCC).
Occupation East India fortune and landowner. (Occupational categories VI.31 and I; venue 29.) In 1883, Edward Owen Hornby of Hook, Hampshire, owned 3,109 acres worth £3,217 p.a. in Hampshire.
Address 'Of Hook [near Fareham], Hampshire and Portland Place, Middlesex' (probate calendar).
Father William Hornby (1723–18 November 1803), who 'entered the East India Company in 1740 and became Governor of Bombay, 1771–84', later of Hook, Hampshire.
Mother Anne Atkin (c. 1740–23 December 1803).
Education Harrow; St John's College, Cambridge.
Marriage In 1794 to Jane (1773–2 November 1832), daughter of William Wynne of Wern and granddaughter of the Dowager Viscountess Bulkeley. (Five sons, one daughter.) (Their daughter married the 6th Earl of Egmont.)

Religion Anglican.
Public None known.
Miscellaneous He apparently inherited an East India and landed fortune and lived quietly as a landowner in Hampshire.
References *GM*, 1832, vol. I, p. 475; *BLG*, 1855, 1937; 'This Is Hampshire', online.

Name **Darby, Zachariah Foxall** 1832/17
Dates 1751–11 August 1832.
Probate £100,000 (PCC).
Occupation 'He acquired a considerable fortune in the firm of Walkden & Darby, writing-ink makers and pen-makers, of Shoe Lane' (*GM*). 'Walkden, Darby & Terry, stationers, of 5 Shoe Lane, Fleet Street, City of London' (1825 directory). (Occupational categories II.11 and IV.20; venue 1.)
Address 'Formerly of Shoe Lane and Bridge Street, Blackfriars, in the City of London, and then Woburn Place and Hampstead, Middlesex' (probate calendar).
Father Unknown.
Mother Unknown.
Education Unknown.
Marriage Unknown.
Religion Unknown.
Public None known.
Miscellaneous Presumably he supplied printer's ink to Fleet Street newspapers, among other activities.
References *GM*, 1832, vol. II, p. 186.

Name **Hobson, George** 1832/18
Dates 1768–21 July 1832, at Portland Place, Middlesex.
Probate £120,000 (PCC).
Occupation 'Merchant' (probate calendar) in the City of London. ('George Hobson, merchants, of 4 Artillery Place, Finsbury Square, City of London', 1803 directory; 'Hobson, Alfrey & Co., merchants, of 34 Great St Helen's, City of London', 1825 directory.) (Occupational category IV.21 or 19? Venue 1.)
Address 'Formerly of Artillery Place, Great St Helen's, City of London, and then of Buckingham Street, Adelphi, Middlesex, and then of Harley Street, Middlesex, and then of Portland Place, Middlesex' (probate calendar).
Father Unknown.
Mother Unknown.
Education Unknown.
Marriage Unknown.
Religion Unknown.
Public None known.
Miscellaneous A merchant in the City but, as with so many other City merchants, exactly what he did is unclear.
References *GM*, 1832, vol. II, p. 92.

1832/19 **Name** **Clarke, Sir Alured**

Dates 24 November 1744–16 September 1832 at Llangollen.

Probate £250,000 (PCC). He 'left £258,229' (*ODNB*, from the Executors' Accounts of his estate).

Occupation Field-Marshal in the Army; also Lieutenant Governor of Jamaica, 1783–90, and Commander-in-Chief, India, 1797–1801. (Occupational category VI.31.)

Address Lived at Mansfield Street, Marylebone, Middlesex, in retirement. He also owned an estate at Rhual in North Wales.

Father Charles Clarke (c. 1702–17 May 1750), Baron of the Exchequer, barrister, and MP. (Sixth child.)

Mother Jane (d. 1751), daughter of (Major) Mullins of Winchester.

Education Eton, 1758–9, then entered the Army as an ensign.

Marriage In 1770, to Elizabeth (d.s.p., 1795), daughter of Thomas Orby Hunter.

Religion Anglican.

Public Created GCB, 1797.

Miscellaneous Ensign, 1759; Lieutenant, 1760; Lieutenant Colonel, 1781; Colonel, 1790; Major-General, 1796; Lieutenant General, 1801; General, 1802; Field-Marshal, 1830. Served in the American Revolutionary Wars, in Canada, 1790–5, where he opened Lower Canada's first legislature, and in India. He captured the Cape of Good Hope for the British, 1797.

References *ODNB*; *GM*, 1832, vol. II, p. 474.

1832/20 **Name** **Higgins, Tully (sic)**

Dates Unknown–11 September 1832 at Bryanston Square, Marylebone.

Probate £140,000 (PCC).

Occupation Unknown. Nothing could be traced about his fortune in any source.

Address 8 Bryanston Square, Marylebone, Middlesex. In 1817 and 1819 he had lived at 23 Manchester Square, Marylebone.

Father Unknown.

Mother Unknown.

Education Unknown.

Marriage Charlotte, surname unknown. His daughter Louisa (c. 1825–84) married, in 1845, Percy, 8th Viscount Barrington.

Religion Unknown; presumably Anglican.

Public None known.

Miscellaneous As noted, he is not listed in any biographical or genealogical source. His surname would suggest an Irish background, but he is not listed in *Burke's Irish Landed Gentry*, etc. Males of this name were christened in London in 1795 and 1800, as well a boy born on 31 August 1762 in Barnstaple, Massachusetts, the son of Zacheus and Mercy Higgins (Family Search).

References *GM*, 1832, vol. II, p. 284.

Name **Ryder, (Hon.) Richard** 1832/21
Dates 5 July 1766–18 September 1832.
Probate £140,000 (PCC).
Occupation 'Registrar of the Consistory Court' (probate calendar); held that post for 'many years' (*ODNB*); barrister and was Home Secretary, 1809–12. (Occupational category VI.29; venues 1 and 2.)
Address 'Westbrook near St Albans, Hertfordshire' (probate calendar).
Father Nathaniel Ryder, 1st Baron Harrowby, MP (1735–20 June 1803). (Second son.) Richard Ryder was the brother of the 1st Earl of Harrowby. In 1883, the Earl of Harrowby owned 12,625 acres worth £20,291 p.a. in Staffordshire, Lincoln, Gloucestershire, etc.
Mother Elizabeth (d. 1804), daughter of (Rt. Revd) Richard Terrick, Bishop of London.
Education Harrow; St John's College, Cambridge (MA). Barrister, Lincoln's Inn. (Bencher, 1811; Treasurer, 1819).
Marriage In 1799, to Frederica (d. 1821), daughter of Sir John Skynner, Chief Baron of the Exchequer. (One daughter.)
Religion Anglican – 'Evangelical' (*ODNB*).
Public MP (Tory) Tiverton, 1795–1831. Served as Lord of the Treasury in 1807 and Home Secretary, 1809–12. PC, 1809.
Miscellaneous A well-connected legal figure. He served as Justice for the counties of Cardigan, Carmarthen and Pembroke, from 1804. He also 'received £2000 p.a. as estate auditor for his brother's father-in-law, Lord Stafford' (*ODNB*).
References *ODNB*; *GM*, 1832, vol. II, p. 572.

Name **Collins, James** 1832/22
Dates 1760–22 November 1832, Stamford Hill, Middlesex.
Probate £120,000 (PCC).
Occupation Solicitor, at 33 Spital Square, Spitalfields, adjacent to the City of London. In 1812, he was a partner there of George Waller. The 1797 directory lists him there as a solicitor and also Secretary to the London Dispensary. (Occupational category VI.29; venue 2.)
Address 'Spital Square and Stamford Hill, Middlesex' (probate calendar).
Father Unknown.
Mother Unknown.
Education Unknown.
Marriage Unknown.
Religion Unknown.
Public None known.
Miscellaneous Nothing further could be traced about him.
References *GM*, 1832, vol. II, p. 483.

Name **Franks, Priscilla** 1832/23
Dates Unknown – probated December 1832.
Probate £400,000 (PCC).

Occupation Described in PROB 11 as a 'widow'. She was presumably the widow of Jacob Franks (d. 10 May 1814; see 1814/22, left £250,000) of Isleworth, whose wife was named Priscilla and who had American and West Indies connections. *The History of Isleworth* (1795, online) notes that a John Franks had a 'seat' there. However, the identity of her husband isn't certain. In her will, she states that her 'late husband's sister' was married to General Sir Henry Johnson, Baronet. According to Johnson's entry in the *ODNB,* he was married to Rebecca (d. 1823), daughter of David Franks of Philadelphia, while she also stated that her husband's brother was named Moses Franks. It appears that these were cousins of Jacob Franks of Isleworth. Priscilla Franks's background thus remains unclear, and her father's name remains unknown. (Nevertheless, occupational category IV.19; venue 29 is very likely.)

Address Isleworth, Middlesex.

Father Unknown.

Mother Unknown.

Education Unknown.

Marriage See above.

Religion She was probably originally Jewish – although this isn't entirely clear – and left a legacy to the Jews' Charity School, Mile End in her will. But she requested that she be buried in the Anglican Church in Isleworth or with her husband in St Michael's Church, Bath.

Public None known.

Miscellaneous The origins and connections of this family are very confused. They appear to have been American loyalists and merchants of Jewish descent who settled in England after the American Revolution. Jacob Franks's uncle Aaron was a wealthy Jewish merchant in London. Nothing could be traced about the background of Priscilla Franks. Confusingly, Family Search notes that a Priscilla Franks was born at Isleworth in 1747, the daughter of Aaron and Bilah Franks.

References Will (PROB 11 online); other sources as above.

1832/24 **Name** **Rickards, George**

Dates 1771–19 November 1831.

Probate £120,000 (PCC).

Occupation His father was a merchant in Leicester. He appears to have lived in London most of his life, but his occupation, if any, is unclear. He is not listed in any trade directory. (Occupational category IV.21? Venue 18.) A firm called Rickards & Hill, distillers, existed at 210 Piccadilly in the Regency period, but it appears to have been founded during the eighteenth century by a Samuel Rickards. It is possible that George Rickards had some connection with this firm, although its association with Leicester, if any, is unclear.

Address He lived in Piccadilly in later life.

Father Thomas Pares Rickards (d. 23 October 1821). 'Merchant' of St Mary's parish, Leicester. (Second son.) The nature of his mercantile activities is unclear.

Mother Hannah (d. 1794), daughter of Thomas Ascough of Leicester.

Education Unknown.

Marriage To Eleanor (d. 1839; marriage date unknown), daughter of Henry Dismorr of Erith, Kent. (One son.)
Religion Anglican – his brother Thomas was an Anglican clergyman. (Revd) Samuel Rickards (1796–1865), apparently his nephew, is listed in the *ODNB* as a 'clergyman'.
Public None known.
Miscellaneous He had lived in Leicester, where he may have been engaged in his father's business, but afterwards lived in the West End of London most of his life.
References *BLG*, 1937.

Name **Tenterden, 1st Baron, Sir Charles Abbott** 1832/25
Dates 7 October 1762, Canterbury–4 November 1832.
Probate £120,000 (PCC).
Occupation Chief Justice of the King's Bench, 1818–death; previously barrister and judge. (Occupational category VI.29; venue 1 and 2, etc.)
Address Lived at 28 Russell Square, Middlesex at death.
Father John Abbot (d. 14 February 1795; *ODNB* states 1785), given in different sources as a hairdresser, 'barber' and 'wigmaker', with a shop adjacent to Canterbury Cathedral. (Second son.)
Mother Alice (d. 1793), daughter of Daniel Bunce of Canterbury.
Education King's School, Canterbury (Scholar); Corpus Christie College, Oxford (BA, 1784; Chancellor's Medal). Barrister, Inner Temple (called 1796).
Marriage In 1795, to Mary (d. December 1832), daughter of John Lagier Lamotte of Basildon Grotto House, Berkshire. (Two sons, two daughters.)
Religion Anglican.
Public Knighted, 1816; created baron, 1827. He was a resolute high Tory, who opposed Catholic emancipation and parliamentary reform but supported some law reforms.
Miscellaneous Practised on the Oxford Circuit and served as Junior Counsel to the Treasury; Serjeant at Law, 1816, although never a KC. He was appointed Puisne Judge of Common Pleas, 1815, and a Judge of the Court of the King's Bench, 1816–18, before becoming Chief Justice. In 1807, his income as a barrister was £8,026. As the son of a hairdresser or wigmaker in Canterbury, he was often highlighted in Samuel Smiles-type accounts as an extraordinary example of upward social mobility.
References *ODNB; GM*, 1832, vol. II, p. 568; *CP; BP.*

Name **Garle, John** 1832/26
Dates Unknown – probated December 1832.
Probate £160,000 (PCC).
Occupation Possibly a sugar refiner in the City of London, although this is not really clear. The 1793 directory lists a Thomas Garle & Sons, sugar refiners, of 17 Bennet's Hill in the City. Despite John Garle's City of London address, Friday Street, no business occupation is listed for him in any directory, and this appears to

have been his private residence. The 1803 directory notes him as of 44 Friday Street in the City but does not give an occupation. (If he was a sugar refiner, then III.12 and 15? Venue 1.) He does not appear in any directory after 1803. In his will, he states that his brother was named Thomas Garle, presumably the sugar refiner noted here. He also left a considerable legacy to John Marshall, a tea dealer of Southampton Street, Strand. He also states that he owned a copyhold in East Barnet.

Address '[44] Friday Street, City of London' (probate calendar). 'Of St Margaret Moses, City of London' (PROB 11).

Father Unknown, but see above.

Mother Unknown.

Education Unknown.

Marriage Unknown. He does not mention a wife or children in his will.

Religion Unknown.

Public None known.

Miscellaneous The *ODNB* states that a John Garle was a 'patron' in Kent of the artist Robert Hills (1769–1844), and that this Garle was FSA. It is unclear whether this was the same man.

References Above sources only, and his will (PROB 11, online).

1832/27 **Name** **Smyth, Alexander**

Dates c. 1754–27 November 1832, in Mark Lane, City of London.

Probate £140,000 (PCC).

Occupation Wine merchant in the City of London (Allan & Smyth, wine merchants, of 12 Mark Lane, City of London – 1803, 1815 directories). (Occupational category IV.20; venue 1.)

Address '[12] Mark Lane, City of London' (probate calendar).

Father Unknown.

Mother Unknown.

Education Unknown.

Marriage Unknown.

Religion Unknown.

Public None known.

Miscellaneous Nothing more could be traced about him. His name possibly suggests a Scottish background.

References *GM*, 1832, vol. II, p. 580.

1832/28 **Name** **Innes, Gilbert**

Dates 7 February 1751–26 February 1832.

Probate £143,486 (Scottish probates).

Occupation 'A banker in Edinburgh' (*BLG*, 1952), and 'Depute-Governor of the Bank of Scotland'. He was also a landowner. In 1883, Alexander Mitchell-Innes, his successor, owned 6,307 acres worth £13,364 p.a. in Berwick and Haddington. (Occupational category IV.16; venue 23.)

Address Lived at Stow, Edinburgh.

Father George Innes (1703–7 February 1780), Director of the Royal Bank of

Scotland and Deputy Receiver-General of HM Land Rents in Scotland, of Stow, Edinburgh. (First son.)

Mother Marian (d. 1780), daughter of David Lauder of Huntley Wood.

Education Unknown.

Marriage Unmarried. His property went to a relative, Alexander Mitchell (later Mitchell-Innes) of Stow, and also to his sister Jane Innes (1748–2 December 1839; see 1839/2), who left £1,043,000.

Religion Church of Scotland.

Public DL, Edinburgh. Freeman of Edinburgh, 1814.

Miscellaneous He was said to be 'the richest commoner in Scotland' and a 'millionaire' (*Burlington Magazine*, 1987), but there is no evidence that he was so wealthy, although his sister left over £1 million. He was also an amateur performer at the Old Edinburgh Club (*Book of the Old Edinburgh Club*, vol. 20, 1933).

References *BLG*, 1952, 'Mitchell-Innes'; Helen Smailes, 'Thomas Campbell and the Camera Lucinda: The Buccleuch Statue of the First Duke of Wellington', *Burlington Magazine*, November 1987.

Name **Cookson, Isaac** 1832/29

Dates 2 August 1745–13 December 1831.

Probate £140,000 (York PC).

Occupation According to the collective entry in the *ODNB* on the Cookson family, he inherited his father's banking interests in Newcastle upon Tyne and retired from the Old Bank in 1796. However, the 1791 Newcastle directory lists him as heading a 'crown glass and bottle warehouse' and the 1827 directory lists 'Isaac Cookson & Sons, glass bottle manufacturers and plate glass manufacturers and iron and steel manufacturers' of Newcastle. (His father was also a mine-owner and glass manufacturer.) (Occupational categories II.3 and 11 and IV.16; venue 9.)

Address 'Whitehill [near Chester-le-Street], County Durham and Newcastle-upon-Tyne' (probate calendar).

Father John Cookson (c. 1712–17 December 1783), merchant, banker, glass manufacturer and mine owner, in Newcastle upon Tyne and Whitehill. (Sixth son.)

Mother Elizabeth, daughter of Walter Lutwidge of Whitehaven, Cumberland.

Education Unknown.

Marriage In 1772, to Margaret, daughter of James Wilkson of Newcastle upon Tyne. (Six sons, two daughters.) Several descendants left large estates, e.g., his son Isaac Cookson, (d. 1851), q.v.

Religion Presumably Anglican.

Public None known.

Miscellaneous The family had multiple interests and was among the industrial and commercial leaders of Tyneside for several generations.

References *ODNB;* Benwell Community Project, *The Making of a Ruling Class: Two Centuries of Capital Development on Tyneside* (1978); *BLG*, 1937.

Name **Clayton, Nathaniel** 1832/30

Dates 1754–20 March 1832.

Probate £160,000 (York PC).

Occupation Solicitor in Newcastle upon Tyne and Town Clerk, 1789–1822. (Occupational category VI.29; venue 9.) The family were also involved as coal merchants, etc., and became landowners. In 1883, John Clayton of The Chesters owned 11,004 acres worth £13,213 p.a., chiefly in Northumberland.

Address 'Newcastle-upon-Tyne and The Chesters, Northumberland' (probate calendar).

Father (Revd) Nathaniel Clayton, BD (c. 1711–10 August 1786), Rector of Ingram, Northumberland. (Second son.)

Mother Grace (d. 1786), daughter of Nicholas Fenwick, a 'merchant' of London.

Education Unknown.

Marriage In 1786, to Dorothy (d. 1827), daughter of George Atkinson of Temple Sowerby. (Six sons, five daughters.) Their son, John Clayton (d. 1890, aged ninety-eight), also a solicitor in Newcastle, left over £500,000.

Religion Anglican.

Public None known.

Miscellaneous Like the Cooksons, they were at the heart of the Newcastle business elite and were among the town's leading solicitors serving its industrial and commercial leaders. Nathaniel Clayton purchased the Chesters estate in 1796.

References *BLG*, 1937; Benwell Community Project, *The Making of a Ruling Class* (1978).

1832/31 **Name** **Hildyard, (Revd) Henry**

Dates 6 August 1752–16 September 1832, at Stokesley, Yorkshire.

Probate £140,000 (York PC).

Occupation He did not practise as a clergyman and was apparently a landowner in the East Riding. In 1883, Thomas Thoroton-Hildyard of Newark owned 2,128 acres worth £2,929 p.a. in East Riding, as well as lands in Nottinghamshire. (Revd) Henry Hildyard's father was a publisher and bookseller, and our man may have inherited clerical money. (Occupational category I?)

Address The Manor House, Stokesley, East Riding.

Father John Hildyard (1710–57), a 'publisher and bookseller' of York. (Only son.)

Mother Honor (d. 1756), daughter of (Revd) Henry Thorpe, Prebendary of Salisbury.

Education Secondary schooling unknown; Queen's College, Oxford (BA, 1773); St John's College, Cambridge (LL.B, 1778).

Marriage In 1780, to Phyllis, daughter of John Westgarth of Unthanks House near Stanhope, Durham. (Three sons, six daughters.)

Religion Anglican clergyman.

Public None known.

Miscellaneous The sources of his wealth are rather unclear. He plainly inherited a good deal, but it is not clear from whom.

References *GM*, 1832, vol. II, p. 579; *Alum. Cantab.*

Name **Goff, Joseph** 1833/1
(*BLG*, 1952 says Joseph Fade Goff; PROB 11 says Joseph Goff)
Dates c. 1756–early 1833 at Newtown Park near Dublin ('died lately', aged seventy-six: *GM*, February 1833); probated February 1833.
Probate £100,000 'within province' (PCC).
Occupation A mercantile family in Dublin. His uncle or great-uncle, Joseph Fade, was a merchant in Dublin and left money to him or his father (Quaker sources, online). A William Goff (d. 1848) was Governor of the Bank of Ireland (*ODNB* for his daughter, Sarah Heckford, 1839–1903). (Occupational category IV.21? Venue 26.)
Address 'Of Mountjoy Square, Dublin and Newtown Park, near Dublin' (*GM*).
Father Joseph Goff (d. 1764) of Dublin.
Mother Elizabeth, daughter of Robert Unthank.
Education Unknown.
Marriage Sarah, daughter of George Clibborn of Moate Castle, Westmeath. (Six sons.)
Religion The family were Quakers.
Public None known.
Miscellaneous He was apparently a Quaker merchant or banker in Dublin, but little could be traced about his career.
References *GM*, 1833, vol. I, p. 382; *BLG*, 1952.

Name **Palmer, Elizabeth** 1833/2
Dates Unknown–31 May 1832, Ham Common. She died in a fire caused by an overturned candle.
Probate £250,000 'within province' (PCC).
Occupation Landowner in Ireland. She was 'the sister and heiress of Roger Palmer of Rush and Palmerstown, Co. Mayo' and had 'a valuable estate in Co.Mayo, worth £30,000 p.a., and large estates in Co. Dublin' (*GM*). In 1883, Sir Roger Palmer Baronet owned 98,954 acres worth £26,661 p.a. in County Mayo and other Irish counties and in Denbighshire, etc. She succeeded in 1811. (Occupational category I.)
Address 'Formerly of Oxford Street, Middlesex, then of West Moulsey, Richmond and Ormley Lodge, Ham Common, Surrey, and Rush House, Dublin and Palmerstown, Co. Mayo' (probate calendar).
Father Roger Palmer (d. 1770) of Palmerstown, County Mayo.
Mother Frances Ellis.
Education Unknown.
Marriage In c. 1786, to (Captain) Joseph Budworth (1756–4 September 1815) FSA, who changed his surname to Palmer. (Their daughter married W. A. Mackinnon, MP, who is in the *ODNB*.)
Religion Anglican.

Public None known.
Miscellaneous Her landed property apparently came to Sir Roger Palmer, Baronet.
References *GM,* 1832, vol. I, p. 574; vol. II, p. 388.

1833/3 **Name** **Elmslie, James**
Dates c. 1762–29 January 1833, Southampton Row, Middlesex.
Probate £180,000 (PCC).
Occupation 'Formerly of Gibraltar and London, merchant' (probate calendar). 'Merchant' of 6 Hunter Street North, Brunswick Square', 1817 directory; 'Elmslie & Stooks, merchant of Old Broad Street, City of London', 1830 directory. In 1825, he was listed as of 'John Elmslie and Thomas Stooks, East India merchant, Winchester House, Old Broad Street'. (Occupational category IV.19; venue 1.)
Address 'Formerly of Hunter Street, Middlesex and Old Jewry, City of London, and then of Woodcote Place, Epsom, Surrey' (probate calendar).
Father Unknown.
Mother Unknown.
Education Unknown.
Marriage Unknown.
Religion Unknown.
Public None known.
Miscellaneous Apparently a merchant connected with the Mediterranean and East India trade, chiefly in London.
References *GM,* 1833, vol. I, p. 187.

1833/4 **Name** **Browne, Francis John**
Dates 4 October 1754–29 March 1833, Weymouth.
Probate £100,000 (PCC).
Occupation A landowner in Dorset. The family was 'seated for many generations at Frampton', Dorset (*HP*). On his death, his lands passed to his brother-in-law, Sir John Colquhoun-Grant, but no one named either Browne or Colquhoun-Grant is listed in Bateman as owning lands in Dorset. (Occupational category I.)
Address Frampton, near Dorchester, Dorset.
Father George Browne (d. 1777) of Frampton.
Mother Mary Kingsbury.
Education Unknown.
Marriage In 1796, to Frances (d.s.p.), daughter of (Revd) John Richards of Long Bridy, Dorset.
Religion Anglican; he left money for the Society for the Relief of Clergymen's Widows and Orphans.
Public MP (pro-Whig) Dorsetshire, 1784–1806. JP, Dorsetshire and High Sheriff, 1783.
Miscellaneous Was a captain in the Dorset Yeomanry.
References *GM,* 1833, vol. I, p. 463; *HP.*

Name **Brune, (Revd) Charles Prideaux** (né Prideaux) 1833/5
Dates 14 June 1760, Bath–28 April 1833.
Probate £180,000 (PCC).
Occupation Landowner. In 1883, Charles Glynn Prideaux-Brune of Prideaux Place owned 8,629 acres worth £10,654 p.a. in Cornwall, Hants, and Dorset. (Occupational category I.)
Address Prideaux Place near Padstow, Cornwall.
Father Humphrey Prideaux (1719–May 1793) of Prideaux Place, High Sheriff of Cornwall, 1750. (First son.)
Mother Jenny, daughter of Neville Morton Pleydell of Beer, Dorset. Her mother was the daughter of Charles Brune of Plumber, Dorset. The son evidently changed his surname to Brune on inheriting this property.
Education Blundell's School, Tiverton; Clare College, Cambridge (BA).
Marriage In 1788 to Frances (d. 1831), daughter of Thomas Patten of Bank Hall, Lancashire. (One son, five daughters.)
Religion Anglican.
Public DL, Cornwall.
Miscellaneous A landowner in Cornwall. He does not appear to have made much from his clerical income.
References *BLG*, 1952; *Alum. Cantab.*

Name **Rawe, Richard** 1833/6
Dates 1743–7 August 1833, Wincanton, Somerset.
Probate £250,000 (PCC).
Occupation Unknown. It has not been possible to trace him in any source. He might well have been a bona-fide landowner or a merchant or East India Company official, or similar, who settled in the West Country. He is not listed in any genealogical guide, and there is no one of his surname in Bateman.
Address 'Of Trevithick, Cornwall and Purse Caundle, Somerset, and then Winchester and Wincanton, Somerset' (probate calendar)
Father Unknown.
Mother Unknown.
Education Unknown.
Marriage Unknown.
Religion Unknown; presumably Anglican.
Public None known.
Miscellaneous Nothing more could be traced about him.
References *GM*, 1832, vol. II, p. 189.

Name **Gray, John** 1833/7
Dates Unknown – probated October 1833.
Probate £180,000 (PCC).
Occupation 'Of the Stock Exchange' (probate calendar). (Occupational category IV.23; venue 1.) He is not listed in any London directory from 1811.
Address 'Formerly of the Stock Exchange and then of Clapham Common, Surrey' (probate calendar).

Father Unknown.
Mother Unknown.
Education Unknown.
Marriage Unknown.
Religion Unknown.
Public None known.
Miscellaneous Nothing more could be traced about him.
References Probate calendar only.

1833/8 **Name** **Rooke, William**
Dates c. 1750–22 February 1833, at the house of (Revd) R. W. Ford, of Little Rissington, Gloucestershire.
Probate £180,000 (PCC).
Occupation Unknown. A William Rooke was admitted to Trinity College, Cambridge in 1772, the son of Henry Rooke of Edmonton. He was educated at Tonbridge School, but was eighteen when admitted (i.e. born about 1754). A William Rookes (sic) was admitted to Gray's Inn in April 1779, the son of William Rookes, a Bencher of Gray's Inn. No other possible candidates have been traced in plausible sources.
Address 'Formerly of Nacton, Suffolk and then of Bulstrode Street, Cavendish Square, Middlesex, and then of Edmonton and then of Little Rissington, Gloucestershire' (probate calendar).
Father Unknown.
Mother Unknown.
Education Unknown, but see above.
Marriage Unknown.
Religion Unknown, probably Anglican.
Public None known.
Miscellaneous He does not appear to have been engaged in any trade in London.
References *GM*, 1833, vol. I, p. 285.

1833/9 **Name** **Watkins, (Revd) John**
Dates Baptised 11 April 1750, Clifton Campville, Staffordshire (Family Search)–19 May 1833, The Rectory, Clifton Campville, Staffordshire.
Probate £100,000 (PCC).
Occupation He was Lord of the Manor of Clifton Campville (near Tamworth), Staffordshire, and presumably a landowner, but no one of his name is listed in Bateman (Occupational category I?) He was Rector of Clifton Campville.
Address Clifton Campville, near Tamworth, Staffordshire.
Father (Revd) Richard Watkins (1702–18 November 1776), Rector of Clifton Campville. He was educated at Wadham College, Oxford and had been Dean of Wadham College. His mother was the daughter of Sir John Pye, 1st Baronet, of Hone, Derbyshire (John Burke, *History of the Extinct and Dormant Baronetcies of England, Ireland, and Scotland,* 2nd edn [1844], p. 433).
Mother Anne, surname unknown (Family Search).

Education Secondary schooling unknown; Wadham College, Oxford (matriculated 1769; BCL).
Marriage Name unknown. His daughter Anne (d. 1781) married (Revd) Robert Taylor, also of Clifton Campville. Their daughter Margaret married, in 1839, Sir John Gaspard LeMarchant (1803–71), in *ODNB* as an 'army officer and colonial administrator'.
Religion Anglican clergyman.
Public None known.
Miscellaneous He might have profited from a clerical or university income but was, it seems, chiefly a landowner. He apparently inherited lands from his Pye ancestors (John Burke, *Extinct and Dormant Baronetcies,* 1844, p. 433).
References *Alum. Oxon.*; above sources.

Name **Cocksedge, Thomas** 1833/10
Dates 15 January 1747, Bardwell, Suffolk–2 February 1833, Bury St Edmunds, Suffolk.
Probate £120,000 (PCC).
Occupation Unknown. He appears to have been a local landowner, but a Sarah Cocksedge (1752–1821), possibly a relative, married, in 1785, Thomas Bignold (1761–1835), founder of the Norwich Union Insurance Company, who has an entry in the *ODNB.* She was the daughter of Samuel Cocksedge of Hopton, Suffolk, and had previously been married to a Mr Long. Their son was Sir Samuel Bignold (1791–1875), in the *ODNB* as a 'businessman and politician'.
Address 'Bury St Edmunds, Suffolk' (probate calendar).
Father Abraham Cocksedge (1713–11 April 1766).
Mother Bridget, née Cocksedge.
Education Unknown.
Marriage Unknown.
Religion Anglican.
Public High Sheriff of Suffolk 1802.
Miscellaneous The fact that he was High Sheriff of Suffolk suggests that he had been accepted by Society as a landowner, but the source of his wealth is unclear. He does not appear to have had a country seat. His address in Bury St Edmunds suggests that he had business interests.
References *GM,* 1833, vol. I, p. 189; online genealogy of the Cocksedge family; *ODNB.*

Name **Tritton, John Henton** 1833/11
Dates 29 April 1755–20 May 1833, Gloucester Place, Middlesex.
Probate £250,000 (PCC).
Occupation Banker of Lombard Street, City of London (Barclay, Bevan & Tritton) – joined in 1782. (Occupational category IV.16; venue 1.)
Address 'Beddington, Surrey; Lombard Street, City of London; and Gloucester Place, Middlesex' (probate calendar). He also had a country house at Lyons Hall, Great Leighs, Essex.

Father Thomas Tritton (1717–13 November 1786). (First son.)
Mother Anna Maria (d. 26 July 1793), daughter of Henton Brown (c. 1697–1775), Quaker minister and banker, in the *ODNB*.
Education Unknown.
Marriage In 1783, to Mary, daughter of John Barclay, banker of Lombard Street. (Three sons.)
Religion Originally a Quaker and appears to have been a Quaker at his death, although his son, (Revd) Robert Tritton (1782–1877), was an Anglican vicar. The Trittons were part of the 'Quaker Cousinhood' of successful banking and mercantile families.
Public None known.
Miscellaneous He was originally given a partnership in the banking firm Henton, Brown & Sons, later Henton & Collinson, of London, founded by his maternal grandfather.
References *GM,* 1833, vol. I, p. 571; BP, Tritton, baronet; *ODNB* for relatives.

1833/12 **Name** **Cadogan, 2nd Earl, Charles Henry Sloane Cadogan**
Dates 18 June 1749–23 December 1832.
Probate £100,000 (PCC).
Occupation Urban property: he owned the Cadogan estate in Chelsea, which was estimated by Lindert to generate an income of £180,122 p.a. in the 1890s. It would have been worth much less in Cadogan's lifetime, but was still lucrative. In 1883, Earl Cadogan owned less than 500 acres of land outside London. (Occupational category I.)
Address It is unclear where he lived, and he was declared legally insane in 1807. A successor lived at 110 Piccadilly in the mid-nineteenth century.
Father Charles Sloane Cadogan, 1st Earl and 3rd Baron Cadogan (1728–3 April 1807), MP, Master of the Mint. (First son.)
Mother (Hon.) Frances (d. 1768), daughter of Henry, 1st Baron Montford.
Education Unknown.
Marriage Unmarried. His property passed to his half-brother, the 3rd Earl.
Religion Anglican.
Public None known.
Miscellaneous He was an army officer and was declared insane in 1807.
References *CP; GM,* 1833, vol. I, p. 80; Peter Lindert, 'Who Owned Victorian England?', *Agricultural History* 61 (1987); online sources.

1833/13 **Name** **Douglas, George**
Dates Unknown – probated July 1833.
Probate £160,000 (PCC).
Occupation 'Merchant' of 45 Chiswell Street, near the City of London (1817 directory); of 3 Finsbury Square, City of London (1803 directory). (Occupational category IV.21? Venue 1.)
Address 'Formerly of Tunbridge Wells, Kent and Finsbury Square, City of London; and then of Chiswell Street, Middlesex and Chilston Park, Maidstone,

Kent' (probate calendar). He was a relative by marriage, although not by blood, of Aretas Akers-Douglas, 1st Viscount Chilston (1851–1926), the Tory politician. In 1883, he owned 15,678 acres worth £13,090 p.a., of which 3,753 acres worth £4,937 p.a. were in Kent. Presumably some of this, including Chilston Park, had been owned by George Douglas.

Father Unknown. An Alexander Douglas, 'merchant' of 3 Finsbury Square, is listed in the 1794 directory. He was presumably George's father or brother.

Mother Unknown.

Education Unknown.

Marriage Name unknown. His daughter Margaret Braziere Douglas (d. 1858) married, in 1830, George Alexander Stodart, who changed his surname to Douglas. Their son, James Douglas (d. c. 1875) of Baads, Midlothian and Chilston Park, left his property to Aretas Akers (later Akers-Douglas), a 'kinsman', later Viscount Chilston. The relationship between Akers-Douglas and George Douglas thus appears to have been based on marriage links.

Religion Probably originally Church of Scotland.

Public None known.

Miscellaneous As is so often the case, the exact nature of his mercantile activities is unclear.

References *ODNB* for Akers-Douglas; online sources.

Name **Heneage, George Robert** 1833/14

Dates 21 December 1768–17 June 1833, Portland Place, Middlesex.

Probate £160,000 (PCC).

Occupation Landowner in Lincolnshire. (Occupational category I.) In 1883, Edward Heneage of Hainton Hall owned 10,761 acres worth £15,527 p.a. in Lincolnshire. George Robert Heneage does not appear to have had any other obvious sources of wealth.

Address Hainton Hall, in Lindsey, Lincolnshire.

Father George Fieschi (sic) Heneage (1730–March 1782). (An ancestor was a count in Genoa.)

Mother (Hon.) Katherine (d. 1783), daughter of Robert, 8th Baron Petre.

Education Unknown.

Marriage (Hon.) Frances (d. 13 March 1807), daughter of (Lieutenant General) George Ainslie. (Two sons, two daughters.) (Their grandson, Edward Heneage, MP [1840–1922], was created 1st Baron Henage in 1896. Their daughter Catherine married in 1833 William Marcus Joseph Beresford [1797–1883], in the *ODNB* as a 'politician'. Another daughter, Frances, married Edward Gyles Howard [1805–40], a nephew of the Duke of Norfolk. Their son Edward Henry Howard [1829–92] is in the *ODNB* as a 'cardinal'.)

Religion Some members of this family appear to have been Roman Catholics, possibly including this man. The first Lord Heneage was, however, certainly an Anglican, and the patron of livings.

Public None known.

Miscellaneous His son George Fieschi Heneage (1800–68) was an MP for many years. He was certainly an Anglican, as he attended Cambridge University and served in Parliament from 1826, before 'Catholic emancipation'.

References *GM*, 1833, vol. I, p. 649; *BP*; *CP*; *ODNB* for relatives; Stenton.

1833/15 **Name** **Westcar, John**

Dates 1749, Cottisford, Oxfordshire–'lately' in June 1833 (*GM*); probated July 1833.

Probate £180,000 (PCC).

Occupation Stockfarmer at Creslow, near Winslow, Buckinghamshire, who 'supplied prize beef to London' and was a founder of the Smithfield Meat Market in 1799. ('John Westcar', Oxfordshire Family History Society, online.) 'To this gentleman is mainly to be attributed the celebrity which Herefordshire cattle have attained throughout the kingdom' (*GM*). (Occupational category I.) No one of his name is listed in Bateman.

Address Creslow, Buckinghamshire.

Father John Westcar (1721–84).

Mother Joanna (or Johanna) Watts, from 'a prominent Northamptonshire family' and a great-aunt of Lord Sidmouth (Oxfordshire Family History, online; *BLG*, 1863).

Education Unknown.

Marriage In 1780, to Mary Hedges (d. 1781). Their grandson was (Lieutenant) Henry Emerson Westcar, later Prescott-Westcar.

Religion Anglican; married and buried at the Church at Whitchurch, Buckinghamshire, with a monument.

Public None known.

Miscellaneous A fairly unusual example of someone who became very wealthy as an innovating farmer rather than as a landowner.

References *GM*, 1833, vol. I, p. 571, which spells his name as 'Westear'; *VCH Buckinghamshire*, vol. 3, pp. 341, 449; online sources.

1833/16 **Name** **Kemble, Thomas Nash**

Dates 1791–20 April 1833, at Moor Hall, Hertfordshire.

Probate £120,000 (PCC).

Occupation Sugar broker in the City of London (Thomas Kemble & Sons, 'sugar brokers' of 10 Mincing Lane, City of London – 1817 and 1825 directories.) (Occupational category IV.21; venue 1.) His father-in-law was also a wealthy City merchant.

Address 'More Hall, Gobions [Gubbins] parish, North Mimms [Mymms], Hertfordshire and [10] Mincing Lane, City of London' (probate calendar). Also 'of Runwell Hall, Essex' (*GM*).

Father Thomas Kemble (1760–23 August 1821), 'sugar broker' of Gobions Park, Hertfordshire and Mincing Lane, City of London.

Mother Arabella Mary Waugh (d. 1820).

Education Unknown.

Marriage In 1814, to Virginia (d. 1870), daughter of Horatio Clagett, merchant of America Square, City of London (see 1816/5, left £180,000).

Religion Presumably Anglican.
Public High Sheriff of Hertfordshire, 1825.
Miscellaneous He presumably was head of the firm, if at all, only after his father's death in 1821.
References *GM* 1833 vol. I, p. 380; *BLG* 1952; *VCH Hertfordshire*, vol. 2, 1908.

Name **Dudley 1st Earl of and 4th Viscount, John William Ward** 1833/17
Dates 9 August 1781–6 March 1833, Norwood, Surrey.
Probate £350,000, 'within province' (PCC).
Occupation Land and colliery owner. (Occupational categories I and II.1.) He also owned canals and was said to have had an income of £120,000 p.a. (*ODNB*). In 1883, the Earl of Dudley owned 25,554 acres worth £123,176 p.a. in Staffordshire, Worcester, and other counties, chiefly the product of his lucrative coalmines.
Address The principal seat was Witley Court, Stourport.
Father William Ward, 3rd Viscount Dudley and Ward (1750–25 April 1823). (Only child.) He was known as a 'brutal' father (*ODNB*).
Mother Julia (1754–23 June 1833), daughter of Godfrey Bosvile of Gunthwaite, Yorkshire (see 1833/27, left £160,000).
Education 'Privately at Paddington' (*ODNB*); Edinburgh University; Oriel College, Oxford (MA).
Marriage Unmarried. Lady Lyndhurst was his mistress, and he apparently had one illegitimate daughter by her. He also had many other affairs, and liaisons with prostitutes (*ODNB*). Most of his property passed to his cousin, whose son, William Ward (1817–85), was created 1st Earl of Dudley of the second creation in 1860. The latter left £1,026,000 in personalty.
Religion Anglican.
Public MP (pro-Whig then pro-Tory) Downton, 1802–3; Worcestershire, 1803–6; Petersfield, 1896–7; Wareham, 1807–12; Ilchester, 1812–18; Bosseney, 1819–23. PC, 1827. Served as Foreign Secretary, 1827–8. Succeeded to the Viscountcy, 1823 and created an earl in 1827.
Miscellaneous He was one of the richest aristocrats in England, was regarded as highly cultured and was an FRS, but had a disappointing political career. He went mad shortly before his death and was placed under restraint in an asylum in Norwood, where he died.
References *ODNB; HP; CP.*

Name **Collett, Ebenezer John** 1833/18
Dates 24 May 1755, Hemel Hempstead–31 October 1833, Lockers House, Hemel Hempstead.
Probate £300,000 (PCC).
Occupation Hop merchant in Southwark – a partner there with Samuel Thorpe. (Occupational categories IV.21 and III.12; venue 2.)
Address Lived at Lockers House, Hemel Hempstead, Hertfordshire.
Father Joseph Collett of Hemel Hempstead.

Mother Mary Smith.
Education Unknown.
Marriage In 1795, to Margaret, daughter of Thomas Alsiger, 'cloth merchant' of Newington, Surrey. (Four sons, two daughters.)
Religion Anglican.
Public MP (pro-Tory) Grampound, 1814–18; Cashel, 1819–30. He was said to have declined a baronetcy.
Miscellaneous He spent part of his early career as a Consul in Charleston, South Carolina. He was a captain in the Surrey Yeomanry and subscribed £3,000 to the Loyalty Loan in 1797.
References *HP; GM,* 1833, vol. II, p. 476; C. E. Collett and H. H. Collett, *The Family of Collett* (1935).

1833/19 **Name** **Perry, John**
Dates Unknown–15 October 1833.
Probate £140,000 (PCC).
Occupation Shipbuilding fortune in Blackwall. (Occupational category II.4; venue 2.) He also 'had been some time in the East India Company's Civil Service in Bengal' (*BLG*).
Address 'Formerly of Montagu Square and then of Bryanston Square, Middlesex, and of Moor Hall, Harlow, Essex' (probate calendar).
Father John Perry (1745–7 November 1810), of Moor Hall, Essex, of the important family of shipbuilders in Blackwall, although he was educated at Harrow and was High Sheriff of Essex in 1818.
Mother Elizabeth Browne (d. 1795).
Education Unknown.
Marriage In 1823, to Maria, daughter of George Watlington of Caldecote House, Aldenham, Prothonotary of the Court of Common Pleas and Recorder of St Albans. (One son, four daughters.) (Their son was John Watlington-Perry; see 1882/119.)
Religion Anglican.
Public None known.
Miscellaneous His brother was Philip Perry; see 1830/25, leaving £250,000.
References *ODNB; BLG,* 1846.

1833/20 **Name** **Birch, Nicholas**
Dates Unknown – probated February 1833.
Probate £180,000 (PCC).
Occupation 'Surgeon' (probate calendar) of Mansel Street, Goodman's Fields, Middlesex (adjacent to the City of London, near what is today Fenchurch Street Station). ('Complin & Birch, surgeons, of 38 Mansel Street', 1803 directory; 'Nicholas Birch, surgeon, of 38 Mansel Street', 1817 directory.) (Occupational category VI.30; venue 1.)
Address '[38] Mansel Street, Goodman's Fields, Middlesex' (probate calendar).
Father Unknown.

Mother Unknown.
Education Unknown.
Marriage Unknown. He was perhaps the Nicholas Birch who married Frances Complin in 1779 at St Mary's, Whitechapel (Family Search).
Religion Unknown.
Public None known.
Miscellaneous Nothing more about his career could be traced, including his education. It appears that he earned a fortune as a surgeon, presumably treating City men, although he might have had other sources of income.
References Probate calendar and above only.

Name **Farquhar, James** 1833/21
Dates 1 August 1764–4 September 1833.
Probate £140,000 'within province' (PCC).
Occupation 'Deputy Registrar of the Admiralty Court' in Doctor's Commons, City of London (probate calendar). 'He formerly held several other appointments connected with the civil law and had a large private practice as a proctor in Doctor's Commons' (*HP*). (Occupational category VI.29; venue 1.) He was also a director of the Crown Life Assurance Company from 1825–death.
Address Doctor's Commons, City of London; Duke Street, Middlesex; Johnston Lodge, Kincardineshire' (probate calendar).
Father John Farquhar (d. 1767), 'stocking merchant' of Aberdeen.
Mother Rachel, daughter of James Young, 'merchant' of Aberdeen.
Education Aberdeen Grammar School; Aberdeen University. Articled at Doctor's Commons after coming to London.
Marriage In 1795 to Helen (d.s.p.), daughter of Alexander Innes of Cowie, Kincardineshire.
Religion Presumably originally Church of Scotland.
Public MP (pro-Tory) Aberdeen Burghs, 1802–6, 1807–18; Portarlington 1824–30. He was also Provost of Inverbervie.
Miscellaneous He was briefly in business as a merchant in London before being articled at Doctor's Commons. He served there as a Proctor from 1788, Deputy-Registrar, 1788–1805, and Deputy-Registrar of the Admiralty Court, 1810–death. His career, moving from Scotland to London, and combining an uncommon court practice with a career in Parliament, was rather unusual.
References *HP.*

Name **Sutherland, 1st Duke of and 2nd Marquess of Stafford, George Granville Leveson-Gower** 1833/22
Dates 9 February 1758, Arlington Street, Middlesex–19 July 1833, Dunrobin Castle, Sutherlandshire.
Probate 'Upper Value' (i.e. over £1 million) (PCC) + £350,000 (York PC) + £77,499 (Scottish probate): over £1.4 million. (He was probably worth about £7 million in all, and was certainly the richest man, in current value terms, who had ever lived in Britain to that point.) In 1883, the Duke of Sutherland owned

1,385,545 acres worth £141,667 p.a. in Sutherland, Shropshire, Staffordshire, Ross-shire and Yorkshire, while the Earl of Ellesmere (see 'Miscellaneous' below) owned 13,222 acres worth £71,290 p.a. in Lancashire, Cheshire, etc.

Occupation 'The leviathan of wealth.' Land, mineral, canal and railway owner. (Occupational category I and IV.25.)

Address His chief residences were Cleveland House and Stafford House, Middlesex and Dunrobin Castle, Sutherlandshire.

Father Granville Leveson-Gower, 1st Marquess of Stafford (1744–26 October 1803), KG, MP, Lord Privy Seal, etc. (First son.)

Mother Lady Louisa (1723–61), daughter of Scroop Egerton, 1st Duke of Bridgewater, and sister of the 'Canal Duke'.

Education Westminster School; Christ Church, Oxford. He went on the 'Grand Tour' in the 1780s.

Marriage In 1785, to Elizabeth, Countess of Sutherland in her own right (1765–1839). She owned over 1 million acres in Sutherland. (Two sons, two daughters.)

Religion Anglican.

Public MP (Whig) Newcastle-under-Lyme, 1779–84; Staffordshire, 1787–99. Joint Postmaster-General, 1799–1801. PC, 1790; KG, 1806. Created 1st Baron Gower, 1799, and 1st Duke of Sutherland, 1833, just before his death. Ambassador to France, 1790–2. He was known as Viscount Trentham until 1786.

Miscellaneous He won the Lottery of Life many times over: he was already enormously wealthy as the Marquess of Stafford, with great holdings in Staffordshire and Shropshire. He then married the Countess of Sutherland in her own right, gaining her more than 1 million acres in northern Scotland. Then, in 1803, he inherited the Duke of Bridgewater's canals and land! (The Duke was his uncle.) The holdings of the famous 'Canal Duke' included the main Manchester–Liverpool canal. Sutherland was regarded as the richest man who ever lived and was said to have had an income of over £300,000 p.a. He also became one of the largest shareholders in the Manchester–Liverpool Railway. But he also became notorious for the 'Highland Clearances', carried out to promote agricultural development on his Scottish lands. Upon his death, most unusually, his holdings were split into two parts, with his elder son, the 2nd Duke, gaining the bulk, but the Bridgewater property coming to his younger son, who was created 1st Earl of Ellesmere.

References *ODNB*; *GM*, 1833, vol. II, p. 175. Eric Richards, *The Leviathan of Wealth* (1972).

1833/23 **Name** **Dundas, James**

Dates 1752–11 April 1831 (not registered until January 1833).

Probate £116,156 (Scottish probates).

Occupation 'Clark [sic] to the Signet' (probate calendar) in Edinburgh – a Writer to the Signet, i.e. a senior solicitor. (Occupational category VI.29; venue 23.)

Address Edinburgh and Dundas Castle, Midlothian, although there were several successful Scotsmen of this name at the time, and another one might have been the owner of Dundas Castle.

Father Ralph Dundas (1709–23 December 1789) of Manour and Edinburgh. (Fourth son.)
Mother Mary, daughter of William Ferguson.
Education Unknown.
Marriage In 1794, to Elizabeth, daughter of William Graham of Airth, Stirlingshire. (Five sons.) One son was Sir David Dundas, QC (1799–1877), in the *ODNB* as a 'politician'. James Dundas's niece was Maria Calcott, née Dundas (1785–1842), in the *ODNB* as 'traveller and author'.
Religion Church of Scotland.
Public None known.
Miscellaneous He was friendly with many writers and intellectuals, including Dugald Stewart and John Playfair (*ODNB* for niece).
References *BLG*, 1952; *ODNB* for relatives.

Name **Preston, Robert** 1833/24
Dates Unknown – probated 1833. He may be the Robert Preston who was born in 1761 and died on 19 November 1833. His will was registered on 27 December 1833.
Probate £250,000 (Consistory Court of Preston probates).
Occupation 'Distiller' (probate calendar) in Liverpool. (Occupational category III.13; venue 5.) 'Wine vaults and commission warehouse' at 22 Castle Ditch and 'Robert Preston, Jr., liquor merchant, of 7 Vernon Street', 1805 Liverpool directory; 'Rectifier', of 7 Vernon Street, Liverpool, 1827 directory; 'distiller', of Vernon Street, 1832 Liverpool Poll Book.
Address Liverpool. The Robert Preston who died on 19 November 1833 lived at Firgrove, West Derby, Lancashire.
Father Possibly Robert Preston (1713–18 March 1788). (First son.)
Mother Possibly Margaret, daughter of Robert Bouker of Broughton (online genealogy souce).
Education Unknown.
Marriage Possibly Jane Wilkinson (date of marriage unknown). (Three sons, three daughters.)
Religion Unknown.
Public None known.
Miscellaneous He apparently evolved from a wine merchant to a distiller. He employed John Gibson (1790–1834) to produce a bust of him (*ODNB* for Gibson, sculptor).
References Above sources only.

Name **Beaumont, Thomas Richard** 1833/25
Dates 29 April 1758–31 July 1829 (not probated until 1833).
Probate £120,000 (York PC).
Occupation Landowner and mineral owner. (Occupational category I.) Husband of Diana Beaumont (see 1831/36). In 1883, Wentworth Blackett Beaumont (later 1st Baron Allendale) of Bretton Park, Wakefield, owned 24,098 acres worth

£34,670 p.a. in Northumberland, West Riding, and Durham.
Address Bretton Hall, near Wakefield, Yorkshire and Hexham Abbey, Northumberland.
Father Thomas Beaumont (1723–6 February 1785) of The Oaks, Yorkshire. He was in 'relatively modest' circumstances (*HP*).
Mother Anne (d. 1778), daughter of Edward Ayscough of Louth, Lincolnshire.
Education Unknown.
Marriage In 1786, to Diana (1831/36), illegitimate daughter and heiress of Sir Thomas Wentworth Blackett, 5th Baronet. According to *HP*, the income from her leadmines and other holdings in Yorkshire were never less than £80,000 p.a. (Five sons, three daughters.)
Religion Anglican.
Public MP (pro-Pitt) Northumberland, 1795–1818.
Miscellaneous He was a colonel in the Dragoons and known for his 'princely' lifestyle. His grandson became 1st Baron Allendale in 1907.
References *HP; BP.*

1833/26 **Name** **FitzWilliam, 4th Earl** (in the Irish peerage and 2nd Earl in the UK peerage), **William Wentworth FitzWilliam**
Dates 30 May 1748, Milton House near Peterborough–8 February 1833, Milton House.
Probate £180,000 (York PC).
Occupation Landowner and mineral owner. (Occupational category I.) In 1883, Earl FitzWilliam owned 115,743 acres worth £138,801 p.a. in Yorkshire, County Wicklow, etc.
Address Wentworth House, Yorkshire and Milton House, Peterborough were the chief residences.
Father John FitzWilliam, 3rd and 1st Earl FitzWilliam (1720–10 August 1756). (First son.)
Mother Lady Anne (d. 1769), daughter of Thomas, 1st Marquess of Rockingham, the Prime Minister.
Education Eton; King's College, Cambridge (DCL, Oxford, 1793). Made the Grand Tour, 1769.
Marriage First, in 1770, to Lady Charlotte (1747–13 May 1822), daughter of William, 2nd Earl of Bessborough. (One son.) Second, in 1823, to Louisa (1749–1824; d.s.p.), daughter of Richard, 4th Viscount Molesworth and widow of William, 1st Baron Ponsonby.
Religion Anglican.
Public Lord Lieutenant of Ireland, 1795. A radical Whig in the House of Lords and a friend of Charles James Fox from Eton. Mistrusted by the King, who refused to grant him a marquessate.
Miscellaneous Inherited the property of the Marquess of Rockingham, his grandfather, in 1782. He had an income of £60,000 p.a. in the 1780s (*ODNB*).
References *ODNB; CP; GM,* 1833, vol. I, p. 365.

Name **Dudley and Ward, Julia Ward** (née Bosvile) 1833/27
Dates 21 July 1754–23 June 1833.
Probate £160,000 (PCC).
Occupation Landed family (see John, Earl of Dudley and Ward; see 1833/17). (Occupational category I.)
Address The principal seat was at Witley Court, Stourport.
Father Godfrey Bosvile (d. 1784) of Gunsthwaite, Yorkshire. (Second daughter.) He was related to Godfrey Bosvile (d. 1658), MP for Warwick in the Long Parliament and a Roundhead colonel.
Mother Diana Wentworth.
Education Unknown.
Marriage In 1780, to William Ward, 3rd Viscount Dudley and Ward (1750–25 April 1823). (One son, the 1st Earl of Dudley, 1833/17).
Religion Anglican.
Public None known.
Miscellaneous Little information could be found about her father. It is also unclear how she could have become so wealthy in her own right. Her portrait was painted by John Singleton Copley.
References *CP; BP;* online genealogy.

Name **Watson, (Hon.) Henry** (Some sources state George Henry.) 1833/28
Dates 18 October 1755–9 March 1830 (sic; not probated until 1833).
Probate £120,000 (PCC).
Occupation Landed, but the precise sources of his wealth are unclear. (Occupational category I.)
Address 'Formerly of Berkeley Square, Middlesex and then of Selden near Hemel Hempstead, Hertfordshire' (probate calendar).
Father Lewis Monson Watson, 1st Baron Sondes (1728–30 March 1795). (Second son.) His mother was the daughter of the 1st Marquess of Rockingham.
Mother Grace (1728–31 July 1777), daughter of (Rt. Hon.) Henry Pelham, Prime Minster.
Education Eton.
Marriage Unknown, probably unmarried.
Religion Anglican.
Public None known.
Miscellaneous Well connected, but very obscure. His executors were his nephews, Lewis, Baron Sondes and (Hon.) George John Miles.
References *GM,* 1930, vol. I, p. 282; *BP.*

WEALTH-HOLDERS, 1834

1834/1 **Name** **Steer, William**

Dates Unknown – probated January 1834.

Probate £250,000 (PCC).

Occupation Stockbroker in the City of London ('Steer & Wakefield, stockbrokers', of 70 Old Broad Street, City of London, 1814 directory; 'William Steers [sic] & Co., stockbrokers', of 70 Old Broad Street, 1803 directory). (Occupational category IV.23; venue 1.)

Address 'Formerly of [70] Old Broad Street in the City of London, and then of [78] Pall Mall, Middlesex and Paris, France' (probate calendar).

Father Unknown.

Mother Unknown.

Education Unknown. A William Steer was married in 1804 in Finsbury to a Maria Hardy (Family Search).

Marriage Unknown.

Religion Unknown.

Public None known.

Miscellaneous Nothing more could be traced about him. He apparently lived in Paris at the end of his life.

References Above sources only.

1834/2 **Name** **de Povia, Count, Henrique Teixera de Sampayo**

Dates Unknown – probated April 1834.

Probate £600,000 (PCC).

Occupation Presumably connected with J. T. Sampayo, Portuguese wine merchant and Consul for Portugal in London ('F. T. Sampayo, Agent to the Royal Wine Company of Oporto', of 15 Great St Helen's, City of London, 1825 directory. 'Sampayo, Palyart & Barrozo, Directors of the Portuguese Administration', were also at this address. 'Sampayo, Pinto & Sampayo, Agents to the Oporto Wine Company' of 20 Great St Helen's, Bishopsgate; and 'J. T. Sampayo, Consul for Portugal', of 30 Great St Helen's, 1827 directory). (Occupational categories IV.19 and VI.31; venues 1 and 29, assuming that the Count had mercantile connections with London). He is noted as an 'Honorary Counsellor of the State' in the probate calendar.

Address 'Lisbon' is the address given in the probate calendar.

Father Unknown.

Mother Unknown.

Education Unknown.

Marriage Unknown.

Religion Presumably Roman Catholic.

Public None known – Portuguese nobility.

Miscellaneous The immense size of his estate in Britain suggests that he was a major merchant in the wine trade, possibly holding a Portuguese government monopoly. Presumably Portuguese sources would contain more about his career.

References Above sources only.

Name **Preston, Sir Robert, 6th Baronet** 1834/3
Dates 4 April 1740–7 May 1834.
Probate £180,000 'within province' (PCC).
Occupation He 'made a fortune in the naval service of the East India Company' and then 'prospered still more as a London insurance broker and shipowner' (*HP*). 'In early life he was a Commander in the service of the East India Company and afterwards for many years was an eminent ships-husband [sic] in London' (*GM*). (Occupational categories IV.25, 22, and 24; venues 29 and 1.) He was a younger son and had to make his own way in the world, although he eventually inherited the family baronetcy. In 1883, a Sir Jacob Preston, Baronet owned 4,800 acres worth £7,000 p.a. in Norfolk. Sir Robert Preston was known as 'Floating Bob' (*HP*).
Address Valleyfield, near Dunfermline, Fife. He also owned the site of what was later the Colonial Office in Downing Street.
Father Sir George Preston, 4th Baronet (d. 1779). (Fifth son.) Sir Robert succeeded his elder brother as 5th Baronet in 1800.
Mother Anne, daughter of William Cochrane of Ochiltree, Ayrshire.
Education Unknown.
Marriage In 1790, to Elizabeth (d.s.p.), daughter of George Browne of Stockton.
Religion Presumably originally Church of Scotland.
Public MP (pro-Government), Dover, 1784–90; Cirencester, 1790–1806.
Miscellaneous He was an Elder Brother of Trinity House from 1781 and a director of Greenwich Hospital. He was also a friend of James Boswell and was famous for his annual whitebait dinners. According to *GM,* he was 'reportedly worth £1 million', but this is clearly an exaggeration.
References *HP; GM,* 1834, vol. II, p. 315.

Name **Breadalbane (or Bredalbane), 1st Marquess and 4th Earl of, Sir John Campbell, 8th Baronet** 1834/4
Dates 30 March 1762–29 March 1834, Taymouth Castle, Perthshire.
Probate £300,000 'within province' (PCC).
Occupation Landowner. In 1883, Lord Breadalbane owned 43,358 acres worth £58,292 p.a. in Perth and Argyllshire. (Occupational category I.) From 1814 he was also a lieutenant general in the Army.
Address Taymouth Castle, Perthshire, was the principal seat.
Father Colin Campbell (1704–30 March 1772). (First son.) Sir John succeeded a distant kinsman as Earl of Breadalbane and 8th Baronet in 1782.
Mother Elizabeth, daughter of Archibald Campbell of Stonefield.
Education Winchester College.
Marriage In 1793 to Mary (d. 1845), daughter of David Gavin of Langton, Berwickshire. (One son, two daughters.)
Religion Church of Scotland.

Public Scottish Representative Peer, 1795–1806. Created Baron Breadalbane of Taymouth (UK peerage), 1806. Created 1st Marquess of Breadalbane, 1831.
Miscellaneous Lived in Lausanne as a youth. Was an army officer – Lieutenant Colonel, 1795; Colonel, 1802; Major-General, 1809; Lieutenant-General, 1814. FRS from 1784.
References *ODNB* for son; *BP; GM,* 1834, vol. I, p. 650.

1834/5 **Name** **Crouch, Charles**
Dates Unknown – probated August 1834.
Probate £160,000 (PCC).
Occupation Presumably a planter or merchant in Antigua. (Occupational category I; venue 29.)
Address 'Formerly of Antigua, and then of Tottenham, Middlesex' (probate calendar).
Father Unknown.
Mother Unknown.
Education Unknown. A Charles Crouch married a Margaret Bynoe in 1818 in Barbados (Family Search).
Marriage Unknown.
Religion Unknown.
Public None known.
Miscellaneous Nothing further could be traced about him. His will is very brief and uninformative.
References Probate calendar only.

1834/6 **Name** **Smith, (Revd) Martin Stafford**
Dates Baptised 27 June 1746, Churchdown, near Cheltenham, Gloucestershire–6 January 1834, Bath.
Probate £200,000 (PCC).
Occupation The source of his fortune is unclear. He may have inherited it from his father, his first wife's first husband or her uncle, or his second wife's father. He was Rector of Fladbury, Worcestershire, from 1792 to 1834. He was 'at the time of his marriage with Mrs. Warburton, Vicar of Langton in Gloucestershire and Rector of Uphill in Somersetshire [sic]. In 1793 [sic] he obtained, from Bp. Hurd, the valuable Rectory of Fladbury' (*Literary Anecdotes of the Eighteenth Century,* vol. 9, 1815, p. 763).
Address Lived at Bath at his death.
Father Martin Smith of Hucclecote, Gloucestershire.
Mother Unknown.
Education Secondary schooling unknown; Corpus Christi College, Oxford (MA, BD).
Marriage First, in 1781, to Gertrude Tucker (d. 1 September 1796), widow of Bishop Warburton (1698–1779) and niece of Ralph Allen (1693–1764), in *ODNB* as 'postal entrepreneur and Bath philanthropist'; Mayor of Bath in 1742. Second, in 1797, to Mary Elizabeth (c. 1758–23 September 1839), daughter of Thomas

Plaisted of Ticehurst, Sussex, Edward Plaisted of Bolehill near Tamworth, Staffordshire, by Joyce, daughter of Stamford Wolfrestan. (She left £120,000; see 1839/9).
Religion Anglican clergyman.
Public None known.
Miscellaneous Inheritance from one or both wives seems most likely, but there is no clear evidence. The *GM* obituary of his widow states that she was 'one of the last links to the classic days at Prior Park'. This reference is unclear, but Prior Park, in Bath, was the home of Bishop William Warburton (1698–1779), who was a friend of Sterne, Richardson, and other writers.
References *GM*, 1834, vol. I, p. 338; *Alum. Oxon.*

Name **Ewart, John Manship** 1834/7
Dates 23 November 1777 (baptised 25 December 1777), Morden, Surrey (Family Search)–19 March 1834 at Brome, near Dorking.
Probate £120,000 (PCC).
Occupation East India Company money from his father and maternal grandfather; probably also a brandy merchant in the City of London ('John Ewart, brandy merchant', of 31 Lower Thames Street, City of London, 1803 directory). (Occupational categories IV.19 and 21? Venues 1 and 29?) His grandfather was described as 'an eminent distiller' (see 'Miscellaneous' below).
Address 'Formerly of Cannon Street, in the City of London, and the Broome, Beckworth, Surrey, and The Beeches, Sussex.' (Nobody of his name could be identified in Cannon Street in London.)
Father Simon Ewart, who 'served in the East India Company in Bengal' (Roots Web). He lived at Horne, Surrey, purchased from R. G. Bulkeley in 1787 (*VCH Surrey*, vol. 4, 1902).
Mother Anne, daughter of John Manship, 'a successful cloth merchant in London, who traded extensively with the East India Company and was a director of the East India Company' (*VCH Surrey*, vol. 4, 1902, and Family Search).
Education Unknown.
Marriage Probably, in 1812, Catherine Bethune (see 1835/30; left £100,000). She is described as a 'widow' of Bloomsbury Square, Middlesex. They had at least two daughters.
Religion Presumably Anglican.
Public None known.
Miscellaneous His occupation has proved difficult to trace. His grandfather, 'the eminent distiller' John Manship, purchased the mansion of Bysse Court, Surrey, to which a manor was attached, in 1788, had it demolished and erected a new mansion in its place, which passed to John Manship Ewart (Thomas Allen, *A History of the County of Surrey*, vol. II [1831], p. 86).
References *GM*, 1834, vol. I, p. 453 and above sources.

Name **Rapp, John** 1834/8
Dates c. 1760–26 April 1834 at Clapham.

Probate £250,000 (PCC).

Occupation 'Merchant' (probate calendar). ('Merchant' of 25 Budge Row, Cannon Street, City of London, 1817 directory; 'merchant' of 17 Budge Row, 1803 directory.) (Occupational category IV.21 or 19? Venue 1.)

Address '[25] Budge Row, City of London, and Battersea Rise near Clapham Common, Surrey' (probate calendar).

Father Unknown. The name suggests a German, Swiss or Swedish origin.

Mother Unknown.

Education Unknown.

Marriage Unknown.

Religion Unknown.

Public None known.

Miscellaneous As is often the case here, the nature of his mercantile activities is unclear.

References *GM*, 1834, vol. I, p. 666, and above sources.

1834/9 **Name** **Wood, Thomas**

Dates Unknown–27 March 1834, Clapham Common.

Probate £120,000 (PCC).

Occupation Unknown. There is no real clue in his will. The 1817 London directory lists a Thomas Wood, 'merchant', of 31 Stamford Street, Blackfriars Bridge, as well as a 'bedstead manufacturer and undertaker' and a 'jeweller'. The 1803 London directory lists a 'T. Wood & Sons, stockbrokers, of Castle Alley, Cornhill'.

Address Clapham Common, Surrey.

Father Unknown. His will notes that his sister was named Anne Thomas and his sister-in-law named Mary Milward.

Mother Unknown.

Education Unknown.

Marriage Unknown. There is no mention of a wife or children in his will.

Religion Probably Anglican; an Anglican clergyman was one of his executors.

Public None known.

Miscellaneous Nothing more could be traced about him.

References *GM*, 1834, vol. I, p. 666; will (PROB 11, online).

1834/10 **Name** **Stephens, Samuel**

Dates c. 1768–25 February 1834, Leamington Spa.

Probate £100,000 (PCC).

Occupation A property owner in St Ives, Cornwall, where his father owned local fisheries and mines, and then a partner in Williams Foster & Co., copper smelters of Swansea. (Occupational categories I and II.2, etc.; venue 19.)

Address 'Formerly of Devonshire Street and then Baker Street, Middlesex, and Treguna Castle, Cornwall and Leamington Spa' (probate calendar).

Father Samuel Stephens (1728–1 March 1794), MP for St Ives, 1751–4; and Mayor of St Ives in 1761, 1763 and 1765. His wealth 'derived from local fisheries and mines' (*HP*), and then he became a leading property owner in St Ives.

(No one of this name is listed in Bateman as having owned land in Cornwall.) (First son.)

Mother Anne, daughter of Richard Seaborne of Bristol.

Education Secondary schooling unknown; St John's College, Cambridge. Barrister, Lincoln's Inn (called 1795, but did not practise).

Marriage In 1796, to Betty, daughter of (Captain) Samuel Wallis, known as 'the circumnavigator', who allegedly 'had a fortune of £100,000' (*HP*). (Five sons, one daughter.)

Religion His ancestors were Presbyterians, but he was an Anglican.

Public MP (Tory) St Ives, 1806–12. JP, DL, Cornwall and High Sheriff, 1805–6.

Miscellaneous His fortune appears to have come from his copper-smelting interests and probably from his father-in-law and father.

References *HP; GM,* 1834, vol. II, p. 110.

Name **Gist, Josiah** 1834/11

Dates c. 1765–25 March 1834, Wormington Grange, Gloucestershire.

Probate £120,000 (PCC).

Occupation Apparently a landowner in Gloucestershire. In 1883, Samuel Gist of Wormington owned 4,020 acres worth £6,893 p.a. in Gloucestershire and other counties. Josiah Gist does not appear to have been related to Samuel Gist (see 1815/17), Lloyd's broker, or to the other Samuel Gist (see 1827/28), tobacco merchant, although the unusual surname suggests some connection. (Occupational category I?)

Address Wormington Grange, Winchcombe, Gloucestershire.

Father Unknown.

Mother Unknown.

Education Unknown.

Marriage To Anne Placeway (d. 1825; marriage date unknown). They had at least two sons, named Samuel and William, and at least two daughters.

Religion Presumably Anglican. He was patron of the living of Wormington.

Public High Sheriff of Gloucestershire at death.

Miscellaneous He is listed in *BLG,* 1894, but with no clue as to his ancestry. This suggests a mercantile background, possibly in Bristol or London.

References *GM,* 1834, vol. I, p. 668; *BLG,* 1894.

Name **Ovey, Richard** 1834/12

Dates 1756–probated June 1834.

Probate £250,000 (PCC).

Occupation 'Furniture printer' (probate calendar) of Tavistock Street, Covent Garden, Middlesex. (Occupational category II.9 or 11; venue 2.) The family became very wealthy as furniture printers. In the 1793 and 1817 London directories, he appears as a 'linen draper' of 22 Tavistock Street, Covent Garden, but as a 'furniture printer' thereafter.

Address 'Tavistock Street, Covent Garden, Middlesex and Northfield, Henley, Oxfordshire' (probate calendar).

Father Richard Ovey (1728–1806) of Northfield, Henley-on-Thames, Oxfordshire, a 'yeoman' (*VCH Oxfordshire,* vol. 6).
Mother Ann Skete.
Education Unknown.
Marriage In 1787 to Mary Vaughan. (At least one son.) Several of his descendants were very wealthy.
Religion Presumably Anglican.
Public None known.
Miscellaneous It is not clear how he achieved such great wealth as a 'furniture printer'. Presumably he was very popular with the upper or middle classes.
References *BLG,* 1952.

1834/13 **Name** **Simpson, Samuel**
Dates Unknown – probated July 1834.
Address £120,000 (PCC). (Fitton says £122,041, citing probate documents.)
Occupation The brother-in-law of Richard Arkwright (d. 1843), cotton-manufacturing millionaire, who, in 1780, married Simpson's sister Mary (d. 1829). Simpson was a cotton manufacturer in his own right, chiefly in Bakewell, Derbyshire, and was closely connected with the Arkwrights. (Occupational category II.7; venue 17.)
Address Lived at Matlock, Derbyshire.
Father Adam Simpson of Bonsall, Derbyshire. He owned leadmines near Matlock, Derbyshire.
Mother Elizabeth, surname unknown, but presumably the Elizabeth Oldham who married an Adam Simpson in 1754 at Shirland, near Alfreton, Derbyshire (Family Search).
Education Unknown.
Marriage Unmarried. He left most of his estate to nephews and nieces, including Francis Arkwright.
Religion Presumably Anglican, like the Arkwrights.
Public None known.
Miscellaneous He was close to his Arkwright relatives but appears to have been a cotton manufacturer on his own, chiefly in Bakewell. He was probably the Samuel Simpson who is listed among the subscribers to *New Experiments in Electricity* by Revd A. Bennet FRS, Curate of Wirksworth, printed at Derby in 1789.
References Will (PROB 11 online); *ODNB* for Richard Arkwright; R. S. Fitton, *The Arkwrights: Spinners of Fortune* (1989); information from Catherine Beale; online sources.

1834/14 **Name** **Wilmot, Sir Robert, 2nd Baronet**
Dates 1752–23 July 1834, at The Parks, Great Malvern.
Probate £100,000 (PCC).
Occupation Apparently a landowner. In 1883, his descendant (Revd) Sir George Wilmot-Horton, Baronet, owned 6,036 acres worth £12,055 in Derbyshire, Staffordshire Northamptonshire, etc. (Occupational category I?)

Address Osmaston, near Ashbourne, Derbyshire.
Father The illegitimate son of Sir Robert Wilmot, 1st Baronet (d. 14 November 1772), Secretary to the Lord Lieutenant of Ireland for thirty years. Sir Robert succeeded to the baronetcy in 1772 by a Special Remainder.
Mother Unknown.
Education Unknown.
Marriage First, in 1783, to Juliana (d. 1788), daughter of (Admiral the Hon.) John Byron and widow of (Hon.) William Byron, MP; she was a cousin of Lord Byron the poet. (One son.) Second, in 1795, to Mariana, daughter of Charles Howard of Pipe Grange, Staffordshire. His son Sir Robert Wilmot-Horton, 3rd Baronet (1784–1841) is in the *ODNB* as a 'politician and colonial governor'.
Religion Anglican.
Public None known.
Miscellaneous He served as Secretary to Earl Harcourt, Lord Lieutenant of Ireland.
References *GM*, 1834, vol. II, p. 431; *Complete Baronetage; BP; ODNB* for son.

Name **Spencer, 2nd Earl, Sir John George Spencer** 1834/15
Dates 1 September 1757, Wimbledon Park, Surrey–10 November 1834, Althorp Park.
Probate £160,000 (PCC).
Occupation Landowner. In 1883, Earl Spencer owned 27,185 acres worth £46,764 p.a. in Northamptonshire, Warwickshire, Hertfordshire, etc. (Occupational category I.)
Address Althorp Park, Northamptonshire, was the chief residence.
Father John Spencer, 1st Earl Spencer (1734–31 October 1783), created an earl in 1765. (First son.)
Mother Margaret (1737–18 March 1814), daughter of (Rt. Hon.) Stephen Poyntz of Midgham, Berkshire.
Education Harrow; Trinity College, Cambridge (MA, 1778; honorary degree, 1793). Made the Grand Tour, 1775–80.
Marriage In 1781, to Lady Lavinia (1762–1831), daughter of Charles Bingham, 1st Baron Lucan. (Four sons, two daughters.)
Religion Anglican.
Public MP (Whig) Northampton, 1780–2; Surrey, 1782–3. Served as Lord of the Treasury, 1782; Lord Privy Seal, 1794; First Lord of the Admiralty, 1794–1801, when he was important in Britain's naval successes; Home Secretary, 1806–7. PC, 1794; KG, 1799. High Steward of St Albans.
Miscellaneous His elder sister was Georgiana, Duchess of Devonshire. He was known as Viscount Althorp from 1765 until 1783. FRS, 1780; FSA. An Elder Brother of Trinity House, etc. He is probably best known for developing one of the greatest private libraries in Europe, of over 40,000 volumes, which later became the basis of the John Rylands Library in Manchester.
References *ODNB; CP; BP.*

1834/16 **Name** **Gosling, William**

Dates 1 January 1765–27 January 1834, Portland Place.

Probate £600,000 (PCC).

Occupation Banker in Fleet Street, London (Gosling & Sharpe, 19 Fleet Street, City of London). (Occupational category IV.16; venue 1.) In 1883, Robert Gosling of Hassobury, near Bishop's Stortford, Essex, owned 5,147 acres worth £6,433 p.a. in Essex and Hertfordshire

Address '[19] Fleet Street, City of London and Portland Place, Middlesex' (probate calendar). He also lived at Putney Park, Surrey (*VCH Surrey*, vol. 4, 1912) and at Roehampton Grove.

Father Robert Gosling (d. 4 January 1794), banker of Lincoln's Inn Fields, and Hassobury, Essex. (First son.) His brother Sir Francis Gosling, a banker, was Sheriff of London.

Mother Elizabeth (d. 1811), daughter of William Houghton of Clapham.

Education Unknown.

Marriage First, in 1793, to Margaret (d. 1803), daughter of Sir Ellis Cunliffe, Baronet, of Liverpool. (Three sons, two daughters.) Second, in 1806, to (Hon.) Charlotte, daughter of Thomas, 2nd Baron Walsingham. (One son, one daughter.)

Religion Anglican.

Public None known.

Miscellaneous An extremely wealthy London banker.

References *GM,* 1834, vol. I, p. 441; *BLG.*

1834/17 **Name** **Pulsford, William**

Dates 1772–17 December 1833, Wimpole Street.

Probate £250,000 (PCC).

Occupation Wine merchant in the City of London ('R. & W. Pulsford, wine merchants', of 7 Great St Helen's, City of London, 1817 directory; 'Latham & Pulsford, wine merchants', of 91 Great Tower Street, City of London, 1794 directory). (Occupational category IV.20 and 21? Venue 1.) The firm was also described in the 1820 directory as West India merchants, of 7 Great St Helen's.

Address 'Formerly of Upper Clapton, Middlesex, and then of Walthamstow, Essex, and then of Great St Helen's, City of London and of Wimpole Street, Middlesex' (probate calendar). He is described in the 1866 *Baronetage* as 'of Linslade, Berks.'

Father Unknown. Probably Robert Pulsford, husband of Mary, whose son William was baptised on 22 May 1772 according to the Protestant Dissenters Registry (Family Search).

Mother Unknown. If Robert mentioned in 'Father' above was the father, she was probably Mary Richards; however, despite the son's registration as a Dissenter, this couple were married in 1770 at St James's, Westminster (Family Search).

Education Unknown.

Marriage Unknown. His daughter Ann married, in 1832, Sir William Goodenough Hayter, 1st Baronet (1793–1878), in the *ODNB* as a 'politician and barrister'. She died in 1889 (see 1889/46), leaving £233,000.

Religion Presumably Anglican, but see 'Father' and 'Mother' above.
Public None known.
Miscellaneous Little could be traced about his career. Robert Pulsford (see 1836/33), who left £450,000, was apparently his brother.
References *GM,* 1834, vol. I, p. 228; online source as above.

Name **Goad, Benjamin** 1834/18
Dates Baptised 17 July 1784, at Walthamstow, Essex–17 February 1834, Upper Harley Street.
Probate £120,000 (PCC).
Occupation Stockbroker in the City of London ('Goad & Hanbury, stockbrokers', of 12 Throgmorton Street, City of London – 1814, 1817 and 1825 directories.) (Occupational category IV.23; venue 1.)
Address 'Formerly of Wimpole Street and then of Harley Street, Middlesex' (probate calendar).
Father William Goad (d. 14 July 1793), skin broker. (Third son.)
Mother Darling (sic) Thomas.
Education Unknown.
Marriage To Anne Eliza (b. 1804), daughter of Robert Hill (1774–1816), Commissary-General. Marriage date unknown. (Three sons, three daughters.) She married, second, in 1840, (General) Sir Thomas Bradford (d. 1853).
Religion Presumably Anglican.
Public None known.
Miscellaneous A W. T. Goad (see 1864/30) was a skin broker, presumably a relative.
References *GM,* 1834, vol. I, p. 450; online Goad family genealogy; H. E. M. and W. A. James, *Pedigrees in the Family of Culgarth* (privately printed, Society of Genealogists), Pedigree 10.

Name **Pomfret, John Butler** 1834/19
Dates 1764–12 February 1834, Tenterden, Kent.
Probate £100,000 (PCC).
Occupation Probably a banker in Ashford, Kent (Pomfret, Burra & Co., bankers, of Ashford). His daughter Mary married William Burra, an Ashford banker. It is not clear, however, whether Pomfret was connected with this bank in his lifetime, and his will gives no indication as to his source of wealth. The family is not listed in Bateman. (If a banker, then occupational category IV.16; venue 14.) He and his third son, Richard Curteis Pomfret, were partners in the firm of Curteis & Co., of Rye, Sussex. T. Twigg, *Twigg's Corrected List of the Country-Bankers of England and Wales* (1830), p. 67.
Address Of Tenterden, Kent.
Father Virgil Pomfret.
Mother Harriot (sic), née Wilson.
Education Unknown.
Marriage Mary (d. 26 December 1804, aged thirty-six), daughter of Richard

Curteis (d. 21 August 1814) and his wife Mary, daughter of Searles Giles (d. 10 April 1806) of Biddenden. (Five sons, two daughters.) The second son, Virgil Pomfret (1795–1875; see 1875/97), left £400,000. John Butler Pomfret's great-nephew, William Pomfret Burra, was a banker and MP from 1886–95.

Religion Anglican; memorial to him and his family in Tenterden Church.

Public JP, Kent; Mayor of Tenterden in 1792, 1801–3, 1815, 1819 and 1827. His son Virgil was also Mayor several times.

Miscellaneous His source of wealth has proved difficult to identify precisely, although he was probably a banker.

References *GM*, 1834, vol. I, p. 341; will (PROB 11, online); other online sources.

1834/20 **Name** **Barton, (Very Revd) Charles, DD**

Dates Baptised 15 September 1766 St Nicholas, Gloucester (Family Search)–6 March 1834.

Probate £120,000 (PCC).

Occupation Dean of Bocking, Essex, from 1816, and also Rector of Bocking and of Monks Eleigh, Essex. (Occupational category VI.30.)

Address Bocking, Essex.

Father William Barton of Gloucester.

Mother Probably Mary Chapman, who married a William Barton in 1765 at St Nicholas's Church, Gloucester (Family Search).

Education Secondary schooling unknown; Corpus Christi College, Oxford (MA, 1789; DD, 1805; Fellow).

Marriage Unknown; probably unmarried since he was a College Fellow.

Religion Anglican clergyman.

Public None known.

Miscellaneous How much of his wealth derived from his clerical income and how much from other sources is unclear.

References *Alum. Oxon.*; online source as above.

1834/21 **Name** **Bridge, John**

Dates 21 January 1755, Piddletrenthide, Dorset–9 April 1834, The Manor House Piddletrenthide.

Probate £400,000 (PCC).

Occupation Jeweller at Ludgate Hill, City of London – partner with the millionaire jeweller, Philip Rundell (see 1827/25). (Occupational category IV.20 and 25; venue 1.)

Address 'Of Wood House, [Wood Lane,] Shepherd's Bush, Middlesex and Ludgate Hill, City of London' (probate calendar).

Father Thomas Bridge (d. 1792). (First son.)

Mother Mary (d. 1779), surname unknown.

Education Unknown. Apprenticed from 1769 to William Rogers of Bath (*ODNB*).

Marriage Unmarried.

Religion Anglican.
Public None known.
Miscellaneous Arrived in London c. 1776 and was shopman at Pickett & Rundell, goldsmiths and jewellers, and partner from 1787 as Rundell & Bridge. They were known as 'Oil' Bridge and 'Vinegar' Rundell from their personalities. The firm had royal patronage as jewellers. He lived at Wood House with his two cousins, Amelia and Maria Bridge.
References *ODNB.*

Name **Dodd, George** 1834/22
Dates 1757–16 April 1834.
Probate £120,000 (PCC).
Occupation Probably a coachmaker at 43 Crawford Street, Montagu Square, Middlesex – 1817 and 1825 directories. (If so, occupational category II.11; venue 2.)
Address '[26] Montagu Square, Middlesex' (probate calendar).
Father Unknown.
Mother Unknown.
Education Unknown.
Marriage Name unknown. His son, George Dodd (d. 1854 or 1864) was a Tory MP from 1841 to 1853 and PC, JP, DL.
Religion Unknown, probably Anglican.
Public None known.
Miscellaneous Presumably catered to the upper-class 'carriage trade' in the West End.
References *GM,* 1834, vol. I, p. 666; Stenton for son.

Name **Mellish, William** 1834/23
Dates Unknown–27 January 1834.
Probate £300,000 (PCC).
Occupation Contractor and shipowner in Shadwell, London. 'He left property, it is supposed, nearly amounting to three million sterling, acquired chiefly by contracts for provisioning the navy during the war, and was also in extensive business as a shipowner' (*GM*). The figure cited appears to have been an exaggeration by 1,000 per cent, although he was very rich. (Occupational categories IV.24 and 25; venue 2.) The 1825 directory also noted a John and a William Mellish, 'merchants', of 112 Bishopsgate Within, City of London, although that William may have been his namesake (see below).
Address 'Shadwell, Middlesex and Dover Street, Middlesex' (probate calendar). He had a house near Shadwell Docks.
Father Unknown.
Mother Unknown.
Education Unknown.
Marriage Name unknown. He had two daughters, one of whom married Lord Edward Thynne and the other the Earl of Glengall.

Religion Anglican; buried in the Wapping Church.
Public None known.
Miscellaneous He should not be confused with William Mellish (1764–1838), in the *ODNB* as a 'banker and politician'. The two do not appear to have been related. In 1832, one of his captains 'attempted an assassination' of our William Mellish (*GM*).
References *GM,* 1834, vol. I, p. 339.

1834/24 **Name** **Wheeler, John Rivington**
Dates 1758–26 April 1834, Gloucester Place.
Probate £180,000 (PCC).
Occupation Solicitor and 'Procurator-General of Arches' (probate calendar). 'Solicitor, Proctor, and Deputy Registrar of the Admiralty Court' of 6 Godliman Street, City of London, 1805 directory. (Occupational category VI.29; venue 1.)
Address 'Doctor's Commons, City of London and Gloucester Place, Middlesex' (probate calendar).
Father Thomas Wheeler, 'surgeon' or 'apothecary' of Basinghall Street, City of London. He was the first cousin of Mrs Cibber, the actress (online biography of John's brother Thomas). He is described as an 'apothecary' in the St Paul's alumni book.
Mother Unknown.
Education St Paul's School (entered October 1766, aged eight).
Marriage Name unknown. His son was Henry James Wheeler; see 1860/53.
Religion Anglican.
Public None known.
Miscellaneous His brother Thomas Wheeler (1754–1847) was an important botanist (online biography).
References *GM,* 1834, vol. I, p. 666, and above sources.

1834/25 **Name** **Allfrey, Edward**
Dates c. 4 November 1770 Westdean, East Sussex (Family Search)–1 June 1834.
Probate £160,000 (PCC).
Occupation Merchant in the City of London ('Blakes, Hooson & Allfrey, merchants', of 34 Great St Helen's, City of London, 1803 directory). He could not be traced in any other directory, although he gave Great St Helen's as his former address in his will. (Occupational category IV.21? Venue 1.)
Address 'Formerly of [34] Great St Helen's, City of London, and then of Stamford Hill and then Fitzroy Square and then Bryanston Square, Middlesex' (probate calendar). In *BLG,* he is noted as of 'Bryanston Square, Salehurst, Sussex, and Banstead'.
Father George Allfrey (d. 1794) of Westdean and Friston Place, Sussex. (Second son.)
Mother Mary (d. 1810), daughter of William Stone of Stonebridge, Sussex.
Education Unknown.
Marriage In 1807, to Margaret, daughter of Robert Shedden of Gower

Street. (Three sons, one daughter.) Their son Robert (1809–75); see 1875/2, left £400,000.
Religion Unknown, presumably Anglican.
Public None known.
Miscellaneous A merchant in London, but, as has proved so often the case regarding other wealth-holders, little is known about his actual activities. In 1839, his nephew William Allfey, fifth and youngest child of his brother George (1769–1802), found 'several gross errors' in Edward Allfey's accounts, and, in 1849, there was a case in the Rolls Court regarding those accounts: see *The Legal Observer,* vol. 37 (1849), p. 395.
References *BLG,* 1846, vol. III; other sources as above.

Name **Fuller, John** 1834/26
Dates 20 February 1757, North Stoneham, Southampton–11 April 1834, Devonshire Place, Middlesex.
Probate £160,000 (PCC).
Occupation Jamaica fortune and landowner. (Occupational category I; venue 29, etc.) He succeeded his uncle, Rose Fuller (1708–77), MP, 'an extremely wealthy Jamaica planter and then an estate owner in Sussex'. John Fuller was 'extremely rich', with estates in Sussex and on Jamaica (*HP*). He left his wealth to his brother and nephews. No one of this name is listed in Bateman.
Address 'Rosehill, Sussex and Devonshire Place, Middlesex.'
Father (Revd) John Fuller (1713–61) of South Stoneham, Hampshire.
Mother Frances (1725–78), daughter of Thomas Fuller of Park Gate, Catsfield, Sussex; she was her husband's cousin.
Education Eton.
Marriage Unmarried.
Religion Anglican.
Public MP (pro-Whig) Southampton, 1780–4; Sussex, 1801–12. High Sheriff of Sussex, 1796–7. Declined a peerage.
Miscellaneous One of the great eccentrics of his time, he was famous for his Cobbett-like attacks on 'Old Corruption', his raucous behaviour in Parliament and his building of follies and mausoleums on his estates, especially the famous 'Sugar Loaf' at Battle. He also founded professorships at the Royal Institution and was a patron of J. M. W. Turner.
References *ODNB* as 'politician and eccentric'; *HP; GM,* 1834, vol. II, p. 106; *BLG.*

Name **Hertford, Dowager Marchioness of, (Hon.) Anne Ingram Shepheard Seymour-Conway** 1834/27
Dates 1760–12 April 1834, Hertford House.
Probate £180,000 (PCC).
Occupation Landed wealth and inherited a 'speculator's' fortune. (Occupational categories I and IV.18; venues 1, etc.) In 1883, the Marquess of Hertford owned 12,289 acres worth £18,392 p.a. in Warwickshire, etc., while Sir Richard Wallace,

Baronet, who also inherited part of the former marquess's estate, owned 72,307 acres worth £85,737 p.a. in County Antrim, Suffolk, etc.

Address Manchester House (later Hertford House), Manchester Square, Middlesex (now the Wallace Collection) was the chief London seat.

Father Charles Ingram, 9th Viscount Irvine (or Irving) (1727–27 June 1778). (First daughter.)

Mother Frances (1734–20 November 1807), illegitimate daughter and heiress of Samuel Shepheard, a 'wealthy speculator' (*ODNB*). She is in the *ODNB* in her own right as a 'landowner and political manager'.

Education Unknown.

Marriage In 1776, to Sir Francis Ingram Seymour-Conway, 2nd Marquess of Hertford (1743–17 June 1822), MP, Lord of the Treasury, KG, in the *ODNB*. (One son.)

Religion Anglican.

Public None known.

Miscellaneous She was 'the intimate friend (but not the mistress) of the Prince of Wales' until 1820 (*ODNB*). She inherited a great fortune in her own right.

References *GM*, 1834, vol. I, p. 564; *ODNB* for relatives.

1834/28 **Name** **Crawshay, William**

Dates 1764–11 August 1834, Stoke Newington.

Probate £700,000 'within province' (PCC).

Occupation Ironmaster – known as 'the iron king' and 'the sole proprietor of the Cyfarthfa and Hirwan iron works in Glamorgan and Brecon' (*GM*). He had also run the mercantile side of the business at George Yard, City of London, before managing Cyfarthfa. (Occupational category II.3 and IV.20; venues 19 and 1.)

Address 'Stoke Newington' was his address at death. He had also lived at Cyfarthfa.

Father Richard Crawshay (1739–27 June 1810) of Cyfarthfa, ironmaster and millionaire (see 1810/15). William was on bad terms with his father and did not sit in the same room as him. He inherited only three-eighths of the father's property, although he was an only son.

Mother Mary Bourne (1745–1811).

Education Unknown.

Marriage In 1785, to Elizabeth Couzens (d. 1825). (Three sons, two daughters.)

Religion Anglican.

Public None known.

Miscellaneous His 'vast iron works' at Cyfarthfa, 'the largest in the United Kingdom', were inherited mainly by his second son.

References *ODNB* as 'ironmaster and merchant'; *GM*, 1834, vol. II, p. 439; J. P. Addis, *The Crawshay Dynasty* (1957).

1834/29 **Name** **Inglish, Benjamin Hanson**

Dates Unknown – probated November 1834. According to Roots Web, he died 14 November 1834.

Probate £100,000 (PCC).
Occupation Patent medicine manufacturer on the Strand, Middlesex ('B. H. Inglish, Proprietor of Scot's Pills, 165 the Strand' – 1814 and 1820 directories). (Occupational category II.11; venue 2.)
Address 'Formerly of [165] the Strand, Middlesex, then of Ray [sic, Wray] Lodge, Woodford, Essex, and then of Stamford Hill, Hackney, Middlesex' (probate calendar). He also lived at The Blue House, Belsize Lane (*VCH Middlesex*, vol. 9, 1989). The Blue House had been owned in 1793 by James Inglish, 'a Hampstead gentleman' (*VCH Middlesex*, vol. 9, 1989). According to *London and its Environs*, 12th edn (1820), p. 373, Benjamin Hanson Inglish had two residences at Woodford Bridge: 'Wray Lodge, the handsome and much improved residence' where he lived and 'a pretty villa' which he had let. In 1801, a thief of four chickens from Inglish's Hampstead home was sentenced to seven years' transportation (*The Proceedings of the Old Bailey*, online).
Father Unknown, but see the previous. It is possible that the father's name was Hanson and that Inglish was added at some point by the son.
Mother Unknown.
Education Unknown.
Marriage In 1825, to Elizabeth (d. 2 August 1836), widow of William Lewis, (Roots Web). The same source gives his address as Sion House, Stamford Hill.
Religion Presumably Anglican; he was married in an Anglican church.
Public None known.
Miscellaneous His must have been an interesting career, and one wants to know what his pills were supposed to cure (and whether they worked, and what was in them), but no further information could be found about him.
References Above sources only.

Name **Dent, Jonathan** 1834/30
Dates c. 1744–26 August 1834, Winterton, Lincolnshire.
Probate £250,000 'within province' (PCC) + £100,000 (York PC): £350,000.
Occupation Apparently a 'large-scale speculator in land' and a money-lender for rural credit in north Lincolnshire. (Occupational categories 18 and 25? Venue 22?) (See Lincolnshire Archive Committee, *Report for 1952–3*, online, and B. A. Holderness, 'Credit in English Rural Society', *Economic History Review*, 1974, citing H. W. Brace, 'Jonathan Dent of Winterton', *Lincolnshire Architectural and Archaeological Society* [1954].) In 1883, John Dent Dent, of Ribston Hall, Wetherby, owned 8,454 acres worth £14,570 p.a. in Yorkshire and Lincolnshire.
Address Winterton, Lincolnshire.
Father Name unknown – he was a 'respectable farmer and left considerable property, but nearly the whole of it was lost through the failure of a bank', so that the son had to build it up again during 'a persevering struggle of 70 years' (*GM*).
Mother Unknown.
Education Unknown.
Marriage Unknown. He left most of his property to his nephew Joseph Tricket, who consequently took the surname Dent.

Religion A Quaker, but not in the *Quaker Monitor* at death. 'As a very wealthy man he was looked up to by a little aspiring community of Quakers in the neighbourhood', who knew him as 'Friend Jonathan'; his seldom-worn 'best suit' was Quaker dress. At his request he was buried in the garden of his home at Winterton. His nephew and heir restored the 'old dilapidated dwelling-house' that Dent in his frugality had neglected (*Notes and Queries* [1853], p. 202).
Public None known.
Miscellaneous Noted for his eccentricity and parsimony and was said to have been worth £500,000 (*GM*).
References *GM*, 1834, vol. II, p. 444; T. W. Beastall, *The Agricultural Revolution in Lincolnshire* (1978), and above sources.

1834/31 **Name** **Biddles, James**
Dates Unknown–4 March 1834, 'at an advanced age' (*GM*).
Probate £120,000 (PCC).
Occupation A 'shoemaker' (sic; probate calendar). He was 'long known as the rich money-lending shoe-contractor of Bishopsgate Street' (*GM*). He had shoe contracts with the Government. (Occupational category II.11; venue 1.) He also owned 'large property in the East India Company and the Chartered Gaslight Company' (*GM*). He is listed in the 1814 directory as a 'shoemaker' of 80 Bishopsgate Without.
Address '[80] Bishopsgate Without, City of London' (probate calendar).
Father Unknown.
Mother Unknown.
Education Unknown.
Marriage Unknown. He was perhaps the James Biddles who married a Lydia Frome in 1789 at St Luke's, Old Street, Finsbury (Family Search).
Religion Unknown.
Public None known.
Miscellaneous He left Mountsorrel, Leicestershire with a basket-weaver, was employed as a journeyman shoemaker, then was a shoe cobbler at Finsbury Square, and then a shoe contractor to the Government (*GM*). He was known as an eccentric and was 'mean in the extreme', with his 'dress that of a labouring mechanic or a charity boy' (*GM*). His brother, T. Biddles, was a sheep-jobber of Mountsorrel.
References *GM*, 1834, vol. II, p. 327.

1834/32 **Name** **Neal, William**
Dates 14 December 1771–1 March 1834.
Probate £300,000 (PCC).
Occupation 'Hemp and flax merchant' of Goodman's Yards, Minories – 1814 and 1817 directories. (Occupational category IV.21; venue 1.) 'Of Little Tower Hill House, City of London' (*BLG*). In 1883, a William Neal (1838–1901) of Kingsdon, Somerset, owned 2,170 acres worth £3,650 p.a. He was the grandson of William Neal's brother. There is no evidence that our William Neal owned this land.

Address 'Little Tower Hill, St Botolph Aldgate, City of London' (probate calendar).
Father William Neal (1748–27 May 1799) of Yeovil. (First son.)
Mother Mary (d. 1777), daughter of John Tatchell.
Education Unknown.
Marriage In 1798, to Mary Elizabeth Hewlett (d.s.p.).
Religion Unknown.
Public None known.
Miscellaneous A London merchant.
References *BLG*, 1952.

Name **Adair, Alexander** 1834/33
Dates c. 1739–17 March 1834.
Probate £700,000 (PCC).
Occupation Army Agent in Pall Mall, Middlesex – 'Adair and Bullock, Agents, of Childley Court, Pall Mall', 1793 directory; of 4 Pall Mall Court, Pall Mall, 1794 directory. 'For many years he was an army agent conducting a very extensive business.' (Occupational category IV.18? and VI.31; venue 2.) In 1799/1800 he paid income tax on an income of £14,000, certainly one of the largest business incomes in Britain at the time. (T. V. Jackson, 'British Incomes Circa 1800', *Economic History Review* [1999]). An 'army agent', presumably contracted for military goods and held and invested monies for army officers.
Address 'Flexton Hall, Suffolk and Pall Mall, Middlesex' (probate calendar).
Father William Adair, who purchased the Flexton estate.
Mother Unknown.
Education Unknown.
Marriage Unknown. He left the residue of his estate to Sir T. Baring, Alexander Baring and Sir Frederick Roe (who hardly needed it!), suggesting that he had no close heirs.
Religion Presumably Anglican.
Public None known.
Miscellaneous His income must have skyrocketed during the Napoleonic Wars.
References *GM*, 1834, vol. II, p. 318; *Times*, 17 April 1834.

Name **Burlington, 1st Earl of, Lord George Augustus Henry Cavendish** 1834/34
Dates 31 March 1754–9 May 1834, Burlington House, Piccadilly.
Probate £140,000 (PCC).
Occupation Landed wealth – inherited £700,000 from Hon. Henry Cavendish (1810/2), the millionaire scientist, in 1810. In 1883, Lord Chesham, who apparently inherited most of his estate, owned 112,487 acres worth £15,628 p.a. in Buckinghamshire, Huntingdon, etc. (Occupational category I.)
Address Burlington House, Piccadilly.
Father William Cavendish, 4th Duke of Devonshire (1720–2 October 1764), Prime Minister, etc. (Third son.)

Mother Lady Charlotte (1731–54), daughter of Richard Boyle, 3rd Earl of Burlington and of the Baroness Clifford in her own right.
Education 'Hackney'; Trinity College, Cambridge (LL.D, Cambridge University, 1811).
Marriage In 1782, to Lady Elizabeth (1760–1835), daughter of Charles Compton, 7th Earl of Northampton. (Four sons, six daughters.) His son Charles (1793–1863) was created 1st Baron Chesham and appears to have inherited most of his land. The present Duke of Devonshire is a descendant of Lord Burlington.
Religion Anglican.
Public MP (Whig) Knaresborough, 1775–80; Derby, 1780–96; Derbyshire, 1797–1831. Created 1st Earl of Burlington of the second creation in 1831.
Miscellaneous He was known as Lord George Cavendish until 1831 and inaugurated the Burlington Arcade, off Piccadilly, in 1817. A premier Whig aristocrat.
References *ODNB*; *HP*; *BP*; *GM*, 1834, vol. II, p. 102.

1834/35 **Name** **Hammond, William**
Dates Unknown – probated July 1834.
Probate £120,000 (PCC).
Occupation Stockbroker of 16 Throgmorton Street, City of London (1817 directory). 'Of Queen Square, Bloomsbury and the Stock Exchange' (*ODNB* for son-in-law). (Occupational category IV.23; venue 1.)
Address '[9] Queen Square, Bloomsbury' (probate calendar); also of Champneys, Tring, Hertfordshire (1824 Court directory).
Father Unknown.
Mother Unknown.
Education Unknown.
Marriage Name unknown. In 1805, his daughter married Sir Thomas Charles Morgan (c. 1780–1843), surgeon, philosopher and writer, who is in the *ODNB*. George Dighton Hammond (see 1862/26), stockbroker of Brighton, left £200,000.
Religion Unknown.
Public None known.
Miscellaneous Little could be traced about his career.
References Above sources only.

1834/36 **Name** **Flower, Sir Charles, 1st Baronet**
Dates 18 February 1763–September 1834, Russell Square, Middlesex.
Probate £500,000 (PCC).
Occupation Merchant and government contractor. 'Made a large fortune by extensive provision contracts during the [Napoleonic] war' (Ormonde). 'Merchant' at Stable Yard, Crescent, Minories (1798 directory); 'Charles Flower, merchant', of 3 Crescent, Minories (1800 directory), and Lord Mayor of London. (Occupational category IV.21? Venue 1.)
Address Lived at Russell Square, Middlesex.
Father Stephen Flower, a 'cheesemonger' at 74 Minories in 1793.

Mother Mary, daughter of William Brazier of Chippenham, Wiltshire.
Education Unknown.
Marriage To Anne (d. 1803), marriage date unknown, daughter of Joseph Squire of Plymouth. (One son, six daughters.)
Religion Anglican; buried Aldgate Church.
Public Sheriff of London, 1799; Alderman from 1801. Lord Mayor of London, 1808–9. Created baronet, 1809. Pro-Tory.
Miscellaneous Noted as 'entirely the architect of his own fortune' (Ormonde).
References B. B. Ormonde, *Some Accounts of the City of London* (1867), p. 2512; *GM.*

Name **Copland, Alexander** 1834/37
Dates 14 May 1774, St Martin-in-the-Fields parish–12 July 1834, Great George Street, Middlesex.
Probate £120,000 (PCC).
Occupation Builder in London. (Occupational category II.10; venues 2 and 1, etc.) According to the *ODNB*, he was 'the earliest of the great building contractors' in London. He also owned 76 acres at Gunnersbury Park in West London.
Address 'Gunnersbury Park, Middlesex, and [29] Great George Street, Middlesex' (probate calendar). His address at Great George Street is now the National Portrait Gallery.
Father Alexander Copland (1736–31 October 1793), 'builder', of St Martin-in-the-Fields, Westminster. He is said to have left £10,000 (*ODNB*). (First son.)
Mother Barbara (1734–91), daughter of Richard Smirke of Wigton, Cumberland, and widow of Richard McCartney. Her father was apparently the grandfather of Robert Smirke, the architect (*ODNB*).
Education At a school in Sowerby, Yorkshire, and then apprenticed to Richard Holland, surveyor at the Stationers' Company. He also entered the Royal Academy Schools (*ODNB*).
Marriage In 1796, to Lucy (d. 1849), daughter of William Giffard of St Paul's, Covent Garden and Turnham Green. (Three sons, one daughter.)
Religion Anglican; buried in St Martin-in-the-Fields.
Public JP, Middlesex. Appointed Sheriff of London, 1820, but paid to be excused from the post.
Miscellaneous He became very successful by building twenty-six large military barracks during the Napoleonic Wars. He was a pioneer of rational management techniques, employing many superintendents to supervise his workmen and keeping to strict schedules. He also built the Duke of York's Asylum in Chelsea; the Horse Guards in Hyde Park; and part of Albany, Piccadilly. It should be noted that he was a builder and building contractor, not an architect.
References In *ODNB* as 'building contractor'; *GM,* 1834, vol. II, p. 219; *BLG,* 1952, 'Copland-Griffiths'.

Name **Lambert, James** 1834/38
Dates Unknown – probated December 1834.
Probate £100,000 (PCC).

Occupation Unknown. There is no clear evidence from his will or any other source regarding his occupation. In his will he noted relatives in Yorkshire and his cousin, John Lambert, an American citizen, but not his own occupation. There were a number of James Lamberts in the London directories of the time, including a hosier of 100 Bishopsgate Within, and Lambert, Princeps & Saunders, 'merchants' of 147 Leadenhall Street in the City, but there is no evidence for a direct linkage between him and any of them.

Address '[7] Bedford Square, Middlesex' (probate calendar). He lived there from c. 1819 or earlier. In 1811 he lived at 27 Great Coram Street, Middlesex.

Father Unknown.

Mother Unknown.

Education Unknown.

Marriage Unknown.

Religion Unknown.

Public None known.

Miscellaneous Nothing more could be traced about him.

References Will (PROB 11, online); above sources.

WEALTH-HOLDERS, 1835

Name **Peel, Jonathan** 1835/1
Dates September 1752–5 December 1834.
Probate £600,000 'within province' (PCC).
Occupation Calico manufacturer in Accrington, Lancashire – brother of Sir Robert Peel, 1st Baronet, cotton millionaire. (Occupational category II.7; venue 4.) In 1883, Jonathan Peel of Knowlmere, Clitheroe, owned 3,019 acres worth £7,086 p.a.
Address Accrington House, Lancashire.
Father Robert Peel (1723–95) calico printer of Burton-on-Trent and Ardwick, founder of the business, who is said to have left £140,000. (Fourth son.)
Mother Elizabeth (d. 1796), daughter of Edmund Howarth of Walmesley Fold, Lower Darwen, Lancashire.
Education Unknown.
Marriage First, in 1773, to Ann (d. 1785), daughter of Giles Haworth. (Two sons, two daughters.) Second, in 1786, to Esther Bolton (d. 1841). (Two sons, four daughters.)
Religion Anglican.
Public None known.
Miscellaneous The brother of the cotton millionaire Sir Robert Peel and uncle of the Prime Minister. He apparently operated his own businesses, very successfully.
References *ODNB* for relatives. Catherine Formby Jackson published *Jonathan Peel (1752–1834): A Memoir* in 1909.

Name **Scarbrough (sic), 7th Earl of, (Revd) John Lumley Savile** 1835/2
(né Lumley-Sanderson)
Dates 15 June 1760 Sandbeck–21 February 1835, in a hunting accident near Markham Moor.
Probate £350,000 (PCC) + £90,000 (York PC): £340,000.
Occupation Landowner and 'Senior Prebend of York Cathedral' (*GM*). (Occupational categories I and VI.30.) In 1883, the Earl of Scarbrough owned 21,698 acres worth £31,597 p.a. in Lincoln, Yorkshire and Durham.
Address Sandbeck Park, Rotherham, was the principal seat.
Father Richard Lumley-Sanderson, 4th Earl of Scarbrough (1725–12 May 1782). (Fourth son.) He succeeded two older brothers, who died in 1807 and 1832.
Mother Barbara (d. 1784), daughter of Sir George Savile, 8th Baronet.
Education Eton; King's College, Cambridge (MA).
Marriage In 1785, to Anna Maria (1766–March 1850), daughter of Julian Herring of Heybridge, Essex and Jamaica. (Three sons, of whom one survived; three daughters.)
Religion Anglican clergyman.
Public None known.

Miscellaneous He took the surname Savile in 1797. A younger son who unexpectedly succeeded his father in the family earldom, he was Rector of Wintringham, Yorkshire, and Thornhill, Yorkshire, and then Prebendary of York from 1785 until his death.
References *GM*, 1835, vol. I, p. 541; *CP*; *BP.*

1835/3 **Name** **Taylor, Michael Angelo**
Dates c. 1757–16 July 1834.
Probate £100,000, 'within province' (PCC).
Occupation Inherited the fortune of his father, the Architect to the Bank of England. Also a barrister, and Recorder of Poole, 1784–death. (Occupational categories II.10 and VI.29; venue 1.)
Address Privy Gardens, Whitehall; Park Hill, Bawtry, Yorkshire and Ledstone Park, Yorkshire.
Father Sir Robert Taylor (1714–27 September 1788), Architect to the Bank of England and Surveyor to the Admiralty; he built Somerset House and was also a speculative builder. He was said to have left £180,000 (*ODNB*). (First son.)
Mother Name unknown; she lived 1722–1803.
Education Westminster; Corpus Christi College, Oxford (MA). Barrister, Inner Temple, 1769, and Lincoln's Inn, 1777.
Marriage In 1789, to Frances (d. 1835), daughter of (Revd) Sir Henry Vane, 1st Baronet, of Long Newton, County Durham. (One daughter.)
Religion Anglican; buried in the church of St Martin-in-the-Fields.
Public MP (pro-Pitt, then Whig) for ten seats between 1784 and 1834. PC, 1831.
Miscellaneous Was an eccentric but useful MP who was responsible for abolishing pillories and for the 1817 Act improving paving in the Metropolis. He was also a 'butt' of jokes owing to his pomposity (*ODNB*).
References *ODNB; GM*, 1834, vol. II, p. 430; *HP.*

1835/4 **Name** **Gloucester and Edinburgh, HRH 2nd Duke of, William Frederick of Brunswick-Lunenberg**
Dates 15 January 1776, Rome–30 November 1834, Bagshot Park.
Probate £100,000 (PCC).
Occupation Royal Duke and Field Marshal in the Army. (Occupational category VI.31.)
Address Chiefly Bagshot Park, Surrey.
Father Prince William Henry, 1st Duke of Gloucester (1715–5 October 1805). (First son.) The father was the son of Frederick, Prince of Wales and the younger brother of King George III.
Mother Maria (1736–1807), daughter of (Hon.) Sir Edward Walpole and widow of James, Earl Waldegrave.
Education Private tutors; Trinity College, Cambridge (MA, 1790; LL.D, 1796).
Marriage In 1816, to Princess Mary (1776–1857; d.s.p.), daughter of King George III, his first cousin.
Religion Anglican.

Public Created PC, KG, 1801, GCB. He was also Earl of Connaught.

Miscellaneous Dubbed 'Silly Billy'. He was Chancellor of Cambridge University from 1811 and an FRS from 1797. He was known as Prince William of Gloucester until 1805. He entered the Army at thirteen with the rank of colonel and became a general in 1809 and a field marshal in 1816. From 1805 he had an official allowance of £14,000 p.a.

References *ODNB; GM,* 1835, vol. I, p. 86.

Name **Hudleston, John** 1835/5

Dates 2 September 1749–6 March 1835, Bath.

Probate £120,000 (PCC).

Occupation 'For many years an East India Company director' (*GM*). 'Served in Madras over twenty years in the Company's service' – rose to be Senior Merchant in 1778 and Resident in 1790. (Occupational categories IV.19 and VI.31; venue 29.) He was an East India Company director from 1803 to 1826.

Address 'Formerly of Down Place, Bray, then Windsor and then Bath' (probate calendar).

Father (Revd) William Hudleston (1716–66), Vicar of St Cuthbert's and Prebendary of Wells.

Mother Mary, daughter of John Burland of Wells.

Education 'By J. Sharpe of Bromley-by-Bow' (*HP*).

Marriage In 1788, to Honoria, daughter of (Revd) John Marshall. (Five sons, two daughters.)

Religion Anglican.

Public MP ('doubtful' pro-Pitt – *HP*) Bridgewater, 1804–6. He was opposed to slavery and to suttee.

Miscellaneous He entered the East India Company as a Writer in 1766 and rose to be a Resident. He retired in 1790 and settled in Bray and then Bath.

References *HP; GM,* 1835, vol. I, p. 445; *BLG.*

Name **Paynter, Francis** 1835/6

Dates Baptised 21 May 1762 at Newlyn, Cornwall–7 (17?) June 1835, Denmark Hill, Surrey.

Probate £120,000 (PCC).

Occupation Apparently a builder in London (F. & T. Paynter, 'builders', of 63 Coleman Street, City of London, 1803 directory). (If so, occupational category II.10; venue 1?) In 1825, there was also a Paynter & Haynes, surveyors, of 60 Coleman Street, which might have been a branch of the builders.

Address Lived at Denmark Hill, Surrey.

Father William Paynter (1726–22 July 1801) of St Issey, Cornwall. (Second son.)

Mother Elizabeth Glanville (1727–98), widow of Anthony Hawkey of Newlyn, with whom she had three sons.

Education Unknown.

Marriage First, in 1783, to Sarah Whidbourne (d. 1810). (Two sons.) Second, in 1811, to Mrs Ann Olding (d. 1851). His son was High Sheriff of Surrey in 1838.

Religion Anglican.
Public None known.
Miscellaneous His occupation is unclear, but he appears to have been a successful builder in the City.
References *GM,* 1835, vol. II, p. 101; *BLG;* Roots Web.

1835/7 **Name** **Tyler, William**
Dates c. 1764–23 October 1835, Petworth.
Probate £120,000 (PCC).
Occupation Solicitor and land agent in Petworth, Sussex. (Occupational category VI.29; venue 14.) He was an 'attorney' (probate calendar) and was steward for the Petworth estate and agent to the Earl of Egremont (NRA online).
Address Petworth, Sussex.
Father Unknown.
Mother Unknown.
Education Unknown.
Marriage Unknown.
Religion Presumably Anglican.
Public None known.
Miscellaneous It is unclear whether he had a separate practice as a solicitor. The size of his estate is very unusual, and he might well have had other interests.
References *GM,* 1835, vol. II, p. 665.

1835/8 **Name** **Castle, Catherine**
Dates Unknown – probated January 1835.
Probate £120,000 (PCC).
Occupation Probably the daughter of Michael Castle (see 1821/31), 'rectifier' or distiller in Bristol, who left £120,000. (If so, occupational category III.13; venue 12.) She is described in the probate calendars as unmarried.
Address Stapleton, Bristol.
Father See above.
Mother Unknown.
Education Unknown.
Marriage Unmarried.
Religion Michael Castle was a Unitarian.
Public None known.
Miscellaneous Nothing more could be found about her.
References Above sources only.

1835/9 **Name** **Smith, George**
Dates c. 1769–28 November 1835, Goldicote House, Worcestershire.
Probate £250,000 (PCC).
Occupation Unknown. He is described as 'an officer in the Horse Guards' in *BLG,* 1914, 'Smith of Walcote House, Leicestershire', but his ancestry and source of wealth could not be traced.

Address 'Formerly of Spettisbury House [near Blandford], Dorset, and then Goldicote House [near Stratford-upon-Avon], Worcestershire' (probate calendar).
Father Unknown. The name of his father could not be traced in any source.
Mother Unknown.
Education Unknown.
Marriage In 1796, to Frances, daughter of Thomas Grace Smith of Normanton Hall, Leicestershire. (Five sons, one daughter.) One son, William Corbet Smith (c. 1811–47), was High Sheriff of Leicestershire in 1845 and married the daughter of Viscount Bolingbroke (*GM,* May 1847). Another son was named Gustavus Thomas Smith.
Religion Anglican.
Public None known.
Miscellaneous A very unusual case. He appears to have been well born, but nothing could be traced about his ancestry or source of wealth. There is obviously a story here. His name, of course, makes tracing him difficult.
References *GM,* 1836, vol. I, p. 101; *BLG,* 1914.

Name **Booth, William** 1835/10
Dates Unknown–17 October 1834, Gunnersbury, Middlesex.
Probate £120,000 (PCC).
Occupation Probably a distiller at Brentford – he was the brother of Sir Felix Booth, Baronet (d. 1850), a wealthy distiller at Brentford. The firm made Booth's Gin. Sir Felix was known for financing Arctic expeditions. (If so, occupational category II.13; venue 3.)
Address Roydon Lodge, near Harlow, Essex.
Father Philip Booth, a distiller of Russell Square and Clerkenwell.
Mother Elizabeth Wallis.
Education Unknown.
Marriage To Mary (marriage date unknown), daughter of John Williamson. (Three sons.) One son, William, succeeded by special remainder to his uncle's baronetcy. Another, Henry Booth (1815–83), was a noted cricketer for Cambridge University.
Religion Anglican; buried in Roydon Church.
Public None known.
Miscellaneous It is not clear whether he was in trade, but it seems very likely.
References *ODNB* for brother; *GM,* 1834, vol. II, p. 556; *BP.*

Name **Kent, Sir Charles Egleton, 2nd Baronet** 1835/11
Dates 4 March 1784–5 December 1834, Peterborough House, Fulham.
Probate £140,000 (PCC).
Occupation Unclear. His grandfather Sir Charles Egleton, Baronet, was a merchant and Sheriff of London. Sir Charles was married to Sarah, the daughter of Samuel Kent, MP, a wholesale malt distiller. Presumably Sir Charles inherited from these sources, but the sources of his wealth are unclear. The family is not listed in Bateman.
Address 'Formerly of Edward Street, Cavendish Square, Middlesex, and then of

Little Ponton House near Grantham, Lincolnshire' (probate calendar). He also had a house at Farnham St Genevieve, Suffolk.

Father Sir Charles Kent (né Egleston), 1st Baronet (c. 1743–14 March 1811), MP 1784–90; Sheriff of Suffolk, 1781–2, of Farnham St Genevieve, Suffolk. (First son.) He was created a baronet in 1782.

Mother Mary (d. 1817), daughter of Josias Wadsworth of Wadsworth, Yorkshire and Sevenoaks, Kent.

Education Secondary schooling unknown; Christ Church, Oxford (MA).

Marriage In 1818, to Sophia (d. December 1834), daughter of William, 1st Earl Beauchamp. (One son.)

Religion Anglican.

Public None known.

Miscellaneous Presumably he lived on inherited capital and land, but the details are unclear.

References *GM,* 1835 vol. I, p. 436; *HP* for father; *Complete Baronetage.*

1835/12 **Name** **Tuck, Thomas**

Dates 1774–9 October 1834, Strumpshaw near Norwich, Norfolk.

Probate £100,000 (PCC).

Occupation 'Farmer and gentleman' (probate calendar). Presumably a landowner and farmer in Norfolk, but little could be traced about him. (Occupational category I?)

Address Strumpshaw, near Norwich, Norfolk.

Father Unknown.

Mother Unknown.

Education Unknown.

Marriage Mary, surname unknown. They had at least one son, Richard. A Thomas Gilbert Tuck lived at Strumpshaw in 1825 (William White, *History, Gazeteer and Directory of Norfolk,* 1845). He was presumably a son of Thomas. Thomas Gilbert Tuck built Strumpshaw Hall in 1835.

Religion Unknown.

Public None known.

Miscellaneous He tore down the ruins of the Chapel of St Clements, Brundall, of which he was then the owner, in 1820 (*Norfolk Archaeology*, vol. 22, p. 197). Nothing further could be traced about him.

References *GM,* 1834, vol. II, p. 556; online sources.

1835/13 **Name** **Bradshaw, Richard Haldane**

Dates 23 August 1759–8 January 1835, Woodmans, Hertfordshire.

Probate £350,000 (PCC).

Occupation Multiple interests: he 'inherited the reversion of the lucrative Auditorship of Plantations'; was Deputy Paymaster in the Pay Office, c. 1780; was the 'man of business to the Duke of Bridgewater' and trustee of his estate, earning £2,000 p.a., and invested in coal and the sale of coal in Lancashire (*HP*). (Occupational categories VI.29 and 30 and II.1; venue 1, etc.)

Address Woodmans, King's Langley, Hertfordshire.
Father Thomas Bradshaw (1733–74) of Hampton Court, Middlesex.
Mother Elizabeth (d. 1812), daughter of Robert Wilson, a corn merchant.
Education Possibly Harrow, but this is unclear (*HP*).
Marriage To Cornelia Thornhill Rowe (marriage date unknown). (Two sons.)
Religion Anglican.
Public MP (pro-Pitt) Brackley, 1804–32.
Miscellaneous It is not clear from whom he 'inherited' the Auditorship of Plantations, nor what portion of his wealth was owed to 'Old Corruption', to estate management, or to coal sales.
References *HP; GM,* 1835, vol. I, p. 536.

Name **Hibbert, Robert** 1835/14
Dates 12 October 1750–24 January 1835.
Probate £250,000 'within province' (PCC).
Occupation West India merchant in Manchester (Hibbert, Purrier & Horton, West Indian traders, of 9 Mincing Lane); also probably a planter in Jamaica. (Occupational category IV.19 and I; venue 4.)
Address 'Birtles Hall [near Macclesfield], Cheshire and Chalfont House, Buckinghamshire' (probate calendar).
Father Robert Hibbert (1717–12 January 1784), a 'wealthy merchant' of Manchester, of Stockfield Hall, Lancashire. (Third son.) His brother Thomas was a prominent planter in Jamaica.
Mother Abigail, daughter of William Scholey of Yorkshire.
Education Unknown.
Marriage In 1785, to Letitia, daughter of John Frederick Nembhard of St Mary's, Jamaica. (Three sons, two daughters.)
Religion Presumably Anglican.
Public None known.
Miscellaneous His brother George Hibbert (1757–1837), MP, is in the *ODNB* as a 'merchant'. He founded the London institution. The *ODNB* also lists Robert Hibbert (1769–1849), probably his cousin, a 'philanthropist', born Jamaica. Our Robert Hibbert was also apparently in Jamaica in early life.
References *ODNB* for relatives; *GM,* 1835, vol. I, p. 331; *BLG,* 1952.

Name **Jones, John** 1835/15
Dates Unknown–2 January 1835.
Probate £160,000 (PCC).
Occupation 'Surgeon and apothecary' (probate calendar), of Gracechurch Street in the City of London. (Occupational category VI.30 and IV.20; venue 1.) The 1808 directory lists Board, Jones & Sons, apothecaries of Gracechurch Street.
Address 'Formerly of Gracechurch Street, City of London, and then of Brunswick Square, City of London; Portland Place, Middlesex; and Dery [Derry] Ormond [near Lampeter], Cardiganshire' (probate calendar).

Father Almost certainly John Jones, apothecary of Gracechurch Street, City of London (d. 21 June 1817) (see 1817/24, left £160,000).
Mother Probably Hannah, daughter of Andrew Smith of Gunston House, Hertfordshire.
Education Unknown.
Marriage Unknown.
Religion Unknown.
Public None known.
Miscellaneous The business must have been very lucrative, but nothing more could be traced about it.
References *GM,* 1835, vol. I, p. 218; *BLG,* 1914.

1835/16 **Name** **Bromhead, (Revd) Edward**
Dates 30 October 1746–16 January 1835.
Probate £120,000 (PCC).
Occupation He was 'for sixty-four years the vicar of Repham near Lincoln' (*GM*). His family was prominent in the development of Lincoln. No one of this name is listed in Bateman. (Occupational categories VI.30 and I? Venue 18.)
Address Repham, near Lincoln.
Father Benjamin Bromhead (d. 21 January 1782) of Lincoln. (Sixth son.) He owned College House, Lincoln (J. W. F. Hill, *Georgian Lincoln,* 1966, p. 22n.). A relative, Sir Edward Bromhead, Baronet, was also prominent in the development of Lincoln.
Mother Margaret, daughter of James Boardman of King's Lynn.
Education Secondary schooling unknown; Corpus Christi College, Oxford (matriculated 1765).
Marriage In 1776, to Catherine (d. 1837), daughter of Thomas Ayre. (One son, two daughters.) His son Thomas Ayre Bromhead (1793–1825) died in Syria (*GM,* February 1826); his daughter Maria married, in 1827, Sir Edward Brackenbury (1785–1864), army officer, in *ODNB;* another daughter, Catherine (1779–1863) married, in 1805, James Edwards (1756–1816), bookseller and book collector, in *ODNB.*
Religion Anglican clergyman.
Public None known.
References The family presumably owned land, but this could not be traced. Presumably most of his fortune came from the inheritance of land and other property near Lincoln, although holding a living for sixty-four years (!) must also have been lucrative.
References *GM,* 1835, vol. I, p. 329; *ODNB* for relatives.

1835/17 **Name** **Garnier, (Revd) William**
Dates 1772–18 March 1835, Grafton Street, Middlesex.
Probate £250,000 (PCC).
Occupation 'Senior Prebendary of Winchester and Rector of Droxford, Hampshire' (*GM*). His family also owned lucrative saltmines, which provided most Epsom

salts. (Occupational categories VI.30 and II.2.) In 1883, John Carpenter-Garnier of Rookesbury owned 4,901 acres worth £5,957 p.a. in Hampshire and Devon.

Address 'Rookesbury, Wickham, Hampshire and Grafton Street, Bond Street, Middlesex' (probate calendar).

Father George Charles Garnier (1739–November 1819) of Rookesbury, Hampshire; High Sheriff of Hampshire in 1766. (Eldest surviving son.) His family owned lucrative saltmines which supplied Epsom salts, and the family 'long held the office of apothecary to Chelsea Hospital' (*ODNB* for brother).

Mother Margaret (d. 1807), daughter of Sir John Miller, Baronet.

Education Secondary schooling unknown; New College, Oxford (MA).

Marriage In 1797, to Lady Henrietta, daughter of (Hon.) Brownlow North, Bishop of Winchester. (Six sons, seven daughters.)

Religion Anglican clergyman. The family was of Huguenot descent.

Public None known.

Miscellaneous A well-connected beneficiary of 'Old Corruption' and of a clerical income. His brother-in-law was the Earl of Guildford. His brother, (Revd) Thomas Garnier (1776–1873), Dean of Winchester, is in the *ODNB*.

References *ODNB* for brother; *GM*, 1836, vol. I, p. 554; *BLG*, 1952.

Name **Smyth, George Watson** 1835/18

Dates c. 1747–8 June 1835, Green Street, Middlesex.

Probate £300,000 (PCC).

Occupation 'Perfumers to His Majesty' (Smyth & Nephews, 117 New Bond Street, 1817 directory); George Watson Smyth, 'Perfumer to His Majesty' of the same address, 1811 directory. (Occupational category IV.20; venue 2.)

Address 'Formerly of [117] New Bond Street, Middlesex, then of Green Street, Grosvesnor Square, Middlesex' (probate calendar). From 1821, he also owned the manor of Manton, Rutland.

Father Unknown.

Mother Unknown.

Education Unknown.

Marriage Unknown. A Phoebe Vain married a George Watson Smyth in 1819 at St Marylebone (Family Search). *A History of the County of Rutland*, vol. II (1935) (online) states that the Manor of Manton, Rutland 'in 1821 came into the possession of George Watson Smyth'. It 'passed in 1830 to Edward Watson Smyth, who died in 1869'. The latter was presumably a son. It is possible that the date of 1830 is inaccurate.

Religion Unknown.

Public None known.

Miscellaneous Presumably he was a very upmarket perfume and spray vendor and possibly manufacturer.

References *GM*, 1835, vol. II, p. 100.

Name **Wormald, John** 1835/19

Dates 1761–21 April 1835, Highbury Place.

Probate £200,000 (PCC).
Occupation Partner in Child's Bank, Temple Bar, Fleet Street, City of London. (Occupational category IV.16; venue 1.)
Address 'Temple Bar, City of London and Highbury Place, Middlesex' (probate calendar).
Father *BLG*, 1952, states he was Thomas Wormald of Gomersal, Yorkshire. The *Handbook of London Bankers* notes that John Wormald, Senior 'retired as a partner in Child's Bank, 1797'.
Mother Martha Sykes of Drightlington, Yorkshire.
Education Unknown.
Marriage To Frances Jones (d. 1857), marriage date unknown. (Four sons, two daughters.) Their son, Thomas Wormald (1802–73), surgeon, is in the *ODNB*.
Religion Presumably Anglican.
Public None known.
Miscellaneous A wealthy London banker.
References *GM*, 1835, vol. I, p. 667; Frederick Price, *Handbook of London Bankers* (1890).

1835/20 **Name** **Wood, Thomas**
Dates c. 1747–7 May 1835, Littleton, Middlesex.
Probate £180,000 (PCC).
Occupation He appears to have inherited money from his father, a barrister and MP, but the source of his wealth is unclear. In 1883, Thomas Wood of Littleton, Chertsey, owned 9,978 acres worth £12,419 p.a. in Brecon, North Riding, Middlesex, etc. (1,428 acres worth £2,633 p.a.) (If he was primarily a landowner, then occupational category I.)
Address Littleton, near Staines, Middlesex.
Father Thomas Wood (1708–25 June 1799 [1790, *HP*]) of Littleton, MP, barrister and Bencher of the Inner Temple. He was educated at Eton and Oxford.
Mother Ann, daughter of Richard Jones.
Education Unknown.
Marriage In 1776, to Mary, daughter of Sir Edward Williams, 5th Baronet. (Six sons, six daughters.) A son, Colonel Thomas Wood, was an MP and married the daughter of the 1st Marquess of Londonderry. Two sons were in the East India Company's service.
Religion Anglican.
Public None known.
Miscellaneous The family appears to have been landed for several generations, but the sources of his wealth are unclear.
References *GM*, 1835, vol. I, p. 669; *BLG*, 1952; *HP* for father.

1835/21 **Name** **Alvarez, Joaquin d'Oliviera**
Dates Unknown – probated July 1835.
Probate £120,000, 'within province' (PCC).
Occupation 'Field Marshal of the Armies of the Brazils' (probate calendar).

(Occupational category VI.31, although he should not be counted with the British statistics since he appears to have had no career in Britain.)

Address 'Formerly of Portman Square, Middlesex, and then of [19] Devonshire Place, Middlesex and of Paris' (probate calendar).

Father Unknown.

Mother Unknown.

Education Unknown.

Marriage Unknown.

Religion Roman Catholic.

Public None known.

Miscellaneous Why he lived in England and left a fortune there is unclear.

References Above sources only.

Name **Banks, Sir Edward** 1835/22

Dates 4 January 1770, Richmond, Yorkshire–5 July 1835, Tilgate Lodge (near Crawley), Sussex.

Probate £250,000 (PCC).

Occupation Public-works contractor (Joliffe & Banks) of London. He built the Waterloo, Southwark and new London bridges, as well as Sheerness Dockyard, river channels, etc. (Occupational category II.10; venues 2 and 1, etc.)

Address He lived at Adelphi Terrace, Westminster, which was possibly also his business address. He also owned country properties in Kent.

Father 'Nothing is known of his parentage' (*ODNB*). He 'began as a day labourer', went to sea for two years and became a sea banking contractor in Holderness in 1769. He 'rose from the humblest beginnings' (*GM*).

Mother Unknown.

Education Unknown, but plainly very little.

Marriage First, in 1793, to Nancy (d. October 1815), daughter of John Franklin. (Five sons, three daughters.) Second, in 1821, to Elizabeth (d. 1836), daughter of Sir Abraham Pytches.

Religion Anglican.

Public Knighted in 1822.

Miscellaneous A true self-made man. He worked for John Rennie with his partner, Revd Mr Joliffe, and then became a large-scale contractor.

References *ODNB*; *GM*, 1835, vol. II, p. 444.

Name **Hanbury, Sampson** 1835/23

Dates 12 March 1769–August 1835.

Probate £120,000 (PCC).

Occupation Brewer in Bethnal Green, Spitalfields (The Black Eagle Brewery, Brick Lane, Bethnal Green, later Truman, Hanbury & Buxton). (Occupational category III.12; venue 2.)

Address 'Spitalfields and Poles near Ware, Hertfordshire' (probate calendar).

Father Osgood Hanbury (d. 11 January 1784) of Holfield Grange near Coggleshall, Essex. (Fifth son.)

Mother Mary, daughter of Sampson Lloyd, banker of Birmingham.
Education Unknown.
Marriage To Agatha (1776–1847), marriage date unknown, daughter of Richard Gurney of Keswick, and sister of Hudson Gurney, the wealthy banker.
Religion Quaker – part of the 'Quaker Cousinhood'.
Public None known.
Miscellaneous He took over the brewery from Sir Benjamin Truman, c. 1790. He was a 'keen sportsman' (*VCH Middlesex,* vol. 2).
References *Survey of London,* vol. 27, 1957; *BLG.*

1835/24 **Name** **Willis, John**
Dates 1751–2 October 1835, Branston near Lincoln.
Probate £250,000 (PCC).
Occupation 'Doctor of Medicine' (probate calendar). He and his father are well known for having attended King George III in his madness – they were doctors to the royal family. (Occupational category VI.30; venue 2, etc.)
Address 'Greatford, Lincolnshire and Tenterden Street, Middlesex' (probate calendar).
Father (Revd) Dr Francis Willis (1718–3 December 1807), MD and Vice-Principal of Brasenose College, Oxford, who was 'justly celebrated' as a physician; in the *ODNB.*
Mother Mary (d. 1807), daughter of (Revd) John Curtois of Branston, Lincolnshire.
Education Unknown – presumably he was educated under his father, but where he received his degree is unclear.
Marriage Unmarried.
Religion Anglican.
Public None known.
Miscellaneous Although his father is listed in the *ODNB* and other sources, he is not well documented. He and his father received substantial pensions for attending the King and are well known, owing to the film *The Madness of King George* and other sources. Several of his relatives are also in the *ODNB.*
References *ODNB* for father; *GM,* 1835, vol. II, p. 549.

1835/25 **Name** **Hall, Richard**
Dates c. 1764–15 October 1835, Totteridge.
Probate £250,000 (PCC).
Occupation Unknown. Owing to his relatively common name he has proved very difficult to trace. His will is unilluminating, although it does mention that his nephew, Charles Gartllor (? the handwriting is not fully legible) was of Gracechurch Street in the City of London. He cannot be precisely identified from any genealogical work. A Richard Hall, 'Manchester warehouseman', of 23 Lawrence Lane in the City, is listed in the 1803 directory.
Address '[28] Portland Place, Middlesex and Totteridge Place, Hertfordshire' (probate calendar).

Father Unknown.
Mother Unknown.
Education Unknown.
Marriage Unknown.
Religion Unknown.
Public None known.
Miscellaneous Nothing further could be found about him.
References *GM,* 1835, vol. II, p. 557; will (IR 11, online).

Name **Churchill, William** 1835/26
Dates Unknown–3 December 1835, Hill Street, Berkeley Square.
Probate £120,000 (PCC).
Occupation He appears to have inherited his money from his grandfather's brother Awnsham (sic) Churchill (1658–1728), a wealthy bookseller and politician, and a friend of John Locke. This great-uncle, who has an entry in the *ODNB,* purchased Henbury, Dorset. The family does not appear to be listed in Bateman, unless George Churchill of Alderholt, Dorset, who owned 2,210 acres worth £2,283 p.a. was a descendant. William Churchill does not appear to be directly related to the dukes of Marlborough or other titled Churchills. His fortune should thus be attributed to bookselling and perhaps publishing, plus land, although this is not clear enough to be more than likely. (If so, occupational categories V.27 and I; venue 2.)
Address 'Henbury [near Wimborne], Dorset and Hill Street, Berkeley Square, Middlesex' (probate calendar). In 1811, he lived at 24 Piccadilly and Henbury, near Wimborne, Dorset.
Father Probably Awnsham Churchill, nephew of the Awnsham Churchill noted in 'Occupation' above.
Mother Probably Sarah Lowndes of Sherperswell, Kent.
Education Possibly Eton and Peterhouse, Cambridge (admitted 1763), but it is not certain that this was the same man.
Marriage Apparently in 1770, to Louisa, daughter of Francis Greville, 1st Earl of Warwick and Broke. (The bridegroom in this case may have been a namesake.)
Religion Presumably Anglican.
Public None known.
Miscellaneous A surprisingly difficult identity to pin down. He may have been the 'Captain Churchill' who raised the Wimborne troop of Dorset Yeomanry in 1794. (*VCH Dorset,* vol. 2, p. 172).
References *GM,* 1836, vol. I, p. 99; *ODNB* for Awnsham Churchill; John Nichols and Samuel Bentley, *Literary Anecdotes of the Eighteenth Century* (1812), online.

Name **Davies, Mainwaring** 1835/27
Dates c. 1744–23 November 1835, Addington House, Buckinghamshire.
Probate £250,000 (PCC).
Occupation Apparently a 'broker' at Little St Martin's Lane, City of London (1808 directory), although this is not entirely certain. (If so, occupational cat-

egory IV.18 or 23? Venue 1?) Despite his uncommon name, he could not be found in other directories or sources. As he died at the age of ninety-one, his business activities might well have occurred before there were many comprehensive directories.

Address 'Formerly of Martin's Lane, Cannon Street, City of London, and then Addington House and Winslow, Buckinghamshire' (probate calendar).

Father Unknown.

Mother Unknown.

Education Unknown.

Marriage Unknown.

Religion Unknown.

Public None known.

Miscellaneous George Carr Glyn, the banker, was an executor.

References Above sources only.

1835/28 **Name** **Keppel, Sir William**

Dates Unknown (c. 1760)–11 December 1834, Paris. Oddly, his date of birth does not appear in any source.

Probate £100,000 (PCC).

Occupation 'General in the Army' (probate calendar). He was also Governor of Martinique in 1796–1802 and of Guernsey in 1827–34. (Occupational category VI.31.)

Address Lived at Bury Street, St James's, Middlesex, at death.

Father Unknown – again, oddly, no trace can be found of his parentage. This suggests that he might have been illegitimate. He is not listed in any genealogical guide as being related to the Keppels, Earls of Albemarle. According to Family Search, a William Keppell (sic) was baptised on 14 September 1756 at the Foundling Hospital in St Pancras.

Mother Unknown.

Education Unknown.

Marriage Unknown.

Religion Anglican.

Public Created GCB, 1815; PC, 1827. Groom of the Chamber to King George IV.

Miscellaneous He entered the Army in the 25th Regiment of Foot, 1777; Colonel, 1794; Major-General, 1796; Lieutenant-General, 1803; General, 1813. Colonel of the 2nd Regiment of Foot, 1828. Governor of Martinique, 1796–1802; Governor of Guernsey, 1827–34.

References Online sources only.

1835/29 **Name** **Thwaytes, William**

Dates 9 February 1748 or 1749 at Crosby, Westmorland–13 December 1834, Fenchurch Street, City of London.

Probate £700,000 (PCC).

Occupation Chiefly a tea merchant in the City of London (Davison & Newman, 44–6 Fenchurch Street, City of London) – described as 'grocers, tea merchants,

and confectioners' (1804 directory). The firm's address was also at Dunster Court, City of London. He is described as a 'grocer' in the probate calendars. His firm appears to have dealt mainly in tea but also provided other produce, clearly on a large scale. He also stated in his will that he owned Rose Hall in Jamaica and owned £20,000 of stock in the Hudson's Bay Company. (Occupational categories IV.19 and 21; venue 1.)

Address 'Fenchurch Street in the City of London' (probate calendar) is the only address given.

Father William Thwaytes, probably a farmer of Crosby, Westmorland.

Mother Ann, daughter of John Harrison of Reagill Grange, a tenant farmer.

Education Reagill Grammar School.

Marriage Married, but name unknown.

Religion Anglican; gave to the Church of England in Crosby.

Public None known.

Miscellaneous He began as a clerk with Davison & Newman in 1774. It was the tea of this firm that was thrown into the harbour of Boston, Mass., during the 'Boston Tea Party' in 1775. He became a partner in 1777 and sole owner in 1799. The firm had warehouses in Fenchurch Street and Lime Street in the City and in Jamaica. It also dealt in confectionery, sugar and other commodities and was apparently one of the largest firms of its kind.

References *GM,* 1835, vol. I, p. 218; Society of Genealogist sources.

Name **Ewart, Catherine** (probably née Bethune) 1835/30

Dates Unknown – probated 5 August 1835.

Probate £100,000 (PCC).

Occupation A 'widow' (probate calendar). She was probably the widow of John Manship Ewart (d. 19 March 1834; see 1834/7, left £120,000), who was probably a brandy merchant, although his occupation is unclear.

Address '[20] Bloomsbury Square, Middlesex' (probate calendar).

Father Unknown.

Mother Unknown.

Education Unknown.

Marriage See 'Occupation' above. According to Family Search, John Manship Ewart married, in 1812, Catherine Bethune.

Religion Unknown.

Public None known.

Miscellaneous Nothing more could be found about her.

References Probate calendar only.

Name **Steele, Joseph** 1835/31

Dates Unknown – probated in November 1835. He died at Hoddeson, Hertfordshire.

Probate £250,000 (PCC).

Occupation A 'surgeon' (probate calendar), apparently at Trinity Square in the City of London. (Occupational category VI.30; venue 1.)

Address 'Acrewalls, St Bees parish [near Whitehaven], Cumberland, and Trinity Square, Great Tower Hill, City of London' (probate calendar).

Father Unknown. His family were apparently gentry at Acrewalls and related to other local gentry. He was a relative of Christopher Steele (1733–67), the portrait painter, listed in the *ODNB*. Christopher Steele's father was John Steele (c. 1700–70), a tallow chandler.

Mother Unknown.

Education Unknown.

Marriage Unknown. According to Family Search, a Joseph Steele married a Sarah Sears in 1781 at St Dunstan's, Stepney, and a Joseph Steel [sic] married a Susanna Deverex [sic] in 1784 at the same church (which is near Trinity Square, where our Joseph Steele lived.)

Religion Unknown, presumably Anglican.

Public None known.

Miscellaneous Nothing more could be traced regarding how he became so wealthy as a surgeon, where he was educated, etc.

References Above sources only.

1835/32 **Name** **Croft, Thomas**

Dates Unknown–25 November 1835, Brighton.

Probate £200,000 (PCC).

Occupation A 'merchant' at 27 Guildford Street, Feundling (sic, i.e. at the Foundling Hospital), Middlesex (1825 directory). (Occupational category IV.21? Venue 2.)

Address 'Formerly of Guildford Street, Middlesex, and then of Montague Street, Middlesex' (probate calendar).

Father Unknown.

Mother Unknown.

Education Unknown.

Marriage Unknown. He may have been the father of Matilda who in 1852 married Sir Charles Felix Smith (1786–1858), army officer listed in *ODNB*.

Religion Unknown.

Public None known.

Miscellaneous Nothing more could be traced about him. His connection, if any, with the Foundling Hospital is unknown.

References *GM*, 1836, vol. I, p. 101.

1835/33 **Name** **Alison, Richard**

Dates Unknown – probated 1835.

Probate £200,000 (Chester Consistory Court).

Occupation A 'corn merchant' in Liverpool (Richard Alison, Senior & Junior, of 45 St Anne's Street, 1827 directory; Alison & Freeman, corn merchants, of 23 Brunswick Street, 1827 directory). (Occupational category IV.21? Venue 5.)

Address Liverpool.

Father Unknown.

Mother Unknown.
Education Unknown.
Marriage Unknown.
Religion Unknown.
Public None known.
Miscellaneous He is described as a 'gentleman' of Chatham Street and St Anne's Street, Liverpool in the 1832 Liverpool Poll Book.
References Above sources only.

Name **Heywood, Arthur** 1835/34
Dates 1753–1835 (probated PCC, October 1836).
Probate £400,000 (York PC) + £70,000 (PCC): £470,000.
Occupation Banker in Liverpool (Arthur Heywood & Sons, bankers, of 5 Brunswick Street, Liverpool, 1827 directory). 'Banker' of 5 Fenwick Street, Liverpool and Larkhill, West Derby (1827 directory). (Occupational category IV.16; venue 5.)
Father Arthur Heywood (1719–11 February 1795), banker of Liverpool. (Third son.)
Mother Hannah, daughter of Richard Milne of Wakefield.
Education Unknown.
Marriage Unmarried. His nephew John Pemberton Heywood (1803–77), who left £1.9 million, apparently inherited most of his estate.
Religion Presumably Anglican.
Public None known.
Miscellaneous He inherited the Larkhill estate in c. 1800. His family was one of the principal bankers in Liverpool and had previously financed slave-trading expeditions.
References 'Heywood-Lonsdale', *BLG*, 1914; family genealogy online.

Name **Thompson, Samuel** 1835/35
Dates 1766–1835 (probated PCC, January 1836).
Probate £100,000 (York PC) + £35,000 (PCC): £135,000.
Occupation Banker in Liverpool: a partner in Heywood & Co. (See previous entry.) (Occupational category IV.16; venue 5.)
Address Liverpool.
Father William Thompson, a 'sailmaker' of Liverpool.
Mother Unknown.
Education Unknown.
Marriage Date unknown, to Elizabeth, daughter of Joseph Brooks Yates of Liverpool. Their son, Samuel Henry Thompson (1807–92) left over £1 million; their grandson, Henry Yates Thompson (1838–1928) is in the *ODNB* as a 'newspaper proprietor and collector of illuminated manuscripts'. The *ODNB* lists a Joseph Brooks Yates (1780–1855), 'merchant and antiquary', but he cannot have been the father of Thompson's wife.
Religion Unknown. Joseph Brooks Yates was a Unitarian.
Public None known.

Miscellaneous Coincidentally, apparently a partner of the previous entry. He was apprenticed to Richard Heywood in 1780.

References Above sources only.

WEALTH-HOLDERS, 1836

Name **Woodhouse, William** 1836/1
Dates Unknown–20 September 1835, Marsala, Sicily (probated March 1836).
Probate £180,000 (PCC).
Occupation 'Wine merchant' at Toxteth Park, Liverpool (1827 directory); also, 'merchants and shipowners' (John, Samuel, and William Woodhouse, of 15 Henry Street, Liverpool, 1827 directory). Listed as a 'wine merchant' of Henry Street, Liverpool, in the 1832 Poll Book. (Occupational category IV.19 and 20? Venue 5.)
Address Ivy Cottage, Toxteth Park, Liverpool and Lodge Lane, Toxteth Park, Liverpool.
Father John Woodhouse (1731–21 December 1812) of Toxteth Park and Bootle, Lanacshire. (Third son.)
Mother Jane Heys (c. 1749–October 1781) of Everton near Liverpool.
Education Unknown.
Marriage To Sarah (1797–3 August 1867), marriage date unknown, daughter of (Revd) Humphrey Henry Clerk, Vicar of Bridekirk, Cumberland. (At least two sons, and one daughter.)
Religion Anglican; buried St Ann's Church, Liverpool.
Public None known.
Miscellaneous His dates could not be traced.
References *BLG*; Society of Genealogists.

Name **Motteux, Robert** 1836/2
Dates Unknown – probated August 1836.
Probate £120,000 (PCC).
Occupation 'Merchant' (Motteux & Co.) of 11 Walbrook, City of London (1824 directory). (Occupational category IV.21 or 19? Venue 1.)
Address 'Banstead, Surrey and [11] Walbrook, City of London, and Paris' (probate calendar).
Father Possibly John Motteux (1737–30 April 1793), Director of the East India Company, of St Stephen's, Walbrook and Beachamwell, Sandringham. He was descended from Anthony Motteux (d. 1718), dramatist.
Mother Unknown.
Education Unknown.
Marriage Unknown.
Religion Of Huguenot descent.
Public None known.
Miscellaneous As with so many 'merchants', what he dealt in isn't clear. His Paris address suggests that he traded with Europe.
References Society of Genealogists' archives.

Name **Naters, Thomas** 1836/3
Dates c. 1786–October 1836, Boldenburg, Switzerland.

Probate £120,000 (PCC) + £120,000 (Chester Consistory Court): £240,000.
Occupation 'Shipmaster and shipowner' (probate calendar) in Liverpool, then New York, and then Switzerland. (Occupational category IV.24; venues 5 and 29.)
Address 'Liverpool, and then Quebec, the New Town, Queen's County, Long Island [New York], and the Switzerland' (probate calendar).
Father Unknown.
Mother Unknown.
Education Unknown.
Marriage Unknown.
Religion Unknown.
Public None known.
Miscellaneous His heir was his kinsman William Mathers (1761–March 1863) and then Charles Thomas Naters Mathers (1822–73; see 1873/85, left £140,000), who lived in Newcastle upon Tyne. According to Newcastle sources, Thomas Mathers 'had assumed the name of Jacob Von Naters upon leaving New York in about 1824'. The details of his strange career are unknown, apart from his having been a successful shipowner, presumably in the Atlantic trade.
References Above sources only.

1836/4 **Name** **Brettle, George**
Dates 1778–1835.
Probate £300,000 (PCC).
Occupation 'Wholesale hosier' of Wood Street, Cheapside (probate calendar). His firm was also a hosiery manufacturer in Belper, Derbyshire. (Occupational categories IV.21 and II.9; venues 1 and 17.) The firm was founded by William Ward in Belper as Ward Sharpe & Co. Brettle joined as a partner in 1803, apparently handling the London mercantile branch as Ward Brettle & Co. and then George Brettle & Co.
Address 'Wood Street, Cheapside, City of London and Raleigh Lodge, Brixton, Surrey' (probate calendar).
Father Unknown.
Mother Unknown.
Education Unknown.
Marriage Unknown.
Religion Unknown.
Public None known.
Miscellaneous The firm supplied London drapers with cloth, hosiery, haberdashery and blankets and was one of the largest of its kind in the country. It continued into the twentieth century, chiefly as a manufacturer of underwear after the late nineteenth century. The George Brettle Warehouse in Church Street, Belper, built in classical style in 1834, still exists.
References Records of George Brettle & Co., 1799–1984, online; Negley Harte, *A History of George Brettle & Co. Ltd., 1801–1964* (1975).

Name **Fielder, Thomas** 1836/5

Dates Unknown – probated January 1836.

Probate £120,000 (PCC).

Occupation 'Stockbroker' (probate calendar) in the City of London. (Occupational category IV.23; venue 1.) He does not appear to be listed as a stockbroker in any London directory. The 1832 directory lists a Joseph Fielder, stockbroker, at 36 Throgmorton Street, City of London.

Address 'Formerly of the Stock Exchange and then of Dover Place, Newington, Surrey' (probate calendar).

Father Unknown.

Mother Unknown.

Education Unknown.

Marriage In 1785, to Jane Berry. Their daughter Jane (baptised 1788) married William Spong (1790–1839), a papermaker (Family Search; Andrew Ashbee, 'The Paper Makers of Snodland, c. 1740–1854', www.kentarchaeology.ac).

Religion Unknown. Presumably Anglican: he married in St Anne's Church, Soho, and his daughter was baptised in an Anglican church.

Public None known.

Miscellaneous Nothing more could be traced about him.

References Probate calendar and above sources only.

Name **Kennaway, Sir John, 1st Baronet** 1836/6

Dates 6 March 1758, Exeter–1 January 1836.

Probate £120,000 (PCC).

Occupation Soldier and official in the East India Company. (Occupational category VI.31; venue 29.) Afterwards, a landowner in England. In 1883, Sir John Henry Kennnaway, Baronet, owned 4,045 acres worth £5,038 p.a. in Devon.

Address Escott Lodge, Ottery St Mary, Devonshire.

Father William Kennaway (1717–93), woollen merchant of Exeter. (Third child.)

Mother Frances (1722–88), daughter of Aaron Tozer of Exeter.

Education Exeter Grammar School.

Marriage In 1797, to Charlotte (1768–1845), daughter of James Amyatt, MP, of Freemantle, Hampshire, a captain and merchant in the East India Company. (Seven sons, five daughters.)

Religion A 'devout' Anglican (*ODNB*). He gave to Anglican charities.

Public Created baronet, 1791.

Miscellaneous He entered the East India Company's military service at fourteen, through the patronage of a relative of his mother. He became associated with Lord Cornwallis and was the first British diplomatic representative at Hyderabad. He was created a captain in 1780, was Aide-de-Camp to Cornwallis and concluded an alliance with the Nizam of Hyderabad and an arrangement with Tipoo Sultan. Kennaway returned to England in 1794 and was blind in later life. He apparently became wealthy as a 'nabob'.

References *ODNB; GM*, 1836, vol. I, p. 313; BP.

1836/7 **Name** **Gandolfi, Joseph Thomas**

Dates Unknown – probated March 1836.

Probate £120,000 (PCC).

Occupation Probably a silk merchant in the City of London (P. & N. Gandolfi, of 30 Throgmorton Street, 1825 directory). (If so, occupational category IV.21? Venue 1.)

Address '[30] Throgmorton Street, City of London and Porto Bello House, East Sheen, Surrey' (probate calendar).

Father Probably Joseph Vincent Gandolfi, Italian merchant of East Sheen (*BLG*, 1846, 'Fitzherbert of Norbury').

Mother Probably Teresa, daughter of Thomas Hornyold of Blackmore Park.

Education Unknown.

Marriage Unknown.

Religion Presumably Roman Catholic.

Public None known.

Miscellaneous What his business dealt in remains elusive. It is possible that he was an import merchant trading with Italy.

References *BLG*, 1846.

1836/8 **Name** **Campion, Henry**

Dates 10 March 1762–'before 8 June 1836' (John Comber, *Sussex Genealogies*, 1931).

Probate £140,000 (PCC).

Occupation Probably a landowner, although his maternal grandfather, and possibly his father, were apparently merchants in Oporto, Portugal. In 1883, William Henry Campion, his descendant, owned 6,832 acres worth £7,891 p.a. in Sussex, Essex and Kent. (Occupational categories I and IV.19; venue 29?)

Address 'The Deanery, South Malling, Sussex' (probate calendar). His ancestor Henry Campion, MP, lived at Danny Place, near Hurstpierpoint, Sussex.

Father William Campion (1738–February 1818), JP, of Lewes, Sussex.

Mother Catherine (d. 1763), daughter of William Dawson of Portugal. She is apparently buried at Oporto, which would suggest that Henry Campion's father was living in Oporto at the time.

Education Unknown.

Marriage In 1807, to Frances (d.s.p., 1843), daughter of (Revd) Henry Watkins, Prebendary of York. (She married, second, Sir Fitzroy Maclean, Baronet.)

Religion Anglican.

Public None known.

Miscellaneous His occupation, if any, is unclear. He may also have been a merchant in Portugal.

References *BLG;* above sources.

1836/9 **Name** **Walshman, Thomas**

Dates 1750–2 April 1836, Kennington Common. According to Family Search, a Thomas Walshman was baptised on 10 June 1750 at Whalley, Lancashire.

Probate £160,000 (PCC).
Occupation 'Doctor of Medicine' (probate calendar). A 'physician and surgeon' of Kennington Common, Surrey (1830 directory). He is described as 'a practitioner in midwifery' in the *ODNB* entry for his partner Ralph Blegborough (1769–1827). (Occupational category VI.30, venue 2.)
Address Kennington Common, Surrey.
Father Unknown. Apparently John Walshman, if our man was the Thomas Walshman baptised at Whalley (see 'Dates' above).
Mother Unknown.
Education Unknown.
Marriage Unknown. His 'coheir' was Helen, daughter of John Aspinall of Standen Hall, Lancashire. She married John Lomax of Clayton Hall, Lancashire (*GM*).
Religion Unknown.
Public None known.
Miscellaneous Little about him could be traced in medical directories or alumni books. His education could not be traced. He was a partner with Blegborough from c. 1804.
References *GM*, 1836, vol. I, p. 564.

Name **Goodchild, Joseph** 1836/10
Dates c. 1756–27 October 1836, Southwark.
Probate £100,000 (PCC).
Occupation 'Window glass cutter' (sic) at 252 Tooley Street, Southwark (1794 directory) and at 2 Tooley Street (1825 directory). Thomas Goodchild is listed at the same address in the 1794 directory. In the *ODNB* entry for his son-in-law, he is described as a 'wealthy lead merchant from Hendon', but there is no other evidence that he was a lead merchant or lived in Hendon. (Occupational category II.11 and IV.20? Venue 2.) Joseph Goodchild, presumably a relative, was a glazier who worked on London churches in the early eighteenth century; a Mary Goodchild, probably that Joseph's wife, was a bricklayer (http://www.british-history.ac.uk/report.aspx?compid; see 38884: 'Minutes of the Commissioners: 1724', *The Commissions for Building Fifty New Churches: The Minute Books, 1711–27, A Calendar*, 1986, pp. 107–19).
Address 2 Tooley Street, Southwark (probate calendar).
Father Unknown.
Mother Unknown.
Education Unknown.
Marriage Name unknown. His daughter Elizabeth (1799–1857) married, in 1820, Thomas Wakeley (1795–1862), 'medical journalist and politician', listed in the *ODNB*, who founded *The Lancet*. (*ODNB* for their son James Goodchild Wakeley.)
Religion Unknown, probably Anglican.
Public None known.
Miscellaneous He was also a governor of St Thomas's and St Luke's Hospitals and several other charities (*GM*). Presumably he sold glass for buildings and windows.
References *GM*, 1836, vol. II, p. 664; *Whistler Studies*, online; *ODNB* as above.

1836/11 **Name** **Stowell, 1st Baron, William Scott**

Dates 17 October 1745, Heworth, Durham–28 January 1836.

Probate £250,000 (PCC).

Occupation Judge of the Court of Admiralty, 1798–1828. (Occupational category VI.29; venue 1.) He was the brother of Lord Eldon (1838/18), the famous Lord Chancellor.

Address 'Doctor's Commons, City of London and Erleigh Court near Reading, Berkshire' (probate calendar). He also bought an estate at Stowell, Berkshire, in 1811, allegedly for £165,000.

Father William Scott (c. 1696–1776), a 'coal trimmer' (coal merchant) in Newcastle upon Tyne. (First son.)

Mother Jane (1709–1800), daughter of Henry Atkinson, a 'coal agent'.

Education Newcastle Royal Grammar School; Corpus Christi College, Oxford (MA, Tutor, BCL; later DCL). Barrister, Middle Temple (called 1780).

Marriage First, in 1781, to Anna Maria (d. 1809), daughter of John Bagnall of Erleigh Court, Berkshire. (One son and one daughter surviving; the daughter married Henry Addington, Lord Sidmouth, the Prime Minister.) Second, in 1813, to Lady Louisa (d.s.p., 1817), daughter of Richard, 1st Earl Howe and widow of John, 1st Marquess of Sligo.

Religion Anglican.

Public MP (Tory) for Downton, 1790–1801; for Oxford University, 1801–21. PC, 1798; a member of the Board of Trade, 1798. Created baron, 1821.

Miscellaneous Advocate at Doctor's Commons, 1779; Advocate-General of the Admiralty, 1782–8; Registrar of the Court of Faculties, 1783–90; King's Advocate, 1788–98. Judge of the Consistory Court, 1788–1820. He was also Camden Reader in Ancient History at Oxford University, 1773–85. He was said to have had an annual income of £17,000 in 1807 from the Bar and Bench.

References *ODNB; GM,* 1836, vol. I, p. 427.

1836/12 **Name** **Haythorne, Joseph**

Dates Unknown – probated June 1836.

Probate £180,000 (PCC).

Occupation Banker in Bristol (Joseph Haythorne, 'banker', of City Bank, High Street, Bristol, 1830 directory). Joseph Haythorne and George Wright were partners in the City Bank, All Saints Lane, Bristol, 1794–1834 (online archives and 1822 directory). (Occupational category IV.16; venue 12.)

Address 'Bristol and Clifton, Gloucestershire' (probate calendar).

Father Unknown. Possibly Joseph Haythorne, who married Hester Taylor in Bristol in 1762 (Family Search).

Mother Unknown. Possibly Hester Taylor. (See 'Father' above.)

Education Unknown.

Marriage Unknown. She may have been the Elizabeth (surname unknown), who, in 1786, married a Joseph Haythorne at St Mary's, Westbury-on-Trym, near Bristol (Family Search).

Religion Unknown.

Public None known.
Miscellaneous Apparently a major banker to the local mercantile community. Haythorne and Wright may have been connected to the Atlantic slave trade. From RBSG/CFG Historical Research Report – May 2006, page 20 (online).
References Above sources only.

Name **Bolton, Sir Robert** 1836/13
Dates Unknown–15 March 1836, Swerford Park, Oxfordshire.
Probate £160,000, 'within province' (PCC).
Occupation 'General in the Army' (probate calendar). (Occupational category VI.31.)
Address 'Swerford Park, Oxfordshire' (probate calendar). He also purchased Little Tew, Oxfordshire in 1835.
Father Unknown. Remarkably, nothing could be traced about Sir Robert's background in any source.
Mother Unknown.
Education Unknown.
Marriage Name unknown. He had one son and one daughter. His daughter Louisa (d. August 1839) married Samuel Davis (d. 1874), who inherited Little Tew (*Notes and Queries* [1909], p. 307).
Religion Anglican; buried Swerford Church.
Public KCH, 1816; Knight Bachelor, 1817; GCH, 1834.
Miscellaneous As noted, nothing could be found in any source about his background or career.
References *Notes & Queries* discusses his church memorial.

Name **Gardner, John** 1836/14
Dates Unknown–1836.
Probate £180,000 (PCC).
Occupation 'Banker and common brewer [sic]' (probate calendar) in Cheltenham; 'brewer and banker' (*GM*, 1847, vol. I, p. 563). 'A country banker and Cheltenham brewer' (*ODNB* for Sir James Agg-Gardner). (Occupational categories IV.16 and III.12; venue 13.) ('John Gardner, brewer, of 160 High Street, Cheltenham' and 'Gardner & Co., bankers, of Cheltenham', 1822 directory.)
Address 'Cheltenham, Gloucestershire' (probate calendar).
Father Unknown.
Mother Unknown.
Education Unknown.
Marriage To Mary (d. 8 April 1847, aged ninety-seven), maiden surname unknown (*GM*, 1847, vol. I, p. 563). His property passed to his nephew, James Agg (sic) (1804–58), who changed his name to Agg-Gardner. The latter's son, Sir James Agg-Gardner (1846–1928), was a well-known, long-serving Tory MP who served for three terms in Parliament between 1874 and 1928, a period of fifty-four years (*ODNB*).
Religion Unknown.

Public None known.
Miscellaneous It isn't clear whether he was primarily a banker or brewer.
References Above sources only.

1836/15 **Name** **Sevier, John**
Dates Unknown–24 August 1836, Clifton.
Probate £160,000 (PCC).
Occupation 'Merchant' (probate calendar) in Bristol. (Occupational category IV.21? Venue 12.)
Address 'Formerly of Bristol and then of Stapleton, Gloucestershire, and then of Clifton, Bristol' (probate calendar).
Father Unknown.
Mother Unknown.
Education Unknown.
Marriage Unknown.
Religion Unknown.
Public None known.
Miscellaneous He is listed as 'gentry' in the Bristol directory for 1830, living at 20 Richmond Terrace. Nothing more is known of his career.
References *GM,* 1836, vol. II, p. 443.

1836/16 **Name** **Browne, Augustus**
Dates c. 1767–19 January 1836, Gretford, Lincolnshire.
Probate £100,000 (PCC).
Occupation A 'refiner' in the City of London ('Augustus Browne, refiner, of 23 Foster Lane, Cheapside', 1794 directory; 'Browne & Brind, refiners, of 30 Wood Street, Cheapside', 1825 directory). (A 'refiner' usually dealt with sugar or metals. It is unclear what Browne's firm actually did. Situated off Cheapside, it is likely that he dealt in metals, but this isn't certain.) (Occupational category II.11? Venue 1.)
Address 'Devonshire Place and [30] Wood Street, Cheapside, City of London' (probate calendar).
Father Unknown.
Mother Unknown.
Education Unknown.
Marriage Unknown.
Religion Unknown.
Public None known.
Miscellaneous Nothing more could be traced about him.
References Above sources only.

1836/17 **Name** **Hollond (sic), William**
Dates c. 1750–14 February 1836, Grosvenor Square, Middlesex.
Probate £1,000,000 (PCC).
Occupation 'Bengal Civil Service' (probate calendar). One of the wealthiest of the 'Nabobs', but virtually unknown, William Hollond was one of the few authen-

tic millionaires in Britain. How he amassed his great fortune is unclear. There is no biography in any obvious source. (Occupational category VI.31? Venue 29.) He is described in the *ODNB* entry for his daughter-in-law as 'a wealthy Bengal civil servant'. In 1883, his son (Revd) Edmund Hollond owned 4,243 acres worth £6,071 p.a. in Suffolk, Norfolk, and Dorset.

Address 'Formerly of Highnam Court, Gloucestershire, and then of West Horsley Place, Surrey and of Grosvenor Square, Middlesex' (probate calendar).

Father (Major) Richard Hollond (d. 1751), Commander of the East India Company's troops in Bengal, formerly of Madras (fourth son). (He is listed as 'John Hollond' in *BLG*, 1837.)

Mother Forename unknown, daughter of Edward Fowke of Horsley, Kent.

Education Unknown.

Marriage To Harriet (marriage date unknown), daughter of Thomas Pope. (Seven sons, four daughters.) A son was Robert Hollond, MP for Hastings, 1837–52, who married, in 1840, Ellen Teed (1822–84), in *ODNB* as 'society hostess'. His son Frederic Hollond (c. 1802–38); see 1838/21.

Religion Anglican.

Public None known.

Miscellaneous The exact nature of his great wealth remains largely a mystery.

References *BLG*, 1937.

Name **Gostling, Nathaniel** 1836/18

Dates 3 February 1758–12 April 1836, Sussex Place, Regent's Park.

Probate £100,000 (PCC).

Occupation 'Proctor of Doctor's Commons and Deputy Registrar of the Peculiar of St Catherine's' (Gostling wills, Society of Genealogists); 'Proctor' (probate calendar); 'N. Gostling & Son, of 7 Godliman Street, Doctor's Commons', 1823 directory; 'Notaries' at 7 Godliman Street, 1834 directory. (A 'proctor' was a solicitor in common or civil law, who generally dealt in cases of divorce or wardship.) (Occupational category VI.29; venue 1.)

Address 'Formerly of Knightsbridge and then of Earle's [sic] Court House, and then of Sussex Place, Middlesex and Doctor's Commons, in the City of London' (probate calendar).

Father Probably George Gostling (1714–82), Proctor to the Admiralty and Deputy Registrar of the Peculiar of St Catherine's. He also owned land in Essex and in Twickenham, Battersea, the Strand, and other parts of London.

Mother Ann Green (1722–97).

Education Unknown.

Marriage In 1785, to Elizabeth Theodosia Vaillant (1762–1818). (Six sons, five daughters.)

Religion Anglican.

Public None known.

Miscellaneous A successful solicitor in the civil courts with a lucrative niche market, apparently hereditary. He also bought a part of Brompton Road in 1803–8 and sold it in 1817 for £1,999! (*Survey of London*, vol. 41, 1983).

References *GM,* 1836, vol. I, p. 564; Society of Genealogists' sources.

1836/19 **Name** **Sparke, (Rt. Revd) Bowyer Edward, Bishop of Ely**
Dates 17 April 1759–4 April 1836, at Ely House, Dover Street, Middlesex.
Probate £140,000 (PCC).
Occupation Bishop of Chester, 1810–12, and Bishop of Ely, 1810–36. (Occupational category VI.30.) In 1883, Edward Bowyer Sparke of Gunthorpe, East Dereham, Norfolk, owned 5,447 acres worth £9,717 p.a. in Norfolk and Cambridge. It is not clear whether the Bishop owned any of this land in his lifetime.
Address Ely and Ely House, Dover Street, Middlesex.
Father William Sparke, a major of the 48th Regiment.
Mother Mary (d. 10 February 1813, aged eighty), surname unknown.
Education Eton; Pembroke College, Cambridge (Scholar; BA, 7th Wrangler; MA, DD).
Marriage In 1790, to Hester (d. 1836), daughter of S. Hobbs of Henstridge. (Two sons, two daughters; a son; see 1870/84 among wealth-holders.)
Religion Anglican clergyman.
Public None known. He sat in the House of Lords and is depicted, with other members, in the painting of the House of Lords during the trial of the Queen Caroline in 1820.
Miscellaneous He owed his advancement to the Duke of Rutland, whose tutor he was. He served as Dean of Bristol, 1804–10. He was an FRS and FSA, and the official Visitor for three Cambridge colleges. It is not clear whether he inherited much money, although his Eton education suggests that he came from a well-off background. He presumably amassed most if his fortune from his clerical income.
References *GM,* 1836, vol. I, p. 657.

1836/20 **Name** **Hartland, 2nd Baron, Thomas Mahon**
Dates 2 August 1766–8 December 1835.
Probate £120,000 'within province' (PCC).
Occupation Lieutenant General in the Army and landowner. (Occupational category I and VI.31.) In 1883, Henry Sandford Pakenham-Mahon of Stokestown owned 28,123 acres worth £15,080 p.a. in Ireland.
Address Stokestown, County Roscommon.
Father Maurice Mahon, 1st Baron Hartland (1738–4 January 1819), Irish MP and landowner; created Baron Hartland (Irish peerage) in 1800. (First son.)
Mother Catherine (d. 1834), daughter of Stephen Moore, 1st Viscount Mountcashell.
Education Portarlington School; Royal School, Armagh; Trinity College, Dublin; St John's College, Cambridge.
Marriage In 1811, to Catherine (d.s.p., 1873), daughter of James Topping, KC, MP, of Whatcrost Hall, Cheshire.
Religion Anglican.

Public MP (Ireland) County Roscommon, 1799–1800; MP (UK) County Roscommon, 1801–2; Governor of County Roscommon, 1819.
Miscellaneous Was a professional soldier in the Army – entered 1784; Lieutenant, 1790; Major, 1794; Lieutenant Colonel, 1797; Colonel, 1805; Major-General, 1811; Lieutenant-General, 1819. Also a great Irish landowner. He was succeeded by his brother. The title became extinct when the brother died in 1845.
References *BP; CP.*

Name **Robinson, Charles** 1836/21
Dates Unknown – probated June 1836 ('lately' – *GM,* August 1836) at Highbury Place, Islington.
Probate £120,000 (PCC).
Occupation 'Merchant' in the City of London. ('Charles and John Peter Robinson, merchants' of 6 Austin Friars, 1820 directory; Robinson, William Tooke & Co. of 5–7 Austin Friars, 1818 directory.) (Occupational category IV.21; venue 1.) He was also Lord of the Manor of Grandborough, Warwickshire, near Rugby.
Address 'Formerly of No. 6 Austin Friars, City of London, and then of Highbury Place, Islington, Middlesex' (probate calendar).
Father Unknown.
Mother Unknown.
Education Unknown.
Marriage Unknown.
Religion Probably Anglican – he left £100 to the vicar of Grandborough.
Public None known.
Miscellaneous As has proved so often the case regarding other wealth-holders, the precise nature of his mercantile activities is unknown. A John Peter Robinson, possibly his partner of the same name, is listed on Family Search as baptised in London in 1770, son of William and Catherine Robinson, and was married in London in 1823 to a Mary Ann Eldridge.
References *GM,* 1836, vol. II, p. 219.

Name **Tomline, William Edward** 1836/22
Dates 27 February 1787–28 May 1836, Great Stanhope Street, Middlesex.
Probate £400,000 (PCC).
Occupation Clerical fortune and landowner. The son of George Pretyman-Tomline, Bishop of Winchester (see 1827/10, left £200,000). In 1883, his successor Colonel George Tomline owned 26,914 acres worth £35,542 p.a. in Suffolk and Lincolnshire. (Occupational categories VI.30 and I.)
Address Riby Grove, Lindsey, near Grimsby, Lincolnshire.
Father (Rt. Revd) Sir George Pretyman-Tomline, Baronet (d. 1827), Bishop of Lincoln and then of Winchester. (First son.)
Mother Elizabeth, daughter of Thomas Maltby of Germans, Buckinghamshire.
Education Educated 'privately'; Trinity College, Cambridge (MA).
Marriage In 1811, to Frances, daughter of John Ambler of Ford Hall, Shropshire. (Three sons, two daughters.) (One son; see 1889/135.)

Religion Anglican.
Public MP (Tory) Christchurch, 1812–18; Truro, 1818–20, 1826–9; Minehead 1830–1. High Sheriff of Lincolnshire, 1824–5. He did not claim the baronetcy; his father inherited unexpectedly late in life.
Miscellaneous He apparently lived as a landowner in Lincolnshire and was a colonel of militia. He was a high Tory and member of the Pitt Club.
References *GM,* 1836, vol. II, p. 107; *BLG.*

1836/23 **Name** **Field, Michael**
Dates c. 1791–24 July 1836, Chester Place, Regent's Park.
Probate £120,000 (PCC).
Occupation Unknown. He may be the Michael Field listed as a 'stockbroker' at 4 Shorter's Court in the City of London (1829 directory). (If so, occupational category IV.23; venue 1.) There is no direct evidence for this, however.
Address 'Formerly of [26a] Bryanston Square, Middlesex, and then of Chester Terrace, Middlesex' (probate calendar).
Father Unknown.
Mother Unknown.
Education Unknown.
Marriage Unknown.
Religion Unknown.
Public None known.
Miscellaneous Nothing more is known about him.
References *GM,* 1836, vol. II, p. 220.

1836/24 **Name** **Holford, John Josiah**
Dates 5 February 1765–29 July 1836, York Place, Portman Square, Middlesex.
Probate £250,000 (PCC).
Occupation Merchant in the City of London ('Merchant' of 36 Old Broad Street, 1794 directory; Holford, Gonne & Co., merchants of 26 Old Jewry, 1815 directory; Holford Gribble & Co., of 26 Old Jewry, 1820 directory). (Occupational category IV.21 or 19? Venue 1.) He was also a landowner. In 1883, James Price Gwynne-Holford, MP, apparently a relative, owned 12,726 acres worth £17,741 p.a. in Glamorgan, Brecon and Carmarthen. Probably much of this was amassed after John Josiah Holford's death.
Address 'Formerly of [26] Old Jewry in the City of London, and then of York Place, Portman Square, Middlesex' (probate calendar). He also had an estate at Kilgwyn, Carmarthenshire.
Father Josiah Holford of Hampstead (will probated May 1817). (First son.)
Mother Magdalena (d. 1812), daughter of William Price.
Education Unknown.
Marriage In 1789, to Jane, daughter of Charles Jackson 'of the General Post Office, London' (sic) (*BLG*). (Four sons, two daughters.)
Religion Unknown.
Public None known.

Miscellaneous As is so often the case among these wealth-holders, the nature of his mercantile activities is unknown. He does not appear to have been related to the well-known Holfords of Weston Birt and Holford House.

References *GM*, 1836, vol. II, p. 331; *BLG*, 1846, 1937.

Name **Rothschild, Nathan Mayer** 1836/25

Dates 19 September 1777, Frankfurt–28 July 1836, Frankfurt.

Probate 'Upper Value', i.e. over £1 million (PCC). Rothschild left 'around £3.5 million' at his death, according to Niall Ferguson, in *The World's Banker* (London, 1998), p. 323. He was worth £1.5 million as his share of the bank and left £1.2 million to relatives in his will. He had also given away over £800,000 to relatives in his lifetime. The figure of £3.5 million excludes his land at Gunnersbury Park and his properties in Piccadilly.

Occupation Merchant banker at 2 New Court, St Swithin's Lane, City of London. (Occupational category IV.17; venue 1.)

Address 107 Piccadilly; Gunnersbury Park, near Acton, Middlesex. (Several Rothschilds later became significant landowners in Buckinghamshire, etc.)

Father Mayer Amschel Rothschild (1744–13 September 1812), antique-coin dealer, bill broker and moneylender in Frankfurt. (Third son.) He was Court Agent to the Landgrave William I.

Mother Gutele (1753–1849), daughter of Wolf Salomon Schnapper, a wealthy Frankfurt merchant.

Education Traditional Jewish education.

Marriage In 1806, to Hannah (1783–1850), daughter of Levi Barent Cohen, a leading merchant in London. (Four sons, three daughters.)

Religion Jewish.

Public Created a baron of Austria in 1822.

Miscellaneous The legendary founder of the English branch of the celebrated banking dynasty. Much of his career, for instance his learning of Wellington's victory at Waterloo ahead of anyone else through a message sent by carrier pigeon, is the stuff of legend. He began as a textile merchant in Manchester and was then a bullion broker in London before becoming a merchant banker. At his death, he was very likely the richest businessman in Britain, his only rival being the banker William Joseph Denison (d. 1849). He was also at the centre of the Anglo-Jewish 'Cousinhood' and was the brother-in-law of Sir Moses Montefiore (d. 1885, q.v.)

References Niall Ferguson, *The World's Banker* (1998); *ODNB; BP;* Chaim Bermant, *The Cousinhood* (1961).

Name **Clifden, 2nd Viscount, Henry Welborne-Agar-Ellis** 1836/26

Dates 22 January 1761–13 July 1836, Hanover Square, Middlesex.

Probate £180,000, 'within province' (PCC).

Occupation Landowner. (Occupational category I). In 1883, Lord Clifden owned 49,017 acres worth £38,915 p.a., chiefly in County Kilkenny and Northamptonshire.

Address Gowran Castle, County Kilkenny was the chief seat.

Father James Agar, 1st Viscount Clifden (1734–1 January 1789) of Gowran Castle, Irish MP; created an Irish baron in 1776 and an Irish viscount in 1781. (First son.)
Mother Lucia (d. 1802), daughter of John Martin of Dublin and widow of (Hon.) Henry Boyle Walsingham.
Education Westminster School; Christ Church, Oxford (BA).
Marriage In 1792, to Lady Caroline (d. 1813), daughter of George, 4th Duke of Marlborough. (One son; three daughters.)
Religion Anglican.
Public MP (Irish Parliament) Kilkenny, 1783–89. MP (UK Parliament; Tory, then Whig) Heytesbury, 1793–1802.
Miscellaneous In 1802, he inherited the barony of Mendip from his great-uncle and added the hyphenated suffix Ellis to his surname. A leading Irish landowner.
References *GM,* 1836, vol. II, p. 219; *CP.*

1836/27 **Name Cadell, Thomas**
Dates c. 1773–26 November 1836, Richmond, Surrey.
Probate £120,000 (PCC).
Occupation Bookseller and publisher on the Strand (Occupational IV.20 and V.27; venue 2.) It was known as Cadell & Davies from 1793. In later life he operated as a bookseller from his house in Charlotte Street.
Address 'Upper Charlotte Street, Fitzroy Square, Middlesex and the Strand, Middlesex' (probate calendar).
Father Thomas Cadell (1742–27 December 1802), an eminent bookseller and publisher of the Strand, London and an Alderman of the City of London. He published Edward Gibbon's *Decline and Fall of the Roman Empire,* as well as Adam Smith, Blackstone and Robert Burns, and was a friend of Dr Johnson.
Mother Forename unknown (d. 1786), daughter of Thomas Jones of the Strand.
Education Unknown.
Marriage In 1802, to Sophia (d. 1848), daughter of Robert Smith of Basinghall Street, City of London. (One son, four daughters.)
Religion Presumably Anglican.
Public None known.
Miscellaneous He continued his father's prosperous and leading business as a bookseller and publisher. He was a Liveryman of the Stationers' Company.
References *ODNB; GM,* 1837, vol. I, p. 110.

1836/28 **Name Johnston, William**
Dates c. 1752–20 October 1836, Muswell Hill, Middlesex.
Probate £100,000 (PCC).
Occupation Stockbroker in the City of London. ('J. Johnston & Co., stockbrokers', of 3 Pope's Head Alley, City of London, 1794 directory, which may refer to him or a relative. No other directory listings could be found.) (Occupational category IV.23; venue 1.)
Address 'Formerly of Tottenham and Stoke Newington, and then of Muswell Hill, Hornsey and the Stock Exchange, City of London' (probate calendar).

Father Unknown.
Mother Unknown.
Education Unknown.
Marriage Unknown.
Religion Unknown.
Public None known.
Miscellaneous His address confirms that he was a stockbroker.
References *GM,* 1836, vol. II.

Name **Craven, John** 1836/29
Dates 1760–4 December 1836, Stamford Hill, Middlesex.
Probate £180,000 (PCC).
Occupation 'Sugar refiner' in Duncan Street, Goodman's Fields (probate calendar). Goodman's Fields is near Fenchurch Street Station in Whitechapel, adjacent to the City of London. ('Craven & Bowman, sugar refiners', of Duncan Street, Goodman's Fields, 1815 directory). (Occupational category III.15; venue 2.) His premises were at 27 Goodman's Fields in 1785 and at Buckle Street, Whitechapel in 1798.
Address 'Formerly of Duncan Street, Goodman's Fields [Whitechapel], and then of [Craven Lodge] Stamford Hill, Hackney, Middlesex' (probate calendar).
Father Unknown.
Mother Unknown.
Education Unknown.
Marriage Married. Had at least one son, Arthur Craven, baptised at St John's, Hackney (Family Search; see also 'Miscellaneous' below).
Religion Unknown. Presumably Anglican.
Public None known.
Miscellaneous Refined sugar was often used in brewing as well as a sweetener. His house in Stamford Hill was noted for its gardens.
References *GM,* 1837, vol. I, p. 108; online sources.

Name **Vaughan, Margaret** 1836/30
Dates Unknown–19 November 1836, Manchester Square, Middlesex.
Probate £120,000 (PCC).
Occupation Unknown. She was apparently a relative, probably a cousin, of George Chapple Norton, MP (1800–75) and his brother Lord Grantley, but she could not be traced in any genealogy. In the *ODNB* entry for Norton's wife, Caroline Sheridan Norton (1808–77), 'author and law reform campaigner', Margaret Vaughan is described as Norton's 'rich cousin', and he was an heir in her will. According to her will, which is unilluminating, she also owned houses in Lower Seymour Street. The source and nature of her wealth remains unclear.
Address '1 Lower Berkeley Street, Manchester Square, Middlesex' (probate calendar).
Father Unknown.
Mother Unknown.

Education Unknown.
Marriage Unmarried.
Religion Anglican; she left legacies to Anglican charities.
Public None known.
Miscellaneous In her will, she left £40,000 to the Marquess of Headfort. She left sums to her brother 'Mr. Vaughan', and her residuary legatee was Lord Grantley.
References *GM,* 1837, vol. I, p. 107.

1836/31 **Name Chaumette, Lewis Andrew de la**
Dates 15 February 1763–1 January 1836, Bedford Place, Middlesex.
Probate £120,000 'within province' (PCC).
Occupation 'Stockbroker' (*GM*) and 'merchant' (1828 directory). 'L.A. De la Chaumette', 12 Angel Court, Throgmorton Street, City of London (1828 directory). He appears to have been chiefly, if not entirely, a stockbroker. (Occupational category IV.23; venue 1.) In 1794, he was a 'merchant' of Little Winchester Street, City of London. He appears in 'A List of the Names of the Members of the United Company of Merchants of England, Trading to the East Indies, 1815' (online) as 'Mr. Lewis Andrew de la Chaumette, Stock Exchange' entitled to two votes.
Address '[29] Bedford Place, Middlesex and Lordship Lane, Tottenham' (probate calendar).
Father Unknown.
Mother Unknown.
Education Merchant Taylors' School, London – attended 1772–8. No other information about him is given in its alumni directory.
Marriage Unknown.
Religion Unknown. He was presumably an Anglican, since he donated a gilt-lined silver chalice to Holy Trinity Church, Tottenham, which had suffered a robbery (William Robinson, *The History and Antiquities of the Parish of Tottenham,* vol. I [1840], p. 127). He was probably of Huguenot descent.
Public None known.
Miscellaneous He 'acquired a considerable fortune most honourably as an Exchange and Stockbroker' (*GM*). He also owned a 'valuable' library. He was an FRS.
References *GM,* 1836, vol. I, p. 563.

1836/32 **Name Lymburner, Adam**
Dates 1745 or 1746, Kilmarnock–10 January 1836, Bernard Street, Russell Square.
Probate £100,000 (PCC).
Occupation A 'merchant' at 157 Fenchurch Street, City of London from c. 1791, permanently from 1807. He went to Quebec in 1772 and became a prominent merchant there, as a whaler, sealer and salmon dealer. (Occupational category IV.19; venues 1 and 29.)
Address Lived at Bernard Street, Russell Square, Middlesex at death.

Father Unknown.
Mother Unknown.
Education Unknown.
Marriage Unknown, apparently unmarried.
Religion Buried St George's Anglican Church, Bloomsbury. Presumably Church of Scotland at birth.
Public None known.
Miscellaneous He was a prominent merchant in Quebec and has an entry in the *Dictionary of Canadian Biography* (but with few details about his background). He went to Canada in 1772 to take over from his brother John who had disappeared at sea. He served in the British militia in 1775 but was later a radical in politics and was an expert in constitutional law. 'A merchant in Quebec, 1791, and a gentleman of rare endowments and high attainments, was principally known as the part selected by the merchants and others of Canada, to proceed to England and advocate their rights before the Imperial government, and for the admirable and lengthy speech he made on behalf of the Canadians at the bar of the House of Commons' (Henry J. Morgan, *Sketches of Celebrated Canadians* [1862], p. 85). He lived permanently in London from 1807, presumably trading with Canada.
References *GM*, 1836, vol. I, p. 211; *Dictionary of Canadian Biography*.

Name **Pulsford, Robert** 1836/33
Dates Unknown – probated January 1836.
Probate £450,000 (PCC).
Occupation 'Robert and William Pulsford, West India merchants', of 7 Great St Helen's, Bishopsgate, City of London (1820 directory). The same firm was described in previous directories as 'wine merchants'. (See William Pulsford; 1834/17). (Occupational category IV.19 and 20? Venue 1.)
Address '[7] Great St Helen's, Bishopsgate Street, City of London' (probate calendar).
Father Unknown.
Mother Unknown.
Education Unknown.
Marriage Unknown.
Religion Unknown.
Public None known.
Miscellaneous See the entry for William Pulsford (see 1834/17), who was apparently his brother. Little more is known about them.
References Above sources only.

A **Levy, Henry Moses (Lyon)**, of Great Alie Street, Goodman's Fields, left £100,000, is listed in the PROB 8 probate calendar. All attempts to trace him have failed. He is not listed in the online comprehensive PROB 11 index of PCC wills. This entry is almost certainly a second, supplementary listing for Moses Lyon Levy (see 1830/37) of the same address and the same probate valuation, although the name has been recorded somewhat differently. 1836/33a

1836/34 **Name** **Farquhar, Sir Thomas Harvie, 2nd Baronet**

Dates 27 June 1775–12 January 1836, King Street, Middlesex.

Probate £120,000 (PCC).

Occupation Banker in Middlesex (Herries, Farquhar & Co., St James's Street, Middlesex). (Occupational category IV.16; venue 2.)

Address 'Polesden Lacey [near Dorking], Surrey' (probate calendar).

Father Sir Walter Farquhar, 1st Baronet (1738–21 March 1819), Physician to the Prince of Wales. (First son.) In the *ODNB.* He had a 'high-class clientele' which included William Pitt.

Mother Anne, daughter of Thomas (Alexander) Stevenson of Barbadoes, and widow of Dr Harvie.

Education Westminster School.

Marriage In 1809, to Sybella (d. 1869), daughter of (Revd) Morton Rockliffe of Woodford, Essex. (Three sons, four daughters.) Their daughter Eliza married, in 1836, Charles Grey (1804–70), 'army officer and courtier' (*ODNB*), the son of Prime Minister Earl Grey.

Religion Anglican.

Public None.

Miscellaneous He was a cousin of Earl Farquhar. His brother Robert Townsend-Farquhar was created a baronet in 1821. He was a colonial governor and has an entry in the *ODNB.* Sir Thomas was also a director of the Guardian Insurance Company, as well as a banker for the affluent in St James's.

References *GM,* 1836, vol. I, p. 314; *BP.*

Name **Davenport, Davies** 1837/1
Dates 29 August 1757–5 February 1837.
Probate £120,000 (PCC).
Occupation Apparently chiefly a landowner, although also from a Liverpool mercantile family. In 1883, William Bromley-Davenport, a successor, owned 15,647 acres worth £26,876 p.a. in Cheshire, Warwickshire, etc. In addition, Davies Davenport's uncle William (1725–97) is in the *ODNB* as a 'merchant and slave trader' in Liverpool, who also made substantial sums supplying bread to slave ships. Davies Davenport apparently inherited nearly half of that uncle's estate (*ODNB*). (Occupational categories I and IV.19 and 20; venue 5.) Davies Davenport's father was a barrister, apparently practising in Liverpool. He was also a barrister, but whether he practised is unclear.
Address 'Capesthorne [Hall], Cheshire; Brooks Street, Westminster, Middlesex' (probate calendar). 'Of Woodford, Marton, and Capesthorne, Cheshire' (*BLG*).
Father Davies Davenport (1723–12 February 1758), barrister of Woodford, Marton, and Capesthorne, Cheshire. Besides William (see 'Probate' above), another of his brothers was Sir Thomas Davenport, MP.
Mother Phoebe, daughter of Richard Davenport of Calverley, Cheshire.
Education Secondary schooling unknown; Brasenose College, Oxford. Barrister, Inner Temple (called 1786).
Marriage In 1777, to Charlotte, daughter of Ralph Sneyd of Keele Hall, Staffordshire. (Three sons, one daughter.) Their daughter Catherine (d. 1861) married Sir John Williams (1777–1846), in the *ODNB* as a judge.
Religion Anglican.
Public MP (—) Cheshire, 1806–30. High Sheriff of Cheshire, 1783–4.
Miscellaneous He inherited a 'handsome' estate in Cheshire (*HP*).
References Whether he was actively engaged in any trade or practised law is unclear. *BLG; HP.*

Name **Clifton, Sir Robert, 7th Baronet** 1837/2
Dates June 1767–26 April 1837.
Probate £160,000 (PCC).
Occupation Landowner. In 1883, Henry Robert Clifton of Clifton Hall owned 4,288 acres worth £8,682 p.a. (Occupational category I.) In addition, Clifton might well have inherited from Sir Thomas Lombe (1685–1739), the inventor of the silk-throwing machine, who left about £120,000. His daughter married Lombe's grandfather Sir Robert Clifton, 5th Baronet (1690–1762) (*ODNB*).
Address Clifton Hall (near Nottingham), Nottinghamshire.
Father Sir Gervase Clifton, 6th Baronet (1744–26 September 1815) of Clifton Hall, High Sheriff of Nottingham in 1767–8.
Mother Frances, daughter of Richard Lloyd of Aberbrachen, Denbighshire.
Education Rugby School.

Marriage Unmarried. He was succeeded by his brother as 8th Baronet.
Religion Anglican.
Public High Sheriff of Nottinghamshire, 1820.
Miscellaneous He may well have owned collieries, given his location.
References *BP; Complete Baronetage.*

1837/3 **Name** **Bold, Everilda** (sic) (probably née Patten)
Dates Unknown – probated November 1837.
Probate £100,000 'within province' (PCC).
Occupation She was probably the sixth daughter of Thomas Patten of Bank Hall, Cheshire (1719–19 March 1806), JP, DL, High Sheriff of Lancashire, 1793, and of Cheshire, 1775. His occupation is unknown, but he might well have been a Liverpool merchant or from a mercantile family. (If so, occupational category IV.19? Venue 5?) If so, she took the name Bold sometime after 1806.
Address Lived in Chester at death.
Father See above.
Mother Probably Dorothea, daughter of Peter Bold, MP.
Education Unknown.
Marriage Unmarried.
Religion Anglican.
Public None known.
Miscellaneous Anna Maria Bold (see 1814/1, left £100,000), who was married to Peter Bold, MP, appears to have been her grandmother. Peter Patten-Bold (c. 1764–1819), apparently Everilda's brother, was an MP, 1797–1818. Anna Maria Patten (see 1838/5) was apparently her sister. John Wilson-Patten, 1st Baron Winmarleigh (1802–92) was apparently her nephew. In 1883, he owned 5,338 acres worth £8,852 p.a.
References *BLG*, 1858; Society of Genealogists.

1837/4 **Name** **Soane, Sir John**
Dates 10 September 1753, probably at Goring-on-Thames–20 January 1837, Lincoln's Inn Fields, Middlesex.
Probate £140,000 (PCC).
Occupation The celebrated architect and Architect to the Bank of England, etc. (Occupational category VI.30; venues 1 and 2, etc.)
Address 'Lincoln's Inn Fields, Middlesex and Chelsea' (probate calendar).
Father John Soane (né Swan, then Soan) (1714–68), 'employed as a bricklayer'.
Mother Martha Marcy.
Education At a school in Reading kept by William Baker; later at the Royal Academy schools.
Marriage In 1784, to Elizabeth Smith (d. 1815), niece of George Wyatt, the 'wealthy builder'. (Two sons.)
Religion Anglican.
Public Knighted 1831.
Miscellaneous A genuine self-made man. Virtually nothing is known of his early

life. He was an errand boy to Charles Dance the younger, then gained 'practical experience' in Mr Holland's office, then studied in Rome. He was Architect to the Bank of England from 1788, Clerk of the Works at Parliament, to Chelsea Hospital, etc. He was Professor of Architecture at the Royal Academy, 1806. He is remembered as one of the most original architects of his time and as the founder of the Soane Museum, his house in Lincoln's Inn Fields.

References *ODNB*; *GM*, 1837, vol. I, pp. 321–5.

Name **Smith, George** 1837/5

Dates 30 April 1765–26 December 1836, Selsdon near Croydon.

Probate £200,000 (PCC).

Occupation Banker (Smith, Payne & Smith of Lombard Street, City of London; also Samuel Smith, Brothers of Hull). (Occupational category IV.16; venue 1, etc.) He was also Deputy Chairman of the East India Company, 1805–6, and involved in other activities in the City.

Address 'Selsdeon, Surrey and Lombard Street, City of London' (probate calendar); also George Street, Mansion House, City of London (*HP*).

Father Abel Smith (1717–12 July 1788), MP and banker, chiefly in Nottingham. (Fifth son.) According to the *ODNB* he left £59,953 and land.

Mother Mary, daughter of Thomas Bird, a 'wealthy silk manufacturer' of Barton, Warwickshire.

Education Unknown.

Marriage In 1792, to Frances (d. 1844), daughter of Sir John Frances Mosley, 1st Baronet, of Ancoats, Lancashire and Rolleston, Staffordshire. (Nine sons, six daughters.)

Religion Anglican.

Public MP (Tory) Lostwithiel, 1791–6, Midhurst, 1800–6, 1830–1, Wendover 1806–30. DL, City of London.

Miscellaneous He was in joint control of Smith, Payne & Smith with his brother John. His elder brother Robert (1752–1838) was created 1st Baron Carrington. George Smith was Director of the East India Company from 1795 to 1833. His bank is now part of National Westminster (NatWest) Bank.

References *HP*; *GM*, 1837, vol. I, p. 319; *ODNB* for relatives; J. Leighton-Boyce, *Smiths the Bankers, 1658–1958* (1958).

Name **Weare, William** 1837/6

Dates c. 1750–24 December 1836, Bristol.

Probate £100,000 (PCC).

Occupation Presumably a merchant in Bristol. (Occupational category IV.19 or 21? Venue 12.)

Address 'Formerly of Abbots Leigh, Somerset and then Bristol' (probate calendar).

Father William Weare (d. 15 January 1785), member of the Bristol Corporation, 1762–85; Sheriff, 1762–3; declined mayoralty, 1776. Warden of the Merchant Venturers, 1771–2.

Mother Unknown.

Education Unknown.
Marriage Unknown.
Religion Anglican.
Public Member of the Bristol Corporation, 1782–1835; declined mayoralty 1795.
Miscellaneous Presumably the brother of John Fisher Weare (see 1816/4).
References Graham Bush, *Bristol and its Municipal Government, 1820–1851* (1976); *BLG*, 1846.

1837/7 **Name** **Chapman, Sands (sic)**
Dates c. 1743–31 January 1837, Horsham, Surrey.
Probate £200,000 (PCC).
Occupation Stockbroker in the City of London. (Occupational category IV.23; venue 1.)
Address 'Formerly of the Stock Exchange, City of London, and then of Horsham, Surrey' (probate calendar).
Father Unknown.
Mother Unknown.
Education Unknown.
Marriage Unknown.
Religion Unknown.
Public None known.
Miscellaneous He does not appear to be listed in any London directory. He died at a very advanced age, and his business career probably occurred chiefly before there were many directories.
References *GM*, 1837, vol. I, p. 333.

1837/8 **Names** **Blair, Sir Robert**
Dates c. 1755–15 July 1837, Harley House, Bath.
Probate £140,000 (PCC).
Occupation 'General in the East India Company' (probate calendar), chiefly at Bengal. (Occupational category VI.31; venue 29.)
Address 'Formerly of Portman Square, Middlesex and then of Harley House, Bath' (probate calendar).
Father Daniel Blair of Burntisland, Fife. The family 'were collaterally related to the Blairs of Balthayock'.
Mother Barbara, daughter of Sir John Whitefoord of Milntown, near Ramsey, Isle of Man.
Education Unknown.
Marriage In 1790, to Herculina (d. 1822), daughter of Hercules Durham. (Two sons, five daughters.) Most of Blair's children were Bengal army officers or their wives.
Religion Presumably originally Church of Scotland.
Public Knighted 1815.
Miscellaneous An ensign in the East India Company's military, 1773. Lieuten-

ant, 1777; Captain, 1781; Major, 1794; Lieutenant Colonel, 1798. Commandant at Delhi and collected 'large sums of revenues' at Delhi. Colonel, 1804; Major-General, 1810. Returned to Britain, 1817. His brother William (1741–82) is in the *ODNB* as a 'naval officer', but with few biographical details.

References *GM*, 1837, vol. II, p. 85. V. C. P. Hodson, *List of Officers of the Bengal Army, 1758–1834* (1927), vol. I, pp. 160–1.

Names **Boileau, John Peter** 1837/9

Dates £180,000 (PCC).

Probate 30 November 1747–10 March 1837, Tacolneston Hall, Norfolk.

Occupation East India Company. He 'filled the highest offices in the Presidency of Madras, and returned to England with an ample fortune in 1785' (*BP*). (Occupational category VI.31; venue 29.) In 1883, a descendant, Sir Francis Boileau, owned 3,652 acres worth £5,146 p.a. in Norfolk.

Address 'Castlenau Place, Mortlake, Surrey' (probate calendar); also Tacolneston Hall, near Wymondham, Norfolk.

Father Simeon Boileau (1717–1 January 1767), a merchant of Dublin. (Second son.)

Mother Magdalen, daughter of Theophilus LaCour Desbrisay.

Education Unknown.

Marriage In 1790, to Henrietta (d. 1817), daughter of (Revd) George Pollen, Rector of Little Bookham, Surrey. (Three sons, one daughter.) Their son Sir John Peter Boileau, 1st Baronet (1794–1869), is in the *ODNB* as an 'antiquary'.

Religion Presumably Anglican; his father was a Huguenot refugee.

Public None known.

Miscellaneous He went to India with a relative, General Cailland. He served in Madras and became a landowner upon his return to England. *Officers of the Bengal Army, 1758–1834, Part One*, lists another John Peter Boileau (1787–1838), who was a colonel in the East India Company army. He was presumably a relative of our man, but not his son, as his father was named Solomon.

References *BP; ODNB* for son.

Name **Jenkins, William** 1837/10

Dates c. 1751–22 January 1837, Shepton Mallet, Somerset.

Probate £120,000 (PCC).

Occupation Unknown. He was probably a relative (nephew?) of Thomas Jenkins (1722–98), who is listed in the *ODNB* as an 'art dealer, painter, and banker'. William Jenkins may well have inherited part of his estate, but the source of his wealth is unclear. No one of this name is listed in Bateman as owning land in Somerset.

Address Shepton Mallet, Somerset.

Father Unknown.

Mother Unknown.

Education Unknown.

Marriage Name unknown. His daughter Marianne Jenkins (d. 1865) married in 1819 Edward Francis Colston (1795–1847). (Online peerage.)

Religion Unknown.
Public None known.
Miscellaneous He may have inherited part of a banking fortune in Shepton Mallet, but this is unclear.
References *GM,* 1837, vol. I, p. 333.

1837/11 **Name** **Verrall, William**
Dates c. 1759–31 January 1837, Southover, Lewes.
Probate £100,000 (PCC).
Occupation Probably a brewer in Southover. (*ODNB* for his grandson.) In 1867, William Verrall was listed in the local directory as a 'brewer and maltster' in Southover. (If so, occupational category III.12; venue 14.) A William Verrall, 'upholsterer' of Brighton and Worthing, was born in July 1755.
Address Southover near Lewes, Sussex.
Father Unknown.
Mother Unknown.
Education Unknown.
Marriage Name unknown. His daughter Sarah married George Grantham of Lewes. Their son was Sir William Grantham (1835–1911), a judge in *ODNB.*
Religion Anglican; buried St Michael's Church, Lewes.
Public None known.
Miscellaneous Nothing more could be traced about his career.
References *GM,* 1837, vol. I, p. 334; *ODNB* for grandson; Percival Lewis, 'The Verrall Family of Lewes', *Sussex Archaeological Collection,* vol. 58, pp. 90–131, which provides no details about this man.

1837/12 **Name** **Mangles, John**
Dates c. 1759–21 February 1837, Bath.
Probate £100,000 (PCC).
Occupation A ship-chandler at 214 Wapping (1773 directory); John & James Mangles, oilmen and ship-chandlers, 272 Wapping (1794 directory); also Mangles, Dutton & Co., wharfingers of Lower Thames Street. (Occupational category IV.21 or 25; venue 2.) The firm was also active as convict-contractors for Australia, and the family was significant in the early settlement of Western Australia. It was also active with the East India Company's trade.
Address 'Formerly of Hurley, Berkshire, and then Bath' (probate calendar).
Father Robert Mangles (1731–88), originally of Newcastle upon Tyne, who came to London about 1750 and established a ship-chandler's business. ('Australia, Ships, and Convicts', online). However, a ship-chandlers' firm of this name appears to be listed in an earlier eighteenth-century London directory.
Mother Unknown.
Education Unknown.
Marriage Name unknown. His daughter Frances married, in 1828, Charles Leonard Irby (1789–1845), naval officer and traveller, listed in the *ODNB.* Irby was the son of Frederick, 2nd Baron Boston.

Religion Presumably Anglican.
Public None known.
Miscellaneous His brother James (c. 1762–1838) was MP for Guildford, 1831–7. They appear to have been the uncles of Ellen Mangles, who married Sir James Stirling, the first Governor of Western Australia.
References *GM,* 1837, vol. I, p. 556; *HP* for brother; online sources.

Name **Parker, Robert** 1837/13
Dates Unknown – probated April 1837.
Probate £160,000 (PCC).
Occupation Unknown. He could not be traced in any source. He was almost certainly the Robert Parker who was the uncle of the poet Percy Bysshe Shelley. His career does not seem to be discussed in any biography of Shelley, although he is mentioned by name in many biographies.
Address 'Formerly Maidstone, Kent, and then Bath' (probate calendar).
Father Unknown.
Mother Unknown.
Education Unknown.
Marriage To Helen Shelley (see 1838/9), marriage date unknown, daughter of Sir Bysshe Shelley, 1st Baronet (1731–1815). She was the cousin of the famous poet and left £100,000.
Religion Anglican.
Public None known.
Miscellaneous He was the uncle by marriage of Shelley, the famous poet. In 1819, Shelley became attracted to Parker's ward Sophia Stacey, but nothing came of it.
References Percy Bysshe Shelley in *ODNB;* Parker's will, PROB 11 online; online sources.

Name **Villebois, John Truman** 1837/14
Dates c. 1769–1 April 1837, at Harmsworth House near Alresford, Hampshire.
Probate £250,000 (PCC).
Occupation Brewer in Brick Lane, London – partner in the brewery with Hanbury and Buxton. (Occupational category II.12; venue 2.) In 1883, Henry Villebois, who lived at Marham, Norfolk, owned 2,370 acres worth £2,171 p.a. in Norfolk. He was probably a descendant of this man's brother.
Address Harmsworth near Alresford, Hampshire (described in *VCH Hampshire,* vol. 5, p. 515, as Preston Candover, Hampshire).
Father William Villebois of Feltham, Middlesex.
Mother Unknown.
Education Harrow; Christ Church, Oxford (matriculated 1790).
Marriage Unknown.
Religion Presumably Anglican; probably of Huguenot descent.
Public None known.
Miscellaneous He inherited his partnership in the brewery from his grandfather,

Sir Benjamin Truman. As a child he was depicted in a famous portrait by Gainsborough. He was a Master of the Foxhounds in Hampshire and lived at Harmsworth from c. 1804.

References *GM,* 1837, vol. I, p. 556.

1837/15 **Name** **Poynder, Thomas**

Dates c. 1751–May 1837, Clapham Common.

Probate £350,000 (PCC).

Occupation Apparently a builder, chiefly in the City of London (Thomas Poynder & Sons, builders, of Bishopsgate Within, City of London – 1808, 1817, 1820 directories). (If so, occupational category II.10; venues 1 and 2.) Poynder & Hobson, 'lime burners' and 'builders' of Earl Street, Blackfriars and other places in London, is also listed in the 1823 and 1826 directories. In 1823, this firm was described as 'lime and Roman cement merchants' of Blackfriars, and, in 1826, as 'builders' of Shad Thames. An online London guidebook to the N7 area of London describes him as the 'chief developer' of Lower Holloway. In 1883, John Dickson Poynder of Hilmarton Manor, Calne, Wiltshire, apparently his grandson, owned 6,908 acres worth £14,928 p.a. in Wiltshire, Kent, etc. It is unclear how much of this was owned by Thomas Poynder.

Address Clapham Common, Surrey (probate calendar).

Father Unknown.

Mother Sarah, daughter of Allen Cooper of the East India Company.

Education Unknown.

Marriage Name unknown. His son T. H. A. Poynder, educated at Charterhouse, who died in 1874, left £100,000. Thomas Poynder's third daughter Sarah married (Rear-Admiral) John Bourmaster Dickson (1815–76). Their son was John Dickson Poynder, 1st Baron Islington (1866–1936), Tory, later Liberal MP and Governor General of New Zealand (*ODNB*).

Religion Anglican.

Public None known.

Miscellaneous He was also Treasurer of Christ's Hospital, 1824–35. His background and career are obscure.

References *GM,* 1837, vol. I, p. 667; above sources.

1837/16 **Name** **Robinson, Matthew**

Dates Unknown–20 July 1837.

Probate £100,000 (PCC).

Occupation Unknown. The most plausible possibility is James & Matthew Robinson, 'grocers and tea dealers' of 64 Red Lion Square, Middlesex (1808 directory). The 1826 directory lists a Matthias (sic) Robinson, 'grocer and patentees and inventors of prepared barley and groats' of 64 Red Lion Square. The 1817 directory also lists an 'M. Robinson, account and general agents', of 2 Mitre Court, City of London. There is no clue as to his occupation in his will, although he appears to have been a merchant of some kind in London.

Address 'Dulwich, Surrey' (probate calendar).

Father Unknown.
Mother Unknown.
Education Unknown.
Marriage Mary, surname unknown. He had a son named Augustus and cousins named Richard and James Robinson.
Religion Unknown.
Public None known.
Miscellaneous His will states that he owned an estate in Ponds End, Enfield.
References *GM,* 1837, vol. II, p. 325.

Name **Carbonell, John** 1837/17
Dates c. 1772–31 August 1837, Haling Park, Croydon.
Probate £140,000 (PCC).
Occupation Wine merchant in Golden Square Middlesex (Carbonell, Moody & Co., King Street, Golden Square, 1793 directory; 'wine and brandy merchant' of 91 King Street, Golden Square, 1837 directory). (Occupational category IV.20; venue 2.)
Address 'Formerly of [91] King Street, Golden Square, Middlesex; then of Golden Square; then of Haling Place, Croydon, Surrey and Regent Street, Middlesex' (probate calendar).
Father Unknown. Records at the Society of Genealogists list a John Cockerell, who died aged seventy-one on 9 April 1801.
Mother Unknown.
Education Unknown.
Marriage Unknown.
Religion Unknown.
Public None known.
Miscellaneous Apparently a successful wine merchant in the West End. As is so often the case, what set him apart from dozens of other wine merchants in London is unclear.
References *GM,* 1837, vol. II, p. 437.

Name **Cockerell, Sir Charles, 1st Baronet** 1837/18
Dates 18 February 1755, Bishop's Hill, Somerset–6 January 1837, Sezincote, Gloucestershire.
Probate £140,000 (PCC).
Occupation Banker in India (Cockerell, Traill & Co., of Calcutta) and then, from 1801 in the Strand, and then Pall Mall, Middlesex, and then at Austin Friars, City of London (Paxton, Cockerell & Traill; later Cockerell & Co.). (Occupational category IV.16; venues 2, 1, and 29.)
Address 'Formerly of Pall Mall, Middlesex, and then of Austin Friars in the City of London, and then of Sezincote [near Moreton-in-the-Marsh], Gloucestershire and Hyde Park Corner, Middlesex' (probate calendar).
Father John Cockerell (1714–67) of Bishop's Hill near Taunton, who had 'interests in the West Indies' (*ODNB*). (Fifth son.)

Mother Frances (d. 1769), daughter of John Jackson of Clapham, Surrey; Jackson was a descendant of the sister of Samuel Pepys.

Education Winchester College; Sharpe's School, Bromley-by-Bow (to learn accounting and bookkeeping).

Marriage First, in 1789, in Calcutta, to Mary (d.s.p., 1789), daughter of Sir Charles William Blunt, 3rd Baronet. Second, in 1808, to (Hon.) Harriet, daughter of John Rushout, 1st Baron Northwick. (One son, two daughters.) His son changed his surname to Rushout. In 1883, his grandson, Sir Charles Rushout, Baronet, owned 3,993 acres worth £4,864 p.a. in Gloucester and Worcester.

Religion Anglican.

Public MP (Tory, but pro-Reform) Tregony, 1802–6; Lostwithiel, 1807; Bletchingley, 1809–12; Seaford, 1816–18; Evesham, 1819–30, 1831–7. Created baronet in 1809. Recommended for a peerage in 1835 but didn't receive it. A Commissioner of the Board of Control, 1835–7. Postmaster-General in Bengal, 1804. Mayor of Evesham, 1810 and 1833. High Sheriff of Gloucestershire, 1814–15.

Miscellaneous Went to India, 1775, with the East India Company; Junior Merchant, 1785; Senior Merchant, 1790. Subsequently, from 1801, a successful banker, dealing mainly with India, in London and a long-time MP. He was also a director of the Globe Insurance Company and other concerns.

References *ODNB;* his brother Samuel Pepys Cockerell (1753–1827), is in the *ODNB* as an 'architect'.

1837/19 **Name** **Sawyer, George**

Dates c. 1764–21 July 1837, Ironhill near Bristol.

Probate £100,000 (PCC).

Occupation Unclear. His father was the Chief Accountant of the Navy Pay Office, and his brother was a 'very considerable landowner' (*HP*). It is unclear how George Sawyer accumulated his fortune. No one named Sawyer, owning land in Gloucestershire, is listed in Bateman.

Address 'Bath and Ironhill, Henbury, Gloucestershire' (probate calendar).

Father Anthony Sawyer (1713–84), Chief Accountant of the Navy Pay Office, of Heywood, Berkshire. His first wife was Anne, Countess of Ruglen, and his grandfather was Sir Edmund Sawyer (d. 1670), MP.

Mother Phoebe (d. 1813), daughter of Richard Harcourt of Wigsell, Essex, MP.

Education Unknown.

Marriage First, to the daughter (d. 1814; name and marriage date unknown) of Baron von Capellan of the Netherlands. (Five sons.) Second, to Marianne (marriage date unknown), widow of (Captain) William Maxwell.

Religion Anglican.

Public None known.

Miscellaneous His brother John (1762–1845) was an MP, 1790–1. He was educated at Eton and, as noted, owned 'very considerable landed property'.

References *GM,* 1837, vol. II, p. 324; *BLG; HP* for brother.

Name **Jones, Thomas** 1837/20
Dates c. 1748–11 October 1837, Stapleton (Bristol), Gloucestershire.
Probate £200,000 (PCC).
Occupation Probably a 'glass bottle manufacturer' in Bristol (Thomas Jones & Co., of Temple Back, 1805 directory). If so, occupational category II.11; venue 12. A Thomas Jones, 'merchant' of Barton Street, Bristol, is listed in the 1793 directory. His name makes a precise identification difficult. (*Alum. Oxon.* lists a Thomas Jones [d. 1848] of Magdalen College and Lincoln's Inn, son of Thomas Jones of Stapleton, Gloucestershire. He matriculated in December 1803, aged seventeen, and was thus born around 1786. He graduated in 1808 and was called to the bar in 1812.)
Address 'Stapleton, Gloucestershire' (probate calendar).
Father Unknown.
Mother Unknown.
Education Unknown.
Marriage To Frances, surname and marriage date unknown.
Religion Unknown, presumably Anglican if the above is his son.
Public None known.
Miscellaneous His executor was Robert Newton Shawe.
References *GM,* 1837, vol. II, p. 548.

Name **Perry, James** 1837/21
Dates Unknown–21 August 1836 (*BLG,* 1937, 'Herrick'), although his estate was not probated until November 1837.
Probate £250,000, 'within province' (PCC).
Occupation Probably ironfounders in Bilston, near Wolverhampton, Staffordshire and possibly related to the family of gunlock-makers of Wolverhampton, founded in 1660, although his occupation is unclear. (If either, occupational category II.3 or 5; venue 8.)
Address 'Wolverhampton' (probate calendar). A local directory lists him as of Graisley near Wolverhampton but does not give an occupation.
Father Unknown.
Mother Unknown.
Education Unknown.
Marriage Probably unmarried. His brother Thomas succeeded to the 112-acre Dippon's Farm (*VCH Staffordshire*). Thomas's daughter and heiress married Thomas Bainbridge Herrick. In 1883, 'Mrs. Perry-Herrick' of Beaumanor Park, Loughborough, owned 13,747 acres worth £22,325 p.a. in Leicester, Monmouth and Hereford. It is unclear how much, if any, of this land had been owned by James Perry.
Religion Presumably Anglican, although there is no direct evidence.
Public None known.
Miscellaneous A surprisingly obscure man to trace. Normally, it would be easy to trace a major wealth-holder in a provincial town such as Wolverhampton, but he has proved elusive. It seems likely that he was involved in engineering or iron-founding, but this cannot be precisely confirmed.
References *BLG,* 1937, 'Herrick'.

1837/22 **Name** **Russell, Sir Robert Greenhill, 1st Baronet** (né Greenhill)

Dates 1763–12 December 1836.

Probate £140,000 (PCC).

Occupation Barrister and Equity draftsman. He also succeeded to the estates of Sir George Russell, 10th Baronet (d. 1815) and took the name Russell. He inherited Chequers, later the official country residence of prime ministers, from his cousin Mary Russell. (Occupational categories I and VI.29; venue 2.) He was succeeded by Robert Frankland, MP, a relative. In 1883, Lady Frankland-Russell, presumably his successor, owned 2,531 acres worth £3,585 p.a., but in Yorkshire. Russell's father's grandfather was John Russell, a governor of Bengal.

Address 'Chequers Court, Ellenborough [Wendover], Buckinghamshire; Lincoln's Inn' (probate calendar).

Father (Revd) John Russell Greenhill, LL.D (d. 1813) of Costisford, Oxfordshire. (First surviving son.)

Mother Elizabeth, daughter of Matthew Noble of Sunderland, Durham.

Education Westminster School; Christ Church, Oxford; barrister, Lincoln's Inn (called 1790).

Marriage Unmarried. As noted, Robert Frankland, MP, inherited the bulk of his property.

Religion Anglican.

Public MP (Whig) Thirsk, 1806–32. (The seat was 'owned' by his kinsman Sir Thomas Frankland, 6th Baronet, MP.) Created baronet, 1831.

Miscellaneous It is difficult to disentangle the several sources of wealth of this long-serving MP. He appears to have been primarily both a landowner and a barrister.

References *GM*, 1837, vol. I, p. 204; *HP; BP.*

1837/23 **Name** **Auldjo (sic), John**

Dates c. 1759–25 January 1837, Mottingham House, Kent.

Probate £140,000 (PCC).

Occupation 'Underwriter and merchant' in the City of London – in the firm of Strahan, Mackenzie & Co., owned by his uncle, of 13 Cannon Street (1793 directory), 41 Finsbury Square (1803 directory) and 41 Cross Street, City of London (1826 directory). (Occupational categories IV.22 and 21; venue 1.)

Occupation 'Formerly of Finsbury Square, City of London, and then of Mottingham House near Eltham, Kent' (probate calendar). He also lived at 7 Lancaster Place, Middlesex.

Father John Auldjo (c. 1710–16 August 1786) of Portlethen, Kincardineshire, and Clayhills (Aberdeenshire?), and Aberdeen, a 'baker' but also Deacon Convenor of Trades. (Fourth son.)

Mother Margaret (d. 1803), daughter of Alexander Mackenzie, a 'merchant' of Aberdeen.

Education Unknown.

Marriage In 1798, to Jane (d. 1861), daughter of John Rose of Clara, Nairnshire and Charleston, South Carolina, a 'shipbuilder' of South Carolina and London. (Four sons, two daughters.)

Religion Presumably originally Church of Scotland; buried as an Anglican.

Public None known.

Miscellaneous Auldjo is a Scottish name. He benefited from the business connections of his uncle and possibly father-in-law.

References *GM,* 1837, vol. I, p. 332; *Scottish Notes & Queries,* 3rd series, vol. 12, no. 8, 1934, pp. 113 ff.

Name **Malcolm, Neil** 1837/24

Dates 26 July 1769–24 January 1837.

Probate £500,000 (PCC).

Occupation Merchant and planter in Jamaica and landowner in Scotland. (Occupational categories I and IV.19; venue 29.) In 1883, his son owned 85,611 acres worth £24,989 p.a. in Argyllshire, Lincolnshire, etc.

Address 'Poltalloch, Argyllshire; Hanover Square, Middlesex; and Lamb Abbey, Kent' (probate calendar).

Father Neil Malcolm (1736–1 April 1802), 11th Laird of Poltalloch, who was a Jamaica planter and merchant and was one of the progenitors of the Crinan Canal. (Only son.)

Mother Mary, daughter of John Brisset and widow of Philip Houghton of Jamaica.

Education Unknown.

Marriage In 1797, to Mary Anne (d. 1830), daughter of David Orme MD, a 'noted physician' of Lamborey, Kent. (Four sons, three daughters.) Their son John Malcolm (1805–93), educated Harrow and Cambridge, is in the *ODNB* as an 'art collector and landowner' and built up a foremost collection of artworks and rare books. He had a 'grand London townhouse' at 9 Great Stanhope Street, off Park Lane. His son was created 1st Baron Malcolm of Poltalloch in 1896.

Religion Presumably Church of Scotland, but his son John Malcolm was buried as a member of the Episcopal Church of Scotland.

Public JP, DL, Argyllshire and Argyle.

Miscellaneous A large-scale Scottish landowner whose family became wealthier as Jamaica sugar planters and merchants. The size of his estate, which excludes land, indicates that his mercantile activities were highly successful.

References *GM,* 1837, vol. I, p. 329; *BP; ODNB* for son.

Name **Robinson, William Tooke** 1837/25

Dates c. 1769–14 February 1837, Portman Square, Middlesex.

Probate £140,000 (PCC).

Occupation Merchant in the City of London ('Merchant of 6 Austin Friars, 1817 directory; 'merchant' of 43 Crutched Friars, 1812 directory). (Occupational category IV.21? Venue 1.)

Address 'Walthamstow, Essex' (probate calendar)

Father Unknown.

Mother Unknown.
Education Unknown.
Marriage Unknown.
Religion Unknown.
Public None known.
Miscellaneous A William Tooke Robinson (1820–84), possibly a nephew or grandson, attended Westminster School. As is so often the case with these wealth-holders, the nature of his mercantile activities is unclear.
References *GM,* 1837, vol. I, p. 330.

1837/26 **Name** **Greville, William Fulk** (sic; the middle name is spelled Fulk, not Fulke, in the probate calendar)
Dates 8 November 1751–14 January 1837 (probated 2 March 1837), Dover.
Probate £160,000, 'within province' (PCC).
Occupation Captain in the Royal Navy, although he had retired from sea duty by 1783. Lieutenant, 1775; Commander, 1782; Captain, 1783; Superannuated, 1804 (David Syrett and R. L. DiNardo, eds., *The Commissioned Sea-Officers of the Royal Navy,* 1994, p. 189). His father, an MP, was an ambassador and may have been a landowner, although there is no evidence that William Fulk Greville owned land. No one by his name of the county of Wiltshire is listed in Bateman. (Occupational category VI.31?, although this may not be wholly accurate.) It is certainly possible that his fortune derived in actual fact from land or another source not traced.
Address 'Formerly of Hanover Square, Middlesex, and then of Dover, Kent' (probate calendar).
Father Fulke (sic) Greville (1717–1806; some sources state 1805), of Wilbury, Wiltshire, MP, 1747–54 and Envoy to Bavaria, 1764–70. (Second son.) He 'gambled away his fortune' (*ODNB* entry on his wife). He was presumably related to the Elizabethan Fulke Greville, but no genealogy could be traced. He was also a patron of the arts and a patron of the musician Charles Burney (*ODNB* for Burney).
Mother Frances (c. 1727–89), daughter of James Macartney, a lawyer and landowner in Ireland, and cousin of Earl Macartney. She is in the *ODNB* as a 'poet'.
Education Unknown.
Marriage To Meliora (marriage date unknown), daughter of (Hon.) and (Revd) Richard Southwell. (Two sons, at least two daughters.) Their daughter Harriet (1788–1858) married, in 1820, James G. Moirier (1782–1849), in *ODNB* as 'diplomat and novelist'. Their daughter Caroline (1793–1837) married, in 1814, Field Marshal Sir Stapleton Cotton, 1st Viscount Combermere (he is in the *ODNB*).
Religion Anglican.
Public MP (—) Granard in the Irish Parliament, 1798.
Miscellaneous As noted, the source of his wealth is not entirely clear. It is possible that, besides any naval income, he was an Irish landowner, although there is no direct evidence. His sister was Anne Greville, Lady Crewe (1748–1818), in the *ODNB* as a 'Society hostess'.
References *GM,* 1837, vol. I, p. 220; David Syrett and R. L. DiNardo, eds., *The*

Commissioned Sea-Officers of the Royal Navy (1994), p. 189, for naval ranks held; *ODNB* for relatives.

Name **Jekyll, Joseph** 1837/27
Dates 1 January 1754–8 March 1837, New Street, Spring Gardens, Middlesex.
Probate £120,000 (PCC).
Occupation Barrister and Master in Chancery, 1815–23. (Occupational category VI.29; venues 1 and 2.) He may well also have benefited from his father-in-law, Hans Sloane, MP, who owned considerable property in west London.
Address '[6 King's Bench Walk], Inner Temple and New Street, Spring Gardens, Middlesex' (probate calendar).
Father (Captain) Edward Jekyll, of the Royal Navy (d. 1776), of Haverfordwest, Pembrokeshire. (Only son.)
Mother Elizabeth, daughter of Thomas Walter of Killiver, Carnarvonshire.
Education Westminster School; Christ Church, Oxford (MA); barrister, Lincoln's Inn (called 1778).
Marriage In 1801, to Maria, daughter of Hans Sloane, MP, of South Stoneham, Hampshire. (Two sons, one daughter.) She 'had a considerable fortune' (*DNB*).
Religion Anglican.
Public MP (Tory) Calne, 1787–1816.
Miscellaneous He became a KC in 1805, and a Bencher (1805), Reader (1814), and Treasurer (1816) of Lincoln's Inn. He served as Solicitor-General (1808–12) and Attorney General (1812–16) to the Prince of Wales, and was noted for his 'ready wit' and 'talent in epigram and repartee' as a barrister.
References *ODNB* as 'lawyer and politician'; *GM*, 1837, vol. II, p. 228; *HP*.

Name **Newton, Susannah Houblon** (née Archer) 1837/28
(sometimes written as Houblon-Newton)
Dates 17 May 1753–14 February 1837, Coopersale, Essex.
Probate £500,000 (PCC).
Occupation Landowner. She succeeded to her father's estates in 1800 and succeeded to her grandmother's estates in 1819 and took her surname, Newton. Her husband, of Huguenot descent, was also a landowner in Essex. In 1883, her descendant John Archer Houblon owned 15,515 acres worth £19,487 p.a. in Essex, Lincoln and Hertfordshire. (Occupational category I.)
Address 'Coopersale House [near Epping], Essex; Culverthorpe, Lincolnshire; and Dover place, Middlesex' (probate calendar).
Father John Archer (d. 1800), a landowner of Coopersale; Welford, Berkshire; and Holme and Highlow, Derbyshire. (Eldest daughter.)
Mother Lady Mary, daughter of John, 2nd Earl FitzWilliam.
Education Unknown.
Marriage In 1770, to Jacob Houblon (1736–14 October 1783) of Great Hallingbury, Essex. He was educated at Harrow and Cambridge; his father, Jacob Houblon (1710–70) was High Sheriff of Essex in 1757. (One son, two daughters.) Their son John Archer Houblon (1773–1831) was an MP.

Religion Anglican.
Public None known.
Miscellaneous The great size of her estate suggests that she had a considerable income, possibly from commercial sources as well as from land, which was reinvested. The Houblon-Newton Scholarship, offered by the Huguenot Society, is named for her family.
References *BLG.*

1837/29 **Name** **Carr, Ralph**
Dates c. 1769–5 March 1837, Park Crescent, Middlesex.
Probate £140,000 (PCC).
Occupation Barrister of 1 Pump Court, Temple (1812 directory); of 4 Essex Court, Temple (1837 directory). In 1812, he went the Northern Circuit. (Occupational category VI.29; venue 1, etc.)
Address 'Formerly Charlotte Square, Bloomsbury and then Park Crescent, Middlesex' (probate calendar). *Alum. Oxon.* states that he lived at Stannington, Northumberland and Barrowpoint Hill, Middlesex.
Father Ralph Carr of Whickham, Durham. He is described as 'Esquire, of Newcastle-upon-Tyne' in the son's entry in the Middle Temple Register. (Second son.) He was presumably Ralph Carr (1711–7 May 1806) who is featured in the *ODNB* as a 'merchant and banker' of Newcastle upon Tyne. He traded extensively with Europe and was one of the founders of the Newcastle Old Bank. He married late, in 1758, and fathered six children.
Mother If the father was the Newcastle banker, then the mother was Isabella (1727–97), daughter of (Revd) Henry Byrne of Pontland, Northumberland.
Education Secondary schooling unknown; Christ Church, Oxford (BA); Merton College, Oxford (MA); barrister, Middle Temple (called 1796).
Marriage Unknown.
Religion Anglican.
Public None known.
Miscellaneous Apparently a barrister in London and on the Northern Circuit, at least for part of his career. He presumably inherited money from his mercantile father.
References *GM,* 1837, vol. I, p. 443.

1837/30 **Name** **Erskine, Mary** (née Reid or Reed)
Dates Unknown – probated July 1837.
Probate £120,000 (PCC).
Occupation Unknown. She was the widow of Stewart Erskine (see 1826/13, left £140,000), probably a landowner.
Address 'Bromley Lodge, near Bromley, Kent' (probate calendar).
Father Forename unknown. His surname was Reid, or Reed (as in her will). His occupation and other details are unknown.
Mother Unknown.
Education Unknown.

Marriage To Stewart Erskine (c. 1751–31 July 1826; d.s.p.), of Park House, Maidstone and then of Bromley Lodge, Kent, a relative of the Earls of Kellie. (Marriage date unknown.) The source of his wealth is obscure, but he was probably landed.
Religion Presumably Church of Scotland or Anglican.
Public None known.
Miscellaneous Nothing more could be traced about her. Presumably she inherited the bulk of her husband's estate.
References *GM,* 1837, vol. II, p. 100.

Name **Oakes, Orbell Ray** 1837/31
Dates 1767–29 July 1837.
Probate £160,000 (PCC).
Occupation The son of James Oakes (1741–1829; see 1829/21, left £180,000), primarily a banker and also a yarn manufacturer in Bury St Edmunds. Presumably his son was involved in the family bank and benefited from it. (Occupational category IV.16, etc.; venue 11.) The son also became a landowner. In 1883, H. H. P. Oakes of Nowton Court, Suffolk owned 2,840 acres worth £4,317 p.a.
Address 'Bury St Edmunds, Suffolk and Nowton Court, Suffolk' (probate calendar).
Father James Oakes (1741–1829), banker, etc., in Bury St Edmunds, JP, DL, as above. (First son.)
Mother Elizabeth (d. 1802), daughter of Christopher Adamson of Wereham, Norfolk.
Education Unknown.
Marriage To Elizabeth (d. 1811), marriage date unknown, daughter of John Plamplin of Chalacre Hall, Shimpling. (Three sons, one daughter.) Her mother was the daughter of (Hon.) and (Revd) H. Hervey, son of the 4th Earl of Bristol.
Religion Anglican; his brother was a clergyman.
Public JP, DL, Suffolk.
Miscellaneous He purchased Nowton Court and other lands from the Earl of Bristol. His unusual name sounds remarkably like that of a contemporary Country and Western singer!
References *BLG,* 1837, vol. II, p. 325; *BLG;* sources in father's entry.

Name **Cardigan, 6th Earl of, Robert Brudenell** 1837/32
Dates 25 April 1769–14 August 1837, Portman Square, Middlesex.
Probate £350,000 (PCC).
Occupation Landowner. (Occupational category I.) In 1883, the Countess of Cardigan (the widow of the 7th Earl) owned 15,724 acres worth £35,357 p.a. in the West Riding, Northampton and Leicester. The 6th Earl's successor in the earldom in 1883 was George Brudenell-Bruce, 8th Earl of Cardigan and 1st Marquess of Ailesbury. In 1883, he owned 55,051 acres worth £59,716 p.a. in Wiltshire, Yorkshire and Berkshire. It is unclear how much of the property of either belonged to the 6th Earl, although he was plainly a great landowner.

Address 'Hambleden, Berkshire' (probate calendar). This appears to have been his principal seat.
Father (Colonel) Robert Brudenell, MP (1726–20 October 1768). (First son.) The 6th Earl succeeded his uncle, James, 5th Earl, in 1811.
Mother Anne (d. 1803), daughter of Sir Cecil Bisshopp, 6th Baronet of Parnham, Sussex, MP.
Education Harrow.
Marriage In 1794, to Penelope (d. 1826), daughter of George John Cooke of Harfield Park, Middlesex, Lady of the Bedchamber to Queen Charlotte, 1818. (One son, seven daughters.) Their son, John, 7th Earl of Cardigan (1797–1868) commanded the Light Brigade in the Crimean War; the cardigan garment is named for him.
Religion Anglican.
Public MP (Tory) Marlborough, 1797–1802.
Miscellaneous He was Equerry to Queen Charlotte, 1791–1810.
References *ODNB* for son; *GM,* 1837, vol. II, p. 421; *BP.*

1837/33 **Name** **Camac, William**
Dates c. 1762–11 August 1837, Harrogate, Yorkshire.
Probate £140,000 (PCC).
Occupation Presumably a merchant or East India Company official in Calcutta, in view of his address, although he is not listed in *Army Officers of Bengal.* Colonel Jacob Camac (1745–89), presumably a relative, led the expedition against the Marathas and made a fortune in India. Our man's brother Turner Camac (1751–1830) owned copper mines in County Wicklow and minted Irish coins. (Online sources). (Occupational category IV.19? and VI.31? Venue 29.)
Address 'Formerly of Calcutta, then Portman Square, Middlesex; then Mansfield Street, Middlesex; and then Hastings, Sussex' (probate calendar).
Father Unknown.
Mother Unknown.
Education Unknown.
Marriage In 1810, to Sarah, daughter of Wastel (sic) Brisco, JP, DL, Sussex and Yorkshire, of Coghurst (Hall, near Hastings), Sussex, a captain in the Coldstream Guards (*BLG*).
Religion Presumably Anglican, although the surname suggests possibly French ancestry.
Public None known.
Miscellaneous Nothing more could be traced about him, although his fortune appears to have been made in India.
References *BLG,* 1846; online sources.

1837/34 **Name** **Trotter, Sir Coutts (sic), 1st Baronet**
Dates 15 February 1767–1 September 1837, Grosvenor Square, Middlesex.
Probate £250,000 (PCC).
Occupation Banker in the Strand, Middlesex: senior partner, Coutts & Co.

(Occupational category IV.16; venue 2.) Thomas Coutts (see 1822/34), the wealthy banker, was his godfather and a relative. In 1883, his grandson, Sir Coutts Lindsay, Baronet, owned 5,288 acres worth £10,449 p.a. in Fife and Hereford. It is unclear how much of this, if any, was owned by Sir Coutts.

Address 'The Strand, Middlesex and Grosvenor Square, Middlesex' (probate calendar). He also had a residence at Westville, Lincolnshire (*GM*).

Father Archibald Trotter of Edinburgh, a banker and relative of Thomas Coutts. His mother was Jane, daughter of Sir Robert Stuart, Baronet, of Allenbank. (Fourth son.)

Mother Jean (Joan?), daughter of Robert Mowbray of Castle Law, Berwick.

Education Unknown.

Marriage In 1802, to Margaret, daughter of (Hon.) Alexander Gordon, Lord Rockville, a Scottish Lord of Session and the son of William, 2nd Earl of Aberdeen. (Four daughters.) Their daughter Susan (d. 1885) married the 6th Earl of Aberdeen. Their daughter Anne married (Lieutenant General) James Lindsay. James's son Robert Loyd-Lindsay, married the daughter of Lord Overstone, the great banker, and was created 1st Baron Wantage.

Religion Presumably Church of Scotland.

Public Created baronet, 1821.

Miscellaneous He was a relative of Thomas Coutts and was a partner in Coutts' Bank from 1793 to 1837 and senior partner upon Coutts' death in 1822.

References *GM*, 1837, vol. II, p. 422; *ODNB* for relatives; *BP*.

Name **Boyd, Walter** 1837/35

Dates 18 November 1753, Scotland–16 September 1837, Plaistow Lodge, Kent.

Probate £180,000 'within province' (PCC).

Occupation Financier and merchant banker in Paris and then of Boyd, Benfield & Co., Old Broad Street, City of London. (Occupational categories 17 and 18; venues 1 and 29.) Boyd's career was very complicated and is set out in his entry in the *ODNB*.

Address 'Plaistow Lodge near Bromley, Kent' (probate calendar); Putney Hill, Surrey (*HP*).

Father Unknown. No account of his life mentions his parentage, other than to say that he was born in Scotland.

Mother Unknown.

Education Possibly in Amsterdam and Switzerland, but this is unclear.

Marriage In c. 1790, to Harriet (d. 1833), daughter of Thomas Goddard of 30 Sackville Street, Middlesex. (Three sons, four daughters.)

Religion Presumably Anglican; presumably originally Church of Scotland.

Public MP (independent Tory) Shaftesbury, 1796–1802; Lymington, 1823–30.

Miscellaneous A brief summary of his complex career would note that he worked as a farm manager in Lincolnshire and possibly for Hope & Co. of Amsterdam, was then a factor to Patrick Herries, MP and worked in his bank. He then founded Boyd, Ker & Co., a merchant bank in Paris, 1785, where he remained until moving to London in 1792 and co-founding Boyd, Benfield & Co.

The bank crashed in 1799, but he re-emerged and was known as 'the dictator of the money market' and an important loan contractor. *GM* described him as 'the famous financier' at his death.

References *ODNB; HP; GM,* 1837, vol. II, p. 548.

1837/36 **Name** **Carr, Thomas**

Dates c. 1767–15 September 1837, Hampton, Middlesex.

Probate £120,000 (PCC).

Occupation 'Formerly Secretary of Lunatics and a Commissioner of Bankrupts' (*GM*), apparently at Bedford Row, Middlesex. He was seemingly a solicitor, since he is listed in the *Law List* for 1805 as a 'Secretary for Lunatics'. (Occupational category VI.29 and 31? Venue 2.)

Address '[1] John Street, Bedford Row, Middlesex and Hampton, Middlesex' (probate calendar).

Father Unknown.

Mother Unknown.

Education Unknown.

Marriage Unknown.

Religion Unknown, presumably Anglican.

Public None known.

Miscellaneous Nothing further could be traced about him.

References *GM,* 1837, vol. II, p. 437.

1837/37 **Name** **Lambert, Charles**

Dates c. 1768–6 October 1837, Eastbourne.

Probate £100,000 (PCC).

Occupation The only Charles Lambert listed in London directories was a 'haberdasher' of 80 New Bond Street (1793), a 'straw hat dealer' of 85 New Bond Street (1815–25), and a 'straw hat manufacturer' of 85 New Bond Street (1826). (If this was the same man, and identical to this wealth-holder, then occupational category IV.20 and II.11? Venue 2.) However, it is not absolutely clear that either or both were identical with the wealth-holder.

Address 'Fitzroy Square, Middlesex and Blendon Hall [near Bexley], Kent' (probate calendar).

Father Unknown.

Mother Unknown.

Education Unknown.

Marriage To Louisa Elizabeth, surname unknown. Their son Henry Thomas Lambert (b. 1812) married, in 1842, Mary, daughter of John Willes of Pembury (*GM,* April 1842). A Frances Thomasine, daughter of Charles Lambert and Frances Dutton, married, in 1800, Charles, 2nd Earl Talbot. But her dates (1785–1819) make it almost impossible for her to have been this man's daughter. *GM* states that he was sixty-nine when he died, suggesting that he was born in c. 1769. It is possible that his age at death was given inaccurately.

Religion Unknown.

Public None known.
Miscellaneous A rather elusive individual.
References *GM,* 1837, vol. II, p. 549.

Name **Fraser, George** 1837/38
Dates c. 1764–2 November 1837, Clifton near Bristol.
Probate £120,000, 'within province' (PCC).
Occupation 'Merchant' (probate calendar) of 8 New City Chambers, City of London (1826 directory). (Occupational category IV.21 or 19? Venue 1.)
Address 'Camden Hill, Kensington, Middlesex and [8] New City Chambers, City of London' (probate calendar); 'The Park, Scotland' (*GM*).
Father Unknown.
Mother Unknown.
Education Unknown.
Marriage Unknown.
Religion Unknown, but probably Church of Scotland.
Public None known.
References A James Fraser (b. 1740) was MP for Gatton, 1787–90. He was a merchant and apothecary of Golden Square, Middlesex, but there is no known connection between the two men. As is so often the case, the nature of our man's mercantile activities is unclear.
References *GM,* 1838, vol. I, p. 108.

Name **Paton, George** 1837/39
Dates c. 1768–5 July 1837, at Upper Gower Street, Middlesex.
Probate £100,000 'within province' (PCC).
Occupation 'Merchant' (probate calendar) of Bucklersbury, Cheapside, City of London (1817 directory) and 12 Pancras Lane, City of London (1826 directory). (Occupational category IV.21 or 20? Venue 1.) His venue near Cheapside suggests that he might have been involved in retailing or wholesaling.
Address 'Formerly of Bucklersbury, City of London, then of Pancras Lane, City of London, and then of Upper Gower Street, Middlesex' (probate calendar).
Father Unknown.
Mother Unknown.
Education Unknown.
Marriage Unknown. His son George (see 1894/95, left £113,000) was educated at Eton and Trinity College, Cambridge and was a barrister, but little could be found about our man in works listing alumni or in other books.
Religion Unknown, presumably Anglican, although the name suggests a Scottish background.
Public None known.
Miscellaneous Nothing more could be traced about him.
References *GM,* 1837, vol. II, p. 211.

1837/40 **Name** **Ashworth, Robert**

Dates Unknown–20 December 1837, Ramsgate.

Probate £120,000 (PCC).

Occupation Unknown. There are two possibilities in *BLG*, 1846: the son of Charles Ashworth, Governor of Oporto, and a Robert Ashworth who married Margaret, the daughter of Sir Benjamin Sullivan (d. 1810) of Wilmington, Isle of Wight, and Madras. No further information is given on either, and there is no evidence that either was this wealth-holder. His will (PROB 11 online) is brief and unilluminating.

Address 'Formerly of Bryanstone Square, Middlesex, and then of Ramsgate, Kent' (probate calendar).

Father Unknown.

Mother Unknown.

Education Unknown.

Marriage Unknown. He had at least two daughters. One was Emily, who married, in 1834, Sydney Cosby (d. 1840) (will). Her daughter Margaret married, first in 1855, John Childers Coote (1816–79), and, second, in 1886, Sir Charles Robert Piggott, 2nd Baronet (*BLG*, and *Visitation of Ireland*). Robert's daughter Marie married, in 1841, Wellesley Pole Cosby (d. 1842) (*BLG*, 1846).

Religion Unknown, presumably Anglican.

Public None known.

Miscellaneous Nothing more could be traced about him.

References *BLG*, 1846, and above sources.

1837/41 **Name** **Carver, William**

Dates Unknown – probated December 1837.

Probate £140,000 (PCC).

Occupation Unknown. Probably a merchant or banker in London, but there is no direct evidence. An executor was Abraham Wildey Robarts, a prominent City banker and wealth-holder. The only Carver listed in any relevant London directory was the firm Carver & Peet, 'Blackwell hall factors' of 67 Basinghall Street, City of London, listed in the 1817 and 1825 directories, but there is no direct evidence that he had any connection with this firm.

Address 'Formerly of Gosport, Hampshire and then of Long Stratton, Norfolk' (probate calendar).

Father Unknown.

Mother Unknown.

Education Unknown.

Marriage To Susannah, surname unknown. According to his will, he had two sons, James and William James. The latter was born c. 1792 and died after 1849. He was educated at Midhurst, Sussex and at Trinity College, Cambridge (BA, 1816) and became a clergyman in Norfolk. He was born in London, suggesting that the father was resident there in the 1790s (*Alum. Cantab.*).

Religion Anglican.

Public None known.

Miscellaneous Nothing more could be traced about him.
References Above sources only.

Name **Fellowes, William Henry** 1837/42
Dates 15 July 1769–23 August 1837.
Probate £140,000 (PCC).
Occupation Landowner. In 1883, his son Edward Fellowes, later 1st Baron DeRamsey, owned 20,021 acres worth £26,203 p.a. in Huntingdonshire, Norfolk, etc. (Occupational category I.)
Address 'Ramsey Abbey, Huntingdonshire and Lower Berkeley Street, Marylebone, Middlesex' (probate calendar).
Father William Fellowes (c. 1726–4 February 1804), MP, of Ramsey Abbey, Huntingdonshire and Nacton, Suffolk, landowner. (First son.)
Mother Lavinia (d. 1827), daughter of James Smyth of St Audries, near Watchet, Somerset.
Education Charterhouse; St John's College, Cambridge.
Marriage In 1805, to Emma, daughter of Richard Benyon, MP, of Englefield House, Berkshire. (Four sons.) Their son Edward Fellowes (1809–87), who served as an MP from 1837 to 1880, was created 1st Baron De Ramsey in 1887. His son Ailwyn Fellowes (1855–1924), MP, was created 1st Baron Ailwyn in 1921.
Religion Anglican.
Public MP (Tory) Huntingdon, 1796–1807; Huntingdonshire, 1807–30.
Miscellaneous He was a cousin of the Earl of Portsmouth and succeeded to Ramsey Abbey.
References *GM*, 1838, vol. I, p. 108; *BP*; *HP*.

Name **Prevost, William** 1837/43
Dates Unknown – probated January 1837.
Probate £100,000 (PCC).
Occupation Unknown. He is listed in only a few London directories, in the 'Court' rather than the 'Commercial' section, i.e. without an occupation; for instance, in the 1805 directory, he is listed as of 8 Red Lion Square. His Bedford Row address might indicate that he was a lawyer, but he is not included in any *Law List*. The 1825 directory lists a G. P. Prevost, stcockbroker, of 13 Copthall Court, City of London.
Address 'Formerly of [8] Red Lion Square, Middlesex, and then of [12] King's Road, Bedford Row, Holborn, Middlesex' (probate calendar).
Father Unknown. According to Family Search, a William Prevost was baptised on 20 March 1774 at St Leonard's, Shoreditch, son of John and Mary.
Mother Unknown. If the father was John Prevost (see 'Father' above), she was probably Mary Abart, who married a man of that name in 1772 at St Matthew's, Bethnal Green, or possibly Mary Magdalen Taunay, who married a John Louis Prevost in the same church the same year (Family Search).
Education Unknown.

Marriage Unknown. Perhaps she was the Mary Steward who married a William Prevost on 30 October 1808 at St Ethelburga's, Bishopsgate.
Religion Unknown. His name suggests possible Huguenot ancestry.
Public None known.
Miscellaneous Nothing more could be traced about him in any source.
References Above sources only.

1837/44 **Name** **Bennet, Elizabeth Amelia** (née Burrell)
Dates Unknown – probated March 1837.
Probate £120,000 (PCC).
Occupation Landed wealth, but probably with other sources. Her paternal grandfather was a 'considerable merchant' and government contractor in London. Her father benefited as Surveyor-General of Crown Lands. Because she was related to so many aristocrats, it is difficult to identify her landed property in Bateman. Bateman lists a Philip Bennet of Rougham Hall, Bury St Edmunds, who owned 3,949 acres worth £4,892 p.a. in Suffolk. Her brother, Peter Burrell, 1st Baron Gwydir (see 1820/23) married Baroness Willoughby d'Eresby in her own right. In 1883, Elizabeth Bennet's successor owned 132,220 acres worth £74,006 p.a., but not any in Hampshire. (Occupational category I, etc.)
Address 'Whitehall Gardens and Beauchamp Cottage, Niton, Isle of Wight, Hampshire' (probate calendar).
Father Sir Peter Burrell (1723–6 November 1775) of Langley Park, Beckenham, Kent; MP, 1759–74; Surveyor-General of Crown Lands, 1769–death; and barrister. His father Peter Burrell (1692–1756) was a 'considerable merchant' and government contractor (*HP*).
Mother Elizabeth, daughter of John Lewis of Hackney, Middlesex.
Education Unknown.
Marriage In 1766, to Richard Alexander Henry Bennet (c. 1742–14 March 1814) of North Court and Shorwell, Isle of Wight, MP, 1770–4. He was the son of Richard Alexander Bennet and Mary, daughter of Benjamin Ash of Ongar. *HP* gives no clues at to his source of wealth. His stepfather was Richard Bull, possibly a relative of the wealthy Bulls among the wealth-holders.
Religion Anglican.
Public None known.
Miscellaneous The Burrells were famous for their 'luck': her sisters married, respectively, the Earl of Beverley, the Duke of Hamilton and the Duke of Northumberland, and her brother was given a peerage and married a peeress with vast landed holdings. But how Elizabeth Bennet became so wealthy is not clear, and neither is her husband's source of wealth.
References *GM*, 1837, vol. I, p. 445; *ODNB* for relatives; *HP; BP.*

1837/45 **Name** **Fettes, Sir William, 1st Baronet**
Dates 25 June 1750, Edinburgh–27 May 1837, Gray Bank near Edinburgh.
Probate £220,374 (Scottish probate).
Occupation Primarily a military stores contractor in Edinburgh, then a land-

owner. (Occupational category IV.21 or 25; venue 23.) He was the founder of Fettes College, the Edinburgh public school.
Address Comely Bank and Redcastle, Edinburgh, and Whamphrey, Dumfriesshire.
Father William Fettes (d. 1750), a merchant of Edinburgh
Mother Margaret (d. 1782?), daughter of James Rae, 'surgeon'.
Education Edinburgh High School.
Marriage In 1787, to Maria (d. 1836), daughter of John Malcolm, MD of Ayr. (One son, predeceased.)
Religion Church of Scotland.
Public Member of the Edinburgh Town Council from 1785 and Lord Provost of Edinburgh, 1800–1. Created baronet in 1804.
Miscellaneous He began as a wine and tea merchant on High Street, Edinburgh c. 1768, became an insurance underwriter and banker, and then a military stores contractor, retiring about 1800 to become a landowner. He is said to have left £350,000–£400,000 to Fettes College, but the *ODNB*, probably more realistically, says that he left Fettes College about £166,000 at his death.
References *ODNB; Book of the Old Edinburgh Club* (1908), vol. V, pp. 152–70.

Name **Winter, Samuel** 1837/46
Dates c. 1771–6 November 1837, St Helen's Place, City of London.
Probate £120,000 (PCC).
Occupation 'Merchant' of 2 St Helen's Place, Bishopsgate Within, City of London. (Occupational category IV.21; venue 1.)
Address 'Of [2] St Helen's Place, City of London and South Wood House, St Lawrence, Isle of Thanet, Kent' (probate calendar).
Father Unknown. *BLG,* 1871, lists a Samuel Winter (d. 1811) who was succeeded by his eldest son, John Pratt Winter (d. 1846), High Sheriff of County Meath, but there is no mention of our Samuel Winter.
Mother Unknown.
Education Unknown.
Marriage Unknown.
Religion Unknown.
Public None known.
Miscellaneous The 1793 London directory notes a Samuel Winter, 'boatbuilder' of 88 Rotherhithe. As is so common in our study, the nature of his mercantile activities is not specified.
References *GM,* 1837, vol. II, p. 656.

Name **Bolton, John** 1837/47
Dates Baptised 13 April 1756, Ulverston–1837 (probated May 1837).
Probate £180,000 (PCC).
Occupation Merchant and shipowner in Liverpool ('Merchant' of 15 Henry Street; lived 98 Duke Street, Hanover Street, 1824 directory; 'Counting House' at 12 Henry Street; lived 88 Duke Street, 1805 directory). He was heavily involved in

the slave trade. (Occupational categories IV.19 and 24; venue 5.)

Address Liverpool and Storrs Hall, Ulverston, Lancashire.

Father Name unknown. Lived in Ulverston; was an apothecary.

Mother Unknown.

Education Unknown.

Marriage Name unknown.

Religion Baptised Anglican.

Public None known.

Miscellaneous At Storrs Hall, which he had purchased in 1806, he entertained Sir Walter Scott, William Wordsworth, George Canning and other notables. He was a large-scale merchant and shipowner in Liverpool and was known as a slave trader.

References Godfrey W. Mathews, 'John Bolton, A Liverpool Merchant, 1756–1837', *Historical Society of Lancashire and Cheshire,* vol. 93 (Liverpool, 1942); online sources.

Name **Lawrence, Robert John Grews** 1838/1
(sic; given as Grewse in *Alum. Oxon.*)
Dates Baptised 20 July 1796, St Marylebone–2 May 1838, Pisa, Italy. According to Family Search, he was born on 13 July 1796.
Probate £140,000 (PCC).
Occupation Unknown. His father was (Revd) Benjamin Lawrence (1759–18 February 1838), but nothing more could be traced about the possible sources of his wealth.
Address 'Gower Place, then No. 48 Montague Square, Middlesex, and then Pisa in Italy' (probate calendar).
Father (Revd) Benjamin Lawrence (1759–18 February 1838), who matriculated at Jesus College, Oxford, in November 1777. His address is given as Marylebone in his son's entry in *Alum. Oxon.*, but he was the rector of Darley Dale, Derbyshire from 1808.
Mother Mary Grews, who married Benjamin Lawrence in 1794.
Education Secondary schooling unknown; Christ Church, Oxford (entered February 1815, aged eighteen).
Marriage Unknown.
Religion Anglican.
Public None known.
Miscellaneous In his will he left a legacy to William Clark Loraine of Bedford Square, Middlesex, and Elm Lodge, Hempstead, Gloucestershire, on the proviso that he changed his surname to Grews. He did change his surname, in 1849.
References *GM,* 1838, vol. II, p. 110; will (PROB 11, online); Family Search.

Name **Kinloch, James** 1838/2
Dates c. 1776–29 August 1838.
Probate £120,000, 'within province' (PCC).
Occupation Presumably a merchant or official of the East India Company in Bombay. (Occupational category IV.19 or VI.21; venuc 29.)
Address 'Formerly of Bombay, and then Jermyn Street, St James's, Middlesex, and then of Fochabers, Morayshire' (probate calendar). He also owned Park House, Drumoak, Aberdeenshire.
Father Unknown.
Mother Unknown.
Education Unknown.
Marriage Unknown.
Religion Presumably Church of Scotland.
Public None known.
Miscellaneous Presumably a merchant or official in Bombay who then retired to London and Scotland. The gardens at Park House, designed by Archibald Simpson in 1823, are well known. An obelisk there records his dates.

References 'An Inventory of Gardens and Designed Landscapes in Scotland', online.

1838/3 **Name Egremont, 3rd Earl of, George O'Brien Wyndham**

Dates Baptised 18 December 1751, St Margaret's, Westminster–21 November 1837, Petworth.

Probate £250,000, 'within province' (PCC).

Occupation Landowner, with 'an annual income estimated at £100,000' and the owner of 110,000 acres (*ODNB*). In 1883, his illegitimate son Lord Leconfield owned 109,935 acres worth £88,112 p.a. in Sussex, Yorkshire, County Clare, etc. (Occupational category I.)

Address Petworth, near Chichester, Sussex was the principal seat. He also owned Egremont House, Piccadilly, but sold it in 1794.

Father Charles Wyndham, 2nd Earl of Egremont (1710–21 August 1763), landowner, in *ODNB*. (First son.)

Mother Alicia (c. 1729–94), daughter of George Carpenter, 2nd Baron Carpenter of Killaghy. (Irish peerage.) She married, second, in 1767, Hans Moritz, Count von Bruhl of Saxony.

Education Winchester; Eton; Christ Church, Oxford (matriculated 1767).

Marriage In 1801, to Elizabeth (d.s.p., December 1822), daughter of (Revd) Iliffe of Westminster School. He also had mistresses and an illegitimate son, who was given a peerage.

Religion Anglican.

Public Sat in the House of Lords for over seventy years, first as a Whig and then as a Tory lord lieutenant of Sussex, 1819–35.

Miscellaneous Was a renowned art collector who owned twenty Van Dycks and was one of the most successful racehorse-owners of his time, winning the Derby five times. FRS, 1787; FSA, 1800. He was one of the richest men of his time and allegedly gave away £12 million to charity. He was known until 1763 as Lord Cockermouth, his courtesy title.

References *ODNB; GM,* 1838, vol. I, p. 89.

1838/4 **Name Baskerville, John**

Dates Unknown–20 December 1837, Bath.

Probate £120,000 (PCC).

Occupation Apparently a landowner. In 1883, J. Baskerville of Crowsley Park, Oxfordshire, owned 2,392 acres worth £2,926 p.a. in Oxfordshire. Walter Thomas Mynors Baskerville of Clyro Court, Hay, owned 6,397 acres worth £6,350 p.a. in Radnor, Wiltshire, and Herefordshire. (Occupational category I.) His location near Bradford, Wiltshire, suggests a connection with the wool trade.

Address 'Formerly of Wooley near Bradford, Wiltshire, then Bath' (probate calendar).

Father John Baskerville (1745–15 March 1800) of Wooley, Wiltshire, JP, DL. (First son.) The family had been settled there since c. 1600.

Mother Hester, daughter of Nicholas Webb of Norton Court, Gloucestershire.

Education Unknown.
Marriage Unmarried. He was 'succeeded' by his cousin, Henry Viveash Baskerville (1793–1877) of Crowsley Park, Oxfordshire.
Religion Anglican.
Public None known.
Miscellaneous The source of his wealth apart from land is unclear. He was apparently unrelated to John Baskerville (1706–75), the famous printer.
References *GM*, 1838, vol. I, p. 220; *BLG*, 1937.

Name **Patten, Anna Maria** 1838/5
Dates c. 1757–10 December 1837, Bath.
Probate £100,000 (PCC).
Occupation Apparently a landed family, although probably with mercantile interests in Liverpool and Cheshire. See her sister Everilda Bold (see 1837/3). (Occupational category I?) The family apparently owned land in Warrington.
Address 'Formerly of the Bank, Warrington, and then Alfred Street, Bath' (probate calendar).
Father Thomas Patten (c. 1719–19 March 1806), JP, DL, of Bank Hall, Lancashire, High Sheriff of Lancashire, 1773, of Cheshire, 1775. (First daughter.)
Mother Dorothea, daughter of Peter Bold, MP.
Education Unknown.
Marriage Unmarried.
Religion Anglican.
Public None known.
Miscellaneous John Wilson-Patten, MP, 1st Baron Winmarleigh (1802–92) was apparently her nephew, the son of her brother Peter (d. 1819), MP. In 1883, he owned 5,338 acres worth £8,852 p.a. in Lancashire, Cheshire and Staffordshire and also land in Warrington.
References *GM*, 1838, vol. I, p. 109; *BLG*, 1846; *ODNB* for Lord Winmarleigh.

Name **Carter, John Bonham** (né Carter) 1838/6
(The name was often given as Bonham-Carter.)
Dates 1788–17 February 1838.
Probate £120,000 (PCC).
Occupation Primarily a barrister on the Western Circuit but also inherited money from his father, a prominent brewer in Portsmouth, and also inherited lands from Thomas Bonham (d. 1827) and added his surname. In 1883, John Bonham-Carter of Petersfield, Hampshire, owned 5,622 acres worth £6,260 p.a. in Hampshire. (Occupational categories I, II.12, and VI.29; venues 14 and 1.)
Address 'Of the Inner Temple, City of London, and then of Duke Street, Middlesex, and of Ditcham Gore, Hampshire' (probate calendar). Lived at 19 High Street, Portsmouth and at 16 Duke Street, Westminster (*HP*).
Father Sir John Carter (1741–1808), 'brewer' (*HP*), Mayor of Portsmouth, knighted in 1773. (First son.)
Mother Dorothy, daughter of George Cuthbert of Portsmouth.

Education 'Unitarian Academy, Cheshunt'; Trinity College, Cambridge (4th Wrangler; BA; Fellow); barrister, Lincoln's Inn (called 1819).
Marriage In 1816, to Joanna (d. 1884), daughter of John William Smith, MP for Norwich. (Four sons, four daughters.) Their son Henry Bonham Carter (1827–1921) is in the *ODNB* as a 'barrister and company director'. The family was well known in twentieth-century Liberal politics.
Religion Unitarian, but John Bonham Carter 'conformed' to Anglicanism upon attending Cambridge.
Public MP (Whig) Portsmouth, 1816–death, a pro-Reformer. Alderman of Portsmouth. Thirty-two members of his family were mayors of Portsmouth between 1747 and 1835.
Miscellaneous An 'eminent' barrister on the Western Circuit, who earned £1,850 p.a. as a barrister. His estates were worth about £4,000 p.a.
References *HP; GM,* 1838, vol. I, p. 429; *ODNB* for son.

1838/7 **Name** **Tritton, Henry**
Dates 26 February 1790–20 April 1838, St John's Hall, Battersea.
Probate £140,000 (PCC).
Occupation 'Banker' of Lombard Street, City of London (probate calendar) (Barclay, Bevan, Tritton, Twells & Co., Lombard Street). (Occupational category IV.16; venue 1.)
Address 'Lombard Street, City of London and St John's Hall, Battersea, Surrey' (probate calendar). He also lived at Lyons Hall, Great Leighs, Chelmsford, Essex (*BP*).
Father John Henton Tritton (1755–1833; see 1833/11), banker of Lombard Street and Battersea. (Second son.)
Mother Mary, daughter of John Barclay, 'banker' of Lombard Street, City of London.
Education Unknown.
Marriage Amelia (d. 1855), daughter of Joseph Benwell of Battersea. (Two sons.) Their son was Joseph Tritton (1819–87); his son Joseph Herbert Tritton (1844–1923) is in the *ODNB* as a 'banker'. The family was given a baronetcy in 1905.
Religion The family had been Quakers, but Henry's brother was an Anglican vicar, and Henry left a legacy in his will to the Minister of the Baptist Chapel in Battersea (*VCH Surrey*, vol. 10, 1912. He died at the age of only forty-eight.
Public None known.
References *GM,* 1838, vol. I, p. 665; *BP.*

1838/8 **Name** **Chalie, Matthew**
Dates c. 1745–22 May 1838. He was perhaps the Mathieu Chalie, son of Jacques and Marianne, who was born on 25 March 1747 and baptised on 15 April 1747 at St Martin Orgar French Huguenot Church, Martin Lane, London (Family Search).
Probate £400,000 (PCC).
Occupation Wine merchant in Mincing Lane, City of London, and the Strand,

Middlesex (John & Matthew Chalie, 'wine merchants', of 29 Mincing Lane, 1793 directory; Chalie & Richards, 'wine merchants', of 8 Wellington Street, the Strand, Middlesex, 1825 directory). The 1794 directory lists John and Matthew Chalie as 'merchants' of 29 Mincing Lane, and also a Francis Chalie, 'merchant' of 14 Mincing Lane. (Occupational categories IV.20 and 21? Venues 1 and 2.)

Address 'Formerly of Mincing Lane, City of London, and then of [8] Wellington Street, the Strand, Middlesex, and of Bolingbroke Grove, Battersea Rise, Surrey' (probate calendar).

Father Unknown. Probably Jacques Chalie (see 'Dates' above).

Mother Unknown. Probably Marianne, maiden surname unknown (see 'Dates' above). Matthew's granddaughter (see 'Marriage' below) was named Marianne Catharine.

Education Unknown.

Marriage Unknown. According to *GM,* 1846, vol. II, p. 207, Jane, the 'daughter and heiress' of Matthew Chalie, married Robert Vaughan Richards (c. 1791–2 July 1846), son of Sir Robert Richards, Chief Baron of the Exchequer. Robert Richards was educated at Oxford and was a barrister and QC. This marriage must have taken place in the 1820s. Matthew Chalie appears to have been around forty-six when the daughter was born. Her daughter was named Marianne, which strengthens the supposition that Marianne Chalie was Mathieu's mother.

Religion Unknown, presumably Anglican but seemingly of Huguenot origin.

Public None known.

Miscellaneous A wealthy wine merchant, but what set him apart from the hundreds of other wine merchants in England at the time is unclear.

References *GM,* 1838, vol. I, p. 666.

Name **Parker, Helen** (née Shelley) 1838/9

Dates c. 1755–probated July 1838.

Probate £100,000 (PCC).

Occupation Probably landed – the daughter of Sir Bysshe Shelley, 1st Baronet, and the aunt of Percy Bysshe Shelley the poet. (Occupational category I?) In 1883, Sir John Shelley, Baronet, of Shobrooke Park, Crediton, owned 6,500 acres worth £7,500 p.a. in Devon, and Lady Shelley of Maresfield Park, Uckfield owned 5,052 acres worth £6,023 p.a. in Sussex and Lancashire. Her husband, Robert Parker (see 1837/13) of Maidstone left £160,000, but the source of his wealth is unclear.

Address 'The Circus, Bath' (probate calendar).

Father Sir Bysshe Shelley, 1st Baronet (1731–6 January 1815) of Castle Goring and Dudley – he was created a baronet in 1806. (First daughter.)

Mother Mary (1734–60), daughter of (Revd) Theobald Michell of Horsham.

Education Unknown.

Marriage In 1782 to Robert Parker of Maidstone (see 1837/13), occupation unknown.

Religion Anglican.

Public None known.

Miscellaneous The poet Shelley was the son of her brother Sir Timothy Shelley,

2nd Baronet. She was also the aunt of Lord De Lisle and Dudley. The source of her wealth is unclear.

References *GM,* 1838, vol. II, p. 108; *BP.*

1838/10 **Name** **Sparkes, Robert**

Dates Baptised 25 December 1773, Wonersh, Surrey (Family Search)–14 June 1838, Stoke, near Guildford, Surrey.

Probate £160,000 (PCC).

Occupation Probably a landowner in Surrey, although this is not entirely clear. No one named Sparkes is listed in Bateman. According to an online genealogy, Richard Sparkes (1715–86), almost certainly this man's father, was a member of a family who were 'large landowners in the Bramley and Wonersh areas in the eighteenth and nineteenth centuries'. Wornesh is three miles from Guildford, Surrey. But the same source states that this man had a son, Richard, who died in 1815, who in turn had a son named Richard who died in 1850, although these dates might be inaccurate. *VCH Surrey* (vol. 3, p. 124) states that a Richard Sparkes bought Rowleys, Blackheath, in 1806 and was succeeded by his son John. The family also owned land near Godalming. The source of their wealth remains unclear. (Occupational category I?)

Address 'Stoke next Guildford, Surrey' (probate calendar).

Father Probably Richard Sparkes (see 'Occupation' above).

Mother Probably Sarah Attfield, who married a Richard Sparkes at Stoke, Surrey, in 1772.

Education Unknown.

Marriage Unknown. A Richard Sparkes married Sarah Ewen in 1806 in Abinger, Surrey. The Richard Sparkes who died in 1815 (see 'Occupation' above) had a wife named Sarah (d. 1837).

Religion Unknown. The Richard Sparkes who died in 1815 was buried in an Anglican church.

Public None known.

Miscellaneous A difficult case to unravel.

References *GM,* 1838, vol. II, p. 109; online sources.

1838/11 **Name** **Gower, Abel Anthony**

Dates 16 August 1748–1 October 1837, Glandovan, Pembrokeshire.

Probate £180,000 (PCC).

Occupation 'An eminent merchant in the City of London' (*GM*). ('A. Anthony Gower & Nephews, Cross Street, Finsbury Square, and 7 South Street, Finsbury Square, City of London', 1825 directory.) (Occupational category IV.21? Venue 1.)

Address 'Formerly of South Street, Finsbury Square, City of London, and then of Glendovan, Pembrokeshire' (probate calendar).

Father Abel Gower (1694–26 March 1788) of Glandovan, who had nineteen children. His occupation is unclear and is not noted in the *ODNB* entry for Sir Erasmus Gower. (Second son.)

Mother Letitia, daughter of (Revd) Erasmus Lewes.
Education Unknown.
Marriage Unknown; probably unmarried.
Religion Anglican.
Public JP, DL, Pembrokeshire; High Sheriff, Pembrokeshire, 1830.
Miscellaneous His elder brother was (Admiral) Sir Erasmus Gower (1742–1814), in *ODNB* as a 'naval officer and colonial governor'. A. A. Gower's property passed to his nephew, Robert Frederick Gower (1794–1884). None of the family appears in Bateman. A. A. Gower apparently made a fortune as a London merchant and then retired to Pembrokeshire. According to C. Gordon Winder, *William Edmond Logan (1798–1875): Knighted Canadian Geologist* (2004, pp. 55–6), it passed to his nephew Abel Lewes Gower (d.s.p., 1849). *GM,* 1839, records death of a namesake, Abel Anthony Gower, on 23 November 1838.
References *GM,* 1837, vol. II, p. 550; *BLG,* 1937; other sources as above.

Name **Longmore, John** 1838/12
Dates c. 1770–14 January 1838, Clifton, Bristol.
Probate £160,000 (PCC). Unusually, his will lists the 'value of his property' as of 1836, a total of £173,100 at that time.
Occupation Apparently a merchant in Bristol, but he does not appear to be listed in any directory. In his will he mentions his 'clerk' and 'bookkeeper'. (Occupational category IV.19 or 21? Venue 12.) He is listed as a 'gentleman' of Clifton Wood, Bristol in the 1830 Bristol directory.
Address 'Clifton, Bristol' (probate calendar).
Father Unknown.
Mother Unknown.
Education Unknown.
Marriage Susannah, surname unknown.
Religion Anglican; buried Clifton Church.
Public None known.
Miscellaneous His will mentions his brothers Joseph and Benjamin, and his nephew Charles Joseph Longmore Joseph apparently lived in Tewkesbury and was a member of its town council.
References *GM,* 1838, vol. I, p. 219; *BLG,* 1952; will (PROB 11, online).

Name **Plowden, Edmund** 1838/13
Dates c. 1755–4 April 1838, Haughton Hall, Shropshire.
Probate £250,000 (PCC).
Occupation Landowner. (Occupational category I.) In 1883, William Francis Plowden of Plowden, Shropshire, owned 5,934 acres worth £6,964 p.a. in Shropshire and Northampton. The family had been landowners in Shropshire since c. 1500. He does not appear to have had any other significant source of wealth.
Address 'Haughton Hall, Shifnal, Shropshire' (probate calendar). He also had a house at Aston-le-Wells, Northamptonshire.
Father Edmund Plowden (d. 9 January 1768), landowner. (First son.)

Mother Lucy (d. 1765), daughter of William Thompson of Leicester Square, Middlesex, and granddaughter of Sir Berkeley Lucy, Baronet.

Education Unknown.

Marriage In 1776, to Anna Maria, daughter of Robert Burton of Lougner, Shropshire. (One daughter.) His chief heir was his nephew William Henry Francis Plowden (d. 1870). Edwin Plowden, Baron Plowden (1907–2001), public servant, was a relative.

Religion Roman Catholic; a prominent Catholic family.

Public None known.

Miscellaneous His religion probably debarred him from serving in official positions, at least before the latter part of his life.

References *GM,* 1838, vol. I, p. 658; *BLG,* 1937.

1838/14 **Name** **Attwood, Matthias**

Dates 1746–24 November 1836. (The estate was not probated until 1838.)

Probate £120,000 (PCC).

Occupation Initially an ironmaster in the Black Country and then a banker (Spooner & Attwood) in Birmingham. (Occupational categories II.3 and IV.16; venue 8.)

Address Hawne House, Halesowen, Shropshire. His father 'purchased the celebrated estate of the Leasowes, near Hales Owen' (*HP*), but no Attwood is listed in Bateman.

Father George Attwood (1721–19 April 1807) of Haden Cross; he purchased Hawne House, but his occupation is unclear. (Third son.)

Mother Rachel, daughter of Samuel Gaunt of Green House, Rowley Regis.

Education Unknown.

Marriage In 1775, to Ann (1752–1835), daughter of Thomas Adams, a 'yeoman farmer' of Cakemore House near Halesowen. (Seven sons, four daughters.) Their son George (1791–1875) is in the *ODNB* as an 'ironmaster'. Their son Thomas (1783–1856), the well-known currency reformer, is in the *ODNB* as a 'banker and radical M.P.'.

Religion Anglican.

Public JP, DL, Worcestershire, Staffordshire, Shropshire.

Miscellaneous He 'made a fortune from steel converting, the manufacture of nails and Swedish iron sales' (T. S. Ashton in *HP*) and then, in 1791, was a founder and partner in Spooner & Attwood's Bank in Birmingham. It had a London branch from 1801.

References *ODNB* for relatives; *HP* for son; *BLG,* 1937.

1838/15 **Name** **Nicholl, Sir John**

Dates 16 March 1759–26 August 1838, Merthyr Mawr, Glamorganshire.

Probate £140,000 (PCC).

Occupation Judge of the High Court of Admiralty, 1809–34, and Dean of Arches and Judge of the Prerogative Court of Canterbury, 1834–5. (Occupational category VI.29; venue 1.) In 1883, John Cole Nicholl of Merthyr Mawr owned 4,894 acres worth £6,565 p.a. in Glamorganshire.

Address 'Formerly of Bedford Square, Middlesex, then of Lincoln's Inn Fields and Bruton Street, Berkeley Square, Middlesex; then of Audley Street, Middlesex and Merthyrmawr, Glamorganshire' (probate calendar).
Father John Nicholl (c. 1726–21 February 1773), of the 'minor gentry' (*ODNB*) of Llanmaes, Glamorgan. (Second son.)
Mother Elizabeth, daughter of James Havard of Herefordshire.
Education Cowbridge Grammar School; Bristol Grammar School; St John's College, Oxford (Founders' Kin Fellow; BCL; DCL). Admitted an advocate of Doctor's Commons, 1785.
Marriage In 1787, to Judy (1760–December 1829), daughter of Peter Birt of Wenvoe Castle. (One son, three daughters.)
Religion Anglican and a member of the committee of the Society for the Promotion of Christian Knowledge.
Public MP (Tory) Penrhyn, 1802–6; Hastings, 1806; Rye, 1807; Great Bedwin, 1813–31. PC, 1809; knighted, 1798.
Miscellaneous Made a King's Advocate in 1798 and then a judge in the Probate and Admiralty Courts. A strong Tory and a lieutenant colonel in the St Giles and Bloomsbury Volunteers. Doctor's Commons had many critics at this time.
References *ODNB; GM,* 1838, vol. II, p. 546; *HP; BLG,* 1937.

Name **Blicke, Charles Tufton** 1838/16
Dates c. 1782–28 July 1837, Park Crescent, Middlesex.
Probate £100,000 (PCC).
Occupation Medical fortune – he was the son of Sir Charles Blicke (see 1816/23), Surgeon to St Bartholomew's Hospital, who left £160,000. (Occupational category VI.30; venues 1 and 2.)
Address 'Regent Street and Park Crescent, Middlesex' (probate calendar).
Father Sir Charles Blicke (1745–30 December 1815), surgeon and physician of London, in *ODNB.*
Mother Unknown.
Education Secondary schooling unknown; Queen's College, Oxford (matriculated 1798; BA, 1802; MA, 1808). Entered Lincoln's Inn, 1808, but does not appear to have been a barrister.
Marriage Unmarried.
Religion Anglican.
Public None known.
Miscellaneous He does not appear to have had any profession or occupation.
References *GM,* 1837, vol. II, p. 323; *ODNB* for father.

Name **Woolmore, Sir John** 1838/17
Dates Baptised 4 May 1755, St Mary's Whitechapel–2 December 1837, Bruton Street, Middlesex.
Probate £180,000 (PCC).
Occupation Shipshusband and shipowner in London. (Occupational categories IV.24 and 25; venues 1 and 2.) and Chairman of the East India Dock Company.

(As a 'shipshusband' he was an agent who managed the affairs of a vessel in port on behalf of the owner.)

Address 'Hampton, Middlesex and [15] Bruton Street Berkeley Square, Middlesex' (probate calendar). In 1802, his addresses were 12 Bishopsgate Street, City of London and Queen Square, Bloomsbury, Middlesex.

Father John Woolmore, an 'innholder' or 'victualler' of Ramsay Lane, Whitechapel (Tony Fuller, online).

Mother Ann, surname unknown.

Education Unknown.

Marriage First, in 1778, to Margaret Wickham, née Mason, of St Dunstan, Stepney (d.s.p.); second, in 1790, to Harriet (d. 1845), daughter of John Turner of Limehouse and sister of Charles Hampden Turner of Rooks Nest, Godstone, Surrey.

Religion Anglican; buried in Poplar Church.

Public MP (pro-Grenville) Westbury, 1806–7. Knighted, 1834; KCH, 1834.

Miscellaneous Entered the East India Company's navy, 1767, retired as a captain and a shipowner, 1782, and was a private shipowner in the Indian trade, 1782–7. Then became a wealthy shipowner and shipshusband in London and was Deputy-Chairman (1803–32) and Chairman (1826–35, over several terms) of the East India Dock Company, and other concerns. He was an Elder Brother of Trinity House from 1803 and its Deputy Master, 1825–34, and a friend of King William IV.

References *HP;* Tony Fuller, 'Mariners', online; *GM,* 1838, vol. I, p. 106.

1838/18 **Name** **Eldon, 1st Earl of, Sir John Scott**

Dates 4 June 1751, Love Lane, Newcastle upon Tyne–13 January 1838, Hamilton Place, Middlesex.

Probate £700,000, 'within province' (PCC).

Occupation Lord Chancellor, 1801–6, 1807–27. He was previously Chief Justice of the Common Pleas from 1799. (Occupational categories IV.29 and 31; venues 1 and 2.)

Address His London residence for many years was 6 Bedford Square, Middlesex, where there is a blue plaque to commemorate this. He later lived at Hamilton Place, Middlesex, and owned estates at Eldon, Durham and at Enscombe, Dorset.

Father William Scott (1696–1776), a 'coal factor' and shipbroker in Newcastle upon Tyne. (Third son.)

Mother Jane (c. 1709–1800), daughter of Henry Atkinson of Newcastle.

Education Newcastle Royal Grammar School; University College, Oxford; barrister, Middle Temple (called 1776; Bencher, 1783; Treasurer, 1797).

Marriage In 1772, to Elizabeth (d. 1831), daughter of Aubone (sic) Surtees, banker of Newcastle upon Tyne. (Two sons, predeceased; two daughters.)

Religion Anglican.

Public MP (Tory) Weobley, 1793–6; Boroughbridge, 1796–9. Knighted, 1788; created Baron, 1799, and Earl, 1821. PC, 1799. Served as Solicitor-General, 1788–93 and Attorney General, 1793–6.

Miscellaneous The celebrated arch-Tory Lord Chancellor, notorious for his

delay in handing down decisions but also lawyer in legal annals. He was said to have made £15,000 p.a. from fees and income as Lord Chancellor (*ODNB*) and was certainly one of the wealthiest legal figures in British history. FRS, 1793, and High Steward of Oxford from 1801 until his death. His brother was William Scott, 1st Baron Stowell (1745–1836; see 1836/11), also a judge.
References *ODNB; BP.*

Name **Morse, John** 1838/19
Dates 13 December 1745–1837 (probated February 1838) at St Bartholomew's Close, Norwich.
Probate £100,000 (PCC).
Occupation Brewer (Morse & Adams) in Norwich. (Occupational category II.12; venue 11.)
Address 'St Bartholomew's Mews Close, All Saints parish, Norwich, Norfolk' (probate calendar). He also lived at Sprowston Manor near Norwich to 1802 and at 7 Upper Surrey Street, Norwich from 1786 to 1806.
Father Unknown.
Mother Unknown.
Education Unknown.
Marriage In 1775, to Elizabeth, daughter of John Boycott of Sprowston Hall. A relative (possibly his son?) was Sir George Morse, a brewer at Norwich during the mid-nineteenth century.
Religion Anglican.
Public Mayor of Norwich, 1781, 1803, and Alderman; Sheriff of Norwich, 1779.
Miscellaneous He was known as the 'Father of the City' of Norwich and presided at a meeting in December 1820 to address the new King, 'expressing attachment to Government, Church, and State'.
References B. Cozens-Hardy and E. A. Kent, *Mayors of Norwich, 1403–1835* (1938).

Name **Grenfell, Pascoe** 1838/20
Dates 3 September 1761, Marazion, Cornwall–23 January 1838.
Probate £140,000 (PCC).
Occupation Primarily a copper merchant at Charlotte Row near the Mansion House in the City of London. (Occupational category IV.21; venue 1.) He was also a partner with Thomas Williams, the 'Copper King' of South Wales, and his father and uncle were also copper-smelters as well as merchants, although he appears to have been primarily a London merchant, dealing in copper and tin ores. He was also a partner in the Chester & North Wales Bank, from 1817, and was Governor of Royal Exchange Assurance from 1829 until his death, having been a director of it from 1789. In 1883, William Henry Grenfell of Taplow House owned 3,195 acres worth £7,224 p.a. in Berkshire and Buckinghamshire.
Address 'Taplow House [near Maidenhead], Buckinghamshire and 38 Belgrave Square, Middlesex' (probate calendar).

Father Pascoe Grenfell (1729–27 May 1810) of Marazion, Cornwall, a copper-smelter and merchant and Consul for Holland (*ODNB*). (First son.)
Mother Mary, daughter of William Tremenheere, a solicitor.
Education Truro Grammar School.
Marriage First, in 1786, to Charlotte Granville (d. 1790), his cousin. (Two sons, seven daughters.) Second, in 1798, to (Hon.) Georgina St Leger (d. 1818), daughter of 1st Viscount Doneraile. (Two sons, nine daughters.) His grandson was William Henry Grenfell (1855–1945), MP, created 1st Baron Desborough, in the *ODNB* as 'politician and sportsman'; Desborough's son was Julian Grenfell (1888–1915), the Great War poet.
Religion Anglican – a 'strong Evangelical' and a friend of William Wilberforce.
Public MP (Whig), Great Marlow, 1802–20.
Miscellaneous The family had strong mining links in Cornwall, but he appears to have been primarily a merchant in London. He began by entering the family firm.
References *ODNB; HP.*

1838/21 **Name** **Hollond, Frederic (sic)**
Dates c. 1802–4 February 1838, at Bond Street, Middlesex.
Probate £160,000 (PCC).
Occupation East India Company fortune – the son of the millionaire William Hollond (see 1836/17). (Occupational category VI.31; venue 29.)
Address 'Upper Spring Street, Baker Street, Middlesex' (probate calendar).
Father William Hollond (c. 1750–14 February 1836), of the East India Company's Civil Service at Bengal and then of England, who left £1 million. (Second son.)
Mother Harriet, daughter of Thomas Pope.
Education Unknown.
Marriage Unmarried.
Religion Anglican.
Public None known.
Miscellaneous He appears to have been a member of the class of the 'idle rich'.
References *BLG,* 1846, 1914; *GM,* 1838, vol. I, p. 330.

1838/22 **Name** **Hewetson, Henry**
Dates 9 May 1755, Ellergill, Westmorland–8 March 1838.
Probate £500,000 (PCC).
Occupation 'Gold and silver laceman' at 30 King Street, Covent Garden, Middlesex – in various directories from 1780 on. He was also 'laceman to His Majesty'. A 'gold and silver laceman' apparently manufactured and retailed high-class lace goods embroidered with gold and silver, but how he made £500,000 out of this isn't clear. (Occupational categories II.9 and IV.20? Venue 2.) The firm 'prospered as a result of the boom in uniforms during the Napoleonic Wars' (K. L. Watson, *The Hewetsons of Ravenstonedale,* 1965), but the size of his fortune still seems extraordinary.
Address 'The Grange, Worth, Sussex and Turnham Green, Middlesex' (probate calendar). He also had lived at 5 Upper Belgrave Place, Middlesex, in 1817.

Father John Hewetson (d. c. November 1798), a 'yeoman' of Ellergill, Westmorland. (Third son.)
Mother Elizabeth née Taylor.
Education Unknown.
Marriage Apparently unmarried – he left his fortune to his six nephews.
Religion A 'Dissenter' at birth, but buried as an Anglican.
Public None known.
Miscellaneous He was apprenticed to his uncle Richard, who had also been a 'gold and silver laceman' at King Street, Covent Garden. He also left legacies to his native parish in Westmorland.
References *GM*, 1838, vol. II, p. 226; K. L. Watson, *The Hewetsons of Ravenstonedale* (1965).

Name **Kirkpatrick, George** 1838/23
Dates 1 June 1762, Madras–16 March 1838, Hollydale near Bromley, Kent.
Probate £100,000 (PCC).
Occupation Apparently an East India Company fortune: he was, it seems, the son of Colonel James Kirkpatrick (1730–1818) of the East India Company, who became wealthy there and later lived in London and in Keston, Kent. (Occupational category VI.31? Venue 29?)
Address 'Formely of Isleworth, Middlesex, and then of Hollydale, Keston parish, near Bromley, Kent' (probate calendar).
Father Probably (Colonel) James Kirkpatrick (1730–1818), of the East India Company. His illegitimate son (George's half-brother) was William Kirkpatrick (1754–1812), in the *ODNB* as an 'army officer in the East India Company and diplomatist'.
Mother Unknown.
Education Unknown.
Marriage To Eleanor (1782–1809), surname unknown; she was perhaps the Eleanor Metcalf who married a George Kirkpatrick on 18 December 1806 at St Marylebone (Family Search). Our George and Eleanor had at least four sons, James, William (d. 1831) who was a lieutenant in the East India Company, George (1809–31), and John.
Religion Anglican; buried at Keston Church, with a memorial inscription.
Public None known.
Miscellaneous He apparently had an Anglo-Indian niece or granddaughter, Kitty Kirkpatrick, who was a friend of Thomas Carlyle. Nothing is known about his career in Britain, although he owned 50 acres at Keston, Kent. He apparently spent his youth in India.
References *GM*, 1838, vol. I, p. 444; will (PROB 11 online); online sources; *ODNB* for William Kirkpatrick.

Name **Farnborough, 1st Baron, Sir Charles Long** 1838/24
Dates January 1760 in the City of London–17 January 1838 Bromley Hill Place, Kent.

Probate £120,000 (PCC).

Occupation Jamaica fortune and land, as well as a steady income from political offices. (Occupational categories I, IV.19 and VI.31? Venues 1, 2 and 29.) His grandfather, Charles Long MP, of Saxmundham, Suffolk, was previously a Jamaica planter, and his father was a West India merchant in the City of London. In 1883, Mrs Long of Bromley Hill, Kent, owned 3,917 acres worth £5,563 p.a. in Fife, Lincoln, etc., and William Beeston Long of Saxmundham owned 3,634 acres worth £4,790 p.a.

Address Bromley Hill Place, Kent.

Father Beeston Long (1710–85) of Carshalton Park, Surrey of 'a well-known firm of West Indies merchants in the City of London' (*ODNB*). (Fourth son.)

Mother Sarah, daughter of Abraham Cropp, 'a wealthy City merchant'.

Education At 'a private school in Greenwich'; Emmanuel College, Cambridge (matriculated 1778); entered the Inner Temple and made the Grand Tour.

Marriage In 1793 to Amelia (1772–1837; d.s.p.), daughter of Sir Abraham Hume, 2nd Baronet. She was a well-known artist and is in the *ODNB* as a 'watercolour painter'. He also had a mistress, Sophia Tarleton.

Religion Anglican.

Public MP (Tory) Rye, 1789–96; Midhurst, 1796–1802; Wendover, 1802–6; Haslemere, 1806–26. PC, 1802; PC (Ireland), 1805; GCB, 1820; created 1st Baron Farnborough, 1826. He served as Joint Secretary of the Treasury, 1791–1801; Lord of the Treasury, 1804–6; Joint Paymaster-General, 1807–17; and Paymaster-General, 1817–26.

Miscellaneous He was also well known and respected as an art collector and connoisseur of the arts whose taste was universally admired. He was a trustee of the British Museum and of the National Gallery and was also a painter. He received an honorary degree from Cambridge in 1833 and was an FRS. He was almost certainly not engaged in any trade but must have made a substantial income from his political offices.

References *ODNB* as 'politician and connoisseur of the arts'; *GM*, 1838, vol. I, p. 425; *BP*.

1838/25 **Name** **Lewis, Wyndham**

Dates 7 October 1778 (1780?)–14 March 1838, Grosvenor Gate, Middlesex.

Probate £120,000 (PCC).

Occupation Ironmaster in South Wales – he owned one-fifth of the Dowlais ironworks (*ODNB* for wife); also a barrister. (Occupational categories II.3 and VI.29? Venues 19 and 1?)

Address '[1] Grosvenor Gate, Middlesex and [Green Meadows,] Cardiff' (probate calendar).

Father (Revd) Wyndham Lewis (b. 1735–probated November 1781), of Newhouse, Gloucestershire; educated at Oxford. (Third son.)

Mother Mary, daughter of Samuel Price of Park and Coity, near Bridgend, Glamorgan.

Education Schooling unknown; barrister, Lincoln's Inn (called 1819).

Marriage In 1816, to Mary Ann (c. 1798–15 December 1872; d.s.p.), daughter of John Evans, Commander RN, of Branceford Park, Devonshire. She married, second, in 1839, Benjamin Disraeli (1804–81), later Prime Minister and 1st Earl of Beaconsfield. She was, remarkably, created Viscountess Beaconsfield in her own right in 1868.
Religion Anglican.
Public MP (Tory) Cardiff, 1802–6; Aldborough, 1827–30; Maidstone, 1835–death. DL, Glamorgan.
Miscellaneous He was a wealthy ironmaster in South Wales who is well known because his widow remarried Disraeli. Lewis helped Disraeli to obtain his first parliamentary seat. Disraeli's wife was renowned for her gaucheness. This Wyndham Lewis does not appear to have been related to either of the two well-known writers of this name of the twentieth century.
References *ODNB* for wife; *GM,* 1838, vol. I, p. 658.

Name **Glyn, Sir Richard Carr, 1st Baronet** 1838/26
Dates 2 February 1755, London–27 April 1838.
Probate £250,000 (PCC).
Occupation 'An eminent banker of London' (*GM*). (Halifax, Mills, Glyn & Milton of 12 Birchin Lane and Lombard Street, City of London, later Glyn Mills & Co.) (Occupational category IV.16; venue 1.) In 1883, Sir Richard Glyn, Baronet, of Gaunt's House, Wimborne owned 9,770 acres worth £12,893 p.a., chiefly in Dorset.
Address 'Gaunt's [near Wimborne] Dorset; Lombard Street, City of London; and Arlington Street, Middlesex' (probate calendar).
Father Sir Richard Glyn, 1st Baronet (1712–1 January 1773), a 'prosperous drysalter and then banker' in London and Lord Mayor, 1758–9. (Second son.)
Mother Elizabeth (d. 1814), daughter of Robert Carr of Hampton, Middlesex, a silk merchant of Ludgate Hill.
Education Westminster School.
Marriage In 1785, to Mary (c. 1760–2 August 1832), daughter of John Plumptre, MP, of Fredville, near Canterbury, Kent. (Five sons, one daughter.) Their fourth son was George Carr Glyn, 1st Baron Wolverton (1797–1873), wealthy banker.
Religion Anglican.
Public MP (Tory) St Ives, 1796–1802. Sheriff of London, 1790–1 and Lord Mayor of London, 1798–9 and Alderman, 1790–1835. Knighted in 1790 and created a baronet in 1800.
Miscellaneous A wealthy City banker from a major banking family.
References *ODNB* as 'banker'; *GM,* 1838, vol. II, p. 211; *BP.*

Name **Taylor, Meadows** 1838/27
Dates c. 1797–18 April 1838.
Probate £120,000 (PCC).
Occupation Solicitor in Diss, Norfolk (20 miles from Norwich). He is listed as a solicitor in the *Law List* for 1836. Judging from his age he almost certainly inherited

wealth, but the source of this wealth is unclear. No one named Taylor with land in Norfolk is listed in Bateman. His father's occupation is unknown. (Occupational category VI.29 +? Venue 11.)

Address 'Diss, Norfolk' (probate calendar). *GM*, states Starston, near Harleston, Norfolk.

Father Meadows Taylor of Diss – described as 'late' in 1838, possibly also a solicitor. (First son.)

Mother Unknown.

Education Unknown.

Marriage Unknown. His sister Ann (1800–93) married, in 1829, Jerom Murch (1807–95), 'Unitarian minister and municipal activist', in *ODNB*. His cousin was Edgar Taylor (1793–1839) 'author', in *ODNB*. He was the son of Samuel Taylor and a descendant of John Taylor (1694–1761), Hebrew scholar and dissenting minister. Meadows Taylor's cousin was Emily Taylor (1795–1872), in the *ODNB* as 'schoolmistress and author'.

Religion Unitarian.

Public None known.

Miscellaneous He is referred to as 'M. Taylor Jr.' in the 1836 Norfolk directory. His source of wealth is unknown, but he and his father appear to have been solicitors. A Meadows Taylor wrote *Confessions of a Thug* (1839), and the *ODNB* lists a Philip Meadows Taylor (1808–76), 'army officer and novelist', the son of Philip Meadows Taylor, a Liverpool merchant, but there is no clear linkage with this man.

References *GM*, 1838, vol. I, p. 669; above sources.

1838/28 **Name** **Fisher, John**

Dates Unknown–28 June 1838, Kensington, Middlesex.

Probate £100,000 (PCC).

Occupation Unknown. His will provides no real clues. The only John Fisher listed in a London directory was a 'Blackwell Hall factor' of 3 Lothbury, City of London, in the 1793 directory, but there is no evidence that he was this wealth-holder.

Address 'Formerly of Downing Street, Middlesex and then of [3] Dorset Square, Middlesex' (probate calendar). The 1819 directory lists a John Fisher of 18 Portman Square, Middlesex. Fisher also owned a 'settled estate' in Southampton (presumably the county, not the city). In his will, he left a legacy to an Arthur Cooper, aged eighteen, who traded with India. This might suggest an East India Company connection for Fisher.

Father Unknown.

Mother Unknown.

Education Unknown.

Marriage Unknown, probably unmarried.

Religion Unknown.

Public None known.

Miscellaneous His will notes that he had a brother named William and sisters named Mary Louisa Fisher, Mrs Sarah Shafto and Mrs Amelia Freeman, but nothing could be traced on these persons.

References *GM,* 1838, vol. II, p. 225; will (PROB 11, online).

Name **Lany (sic), Elizabeth** 1838/29

Dates Unknown – probated August 1838.

Probate £120,000 (PCC).

Occupation Unknown. She is described in her will as a 'spinster' of Norwich and formerly of Queen Anne Street, Middlesex, but she is described as 'Mrs. Lany' in the 1811 London directory and the 1836 Norwich direcrory. A Moses Lany (c. 1737–8 August 1808), 'lace merchant' of 11 Tavistock Street, Covent Garden, Middlesex, is listed in the 1795 London directory and as a 'lace warehouseman' of the same address in the 1805 London directory (*GM,* 1808, vol. II, p. 757). This was possibly her father, although there is no direct evidence. (If so, occupational category IV.20 or 21; venue 2?)

Address 'Formerly of Queen Anne Street West, Holborn, Middlesex, and then of All Saint's Green, Norwich, Norfolk' (probate calendar).

Father Unknown – see above.

Mother Unknown.

Education Unknown.

Marriage Unmarried, but see 'Occupation' above.

Religion Probably Anglican; in her will she left a legacy to her cousin, (Revd) Augustus Cooper, an Anglican clergyman.

Public None known.

Miscellaneous (Revd) Augustus Cooper was the son of Robert Cooper of Woodbridge, Suffolk. He was born c. 1790 and educated at Pembroke College, Cambridge and was a cleryman in Norfolk. Other relatives to whom she left legacies were her cousins (Captain) Edmund Stoppard, Edmund Frodair (?) Stoppard, a solicitor, Dr William Salmon, Mrs Anne Cooper and Anne Cooper's son (Captain) Robert Brown Cooper. Little could be traced, however, about her source of wealth.

References Will (PROB 11 online); above sources.

Name **Poulett, Dowager Countess, Margaret Poulett** (née Burges) 1838/30

Dates c. 1753–28 May 1838, Brighton.

Probate £100,000 (PCC).

Occupation Landed and East India Company fortune. (Occupational categories I and VI.31; venues 1 and 29?) In 1883, Earl Poulett owned 22,129 acres worth £21,998 p.a. in Somerset. She inherited her father's estate in East Ham, Essex, of 410 acres worth £1,549 p.a. at that time (*VCH Essex,* vol. 6, 1973, pp. 8–14).

Address She lived at Brighton and inherited her father's homes in Essex. Earl Poulett's principal seat was at Hinton House, Somerset.

Father Ynyr (sic) Bugess (or Burgess) (buried 31 December 1793) of Thorpe Hall and East Ham, Essex, 'Paymaster of the East India Company'. His address was given as 'of St Lawrence Jewry' at the time of his marriage in 1747.

Mother Margaret Browne, 'of St Margaret's near Fish Street, City of London' at her marriage. According to Family Search, that took place in 1747 at Gray's Inn Chapel, London.
Education Unknown.
Marriage First, in 1771, to Sir John Smith-Burges(s), 1st Baronet (1734–1803), né Smith, the son of a City merchant who was a lieutenant colonel in the East India Company and added his wife's surname. He received a baronetcy in 1793; second, in 1816, to Sir John Poulett, 4th Earl Poulett (1756–14 January 1819; d.s.p.), KT, Lord of the Bedchamber, 1795–1819.
Religion Anglican; she has a monumental inscription in East Ham Church.
Public None known.
Miscellaneous She inherited East India and landed money from her father and presumably benefited from her marriages.
References *GM,* 1838, vol. II, p. 109; *BP; Complete Baronetage;* online sources.

1838/31 **Name** **Sowerby, Elizabeth Ann**
Dates c. 1770–18 August 1838, Blackheath Park.
Probate £120,000 (PCC).
Occupation She was the 'widow' of Robert Sowerby. The only Robert Sowerby listed in PCC, PROB 11, online, was a 'wine merchant' of Broad Street, City of London, probated December 1811. (If she was his widow and derived her wealth from him, then occupational category IV.20 or 21; venue 1.) She has no discernible connection with John Sowerby (1745–1823; see 1823/17), a 'warehouseman and insurance broker' in the City of London who left £500,000, but who lived at Putteridge Bury, Hertfordshire. However, since he had ten sons it is possible that Robert was one of them.
Address 'Blackheath Park, Kent' (probate calendar).
Father Unknown.
Mother Unknown.
Education Unknown.
Marriage To Robert Sowerby (see above), marriage date unknown.
Religion Unknown.
Public None known.
Miscellaneous Neither she nor her husband are listed in the *BLG* entry for the Sowerby family, which includes John Sowerby the wealth-holder, but not all of the latter's sons are listed by name.
References *GM,* 1838, vol. II, p. 449. She is not listed in Arthur DeCarle Sowerby, *The Sowerby Saga* (1952).

1838/32 **Name** **Kay, William**
Dates 13 March 1777, Wigton, Cumberland–15 September 1838, York Terrace, Middlesex. He was knocked down by a cart in the New Road and died shortly after (*GM*).
Probate £120,000 (PCC).
Occupation Probably a 'merchant' at 14 Angel Court, Throgmorton Street,

City of London (1825 and 1828 directories). (If so, occupational category IV.21? Venue 1.) However, in an online description of Tring Park, Hertfordshire, which he owned, he is described as a 'Northern businessman' who built a silk mill at Tring Park.

Address 'Tring Park, Hertfordshire and York Terrace, Middlesex' (probate calendar). He also owned an estate at The Mains, Cumberland.

Father John Kay, a 'joiner' of Wigton, Cumberland.

Mother Mary, surname unknown.

Education Unknown.

Marriage To Elizabeth, surname and marriage date unknown. (They had at least one son, William.)

Religion Baptised Anglican.

Public None known.

Miscellaneous He bought Tring Park, Hertfordshire, from Sir Drummond Smith's executors in 1823. After the death of his son, who inherited it, it passed to his great-niece, Lady Barnes, who sold it to the Rothschilds as one of their principal mansions. He does not appear to have been related to the Kay-Shuttleworth family. It is possible that he was a Northern silk manufacturer (?) who retired to London, rather than a London merchant.

References *GM,* 1838, vol. II, p. 450; *Cumberland News,* 17 August 2007, online; online sources about Tring Park; *VCH Hertfordshire,* vol. 3, p. 283.

Name **Carrington, 1st Baron, Robert Smith** 1838/33

Dates 22 January 1752, Nottingham–18 September 1838, at 26 St James's Place, Whitehall, Middlesex.

Probate £120,000 (PCC).

Occupation Banker (Smith, Payne & Co.), chiefly in Nottingham, but also in London. (Occupational category IV.16; venues 17 and 1.) He was the head of the firm from 1780.

Address 'Dulcote Lodge, Nottingham and 26 St James's Place, Middlesex' (probate calendar). He also owned an estate at Wycombe, Buckinghamshire, which he bought from Lord Lansdowne. In 1883, Lord Carrington owned 25,809 acres worth £42,254 p.a. in Buckinghamshire and Lincoln.

Father Abel Smith (c. 1717–12 July 1788), 'Banker and merchant' of Nottingham and later London, and MP, 1774–88, in *ODNB.* (Third son.) He left £59,753, plus much land and an estate in Jamaica (*ODNB*).

Mother Mary, daughter of Thomas Bird, a 'silk manufacturer' of Barton, Warwickshire.

Education Unknown.

Marriage First, in 1780, to Anne (d. 1827), daughter of Lewyns Boldero Barnard of South Cave, Yorkshire. (One son, eight daughters.) Second, in 1836, to Charlotte (d.s.p., 1849), daughter of John Hudson and widow of (Revd) Walter Trevelyan.

Religion Anglican; a 'generous benefactor'.

Public MP (Tory) Nottingham, 1779–97. A member of the Board of Agriculture

1793 and President of the Board of Agriculture, 1800–3. Created Baron Carrington (Irish peerage), 1796, and Baron Carrington (UK peerage), 1797.

Miscellaneous One of the first bankers still in trade to become a government minister and a peer. His bank is now part of National Westminster. He was the ancestor of the recent Foreign Secretary Lord Carrington.

References *ODNB*; *HP*; *BP*; *GM*, 1838, vol. II, p. 545.

1838/34 **Name** **Thomas, Thomas (sic)**

Dates c. 1756–17 November 1838, at Charles Street, St James's Square, Middlesex.

Probate £140,000 (PCC).

Occupation 'Doctor of Medicine' (probate calendar). 'M.D., formerly of Tunbridge Wells' (*GM*). (Occupational category VI.30; venue 3?)

Address 'Formerly of Tunbridge Wells, Kent and then of Charles Street, St James's Square, Middlesex' (probate calendar).

Father Unknown. His name obviously suggests a Welsh background.

Mother Unknown.

Education Secondary schooling unknown; he was possibly the Thomas Thomas who matriculated at St Andrews University in 1781–2.

Marriage Unknown. In 1795, a Thomas Thomas married an Elizabeth Greensted in Borden, near Sittingbourne, Kent, but there is no indication that this was the same man (Family Search).

Religion Unknown.

Public None known.

Miscellaneous Nothing further could be traced about his career. He may have been a successful Society doctor.

References *GM*, 1838, vol. II, p. 668.

1838/35 **Name** **St Albans, Duchess of, Harriot (sic)** (née Mellon, then Coutts, and then Beauclerk)

Dates 11 November 1777, Lambeth (?)–6 August 1837, 8 Piccadilly, Middlesex.

Probate £600,000 (PCC). She was widely believed to have left £1.8 million, but there is no evidence for such a large figure.

Occupation Banking fortune – she inherited £600,000 and a partnership in Coutts's Bank from her husband Thomas Coutts, millionaire banker (1822/34). (Occupational category IV.16; venue 2.)

Address 80 Piccadilly, in addition to another house in London and one at Highgate (*ODNB*).

Father Unknown, but she claimed to have been the daughter of (Lieutenant) Matthew Mellon of the Madras Infantry, who 'was not seen by his wife after March 1777', (*DNB*) but there is no real evidence for this.

Mother Sarah, daughter of an Irish cottier. She became a milliner at Cork and later a wardrobe-keeper in Kena's Company of strolling players. She married, in 1792, Thomas Entwistle, a musician in Kena's Company.

Education 'In Lancashire' (*ODNB*).

Marriage First, in 1815, to Thomas Coutts (d. 1822), the millionaire banker; second, in 1827, to William Aubrey DeVere Beauclerk, 9th Duke of St Albans (1801–49) (d.s.p.)
Religion Anglican.
Public None known.
Miscellaneous One of the most remarkable and extraordinary of all the wealth-holder sagas. Harriot Mellon, the illegitimate daughter of a strolling actress, began acting at ten and was noticed by Sheridan, who took her to London. There she became a well-known actress and was earning £12 per week when, in 1815, she married the phenomenally wealthy banker Thomas Coutts, inheriting most of his fortune and a partnership in his bank – possibly the first woman partner in a major British enterprise. After his death, she married the (relatively impecunious) 9th Duke of St Albans! She proved an astute businesswoman, although shunned by much of Society and Coutts's own daughters. Harriot Mellon left most of her fortune to Coutts's granddaughter Angela Burdett-Coutts, later Baroness Burdett-Coutts (1814–1906), the celebrated philanthropist – Mellon's generosity to her, never fully acknowledged, was the basis of Angela's own fortune.
References *ODNB; GM.*

Name **Ray, Robert** 1838/36
Dates Unknown–24 December 1837, Edmonton.
Probate £120,000 (PCC).
Occupation Prothonotary of the Court of Common Pleas and 'a Bencher and one of the Masters of the Library of the Temple' (*GM*) – barrister of Lincoln's Inn and of the Middle Temple. (Occupational category VI.29; venues 1 and 2.)
Address 'Lincoln's Inn and [Tanfield Court,] Middle Temple' (probate calendar). He also lived at Montague Place, Middlesex, and at The Grove, Edmonton, Middlesex.
Father Henry Ray of Bovingdon, Hertfordshire (possibly 1677–June 1763), formerly of Montague Place, Russell Square, Middlesex, and possibly a former grocer of London. (Only son.) (Lincoln's Inn Admissions Book.)
Mother Unknown.
Education Unknown; barrister, Lincoln's Inn (admitted 1780, called 1785).
Marriage Name unknown. Their daughter Lucy (d. 1879) married, in 1838, Claude Wilde, son of Mr Sergeant Wilde, MP (*GM*).
Religion Anglican.
Public None known.
Miscellaneous A high-ranking legal official and barrister. He was an FSA and 'possessed a valuable library' (*GM*).
References *GM,* 1838, vol. I, p. 217; G. Milner-Gibson-Cullum, 'Pedigree of Ray of Denston' (Society of Genealogists).

Name **Attwood, Phebe** (sic) (née Cox) 1838/37
Dates Unknown – probated April 1838.
Probate £250,000 (PCC).

Occupation Ironmastery fortune in the West Midlands. (Occupational category II.3; venue 8.) She was the widow of James Attwood, an ironmaster of Halesowen, and the brother of Matthias Attwood (see 1838/14). She mentions her shares in the British Iron Company in her will. Matthias Attwood was also a banker, but she does not appear to have profited from his bank.

Address 'Formerly of Cheltenham, Gloucestershire and then of Baker Street, Portman Square, Middlesex' (probate calendar). She had presumably lived with her husband at Halesowen, Staffordshire.

Father Forename unknown, surname Cox. She was perhaps the Phebe (sic) Cox baptised at Halesowen on 11 October 1747, daughter of Abraham and Sarah (Family Search).

Mother Unknown. Possibly Sarah Heykin, who married an Abraham Cox at Halesowen in 1743 (see 'Father' above).

Education Unknown.

Marriage In 1779, to James Attwood, ironmaster of Halesowen, Staffordshire. This was probably the James Attwood (b. 1744) of Rowley Regis, Staffordshire, whose estate was probated in November 1821. (Two sons, two daughters; one son was John Attwood, MP [d. 1865].)

Religion Presumably Anglican.

Public None known.

Miscellaneous It was unusual for a woman to inherit such a large fortune in her own right. *BLG* gives the date of her death as 2 August 1835 (sic), but this is likely to be wrong.

References *BLG*, 1937, 1952.

1838/38 **Name** **Constable, George**

Dates Unknown–12 July 1838, New Road, Marylebone, Middlesex.

Probate £100,000 (PCC).

Occupation 'Lieutenant Colonel, East India Company' (probate calendar). 'Late of the Bengal Army' (*GM*). (Occupational category VI.31; venue 29.)

Address 'Park Cresent, Marylebone, Middlesex' (probate calendar).

Father Unknown.

Mother Unknown.

Education Unknown.

Marriage Unknown. His daughter was a Mrs Nicoll.

Religion Unknown, presumably Anglican.

Public None known.

Miscellaneous He fought in the Mahratta War and was seriously wounded at Agra. He served in the Bengal Artillery. How he accumulated his fortune is unclear. *GM* notes that he was the nephew of George Constable, the original of Sir Walter Scott's *The Antiquary*.

References *GM*, 1838, vol. II, pp. 337 and 678.

1838/39 **Name** **Chisholm, George**

Dates Unknown–1833 (?). Probated February 1838.

Probate £120,000 (PCC).
Occupation 'Merchant' (probate calendar) in Calcutta. (Occupational category IV.19; venue 29.)
Address 'Calcutta, East Indies' (probate calendar). He does not appear to have resided in Britain at his death.
Father Unknown.
Mother Unknown.
Education Unknown.
Marriage Unknown, but probably unmarried.
Religion Unknown, but probably a 'Dissenter'.
Public None known.
Miscellaneous He appears to have been the George Chisholm who was born in Leith in 1754 and went about 1776 to Calcutta, where he was a 'merchant'. That man died in 1833 and was buried in the Dissenters' Burial Grounds in Calcutta. He died unmarried but had an illegitimate son, George Wilding Chisholm (1777–April 1843) (online genealogical inquiry). According to *GM*, March 1823, he was a partner of 'Mr. Hay'.
References Above sources only.

Name **Wyndham, Laetitia** (née Popham) 1838/40
Dates Unknown–7 December 1837, Dinton, Wiltshire.
Probate £100,000 (PCC).
Occupation Landed and legal fortune. Her father was a master in Chancery, 1786–1802, and Auditor of the Duchy of Lancaster. Her husband was a major landowner. (In 1883, William Wyndham of Dinton, Wiltshire, owned 23,708 acres worth £37,420 p.a. in Somerset, Wiltshire and Devon.) (Occupational categories I and VI.29; venue 1 and 2.)
Address Dinton near Salisbury, Wiltshire, was the main estate.
Father Alexander Popham (1729–13 October 1810), educated at Oxford; barrister and bencher of the Middle Temple, MP, 1768–96; Master in Chancery, 1786–1802, and Auditor of the Duchy of Lancaster from 1802. (Only daughter.)
Mother Unknown.
Education Unknown.
Marriage In 1794, to William Wyndham (1769–19 September 1841) of Dinton, Wiltshire, and Norrington, Wiltshire, landowner. (Six sons, six daughters.) Their son George Wyndham (1801–70) moved to New South Wales, where, from 1828, he developed the famous Wyndham vineyards (*Australian Dictionary of Biography*).
Religion Anglican; there is a memorial at St Mary's Church, Dinton, to William and Laetitia Wyndham.
Public None known.
Miscellaneous Presumably she inherited most of her fortune from her father. Her husband was still alive when she died; nevertheless, she managed to leave £100,000 in her own right.
References *GM*, 1838, vol. I, p. 110; *BLG*, 1871 and 1937.

1838/41 **Name** **Hope, Samuel**

Dates 1 February 1781–15 October 1837.

Probate £250,000 (York PC).

Occupation Cotton broker (13 Hope Street and 3 Water Street, Liverpool, 1813 directory) and the banker (Samuel Hope & Co., bankers, of 4 Water Street) in Liverpool. He was apparently only a banker from 1833. (Occupational categories IV.16 and 21; venue 5.)

Address Lived at 23 Everton Terrace, Liverpool.

Father William Hope (1751–20 March 1820), merchant, banker and landowner in Liverpool. (Second son.)

Mother Mary née Jones (1753–1836).

Education Unknown.

Marriage In 1816, to Rebekah (1794–8 October 1836), daughter of Thomas Bateman of Middleton, Derbyshire. (Ten children.) Their daughter Charlotte married, in 1852, George Denman (1819–86), 'judge and politician' (*ODNB*); their daughter Rebekah married, in 1841, Samuel Morley (1809–80), the businessman and MP; their son was Samuel Hope Morley, created 1st Baron Hollenden (*ODNB*). Alfred Holt (1829–1911), the well-known shipowner, was his nephew (*ODNB*).

Religion The parents married as Anglicans, but he was apparently a Congregationalist or a Unitarian.

Public JP, Lancashire.

Miscellaneous He was apprenticed to Nicholas Waterhouse and began as a cotton broker and partner with his brother George from 1807. He was also a banker and was wholly a banker from 1833. The Holts became leading shipowners and were part of the Unitarian 'Cousinhood', but it is not clear whether he was a Unitarian.

References *ODNB* for relatives; Hope Harding, *But My Hope's Not Broken* (1967); online sources.

Name **Yates, William** 1839/1

Dates c. 1796–28 February 1839, Rome.

Probate £120,000, 'within province' (PCC).

Occupation Cotton-manufacturing fortune, chiefly in Bury, Lancashire. His father was the partner, and probably brother-in-law, of Sir Robert Peel, 1st Baronet (1830/17), the cotton millionaire, in Bury, Lancashire. (Occupational category II.7; venue 4.) William Yates was probably not directly involved in trade, although this isn't entirely clear.

Address Hoole Hall, near Chester, Cheshire.

Father Thomas Yates (probated July 1815) of Irwell House and Tenters, near Bury, Lancashire, partner of Sir Robert Peel, 1st Baronet in Bury around 1800. (First son.)

Mother Elizabeth, surname unknown, but possibly Bayly (c. 1777–1840) (*GM*, 1840). According to Family Search, a Thomas Yates and an Elizabeth Allen married at Manchester Cathedral in 1791. Yates is a fairly common Lancashire surname, however, and there are no indications that this couple were the parents.

Education Secondary schooling unknown; Brasenose College, Oxford (matriculated 1819; BA, 1823).

Marriage Unknown, probably unmarried.

Religion Anglican.

Public None known.

Miscellaneous He died in Rome and is buried in the Protestant cemetery there, where he has a memorial inscription.

References *BLG*, 1855; *ODNB* for relatives; *Alum. Oxon.*; online sources; *Notes & Queries*, January 1958, p. 35.

Name **Innes, Jane** 1839/2

Dates 13 August 1748–2 December 1839, Edinburgh.

Probate £800,000, 'within province' (PCC) + £242,667 (Scottish probate): £1,042,667.

Occupation Inherited from her father, a banker and placeman in Edinburgh. (Occupational categories IV.16 and VI.31; venue 23.) She also inherited, probably as much or more, from her unmarried brother, Gilbert Innes (see 1832/28), Director of the Royal Bank of Scotland, who left £143,000.

Address 'Formerly of Piccadilly Place, Edinburgh, and then of Stow, Midlothian, Scotland' (probate calendar).

Father George Innes (1703–80), banker in Edinburgh and Receiver of HM Lands and Rents in Scotland. (Third daughter.)

Mother Marian (d. December 1780), daughter of David Lauder of Huntly Wood.

Education Unknown.

Marriage Unmarried.

Religion Presumably Church of Scotland.
Public None known.
Miscellaneous Her enormous estate was one of the largest left by a woman in the early nineteenth century. Her personalty came to William Mitchell of Parsons Green and her land to Alexander Mitchell, later Mitchell-Innes. In 1883, Alexander Mitchell-Innes owned 6,307 acres worth £13,364 p.a. in Berwick and Haddington.
References *BLG*, 1937; *GM*, 1840, vol. I, p. 222.

1839/3 **Name** **Reynolds, William Foster**
Dates c. 1768–19 November 1838 at Carshalton House, Surrey.
Probate £140,000 (PCC).
Occupation His father was 'an eminent linen bleacher' (*GM*, 1797, vol. II, p. 1077) at Carshalton; he was also described as a 'whitster'. It is not clear whether the wealth-holder was active in this trade or not. In 1811, Thomas and Jacob Foster Reynolds, presumably his brothers, were in charge of the Carshalton bleaching works. (Occupational category II.6; venue 3.) There is no evidence that he was engaged in any other trade or profession.
Address 'Carshalton House [near Sutton], Surrey' (probate calendar).
Father Foster Reynolds (d. 16 December 1797), linen bleacher of Carshalton.
Mother Deborah, surname unknown.
Education Unknown.
Marriage To Esther (d. 28 October 1857, aged eighty-four), surname unknown (*GM*, 1857, vol. II, p. 687). (At least four daughters and apparently at least one son.) Daughter Esther married, in 1824, a son of Robert Barclay (1758–1816), while a Jacob Foster Reynolds married a daughter of Robert Barclay (1751–1830), also of the Barclay/Gurney clan (www.Stirnet.com). Another of William Reynolds's daughters, Elizabeth, married, in 1823, William Prideaux, of a gentry family in Devon (*BLG*, 1838, p. 534, 'Prideaux, of Luson'); in 1844, her sister Marianne married Joseph James of Surrey (*GM*, 1844, vol. II, p. 312). In 1828, Foster Reynolds (b. c. 1805), apparently William's son, married Richenda (1808–84), daughter of the Quaker philanthropist Elizabeth Fry, who described the event in her diary (Gil Skidmore, ed., *Elizabeth Fry: A Quaker Life*, 2005, pp. 158–9). Yet another daughter, Ellen, married, in 1837, Samuel Gurney (1816–82), in the *ODNB* as a 'Quaker philanthropist and discount banker'.
Religion His father was a Quaker. William Foster Reynolds was a member of the Committee of the Anti-Slavery Society, which included many Quakers, and was married into the Gurney family.
Public None known.
Miscellaneous The firm was known as Reynolds & Cookson in 1792 and had 'extensive' works.
References *GM*, 1837, vol. II, p. 670; *VCH Surrey*, vol. 2, p. 376.

1839/4 **Name** **Poore, Sir Edward, 2nd Baronet**
Dates 4 December 1795–13 October 1838, at Norfolk Street, Park Lane, Middlesex.

Probate £120,000 (PCC).
Occupation Presumably a landowner and was High Sheriff of Wiltshire, but no one of this name appears in Bateman. Who owned his land in 1883 is unclear. (Occupational category I?)
Address 'Formerly of Rushall, Wiltshire, and then of Cuffnells, Hampshire' (probate calendar).
Father Edward Poore (1773–17 July 1817), presumably a landowner. (First son.) Sir Edward succeeded his great-grandfather's younger brother, Sir John Methuen Poore, 1st Baronet (c. 1744– 1 June 1820), who was created a baronet in 1795, was High Sheriff of Wiltshire in 1797–8 and died unmarried. The family had owned land in Wiltshire for three generations.
Mother Martha Anne (d. February 1801), daughter of George Wolfe, Consul-General for Denmark.
Education Secondary schooling unknown; Magdalene College, Oxford (matriculated 1814).
Marriage In 1818, to Agnes (d. 1868), daughter of Sir John Marjoribanks, Baronet. (One son, five daughters.)
Religion Anglican.
Public High Sheriff of Wiltshire, 1824–5.
Miscellaneous He died at the age of only forty-two. His career and what became of his lands are obscure.
References *BP.*

Name **White, Charles Nicholas** 1839/5
Dates c. 1753–20 February 1839 at Bognor Lodge, Sussex.
Probate £120,000 (PCC).
Occupation 'Of the Madras Civil Service' (*GM,* 1822). (Occupational category VI.31; venue 29.)
Address 'Formerly of Datchett [sic; near Windsor], Buckinghamshire, and then of Bognor, Sussex' (probate calendar).
Father Unknown. A Charles Nicholas White, son of John and Joanna, was baptised at Alphington, Devon, on 18 June 1755 (Family Search); there is no way of knowing whether this was our man.
Mother Unknown.
Education Unknown.
Marriage To Letitia, daughter of John Mytton of Halston Park, Shropshire, marriage date unknown. She died in 1822 at Datchet House (*GM,* 1822, vol. I, p. 517).
Religion Presumably Anglican.
Public None known.
Miscellaneous Details of his career in India are unknown, but that career was presumably the source of his wealth. The date of his return to England is unknown.
References *GM,* 1822, vol. I, p. 517; 1839, vol. I, p. 445.

1839/6 **Name** **Fuller, John**

Dates 1762–31 March 1839, at Neston Park.

Probate £120,000 (PCC).

Occupation He was apparently a landowner in Wiltshire. In 1829, he became extensively involved with what became Fuller, Smith & Turner's Brewery in Chiswick, later known as Fuller's, as it is today. His family apparently did not have any connection with the brewery before then (but see below). (Occupational categories I and II.12; venue 2.) The family is not listed in Bateman.

Address 'Neston Park, Corsham, Wiltshire' (probate calendar).

Father *BLG*, 1855, states that the father was named John Fleetwood Fuller, although no one of that name is listed in PROB 11. *GM* states that John Fuller 'succeeded to the estate in Sussex on the death of Gerald Dutton Fleetwood, who claimed to be the direct descendant of General Charles Fleetwood, who married in 1652 Bridget, the daughter of Oliver Cromwell [and widow of Henry Ireton]. John Fuller came to reside in Wiltshire in 1801.' His estate was probated in December 1795, where he is described as 'of Leatherhead, Surrey'.

Mother Unknown.

Education Unknown.

Marriage In 1788, to Dinah (d. 1856), daughter of Jacob Jeans. (Two sons, two daughters.) Their son John Bird Fuller (1801–72), JP, DL, ran the brewery and was also High Sheriff of Wiltshire in 1852. A descendant, Sir John Fuller, 1st Baronet (1864–1915), was a Liberal government minister and was Governor of Victoria, Australia, 1911–14 (*Australian Dictionary of Biography*).

Religion Anglican.

Public JP, DL, Wiltshire; High Sheriff, 1823.

Miscellaneous Pepys noted in his Diary (April 1660) that Fuller's was 'the famous place for ale' in London, but this is apparently a coincidence. Whether John Fuller was wealthy before 1829 is unclear, and his career before then is obscure. Fuller's beer is still well known today.

References *GM*, 1839, vol. I, p. 557; *BP*; online history of Fuller's Brewery.

1839/7 **Name** **Farmer, Samuel**

Dates c. 1747–14 May 1839, at Nonsuch Park, Surrey.

Probate £120,000 (PCC).

Occupation Scarlet dyer at Worship Street, Finsbury – he inherited this business around 1790. He was also the residual legatee of his brother William Gamul Farmer, Chief of Surat in the East India Company, and held East India Company stock. (Occupational categories II.6 and VI.39; venues 2 and 29.) He also invested in land in Surrey and elsewhere. In 1883, William Robert Gamul Farmer of Nonsuch Park, owned 9,495 acres worth £8,377 p.a. in Suffolk, Surrey, etc.

Address 'Nonsuch Park [Epsom,] Surrey and Langham Place, Middlesex' (probate calendar). He also had property at Somersham Park, Huntingdonshire.

Father George Farmer, 'merchant', of Hog Lane, Shoreditch. (PROB 11 lists three possibilities: a George Farmer of St George Hanover Square, probated in July 1797; a 'hop factor' of Southwark, probated in December 1797; and a George Farmer of St Mary, Whitechapel, probated in July 1806.)

Mother Unknown.

Education Unknown.

Marriage In c. 1795 to Elizabeth, daughter of Joseph Easton Meeke of Rotherhithe and sister of William Meeke, MP. (One son, William Meeke Farmer, MP, d. 1836.)

Religion Anglican.

Public MP (Tory) Huntingdon, 1809–18.

Miscellaneous He 'inherited the scarlet dyeing business at Worship Street, Finsbury', but it is unclear from whom. This was apparently the main source of his wealth, although he also inherited an East India fortune. In 1799, he purchased Nonsuch Park in Epsom, Surrey, adjacent to the former royal residence Nonsuch Palace.

References *HP; GM,* 1839, vol. I, p. 669; *BLG,* 1937.

Name **Ricketts, Jacob Wilcox** 1839/8

Dates c. 1755–29 August 1839, Redland, Gloucestershire.

Probate £250,000 (PCC).

Occupation 'Wholesale and retail tobacconist' at 33 Maryport Street and 112 Redcliff Street, Bristol (1838 directory). In 1793, he was listed as a 'tobacconist' of Old Market, Bristol. His firm amalgamated in 1833 with W. D. & H. O. Wills, and the new firm was known as Ricketts & Wills until 1847, when the Ricketts family retired from the business. This became the basis of Imperial Tobacco and the great fortune of the Wills family. Presumably Jacob Ricketts was a tobacco importer and manufacturer in Bristol, as well as a retailer. (Occupational category II.14 and IV.20; venue 12.) His career has been outlined by B. W. E. Alford (see 'References' below). He took over his father's business interests in 1787 together with his brother Richard. The brothers acquired interests in a number of firms, becoming partners in James Stansfield & Co. On Richard's death, without sons, in 1818, all his interests passed to Jacob Wilcox Ricketts and his two sons, Henry and Frederick. At some stage, Jacob also took over a tobacco company called Ricketts & Davis, with which another relative had been associated. In 1810, he helped to found the Castle Bank and was its senior partner until 1826, when it was taken over by Stuckey's Bank. He gradually relinquished his business interests to Henry and Frederick.

Address 'St Vincent Lodge, Westbury-upon-Trym, Bristol' (probate calendar).

Father Unknown. Jacob Ricketts (d. 1787), who in 1774 became a partner in the Bristol firm Williams, Evans & Co. (Alford, *W. D. and H. O. Wills,* p. 65). On his death, his business interests were taken over by his sons Jacob Wilcox and Richard (c. 1746–5 June 1818).

Mother Probably Hannah, maiden name unknown.

Education Unknown.

Marriage In 1778, to Rachel Murliss (1756–12 March 1820). At least two children, Henry and Frederick.

Religion Probably Anglican although apparently from a Dissenting background. Married at St Mary Magdalen, Taunton. Buried Anglican with a memorial inscription (online). His brother Richard, also buried Anglican, appears to have started life as a Nonconformist, since he is probably the Richard Ricketts, son of Jacob and Hannah, baptised on 18 November 1747 at 'Lewins Mead Presbyterian or Unitarian, Bristol' according to Family Search.

Public None known. He was a 'staunch Whig' (Alford, *W. D. and H. O. Wills*, p. 70).

Miscellaneous The size of his Bristol tobacco fortune this early is somewhat surprising. His grandson Richard reflected in the 1850s: 'Grandfather J. W. Ricketts left about £250,000 behind him but this is nearly all gone, the Ricketts were too grand and lived in too fine places ever to be rich' (Alford, *W. D. and H. O. Wills*, p. 70).

References *GM*, 1839, vol. II, p. 435; *ODNB* for Wills family; B. W. E. Alford, *W. D. and H. O. Wills and the Development of the UK Tobacco Industry, 1786–1965* (2006); online sources.

1839/9 **Name** **Smith, Mary Elizabeth** (née Plaisted)

Dates Baptised 4 October 1758 (Family Search)–23 September 1839, Queen's Square, Bath.

Probate £120,000 (PCC).

Occupation The widow of (Revd) Martin Stafford Smith (see 1834/6), who apparently inherited money from his first wife, the widow of Bishop Warburton and the niece of Ralph Allen, a Bath postal entrepreneur. He was also Rector of Fladbury, Worcestershire, for over forty years. Since the source of his wealth is unclear, he has not been classified by occupational category. It is not clear whether Mary Elizabeth Smith inherited wealth from any other sources.

Address Queen's Square, Bath.

Father Edward Plaisted of Bolehill near Tamworth, Staffordshire (d. 1 December 1761). (Third child and second daughter; her two older siblings died in infancy.)

Mother Joyce (16 June 1716–11 October 1775), daughter of Stanford Wolferstan, 'an active magistrate for the counties of Stafford and Warwick' (Burke), and widow of Edward Littleton (d.s.p.).

Education Unknown.

Marriage In 1797, to (Revd) Martin Stafford Smith (1747–6 January 1834; q.v.).

Religion Anglican.

Public None known.

Miscellaneous GM noted that her death ended 'one of the last links with the classic days of Prior Park'. This is an apparent reference to the home of Bishop Warburton, who was a friend of Sterne, Richardson, etc. Prior Park is in Bath, and later became a Roman Catholic college.

References *GM*, 1839, vol. II, p. 544; John Burke, *A Genealogical and Heraldic History of the Commoners of Great Britain and Ireland*, vol. I (1835), p. 189; Marquis de Ruvigny, *The Plantaganet Roll of the Blood Royal* (1908), p. 247.

1839/10 **Name** **Hill, Thomas**

Dates c. 1762–14 October 1839, Surbiton, Surrey.

Probate £120,000 (PCC).
Occupation Formerly of 'the firm of Hill & Rickards' (*GM*), distillers of 210 Piccadilly, Middlesex. It was also known as Rickards & Hill (1794, 1803 and 1810 directories). (Occupational category II.13; venue 2.)
Address 'Formerly of South Lambeth, and then of Surbiton near Kingston, Surrey' (probate calendar).
Father Unknown.
Mother Unknown.
Education Unknown.
Marriage He is described in *GM* as 'a widower without any relatives whatever'.
Religion Anglican; left money to the Church Missionary Society.
Public None known.
Miscellaneous Nothing more could be traced about him.
References *GM*, 1839, vol. I, p. 549; 1839, vol. II, p. 671.

Name **Thompson, James** 1839/11
Dates c. 1750–11 July 1839 at the Old Bank, Oxford.
Probate £180,000 (PCC).
Occupation 'Banker' (probate calendar) in Oxford – presumably connected with the Old Bank, Oxford (see 'Father' below). (Occupational category IV.16; venue 14.)
Address 'The Old Bank, Oxford' (probate calendar).
Father Unknown. Our man may have been related to banker and former mercer John Parsons (1752–1814), twice Mayor of Oxford, whose mother (née Godfrey) had a sister, Deborah, who married James Thomson (sic), a local gunsmith. Parsons, whose firm Fletcher & Parsons developed into Oxford's Old Bank, married his cousin Elizabeth Thomson (1796–1829), presumably their daughter (www.headington.org.uk/oxon/mayors).
Mother Unknown.
Education Unknown.
Marriage Unknown.
Religion Unknown.
Public None known.
Miscellaneous Nothing more could be traced about him.
References *GM*, 1839, vol. I, p. 213.

Name **Evans, Walter** 1839/12
Dates Unknown – probated October 1839. He died at Darley Abbey, Derbyshire (*GM*).
Probate £200,000 (PCC).
Occupation Cotton manufacturer ('Walter Evans & Co., cotton spinners of Darley, Derbyshire', 1829 directory) and banker (Crompton Evans Bank of Derby) in Derby. (Occupational categories II.7 and IV.16; venue 17.) In 1883, Thomas William Evans of Allestree Hall, Derby, owned 8,126 acres worth 312,721 p.a. in Derbyshire and Staffordshire.
Address 'Darley Abbey, St Alkmund [Derby], Derbyshire' (probate calendar).

Father Thomas Evans (1723–1814; see 1814/12), cotton spinner and banker at Derby. (Third son.) He left £300,000.

Mother Barbara, daughter of John Stubbs of Ranton Abbey, Staffordshire.

Education Unknown.

Marriage In 1798, to Elizabeth, daughter of Jedediah Strutt and widow of William Evans, Walter's elder half-brother.

Religion Anglican – built a church at Darley and founded a Free School there. He was charitable towards his workmen.

Public Unknown.

Miscellaneous He was apparently primarily a banker, although he continued as a cotton spinner. The family received a baronetcy in 1887.

References *GM,* 1839, vol. II, p. 546; *BLG,* 1846; *BP;* Jean Lindsay, 'Early Industrial Community: The Evans' Cotton Mill at Darley', *Business History,* Autumn 1960.

1839/13 **Name** **Prosser, (Revd) Richard**

Dates Baptised 26 July 1747, Market Drayton, Shropshire–8 October 1838, Belmont, Herefordshire.

Probate £250,000 (PCC).

Occupation Archdeacon of Durham from 1808 till his death. (Occupational category VI.30; venue 22.)

Address 'Belmont [Clehonger], Herefordshire' (probate calendar).

Father Richard Prosser (1674–1781) of Market Drayton, described in *ODNB* as a 'gentleman'. (Third son.)

Mother Eleanor Witherson (1708–79).

Education Secondary schooling unknown; Balliol College, Oxford (matriculated 1767; BA, MA, BD, DD, 1797).

Marriage In 1796, to Sarah (1753–1824), daughter of Samuel Wegg, FRS, a 'wealthy barrister'. Prosser's estate passed to his nephew, Francis Richard Haggit, MP (1824–1911), who changed his name to Wegg-Prosser, converted to Catholicism and founded a Benedictine community. (*ODNB* for Prosser.)

Religion Anglican clergyman.

Public None known.

Miscellaneous He was Rector of All Saints, Colchester, 1792–6; of Gateshead Durham, 1796–1804; Prebendary of Durham, 1804–8; and then Archdeacon for thirty years. The *ODNB* describes him as 'the golden canon of Durham'. Prosser had a large library and is remembered for endowing six exhibitions at Balliol College which were among the first to be based on intellectual ability; these greatly improved Balliol's standing.

References *ODNB;* 'Wegg-Prosser', *BLG.*

1839/14 **Name** **Remnant, Samuel**

Dates c. 1755–24 December 1837, Hampstead.

Probate £140,000 (PCC).

Occupation 'Builder and timber merchant' (probate calendar). Samuel Rem-

nant, 'timber merchant' of High Street, St Giles – 1802 and 1811 directories. (Occupational categories IV.21 and II.10; venue 2.)

Address 'High Street, St-Giles-in-the-Fields, Middlesex and Pond Street, Hampstead, Middlesex' (probate calendar).

Father Unknown. The 1793–1800 London directories list a Richard Remnant, timber merchant of High Street, St Giles, who may have been the father. PROB 11 lists two men of this name, a 'timber merchant and carpenter' of St Giles-in-the-Field, probated July 1784; and a 'gentleman, late timber merchant' of Kentish Town, Middlesex, probated May 1813. An inference is that the first of these was the father and the second his brother.

Mother Unknown. Possibly Sarah Wellbeloved, who married a Richard Remnant (see 'Father' above) in 1747; they had at least one son, Richard, born in 1752 (Family Search).

Education Unknown.

Marriage Unknown.

Religion Unknown.

Public None known.

Miscellaneous He appears to have been primarily a timber merchant – the nature of his building activities is unknown.

References *GM*, 1839, vol. I, p. 217.

Name **Hammond, George** 1839/15

Dates c. 1750, Northallerton–7 February 1838, Upper Homerton.

Probate £140,000 (PCC).

Occupation 'Cheesemonger' (probate calendar) in Eastcheap and Whitechapel and also a shipowner (sic) in London. (Occupational categories IV.20, 21 and 24; venues 1 and 2.) ('Wholesale cheesemonger' at 145 Whitechapel, 1815 directory; 'cheesemonger' at 145 Whitechapel, 1793 directory).

Address 'Formerly of Whitechapel, and then of Homerton, Middlesex' (probate calendar).

Father Unknown. He 'came to London as a poor lad and entered the service of a cheesemonger in Eastcheap' (*GM*).

Mother Unknown.

Education Unknown.

Marriage Unknown. According to *GM*, he 'had no near relatives'.

Religion Congregationalist; he was a member of the 1827–8 Committee for the Repeal of the Test and Corporation Act and donated to Congregationalist chapels.

Public None known.

Miscellaneous According to *GM*, he was lent £1,000 to start out by a 'benevolent Quaker gentleman' who was impressed by him. Possibly he was a contractor of foodstuffs to the Government; otherwise, it is difficult to account for the size of his fortune. According to *GM*, he 'subsequently' became a shipowner.

References *GM*, 1839, vol. I, pp. 329 and 549; online sources.

1839/16 **Name** **Redhead, Thomas**

Dates c. 1755–c. 20 January 1838, at Snare Hill, Norfolk.

Probate £160,000 (PCC).

Occupation Apparently a landowner, although the source of his fortune is unclear. In his will he mentions estates in Cambridge, Norfolk, Devonshire and Marylebone. The Norfolk directory for 1836 notes his 'beautiful park' of 350 acres at Snare Hill. But the origins of his wealth are unclear. In his will he left a legacy to a servant described as a 'man of colour', suggesting, at least tentatively, activities in the West Indies or the American South. His father-in-law was Charles Baring (1742–1829), the nephew of Sir Francis Baring, the wealthy merchant banker. There is no evidence that Redhead had any direct connection with the bank, but the Barings had close American connections at this time. (Occupational category I? +?.)

Address 'Nottingham Place, Marylebone, Middlesex and Snare Hill House [near Thetford], Norfolk' (probate calendar).

Father Unknown. *BLG*, 1855, does not list his antecedents.

Mother Unknown.

Education Unknown.

Marriage In 1804, to Eleanor (b. 1771), daughter of Charles Baring (see above). Her mother was Margaret, daughter of William Drake Gould. Their daughter Elinor (sic) married, in 1828, Charles Porcher of Clyffe, Dorset, JP, DL (*BLG*, 1855). Redhead also left a legacy in his will to his illegitimate son, Charles Smith Redhead.

Religion Presumably Anglican; an Anglican clergyman was an executor.

Public None known.

Miscellaneous A rather mysterious case.

References *GM*, 1839, vol. I, p. 220; *BLG*, 1855; will (PROB 11).

1839/17 **Name** **Thompson, Peter**

Dates c. 1765–19 January 1839, Enfield, Middlesex.

Probate £140,000 (PCC).

Occupation Unknown. According to his will, he owned land in Enfield; Woolwich, at Church Street, Croydon; at Queen Street and Meard Street, Soho Square; at Normanton, Nottingham; at Tibsworth, Derbyshire; and at an indecipherable place in Yorkshire. Despite this impressive list, it is unclear how he accumulated this property or the source of his wealth. No one named Thompson and owning property in these places is listed in Bateman. (Occupational category I?)

Address 'Enfield, Middlesex' (probate calendar).

Father Unknown.

Mother Unknown.

Education Unknown.

Marriage To Fanny, surname and marriage date unknown. He had two sons, (Revd) Edward and Peter, and two daughters, Anne, who in 1827 married (Revd) Daniel Cresswell (1776–1844), in *ODNB* as a 'Church of England clergyman and mathematician', and Elizabeth. *Alum. Cantab.* lists two (Revd) Edward Thompsons, one admitted to St Catherine's College in 1830, dying in 1891; and the other admitted to Clare College in 1828, dying in 1860. No information is given about the father of either. No one of this name attended Oxford in this period.

Religion Anglican; he owned an advowson in Nottingham.

Public None known.

Miscellaneous A Peter Thompson (1698–1770) was MP for St Albans in 1747–54, but there is no evidence of any connection.

References *GM,* 1839, vol. I, p. 220; will (PROB 11 online); above sources.

Name **Labouchère, Peter Caesar** (né Pierre Cesar) 1839/18

Dates 1772, The Hague–16 January 1839.

Probate £300,000 (PCC).

Occupation First a merchant and merchant banker and partner in Hope & Co. of Amsterdam, and then a banker (Williams, Deacon & Labouchère & Co. of Birchin Lane, City of London) and a brother-in-law of the Barings. (Occupational categories IV.16, 19 and 17? Venues 1 and 29.) In England he was primarily a banker.

Address 'Formerly of The Hague, Netherlands and then Hamilton Place, Piccadilly, Middlesex and Hylands, Essex' (probate calendar). According to the *ODNB,* he purchased the Hylands estate, but the family is not listed in Bateman.

Father Name unknown, a 'Huguenot cloth merchant' in Nantes and Amsterdam.

Mother Unknown.

Education Unknown.

Marriage In 1796, to Dorothy Elizabeth (b. 1771), daughter of Sir Francis Baring, Baronet (see 1810/10), the wealthy merchant banker. (Two sons.) Their son Henry (1798–1869) was created 1st Baron Taunton (see 1869/74).

Religion The family were Huguenots. He was almost certainly an Anglican at death. In Amsterdam, he gave money to the Presbyterians and Jews.

Public None known.

Miscellaneous He was the first of his family to settle in England. His family had left France at the revocation of the Edict of Nantes but apparently later returned. He began in a mercantile house in Nantes, then joined the great mercantile and banking house of Hope & Co. in Amsterdam, and then went to London as a banker. His descendants were prominent in Whig and Liberal politics.

References *ODNB:* his entry is included with the entry on the Hope family; *ODNB* for relatives; *GM,* 1839, vol. II, p. 669; *BP; BLG.*

Name **Minet, Isaac** 1839/19

Dates 10 November 1767–14 March 1839, Maidstone.

Probate £160,000 (PCC).

Occupation Merchant in the City of London (Minet & Fector [sic], of 21 Austin Friars – 1793 and 1803 directories; Minet & Stride of the same address, 1817 directory). (Occupational category IV.21? Venue 1.)

Address 'Formerly of Austin Friars in the City of London, and then of Baldwyns, near Dartford, Kent' (probate calendar).

Father Hughes Minet (1731–23 December 1813), merchant of Austin Friars. He owned lands in Lambeth and Camberwell.

Mother Mary Loubier (d. November 1768).

Education Unknown.

Marriage In 1802, to Susannah (1779–1869), daughter of Sir Charles Pole, Baronet. Their son was James Louis Minet (see 1885/78).

Religion Originally Huguenot family. He was probably an Anglican.

Public High Sheriff of Kent, 1827.

Miscellaneous The firm was founded in 1746. The first of his family in England was Isaac Minet (1660–1745), who became a shipowner and agent in Dover for the East India Company. He apparently fled to England in 1685.

References *GM,* 1839, vol. I, p. 444; *Burke's Family Records;* online genealogies and sources; PROB 11.

1839/20 **Name** **Pryor, Robert**

Dates 6 May 1778–1 March 1839, Leamington, Warwickshire.

Probate £200,000 (PCC).

Occupation Brewer – a senior partner in Truman, Hanbury & Co., of Brick Lane, Spitalfields. (Occupational category II.12; venue 2.) He had previously been the owner, with his brother Thomas Marlborough Pryor (d. c. 1821), of the Shoreditch Brewery.

Address 'Brick Lane, Spitalfields' (probate calendar).

Father John Pryor (1741–8 September 1819), brewer in Baldock, Hertfordshire. (Second son.)

Mother Martha (d. 1819), daughter of Thomas Marlborough of Hertford and widow of John FitzJohn of Baldock.

Education Unknown.

Marriage Unknown. The brewery was inherited by his nephew Robert Pryor (1889/108).

Religion He was from 'an old Quaker family' (Martin Cornell). It is not clear whether he was a practising Quaker at death.

Public None known.

Miscellaneous His uncle Vickris (sic) Pryor was malt provider to Truman, Hanbury & Co. In 1816, he and his brother became partners in Truman, Hanbury & Co. by purchasing shares in the company for £47,350.

References *GM,* 1839, vol. I, p. 557; Martin Cornell, 'Porter Myths and Mysteries', *Brewery History,* vol. 112 (2004); *VCH Middlesex,* vol. 2 (1911).

1839/21 **Name** **Essex, 5th Earl of, George Capel (or Capell)-Coningsby** (né Capel or Capell)

Dates 13 November 1757–23 April 1839.

Probate £120,000 (PCC).

Occupation Landowner. In 1883, the Earl of Essex owned 14,870 acres worth £18,936 p.a. in Hertfordshire, Essex, Ireland, etc. (Occupational category I.)

Address Cassiobury Park, near Watford, Hertfordshire, appears to have been the main residence.

Father William Anne (sic) Capel (Capell), 4th Earl of Essex (1732–5 March 1799), landowner, Lord of the Bedchamber, etc. (First son.) The 5th Earl suffixed 'Coningsby' to his surname on inheriting the estates of his maternal grandmother.
Mother Frances (d. July 1759), daughter of Sir Charles Hanbury Williams, KB.
Education Secondary schooling unknown; Corpus Christi College, Cambridge (MA).
Marriage First, in 1786, to Sarah (d. January 1838), daughter of Henry Badgett of St Helena and widow of Edward Stephenson; second, in April 1838, to Catherine ('Kitty', a singer, d.s.p., 1882), daughter of Edward Stephens of Leadwell, Oxfordshire.
Religion Anglican.
Public MP (Tory) Westminster, 1779–80; Lostwithiel, 1781–4; Oakhampton, 1785–90; Radnor, 1794–9. Lord Lieutenant of Hertfordshire.
Miscellaneous His surname was spelled as either 'Capel' or 'Capell'. He was Recorder and High Steward of Leominster.
References *GM*, 1839, vol. I, p. 652; *HP; BP.*

Name **Hebbert, Charles** 1839/22
Dates Unknown – probated July 1839.
Probate £120,000 (PCC).
Occupation 'Army and police clothier, and army cap and accoutrement maker' (probate calendar). ('Hebbert & Hume, helmet, army cap and accoutrement makers, of 30 Princes Street, Soho', 1814 directory). (Occupational categories II.11 and 9 and IV.20; venue 2.)
Address 'Pall Mall East, Middlesex' (probate calendar).
Father Unknown.
Mother Unknown.
Education Unknown.
Marriage Unknown. Perhaps to Mary Williams, who married a Charles Hebbert on 21 December 1800 at St Anne's Church, Soho (Family Search).
Religion Unknown.
Public None known.
Miscellaneous He presumably prospered as a result of the wars with France. He later became the 'first clothing contractor' for the Metropolitan Police when it was formed in 1829 and complained about the additional cost of altering the uniforms of the police, because of their very high initial turnover of personnel ('History By the Yard', online).
References Above sources only.

Name **Powis, 1st Earl of, and 2nd Baron Clive of Plessey, Edward Clive** 1839/23
Dates 7 March 1754, Queen Square, Middlesex–16 May 1839, 45 Berkeley Square, Middlesex.
Probate £120,000 (PCC).
Occupation Indian 'nabob' fortune, Indian administrator and landowner-

inherited from his father-in-law. (Occupational categories I and VI.31; venue 29.) In 1883, the Earl of Powis owned 60,559 acres worth £57,024 p.a. in Montgomery and Shropshire.

Address Powis Castle near Welshpool and 45 Berkeley Square, Middlesex.

Father Sir Robert Clive, 1st Baron Clive of Plessey (Irish peerage), KCB (1725–22 November 1774, suicide). In the East India Company: 'Clive of India', the avenger of the Black Hole and Governor of Calcutta; MP. (First son.)

Mother Margaret (d. 1817), daughter of Edmund Maskeleyne of Madras and Puriton, Wiltshire.

Education Eton; Christ Church, Oxford (matriculated 1771).

Marriage In 1784, to Henrietta (d. 1830), daughter of George, 1st Earl of Powis of the first creation. (Two sons, two daughters.)

Religion Anglican.

Public MP (Tory, then Whig, then Tory) for Ludlow, 1774–94. Inherited an Irish peerage and created 1st Baron Clive of Plessey (UK peerage), 1794, and last Earl of Powis of the second creation, 1804. PC, 1805; Lord Lieutenant of Shropshire, 1775–98, of Montgomeryshire, 1804–30. Recorder of Shrewsbury, 1775, and of Ludlow, 1801. Nominated Viceroy of Ireland, 1805, but never served there.

Miscellaneous He was a colonel in the Army and served as Governor of Madras, 1793–1803, expanding British influence. He added an old landed fortune to his father's 'nabob' fortune.

References *ODNB* as 'administrator in India'; *GM,* 1839, vol. II, p. 85; *BP; CP.*

1839/24 **Name** **Alexander, Josias DuPré**

Dates c. 1771–20 August 1839, Stone House near Broadstairs, Kent.

Probate £250,000 'within province' (PCC).

Occupation 'A Director of the East India Company' (*GM*). He was also the nephew of James Alexander, MP and 1st Earl of Caledon (1730–1802), who acquired a fortune estimated at £500,000 (*ODNB*) in the East India Company and became a large-scale Irish landowner. In 1883, the Earl of Caledon owned 34,060 acres worth £22,321 p.a. in County Tyrone, Armagh and Hertfordshire. The family had many ties with the East India Company. (Occupational category IV.19? and VI.31; venues 1 and 29.) Josias Alexander does not appear to have been a landowner on a large scale.

Address 'Formerly of Grosvenor Square, Middlesex, and then of Grosvenor Place, Middlesex.'

Father Robert Alexander (d. 27 March 1790) of Boom Hall, County Derry. (Fifth son.) Robert was the younger brother of the 1st Earl of Caledon.

Mother Anne (d. 1817), daughter of Henry McCullogh of Chadymore and Ballyarton, County Derry.

Education Unknown.

Marriage In 1809, in Calcutta to Mary, daughter of (Revd) Thomas Bracken. (Two sons, eight daughters.) Their son was Caledon DuPré Alexander; see 1884/2.

Religion Anglican.

Public MP (—) Old Sarum, 1820–8, 1830–2.
Miscellaneous It is unclear whether he was ever in India.
References *GM*, 1839, vol. II, p. 435; *BP.*

Name **Bacon, Peter** 1839/25
Dates c. 1765–23 September 1839, Union Row, Mile End.
Probate £100,000 (PCC).
Occupation 'Stockbroker' (probate calendar) of the Stock Exchange, City of London. (Occupational category IV.23; venue 1.)
Address 'Of the Stock Exchange, City of London, and Union Row, Mile End, Stepney' (probate calendar).
Father Unknown.
Mother Unknown.
Education Unknown.
Marriage Name unknown. His wife survived him. They had no children (*GM*).
Religion Unknown, but probably a Dissenter. He gave £10,000 to University College, London, after the death of his widow, suggesting that he may have been a Nonconformist. He left £1,000 each to Homerton College, Highbury College and the Congregational School at Lewisham and £100 each to a local minister and to the Independent Meeting at Stepney. His estate consisted principally of India Stock and government securities (*GM*, 1840, vol. I, p. 670).
Public Unknown.
Miscellaneous He 'retired' with a 'very large fortune' and was devoted to 'promoting education' (*GM*). He is not listed in any London directory as a stockbroker.
References *GM*, 1839, vol. II, p. 545.

Name **Bergareche, Don Manuel de** 1839/26
Dates Unknown–10 October 1839, Islington 'aged 79' (*GM*, 1839, vol. II, p. 546, in which his name was given as 'Emanuel de Bergareche, esq.').
Probate £100,000 (PCC).
Occupation 'Merchant' (probate calendar) in the City of London ('Bergereche & Co., merchants', of Old Pay Office, Broad Street, City of London, 1803 directory; of 33 Winchester Street, City of London, 1825 directory). (Occupational category IV.19 or 21? Venue 1.)
Address 'Of Duncan Terrace, Islington and [33] Great Winchester Street, City of London' (probate calendar).
Father Unknown.
Mother Unknown.
Education Unknown.
Marriage Unknown.
Religion Unknown. The name obviously suggests that he was a Roman Catholic, but there is no direct evidence.
Public None known.
Miscellaneous The probate calendar states that he was 'Don Manuel otherwise Emmanuel de Bergareche, merchant of Islington'. His nationality – presumably

Spanish or French – is not entirely clear, and neither is the nature of his mercantile activities.

References Above sources only.

1839/27 **Name Zetland, 1st Earl of, and 2nd Baron Dundas of Aske, Lawrence Dundas**

Dates 10 April 1766 at St George's Hanover Square, Middlesex–19 February 1839.

Probate £113,781 (Scottish probate).

Occupation Landowner and inherited fortune made in government contracting and finance. (Occupational categories I, IV.16 and 25, VI.31; venues 23 and 2.) In 1883, the Earl of Zetland owned 68,170 acres worth £49,324 p.a. in Yorkshire, Fife, etc.

Address Aske Hall, Richmond, North Riding, and Dundas Houe, New Square, Edinburgh.

Father Sir Thomas Dundas, 1st Baronet, created 1st Baron Dundas of Aske in 1794 (1741–14 July 1820), MP and landowner. (First son.)

Mother Lady Charlotte (d. 1833), daughter of William, 3rd Earl FitzWilliam.

Education Harrow; Trinity College, Cambridge (MA, Hon. LL.D, 1811).

Marriage In 1794, to Harriot (sic) (d. 1834), daughter of (General) John Hale of Plantation near Guisborough. (Four sons, three daughters.)

Religion Baptised as Anglican.

Public MP (Whig) Richmond, North Riding, 1790–1802, 1802–7, 1808–11; York, 1811–20. Lord Mayor of York, 1811–12; Lord Lieutenant of Orkney, 1831 until his death; created an earl in 1838.

Miscellaneous He was a prominent Whig politician, pro-Reform, and a Grand Master of the Freemasons. The Dundas fortune was begun by his self-made grandfather Sir Lawrence Dundas (1712–81), who allegedly made over £1 million as a government contractor and financier.

References *ODNB* for family; *GM*, 1839, vol. I; *BP*; *CP*.

1839/28 **Name Raikes, Robert**

Dates 31 August 1765–20 August 1837, Bridlington, Yorkshire. (The estate was not probated until February 1839.)

Probate £100,000 (York PC).

Occupation Mercantile family in the City of London. He is described as a 'banker' in Duncan Raikes's book, but he is not listed in any London directory. (Occupational category IV.21? and 16? Venue 1.) The family firm was W. Raikes & Co., 'merchants', of Bishopsgate Churchyard, City of London (1803 directory). In 1793, it was known as William Thomas Raikes & Co., 'merchants'. The family is not listed in Bateman.

Address Welton House, near Hull, East Riding, and Cranbrook House, Essex.

Father William Raikes (1737–15 October 1808), an 'eminent merchant' of London and Woodford, Essex. His dates here are from *BLG*, 1937. The *ODNB*, in its article on Raikes Currie, states that he lived from 1738 to 1800 and that he was a 'prominent East India merchant'. Those life dates would appear to be correct, since the estate of William Raikes of Woodford, Essex, was probated in November 1800 (PROB 11). (Second son.) Robert Raikes may have been the nephew of Thomas Raikes (1741–1813; see 1814/18), a wealthy merchant and banker in the City of London.

Mother Martha (d. 1797), daughter of Job Mathew of West Ham, Essex.

Education Unknown.

Marriage In 1789, to Anne (d. 1848), daughter of Thomas Williamson of Welton House, Yorkshire. (Two sons, two daughters.)

Religion Anglican.

Public JP, DL, Essex; High Sheriff of Essex, 1802.

Miscellaneous His sister Mary (d. 1834) married, in 1789, Isaac Currie (1760–1834), banker. Their son was Raikes Currie, a well-known banker, in the *ODNB*. It is possible that Robert Raikes was connected with Currie's bank.

References *BLG*, 1937; Duncan Raikes, *Pedigree of Raikes* (1980).

Name **Sefton, 2nd Earl of, William Philip Molyneux** 1839/29

Dates 18 September 1772, St George's, Hanover Square, Middlesex–20 November 1838.

Probate £100,000 (York PC).

Occupation Landowner in and around Liverpool. (Occupational category I.) In 1883, the Earl of Sefton owned 20,250 acres worth £43,000 p.a. in Lancashire, which, according to Bateman, did not include building land in and around Liverpool.

Address Croxteth Hall, Liverpool, was the principal seat.

Father Charles William Molyneux, 7th Viscount Molyneux of Maryborough (1748–31 January 1795), in the Irish peerage, who was created 1st Earl of Sefton (Irish peerage) in 1771, landowner and MP. (Only child.)

Mother Isabella (d. 1819), daughter of William, 2nd Earl of Harrington.

Education Secondary schooling unknown; Christ Church, Oxford (matriculated 1779).

Marriage In 1792, to Maria (d. 1851), daughter of William, 6th Baron Craven. (Four sons, four daughters.)

Religion The father had been a Roman Catholic until 1768 and then became an Anglican. The 2nd Earl was always an Anglican.

Public MP (advanced Whig) Droitwich, 1816–31. Created a UK peer as 1st Baron Sefton in 1831.

Miscellaneous He was known as a gambler and gourmand. The Seftons became one of the wealthier peerage families during the nineteenth century as a result of their ownership of land in and around Liverpool.

References *GM*, 1838, vol. II, p. 657; *BP*; *CP*.

INDEX